M000307136

BRAVE

YOUNG
WOMEN'S
GLOBAL
REVOLUTION

BRAVE

Vol. 1

*Global
Themes*

Gayle
Kimball,
Ph.D.

Dedicated to the Youth Editorial Board who critiqued chapters and answered many questions.

The cover photo is a poster in Tahrir Square, taken by the author July 2011. The protesters' tents are in the background. Appreciation to Morgan Brynnan and Jesse Poe for critiquing chapters and Miles Huffman for formatting and designing Brave.

© *Gayle Kimball 2017*

No part of this publication may be reproduced, distributed, or transmitted in any form or by any means, including photocopying, recording, or other electronic or mechanical methods, without the prior written permission of the publisher, except in the case of brief quotations embodied in critical reviews and certain other noncommercial uses permitted by copyright law.

Other Books by the Author

50/50 Marriage (Beacon Press)

50/50 Parenting (Lexington Books)

Ed. Women's Culture (Scarecrow Press)

Ed. Women's Culture Revisited. (Scarecrow Press)

The Religious Ideas of Harriet Beecher Stowe (Edwin Mellen Press)

Essential Energy Tools book and 3 videos. (Equality Press)

21st Century Families: Blueprints for Family-Friendly Workplaces, Schools and Governments. (Equality Press)

The Teen Trip: The Complete Resource Guide (Equality Press)

Ed. Everything You Need to Know to Succeed After College (Equality Press)

How to Survive Your Parents' Divorce (Equality Press)

Ed., Quick Healthy Recipes: Literacy Fundraiser (Equality Press)

Your Questions About Love and Family (Equality Press)

Your Questions About Mental and Physical Health (Equality Press)

Your Mindful Guide to Academic Success: Beat Burnout (Equality Press)

Ageism in Youth Studies: A Maligned Generation (Cambridge Scholars Publishing)

Global Youth Values Transforming Our Future (Cambridge Scholars Publishing)

In Process

Democracy Uprisings Led by Global Youth

Tactics and Goals for Changemaking

CONTENTS

INTRODUCTION

Youth Viewpoints from 88 Countries

Our human future is precarious due to our self-centeredness and shortsightedness in not meeting the challenges of climate change and growing inequality between rich and poor. Even Christine Lagarde, head of the International Monetary Fund-- not regarded as a liberal institution, is concerned about these huge problems. This book explores the ideas and actions of young people from 88 countries. Their electronically connected activism is transforming global culture. My surveys of 4,149 young people from 2004 to 2016 aimed to see how they are transforming our lives and planetary future, as I summarize in a TED-style slide show.[1] The survey questions, main answers, and list of the 88 countries are listed on the book webpage, links listed below. I aimed to survey people under age 20 because of their frankness and interviewed activists in their 20s. The surveys and interviews indicate that the new generation is uniquely altruistic, committed to peace and collaboration, and interconnected. Exceptionally brave girls and young women lead uprisings for democracy in tackling major political issues, as highlighted in the list of recent youth-led uprisings that follows this introduction.

Young people are the large majority in developing nations and the best-educated generation in history. Yet half of the new generation is poor and one fourth live on less than $1 a day.[2] With the power given them by their numbers and their ability to communicate electronically with a global network, they catalyzed global uprisings. What I call the Relationship Generation tends to defy or ignore large bureaucratic institutions including government and religion, leading to the false charge of being apathetic, but they focus instead on direct democracy on the local level and loving their family and friends.

The dozen books I've written may seem to be on very different topics, but the common theme is exploring the ideas of groups who were neglected by researchers, writing among the first books on women's culture, egalitarian couples and global (rather than regional) youth activism. I taught Women's Studies and Sociology courses such as "Women Internationally" at California State University, Chico (CSUC) and struggled to find an interesting text on global women's issues that wasn't a disconnected anthology of ethnographies. Doing research on global youth activism, I especially searched for young women activists. Videos shown on TV news usually feature young men protesters on the streets but women lead or are important partners in fomenting global change. The book includes the sexist and ageist obstacles that girls face and their courage in challenging religious and political authorities. It's part of a series of four, listed above in other books by the author.

Young people want to be heard with an open mind; this book provides a forum for the insights of the largest youth generation in history—1.5 billion ages 10 to 24, given various names such as the Millennial Generation or Generation Y and Z. In his most recent work, generations expert Neil Howe defines Gen Y as people born from 1982 to 2004. The period between childhood and adulthood is expanding as "tweens" are stimulated by media to act like teens, youth enter biological adolescence earlier, spend more time in school and therefore delay job seeking and marriage. The United Nations defines youth as ages 15 to 24 and adolescents as ages 10 to 19; I surveyed and interviewed young people younger than 20 and interviewed activists in their teens and 20s.

To learn how Generations Y and Z are shaping our future, I discovered a worldwide source of youth informants, many of them contacted through their teachers. I visited them in their homes and schools in Brazil, China, Cuba, Egypt, England, Greece, India, Indonesia, Japan, South Korea, Mexico, Switzerland and Tanzania, and Turkey, as well as in all regions of the US. Dialogues ranged from Tahrir Square in Cairo; to Rio slums; to remote villages in Tanzania, India and Indonesia; to middle-class London and Shanghai homes; and Japanese and Turkish schools.

The best part of globetrotting was talking with young people in places as varied as Tahrir Square, tiny apartments in China, a colorfully painted home in Brazil, and large two-story homes in London and Northern India as well as email and Skype dialogues. Photographs of some of the young people can be seen on our Facebook Global Youth SpeakOut page and videotaped interviews are on YouTube's "The Global Youth" channel (links below).

Any time I met people from another country, I asked them if they knew youth or their teachers in their country of origin. Over 80 teachers mailed or emailed their students' responses to the 12 book questions, acknowledgements and questions are on the book webpage. I met some of the educators when they came to CSUC for a six-week study program for English teachers offered several times a year. People I meet at the gym led me to contacts in Korea, Brazil, and Mexico. I attended a Global Uprisings conference in Amsterdam in November 2013 where activists, journalists and academics presented their analysis of the upheavals that started with the Arab Spring in 2010. I interviewed activists there and continued discussion with them via email.

Snowball sampling was used when some teachers and students referred others. It's a convenience sample rather than a statistically random sample, but respondents includes a wide variety of backgrounds: hundreds of rural Chinese students (see photos[3]) village youth from Tanzania and Indonesia, students in a village in Northern India so remote the teacher has to walk an hour up hills to reach his classroom, kids from Rio and Shanghai slums, and demonstrators in Cairo, Athens, and Istanbul and in my hometown in Chico, California. In Tanzania, for example, a young guide I met there interviewed rural village youngsters in the north and the principal of a Muslim school I visited in Dar es Salaam assigned the questions to some of his students.

About 500 respondents came from Internet sites such as Sit Diary and Our Shared Shelf feminist book club on Goodreads, youth groups like Students Against Violence Everywhere, and educational organizations like the Yellow Sheep River Foundation that assists poor rural Chinese students. Various friends or language majors at CSUC translated the questions. I posted on all the Facebook pages listed under global youth but only got a few replies, as when Kevin in Trinidad introduced me to Taika in Ethiopia who recruited respondents at her school.

My main contact in China is Yuan whose English teacher (a former student of mine) gave the book questions to her university freshman in Wuhan. His answers were so thoughtful I followed up with more questions. We've been in close contact for almost a decade. He and his friends translated hundreds of surveys I got from an educational organization for rural students I found online. A friend of an Indian woman in Chico where I live in Northern California introduced me to a friend who I met in Singapore who gave me the name of his friend, a high school administrator in Southern India. An Indian student responded to an Internet post I made asking for input and he asked his father, a principal in Central India, to assign the book questions. I met principals when I was in Northern India and other principals through them, and got several Indian names from *Youth-Leader* magazine headquartered in Berlin.

The editor of the magazine, Eric Schneider, commented, "This huge study, with elaborate analysis of the early 21st Century youth environment is massive. We have not come across anything like it, before, and--no wonder, considering Kimball quoted voices of 4,000 youth." Each of the 88 countries has a different access story, so this is not a uniform sample of middle-class youth answering multiple-choice questions on the Internet. For those who did have Internet, I was able to follow-up with more questions.

For the quantitative approach, over 4,000 written surveys were coded by frequency of response with 57% female respondents. All of the answers were quantified by creating categories based on frequency of the answer, summarized in the book website.[4] The questions are open-ended. Rather than starting with a thesis, I used Grounded Theory in that I collected the data, then coded it myself to be consistent as themes and patterns appeared after the fact, to develop a conclusion—globally, girls are bravely stepping out of old gender straightjackets. The data was analyzed using the Statistical Package for the Social Sciences. SPSS was used to see differences based on gender, age, and region—more differences showed up in the latter as gender differences were small.

Staying in family homes can be referred to as a form of ethnographic fieldwork. Qualitative insights were gained from in-person, Skype, and email interviews with young people as revealed in quotations throughout the book. Our dialogues were sometimes supportive as when a gay Chinese youth felt safe to talk to me and a Pakistani girl I've talked with since she was in high school emailed on her graduation from medical school, "Gayle Kimball, thank you for making me realize the light in me." As Professor Jeffrey Jensen Arnett pointed out, we learn more from interviews than survey questions with determined responses, although current research is "heavily in favor of quantitative methods." From the point of view of the study of social movements, I examined what resources enable an uprising to succeed. From the feminist point of view, I sought out female viewpoints and leadership in researching social movements and interviews with young changemakers. "History from the bottom" and feminist Standpoint Theory starts with the voices of un-famous young people, rather than famous "great men." These approaches value and listen to unknown and oppressed groups, rather than studying powerful men or women who act like them such as Margaret Thatcher. Grounded theory is similar in valuing research drawn from the lived experiences of the target group. Chapters include many quotes in order to communicate the actual voices of youth who are usually discounted, as primary sources are the most innovative form of research.

Researchers Neglect Global Youth

Other large global youth studies often draw from young people who have access to

Internet, as listed on the book webpage. Many are conducted for marketing research. For example, Don Tapscott surveyed youth from 12 countries but most of his book quotes from the Digital Generation are North Americans, mainly his children. Other marketers are Habbo and InSites Consulting virtual world surveys, Martin Lindstrom's *BRANDchild*, and Elissa Moses. The Varkey Foundation released a study that claims to be the first and largest global survey of Generation Z attitudes in 2017 because there's "very little in-depth reputable polling on the opinions and attitudes of Generation Z."[5] It surveyed 20,088 young people with Internet access, ages 15 to 21 from 20 representative countries in 2016. It confirmed my survey findings that youth have a global culture. The lead researcher of a global marketing survey of kids aged six to 12 replied to my question about their respondents, "The survey was an online study, which means that respondents in all of the countries have sufficient income to have a computer/mobile device and internet service. Also, our research vendor screened out the lowest incomes, because the consumer group we are interested in marketing to is not at poverty level." In contrast, this book includes slum dwellers and rural youth who may not have electricity. Surveys are also conducted by non-government agencies like UNICEF or *Fondation Pour L'Innovation Politique* whose findings are not available in books. Many of these NGO global youth surveys are about tobacco use or other health issues.

Youth Studies have been published in The *Journal of Youth and Adolescence* since in 1972, followed by *Youth Studies* in 1998, the *Journal of Youth Studies* in 2000, and *Youth Voice Journal* since 2010 and others.[6] Universities like the University of Minnesota offer a major in Youth Studies, but "youth-centered definitions of their lives remain largely absent. Young people have not been enfranchised by the research conducted on their lives."[7] Youth studies focused on developmental stages in the transition to adulthood, with the more recent stage of "emerging adulthood," as young people delay marriage and careers. Australian youth studies professor Anita Harris advocates that youth researchers do "participatory action research" and become less fixated on linear developmental stages, work and employment, because youth are interested in culture, leisure and sexuality.[8] The focus on youth development as influenced by their particular generation is called the social generational paradigm, which some scholars criticize as the "new orthodoxy" in Youth Studies.[9]

Another approach, used in this book, looks at social generations as influenced by their particular historic circumstances, such as recession and the Internet for the current "App Generation" (the title of a 2014 book).[10] The focus on youth development as influenced by their particular generation is called the social generational paradigm, which some scholars criticize as the "new orthodoxy" in Youth Studies.[11] Sociologist Karl Mannheim discussed "The problem of generations" in a 1923 essay. Other scholars like Canadian James Côté emphasize the negative impact of neoliberal capitalism and growing inequality with high youth un- or under-employment that impacts various generations. Along this line, British scholars like Alan France and Steven Roberts think class is an important determinant of youth issues rather than generational differences, similar to the earlier interest in subcultures of working class boys at the influential Center for Contemporary Cultural Studies at the University of Birmingham in the 1970s. I don't see any conflicts, just different focal points as class and precarious employment are both influential.

My scan of the *Journal of Youth Studies* from 2011 to 2014 found only 26 titles on youth activism or political attitudes out of 224 articles and 10 of the titles were about youth attitudes towards traditional politics.[12] Amazingly, not one article was about the uprisings that started in 2011 discussed in this book. A similar search of the *Journal of Adolescence* found only one issue on political engagement but not rebellions (June 2012), with no other such articles in other issues.[13] *Current Sociology* published an issue on "From Indignation to Occupation" in 2013 reporting on the 2011 uprisings but without focus on youth.[14] Online journals--*Interface: A Journal For and About Social Movements* and *ROAR,* do provide current information about social movements but not specifically about youth. A scholarly publication about social movements is *Mobilization* and its blog *Mobilizing Ideas.*[15] *Reflections on a Revolution (ROAR)* is more international and less academic than the US-dominated *Mobilization.*

Psychologist Jeffrey Jensen Arnett pointed out that the study of adolescence began in the US early in the 20th century and the study of US adolescents still dominates the field.[16] He reports that most of the scholarly journals devoted to the age group 10 to 25 are mostly from the US with an occasional European researcher. The *Journal of Youth Studies* includes studies from Canada, Australia, Germany and Sweden, as well as the US and the UK. Girls Studies includes courses, an international association, online faculty discussion group, and *Girlhood Studies* journal, with especially active British Commonwealth researchers.[17] Women's Studies has spread to over 600 universities around the world, with an National Women's Studies Association headquartered in Maryland.

Brave focuses on countries where most young people live because many of the books about Generation Y describe how to manage them in the US workforce. Much of the generational research is done in the US and the UK. Most of the academic books on global youth are anthologies of specialized ethnographies about small groups of young people in various regions without much connection between chapters. While these anthologies have opened important conversations, one such book includes chapters on Thai makeup saleswomen, former child soldiers in Sierra Leone, Latino use of political graphic art, a Sri Lankan refugee, etc. Searching through 15 pages of Amazon.com books listed under "global youth," I found anthologies, youth ministry, how to market to youth, deviant behavior, by country (such as youth in China), or unemployment, but no overviews of global youth activism except this series.

Books that report on young feminists include *Defending Our Dreams: Global Feminist Voices for a New Generation* (2005*)*, an anthology written by transnational feminists in their late 20s and early 30s.[18] They emphasize international human rights law as the key to women's liberation in the only book I found representing young feminists from many continents. *Half the Sky*, a book and video by Nicholas Kristof and Sheryl WuDunn, tells the story of women activists of various ages in Africa and Asia (2010). Three books interviewed urban youth activists in the Americas before the global uprisings of 2011: Jessica Taft, *Rebel Girls: Youth Activism and Social Change Across the Americas,* 2010; Hava Rachel Gordon, *We Fight to Win: Inequality and the Politics of Youth Activism* (2010); and Maria De Los Angeles Torres, Irene Rizzini, and Norma Del Rio, *Citizens in the Present: Youth Civic Engagement in the Americas*, 2013. US feminists report on their activism in Mary Trigg's *Leading the Way: Young Women's Activism for Social Change* (2010). Girls' media activism in Australia, England and the US is discussed in *Next Wave Cultures: Feminism, Subcultures, Activism* (2008), edited by Australian Anita Harris. She pointed out, "Very little has been said about either the political participation or nonparticipation of young women in particular," with the exception of feminist "generation wars" and criticisms of the quieter political activism of the Third Wave of young feminists.

Similar to Harris, Taft reported in *Rebel Girls* that, "Despite their activism, girls are rarely considered and written about as significant political actors. They appear but do not speak." They're left out of academic research on girls' studies and on youth movements. Taft says that the focus is on college students rather than teenagers. Despite the increasing interest in girls' studies over the last two decades, Emily Bent agrees that "the research on girls and politics is surprisingly incomplete" and invisible.[19] Most of the interest in girls' studies, youth studies, and children's rights focuses on their future impact on politics when they can vote rather than girls' current activism. Youth want to be leaders now. However, several international studies cited by Bent found that girls valued political participation as much or more than boys, although some of them view

it as a masculine arena. Girls were more likely to imagine themselves becoming politically involved in the future if the media discussed women politicians. Anita Harris
points out that some girls are interested in politics, but consider the traditional forms
corrupt and dismissive of their views. An editor of *We Got Issues! A Young Woman's
Guide to a Bold, Courageous and Empowered Life* (2006), reported, "Young women in
this country expect to be ignored. Most young women believe that people don't really
want to know what we think."[20]

The editors of a book on *Student Activism in Asia* (2012), like the few other researchers on youth activism, complain that despite the visibility of student protests and
their vanguard actions, because it is so common, "It seems to require no explanation."[21]
They point out the lack of comparative research on the causes and effects of student
activism, with the exception of some interest in specific local uprisings in the 1960s and
70s. I in turn wonder about their lack of mention of young women's roles or feminism.
Editor Meredith Weiss kindly emailed in 2015, "You will find women involved along-
side men in activism in all states in the region, across periods, but I can't think off-hand
of any Asian (or other) state in which feminism per se has been a guiding frame or
objective for student mobilization overall. "

The only books specifically about youth and the recent uprisings are about the
Middle East: Maytha Alhassen and Ahmed Shihab-Eldin, editors, *Demanding Dignity:
Young Voices from the Front Lines of the Arab Revolutions*, 2012; Alcinda Honwana,
Youth and Revolution in Tunisia, 2013; Juan Cole, *The New Arabs: How the Millennial
Generation is Changing the Middle East* (2014); and Ahmed Tohamy Abdelhay's Youth
Activism in Egypt: Islamism, Political Protest and Revolution, 2015. *Youth Activism in
Egypt: Islamism, Political Protest and Revolution*, 2015. The book is $104, inaccessible to
most. I turned down book contract offers from two academic publishers who intended
to charge $100 for a hardback book.

Four books published from 2012 to 2016 cover the global uprisings but not with
analysis of the role of young people: Paul Mason, *Why It's Still Kicking Off Everywhere:
The New Global Revolutions*; an anthology by Anya Schiffrin and Eamon Kircher-Allen, *From Cairo to Wall Street: Voices From the Global* Spring including activists in their
20s and 30s. Internet ebooks by Werner Puschra and Sara Burke are titled *The Future
We the People Need: Voices from New Social Movements* and *World Protests 2006-2013*.
The latest books are *They Can't Represent us! Reinventing Democracy from Greece to
Occupy* by Marina Sitrin and Dario Azzellini (2014) and *Occupy! A Global Movement*
(2014), a $150 anthology edited by Jenny Pickerill, et al. In *Youth Rising? The Politics of*

Youth in the Global Economy (2015) Mayssoun Sukarieh and Stuart Tannock do focus on the portrayal of youth in global uprisings, but acknowledge that they too do not include their actual voices. Their thesis is that although youth played a vital part as activists, their role is exaggerated in order to benefit the interests of neoliberal elites to deflect attention from the structural problems in the existing capitalist system. They don't consider sex roles in activist groups: Fascism is included in the index but not feminism. The 2016 book *This is an Uprising* by Mark Engler and Paul Engler focuses on nonviolent direct action but barely mentions youth leadership. I advocate that researchers address ageism and change the common practice of speaking about youth without including their voices.

Viewpoint

This book contributes to Women's Studies, Girls' Studies, Youth Studies, Global Studies and International Education. My perspective fits with Women's Studies (my teaching background), Cultural Studies, public sociology advocacy and Political Science's Social Movement Theory. My interviews with youth are oral history, first-person narratives with people who participated in or observed uprisings. Feminism can serve to "undermine what has been the dominant tendency of academic and organization thought: a strongly objectivist tendency, uncomfortable with the modes of intuitive observation and ambiguous responses." [22] The pretense of an objective observer is replaced with an activist scholar who aims to be of use to the people she or he studies. Both the study of art and feminism "subvert the very structure of thought."

Feminist scholarship takes seriously the lives of the undervalued and marginal, such as youth or lower classes, and facilitates working for social transformation, creating "history from the bottom up." Feminist interest in marginalized people as the focus of study is called Standpoint Theory where the observations of the grassroots and marginalized are valued. It developed in the 1970s out of Marxist feminist thought, maintaining that research that focuses on power relations should start with the oppressed. I agree with Chandra Talpade Mohanty who advocates that feminists should focus on activism in opposition to neoliberal capitalism and use advocacy research or "militant research," defined as the place where academia and activism meet. Rather than just observe, activist scholars participate in political movements that create new values and relationships. My research, for example, led me to start a literacy program for Pakistani girls including a fundraiser cookbook of quick healthy recipes, and assist some of the book respondents with college applications, as a sounding board for personal issues. What motivated me to research for a decade was being on a treasure hunt. With such a paucity of research on youth activism, I relished each discovery and each new activist who shared her experiences with me.

The main theoretical approaches to studying girls and young women are feminism and youth subcultures like punks or hip-hop that both involve resistance to dominant authorities.[23] Youth subcultures were first studied at the University of Chicago starting in the 1920s with a focus on street gangs as a strategy to cope with poverty. Youth subcultures were made famous at the University of Birmingham's Centre for Contemporary Cultural Studies starting in 1964. Their early studies were criticized by feminist scholars for focusing on class conflict among working class "lads" and their use of public spaces, ignoring what girls did in more private spaces at home. With the development of global marketing aimed at youth and neoliberal individualization, class became less relevant. Instead, scholars discussed nonactivist neotribes such as club scenes, lifestyles, networks, communities, etc. Anita Harris stated in 2008, "There is no longer any such thing as the truly 'resistant' youth subculture, because youth style and cultures have been appropriated by the consumer industries, depoliticized and packaged back to youth."

In the focus on subcultures, youth social action was left out of the Birmingham School approach.[24] Sociologists have been criticized for neglecting the tactics of social movements "with their emphasis upon structural strain, generalized belief, and deprivation."[25] "Post-subcultural" debates ensued, interested in multinational and cross-generational projects. Professor Peter Kelly cautions against the influence of "governmentalized" studies of interest to government departments, corporations and NGOs, who are interested in topics like consumption preferences and youth alcohol and drug use.[26]

Canadian James Côté explained that since the 1980s youth studies has focused on working class youth cultures, "increasingly preoccupied with subjectivities," rather than approaching youth as a whole as a disadvantaged class or proletariat, to use Marxist terminology, disadvantaged economically as a class.[27] He argues for "a new political economy of youth," a conflict theory that generates radical solutions to these material problems. He opposes liberal reformist structural approaches that accept the neoliberal status quo. Côté faults youth studies for ignoring the negative impact of neoliberalism on youth who face an uncertain future while the number of very rich families that can pay for their children to attend expensive universities increases. Additionally, he warns of "growing stigmatization of youth over the past century," especially in terms of claims of "biological inferiority" regarding the adolescent brain as being less rational and more impulsive than adult brains. Schools perpetuate subordination by teaching obedience to hierarchical authority. Côté said the flip side of this trend over the last two decades is increasingly painting adults as superior, responsible, and mature, although I would add that an objective look at the news does not back up this belief. As 13-year-old SpeakOut respondent Lia said in California, "For those who created this mess in a world of chaos, just like you said to us about our rooms, "Clean it up!"

Globalization and new media changed girls' way of doing politics starting in the late 1980s in North America with grrrl power media, including zines, music like punk and rap, the Internet and its blogs and webcams opening up since 1991. Young women engage in culture jamming of commercial media and graffiti, creating a "new form of citizenship" and a new form of cultural politics in postmodern subcultures. The editors of *Riot Grrrl* zine wrote in 1992, "We're tired of being written out--out of history, out of the 'scene', out of our bodies ... for this reason we have created our zine and scene ... be proud of being a grrrl." Feminist girls around the world created a Third Wave partly in reaction to the Second Wave and social media, discussed in Volume 2 Chapter 1. This wave was based on a more fluid and hybrid notion of gender and resistance to multinational corporations' power, sometimes surpassing national governments as the target for resistance.

Since the beginning of the 21st century, Youth Studies has been interested in transition to adulthood; characteristics of Generations X, Y, and Z; and adolescent brain development's influence on risk taking, as seen in Australian Andy Furlong's *Youth Studies: An Introduction* (2012). The newer concerns of youth studies are the complexity of the creation of youth identity and culture, international influences with global media and migration, and identifying ways to support positive youth development, as with school-based health centers.

The developmental approach is criticized for a myopic focus on economic transition from school to workplace and for assuming that the process of individualization is similar for adolescents everywhere. Definitions of youth behavior are socially constructed, thus relative. For example, children used to be viewed as little adults and still are in cultures that send children to hard work in mines, construction, sorting landfills and other dangerous jobs. In some cultures children are treated as little animals, as explained by Ayaan Hirsi Ali in her biography *Infidel (2007)*, about growing up in Somalia. The focus on child development in stages that we accept as obvious began in the 19th century as a spin off of Darwin's theory of evolution.

As relativists, recent theorists believe that the writer and reader are subjective rather than objective and concepts change over time. Not just class, but gender, race, ethnicity, and sexual preference shape intersecting hybrid (a frequent concept about youth cultures) youth identities, as well as the influences of an adolescent's home, school and work. Australian Johanna Wyn observes that ideas about youth as a social category are "likely to be at odds with young people's own perceptions and experiences."[28] Hence the need to consult with youth about policies that affect them, which seems obvious, but an ageist blind spot about youth concerns often gets in the way. (More on scholars' ageism is discussed in *Ageism in Youth Studies*.)

The postmodern subcultural approach is more interested in the individual and intersecting categories. Moving away from the dualistic notion of male and female, for example, Facebook responded by adding 50 choices for gender preference for English-speaking users, including categories like androgyny, intersex, transgender, neither, gender questioning and pangender. It's no longer cool to do binary thinking as in female and male, he or she. "Genderqueer" or "agender" people use pronouns like "ou" to replace he and she. Youth identity is shaped by gender, class, ethnicity, sexual preference, etc. This approach in turn created criticism in a dialectical process. Critical of postmodern or poststructural approaches, UCLA philosophy professor Douglas Kellner faults academics for "subjectivism and relativism, often bordering on nihilism," and advocates instead critical theory associated with the Frankfurt School, a German Marxist-oriented research center.[29] This approach aims to be applicable to social change that can emerge from contradictions and crisis in capitalist societies and faults social theory today for being in "acute crisis" with its "fragmentation, trivialization, and academicization."

Format

Young people's own words and thoughts weave through every chapter of *Brave*. Young people critiqued every chapter. My main intent is to facilitate their voices being heard as they requested, to reveal their lived experiences of being female in a patriarchal global culture. To give a feeling for daily life in different countries, I refer to photographs and videos I've taken as well as commercial media. A filmography is listed in book webpage. Each chapter ends with discussion questions to ponder, activities, and films to watch.

Student comments are organized by age, with younger ones first. Some of the ages for the same person change throughout the book as we've corresponded for years. They're identified by their first name or nickname-- what ever they selected, age and gender as in "Chris, 16, f, England." I corrected spelling and punctuation. Respondents are referred to as SpeakOut youth. They're divided into "kids" 12 and younger, and "teens" 13 and older. I avoid "American" to describe people from the US, because a teacher from El Salvador pointed out he's a Central American, Canadians are North Americans, and so on. The youth advisory board critiqued chapters and answered my questions. Anyone I quoted was emailed a copy of how I wrote about his or her statements or a follow-up question, if an email was available

Volume 1 looks at global issues that impact girls and women such as consumerism and media and the desire for equality and equal rights. Volume 2 discusses regional issues and activism in Muslim countries, developing countries in Latin America, Sub-Saharan Africa, India, and former communist countries of China and Russia.

Findings

Khue, a 16-year-old from Vietnam, asked me, "I would love to know your opinion of us, of people from my generation. During your journey did you find any new perspectives? Does your journey affect you in some ways?" I told her that traveling and talking to young people face-to-face and establishing relationships touched my heart and earned my respect for their openness and willingness to question authority. Teachers and students around the world are enduring friends who answer my unending questions, including book board member Hassan. Like Yuan in China, his answers to the book questions were so thoughtful, we engaged in long-lasting dialogue. He and I started a literacy program where he goes to villages near Peshawar, Pakistan to teach illiterate kids. Maheen, a young woman student at Hassan's university, started teaching in our Open Doors Literacy Program in 2014. I'm impressed by young people's wisdom and insights, but there seems to be a gulf between thoughtful caring ones who criticize their superficial peers who care about material things too much and ignore critical issues like climate change and inequality.

What surprised me was the similarity of urban youth viewpoints. Geographical differences did appear, such as concern about pollution in Eastern Europe, violence in US schools, the importance of having children in Sub-Saharan Africa, and anxiety about the college entrance exam in Asia. There's a large difference in developed and developing nations on a continuum of individuality (valued in the West) and group identity and respect for elders valued in more traditional societies. I was interested to talk with highly educated young adults who expect their families to select their spouses, as in India, Pakistan, and Egypt. However, the Internet connects a global youth culture that shares a common slang, clothes, and music such as hip-hop with local variations. Youth activists I interviewed in places as far apart as Egypt, Brazil, Greece, Turkey and California prided themselves on being leaderless, operating with a new model. Influenced by their frequent contact with the decentralized and democratic World Wide Web, the old model of a pyramid with its hierarchy of power is irrelevant to many young people. This more democratic model will no doubt change the world as we know it, as practiced earlier in the global justice movement, feminism, and anarchist societies.

SpeakOut respondents are "green," concerned about saving the planet from global warming and other human destruction, as they mentioned in their written responses. The exception is village youth like those I talked with in Indonesia and Pakistan who don't know about climate change. Middle-class youth share being "wired" in frequent contact using their electronic devices and the Internet. "Sometimes I spend my time in front of laptop from afternoon until night. I really would like to change my bad habit," reports Annisa in Indonesia (age 16). Some urban youth who can't afford to buy computers or have access to them in school use Internet cafes and rent inexpensive cell phones with Internet access. They're more egalitarian and accepting of diversity than older generations, less trusting of politicians.

I realized more fully that many people around the world do not share beliefs I accept as given. I think of marriage as based on falling in love; in Muslim and Hindu parts of the world, "love marriages," are not the norm. A Saudi girl told me "they don't work" and Indian teens said they're based on lust. I don't think of women's hair as indecent, while some Muslim women are harassed if they don't wear a headscarf. I'd never known an illiterate person, but some rural Chinese and East African students commented about their illiterate parents and a compelling interview with an illiterate village girl included in Chapter 3. I spoke with a West African who grew up routinely eating only every three days in the dry period of the year, making hunger more than an abstract concept. What SpeakOut young people and I share is a desire to end poverty, protect the environment, and to have peace.

Please respond with your comments and observations on the book website or to gkimball@csuchico.edu. I'm especially interested in your ideas about solutions to global economic, environmental and social problems for a future solutions book. Photos mentioned in the text are found on Facebook and the book website and video interviews are on YouTube.

Media Sites

This website lists free videos about girls internationally: http://dayofthegirlsummit.com/wp-content/uploads/2012/07/DayoftheGirl-resourceguide.pdf
*Films about global youth: http://wp.me/p47Q76-3J
*Supplemental information and sites to add your add comments on the book webpage: http://globalyouthbook.wordpress.com/
https://www.facebook.com/search/top/?q=global%20youth%20speakout
*My photos of global youth and their homes: http://www.facebook.com/media/set/?set=a.348956001796264.91437.160382763986923&type=1
*Over 100 video interviews with global youth: https://www.youtube.com/user/TheGlobalyouth
*Literacy project in NW Pakistan: http://opendoorsliteracyproject.weebly.com.

Abbreviations and Definitions

A Globalization Glossary is available on the Emory University globalization website.[30] Definitions of political terms and social movement theory are found on the book website along with global studies centers.[31]

Alterglobalization: also called anti-globalization (but activists say they're not anti-globalization except for neoliberal capitalism), and the global justice movement.

Arab Spring: refers to the series of revolutions starting with Tunisia in 2010. Some Arabs consider this a Western or "Orientalist" term and prefer Arab Awakening or Arab Revolutions.

Civil Society: The third sector outside of government and business, including volunteering groups and other NGOs.

EU: European Union of 28 member states

LGBT: Gay, lesbian, bisexual, and transgendered sexual preference

GA: General Assembly

GDP: Gross Domestic Product is the value of a country's production

Globalization: Transnational exchanges of information, money, products, labor, people, goods, resources, diseases, culture, and media.

GMO: Genetically modified food organism

Hajib: Muslim women's hair covering sometimes worn in layers of scarves.

ICT: Information and communication technology including the Internet

IMF: International Monetary Fund

Intersectionality: considers not just gender but systems of power around sexual preference, ethnicity, religion, class, region, migration,

MENA: Muslim countries in the Middle East and North Africa

Neoliberalism: The dominant global economic policy advocating privatization, deregulation and free trade. It's associated with Professor Milton Friedman of the University of Chicago, who influenced President Ronald Reagan and Prime Minister Margaret Thatcher. It's criticized by the global justice movement and is the main enemy of the global uprisings.

NEETs: Young people not in education, employment or training

NGO: non-profit, non-governmental organization, part of Civil Society

Niqab: Muslim women's face covering except for the eyes.

NPR: National Public Radio broadcast in the US

Sharia: Islamic law governing secular and moral matters. For example, criminal law in Saudi Arabia is based on Sharia law.

Social Media: Internet applications built on Web 2.0 that allows users to generate content.

Standpoint Theory: Focus on attention to the realistic perceptions of marginalized people in comparison with privileged classes and the ways communication is shaped by the social environment. Feminists are especially interested in this approach, which is criticized for "essentialism," overgeneralizing about a group of people.

Transnational feminisms: Also called global feminisms and international feminisms, using the plural to indicate Global Sisterhood is intersectional, with many different points of view.

UNICEF: The United Nations Children's' Fund

UNDP: United Nations Development Program

USAID: US Agency for International Development

WHO: World Health Organization

WTO: World Trade Organization

21st Century Youth-Led Uprisings

*Note: *indicates the protests including an ongoing tent city in a city square. Underline indicates a country with prominent women initiators. Youth started these rebellions but were joined by masses of people of different ages and backgrounds. In some cases, youth includes people in their early 30s. See photos of uprisings.*

Serbia: 2000. President Slobodan Milošević was ousted by a group called *Otpor* (Resistance). The rebels provided a model for later uprisings, including Kyrgyzstan, Azerbaijan, Belarus, Georgia, Ukraine, and Egypt.

Philippines: 2001. People Power II protests led by university students ousted President Joseph Estrada who was accused of corruption.

Malaysia: July 2001-2015: The "freedom generation" led the Bersih (means clean) campaign for democracy using social media and mobile phones, building on Bersih 2.0 in 2007, and followed by Bersih 3.0 in 2012 and Bersih 4.0 in 2015. Demonstrators wearing yellow T-shirts called for an end to "money politics," united various ethnic groups chanting, "We are the Children of Malaysia" (*Kita Anak Malaysia*). As usual, police used excessive force against the crowds, which attracted more supporters. In 2013, the opposition won the popular vote by advocating government transparency. Similar to other global youth protests, Malaysian activists believed in non-violence, humor, generations working together and use of social media.

Georgia: 2003. *Kmara* (Enough) protests against rigged elections led to the resignation of President Edward Shevardnadze in the Rose Revolution. Youth accomplished this by building on earlier organizing against the corrupt education system in 2000 and by learning from Otpor.

*****Ukraine**: 2004, *Pora* (It's Time). Thousands of young protesters organized against rigged elections in the Orange Revolution. Young people from other former Soviet countries came to observe how to make a "Color Revolution."

Zimbabwe: 2004. *Sokwanele* (enough!). Youth protesters distributed CDs and condoms with Bob Marley lyrics on them, painted graffiti, and continued campaigning against President Mugabe until the present. Their focus is on fair elections, "Campaigning non-violently for freedom and democracy in Zimbabwe."

*****Lebanon**: 2005. Cedar Revolution protesters blamed Syrians for the assassination of Prime Minister Rafik Hariri on February 14 and protested the 15,000 Syrian troops stationed in their country. Well-connected and media savvy young people organized large demonstrations resulting in the withdrawal of Syrian troops, the resignation of the government, and the first free parliamentary elections since 1972 (see photos).

Chile: 2006-2016. Starting in 2006, the Penguin Revolution mobilized hundreds of thousands of demonstrators to protest privatization of the education system, with another wave in 2011 that continued to the present.

Venezuela: 2007. The catalyst for student organizing occurred when the government shut down their favorite TV station, a voice of opposition to the government. Their demonstrations in turn shut down the city but the station wasn't reopened. Next, students mobilized for a "no" vote against Hugo Chavez' 44-pages of 69 constitutional amendments that would have permitted him to be president for life and enlarge his powers. They defeated his proposals.

Burma/Myanmar: 2007. In the Saffron Revolution, students and thousands of Buddhist monks and nuns organized non-violent resistance against military rule. A 24-year-old Burmese monk named Ashin Kovida started the Saffron Revolution. He saw a clandestine film *Bringing Down a Dictator* about Otpor's success in Serbia. Ruling General Thein Sein gave up his military rank to become civilian president in 2011. Famous democracy advocate and Nobel Peace Prize winner Aung San Suu Kyi was released from almost 15 years of house arrest in 2010 and was elected to parliament in 2012. Some argue that her campaign was funded by the US State Department, similar to other Color Revolutions.

Moldova: 2009. Natalia Morar, a 25-year-old journalist, organized a protest against rigged elections that attracted 20,000 people to storm the parliament building in the first Twitter Revolution.

Iran: 2009. The Green Movement protested rigged presidential elections but didn't succeed in removing President Mahmoud Ahmadinejad (documented in the 2012 film *The Green Wave*). A common slogan was, "Where is My Vote?" The regime said the uprising was instigated by the US, UK and Israel. Many of the activists and journalists are still in jail. The government monitored social media use, indicating that it is a resource for oppressors as well as rebels.

Portugal: 2010-2011. "Referred to as "A Generation in Trouble," and a "Desperate Generation," young people organized protests against austerity cuts, inspiring later European protests. Portugal's public debt was equal to 90% of its GDP, leading to budget cuts in 2010. Austerity measures didn't solve the problem so a bailout was agreed upon with more budget cuts. Youth wrote their "Manifesto of a Generation in Trouble. "In March 2011 about 300,000 protesters demonstrated on the streets in the 12 March Movement.

***United Kingdom**: 2010-2011. University students organized about 50 campus occupations to protest tuition increases and other austerity measures.

In August 2011 riots started after a young black man was shot by police and protests against racism spread throughout England. Occupy London began on October 15 at St. Paul's Cathedral to protest economic inequality, lasting until the police removed the tents in February 2012 (see video).

2011

Tunisia: In the Jasmine Revolution, President Ben Ali resigned and fled to Saudi Arabia after a fruit vender set himself on fire to protest police corruption. The first democratic elections were won by the Islamist Ennahda Party. Party heads resigned in 2013 so new elections could be held, fearful of incurring the same fate as the outlawed Muslim Brotherhood in Egypt (photos online). Tunisia is the success story of the Arab Spring revolts that started in Tunisia and spread to Egypt, Yemen, Syria, etc., discussed fully in my *Global Youth Uprisings*.

***Egypt**: The revolution in Tahrir Square began on January 25. President Hosni Mubarak resigned only 18 days later. In July 2013, after a year in office, the first freely elected president, Mohammed Morsi was ousted in a military coup backed by large demonstrations due to his attempts to abrogate power and Islamize the government with the Muslim Brotherhood. The military retained power through the election of General Sisi as president in 2014. He outlawed freedom of speech and assembly and jailed youth demonstrators, called worse than Mubarak.

***Yemen**: In January demonstrations against President Ali Abdullah Saleh were led by a woman named Tawakkol Karman. Saleh resigned in November but manipulated behind the scenes. Elections were held in February 2014 but religious factions divided the country, led by Shia Houthtis rebels. They began as the "Believing Youth" in 1992 by organizing school clubs and summer camps. Saleh and the Iranians supported the Houthtis, while the Saudis entered the war against them in favor of President Abd Rabbuh Mansur Hadi in 2015, joined by US support. Much civilian damage and loss of life resulted from Saudi bombing and civil war. Children who survived lost out on their schooling.

***Oman**: January 17-April. Protesters demanded lower costs of living, salary increases, end to corruption, and more free speech. Sultan Qaboos responded by raising the minimum wage, changing cabinet positions, and with new government jobs and stipends for students at the Higher College of Technology. Separate tents for women and men were put in front of the legislature in demonstrators camped for three days in Sohar's main square. Slogans were included in foreign languages for the media. A Facebook page was titled "March 2 Uprising for Dignity and Freedom."

Libya: Uprisings began on February 15 after security forces opened fire on a protest in Benghazi. Demonstrators chanted, "No God but Allah, Muammar is the enemy of Allah" and "Down, down to corruption and to the corrupt." Muammar Qaddafi was killed in August while hiding in a drainpipe. In July 2012 elections a secular party won over the party aligned with the Muslim Brotherhood, but chaos continued with competing militias of mostly young men causing Libya to be a failed state and haven for ISIS terrorists.

Bahrain: Protests began on February 17 against the royal family's monopoly on the economy and government. Sunni King Hamad brought in Saudi Sunni troops against the majority Shia population. Angry Shia youth protested but dissent was stifled and the government tore down the Pearl Roundabout main demonstration site.

Morocco: On February 20, demonstrators took to the streets to limit some of the powers of the monarchy. What was called the February 20th movement was initiated by Amina Boughalbi, a 20-year-old journalism student, similar to Asmaa Mahfouz' call for protest in Tahrir Square in Egypt the previous month. They used horizontal rather than hierarchical organizing and shared roles for men and women. The youth-led February 20 Movement wanted a constitutional monarchy. The king offered reforms including giving up his claims of divine rights to rule and nominating a prime minister from the largest party in parliament but not a constitutional monarchy. Moderate Islamists won the November elections. The protests opened up free speech to criticize the government.

Mauritania: Youth led the February 25 Movement to protest poverty and corruption, posting on Facebook. It followed the January 25 "Day of Anger" organized by students at the Advanced Institute for Islamic Studies and Research to protest the closure of their school.

Syria: In March youth (ages 10 to 15) wrote the slogan of the Arab Spring, "The people want the regime to fall" on a wall in Daraa in southern Syria. Fifteen of them were jailed and tortured. Protests began to demand the release of political prisoners that month. The ongoing civil war between Muslim sects and President Bashar Assad displaced about half of Syrians from their homes as Russians and Americans got involved on opposite sides in a bombing campaign.

*Spain: Beginning in May, the 15-M movement of *indignados* started in Madrid and swept around the country to protest the 50% youth unemployment rate and austerity measures. Protesters occupied the Puerta del Sol until June, and then spread out in neighborhood assemblies. Austerity measures continued under a conservative government, opposed by new Indignado-inspired political parties like Podemos.

*Portugal: In May, inspired by the Spanish Indignados, the "precarious generation" protested unemployment and high cost of living for 15 days, organized as 15O. They chanted "Spain! Greece! Ireland! Portugal! Our struggle is international!"

*Greece: On May 25, "The Squares," the Direct Democracy Now! movement, was sparked by the Spanish protests. Suffering from the most severe austerity cuts, the *aganaktismenoi* (indignants) occupied Syntagma Square until August. General strikes brought out the largest crowds in June.

*****Malaysia**: 2011-2015. On July 30, inspired by the Spanish protests, Occupy Dataran was held every Saturday night in Kuala Lumpur from 8:00 PM to 6:00 AM. Like other Occupy groups, they held large assemblies communicating with hand signals and aimed to create real democracy, as stated on their Facebook page. The movement spread to other cities and continued in the following years with students in the vanguard. On New Year's Eve, 2012, hundreds of protesters wearing Guy Fawkes masks held a "V For Freedom" protest against restriction on protest marches in the capital. In April 2012, more than 300 students set up tents in the square to call for free university education and ending the student loan program. In May 2014, activists occupied the square to protest a new Goods and Services Tax that increased the cost of living. In 2015, students in yellow shirts and some wearing the Guy Fawkes masks demonstrated for the prime minister to resign due to corruption charges.

*****Israel**: A September tent occupation of Tel Aviv's ritzy Rothschild Boulevard demanded social justice. It was triggered by the high cost of housing and high taxes for the middle class. Daphni Leef, 25, was tired of high rents, so she used to Facebook to ask other young people to join her on the streets. Similar to other initiators, she was surprised by the hundreds of thousands who joined her in Tel Aviv and then in other cities across the country. The national student association joined in, along with other youth movements. They avoided the elephant in the room, the dispute between Palestinians and Israelis for land. Conservatives remained in power and property costs continued to rise.

Oman: In the summer youth groups demanded the resignation of the prime minister, a nephew of the Emir. He was replaced in November.

*****US**: In September, the Occupy Wall Street protests began in the financial district of Manhattan. The call to occupy was initiated by the Canadian magazine *Adbusters* and Egyptian leaders came to encourage them in an international effort. Occupy sites spread to cities across the US and the world, with the most publicity given to New York City and Oakland because of police violence. *The Guardian* listed and mapped 746 Occupy sites around the world in 2011. The sites cluster in North America and Europe.

Italy: On October 7, the national student union called a national strike, putting up tents in a square in Bologna. They were referred to as Indignados. On October 12 student and other groups protested in front of the national bank in Rome. On October 15 they marched on the day of global Occupy demonstrations initiated by Spanish rebels. Italian students weren't able to camp in Rome's Piazza San Giovanni because several hundred Black Bloc demonstrators (an anarchist group known for wearing black hoodies and throwing rocks in various countries) initiated a violent riot there and students lacked effective organization.

2012

Canada: In February's Maple Spring, in the *casseroles* (banging pots and pans) protest movement, Quebec students voted to walkout to protest tuition hikes. The strike lasted for 100 days (photos and video online). Martine Desjardins chaired the largest student group in Quebec, the Student University Federation of Quebec from 2012 to 2013. She also served as a political commentator and columnist, and ran for provincial office in 2014 but lost.

Later in the year Idle No More was started by three indigenous women and a non-native woman to protest proposed changes in environmental protection laws. They drew from their culture doing round dances to gather support for their movement. In January 2013, six young indigenous men walked for two months and 1,600 kilometers to parliament. They called it the Journey of Nishiyuu (human beings) for equal rights for all the reserves. Others joined them along the way. The movement was replicated by other occupied indigenous people around the world, including those in Palestine, Australia, New Zealand, and the US.

Mexico: In May, Mexican students in Yo Soy 132 demonstrated against media bias in the upcoming presidential elections. They called for fair elections and spoke against corruption in the narco state and neoliberal policies. Large protests occurred in 2014 after 43 normal school students disappeared. Some accused the PRI government of involvement in their disappearance.

Hong Kong: In May, secondary students formed an activist group called Scholarism to protest the mainland's efforts to impose patriotic education in schools. They led a sit in and a hunger strike in front of government offices, a precedent for their demonstrations in 2014.

2013

*Turkey: May 2013. The occupation of Gezi Park by environmentalists and critics of the prime minister started as a protest against Prime Minister Recep Tayyip Erdoğan's plan to cover the rare urban green space with commercial buildings, and expanded to protest his increasingly autocratic attempts to instill Islamic values. Gezi remained green but President Erdoğan continued with building projects that demolished other green spaces and increased authoritarian rule and attacks on Kurdish villages.

*Brazil: Youth-led protests against fare increases for public transportation in June expanded to protests against government spending on world athletic events rather than for social programs and against corruption. The fare increases were rescinded in São Paulo.

*Ukraine: 2013-2014. Protesters occupied Independence Square for three months to protest the president's delay in aligning with the European Union. President Viktor Yanukovych fled to Russia in February 2014, leaving behind a bankrupt country. Protesters in the western part of the country were angry about his reneging on an alliance with the European Union, under Russian pressure, and government corruption. Civil war broke out in Eastern Ukraine led by pro-Russian rebels.

2014

Bosnia: The Bosnian Spring occurred in February with demonstrators aiming to overthrow the corrupt government and to protest unemployment caused by privatization in one of Europe's poorest and most divided countries. Violent riots took place to protest unemployment (over half of the youth were unemployed) and lasted for several months with some youth burning government buildings. Protesters went on to organize assemblies in about 24 cities led by intellectuals. Prime Minister, Nermin Niksic called youth protesters hooligans, similar to Turkey's prime minister. Activists organized an independent trade union called Solidarity (*Solidarnost*) and the Movement for Social Justice to create direct democracy, but lacked large enough membership to make much change.

*Venezuela: In February, student protests at the University of the Andes in San Cristóbal spread around the country protesting police detention of students. Middle-class neighborhoods in Caracas protested the high inflation rate, shortage of basic goods like flour, and high crime rate. Opposition leaders were jailed. They wanted socialist President Nicolas Maduro to resign. The protests continued for months, with students camping in three plazas in the capital and in front of the United Nations office. The opposition aimed to remove President Nicolas Maduro from office.

*Taiwan: Students occupied the legislative building in March and April to protest a trade agreement with China. The Sunflower Revolution protesters carried banners stating, "If we don't rise up today, we won't be able to rise up tomorrow," "Save democracy," "Free Taiwan," and "We will let the world know you suck [President Ma Ying-jeou]." Their nationalism contributed to the election of a nationalist woman president in 2016.

*Hong Kong: In June and September to December, a movement for democracy organized an unofficial referendum to give voters the right to choose their leaders without Beijing's vetting the nominees, resulting in the largest demonstration in a decade. Occupy Central with Love and Peace was led by professors and students from various universities. Student organizations including Scholarism and The Hong Kong Federation of Students organized an overnight sit-in after the march until police removed them. They used familiar slogans such as, "power to the people" from the 1960s and "the people want…." used in the Arab Spring. A student leader explained, "Students hold the key to future" and asked, "If students don't stand on the front line of democracy, who else can?" In September, the Umbrella Revolution used umbrellas to protect from police tear gas attacks, hence their symbol of yellow umbrellas. Police cleared out the occupations on December 15. Thousands of protesters protested Beijing's November 2016 ruling to prevent two pro-independence legislators from taking their seats. They revived the use of yellow umbrellas. Some frustrated with lack of results from previous protests threw bricks.

*United States: 2014-2016. Black Lives Matter protests against police violence against young black people started in Florida when George Zimmerman was acquitted of the murder of black teen Trayvon Martin. Dream Defenders occupied the Florida state government during July to protest. Protests ignited next in Ferguson, Missouri, then New York City, and Baltimore when black men died at the hands of police in 2015. The hashtag #BlackLivesMatter was popularized by a woman activist in Oakland. Other women, many of whom identified as queer, organized marches and organizations in various cities, typical of the more inclusive leadership of youth organizing.

*North Dakota, United States: Standing Rock Sioux "water protector" Native American and allies occupied camps to protest an oil pipeline in North Dakota. Indigenous Youth Council members, youth runners, and youth who occupied Hillary Clinton's campaign headquarters were joined by protesters such as young actor Shailene Woodley. Arriving on horseback, youth set up the spiritual Sacred Stone camp on April 1, 2016, and were often on the front line of conflict with police and national guard.

Endnotes

1 https://www.youtube.com/watch?v=znYyB4cQ1mY

2 www.unfpa.org/swp/2004/english/ch9/page8.htm

3 www.ysriver.com

4 https://globalyouthbook.wordpress.com/2014/04/25/top-4-responses-to-global-youth-survey/
   http://globalyouthbook.wordpress.com/2014/07/04/social-movement-theories/
   https://globalyouthbook.wordpress.com/2014/07/04/global-youth-activism-definitions/

5 Emma Broadbent, et al., "Generation Z: Global Citizenship Survey," Varkey Foundation, January 2017.
   https://www.varkeyfoundation.org/sites/default/files/Global%20Young%20People%20Report%20%28digital%29%20NEW%20%281%29
   .pdf

6 Geraldine Pratt and Victoria Rosner, **eds**. *The Global and the Intimate: Feminism in Our Time*. Columbia University Press, 2012, p. 3.

7 Ibid, p. 21.
   http://www.youthpolicy.org/research/journals/
   http://arcyp.ca/archives/2421
   Journal of Research on Adolescence
   Journal of Adolescence
   Journal of Adolescent Research
   Youth & Society
   Journal of Youth and Adolescence
   Journal of Youth Development

8 Anita Harris, **ed**. *Next Wave Cultures: Feminism, Subcultures, Activism*. Routledge, 2008, Introduction. p. 190.

9 Alan France and Steven Roberts, "The Problem of Social Generations: a Critique of the New Emerging Orthodoxy in Youth Studies," *Youth Studies*, August 20, 2014, pp. 215-230.
   DOI: 10.1080/13676261.2014.94412

10 Dan Woodman and Johanna Wyn, "Class, Gender and Generation Matter," *Journal of Youth Studies*, Vol. 18, No. 10, July 2015.
   DOI: 10.1080/13676261.2015.1048206

11 Alan France and Steven Roberts, "The Problem of Social Generations: a Critique of the New Emerging Orthodoxy in Youth Studies," *Youth Studies*, August 20, 2014, pp. 215-230.
   DOI: 10.1080/13676261.2014.94412

12 http://www.tandfonline.com/loi/cjys20?open=16&repitition=0#vol_16
   Following are the topics and date posted online that pertain to young women: how to involve young Canadian women in provincial public police development (August 2012), Peruvian youth activism for sexual health (November 2012), Australian girls' attitudes towards women leaders (January 2013).

13 http://www.sciencedirect.com/science/journal/01401971/35/3

14 DOI:10.1177/0011392113479748
   http://csi.sagepub.com/content/61/4/491.short

15 http://mobilizingideas.wordpress.com/category/essay-dialogues/

16 Jeffrey Jensen Arnett, **ed**. *Adolescent Psychology Around the World*. Psychology Press, 2012, p. IX.

17 www.uleth.ca/conreg/icys/call-for-papers

18 Shamillah Wilson, Anasuya Sengupta, Kristy Evans, **eds**. *Defending Our Dreams: Global Feminist Voices for a New Generation*. Zed Books and AWID, 2005.

19 Emily Bent, "The Boundaries of Girls' Political Participation: A Critical Exploration of Girls' Experiences as Delegates to the United Nations' Commission on the Status of Women," *Global Studies of Childhood*, Vol. 3, No. 2, 2013, p. 174.

20 Rha Goddess and JLove Calderón. *We Got Issues! A Young Woman's Guide to a Bold, Courageous and Empowered Life*. Inner Ocean Publishing, 2006.

21 Meridith Weiss and Edward Aspinall, **eds**. *Student Activism in Asia: Between Protest and Powerlessness*. University of Minnesota Press, 2012, p. 1.

22 Shamillah Wilson, Anasuya Sengupta, Kristy Evans, **eds**. *Defending Our Dreams: Global Feminist Voices for a New Generation*. Zed Books and AWID, 2005, p. 205..

23 Anita Harris, **ed**. *Next Wave Cultures: Feminism, Subcultures, Activism*. Routledge, 2008, Introduction.

24 Mary Bucholtz, "Youth and Cultural Practice, "*Annual Review of Anthropology*, June 14, 2002, p. 539. 31: 525-552, 2002. http://www.linguistics.ucsb.edu/faculty/bucholtz/node/1

25 John McCarthy and Mayer Zald, "Resource Mobilization and Social Movements: A Partial Theory," *AJS*, Vol. 82, No. 6, p. 1212.

26 Peter Kelly, "An Untimely Future for Youth Studies," *Youth Studies Australia*, 2011, Vol. 30, Issue 3, pp. 47-53.

27 James Côté, "Towards a New Political Economy of Youth," *Journal of Youth Studies*, 2013.
   https://www.researchgate.net/publication/257365589_Towards_a_new_political_economy_of_youth

28 Samir Khalaf and Roseanne Saad Khalaf, *Arab Youth: Social Mobilization in Times of Risk*.

[29] Saqi Books, 2011, chapter by Johanna Wyn, p. 45.

Douglas Kellner, "Critical Theory and the Crisis of Social Theory," date unknown.

[30] http://www.uta.edu/huma/illuminations/kell5.htm

[31] http://sociology.emory.edu/faculty/globalization/glossary.html

http://wp.me/p47Q76-52

Yale Center for the Study of Globalization, Yale University

The Globalization Website, Emory University

The Institute for Research on World-Systems (IROWS), University of California at Riverside

New Global History, Massachusetts Institute of Technology

GW Center for the Study of Globalization, George Washington University

Globalization and Democracy Research: Responding to Globalization, Colorado University

Center for Global, International and Regional Studies, University of California Santa Cruz

Environmental demonstration, Chico, California

Chapter 1

THE FUTURE IS FEMALE

God gave us gifts; mine is to be a professional and well known throughout life, and prosper.
Aleja, 12, f, Columbia

We are smart people; we will change the world.
Sara, 12, f, California

In the case of women of the yesteryears and girls of the 21st century, there is a wide gap. The women in olden times never used to raise voice against injustice except a few, but today's generation has learned to revolt against the evil done to them.
Gunveen, 13, f, India

Girls are going to change the world. I promise. We are a product of the digital revolution, and with the tools of social media at our disposal, we can get the message of global change across the world.
Jules Spector, 14, in her blog Teen Feminist

I want to make mistakes so I can learn from it and others can learn from it. I want to be noticed, not just someone you walk past in the street. I want to make something of myself.
Talia, 15, f, Australia

I'd like to be the first Kenyan leader who completely eradicated corruption and poverty.
Lylac, 16, f, Kenya

The world will be saved by the Western woman. I could be reincarnated as a mischievous blond woman. He also joked that a female Dalai Lama would have to be very attractive.
The Dalai Lama

We've produced the most uppity generation of young women in history.
Gloria Steinem, feminist author

Women will run the 21st century…This is going to be the women's century, and young people are going to be its leaders.
Bella Abzug, Congresswoman, 1997

Contents: Young Women Leaders, Why so Brave?; What Motivates a Youth Activist?; the Future is Female; Uppity Girls' Activist Tactics; Feminism, the United Nations and Scandinavian Governments Stimulate Equality; Young Men's Viewpoints

On one level *Brave* explores global young women's recent courageous activism and the obstacles that remain for the world's over one billion young women born from 1980 to 2000.[1] Of the 600 million girls between the ages of 10 and 19, one-third of them live in India and China.[2] Another layer exposes unrecognized ageism and sexism on the part of scholars and other adults who discuss young people. A third layer looks at how girls and women organize democratic changemaking differently from males and how this will impact our future. There's never been a better time to be born female with women's rights guaranteed by many countries, especially after the United Nations' Beijing Platform for Action signed by 189 nations in 1995. The former president of Brazil, Dilma Rousseff told the UN General Assembly, "I am certain that this will be the century of women. In Portuguese, words such as life, soul and hope are feminine nouns. Two other words that are very special to me are also feminine: courage and sincerity."[3]

Brave asks why young women globally have higher aspirations and achievements than in the past and how their leadership will change our world. It also examines the forces that aim to keep them in their traditional subordination. This chapter examines how and why girls excel globally in educational achievement and horizontal organizing. Explanations for why girls now aspire to education and equality are considered, including the impact of transnational feminism, the United Nations and the model of progressive egalitarian countries.

Global attention to young women's issues and activism was ignited by Pakistani Malala Yousafzai's advocacy of education for girls since she was 11, awarded the Nobel Peace prize at age 18. Other well-known feminist activism includes protests against the gang rape of a New Delhi student referred to as Braveheart who one of the rapists criticized as unfeminine for fighting back and the "Bring Back Our Girls" protests against the kidnapping of Nigerian school girls by Muslim extremists Boko Haram. In the Americas, protests in the news oppose the murder of hundreds of girls and women in northern Mexico and indigenous girls in Canada. Globally, SlutWalks, Take Back the Night marches, and young women's leadership in the global wave of uprisings since 2011 indicate young women are taking action about their issues. Paul Mason observed that the activist political involvement of so many young educated women is new.[4] In a TEDxYouth talk Canadian Anjali Appadurai defined activism as challenging rotten systems of power in the interests of justice.[5] Born in India and raised in Canada, Anjali Appadurai began her activism at age 15 with the Red Cross, ran a Global Issues club in high school, and worked on climate change in college as she discusses in a TED talk.[6]

The Kenyan editor of *Pambazuka News: Pan-African Voices for a Better World*, Firoze Manji observed that young women are the most dynamic activists and predicts they'll be the leaders of the future, as does Micah White in his book *The End of Protest: A New Playbook for Revolution* (2016).[7] White points out that about 7,000 women entered the palace at Versailles in October 1789, in the first such march of women in recent history. They forced King Louis XVI to march back with them to Paris, a precursor to the French Revolution. A women's march was also influential in the Russian Revolution of 1917, according to Leon Trotsky.[8] He wrote, "A great role is played by women workers in the relations between workers and soldiers. They go up to the cordons more boldly than men, take hold of the rifles, beseech, almost command, 'Put down your bayonets; join us!'" Both marches were motivated by hunger and a bread shortage. In Saint Petersburg, women led over 100,000 workers on strike, chanting "Bread" and "Down with the Czar."

The most interesting gender finding of my survey of over 4,000 young people from 88 countries is that few differences exist between females and males and kids and teens.[9] The respondents are more likely to differ by region than by gender. Some of the small gender differences are girls are more likely to mention sports when asked what they do for fun, they're more critical of adult bad behaviors and would like them to be more understanding. They feel more loved in difficult times and for their successes than boys do; in rating their school they think good teachers are more important; they're more likely to want a business career, and girls are more likely to want their government to develop the economy. Studies generally show that females are more liberal than males.

Despite decades of feminist activism to empower girls, enormous obstacles remain as discussed in the unaffordable text *The Oxford Handbook of Transnational Feminist Movements* (2015, $210). "The abuse of women and girls is the most pervasive and unaddressed human rights violation on earth," stated former President Jimmy Carter in *A Call to Action: Women, Religion, Violence and Power* (2014). He faulted abuses against women committed in the name of religion, the tragedy that more girls are killed at birth than soldiers were killed in World War II, the fact that one in four US college women are sexually abused, and that more slaves are in bondage now than in the 19th century—80% of them are girls. He left the Southern Baptist Church (the largest Protestant church in the US) because women can't be pastors. The status of girls and women is the "great unfinished business of our time," agreed Hillary Clinton in *Hard Choices* (2014). Secretary of State John Kerry said at the World Social Forum in 2016 that the greatest barriers to economic progress are inequality faced by girls and women in their struggles to innovate and start a business.

Women and girls are not usually taken seriously as political actors, with few exceptions like Chancellor Angela Merkel. Based on her interviews with teen activists in the Americas, Jessica Taft reported in *Rebel Girls* (2010) that despite their activism and independence from adults, girls "are rarely considered and written about as significant political actors. They appear but do not speak." They're often left out of academic research on youth movements. Taft also reported that the research focus is on college students rather than teenagers. Although adolescents are the least studied age group, they're the most interesting to me. Like the boy in the "Emperor's New Clothes" tale, they're more likely to tell the uncensored truth about what they see.

Girls and women are also neglected in studies of globalization: Feminist and queer scholars point out "the near total absence of any references to women or feminism" in scholarly analyses of globalization.[10] An exception is the book *Gender, Youth and Culture* (2007) that explores gender sex-role socialization in contemporary global culture.[11] Globalism is defined as the transnational exchange of information, labor, people, resources, products and marketing, diseases, culture, and media. Some of the feminist issues that arise from globalization are poverty and the impact of government austerity programs on girls and women, sweatshop labor, domestic work in foreign countries (like Phillipina maids in Saudi Arabia), trafficking of sex slaves, new technologies and Internet activism, religious fundamentalism, and media portrayals of girls and women.

Growing awareness of these problems as shown on online videos resulted in what a British reporter called a feminist revival in 2013.[12] McVeigh observed,

> ...*a growing digital network of women who are part of the "great feminist revival." Spare Rib magazine is soon to relaunch, women's groups are enjoying a growth in interest, and online feminism is flourishing in blogs and tweets. Beyoncé and Madonna were in London for the Chime for Change concert, promoting global empowerment for women and girls. The F-word is back, with digital-savvy young women joining forces online.*

A British development charity started the #InternationalSisterhood campaign in 2016 where women shared on social media what led them to embrace international sisterhood, ranging from tampon taxes to the Taliban shooting of Malala.[13] An Indian high school blogger in Chennai, Vaishnavi, 16, explains what feminism is and the effect of traditional gender roles on both sexes in her country.[14]

International Women's Day on March 8 has been observed globally since the early 1900s, leading a reasonable person to think that problems like the following would no longer be pertinent in 2017: A UN fact-finding mission in the US in 2015 reported a shocking gap between rhetoric and the facts of "women's missing rights" in the US. They said, "In global context, US women do not take their rightful place as citizens." The report specifically pointed to the increasing barriers to abortion and other reproductive health care, low numbers of women legislators (the US ranks number 72 globally), a 21% gender wage gap, and cuts to social safety net programs. Many Trump cabinet appointees voted against the Violence Against Women Act and the Fair Pay Act, as well as being anti-choice and climate change deniers. The cabinet is the most dominated by white males since President Reagan, in an era when the Canadian and French cabinets are half female (albeit not in the power positions).

The silver lining of the Trump Administration is that women are in the forefront of standing up for human rights, including Senator Elizabeth Warren and Acting Attorney General Sally Yates, plus the large numbers of unknown women who show up at townhalls around the country and are running for local office. Representative David Brat told a meeting of conservatives in Virginia, "We're getting hammered. Since Obamacare and those issues have come up, the women are in my grill, no matter where they go. They come up to me: 'When is your next town hall?' And believe me, it is not to give positive input."[15] When the Senate prohibited Elizabeth Warren from continuing to read Coretta Scott King's letter protesting racist Jeff Sessions appointment as Attorney General, a Twitter storm resulted with the hashtag #shepersisted. Women posted pictures of heroines who persisted like Coretta Scott King, Rosa Parks, Margaret Sanger and Ruby Bridges. Tough Girl posts interviews with courageous women online.[16] The US State Department has awarded annual Women of Courage awards to over 86 women from 50 countries; "recipients reflect women's roles as agents of change and leaders in many of the crises and challenges facing the world today, from countering violent extremism to promoting security and recovery from the Ebola Virus Disease," the State Department said.[17]

Young women globally exhibit great courage in fighting for their fights. Think of Pakistani Malala Yousafzai's advocacy of education for girls since she was 11. As a Muslim, would Trump want to ban her from our country? Young women led more recent uprisings in Lebanon, Egypt, Yemen, Morocco, Israel, and Chile; the list is available on the sidebar that begins this book. Women and allies will continue to be in legislators' grills.

Examples of progressive aspirations from global SpeakOut girls follow.

I think that I born to be an important person to do what I intend in my life—be an engineer of nanotechnology on the NASA. Then put a company of Nanotechnology in Ecuador.
   Camilla, 11, Ecuador

I want to become a blacksmith.
   Nikita, 14, Netherlands

I'd like to be an explorer. Although it's dangerous, and I might have to pay my life for it, I still love it. To get close to nature, to listen to the harmonious sound of it, to go to the animal world to feel their special skills for survival, these are all interesting although I have to take risks.
   Zhangqihong, 15, rural China

I have a dream and one day it's going to be real. After I finish high school I want to be the first Palestinian girl pilot.
   Rafeef, 16, Palestine

Realize that girls have the same rights as boys. Some adults think that girls' duty is taking care of family. I would make them realize time has changed and goes with technology.
   Unknown, 17, Tanzania

I'd like to be the mayor of my village.
   Eman, 17, Bedouin Israeli

I want to be somebody who does what no woman did or only few do in my work. To be different in this way I need to be well educated and literate. I should have the feelings of equality between a man and woman like I can be equal to a man. I should have the ability to compete. Right now I have no interest in marriage. I am thinking to remain single in the future but if at all I am to marry, I would prefer to go by my choice. We don't have custom of selecting groom by the parents.
   Chutney, 17, Bhutan

What Motivates a Young Activist?

Why would Yara, a middle-class girl living in Cairo, risk her parents' disapproval and worry, as well as her life, by demonstrating daily in Tahrir Square in 2011? Conducting "history from the bottom," that is, listening to those who are not famous "great men," to find out what influenced an activist teenager, I interviewed Yara on Skype and in emails in 2013 and 2014 (see video[18]). She describes her experiences as a revolutionary. Yara's mother is very religious and wears *hajib* headcovering, but Yara is an agnostic who doesn't cover her hair, and is not constrained by traditional religious beliefs that girls should stay at home (influence 1). She doesn't think it's fair to condemn someone to hell just because they don't have certain religious beliefs. As a scientific person, she believes in Newton's law of conservation of energy, which she says can be called God. Her parents' education and class status enabled her to get a good education what supported her activism (her class background and education is influence 2). Yara's father is a journalist and her mother is an elementary school science teacher. Like her mother, Yara is a "science geek" who would like to major in physics or astronomy when she enters university.

Yara said the January 25 revolution wasn't made by the hungry, but was led by well-educated people like herself in a country where over a third of females and 18% of males are illiterate.[19] More than 35% of middle-school students ages 12 to 15 are illiterate due to large class sizes and inadequate teacher education. In rural areas girls leave school early to get married, which is in stark contrast to Yara's urban education, and two million women have never been in school. Unlike village girls, her father keeps Yara informed about political issues, and most of her school friends also had no idea what was going on; they didn't even know about leaders like Mohamed ElBaradei who floated the idea of a presidential campaign. Her friends simply talked rather than acting, so she thought she would have to leave Egypt to order to make a difference. She said many people supported dictator Hosni Mubarak because he was a familiar father figure.

Yara was 14 and 15 when she went to the streets and slept in a tent in Tahrir Square during the January 25 revolution, although Egyptian girls do not sleep in mixed sex gatherings. She knows martial arts, so the last man that tried to sexually harass her ended up with a broken hand (not being afraid and being angry is influence 3 on Yara's brave activism). She saw people killed by police gunfire, including one of her friends. Their deaths made her want to complete their goals even if it meant she would also be killed.

Yara and many of her peers around the world abhor the traditional cycle they are taught to follow: go to school, get into a good college, do a boring job, marry and have kids. They're ambitious and give each other courage to rebel through their global social networks (influence 4 on her motivation). Yara is deeply involved in *Harry Potter* books and films, the British hero and role model who routinely defies authority and succeeds.

Yara views herself as strong-willed and altruistic: "I'm the passionate outspoken girl, who will tell you exactly what's on my mind." She views herself as full of contradictions such as, "I'm the shy, awkward kid, who still steps up to steer. I'm the introverted social butterfly. I'm the girl who believes that helping people is her solitude. I'm the hotheaded politician who still believes in Utopia. I'm the down-to-earth type of person who refuses to take a back seat." As the first-born in her family with a younger sister and brother, Yara is expected to achieve (influence 5). She's determined to do well—a trait often associated with high-achieving firstborns.

A pattern for successful women is having an appreciative father whom the girl identifies with, rather than the mother. Yara's encouraging relationship with her father is similar to Malala Yousafzai, as described in her autobiography *I Am Malala* (2013).[20] Malala's father said in the feature film *He Named Me Malala* (2015), "We're one soul in two bodies." Yara describes her father:

> *My mom and dad were high school sweethearts. Their story as told by my dad is, "Fell in love, got hitched, left the small countryside for Cairo, and never looked back." I think it's something that affected me a great deal. Despite the fact that we live in Cairo, we never really lost that connection with the countryside. We go there all the time and the simplicity and beauty of the people and the life here made me appreciate this country a whole lot more. My dad is a journalist. He's basically an Arabic literature god! He taught me a lot. I remember one time when I was extremely nervous about my 6th grade exams (I am crazy when it comes to exams; I get really nervous), he stayed with me up all night reading me poetry. Just this year in my 12th grade I realized that I know and memorized poems that most of my colleagues have never heard of.*

> *Dad likes to talk. We talk about politics, Egypt, literature, music, and video games. I feel like dad gave me the basics and he let me build upon them whichever way I see fit. He didn't teach about the revolution, but he taught me about justice, peace, and love. He taught me to appreciate the little things, and see the*

beauty in the simplicity. He taught me that a walk down the Nile is not to be taken as mundane. He taught me to see Egypt in a farmer working in the field; in an old, decrepit family house; in a weird accent; in a pharonic temple and in Tahrir. I first went to Tahrir with him. He was crying all through and tried his best to hide it. Every time we chanted or screamed or sang in the square, my dad would cry a little harder. He's a sweetheart. He is my dad. I want a lot of things, but above all else, I want my daddy to be proud of me.

After the Tunisians succeeded in expelling their corrupt president, Egyptian youth gained the confidence to take action. Yara reported, "People felt and understood we are the power." (Hope is influence 7.) She thought of the Egyptian people as uneducated, but after the demonstrations she saw a different side of people as she stood side by side with girls who were on the front lines and with Christians and Muslims guarding each other during prayers. After January 25 she witnessed great positive energy as people cleaned up the square and painted the walls; she observed, "Everyone was trying to do something."

Yara was in Tahrir Square on January 25th, the first day of the 2011 revolution, right after she took an exam in her high school. She was involved previously with political groups like the April 6 Youth Movement and had some connections with the administrators of the We Are All Khaled Said Facebook page. That page changed public opinion with its photos of the battered young middle-class man killed by police. She said a lot of people administered the Khaled page. Her group of activists thought about 200 people would show up in Tahrir Square on January 25, but by around 3:00 PM they heard the ground shaking and were shocked when 80,000 people came to the square. (More on the Egyptian revolution in Volume 2 Chapter 3 and in *Democracy Uprisings*.)

In 2013, Yara joined approximately 100 people who organized a petition-drive led by a youth group called Tamarod to unseat President Mohamed Morsi after a year of his presidency. Initially, a group of about 15 unaffiliated youths frustrated with the Muslim Brotherhood's control over Morsi got together and contacted other activists they knew. They created a circle of over 1,000 people around the country to collect signatures on petitions for Morsi to resign. Yara said about 40% were girls. She explained that Egyptians are not extremist Muslims, so they got tired of the Muslim Brotherhood accusing people of being atheists. Her mother doesn't cover her face with a *niqab* that only shows the eyes and was therefore accused by some of being an atheist.

Tamarod's plan was to show the people that "a bunch of kids" could challenge the Muslim Brotherhood's long-established structures and weaponry (founded in 1928).

The youth group gathered more than 22 million signatures, although they didn't expect to influence Morsi who they said did not follow the constitution. Youth activists were unhappy to discover that Tamorod had been infiltrated by military intelligence in March and funded by the security forces to use Tamorod to oust Morsi. Tamorod wanted to show that the people owned the streets and Tahrir Square, but during the July 2013 demonstrations that ousted President Morsi, sexual harassment was worse than ever. Yara went to the square with her father but demonstrators begged him not to go into the square because of the violence. After the military coup and rule by General el-Sisi who was elected president in 2014, she's discouraged and believes that the people want a strongman ruler rather than democracy. She went to the US to attend university.

We can apply Social Movement Theory to understand Yara's activism. A movement succeeds when it makes better uses of its resources than the opposition (usually an autocratic ruler). The oppressive government utilizes its resources such as security forces and propaganda in portraying youth activists as hooligans or terrorists. The resources of young middle-class rebels include having the time, energy and ICT connections to organize with many others without much police interference. In a study of Asian student movements, the editors reported that student power is strengthen by self-identity as an activist, the university system, the government, other social movements and allies, and the stage of national economic development.[21] Yara's intelligence and school success gave her confidence to speak up against injustice. This served as a resource along with support from her generation of global Internet friends that refuses to accept the status quo.

Social Movement Theory emphasizes the importance of resources to be successful, including organizations, material such as money, moral advantages, and human volunteers. Yara didn't act alone, but was part of revolutionary youth groups such as the April 6 Youth Movement and Tamorod. She's currently discouraged about being a changemaker, but just as rain fills a previously dry riverbed, she's built a habit of activism that can be renewed. After the revolution, she started teaching low-income girls, typical of her generation's altruism. Yara illustrates the factors that encourage contemporary youth activists including: education, middle-class, a feminist parent, media role-models of rebels, easy communication with peers, feeling deserving of human dignity and anger about injustice.

To compare these young women activists with a male point of view, I asked a Pakistani university student what motivated him to be a changemaker. He teaches illiterate village girls in our Open Doors Literacy Project and has led various volunteer activities. Hassan's initial motivation was less idealistic than Yara's, more egotistical, and more reactive against his less supportive parents—at one point his mother wouldn't speak to him or serve him food:

> *I wanted to get away, make a name for me, remain engaged in any activity that would put me somewhere away from my family since I was getting a lot of shit from them as I was growing up. In the beginning, it was only community service projects for me, some time with friends and hangouts. Gradually, it turned into something more meaningful as I began to understand the community, the people and the needs. If I were more well-off, I wouldn't have ever opted for studying social science in university. The fact that I have been through all kinds of times makes me understand the lives of the individuals in comparatively backward backgrounds. Hence, it gives me a boost each time I am on the field and ensures I give my hundred percent. It has been a fantastic journey altogether!*

Conversations with brave girls like Yara and Sahar motivated me to write this book about their courageous and thoughtful activism and to do fundraising for my Open Door Literacy Project for girls in Pakistan and India. We've seen that incentives for activist girls include: religious and political beliefs, education, being the first born (they're more likely to be more highly educated[22]), having encouraging fathers, anger about injustice, courage modeled on media stories of fictional and actual rebels, and support from virtual and actual social media peers and friends.

Young Women Leaders

Feminist Standpoint Theory maintains that social research should begin from the bottom up, with marginalized people's lived experiences. In Marxist theory, a standpoint is a collective identity or voice gained through collective political struggle. Knowledge is grounded in a social context rather than in abstract universal truth. That approach believes that marginalized and oppressed people know the most about their situation and is touted as "one of the most influential and debated theories to emerge from second-wave feminist thinking."[23] This theory evolved from Marxist feminism along with the Third Wave focus on intersectionality. In addition to our gender, we're influenced by the intersections of our class, ethnicity, nationality, age, religion, and sexual orientation. As feminist philosopher Sandra Harding explained, "Standpoint theories map how a social and political disadvantage can be turned into an epistemic, scientific and political advantage."[24] Hence this book reveals the voices of unknown young women activists, while my *Democracy Uprisings Led by Global Youth* reports on both female and male youth leadership in recent uprisings.

Even many youth-serving organizations ignore youth or parade them as occasional tokens, according to Sacha Green-Atchley, coordinator for the Coalition for Adolescent Girls.[25] She told me that girls she dialogues with from various countries want to be respected and listened to, rather than patronized or ignored. As bright and informed people, they want to be included in the discussion of social issues and are frustrated with adults' excuses for not including them. British academic Karen Wells observed that the term "youth" usually refers to boys and young men because many young women in developing countries are not allowed to be independent adults and they're defined by the goal of becoming married mothers.[26]

Girls' aspirations are becoming similar to those of boys; they excel in school, and we see brave girls on the front lines of recent global revolutions. Young women's courage is astounding. In Egypt, SpeakOut student Yara (age 17) wrote in an email, "We learned a long time ago to not fear bullets, sticks, fires, or jail. We seek freedom and death with the same zeal that 'they' seek life in ignominy." (Her high school English teacher introduced us online.) I mentioned her to a *Guardian* reporter who included her and her photo in an article on young female activists in the developing world and our video interview is on the book YouTube channel.[27] Another young Egyptian activist, Kholoud reported about the revolution that unseated President Mubarak, "The leaders of the parties dress in suits and talk. The youth are out on the street acting. The young members of the parties are critical. They know how to team build."[28]

Like Malala, uppity girls challenge the education system. Yara reported, "My school doesn't have the newest appliances or the most advanced labs. Loads of things are wrong and the system of bureaucracy is stifling at times. However, once you learn how to circumvent the system and take the initiative yourself, it can be very rewarding." She reported, "In my school I'm not allowed to voice my thoughts; I get in trouble because of it. I refuse to let my voice not be heard. I'm a straight A student, so teachers are more or less tolerant." She earned a score of over 2100 on the SAT college entrance exam out of a possible 2400 points. In Ethiopia, Abeda (age 18) is similar in her willingness to question school authorities. Both got in trouble from teachers and their parents for asking challenging questions in class, as Abeda explains:

> *Education doesn't let you explore or ask questions, just read and follow the*

teacher. Don't ask challenging questions, don't ask why or think outside the box of our culture. Or you can ask about facts. I got B in conduct and didn't get the proper marks; teachers didn't appreciate, hate me, sent me into the office. My parents said this is about marks, so shut up, but I didn't. [Skype interviews with both girls are posted on the Global Youth YouTube channel.[29]]

Anyone who follows world news has heard of Malala Yousafzai, the Pakistani advocate for girls' education who started writing a blog for the BBC at age 11. She addressed the UN on her 16th birthday, wrote her autobiography *I Am Malala* (2013), is featured in a feature film of her life called *He Named Me Malala* (2015), and traveled to Syria and Kenya to meet with refugee children.[30] Craig and Marc Kielburger, Canadian youth activists in WE.org and Free the Children, invited her. She became a millionaire through book sales and public speaking fees and was able to donate around $1 million for education. The Malala Fund helps with her goal to educate children, especially the 67 million girls out of school. In an interview with feminist actress Emma Watson, Malala told her that she started identifying as a feminist after hearing Watson's talk to the UN about her HeforShe campaign. Watson advocated, "Let's not make it scary to say you're a feminist."[31] Watson appeals to boys to join the cause of gender equality and to speak up about it. Malala advised young people during the interview, "Don't think your age can stop you from moving forward and thinking your ideas won't work. Don't wait until you're grown up; that's too late." Watson agrees that ageism is a problem of discrimination similar to sexism.

Malala is the youngest person to receive a Nobel Peace Prize, shared with an Indian advocate for child safety, Kaliash Satyarthi, author of *The Light of the Same Sun* (2017). In his TED talk he urges listeners to make peace by getting angry about injustice. Malala celebrated her 18th birthday in 2015 by opening a girls' school for Syrian refugees in Lebanon paid for by the fund established in her name. Assertively, she demanded that world leaders buy books instead of bullets. She said, "We children should not wait for someone else to speak up. Stand up for your rights." She represents a pattern of successful first-born young women encouraged by their fathers, who are models of feminist parenting. When her teacher father was asked about his influence on Malala, Ziauddin said, "You should not ask me what I have done. Rather you ask me, what I did not do. I did not clip her wings to fly. I did not stop her from flying."[32] She was accepted as a student at Oxford College in 2017.

Another example of a high-achieving daughter encouraged by her Muslim father, SpeakOut student Sahar is in medical school in Pakistan where she is an advocate for women burdened by frequent pregnancies. Her father allowed her to be a high school exchange student in Oregon, while other members of the family were appalled at the thought of her traveling alone to the US to stay with a strange family. Sahar says about her father,

> *A man who always stood with his daughter against society, he has always been a perfect ideal since my childhood, making me believe in myself by trusting me blindly, a man who called me "Baba's Princess." If every daughter could have a father like him, no girl would ever be looked down upon. A barely literate man, he taught me the meaning of Education. He taught me helping poor people doesn't end at lending them with money or goods, but to sit with them as part of their family, tell them how similar we are, and generously give them the love.*

A third Muslim father-daughter team, Ayed Morrar and his daughter Iltezam organized a peace initiative in a West Bank town called Budrus. The Palestinian activist worked with Fatah and Hamas political parties and Israeli supporters to save his village from being destroyed by Israel to build its Separation Barrier. A DVD documentary (2009), *Badrus* tells their story, as its website explains, "Success eludes them until his 15-year-old daughter, Iltezam, launches a women's contingent that quickly moves to the front lines."[33]

Another documentary about a supportive father who encourages a rebel first-born girl, *The Eagle Huntress* (2016) tells the story of a Kazakh girl named Aisholpan, age 13, who lives in Mongolia. Her parents support her goal to become the first female eagle hunter in 12 known generations, although some of the older men say women should be home making tea because they get cold and they're not strong enough to withstand hunting for foxes in the snowy mountains. Aisholpan is the oldest child whose father believes girls and boys are equal. Her mother said she wishes she had more time with her daughter but she wants her to be happy. (They're nomadic herders but carry a solar array for electricity, have a motorcycle and truck, and get news on their radio. The children go to boarding school five days a week.) Aisholpan would like to be a physician but now her focus is on her eagle.

Young women led recent uprisings in Lebanon, Egypt, Yemen, Morocco, Israel, and Chile; the chronological list is in the Introduction and on the book website.[34] Young women protesters are on the street, rotating to the front lines against police attacks, as Yara was at age 15 in Cairo's Tahrir Square in 2011 (described in Volume 2, Chapter 5). Egyptian activist Jawad Nalbusi said the women in Tahrir were amazingly brave: "If there is to be a renaissance in this part of the world, it will be from women, not men. The women will lead."[35] Leader Asmaa Mahfouz reported, "Women participated, no different from men, in all aspects of the revolution. Women fought with police in Tahrir Square throughout the 18-day rebellion, and have continued to take part in street activism into the post-Mubarak era."[36] In the 2013 uprisings in Turkey, women were over half of the demonstrators.

Asmaa Mahfouz, 26, is called the Leader of the Revolution in Egypt because of her famous video appealing to men's honor to come to Cairo's Tahrir Square on January 25, 2011. Her parents forbade her to demonstrate on the street or use the Internet, so she used her phone to organize from her bedroom. In a similar role a month later, Amina Boughalbi initiated the February 20th movement in Morocco when she was a 20-year-old journalism student. She said, "I am Moroccan and I will march on February 20th because I want freedom and equality for all Moroccans." Libyan women lawyers like Salwa Bughaigis organized against Gaddafi in Benghazi. She was a founding member of the National Transitional Council and alienated Islamists by opposing making wearing the *hajib* headscarf mandatory for women because men are too weak to withstand the sight of alluring hair. This mother of three was killed by Muslim extremists in 2014.

When she was 25, journalist Natalia Morar organized a protest in Moldova in eastern Europe against the rigged elections that kept communists in power. Her campaign attracted around 30,000 people who stormed the parliament building in 2009 in the first "Twitter Revolution." She led the protest movement called "I am not a Communist" on her blog "ThinkMoldova." Like later organizers in Egypt and other countries, she was surprised at the massive turnout of young supporters. Other women also used blogs, videos and cell phones to publicize events and educate people about revolutionary issues. For example, blogger Lina Ben Mhenni (born 1983) used social media to spread news of the Tunisian protests started by the mother of the martyr who self-immolated to protest corruption in 2010.

A young Israeli woman, Daphni Leef, started the massive tent city protests in Tel Aviv in September 2011 against high costs of living, preceded by a movement of Mizrahi (non-European Jews) single mothers in the summer of 2003.[37] The September 3rd protest was the largest in Israeli history and spread from Tel Aviv to Jerusalem and Haifa. Protester signs stated "Walk like an Egyptian." Nobel Peace Prize winner Tawakkol Karman, age 34, is called the mother of the Yemeni youth revolution. When she accepted her prize in Oslo in 2011, she accurately predicted, "The revolutions of the Arab spring will continue through the effort of youth, who are ready and prepared to launch each stage and to fully achieve its objectives." Young women like Camila Vallejo are spokespersons for student rebellions; she was president of the Chilean university student union that took control of 300 schools. She said they wanted radical restructuring rather than reform, although she became a member of parliament in 2014, along with another Communist woman and two independent young male activists—all in their 20s.

Chile and Quebec have the longest and best organized activist student organizations. In the 2012 Maple Spring, Quebec students voted to strike to protest the proposed 75% tuition hikes. The strike lasted for 100 days (photos and video online), as discussed in Volume 2 Chapter 1.[38] Martine Desjardins chaired the largest student group in Quebec, the Student University Federation of Quebec, from 2012 to 2013, and then served as a political commentator and columnist. She ran for provincial office in 2014 but lost.

Despite women's leadership, a study of 843 protest movements from 2006 to 2013 reported that only 50 focused women's rights and 23 on LGBT rights.[39] The main protester themes were economic inequality and real democracy. Leftist groups often say women's issues and class inequality will be addressed after the revolution. This problem surfaces even in progressive Scandinavia: Graduate student Katarina Tulia von Sydow reported from Sweden, "Too often women's oppression is sidelined as a lesser cause, and women's experiences dismissed." She advocated that the international left "needs to believe women's narratives and support feminism—before the revolution. Now."[40] How a group responds to sexual violence such as occurred in Occupy camps in the US in 2011 is a test of which alliances are positive; do they blame the victim or the perpetrator?[41] Feminists critiqued male dominance in group discussions in Occupy demonstrations as in New York City and Madrid in 2011, as well as problems with sexual harassment. They formed their own associations and "safe spaces" because patriarchal hierarchy remains problematic and women continue to oppose it.

Even in countries with ancient patriarchal traditions like Egypt, China, Pakistan and India, educated girls advocate for equal rights. Dhwani (13, f, India) observes a decline in sexism among her peers, influenced by "Western culture." The Indian government established the National Policy for Empowerment of Women in 2001. Some young women associate the woman's movement with man-hating while others embrace the "f" word, as discussed in Volume 2 Chapter 9. An ambitious SpeakOut student wrote, "I want to eradicate the evils mainly faced by girls and solve the problems of girls" (Sunihta, 16, f). Another confident Indian girl states: "I think that I have the talent to achieve all these things: I'm here on earth to vanquish corruption, help people and make myself an honest memorable person in the world" (Rita, 17, f). A Pakistani girl, age 18, was a victim of attempted honor killing by her father and uncle because she married a man without their permission. Saba said in *The Girl in the River* documentary (2015) that she hoped for a daughter so the girl could be brave, get an education, work if she wants to, stand up for herself and do what she wants. It's profound that a girl from such a traditional patriarchal family thinks in terms of female bravery and freedom.[42]

When encouraging youth engagement and participation in their communities, adult leaders recognize that girls face gender-specific obstacles in both developed and developing nations such as the need for permission from their families to leave home for meetings, safety, peer pressure, and loss of confidence in their self-expression in adolescence. The girls living in developing countries who were interviewed in "Girls Speak: A New Voice in Global Development" (2010) agreed they lacked power to act on their wishes, such as to go to school and delay marriage and childbearing. The International Center for Research on Women researchers found that girls know what they want but often lack the power to make their own decisions.[43] They suggested that adults who work with youth need training on how to empower girls because engaged youth have better outcomes and self-confidence.

Girl power is put on the pedestal in development programs, as the saviors of their communities due to their individual hard work, instead of focusing on feminist movement building. The Association for Women's Rights in Development (AWID) pointed out that collective organizing is key to successful movements, such as women's suffrage and civil rights. An example of pretending that girls have more power than they actually do in a neoliberal global economic system is *The Girl Effect* campaign. It uses short videos, produced by the Nike and NoVo Foundations, to encourage funding for girls in development. The videos points to the 600 million girls in developing nations as the solution to poverty, the way to "change the course of history;" and "The most powerful force of change on the planet is a girl."[44] Common sense and a little investigation tells us that girls have very little power, so the Girl Effect campaign is not based on reality but an emotional need for a symbol of goodness and self-creation. Girls are stereotyped as less dangerous and aggressive than boys, although decades of studies show that girls' aggression is just indirect; for example, they get the teacher to punish an enemy rather than hit him or her.

Of course this fantasy obscures the reality of the 1% of the very wealthy elite and increasing inequality, reduced government support, and youth unemployment that individual entrepreneurs can't solve. Because of economic problems, almost 32% of Americans ages 18 to 34 live with their parents--51% of men ages 18 to 24 and 47% of women.[45] About seven million men ages 25 to 54 were not in the in labor force in September 2016, many suffered from chronic pain and took painkillers daily.[46] In Europe, almost half of young adults ages 18 to 30 live with their parents, including 26% of women ages 25 to 29, compared to 34% of men.[47] More than a fifth (22%) of European young adults suffer "serious [economic] deprivation." Peter Matjašic, president of the European Youth Forum, said the reality that high youth unemployment is over 50% in some Southern European countries, means youth are still in the "full force of the storm" that followed the Great Recession of 2008.

The most researched areas about girls in developing countries are how to involve them in Participatory Action Research, such as by youth-serving organizations such as Youth on Board, founded in 1994 by student organizer Karen Young for high school students. A useful publication for youth leadership is "15 Points to Successfully Involving Youth in Decision-Making."[48] Increasing numbers of studies report on how to involve girls in being changemakers.[49] Girls create their own tactics as activists, using art and dance and music, working with student or youth groups and NGOs. Girls' appreciate adult mentorship but criticize being disrespected and marginalized as future leaders.

An example of research about the benefits of empowering women is the World Bank's "Voice and Agency" for girls and women.[50] They report on the multiplier effect, in that education for girls increases their earning ability and inhibits child marriage and too early childbirth. When women do paid work, poverty decreases and the GDP increases. The UN Food and Agriculture Organization report "Women—Key to Food Security" concluded that if women farmers had access to the same resources as men, the number of hungry people would be reduced by 150 million.[51] Despite lip service by development experts to the importance of including girls and women in development programs, a small percent is spent on gender equality in these programs funded by the UN, NGOs and governments.

North American-based leadership programs for girls are listed in the endnote.[52] The Free Child Project gives many examples of youth activism programs and resources around the US, a useful site for learning about how to encourage youth activism.[53] Cascading Leadership trains older adolescent girls and young women to teach younger girls. Another organizing tool is Hart's Ladder that diagrams the levels of youth participation from being manipulated by adults and tokenism to youth-led activities.[54]

To me, the most important issue of our time is climate change, also called "climate weirdness." Young environmentalists agree: A 17-year-old environmental activist from New Zealand addressed the Rio+20 Earth Summit in 2012. Brittany Trilford's message was similar to that given 20 years previously at the first Rio Summit by 12-year-old Severn Suzuki from Canada. She told adults, "You must change your ways. I'm losing my future." Both girls' speeches are on YouTube.[55] Trilford told representatives of 188 nations at the largest-ever environmental summit that she represented the world's three billion children who demand action so they can have a healthy future. In an interview with radio host Amy Goodman, Triford said that youth are a powerful force, but they sometimes underestimate their strength and should "take power" as "the voice of youth is so strong, so clear, so truthful."[56] The UN compiled a report on "Youth in Action on Climate Change: Inspirations from Around the World" (2013), available online.[57]

Why so Brave?

Academic Charles Kurzman highlights youths' "sudden prominence of bravery" and willingness to engage in "risky protest," as in the Arab Spring. A reason for their courage is that youth under 30 are about half of the world's population. Youth are a powerful force, because of their numbers (about 1.8 billion aged 10 to 24 and another quarter of the world's population under age 10[58]) and ICT communication skills.[59] Media plays a part in this increase in young people's bravery because it connects them in a network of information and encouragement. Fearlessness characterizes young activists today, both women and men, partly because middle-class youth grew up playing fierce video games and were desensitized by violent movies. Teen Egyptian activist Yara is inspired by Harry Potter movies and books in which Harry, Hermione and Ron defy authority--the most widely read book series in history.

Historically, women's leadership was inspired by the belief that the Holy Spirit guided them, like the teenage Joan of Arc, or the 19th century women founders of US religions including Christian Science, Shakers and Seventh Day Adventists. Some Muslim women said Allah guided them: A Libyan rebel against Muammar Gaddafi, Mervat Mhani said she and other women rebels didn't think, they just acted, because they had to and Allah was on their side.[60] Today the inspiration for young activists is more often justice, freedom, and human dignity rather than the Holy Spirit, political party, union or class.

Gen X has liberal viewpoints: The Varkey Foundation released a study that claims to be the first and largest global survey of Generation Z attitudes in 2017 because there's "very little in-depth reputable polling on the opinions and attitudes of Generation Z."[61] It surveyed 20,088 young people ages 15 to 21 from 20 representative countries in 2016. They were part on online research panels, meaning they all had access to the Internet. Their results reinforced the Global SpeakOut survey findings that youth attitudes are "remarkably similar" globally: They're generally happy, comfortable with diversity, value helping others, are not religious, and are most influenced by their parents. Opposing prejudice, 89% believe men and women should be treated equally (especially in Canada and China), 74% believe that transgender people should have rights, 66% believe in safe and legal abortion, 63% believe same-sex marriage should be legal, but only about half believe in free speech if it's offensive to religion or minority groups. Support for free speech is highest in Turkey and Argentina--countries with a history of authoritarian governments, and lowest in Nigeria and China. Young people in 14 out of the 20 countries are supportive of immigrant rights in their country. Few think a person's religion is an important factor in selecting a friend. Only 3% think fame is the most important factor in choosing a career. It's hopeful for our planetary future that Gen X cares about relationships and doing service more than making money or becoming famous.

Young women today have potential role-models in older female writers who courageously pioneered major social movements, including American environmentalist Rachel Carson (*Silent Spring*), Indian environmentalists Vandana Shiva (*Biopiracy*) and Arundhati Roy (*The God of Small Things*); and French philosopher Simone de Beauvoir (*The Second Sex*). Second Wave feminists Betty Friedan (*The Feminine Mystique)* and Gloria Steinem (*Outrageous Acts and Everyday Rebellions)* led the movement for gender equality. Canadian Naomi Klein (*No Logo* and *This Changes Everything: Capitalism and the Climate*) and Annie Leonard (*The Story of Stuff* and her film *The Story of Change*) write about the global justice movement and environmentalism. (Canadian Chris Dixon compiled a social movement research bibliography.[62])

Global feminist organizations spread the belief in gender equality,[63] as do current female role models. British professor Anthony Giddens argues in *The Transformation of Intimacy* (1993) that increasing equality for women, initiated by women, is the most radical recent social change that expands from women's rights to broader social, sexual and family spheres. Angela Merkel tops *Forbes'* list of the world's 100 most powerful women.[64] The list includes nine heads of state, 28 CEOs, heads of important institutions like the IMF, and a few entertainers like Oprah Winfrey. Their combined social media followers add up to over 812 million.

Feminists have male allies like Jimmy Carter and former Socialist Spanish Prime Minister Jose Zapatero who declared,

> *I'm not just antimachismo, I'm a feminist. One thing that really awakens my rebellious streak is 20 centuries of one sex dominating the other. We talk of slavery, feudalism, exploitation, but the most unjust domination is that of one half of the human race over the other half. The more equality women have, the fairer, more civilized and tolerant society will be. Sexual equality is a lot more effective against terrorism than military strength.[65]*

Under Socialist Prime Minister Zapatero, Spain required that women make up half of its cabinet and half of all company boards. Zapatero appointed 31-year-old Bibiana Aído, head of a new Ministry for Equality although she was removed after three years due to budget cuts. Neus, a SpeakOut Spanish graduate student, commented:

> *Yes, equality in the government cabinet is what he promised that would do if he got elected. It is the first step towards a more egalitarian job market, since we still have lower salaries for the same position that a man has in the private sector and most of the high position jobs are given to men. I guess that the public sector is the one that has to model and demonstrate women's abilities and then the private may follow. We are in the very beginning, but things are changing; we have to keep pushing for our rights!*

As an egalitarian generation, both boys and girls are less tolerant of racism, sexism, classism and homophobia than their elders. Other characteristics of young generations are discussed in *Global Youth Values Transforming the Future* and on the book website.[66] In contrast, radical student groups in the 1960s were infamous for relegating young women to clerical work and to the bedroom. When Stokely Carmichael was asked about the role of women in SNCC (Student Nonviolent Coordinating Committee) in 1964, he answered their position is "prone." A few alpha males ran the show then, while today leaderlessness is valued and women are more often accepted as equals. Spanish professor Raimundo Viejo explained in the Canadian *Adbusters* magazine, "The anti-globalization movement was the first stop on the road. Back then our model was to attack the system like a pack of wolves. There was an alpha male, a wolf who led that pack, then these who followed behind. Now the model has evolved. Today we are one big swarm of people."[67] This trend favors gender equality.

AIESEC's large 2015 YouthSpeak survey confirmed that Millennials are more indi-vidualistic, more confident, and globally minded than previous generations.[68] The larg-est global organization for university students, AIESEC (their formal title) surveyed 42,000 young adults, ages 18 to 25, from 100 countries and territories. The countries with the most respondents were China, India, Indonesia, Algeria, and Poland. Most respondents were students, over half were AIESEC members, most lived outside North America, and 59% were female. Many respondents want to see YouthSpeak develop into a youth movement in order to influence decision-makers.

A confident generation, over two-thirds (64%) of the AIESEC respondents intend to be leaders or senior decision-makers. Very entrepreneurial, the majority of the re-spondents are business students, followed by social sciences and engineering. Amaz-ingly, only 9% don't have plans to become entrepreneurs. Their career goals involve business and meaningful work in this order: work for a multinational company, head their own businesses, and work for an NGO. They like to have fun and value mean-ingful work and their media exposure to global issues leads them to care about social problems. A high salary is not typically as motivating to them as creative work for an employer who makes a positive contribution, in addition to providing ongoing learn-ing opportunities--preferably global.

When asked by AIESEC who influences you in your career decisions, friends were cited much more often than adult family members or professors. SpeakOut student Sneha (16) confirmed from India, "Our generation mostly values friends higher than family, which has both positive and negative sides. We also know how to live and not just merely survive. But in that process we have lost all the worth we had for health and wealth. We also don't know what real love is." When asked by AIESEC, "What is most important to you in the first five years of your career?" the top responses were global opportunities, constant learning, meaningful work, and challenging work. Their ideal workplace is creative, challenging, fun, global, dynamic and purposeful—in that order. They value experimentation over following rules. The idea of earning a high salary in a 9 to 5 job is outdated because Millennials want to grow and learn at work as well as outside of work. Since they'll soon dominate the workforce, work should become more horizontal and less hierarchical, as well as more experimental and flexible, and more creative, with fewer rules. A high salary is not enough to motivate a typical university graduate today.

Not surprising for students, when asked what is the most serious global issue, AIESEC respondents focused on better education, followed by poverty issues. I was surprised that only 9% mentioned climate change. They like to learn online, from peers and experientially and are critical of formal education. They trust peers more than authority figures. In a UN My World survey with 4.4 million respondents ages 16 to 30, they also picked a good education as the most important global issue, followed by better healthcare, better job opportunities and an honest government.[69] Climate change was at the bottom of the list.

Media Influence on Girls

Media is highly influential in shaping contemporary attitudes since middle-class children spend many hours a day in front of a screen, as discussed in the global media chapter. Even some rural villages have battery-powered TVs and hand cranked radios. Young children in North America and abroad watch TV cartoon series with girls portrayed as the smart ones, including *Word Girl*, *Peg + Cat*, *Olivia* the pig, African-American *Doc McStuffins*, and Latina *Dora the Explorer*. *Kim Possible* is another Disney TV superhero, a high school girl who saves the world from bad guys, like Word Girl. Disney TV cartoon princesses portray more traditional femininity including the Princess Sophia TV series that features tea parties (see their photos and books about these characters such as *Cinderella Ate My Daughter* and *The Princess Problem*[70]).

In contrast, young male main TV characters often fight with each other not just villains, like *Mike the Knight*, *Kung Fu Panda*, *Jake and the Neverland Pirates*, the *Teenage Mutant Ninja Turtles* and *Avatar: The Last Airbender*. I asked SpeakOut student Aishwarya about what Indian kids view: "Children here watch *Tom and Jerry*, *Powerpuff Girls* and all sorts of the cartoons coming from overseas. Of the new Indian ones, most notably *Chotta Bheem* is a favorite among kids these days. Bheem was a mythological character who was very strong.[71] With the help of his wit and strength he helps his friends and villagers."

An exceptional princess is Merida whom Disney Studios describes as "an adventurer by spirit." She's an archer and horseback rider who "wants to control her own destiny." Her movie *Brave*, was released in 2012. The rebellious Scottish princess who refuses to be married, competing for her own future with her bow and arrow. Another fearless princess is portrayed in *Frozen* (2013). A popular animated film titled *Inside Out* (2015) explores the emotions of an 11-year-old girl as she learns how to cope with the grief of moving from Minnesota to California because of her father's new job. *Epic* (2013) also features a girl forced to make a move, how she copes and becomes a hero.

All these heroines are from privileged families but teach girls that they can be strong and conquer difficult challenges.

Although I didn't find reviews that emphasized this central theme, a girl as the savior of the world is portrayed in the 2015 Disney film *Tomorrowland*. In the movie, high school student Casey Newton is brilliant, brave and optimistic like Athena, a human–like android (played by a 13-year-old) who recruits her to stop the destruction of the earth. Casey's NASA engineer father's motto was, "If two wolves always fight, one is despair; the other is hope, which wins? The one you feed." George Clooney's character Frank realizes that Casey's optimism is the key to victory because as a science geek she knows how things work and takes risks. Because the girls don't accept the inevitability of destruction, they change the future. They recruit young androids to find other dreamers in order to foil the pessimists' plot to harm the world.

Windows 10 software ads played on this theme the same year, showing children from different countries with the voice-over, "One of these kids might be the one to change the world. We just need to make sure she has what she needs."[72] In one ad a girl uses the software to suggest how to save the oceans from pollution. Another ad shows an African-American girl drawing while the voice over suggests, "Who knows, she could create the next masterpiece." The emphasis on including girls in developing countries plays on the same theme of the innocent girl as savior.

Another example of the brave, smart, young heroine is in *The Hunger Games* young adult novels and films (2012-2015) featuring Katniss, age 16, a clever and compassionate warrior-savior in a dystopian world. When young Hong Kong student activists launched a political party of their own, their poster featured co-founder Agnes Chow shooting an arrow with flames behind her, shown on the cover. The poster says in English "The Younger Games." Another teenage female fighter is Tris in *Divergent* (played by an actor who said she is not a feminist because she wants balance[73]), part of another young adult dystopian series of four films (2014 to 2016). The series is set in a post-war Chicago where people are grouped in factions by emotional type; the government fears and outlaws Divergents because they think independently. Dystopia is a common media theme in an era that journalist Roger Cohen described as "The Great Unraveling" in need of salvation.[74]

Other examples of principled, smart and fearless girl movie characters are Hermione in the eight *Harry Potter* film series (2001-2011); Mattie, age 14, in *True Grit* (2010); Hit-Girl Mindy in the *Kick-Ass* series comics and films (2010 and 2013; and Teresa, age 15, in *The Maze Runner* (2014). *Veronica Mars, and* Max in *Dark Angel.*

Buffy the Vampire Slayer fought evil in a TV series. (Teens voted on their favorite TV shows, selecting the top five shows: *Pretty Little Liars, The Vampire Diaries, Teen Wolf, The Secret Life of the American Teenager, and The Fosters.*[75])

A DC Comics series called *Pres* portrays Beth Ross as the first female teen (age 18) president, elected on Twitter in 2036.[76] A feminist Indian comic book series called Priya's Shakti portrays a girl who is shamed after being raped, retreats to the forest, where she is given magical powers by the goddess Parvati and rides on the back of a tiger to assist other victims. Goddess imagery is still used in China where the 30 foot tall Goddess of Democracy statue motivated Tiananmen Square democracy demonstrations in 1989 and recently when social media in China refers to Ivanka Trump as a goddess and follows her self-help guides. Business woman Li Moya, 31, reported, "A lot of people think Ivanka is the real president. We think she has the brains, not her father."[77]

On the other side of idealization of heroic femininity is a series of American books and media about mean and aggressive girls who bully and terrorize other girls: *Fast Girls: Teenage Tribes And The Myth Of The Slut* (2003), *Queen Bees and Wannabes* (2002), which inspired the TV series and film *(2004)*; and *Little Girls Can Be Mean: Four Steps to Bully-Proof Girls in the Early Grades* (2010). Jessica Poe, who critiqued this book, reported that the theme of *Mean Girls is* "actually that girls should not be mean to one another, a cult classic among girls in their 20s." The globally popular HBO series *Game of Thrones* features tomboy Arya Stark who disguises herself as a boy, trains in sword fighting, and is disgusted by traditional feminine pursuits. She makes a list of the people she intends to kill during Season 4, when she is 14 and has already killed numerous men. She continues to kill men on her list in Season 6, serving an enemy his dead sons cooked in a pie. (The actor who plays Arya, Maisie Williams campaigned for refugees stranded in Greece when she was 19, visiting camps to publicize their plight.)

Twenty other TV mean girls and women are listed in the article cited in the endnote.[78] An example is a teen movie called *Sleepover (2004)* about the good girls against the mean girls, where of course the good clique wins. All the girls are focused on being popular, looking attractive, and getting to sit at the exalted lunch spot by the fountain at the high school. One of the girls who is heavier than the others frequently puts herself down for her weight and says that guys aren't attracted to her because of it.

The wicked sexual temptress is the flip side of the good virgin girl and the compliant wife and mother satirically portrayed in the film *Stepford Wives* (2004). She appears in the Old Testament as Eve, Delilah, and Jezebel who lead men astray and in modern films as Alex in *Fatal Attraction* (1987) and the witch in *The Little Mermaid* (1989).[79]

Fear and resentment of women as sexual seductresses is an ancient fear, rooted in the Abrahamic religions. It's still alive, as SpeakOut respondent Emmanuel illustrates. An Ethiopian, age 17, he attends a Catholic boys' school. He states, "Most men suffer from an imperfection, seduction from a woman. I would like the skill of being immune to the seductive ways of a woman."

Over 2,000 women were killed in India in the last 15 years for being witches, often really over property disputes or blamed for illnesses; a video shows an activist in Assam State who opposes the tradition.[80] Australian Prime Minister Julia Gillard was greeted with "ditch the witch" signs, used again for another member of parliament, Sophie Mirabella. In Spain, Anna Gabriel is a leader in the Catalonian independence movement in a party called CUP (it translates as the Popular Unity Candidacy). Members of her own party attack her as a witch and whore.[81] Zimbabwe's President Robert Mugabe fired Vice-President Joice Mujuru in 2014 for using allegedly using witchcraft in a plot to assassinate him in rituals while "topless and with breasts hanging."

This glorification of feminine salvation and fear of the sexual temptress is not new. Western theology idealized the self-sacrificing virginal mother; therefore Catholics insist that Mary, mother of Jesus, was perpetually a virgin, and pray to her to intercede with her son for their salvation. Orthodox Christians believe that Mary maintained her virginity, but that she was not immaculately conceived like Jesus. Accounts of Mary's grace-giving appearances continue to surface around the Catholic world.[82] Muslim male terrorists believe they will be rewarded with the company of perpetual virgins in heaven, although some scholars believe "white grape" is a more accurate description of the term. It's easy to associate girls with virginity, meaning safe, not threatening men with their sexuality, controllable symbols of capitalist success with their diligence. I wrote my Ph.D. dissertation on 19th century Protestant ideas that glorified the pious pure feminine woman as the key to the salvation for the men in her family and circle of acquaintances. This is clearly the case in all of Harriet Beecher Stowe's novels, including *Uncle Tom's Cabin*. Although this theme is obvious, I was the first to write about it because of blind spots about studying women and girls, similar to the blind spot about the ageist neglect of youth.

Eve Ensler, of *Vagina Monologues* fame, wrote a book for girls titled I Am an Emotional Thinker (2010). After traveling around the world performing her play she apologized to girls; "I know we make you feel stupid, as if being a teenager meant you were temporarily deranged. We have become accustomed to muting you, judging you, discounting you, asking you—sometimes even forcing you—to betray what you know and see and feel." She told girls, "You scare us. You remind us of what we have been forced to shut down or abandon in ourselves in order to fit in."

Anti-Neoliberal Inequality

Girls are the symbol of their family's honor and the new neoliberal symbol of "Girl Up" power through consumerism and entrepreneurship. Neoliberal capitalism is defined by Henry Giroux as an economic and political policy that enables "elites to consolidate political and economic power in their own interests."[83] In the late 1990s, feminists increasingly attacked this capitalist system, realizing that austerity program cut-backs on social programs to pay interest on loans especially harmed women and children. (Chapter 5 is all about media influence.)

Some argue that feminist theory should be used as a strategy to topple global capitalism because it exposes the "hidden relations of oppression," the power structures within and between movements, the focus on the male heroes' direct actions, and what's omitted from social histories such as black women's role in the US Civil Right Movement. Building effective alliances "proceeds from the feminist practice of listening closely to and learning from the experiences of others, past and present."

Our worldview is no longer limited to our nationality or birthplace as people migrate and consume the same media (i.e. MTV, BBC, CNN, Al Jazeera, and Disney). The collapse of US investment banks in 2008 caused worldwide suffering since they sold bundled mortgages globally. Commodity chains like the one that produced your T-Shirt are a transnational product described in *The Travels of a T-Shirt in the Global Economy*.[84] Global organizations provide research on how to implement gender equality, including the UN, World Bank, International Monetary Fund, and the Organization for Economic Co-operation and Development (ODCD). Usually, the greater the power of women, the greater is a country's economic success, according to the OECD. The evidence is clear that women in government improve the quality of life of their constituents.

The New Global Left opposes neoliberal capitalism and the resulting increasing inequality between rich and poor. It includes movements that started in the 19th century (labor, feminism, anarchism, environmentalism, peace and human rights), plus newer movements for LGBT rights, fair trade, indigenous rights, global justice/anti-neoliberalism, food sovereignty, and development in the Global South (sometimes called the Planet of Slums) unified by new technologies.[85] Latin America's "Pink Tide" socialist governments led by Hugo Chávez in Venezuela are a central part of the leftist countermovement. A central meeting space is the annual World Social Forum, but most communication is on social media. A survey of attendees at the Forum held in Brazil in 2009 reported their top issues were, in this order: alternative media (194 responses), human rights, environmentalism, peace, anti-globalization, and feminism (117 responses).[86] Italian feminists coined the phrase "double activism" to describe feminists who are involved in women's organizing and other leftist organizations along with causes like environmentalism.

Young Women's Activist Tactics

In general, what's driving the recent cycle of activism are the effects of the recession of 2008 on increasing youth unemployment and growing awareness of increasing inequality with the 1% versus the 99%. Six men own as much wealth as half the world; in the US the 40 richest people own as much as half of all the others.[87] They don't feel obliged to share the wealth: Billionaire Charles Koch said, "I want my fair share and that's all of it." The Internet provides motivation for protesters, as with videos of police brutality and climate weirdness, or WikiLeaks reports of government corruption shared on the Internet. Slogans used by activists are shared on social media like brand names: "Enough!" "Democracy Now," "Peaceful, peaceful," and "The people want the end of the regime." Practical information is passed along such as how to counteract tear gas with onions, lemon juice or vinegar, as in Brazil's so-called "Vinegar Revolution" where police in São Palo outlawed carrying vinegar in demonstrations.

Activist academic David Graeber explained that "the enemy is becoming increasingly globalized and the only way it can be challenged is by global movements."[88] He believes that the global revolutions that started in 2011 "permanently changed the very language of popular democracy." Different from past movements, the new ones don't aim to take over the system from within or use force. They aim to "create a territory outside the system entirely," in what's called prefigurative politics that include awareness of feminist issues such as who speaks at meetings. Recent feminist activism is described in *Social Sciences For an Other Politics: Women Theorizing Without Parachutes* (2017) as "plural, prefigurative, decolonial, ethical, ecological, communal and democratic."[89] Women are the main leaders of prefigurative politics experimenting with creating concrete utopias, according to British academics Ana Dinerstein and Sarah Amsler. They describe these experiments: "From projects in cooperative production to anti-oppressive education, from radical ecologies and pedagogies to experimentation with new economic possibilities, concrete processes of prefiguration now clearly anticipate a better future in the present." This effort is in opposition to patriarchal, authoritarian, capitalist, violent and colonial structures.

Globally, young women are taking a stand. For example, 30 global feminist initiatives led by young women are listed at the Young Feminist Wire site.[90] Books written for secondary school students urge them to get involved, such as *Activism: Taking on Women's Issues* (2012) by Alexandra Hanson-Harding. However, women are often told to wait until the revolution occurs to push for gender equality. A study of 843 protests that occurred from 2006 to July of 2013 in 87 countries found campaigning for women's rights was featured in only 6% of the protests.[91] The main causes of discontent were in this order: anti-austerity and economic justice problems (such as rising food price that contributed to the Arab Spring revolts), lack of democracy, protests against international financial organizations such as the IMF, and human rights.

The first study of global young feminist organizing was conducted from 2014 to 2016, by The Young Feminist Fund (FRIDA) and AWID's Young Feminist Activism Program.[92] Most of the 1,500 organizations are from Sub-Saharan Africa (41%), Latin America and Caribbean (25%), and Asia and Pacific (16%). The survey found that 91% the young feminist organizations struggle with funding as their main problem. Half of the organizations had incomes under $5,000 in 2014 and 46% had no paid staff. Few are funded by local and national governments. Only one-sixth of them have existed for more than 10 years and most are small. Examples of groups are a radio show run by young women in Nepal, Beyond Borders uses art to empower feminism in Armenia, CHOUF works for LGBT women in Tunisia, and Salud Mujeres educates for access to abortion in Ecuador.

The young feminist groups often use majority rule (71%) and consensus (45%) organizing methods, but 38% report the leader of the organization makes decisions based on advice from the group and 23% rely on their board of directors (respondents listed more than one answer). Africans are more likely to rely on boards of directors and membership groups. The groups use innovative intersectional strategies, including "colorful and creative" "artivism" (art, theater, film, graffiti, social media, street mobilizations, school occupations, and so on) and street mobilization to assist other women. The most common strategies for changemaking are advocacy and lobbying (71%), education and training (61%), and "awareness raising" (51%). More than half of the respondents said they often feel unsafe because of their work, faced with backlash against feminism and religious fundamentalism (54%)--especially in MENA and Asia-Pacific, opposition from governments (39%), police (38%), community authorities (36%), and organized crime (23%). Only 12% had difficulty working with older generations.

The activists' goals are first to build knowledge and share information and second to build leadership and movements, rather than to provide services. They usually collaborate with other social movements and generations, but 47% are not officially registered. The four populations they focus on helping are like the organizers themselves, in this order, grassroots women, women human rights defenders, students, and LGBTQI. Some of their issues are violence against women (55%, a problem across all regions), sexual and reproductive rights (52%), empowering women politically and economically (56%), and access to education (18%). Other concerns are climate justice, sex workers, indigenous people, and disability rights. (Africans are most likely to mention AIDs.)

Global feminist groups work together in organizations such as The World March of Women, which unites over 6,000 grassroots groups working to end women's poverty and violence against women.[93] It was proposed by feminists from Quebec at the UN Beijing Conference on Women in 1995 and is highly visible at annual World Social Forums. Its International Committee meets to coordinate their groups. For example, in Geneva in 2015, representatives discussed migrant women, climate change, unsafe factory working conditions, and other problems created by a "patriarchal, capitalist and neo-colonial system that keeps using women, peoples and nature as objects and chattel for exploitation and the accumulation of wealth, which creates and deepens inequalities between counties and regions."[94]

Other feminist movements boil up with an organizational structure, such as strikes and marches. Iceland's "Women's Day Off" in 1975 got results when about 90% of women went on strike to protest economic inequality. The majority of Polish women went on strike in October 2016. In a Catholic country, the Polish legislature tried to outlaw all abortion, with penalties of up to five years in jail for the woman in the Fall of 2016. In response, over 60% of women surprised the government by going on strike on October 3 in over 50 cities, boycotting work and school, wearing black and carrying black flags in demonstrations in large cities. Informed by social media such as Facebook, they chanted "Stop the fanatics!" and "My body, my choice," "My Uterus, My Opinion," and "Women Just Want to Have FUN-damental Rights." One of the protesters explained, "You cannot change the world from your couch, you know." A Millennial protester observed, "In previous anti-government protests, it was our parents" generation on the streets. But with this, they have managed to mobilize the young, and we are very angry."[95] Many men joined in the protests and solidarity protests were held in other European countries and the US, as seen in a video.[96]

Foreign Minister Witold Waszczykowski commented derisively, "Let them have their fun."[97] He added, "There is no such problem as a threat to women's rights." However, the ruling Law and Justice Party backed down three days later when Jaroslaw Gowin, Minister of Science and Higher Education, said the Black Protests "caused us to think and taught us humility." The government was "scared by all the women who hit the streets in protest, " said former female Prime Minister Ewa Kopacz. However, lawmakers also voted down legislation that would have liberalized the restrictive abortion laws on the books. A 1993 law dictated that women are only allowed an abortion if the pregnancy is a threat to their health, if they were raped or the victim of incest, or if the fetus is defective. In the same month as the Polish strikes, tens of thousands of women also went on strike and marched in Argentina to protest violence against women and girls. The election of sexist Donald Trump fomented strikes around the world on International Women's Day, in a "new international feminist movement for the 99%," according to a US strike organizer Tithi Bhattacharya.[98]

Some activists use distinctly female tactics to be changemakers. During the Yemen revolution led by journalist and mother Tawakkul Karman in 2011, women used the tribal norm against violence against women in battle by sitting on the floor and reciting the Quran to keep soldiers at bay. In the 2007 international "Panties for Peace" campaign against military rule of Burma/Myanmar, women coordinated by a Thai group sent underpants to Burmese embassies because the generals believe that contact with women's underwear robs them of their power. The junta believed that touching a woman's pants or sarong saps their strength. Panties were also used in protests in India. Threatening female nudity jump started Liberian peace talks.

Withholding sex is another women's tactic as in the recent Ukrainian "Don't Give it to a Russian" T-shirt and Facebook campaign in 2014. Proceeds were donated to the Ukrainian army. Co-founder Irina Rubis said, "Sex is known for being one of the most effective elements of drawing substantial attention to campaigns. For us the slogan on the T-shirts is not about sex."

Because of these uniquely female strategies, Kavita Randas observes that the Second Wave feminist slogan "the personal is political" is still effective. Randas, former head of the Global Fund for Women, became a feminist at age 11 while growing up in India. When her aunt was widowed at a young age, relatives took away her colorful saris, gave her white ones to wear for the rest of her life, and broke her bangles.[99] Randas gradually changed from thinking old traditions must be eradicated to realizing there's a "third way" where women can use tradition to move towards equality. She gave the examples of the Quran's teaching of the importance of reading scripture being applied to female literacy and the use of old taboos such as the Liberian belief that seeing a woman remove her clothes in public is a curse. Women demonstrators used this belief as a tactic to pressure men to engage in peace talks.

Several Ugandan women carried on the tradition of nude protest: Dr. Stella Nyanzi protested at the research center where she works, explaining, "The weapons of the powerless never make sense to the powerful. You can laugh at and mock me for using my nudity against the illegal eviction from my office, but it was the only weapon I had in my battle..." Activist Dr. Laila Soueif reported that being a woman helped in some of their political protests in Egypt because, "In this culture, women just aren't taken that seriously, so it allows you to do things that men can't."[100]

In a campaign in Ecuadorian Amazon against oil companies clearing rainforests on Sarayaku indigenous people's land, the women brewed fermented cassava and gave it to the oil workers in their camp who passed out again utilizing traditional women's work. When the workers woke up, their guns were facing them in the hands of the Sarayaku women and men who ordered them off their land. They never returned. The activists reached out to other indigenous people and used media like their film *Children of the Jaguar* (2012) "to propose an alternative development—the development of life." Women stood against negotiations with the enemy. Patricia Gualinga has traveled around the world for indigenous rights, teaching, "We want to be a model that could be replicated."[101]

Some women activists use their bodies to make political statements because the female body has been covered and protected, sexualized, raped, sold, hit, hair covered or hair shaved, and seen as the temptress source of sin or the fertility goddess source of life and feminine values. A young woman in Turkey's Gezi Park occupation in 2013, Elif, age 20, said, "To feel that I am here with my body gives me power."[102]

Contemporary social movements often "organize around identity, 'values,' bodies and emotions," rather than emphasizing organizations or class.[103] Women write on their bodies or display them to make a point, as FEMEN does. Active in Europe, the group writes slogans on their bare torsos to call attention to their causes. Tunisian topless protester and blogger Amina Sboui posted topless photos when she was 19 with "Fuck your morals" written on her chest inspiring the formation of a Moroccan branch of FEMEN in 2013. In SlutWalks some women write words like "slut pride" on their skin.[104] I saw "Slut Pride" graffiti at a university in Athens, Greece, written in English, shown on the Global Youth SpeakOut Facebook page.[105]

In Brazil, Carol Rosetti is a "body positive" feminist artist who paints women comfortable with body hair, green hair, casual sex, weight, using a wheelchair, and other choices outside of the norm shown on her Facebook page.[106] Similar exploration of the unshaven female body is seen in paintings by young Pakistani American artist Ayqa Khan. She also portrays a woman roller-skating while wearing a niqab.[107] During Uganda's first "Gay Beach Pride" parade of men and women, some demonstrators wore only rainbows to protest anti-gay legislation in 2012. In *Girls Will Be Girls: Dressing Up, Playing Parts and Daring to Act Differently* (2015), Emer O'Toole explores the female body modification as performance.

The Women's Studies journal *Signs* collected essays on "Gendered Bodies in the Protest Sphere."[108] Sherine Hafez suggested that the female body is "a fluid and culturally mediated form with the potential to be continually disruptive, destabilizing, and transformative." Ratna Kapur asked as women create new protest tactics, "Can gendered bodies in the protest sphere ever be an exercise moving towards freedom?" Examples of "distinctly gendered uprisings" presented in the *Signs*' "Gendered Body" issue were the protests against the gang rape of a young woman on a Delhi bus in December 2012 and the SlutWalks the previous year where the female body became a "political body." Irish women tweeted details of their menstrual cycles to their prime minister in 2015 and 2016 as part of a campaign to get rid of the eighth amendment of the constitution that gives fetuses the same rights as their mothers. They used the hashtag #repealthe8th to respond to the focus on their "reproductive parts."

Chinese Olympic swimmer Fu Yuanhui made news by discussing the impact of her menstrual period on her performance, a previously taboo topic.[109] In China women may allude to "a visit from my aunt" to avoid the taboo and the country didn't manufacture tampons until 2016. Fu's comment generated millions of comments on China's social media platform Weibo. In a similar vein, American musician Kiran Gandhi ran the London Marathon without a tampon in 2015 to confront "period-shaming."

Young women in Kerala, India, were arrested in a demonstration in 2014 for allowing their shoulders and lower legs to be seen as they were wrapped in cloth banners with anti-rape slogans during a demonstration. They were protesting the lack of outrage about the rape and murder of two Dalit (outcaste) girls, explaining,

We used our bodies to protest against people who are using women's bodies as a political weapon. Without hearing our voices of protests and slogans, without understanding the apolitical climate, which is permeating in the society, people are more worried about our bare shoulders and legs. To those people who still think female bodies are the reason for rape, we mock all those people, in the name of those girls who were raped and lynched in Uttar Pradesh.[110]

Indian media ran false headlines reading "Protest by Naked Women." Other women joined them by posting similar photos of themselves on Facebook. Earlier, Manipur women protested naked with a banner held in front of them saying "Indian Army Rapes Us" in front of an army base in 2004. They protested the rape and murder of a local woman by soldiers and weren't arrested, unlike the Kerala women.

Jessica Taft interviewed 75 girls in Vancouver (British Columbia), San Francisco, Mexico City, Caracas and Buenos Aires.[111] Taft found the common pattern in girls' organizing is aiming for a positive and optimistic feeling in their groups, and emphasizing ongoing learning and discovery with horizontal consensus decision-making. Their groups often provide them with the resource of a network of friendship and support, especially when other girls in their schools think activism is "nerdy or boring." Social movement theorists point out that collective identity generates support for movements like these activist girls who identify as politicos.[112] Taft's interviewees work together to create social change and express their style with Che Guevara T-shirts and political music (Che is the most popular male rebel icon, perhaps Frida Kahlo for women?). They're opposed to consumer media that portrays the ideal girl as loving to shop, her identity expressed by being a fashionista. The "can-do" girl in the "treacherous neoliberal terrain of the new girlhoods" is an individual achiever rather than active in a social movement, so it takes courage to be an activist teen feminist.[113]

In her studies of activist teens in the US, Hava Rachel Gordon found gender differences in the ability to organize. She conducted ethnographic and intersectional feminist studies of high school activist groups in Oakland, California, and Portland, Oregon. She found that limitations on girls' freedom of movement interfered with their ability to attend meetings and demonstrations, what she refers to as "the key issue of spatial and civil mobility."[114] Parents placed more restrictions on girls than boys, causing girls to express more irritation with their parents' opposition to their activism than boys, although both sexes often described their parents as major influences on their activism. A high school girl named Zoe told Gordon, "I've had to keep stuff secret from my parents though, actually. Like, I don't tell them I am going to sit down in the streets." Most of the girls left the Portland group because, as Alana stated, "SRU was started by white, middle-class boys and now it's led by white, middle-class boys," some of whom viewed themselves as secret superheroes. [115] The Oakland group stayed together because feminist young adult allies encouraged girls' leadership, interrupted boys' domination of discussions, and served as intermediaries with parents.

United Nations and Governments Stimulate Equality

Globalization

Why do we witness more uppity girls speaking out and taking action? Globalization and international feminist and development organizations have made a difference, along with female leaders and sports heroes. [116] SpeakOut girls aspire to be pilots, blacksmiths, mayors, and explorers, to do what no other woman in their country has done. "The women in olden times never used to raise voice against injustice except a few, but today's generation has learned to revolt against the evil done to them" (Gunveen, 13, f, India).

Feminist publications and organizations help promote belief in equality and equal rights. The Second Wave of feminism brought about major changes in attitude in developed countries, raising consciousness about hazards of gender roles and teaching that the personal (beauty standards, sex, housework, reproduction, and childcare) is a political power issue. The waves are described in Volume 2 Chapter 1: the first wave fought for the right to vote while the second wave began in 1963 with the publication of Betty Friedan's *The Feminine Mystique* and the formation of the National Organization for Women three years later. The third wave began in the 1980s with an emphasis on interlocking oppressions, and the fourth wave after 2000 has a focus on cyberfeminism and, as Gloria Steinem said, we raised "uppity" girls. The fourth wave is known for its "SlutWalks" that spread from Canada to the US, Europe, India, Brazil, and South Africa in 2011. The catalyst was a Toronto policeman who told female law school students to "avoid dressing like sluts" to prevent being victimized.

United Nations Programs

Some countries had early women's movements as part of their nationalist struggles against colonial rule, as in Egypt and India. The UN Charter of 1945 was the first international declaration to guarantee women's rights, due to lobbying by communist states and other activists since only 17 of the delegates were women.[117] They created a Commission on the Status of Women and guaranteed rights to all human beings. UNICEF was created in 1953 to assist children and was augmented by the Convention on the Rights of the Child in 1990. The US is the only UN member state not to ratify it, partly because it is the only country to sentence children to life in prison without the possibility of parole, which is prohibited by the Convention. A formal Declaration on the Elimination of Discrimination against Women was written in 1967. Feminism spread around the globe in the 1970s spurred on by the UN's International Year of the Woman in 1975, the 25th anniversary of the Commission on the Status of Women in charge of global women's issues.

The United Nations draws the most attention to the status of women through its conferences on the International Decade for Women, in Mexico City (1975), Copenhagen (1980), Nairobi (1985) that revived the international women's movement, and Beijing in 1995. I attended the Copenhagen conference where I was shocked to see that most of the official UN delegates were men. The lively activity was in the unofficial NGO Forum discussions. While we were there, my baby and his dad made the TV news in Copenhagen waiting for me to come out from the conference, as it was still unusual to see a father caring for his child without the mother to watch over him. The Nairobi conference was credited with the birth of global feminism with its call for "gender mainstreaming" to analyze the gender implications of all UN programs, similar to the African Union's platform.[118] Motivated by UN leadership, governments set up ministries for women's issues in the 1970s. Universities set up Affirmative Action programs and Women's Studies programs in the 1970s—I was the first coordinator at CSUC.

I also attended the NGO women's studies conference in Beijing, with the All China Women's Federation presenting mainly facts about Chinese women without suggestions for improvement. (A side trip to Tibet revealed the tragic Chinese destruction of local culture, as well as the stark beauty of the Himalayas.) The resulting Beijing Platform for Action declared "gender equality was an issue of universal concern, benefiting all." Hillary Clinton's statement to the conference that "women's rights are human rights," seemed revolutionary then, but is widely accepted today.[119] (The previous endnote includes a UN film that includes Clinton's speech and images of global women.) Conservatives in the US asked the First Lady not to attend and not to send a delegation to Beijing because the conference was radical and anti-family, as Senator Bob Dole said. Clinton gave her speech in a pink suit, perhaps to signal she wasn't anti-feminine.

The 1995 Beijing Platform for Action adopted by 189 nations in 1995 is a major tool for gender equality and has shaped global gender policies. Despite a focus on being inclusive and its platform, the Beijing conference was criticized for its lack of representation of poor women and the assumption that the global South was not capable of governing itself.[120]

The UN established a Commission on the Status of Women (CSW) in 1946. The CSW currently states it provides one of the largest annual conferences of women's rights activists and worked to include women's goals in the Post-2015 Millennium Goals Agenda.[121] Criticism ensued from voting for Saudi Arabia to join the CSW in 2017, despite its policy of requiring women to have a guardian to approve their actions, extreme sex segregation, and not permitting women to drive. The UN's Working Group on Girls is a coalition of NGOs that advocate for girls and their rights. A teen named Rachel said in the coalition newsletter that as a passionate feminist, "I believe that empowering women and girls is the only way to change the world." In their July 2015 newsletter, they advocated that girls should specifically be included in the Sustainable Development Goals (SDGs) that replaced the Millennium Development Goals because girls have different needs than adults. Goal 5 is gender specific: "Achieve gender equality and empower all women and girls."

Gender data advocates emphasize the importance of collecting data separated by gender to remedy the existing data gap in order to measure progress on the UN goals. Advocates succeeded in their request that the Gates Foundation fund $40 million for this data collection. The non-profit Flowminder Foundation based in Sweden creates "geospatial data" showing hot spots to make visible where girls' issues need the most attention.[122] Melinda Gates advocates the importance of data collection by gender and age, stating, "Women's and girls' empowerment is no longer on the global agenda—it is the global agenda."[123]

Emily Bent interviewed girls involved in CSW programs in New York City.[124] Bent applies standpoint theory to her research about girls who are active in the CSW. The girls told Bent they didn't have actual input into UN policy-making. A teen named Jessica reported that when they tried to say something that wasn't strictly on the agenda, the adults took the microphone away. Young women representing indigenous youth in Latin America to the UN reported that everything is in English, which means an interpreter is always speaking for them instead of others' hearing their own voices.[125] Youth-serving agencies need to respect young people. The 2016 meeting of the CSW finally acknowledged that the missing link in the fight for gender equality is the youth voice and organized the Youth Forum CSW. It published "A Declaration on Gender Equality" that features these youth issues: decision-making, climate change, sexual and reproductive health, violence, economic empowerment, migration, access to media, religion, sports, and engaging young men.[126]

The UN Convention on the Elimination of All Forms of Discrimination Against Women (CEDAW) is considered the most important international agreement on the rights of women and girls and has been ratified by 188 nations. "The CEDAW Convention is at the core of our global mission of peace, development and human rights," observed former U.N. Secretary-General Ban Ki-moon. CEDAW "gave women's rights activists what they needed most: a point of reference, a language and the tools to resist and challenge patriarchy," reported professor Deniz Kandiyoti.[127] Adopted in 1979 by the UN, the US is the only industrial nation that hasn't ratified CEDAW, as the Senate won't even bring it to a vote. CEDAW was expanded in 1992 to include gender-based violence as a violation of human rights.

Emphasizing the importance of women's issues for his international agenda, President Obama appointed Melanne Verveer as the first ambassador-at-large for the Office of Global Women's Issues in 2009 with a blog about international news.[128] At the same time his administration established the White House Council on Women & Girls with a Girls' Research portal as a resource for girls' studies.[129] Trump appointed anti-reproductive choice and anti-feminists to health positions in his administration. For example, he selected anti-birth control delegates to the UN Commission on Women meeting in 2017 and his choice for his administration family planning program said contraceptive use is "medically irresponsible."[130] He also put a freeze on US funding for global health centers that inform women about the possibility of abortion, the "gag rule," greatly diminishing health care for poor women.

In 2010 the UN merged different agencies into one called the UN Entity for Gender Equality and the Empowerment of Women, referred to as UN Women.[131] Former Chilean president Michele Bachelet was its first director, followed by Phumzile Mlambo-Nguka from South Africa, also a politician, and Lakshmi Puri. She worked to get heads of state and other powerholders to sign a pledge to work for gender parity by 2030 and aims to do more movement building and to involve faith-based groups in equity. UN Women started a global campaign on the 20th anniversary of the Beijing conference called "Empowering Women, Empowering Humanity," to inform young women about structural barriers to equality and it publishes frequent reports on the status of women.[132] UN Women adopted youth and gender equality strategy called "LEAPs

Framework and partnered with Plan International girls' rights movement called "Because I am a Girl" in 2016. It claims to have launched more than 500 projects for girls by 2016. WUNRN, Women's UN Report Network provides a ListServ, numerous articles, conferences, and tool kids on issues like ending gender-based violence.[133] Two years later the UN adopted the first International Day of the Girl Child, motivated by a campaign led by School Girls Unite (based in Washington, DC) and Plan International, a Canadian children's development organization. The Girl Child webpage includes fact sheets and information about task forces.[134]

The UN Secretary-General appointed a young Jordanian named Ahmad Alhendawi as the first Envoy on Youth in 2013. He reported on his activities in a 2015 report, stating that the 20th anniversary of the World Programme of Action for Youth was one of the largest gatherings and the #YouthNow campaign got over two billion social media responses.[135]

The United Nations Girls' Education Initiative is a coalition of regional and international groups, as well as UN agencies: UNESCO, UNFPA, WFP, and UNICEF. It was launched in 2000 by the Secretary-General to assist national governments to educate all children. The Initiative's priorities are to increase the number of girls continuing their education after primary school, reduce violence against girls in schools, and to include excluded groups.[136] The Working Group on Girls of the NGO Committee on UNICEF works for girls' rights, the inclusion of girls in UN agencies and international agreements, and for girls as change makers. The Working Group on Girls conducted a survey of girls 18 and younger in 2015 as part of the UN's fourth World Conference on Women in Beijing.[137] The UN also hosts "The Girl Fund" to assist the more than 600 million adolescent girls. The UN Population Fund, UNFPA, provides online resources for how to involve youth in activism, including a manual compiled with the YWCA to train young women to lead.[138] UN Youth of course has a Facebook page.[139]

The eight UN Millennium Development Goals (MDGs) adopted in 2000 aimed for implementation by 2015 had unequal results. The MDGs deal with problems like poverty, violence, AIDS, and access to representation in government.[140] Only eight nations didn't sign on to the MDGs. The US is again the only developed nation that didn't ratify the goals because conservatives oppose following UN regulations. The UN views them as the most successful anti-poverty movement in history because from 1990 to 2010 poverty was reduced by half. However, 836 million people still lived in extreme poverty and suffered from hunger in 2015. By 2012 the number of children not in school decreased by two million, but 120 million youth were illiterate. Global carbon dioxide emissions increased by more than half and 40% of people suffer from water scarcity. The MDGs recognized the fundamental role of women in development, aimed to improve women's health and education, and encourage other UN agencies to work on girls' education.[141] Goal 3 was to "promote gender equality and empower women" and Goal 5 aimed to "improve Maternal Health."

The UN's Millennium Development Goals included gender equality but girls weren't specifically mentioned, so the Nike Foundation funded a campaign linked to the goals called The Girl Effect. It brought together 508 girls living in poverty in 14 countries to write the Girl Declaration in regards to the post-2015 agenda when the goals expired. They wrote statements like, "I was not put on this earth to be invisible," "I was not given life only to belong to someone else," "I have a voice and I will use it," and "I am key to all solutions."[142]

Because the MDGs expired in 2015, new Sustainable Development Goals (SDGs) were formulated based on input from around the world. A feminist declaration for the Post MDG 2015 Agenda was backed by over 340 organizations, demanding a paradigm shift from the current neoliberal economic system that places profits over people.[143] Updates are on GlobalGoals.org. The UN Foundation and the Nike Foundation launched the Girl Declaration to make sure girls are included in the SDGs.[144] Children and youth were included in formulating the new goals after representatives from the Netherlands suggested the need for youth input, which should have been obvious.

The UN World Children Want Internet platform solicited responses about the new goals in 2015 from thousands of youth from over 47 countries.[145] Young respondents believe that humans have a right to food, water, health, and protection of the planet. Their top priority is education, which repeats results of the My World global survey that collected over 7.6 million votes after it was launched in 2013. Ending hunger received as many votes as education. The young UN respondents said that current problems are discouraging as almost half of the people living in extreme poverty are 18 years or younger, so they're glad to have the hopeful SDGs.

The new UN Sustainable Development Goals (SDGs) released in September 2015 are titled "Transforming Our World," consisting of 17 goals with 169 targets to end poverty by 2030. Goal 5 is a stand-alone goal on general equality to empower girls and women.146 It will cost $3 trillion to reach the goals, but US professor Glen David Kuecker calls them lipstick on a pig because the same power broker corporations, NGOs and consultants are in line for the development funds. 147 Kuecker predicts that, "The SDGs will provide just enough growth so that just enough food, medicine, and education are available for the multitudes to ensure the system remains seamless in its reproduction and that capitalism remains non-negotiable," therefore controlling the system from behind the scenes similar to the *Matrix* films. Another criticism is the new goals seldom mention children and youth. In addition, adults in charge of implementing the goals too often approach youth as beneficiaries in need of help rather than as partners.

AIESEC, the largest association of global university students, surveyed 160,292 global youth, 55% female, most ages 16 to 24, which they summarized in a 2016 Youth-Speak report.[148] The AIESEC respondents selected the most important UN goals as to ensure quality education and reduce poverty, which are typical responses for global youth. Western Europeans and North Americans put protect the planet in second place rather than poverty and Africans put poverty as their number one problem, as usual. Youth are also concerned about the 50 million child refugees, including over a 100,000 unaccompanied by an adult.

During the opening of the 59th session of the Commission on the Status of Women in 2015, Secretary-General Ban Ki-moon condemned the fact that, although 189 countries endorsed the Beijing Platform for Action in 1995, no country had achieved gender equality. (He listed his priorities for UN youth programs at the end of his term in 2016 and the endnote includes youth policies by country.[149]) Five countries don't have women in their parliaments. His report identified barriers to equality as wars, climate change, increasing extremism, increasing costs of living, and the backlash against women's rights. He also noted progress such as the facts that girls are almost half of the world's elementary students, maternal mortality rates are falling, and countries are passing more progressive equality legislation. In 2015 UN Women launched a campaign called "Planet 50-50 by 2030: Step It Up for Gender Equality" to energize the Beijing+20 campaign.[150] Over 90 countries signed the initiative.

In spite of these UN programs devoted to gender equality, because of growing fundamentalist attacks on women's and LGBT rights and attacks on reproductive choice the UN didn't opt for a Fifth World Conference on Women for fear of weakening international agreements on women's rights.[151] (The UN's first resolution on the human rights of LGBTI people was adopted in 2011, followed up by a second resolution in 2014, and a third in 2016. The latter was proposed by a group of Latin American countries.)

The same fear of conservatives led to negotiating a bland outcome report on the UN Commission on the Status of Women meeting in March 2015 that attracted nearly

9,000 participants.[152] The report left out strong statements on human rights and reproductive rights for adolescent girls and included an upbeat report on international progress for women.[153] Young feminists from AWID's Young Feminist Wire protested; "We express our deep disappointment at the exclusion of the majority of Civil Society Organizations (CSOs), women's rights and feminist organizations from the process of negotiating the political declaration."[154] They asked governments to include at least two young women in their delegations and to protect young feminist activists from violence. They called for a gender equality goal because the UN Secretary General's report for the post 2015 SDGs left out a specific goal for gender equality and failed to mention adolescent girls. Despite its problems, the UN has provided important data collection, studies, conferences, and workshops where feminists from around the world can learn from each other.

Regional Associations

The African Union (AU) provides a model policy on how to "function in accordance with the promotion of gender equality."[155] However, its 2009 policy reports: "70% of member states currently have gender policies and yet few of them have been implemented." A few of the member nations established Gender Management Systems (GMS), which the AU would like to see adopted in all member states. GMS plans are used by gender issues in public policies such as finance or health, by providing training governments globally to mainstream resources.[156] The European Women's Lobby (EWL) began a campaign for "50/50 for Democracy" in 2008. The EWL is the largest coalition of women in the EU working to promote women's rights and equality and represents more than 2,000 organizations.[157]

Other regional organizations working on gender equality are the Asia-Pacific Economic Cooperation Forum and the African Development Bank. The Young Feminist Fund, formed in 2010, assists young feminist activists with grant writing and "knowledge-building." It was formed by The Association for Women's Rights in Development (AWID), The *Fondo Centroamericano de Mujeres*/Central American Women's Fund (FCAM) and young feminist activists from around the world.[158] Members define feminists as "individuals working within women's movements or in other social movements to advance the rights of equality, justice, dignity, freedom and safety of women, girls and marginalized groups."

Public-private programs also assist women to advance in the workplace; Mexico's federal program, *Generosidad*, awards the Gender Equity Seal to private employers who do an excellent job of promoting gender equity. It inspired similar programs in Brazil, Costa Rica, and Egypt.

Government Models of Equality

Scandinavian countries like Sweden and Norway provide models of how to create equality and break the power of the oligarchic 1%, while also encouraging private enterprise. Education and health care are free and they aim for full employment and gender equality. These Scandinavian countries are small, with a homogenous population (but with increasing numbers of Muslim immigrants), and a historical commitment to equality. Their equality and social welfare programs provide models for other nations, providing youth with free childcare, healthcare and education through university. (See interview with Ylva, 19, from Southern Sweden.[159])

The countries that have the best equality programs are in Scandinavia, according to the Global Gender Gap Index created by the World Economic Forum in 2006.[160] The 2016 report found that the most equal countries were Iceland, Finland, Norway, Sweden and the Philippines. The US was in 23rd place.[161] The Index reported global progress in 2014, with Scandinavians at the top, as usual with Iceland, Finland, Norway, Sweden and Rwanda in that order. Yemen, Pakistan and Chad were at the bottom. Norway is at the top of an index of best countries for mothers, with the US much lower at 31 out of 44 developed nations, partly due to its lack of paid parental leave.[162]

In Sweden, both men and women are entitled to 480 days of paid parental leave between them for childcare and elder care.[163] The economy is growing while workers have five weeks of vacation, health benefits, subsidized childcare, and free education through university.[164] The Social Progress Index ranks countries, not by GDP, but by quality of life factors such as health, access to education, religious freedom and personal safety.[165] In 2013 the top countries were New Zealand, Switzerland, Iceland and the Netherlands with Scandinavians again in the top ten. Various African countries were in the bottom. In the 2015 Social Progress Index the best countries for social progress were Norway, Sweden and Switzerland, in that order, followed by Iceland, New Zealand, Canada, Finland, Denmark, Netherlands, and Australia.[166]

The Scandinavia countries named the "caring state" by economist Hilkka Pietila, also called "nanny states," do the best job of having the most people in the middle class and aiming for gender equality. These countries have private ownership of industry but many government programs to insure that citizens have free education through university, healthcare, and affordable housing. In Denmark, SpeakOut student Carl (age 15) reports that university students get paid to get an education, about the equivalent of $1,500 USD a month. However, he thinks the payment should be reduced and more spent on social welfare and defense.

In Sweden the average individual tax rate for cradle-to-the-grave security is 58%, compared to 40% in the US where these benefits like free university are lacking.[167] Only the Netherlands, Sweden, Norway and Denmark have consistently met the target of 0.7% of national GNP for aid for children internationally, despite other nations' promises at the World Summit on Children and at other summits.[168] Nordic nations have about 40% female legislators, compared to the global average of 22%, shown on the Women in Politics: 2015 Map.[169] Norway passed legislation that requires women to join men in 19 months of military service.

Borgen was a fictional Danish TV series about Birgitte Nyborg, the first female Prime Minister. It aired from 2010 to 2013 and was broadcasted globally.[170] (I learned about it from Kevin, a SpeakOut teen in Trinidad who loved it, part of the books global network of young correspondents.) The actual election of Denmark's first female Prime Minister, Social Democrat Helle Thorning-Schmidt (age 44) occurred during *Borgen*'s second season in 2011. The Prime Minister stated, "We can say farewell to 10 years of bourgeois rule." The show also features Katrine, a female political journalist who is another strong female character in a Scandinavian society that values equality. In Katrine's small apartment, she has a poster of Robert Redford and Dustin Hoffman as reporters in *All the President's Men* (1976). Despite the ideals of shared roles, the show explores the drain on dual-earner families with young children. Katrine is a single parent because her son's father's childhood abuse left him unable to stay in a committed relationship, so their son goes back and forth.

The Prime Minister's marriage falls apart too as her husband does most of the family work in a reversal of traditional roles. Her husband divorces her, saying, "You were never home and it was chaos." Her teenage daughter feels ignored by her mother and falls apart with anxiety attacks that place her in a treatment facility. Nyborg's ex-husband has an affair with a physician, but doesn't feel ready to commit to her. In the third and last season Brigitte's children are doing fine, she has a devoted lover who is a British architect, and she successfully forms a new party, all the while undergoing radiation treatments for breast cancer, so she does manage to have it all.

Unlike *Veep*, the lightweight and silly US show about a woman vice-president (who briefly became president) who swears a lot and makes off-color remarks like "that's like trying to use a croissant as a dildo," *Borgen* seriously explores current issues on each show. The series explored how to fund the welfare state that the PM says is central to Denmark's self-image, the war in Afghanistan, agricultural pollution and the environment, prejudice against immigrants, mental illness and child abuse. It's also striking that the PM does her own cooking, does her own repairs, answers her door at home with no guards, and has a very small entourage. She does have a driver--who she seduces one night while drinking--drowning her sorrow over her divorce, so she's human, as well as being a decisive skilled politician.

Early in the show critics raised the question of whether Nyborg could be both an effective mother and prime minister, but the second season ended with the announcement that she was running again for prime minister and wasn't going to stay home to be a housewife. If her husband was the prime minister, it's unlikely his wife would divorce him or blame him for his daughter's mental health problems. Her husband eventually became a supportive good friend, indicating that women can have it all, just like men. The actual Danish Prime Minister Thorning-Schmidt is married to a British politician and they have two children. Their daughters were 14 and 11 when she became prime minister. When her husband Stephen Kinnock was asked what he was doing while she campaigned for office, he said, "I'm taking care of the children, doing a bit of cooking and trying to do a bit of DIY around the house. But that's not going too well."[171] They're still married and juggling two careers and parenting.

A British critic married to a Dane says of the Nordic countries, "These societies function well for those who conform to the collective median, but they aren't much fun for tall poppies. Schools rein in higher achievers for the sake of the less gifted; 'elite' is a dirty word; displays of success, ambition or wealth are frowned upon."[172] Yuan is a Chinese SpeakOut student doing graduate work in Finland. In a Skype interview he reported about their belief in equality,

> *Equality is the key characteristic, like men don't hold out a chair for women or open doors just for them. You see women on the side of the road fixing their bikes and men don't stop to help because they're assumed to be equal. They practice positive discrimination, so If two people compete for job, they give it to the less capable because the other one can find a job elsewhere. If you get a speeding ticket, wealthy people pay more.*
>
> *People are so modest so there's much under the tip of the iceberg that you can't*

see: People have poker faces. They always talk about being shy. In my college classes, no one raises their hand unless the teacher asks the class a question. They don't want attention. Nobody is trying to impress somebody. Everybody should be the same. Teachers don't think one student is smart or dumb. As a guest in a high school Mandarin class, I asked if they had any questions, but no one raised their hands. You don't show you know more or show off talents, or show you're rich as everyone should be on the same level. Rich people don't buy a fancy car or big house. All the houses are almost the same, without rich neighborhoods.

A Finnish woman commented on Yuan's observations on the Our Shared Shelf bookclub in the thread I started on actual feminist societies, contradicting some of his points and confirming others.[173] The main takeaway is Finland is a model of gender equality, as are other Nordic countries. Birgitta Jonsdottir founded the Pirate Party in Iceland in 2012, is a member of parliament and would be prime minister if her party won an election. She calls herself a "poetician," hacker, supporter of WikiLeaks, and chair of the International Modern Media Association.

Although university is free in Sweden, graduates accumulate debt to pay for living costs as most don't live with their parents, and youth unemployment is higher than in the UK.[174] Swedish professors acknowledge that because of neoliberal policies, "even the Swedish welfare state 'shed its skin' in an "epoch shift.""[175] Although Sweden is a leader in equality, oppression of women exists if there's any truth to the disturbingly violent 2009 films *Millennium Trilogy* based on novels. They reveal the ugly underbelly of Swedish corruption, prostitution, and violence against women displayed in the life of the tough punk character, Lisbeth Slander. An article on "Sweden's Gender-Violence Shame" reported that in 2012, 35,000 cases of violence against women were reported and every three weeks a woman is killed by a man close to her. More than a third of women aged 18 to 29 have been sexually assaulted, so Slander is not just a fictional problem.[176]

Swedish feminists created the Feminist Initiative Party (FI) in 2005, led by politician Gudrun Schyman.[177] Within six days they attracted over 2,500 members, mostly young people who were new to politics. In 2010, the party gained media coverage for burning money equal to the amount employed women don't earn compared to male peers ($15,000). The party had the votes to secure local council seats and a seat in the European Parliament (EP) in 2014, which had over one-third female members. A slogan was "Put the feminists in their place" accompanied by indie music and pink chairs placed on the streets to symbolize parliamentary seats. Schyman said they have the best social media platform, necessitated by their lack of financing.

Her goal is to decompartmentalize women's issues in intersectional postmodern politics explaining, "The big mistake in most politics is not seeing this—how gender, class, ethnicity, sexuality and everything else is related, and there are power structures that perpetuate on another. That's the heart of the feminist analysis we have." She thinks other Swedish parties are too stuck in class analysis. She reported that many young people have a feminist perspective and that FI influenced the 2013 elections that elected a self-proclaimed feminist government and selecting a feminist foreign minister Margot Wallström who advocates a "feminist security policy." She explained that a feminist foreign policy—which was met with derision internationally, is an "analysis and also a practical tool" rather than a set of political views. It acknowledges sexist discrimination as when Wallström spoke out against Saudi sexism.[178]

Soraya Post, the FI party's European Parliament representative, said the FI Party attracts voters who are worried about the rise of European anti-immigration parties and the success of fascist parties that did well in the EP elections in 2014. The party uses small meetings in homes called "Home Parties" to organize young activists. Most of its supporters are under the age of 25.[179] The FI party model spread to Norway, Finland, Denmark, Poland, Spain, and to Britain's Women's Equality Party. Many other women's parties are listed online.[180] Feminist candidates also ran for the EP from France and Germany, resolving to oppose Spain's reactionary move to restrict abortion only to cases of rape or danger to the mother's health, a move that eventually failed. A young Portuguese member of the Communist Party drafted a report on equality in 2014 for the EP, recommending abortion rights, recognition of same-sex marriages, and compulsory "gender education" in schools, but it was not accepted.

How was this Scandinavian model of egalitarian policies achieved? In the 1930s, labor movements organized general strikes and boycotts. Social Democrats were elected to lead parliament for three decades before conservatives returned to the ruling coalition in Sweden and Norway.[181] Many European youth would like to experience the Scandinavian model, despite high youth unemployment in countries like Sweden (20% in 2016, up from a low of 3% in 1990[182]). However, the recession doesn't allow replication of the nanny state of cradle-to-grave security, as the Scandinavian model is "based notably on high employment rates and huge state-financed aid for students."[183] Unemployed immigrant young people rioted in Stockholm, showing cracks in the nanny state. Sweden depended on a growing economy and a homogeneous well-educated population, set back by recession and large numbers of immigrants. Hillary Clinton told Bernie Sanders, "We're not Finland," but many Scandinavian programs could be adopted in the US if the $773.5 billion military budget for fiscal year 2017 was cut.[184] What does the US have to show for the trillions spent on wars in the Middle East and Afghanistan that only led to the rise of ISIS?

Another model of a state making an effort to install equal opportunity, France has a reputation for enabling working women to "have it all," with national subsidized child care and free preschool. Mothers and fathers with one child can take six months of unpaid leave, while families with two children can take three years as long as six months of leave is reserved for the other parent; this is in order to encourage men to spend time with their children. Being able to work and have children is highly valued in France, according to Gender Studies professor Hélène Périvier.[185] She contrasts France with Germany that lacks supports for working mothers, although parents can get up to 24 months of paid leave or 28 months if it's shared by the parents. A problem German mothers told me about is that school gets out earlier than in the US (11:30 for elementary school and 1:00 for secondary school) making it difficult to find childcare.

Socialist President Francois Hollande restored the government office of Minister for Women's Rights after a 30 years hiatus. His cabinet was half female (like Emmanuel Macron who followed him as President and Liberal party Prime Minister Justin Trudeau's cabinet in Canada—both men are young). He sent his ministers to a 45-minute anti-sexism class. A sexual harassment law in 2013 raised the fine for perpetrators. The French legislature approved a 2014 bill to improve gender equality, including outlawing beauty pageants for girls under 13 to prevent "hypersexualization" of girls. The bill also sought to raise women's wages, strengthen laws against domestic violence, offer six months of additional paid leave if taken by the other parent, and provide more support for single mothers.

The young head of the European Association Against Violence Toward Women at Work said they are accused of "wanting to sanitize the relationships between men and women…a puritanical feminism…an American type of feminism." But when former French First Lady Carla Bruni-Sarkozy (born in 1967) told *Paris Vogue*, "My generation doesn't need feminism," a group called *Osez le Femininisme* (Dare to be Feminist) organized a Twitter campaign, "#DearCarlaBruni, we need feminism because…" Women responded with comments like, "people always assume I'm the secretary" and Bruni apologized.

However, "Bou" reported on the Our Shared Shelf bookclub that street harassment is "is the everyday life of many women in France" and that women don't have equal wages because of fear they will take maternity leave. It's possible to combine free enterprise and social supports for citizens who need it but difficult to change traditional behavior.

Is the Future Female?

Ford Motor Company studies future trends because it takes years for a new car to reach the assembly line. Sheryl Connelly, Ford's manager of Global Trends and Futuring, identified the "Female Frontier" as an important trend.[186] She said, "Women around the world are rising in terms of their prominence, their influence, their success, their personal achievements. . . ." Kip Tindell, the CEO of The Container Store with annual sales of nearly $800 million, agrees, so he hired about 70% female top executives.[187] Tindell is "glad to see the feminization of American business" because women tend to understand "communication, empathy, and emotional intelligence" leading to "conscious capitalism" (the title of a 2014 book by John Mackey and Rajendra Sisodia). He quoted the cofounder of Southwest Airlines, Herb Kelleher, who said, "You can build a much better organization on love than you can on fear."

Girls are often seen as more competent than boys: Millennials have more faith in women's ability to lead change than men's, described in an international Euro survey of Millennials in France, China, India, the UK and the US.[188] A pastor of a Catholic church in San Francisco said he stopped training girls to be altar servers because "Boys usually end up losing interest, because girls generally do a better job."[189] A study of social action in the UK found that young women were more active in community-based actions and volunteering, and they viewed boys as less mature.[190] These British girls interviewed by Debi Roker told her their activism developed their skills, changed their identities, garnered social support from other group members, and was fun. Millennial women in the US are also much more likely to volunteer and donate to charities than men, according to The Millennial Impact Report—91% of females had donated to charities compared to 84% of men.[191]

Social scientists point out that in the science of cooperation "tend and befriend," is associated with female animals and humans as significant a part of human survival and evolution along with "fight or flight."[192] Research suggests that women leaders are more likely to collaborate rather than to dictate.[193] For example, a Girl Scout USA study of teen girls found they thought of leadership as shared rather than authoritative in contrast to their view of boys' leadership being characterized by control and ego. FRIDA, a funding organization for young feminists globally, observes that they're typical of women's organization in using co-leadership to share power, moving away from focus on the individual leader to the collective.[194]

Testosterone increases aggressiveness: In a study following 250 youth, baseline testosterone predicted future violent behaviors.[195] However, most of our gendered behavior is socialized, as evidence by sex roles being different in various cultures. "Masculinity is a socially learned construct" that teaches men to be risk takers, impulsive, and to seek sensation; hence men die earlier than women globally. Men have more accidents, are more often drug abusers and drunk drivers, but less likely to seek treatment. This male-sensation seeking is part of learned masculine roles. These traits are also true of adolescents, but women as a group are more likely to grow out of them. Researchers such as Professor Shervin Assari conclude that men need more self-control and to learn from women how to talk about emotions and seek help.[196]

Boys are more likely than girls to commit gun violence and commit suicide in the West, leading some to call for a movement to encourage boys to express feelings other than anger. A neuroscientist, Frances Jensen explained that teenage girls' brains are more connected across hemispheres and that they have superior language abilities compared to boys, placing them about a year and a half ahead in their development. Girls may be ahead in the connections between the emotional and intellectual parts of the brain; they do as well as boys on math tests and have higher average SAT scores.[197] However, Cordelia Fine argues against sex differences in the brain in her book *Delusions of Gender* (2011). For both sexes, the teenage brain is more plastic, able to learn more quickly, is also more impulsive with fewer inhibitions, and is susceptible to addiction and stress that can cause depression later on in life. In a *Doonesbury* cartoon by Gary Trudeau, a little girl in her childcare center tells feminist Joanie Caucus, "It's more 'in' to be a female than a male these days! Much more fashionable." Her statement is backed up by the fact that couples using invitro fertilization in the US more often chose to have a girl baby.

Girls outperform boys in terms of educational achievement in 70% of the 75 countries studied between 2000 and 2010; the study analyzed 1.5 million 15-year-olds.[198] Girls' achievement holds true even in countries with low gender equality ratings. Boys outperform girls only in Colombia, Costa Rica and the Indian state of Himachal Pradesh and among the highest-achievers. That is, boys are more likely to be at the top and bottom of achievement tests. The achievement of boys and girls was similar in the US and UK. Overall, the study reported children think boys are academically inferior to girls and they believe adults share their perception. Boys have more permission not to conform to norms, as in the statement that "boys will be boys."

Around 84% of today's young people will complete upper secondary education with young women now more likely to do so than men in most countries, a reversal of the historical pattern.[199] In the US, women get more undergraduate and graduate degrees than men. In the UCLA CIRP annual national survey of over 150,000 college freshmen, the 2014 students were much more likely to plan on getting a graduate degree (44%) than previously, with women more likely to plan on continuing after the bachelor's degree (36% of women vs. 29% of men).[200]

A key factor shaping the future is the increasing number of women graduates and women workers in the new knowledge economy, many of whom delay marriage and parenting to establish their careers. (Half of US adults are single, while most Chinese adults are married.) The World Bank reports that the ratio of university graduates is 93 men to every 100 women, including the majority of Saudi, Iranian and Nigerian students.[201] In the US, 140 women enroll in higher education every year for every 100 men and women are 58% of the graduates. In Sweden women comprise 60% of university students. Even in conservative Japan, there are 90 females for every 100 male students.

The Silent Sex: Gender, Deliberation and Institutions (2014), reported that when numbers of women increase to a critical mass their participation grows rapidly and men behave in less stereotypically male ways.[202] Universities where young people live on campus are the home of uprisings, like the Free Speech Movement that spread from the University of California, Berkeley in 1964 and on around the world. Since 2009, over 50 countries have experienced student demonstrations.[203] As more girls enter university, they will change how social change occurs in these centers.

The largest countries are moving towards equality as well. In China, young women comprise 48% of university students and in India, young women are 42% of the students. Europe, Latin America and North America enroll more female university students than male. An exception is poverty-stricken Sub-Saharan Africa; it enrolls only about six women for every 10 university students.[204] Women are still the minority of STEM students studying science and technical fields (the gap has widened in the US in computer science degrees since a high point in 1984). Tech programs with equal or more women students are the ones that attract women who feel they can do socially meaningful work, such as at a UC Berkeley graduate program in development engineering that creates solutions for low-income communities and the international engineering minor at the University of Michigan.[205] An online slide show features 21 women from various countries who have achieved excellence in STEM and other fields.[206]

Girls who Code teaches girls to be computer programmers, Reshima Saujani found that perfectionism, a fear of not getting it right, kept the girls from being brave enough to show their attempts at coding.[207] A professor friend of hers also reported that male students will say, Professor, there's something wrong with my code," while the young women say, "Professor, there's something wrong with me." She referred to a Hewlett Packard study that reported men will apply for a job if the meet 60% of the qualifications, while women think they have to have 100% of them, as discussed in a *Harvard Business Review* article.[208] She teaches girls to be brave enough to take the risk of being wrong. Encouraged, two of her high school students built a game called Tampon Run to oppose sexism in gaming.

A UK study of college student protests against proposed tuition hikes in 2019 found that the women students were less likely to feel confident to discuss politics or to feel informed about politics.[209] This research also found that students were more likely to be activists if they grew up in families where their parents frequently discussed politics, if they were politically involved before attending university, and if their friends were involved. It looks like special outreach needs to be made to increase girls' interest in and confidence about their political analysis and interest in science and technology.

Girls perform better on math and science assessment tests in many MENA (Middle East and North Africa) countries. In the Middle East, women outnumber men as tech students and tech entrepreneurs.[210] Rather than struggling with discrimination in the workplace, they start their own companies. They're 35% of MENA tech entrepreneurs compared to the world average of only 10% of women techies. A Syrian woman explained that the Middle East doesn't have the bias against women in STEM jobs and women appreciate the flexibility to be able to work from home because the Internet is a more meritocratic space.

Women are the "most powerful engine of global growth," according to the *Economist* magazine.[211] Utilizing women's skills as workers would add $12 trillion to global growth, according to a report by the McKinsey Global Institute.[212] In many countries the percentage of men with jobs has fallen with the "feminization of the workplace" due to the shift from manufacturing to service and information jobs. In Asia, women are a majority of workers in export industries such as textiles and clothing. In Britain more women than men are studying to be doctors and lawyers. Women are about half of these students in the US, but few women are in high-level positions in those fields. Thus, women's skills are underutilized globally.

The authors of *The Athena Doctrine: How Women (and the Men Who Think Like Them) Will Rule the Future* (2013) share former Brazilian President Rousseff's prediction of a female ascendency in a world that's increasingly interdependent. John Gerzema and Michael D'Antonio surveyed 64,000 people in 13 countries around the world to discover the traits associated with success and effective leadership. Gerzema and D'Antonio state that feminine traits are not just associated with success, morality, and happiness, but also with business success. Countries with more feminine traits have higher per capita GDP and higher reported quality of life. Hedge funds run by women outperform those run by men, and large companies with women board members outperform similar companies with no women.[213] The authors predicted, "feminine values are the operating system of twenty-first-century progress."[214]

Gerzema and D'Antonio conducted interviews in 26 nations for the *Athena Doctrine*. They found that both men and women were dissatisfied with male leadership in the era of neoliberal capitalism and greed. In response to the question, "I'm dissatisfied with the conduct of men in my country," 54% of men agreed along with 59% of women and two-thirds of Millennials.[215] Young adults agreed even more in "highly masculine societies" in China, Japan, South Korea, and India and were less rigid in their definitions of femininity and masculinity than their elders. These traits are socialized rather than innate, so they can change especially when men are more involved in parenting. An example of an outdated and adolescent machismo debate during the Republican presidential contest is when Donald Trump and Marco Rubio engaged in debate about the size of their hands and by implication their genitalia. Trump said in a March 3, 2016, debate about the size issue, "Something else must be small, I guarantee there's no problem there." I've never heard a woman politician engage in an election debate about their bodies; the closest is in Britain's 2016 contest for prime minister, when a female opponent, Andrea Leadsom, said not being a mother limited Theresa May's capacity to have an emotional stake in the future.

Globally, 66% of women and men surveyed for *The Athena Doctrine* agreed that the world would be a better place if men thought more like women do and 81% said everyone needs both masculine and feminine traits to succeed today, an androgynous approach. Millennials were especially supportive of androgyny: Of the 13 countries cited, only Indonesia lacked a large percentage that agreed that both traits are needed to succeed (only 45% agreed). In their previous book, *Spend Shift,* Gerzema and D'Antonio found that young people were more interested in connection and community and less focused on money and status than were older adults. Gerzema and D'Antonio think a global referendum on men is occurring, with Millennials especially dissatisfied with patriarchy. The authors believe this shift in values is driven by technology, the financial crisis and globalization of the new knowledge and service economy.

Other provocative authors maintain that the future trend is the ascendancy of women--Guy Garcia's *The Decline of Men* (2009) and *The Richer Sex* by Liza Mundy (2013).[216] Hanna Rosin's *The End of Men* (2012) points out that in the US women make up the majority of the workforce, undergraduate and graduate university students, and workers with managerial and professional jobs. In a rebuttal article responding to Hanna Rosin's book about women's ascendancy, Andrew Moore states that men are risk takers and innovators and lead in technology fields.[217] Women comprise 54% of young professional workers, but the 23 cents gender pay gap persists and Congress hasn't passed the Paycheck Fairness Act.[218] Girls outnumber boys in high school advanced placement classes, student government, school newspapers, and debate clubs.[219] The gap in gender achievements began in the early 1990s and has been growing ever since then. Men's college graduation rates stopped growing after the Vietnam War ended in the late 1970s.[220] Women undergraduates started outnumbering men in the late 1970s and since 1988 women comprise the majority of graduate students. In 2012, women were 56% of the undergraduate students and are less likely to drop out: 39% of men complete their degree by age 27 compared to 46% of women.[221] Women own an estimated 8.6 million US businesses.[222]

Advertisers manipulate men's fear of losing control. Rosin refers to a Super Bowl ad for Dodge Charger titled "Man's Last Stand," in which a hen-pecked man says, "I will put the seat down, I will separate the recycling, I will carry your lip balm," until empowered by owning the car. Being in charge brings difficulties for men. Richard Reeves and Isabel Sawhill argue that the gender revolution liberated some women from traditional roles, but not men: "Now men need to learn to become more like women," as in training for jobs in health and education and doing more family work, rather than trying to return to patriarchy and "hyper-masculinity."[223]

Gloria Steinem agrees that the way to liberate boys is to involve them in tasks like childcare, modeled by the former Oh Boy, Babies program in New York City.[224] The director of the Center for the Study of Men and Masculinities, Michael Kimmel says that about two-thirds of men still think masculinity requires emotional reserve and "most men still cling tenaciously to an ideology of masculinity that comes off the set of *Mad Men*."[225] US TV shows portray the "toxic bachelor" who can't commit to a relationship as well as men who want commitment: In a *Broad City* show, Hannibal asks his sexual partner, "What are we?" She says it's purely physical and he wonders, "Why does this always happen to me?"[226] Another vulnerable and sensitive man is Gus on the show *Love* representing "the genial, meek façade of the domesticated Millennial guy." Kimmel does see improvement in young men's belief in equality and having friends of the opposite sex. They expect to be in dual-earner families and to be involved fathers.

"Girl Power" is a popular concept, discussed in Chapter 4 and in *Growing up with Girl Power* (2012) by Rebecca Hains. The author of *Parenting Beyond Pink and Blue* (2014). Christa Brown describes girl power as the new "It" movement. Australian Anita Harris defined the grrrl power of the 1990s as, "A loose, global network of predominantly white young women interested in feminism, youth politics, punk and other alternative cultural practices, and a range of left-wing political interests (for example, anarchism, vegetarianism, and environmentalism)."[227] Harris believes that girls are used by Western commercial interests to symbolize the self-made "can-do" girl of the future, mixing feminism and the concept of "grrrl power" with neoliberal capitalist individualism. Girls are portrayed as the "poster girls for success in neoliberal times" and "the ideal citizens of the future."[228]

"A Mighty Girl" Facebook page has over a million likes, providing models of achieving women and girls on its website for "smart, confident and courageous girls."[229] The Wall Street McCann Ad agency installed a statue of a girl facing off the famous Wall Street bull statue in 2017, not a woman but "The Fearless Girl." The sculptor of the "Charging Bull" asked in April 2017 that the girl statue be moved because she insultingly made his bull seem like a threat rather than a positive symbol of strength. "It's really bad," said sculptor Arturo Di Modica, 76, who threatened to sue the city. Mayor Bill de Blasio supported the girl because people need inspiration in the Trump Administration and tweeted, "Men who don't like women taking up space are exactly why we need the Fearless Girl."[230] A Harvard University health curriculum to develop girl power, health and leadership is described in *Full of Ourselves* (2005) by Catherine Steiner-Adair and Lisa Sjostrom.

By making good choices as savvy consumers, smart girls succeed in being "winners in a new world" of late modernity, which results in success stories in contrast to "at-risk" girls who make poor choices and therefore aren't able to consume very much.[231] In an insecure era of global change from industrialization to information economies, girls are "constructed as the ideal new citizens" in their individual work and consumerism.[232] Social media "influencers" or "haulers" on sites like Instagram collect thousands of followers by instructing them about the latest and coolest consumer trends, while at the same time TV reality shows and teen magazines replace the goal of love and marriage with the desire to be famous in girls' fantasies. [233] The approach is parodied in an Australian girl's zine of the 1990s called "My Life as a Mega-Rich Bombshell." However, a global study of over 20,000 Gen Z young people in 2016 found that only 3% were motivated by the desire to be famous. [234]

In Egypt where women are barely represented in government, Asmaa Mahfouz, of YouTube fame for calling Egyptians to Tahrir Square for the revolution, observed, "Women in Egypt have more spirit to persevere. They're more manly than men. People always ask me, 'Why don't you work on women's rights?' I say, 'Men should be looking to protect their rights, because we're doing better than they are now.'" [235] I see no evidence of her optimism. The new electoral law of 2014 guaranteed women only 12% of seats in the legislature, albeit better than the previous parliament's 1.6%. [236] President Abdel Fattah el-Sisi appointed only four women out of 34 ministerial heads and sexual harassment continued on the streets, so there's no evidence of improvement for women. Having "spirit" is different from the reality of violence against women.

Concern for women's rights as human rights is spreading around the world promulgated by the UN and NGOs. A young Tunisian teacher of 18 to 20-year-olds, Khouloud Khammassi said in a Skype conversation that, "I make sure I let people know about women's issues. I have zero tolerance for guys who try to make jokes about women in my class." She said Tunisia is the first and best country in the Arab world to make laws protecting women and children couched in terms of women's legal rights rather than feminism, which is more inclusive of changes in gender roles. She's relieved not to have the Islamic Ennahda party in power because Muslims preach in mosques that a woman's place is in the home. Although she doesn't call herself a feminist, she knows the main issue for her female students is fear of sexual harassment or rape on the streets. Khammassi said of her students,

> *My girls are very aggressive; they yell at the guys in class if they piss them off. They tell me, "Oh, Madame, their questions are stupid, why don't they study at home?" The dean of our school gave a good talk about how the girls perform better than the guys. I was born in 1983; by the time I was 13, I started to be aware of gender issues. I took it for granted that I had the right to do whatever I wanted to do. Because my family is very liberal, I could talk with boys and wear a swimming suit.*

Studies confirm that girls are more self-disciplined. A Magid survey of US "Plurals," ages 8 to 15, reported that the girls were much more likely than the boys to expect to change the world, to care about their grades (66% vs. 47%), and to want feedback from teachers and parents (50% vs. 40%).[237] Girls valued being respectful, ethical and trustworthy, while boys valued loyalty and being fun to be with. Their Generation X mothers were less likely than Millennial or Baby Boomer wives to report that their husbands were very involved in family care. This dynamic, coupled with the fact that girls are just as likely as adult women to say they've experienced sexism (38%), encourages girls to be independent and not to expect Prince Charming to take care of them. A Pew Research Center survey of young adults 18 to 24 found that 66% of women think that career success is very important, compared to 59% of men.[238] What's most important for both sexes is being a good parent, with a successful marriage in second place, and a high-paying career in third place. Young women place a higher value on achieving all three goals than young men.

Antonio De Walk is a 24-year-old California writer who faults media for its outdated stereotypes, saying he doesn't recognize the independent and motivated women of his generation in films such as *Twilight* where the heroines have power only because several men are in love with them. The films don't reflect the fact that "the women of my generation are forces to be reckoned with." He sees his female peers as more likely to succeed in university and their careers; "I don't know a single woman my age sitting on her parents' couch—something I cannot say for my male friends."[239]

Young Men's Issues and Viewpoints

Boys and men have higher status and more power as evidenced in their control of governments and large corporations and their rampant violence against women. Women generally have lower status: A Bangladeshi young feminist reported in her country, "They are not regarded as human beings." An Indian SpeakOut girl, 15, reports, "People think women are for making food for men. They have no respect." Her life purpose is to "save the girl child and motivate girls and enjoy my life." An Egyptian woman, Mona Eltahawy, asked in her article about Arab men, "Why Do They Hate Us?"[240] She favors a global feminist movement in response. However, many younger men favor equal opportunity for women, want their future wives to do paid work, and are allies with their female peers in groups such as UN Women's HeForShe and many anti-violence groups.[241]

Men control public space in many countries. The focus on women as sexual temptresses increases with separation of the sexes. "My Catholic high school is a boys' school so my perspective towards girls is different and not good," revealed Nahom, 18, m, Ethiopia. In Egypt I saw men sit and talk with each other, play board games, pray towards Mecca, smoke water pipes on the sidewalks, and do jobs that women do in the west do like clean hotel rooms. Boys swim in the Nile and control the sports fields. Women on the streets move directly to their destination without any playtime. When I interviewed three women demonstrators in Tahrir Square, a nurse told me men want to keep women looking down rather than straight ahead. Being required to wear *hijab* and *niqab* may also bind women. Walking over a bridge in Cairo, a group of young men looked at and commented on a bit of a strap of my orange sports bra they could see around the neckline of my long-sleeved shirt; in a culture where women must cover up that smidgen of fabric that seemed worth discussing.

I asked Yara about interaction of girls and boys in Cairo. She said gender segregation starts in some schools from the age of seven.

> *My [government] school is a bit more progressive so boys and girls take their classes together, they sit for lunch together, they hang out in and out of school all the time. Too much mingling is still frowned upon at my school but it's not as strict as other schools. My mom and dad are completely fine with me visiting boys in their homes, since I've had male best friends my entire life. But I do know other families were this might be a taboo. The social and economical state of the family determines a lot as well. The better the economic and social state, the more mingling is allowed.*

Hassan, a Pakistani student teacher in our Open Doors Literacy Project, video-taped public space for me near his home in Peshawar. I didn't see any girls playing sports like the boys playing cricket, or women hanging out. The few women I saw in Hassan's video were walking directly to their destination, as in Egypt, covered in white chadors. Sex segregation is still prevalent in the West as well. Look at school playgrounds near you or university STEM classes. However, rigid sex role divisions hurt both sexes. "The Man Box" is the term used to describe the restrictions placed on boys and men, described by US educator Tony Porter in his "Call to Men" TED talk.[242] The documentary *The Mask You Live In* (2013) also explores the rigidities of the male role.[243] An article by Elizabeth Plank lists "23 Ways Feminism Has Made the World a Better Place for Men."[244] Adarsh, 19, m, India, wrote about why he's a feminist on Our Shared Shelf book club on Goodreads:

I'm a feminist because I too have heard that women belong in the kitchen, boys don't cry (heard this one from girls!), and after she get married she won't get to work. I felt like if I don't speak up, I'll be shut down like the rest of them. I'm a rebel. If I don't like the way things are in our society, I'm going to change it and that's how I became a feminist.

The Boy Crisis

In a postmodern "feminized" era in the West, some believe that cultural construction of gender favors female educational achievements and affiliational style. In 2014, Fox News anchor Brit Hume commented about New Jersey Republican Governor Chris Christie: "In this sort of feminized atmosphere in which we exist today, guys who are masculine and muscular like that in their private conduct, kind of old-fashioned tough guys, run some risks."[245] (In his last year as governor Christie had a 15% approval rating.) Other authors also worry that feminism is undermining masculinity, as elucidated in Christina Hoff Summers' *The War Against Boys* (2001), *Boys Adrift* (2009) by Leonard Sax, and Kay Hymowitz' *Manning Up* (2012). These traditional role reversals alarm elders. In Japan, aimless young men who reject the work ethic of their fathers are called "herbivores," while their female peers are "carnivores" or "hunters." The new young man who rejects traditional gender roles is represented by Ken, in the film *How to be Single* (2016). He is a younger man who is in love with an older woman, who doesn't date. Meg is an OB/GYN who got pregnant through artificial insemination by an anonymous donor. Uninspired by his job as a receptionist, Ken wants to stay home with the baby while Meg works, saying that it was a boyhood dream. The actor who plays Ken, Jake Lacy, describes Ken as a "sweet laid back guy."[246]

Chinese boys unanimously told an American teenage interviewer for his book that girls are better students and Chinese experts refer to a "strong female, weak male" phenomenon.[247] A student activist fighting discrimination against women's admittance to majors such as mining engineering, Xiao Meili told the BBC's "100 Women" series, "Sexism is in every corner of life in China, and people get so used to it that it's easy to ignore it. People got used to the idea that men did things better than women. But when women started to excel [in university admissions], people got scared and thought of that as a problem," similar to the US.[248] We've seen that globally more women than men are university students (51%)--31% of females and 28% of males are enrolled in higher education, although about 8% of boys are illiterate compared to 13% of girls.[249] Thus women are both the majority of illiterates and university students, depending on where they live. Girls are more educated than boys in Argentina, Brazil, Indonesia, Iran, China, Saudi Arabia, and the US.[250]

Although boys are more likely to attend school, girls have lower dropout and repetition rates in all developing regions and the gender gap has closed in most countries.[251] In almost one-third of developing countries, girls outnumber boys in secondary school but that means boys outnumber girls two-thirds of the time. Teachers and students I've interviewed globally often report that girls work harder in school, while boys are more distracted by games. In India, boys told me they play better than girls and a boy joked that girls do better in school because the boys help them; these comments generated laughter in the classrooms I visited. A 16-year-old blogger from Chennai, Vaishnavi has empathy for boys: "Traditional families say about boys to girls: they take advantage of you, all boys are bad and cunning, they always have an ulterior motive while interacting with you etc. All these judgmental comments create a long-lasting prejudice against men."[252]

In his classic book *Love and Death in the American Novel* (1960), Leslie Fiedler shows that American fiction centers on boys and men running from the civilizing control of virtuous girls like Becky Thatcher, epitomized by Huck Finn, Tom Sawyer and Holden Caulfield and other books found in the children's section of the library. *New York Times* film critic A.O. Scott updated Fiedler, maintaining that the popularity of comics and young adult fiction like *The Hunger Games* for adults indicate the continuation of juvenile entertainment that doesn't address adult issues like marriage.[253] He thinks TV and films show the allegorical decline of the adult white male; "It seems that, in doing away with patriarchal authority, we have also, perhaps unwittingly, killed off all the grown-ups."

Scott's examples of bad men who don't make it are Tony Soprano in *The Sopranos*, Don Draper in *Mad Men*, and Walter White in *Breaking Bad*. Scott concludes that TV shows like *Girls* and *Masters of Sex* indicate "nobody knows how to be a grown-up anymore." Actress Frances McDormand, age 57, added to the discussion about the US fear of aging; "There's no desire to be an adult. . . . No one is supposed to age past 45 — sartorially, cosmetically, attitudinally. Everybody dresses like a teenager. Everybody dyes their hair. Everybody is concerned about a smooth face," except for her. Superbowl ads are an index of negative attitudes towards both sexes, as in a 2016 ad for a snack chip where the very pregnant wife is getting a sonogram. She gets angry at her slob of an immature husband for crunching on Doritos instead of focusing on their baby.

Scott warned that film characters played by actors like Adam Sandler and Seth Rogen and "bro comedy" films like *The Hangover* series portray "the rebellious animus of the disaffected man-child directed not just against male authority but also against women," finding solace in male buddies. Examples of movies that illustrate boorish male buddies who get drunk together and do stupid things are *The Comedy* (2012), as well as the TV series *Entourage* and *Silicon Valley*. The immature bros are not confined to the US. An Indian film called *Dil Chahta Hai* (2001) shows four male friends who are also confused about their futures and make some bad decisions. The extreme end of the "crisis of masculinity" is young lonely men who commit mass shootings in public places like a school, theater or church. The US averages a shooting every five weeks, usually by a young man.[254] The only shooting I know of committed by a two friends occurred in Columbine, Colorado, in 1999. These incidents also occurred in Finland, Germany, Australia, England, and France.

Professor Michael Kimmel describes "guyland" as a stage of development from adolescence to manhood inhabited by young men, referred to as "laddism" in the UK and Australia.[255] Kimmel says their sexist motto is simple, "Bros before Hos." Their world revolves "almost exclusively around other guys." These young men feel entitled as males but realize male privilege is eroding. They tend to be homophobic, anxious, competitive, lonely, confused, aimless, and desperate to prove their manhood, without adequate male guidance. Kimmel advocates that a new model of masculinity is needed that involves the courage to stand up for what's right rather than conforming to their band of brothers.

Niobe Way's study of boys in the US and China found that boys tend to lose the close friendships they say kept them from going "wako" as they pass through adolescence. During this difficult time they became more distrustful of other boys, fearful of homosexuality—"no homo" was a frequent phrase, as the boys felt increasingly isolated and alone due to the pressure to become men.[256] Way states that close friendships are important for self-worth and feeling connected to others, which leaves boys in a "crisis of connection" as they grow older. Way advocates programs like "Roots of Empathy" used in Canadian schools to help boys develop emotional well-being and critique gender role stereotypes of connection as feminine.[257]

Men's liberationist author Warren agrees there's a boy crisis in the US, as boys are addicted to video games, and too often lack enough contact with their fathers (one-third of children are raised in father-absent homes[258]). In addition, he says boys are not doing as well as girls in school and they're more medicated; for example, with drugs for Attention Deficit Disorder.[259] The award-winning film *Boyhood* was filmed over 12 years as the actor and the girl who plays his sister grew up (2014). It illustrates a boy growing up in a single-parent family without consistent contact with his father, and with two successive, abusive stepfathers. The film is not far from the norm. In 2013 only 19% of households consisted of a married couple and their children; 25% of mothers with children under 18 didn't have a partner, and 41% of births in 2012 were to unmarried women.[260]

Farrell advocated a White House Council on Boys and Men to study the problem, which President Obama created in 2014, along with a program called "My Brothers' Keeper" to encourage men to mentor boys of color. Youth are more likely to commit assaults in areas where men are scarce, according to a University of Michigan study.[261] Young black men are especially at risk of absentee fathers, resulting in the boys more likely to be out of school, out of work, or incarcerated. The US was the first country to organize a Strategy for Adolescent Girls, launched by Secretary of State John Kerry.[262] The International Center for Research on Women, Millennium Challenge Corporation, and Girls Not Brides lobbied for the policy. Kerry explained, "This plan brings together resources and expertise from all of the agencies [USAID, Peace Corps, etc.]" The State Department planned to focus on laws and polices such as assisting girls to go to school, ending child marriage and stopping genital mutilation.

Other authors bemoan *The Demise of Guys: Why Boys Are Struggling and What We Can Do About It* (2012). Authors Philip Zimbardo and Nikita Duncan write that addiction to video games and online pornography created a generation of shy, risk-averse and emotionally unexpressive boys. The prevalence of porn viewing is the confirmed by Peggy Orenstein based on her interviews with girls, summarized in her *Girls and Sex: Navigating the Complicated New Landscape (2016)*. David Benatar argued in *The Second Sexism: Discrimination Against Men and Boys* (2012) that "second sexism" needs to be acknowledged. *Men on Strike: Why Men Are Boycotting Marriage, Fatherhood, and the American Dream--and Why It Matters*, written by Helen Smith in 2014, also argues that the US culture is anti-male.

Another book that addresses boys' problems is *Masterminds and Wingmen: Helping Our Boys Cope with Schoolyard Power, Locker-Room Tests, Girlfriends and the New Rules of Boy World* by Rosalind Wiseman (2013). *In Hollowed Out: Why the Economy Doesn't Work Without a Strong Middle Class* (2015), David Madland argues that male unemployment is higher than female unemployment and male's education attainment is lower, "which doesn't bode well for the future." As a consequence, the Pew Research

Center reported that 40% of Millennial men live with the parents, compared to 32% of young women.[263] One-third of these young men are unemployed, many others work part-time, and two-thirds haven't married.[264] One in three men ages 25 to 54 has a criminal record and three in 10 men over 20 don't work, compared with one in 10 in the 1950s. One in three men between the ages of 18 and 34 live near the poverty line. The median income for men under 34 is only $10,400 according to the Census Bureau.

Author Gary Cross calls male slackers "boy-men," Andrew Yarrow calls them Peter Pans, and others refer to Millennials' delayed adulthood. In the film *The Intern* (2015), Anne Hathaway plays a successful young entrepreneur, Jules, with a stay-at-home husband taking care of their daughter (he is also having an affair). Jules tells her young male interns that girls grew to be women but men devolved to boys, with no current Harrison Fords. She explains that girls had encouragement like Take Your Daughter to Work Day and slogans like "you go girl," but boys had nothing to help them be gentlemen like the kind and wise older man (age 70) played by Robert De Niro.

TV sitcoms explore the "battle of the straight white man to assert his masculinity in an increasingly alien world" that they no longer control, as highlighted in a sign slamming Hilary Clinton's "vagenda of manocide," according to James Poniewozik.[265] His examples of TV shows that struggle to find a place for men in 2016 are: *Kevin Can Wait* (about a retired policeman who goes back to work to prevent his daughter from dropping out of college to support her designer fiancé), *Man With a Plan* about a contractor who unhappily quits work to care for his children while his wife goes back to work, and *The Great Indoors* that explores generational conflict between an older journalist and Millennial workers he views as coddled. *Son of Zorn* is about a macho animated warrior and his ex-wife and son who live in present day Orange County, California. In 2012, *Work It* featured two unemployed men who dress as women to find work in a job market they feel favors women.

Unemployment rates for US men aged 25 to 54 tripled to 16% since the late 1960s. Their children are less likely to succeed, leading a Harvard economics professor to warn, "We could be losing the next generation of kids."[266] Three-quarters of the eight million jobs lost in the US Great Recession were men's jobs, mostly in manufacturing.

With the disappearance of manufacturing jobs for men in the US, women-headed families dominate working-class families and 40% of babies are born to unmarried mothers. In 2011, only 81% of working-age men were employed, compared to 95% of men in 1969, and they're earning less than before. One in six men of prime working age are unemployed, and more than two million are in prison.[267] One in eight men is an ex-felon.

A Brookings Institution study found men's earnings have fallen more than women's and increase in income inequality has become permanent for decades now that the 1% owns 38% of the US wealth and the bottom 40% own less than 1% of wealth.[268] In most of the biggest US cities, young childless women earn 8% more a year than men, 17% more in New York City.[269] "These women haven't just caught up with the guys; in many cities, they're clocking them," says James Chung of Reach Advisors, which analyzes Census Bureau data. However, overall even young single women's earnings lag behind men's salaries. Women cluster in traditional female university majors and jobs, so that women with doctorate degrees earn 77% of what their male colleagues earn. Older men rule government and the work world but younger men are not in the pipeline in the same percentages as in the past, now that more women graduate from university. The UCLA CIRP annual national survey of college freshmen in 2014 reported that women were more likely to plan on earning a graduate degree than men were (36% vs. 29% of men).[270]

Are men expendable for educated career women, as some feminist Second Wave separatists advocated? A growing global phenomenon is well-educated employed young women who remain single either for lack of an equally successful partner or because they prefer being single. Researchers named this the "first new global sociological phenomenon of the 21st century."[271] These single women are often disparaged for not conforming to traditional roles. This trend occurs not only in Asia (China's "left-over women") and the West, but in the Middle East as well.[272] Japan's "single parasites" in their 20s live with their parents and enjoy spending their earnings without having to pay for living expenses. The phenomenon hasn't hit India yet. The BBC interviewed a single 28-year old woman who faces discrimination in India, stereotyped as having a "bad character."[273] She said she's scared all the time and has trouble finding a landlord who will rent to a single woman. (They also don't like to rent to unmarried couples.)

China's one-child policy led to around 50 more million men than women, but it's difficult for successful women to find a partner. The phrase *yin sheng, yang shuai* means the female is going up while the male is going down. Because a couple is expected to support both sets of parents, having a good job is a top draw in a marriage partner. The head of the largest matchmaking site said men want a traditional woman, a teacher or nurse who would be a good mother, hopefully with large breasts.[274] A male marketing consultant in Shanghai revealed, "I would feel ashamed if the woman I'm with is on my level. I would lose my confidence and male status."[275] What women want in a mate is height, salary, and ownership of car or house. A female marketing director said, "I want equality from a marriage and it's hard to find Chinese men who offer that. I've been at work all day, too, so why should I do the washing-up, the cooking and look after the baby as well?"

Hopefully we're moving towards equality rather than a reversal of power and motivation to succeed. Zoe, 17, (California) doesn't think men have anything to worry about:

> *I've noticed that unmotivated young men is the case sometimes at the high school level, but I don't think that's going to be a problem. I think boys will grow out of it. We hit our primes at different times. Women are 51% of the population so they should be that percentage in the Senate and House, but there's no danger of having women take over every sphere of life.*

What Boys Think About Feminism

I would like to stop the dowry system and corruption.
   Bhat, 16, India

Sadly, women in my country are very oppressed and discriminated against by both society and government, so I'll start by giving them back all their rights (right for freedom, right of education, right of thinking, right of speech and opinion, right of participation). Like they say "You educate a man; you educate a man. You educate a woman; you educate a generation."
   Ahmed, 17, Egypt

Most of the parents, with much fear towards their daughter, do not give much freedom to her. Instead, they treat her as a prisoner. This has to be changed and every girl given sufficient freedom to be friendly with others and to do jobs without wasting her 22 years of valuable education.
   Abhinar, 18, India

Equality must be given to every one in the societies because in different tribes women have no say or do not participate in decision-making. I will give first priority to women in employment opportunities in order they will not discriminated by their husbands. Also I will try my level best to help children who are orphans, so I will try to make funds for them to survive like other kids.
   Sarrwatt, 19, Tanzania

The law should be the same for women and men, like a man can't enter a mall in Saudi Arabia at night without a woman. [Single men are frowned on, in fear they're in the mall to meet women, so they have to attend with a family member.]
     Mohammed, 19, Saudi Arabia

I feel more and more clarity that it is my karma to fight for women's equality in education in developing countries. I see more and more clearly how the women in my family react to their fate and how their lives are different because their education. I see how a women's education impacts her whole life, her whole family--and that impacts her society.
     Yuan, 25, China

Young men tend to be more egalitarian than their fathers, comfortable with girls as friends and equals. Feminist actress Emma Watson kicked off a UN campaign called "HeForShe" in 2014 to galvanize boys and men to "be advocates for gender equality."[276] Watson said of the website launched in 2016, "It's important because we want to be the first and largest crowdsourcing tool for solutions to gender inequality." She gave examples of HeForShe solutions, including a husband school in Zimbabwe, the annulment of over 300 child marriages by the President of Malawi, and the Canadian University of Waterloo giving scholarships to young women in engineering programs. She also started a feminist book club on the Goodreads platform called Our Shared Shelf in 2016. Despite her recognition that feminism is an unpopular word, she said she's like Hermione the character she portrayed in the Harry Potter films, "I'm a bit of a feminist. I'm very competitive and challenging." She said by the time she was 18 her male friends weren't able to express their feelings. She pointed out that feminism is not man-hating but about equal opportunities: "We don't often talk about men being imprisoned by gender stereotypes but I can see that they are and that when they are free, things will change for women as a natural consequence. . . If men don't have to control, women won't have to be controlled."[277]

An organization that began in Brazil in 1997, Promundo encourages young men to be non-violent and to support gender equality. It works with the global MenEngage campaign to promote good caregiving practices that prevent domestic violence. An Indian program educates boys to stand up for their sisters' rights in village areas where early marriage for girls is the norm.[278] President Obama launched a similar campaign called "It's On Us," to encourage bystanders, especially men, to prevent assaults on young women on college campuses. Many young men oppose the mistreatment of women. The youngest member of the South African parliament, Mkhuleko Hlengwa, age 25, arrived the first day wearing a button stating "No to rape." He wants to change the high rape rate (64,000 reported cases in 2012) and also to get young people more active in politics to fight unemployment (50% for youth), as well as improve education and recreation.

A true feminist hero is 12-year-old Oli Ahmed who campaigns against child brides in the Dhaka slum where he lives in Bangladesh.[279] Parents marry off young girls so they won't have to pay a dowry and school expenses. Ahmed was motivated by sadness and anger when a girl who was like an older sister to him was forced to get married, sent off to another family never to be seen again. Ahmed spoke with the NGO Plan International workers to propose that he set up a children's group to go door or door "persuading, scolding, and hectoring parents." He and other volunteers ask parents to wait until the legal marriage age of 18. Oli reports, "I think we do a better job than the adults... the adults think we're so young and yet we know so much... we're more enthusiastic than the older people. I feel very good that a girl's life has been saved because of the work that I've done." An NGO worker says that since the children started work on Oli's suggestion, the number of child marriages in that area has dropped by as much as half.

Some young fathers are speaking up about US workplace culture that equates a man taking parental leave or resisting long work hours as feminine. An engineer reported, "There's a lot of competition to see how many hours I can work, whether or not you have a kid."[280] A study found that men who requested a 12-week family leave suffered at work because they were viewed as more feminine than other men. Ram, age 21, posted from California on Our Shared Shelf in 2016:

> *Growing up as a guy, you are always told not to cry, not to be caring, to not show emotions, to not be soft, to not like art because that's a girl thing, to not bake because that's a girl thing. And then there are some choices you have that people question like, "Why do you like cats? That's a girl's pet." "Why don't you hook up? You're a guy. You can get away with it." Those things, for a while, I did not question. They were somewhat basic rules in the society that has been implanted on you since birth that people don't question it. Becoming a feminist, you question those things.*

> *I would like my son in the future to grow up to not think that crying makes you gay. And I would not like my daughter to grow up thinking she's always going to*

earn less than a man even though she works hard. Feminism is such a wonderful thing that we should not be avoiding.

Generational expert Neil Howe observed that US Millennial male rappers don't posture and "swag" like Gen X rappers and are more likely to reveal their vulnerabilities. For example, a rapper named Macklemore talks about his problems with addiction and doesn't denigrate women. Other young rappers delight in their thrift store finds like "wearing your granddad's clothes" rather than expensive gold jewelry. SpeakOut boys care about the status of girls from around the world.

When I asked seniors in a Chico, California high school about equal rights their responses were probably more typical than a young man who would join a feminist book club. The high school senior boys said they were sick and tired of reverse discrimination, as when minorities are favored in college admission. White males are the only ones not allowed to discriminate, they said, as women can sue for sexual harassment at work and get millions of dollars. They don't feel their generation discriminates on the basis of gender or ethnicity as their female peers are likely to excel. Feminism doesn't seem relevant to them, despite public comments like this one in 2009, when the Governor of Virginia remarked, "The dynamic new trend of working women and feminists ... is ultimately detrimental to the family."

A Pakistani high school student and an Indian graduate student have the same fear that women get unfair advantages from affirmative action programs:

I do agree that men dominate most fields in life and women should be given EQUAL opportunity. But if this term of GENDER DISCRIMINATION is altogether ignored, there would be proper equality between the two genders. Media and people have made such big deal out of FEMINISM and DISCRIMINATION that these terms are enough to make a dividing line between females and males. I would give you an example: In a local office of an NGO, all the staff was male. One day a female worker was added to the staff for the sake of giving "equal opportunity to females" and was preferred over a better-qualified male applicant. Now, she may be good but the other male applicant was better than her and now the whole office is fed up.
  Shehroz, 17, Pakistan

I do have questions for which I have never really had any convincing answers in India. Someone reading my questions need not assume that these are coming from a chauvinist.

1. *If women are self-sufficient and strong enough, why do they seek reservations in colleges and schools and work places?*

2. *How much percent of independent women would be willing to marry a man who is less educated and earned less than them?*

3. *How come I become a better potential groom for girls after moving to USA to study even though I am the same person as I was back home?*

4. *Why would an independent girl seek to marry an NRI* [Non resident Indian] *and look for a job in USA and not independently look for better jobs in the world on her own?*

    Jayesh, a graduate student from Mumbai studying in California

If girls as a group are more focused on getting an education, we can speculate about the changes they'll bring as they enter professions and government in greater numbers and change patriarchal attitudes. As women are the majority of university graduates, indicating they'll be more of the professionals and politicians, their inclusive, relationship-oriented, liberal, and non-conforming tendencies should change our future. The next chapter reports that many view women leaders as more peace loving and cooperative. Studies report that girls and women are more supportive of equality, suggesting that the future will be more egalitarian as women exert power, or as Facebook COO Sheryl Sandberg advised them, "lean in" to be more assertive at work and sharing family work at home.

Chapter 1 Discussion Questions and Activities

Questions

1. What do you think are the strongest influences on Yara's willingness to risk her life in Tahrir Square? Look at my YouTube interview with Yara to help you answer the question. Do you have any causes that you'd be willing to die for?

2. Did you know about women's leadership in the uprisings since 2011? If not, why not? You read in the Introduction about scholars' blind spots about youth activism, as author Jessica Taft mentioned in this chapter. Why do you think academics don't have more actual dialogues with young people they write about?

3. Globally young women are the majority of university students. What impact will that have as women assume more leadership and power as a result of their edu-

cation?

4. Do you think class, religion, sexual preference or gender attitudes are more likely to keep young people from progressing? Or is the feminist concept of intersectionality (acknowledging multiple oppressions in addition to gender) the key to understanding the lack of opportunity for many girls?

5. What influences explain girls' increasing aspirations and activism? What roles do you see girls and young women playing where you live? Are there remnants of traditional roles that girls are supposed to let boys lead?

6. Do you think there's a "crisis of masculinity" and "feminization of work?" If so, what consequences can you predict?

Activities

1. Interview the oldest people you know about how and why attitudes towards gender roles have changed since they were young. Ask them if their attitudes have changed and why.

2. Search the Internet for youth activism and girls' activism and report on patterns in what you find.[281]

3. What do you learn from looking at a collection of photos of global women available online?[282] Also look at Girls' Globe blog that aims to "raise awareness about the rights, health and empowerment of women and girls worldwide." [283]

4. See the Australian film *Whale Rider* (2002) and discuss changing gender attitudes. The Whangara Maori people believe their savior ancestor rode home on the back of a whale and that leadership goes to first-born males believed to be his descendant. A young girl, Pai, challenges this tradition.

5. Connecther, founded by Harvard University women students in 2011, organizes an annual Girls Impact the World Film Festival.[284] It also offers crowdfunded projects for girls. What themes do you see in the films and projects?

6. A slide show about gender equality for boys and men is available online.[285]

Endnotes

[1] Why Millennial Matter consulting firm http://whymillennialsmatter.com/

[2] John Poole, "Where the Girls Are (And Aren't): #15Girls. National Public Radio, October 20, 2015.

http://www.npr.org/sections/goatsandsoda/2015/10/20/448407788/where-the-girls-are-and-aren-t-15girls

[3] http://gadebate.un.org/sites/default/files/gastatements/66/BR_en_0.pdf

[4] Paul Mason, "From Arab Spring to Global Revolution," *The Guardian*, February 5, 2013.

5   http://www.theguardian.com/world/2013/feb/05/arab-spring-global-revolution

6   https://www.youtube.com/watch?v=zDVA7r7r0d0 (2013)

7   https://www.tedxdirigo.com/speakers/anjali-appadurai/

Firoze Manji on Real News Network, 2011.

8   http://wn.com/water_privatization_in_morocco

Micah White. *The End of Protest: A New Playbook for Revolution*. Knopf Canada, 2016, p. 198.

Carolyn Harris, "Russia's February Revolution was Led by Women on the March," Smithsonian.com, February 17, 2017.

9   http://www.smithsonianmag.com/history/russias-february-revolution-was-led-women-march-180962218/

https://globalyouthbook.wordpress.com/2014/04/25/top-4-responses-to-global-youth-survey/

10   https://globalyouthbook.wordpress.com/2014/04/25/statistics-global-youth-survey-frequencies-4149-from-88-countries/

11   Geraldine Pratt and Victoria Rosner, **eds**. *The Global and the Intimate: Feminism in Our Time*. Columbia University Press, 2012, p. 3.

12   Anoop Nayak and Mary Jane Kehily. *Gender, Youth and Culture: Young Masculinities and Femininities*. Palgrave Macmillan, 2007.

Tracy McVeigh, "Meet the New Wave of Activists Making Feminism Thrive in a Digital Age," *The Guardian*, June 1, 2013.

13   http://www.theguardian.com/world/2013/jun/01/activists-feminism-digital

Jasleena Grewal, "What Moment Sparked Your #InternationalSisterhood?," *Yes! Magazine*, April 1, 2016.

http://www.yesmagazine.org/people-power/what-moment-sparked-your-internationalsisterhood-20160401?utm_source=YTW&utm_medi-um=Email&utm_campaign=20160401

14

15   http://outspokenspeakers.blogspot.com/2016/02/what-being-feminist-really-means.html

Taylor Link, "Virginia Republican on Obamacare Protesters," *Salon*, January 31, 2017.

16   http://www.salon.com/2017/01/31/virginia-republican-on-obamacare-protesters-the-women-are-in-my-grill-no-matter-where-i-go/

17   www.toughgirlchallenges.com (many of the women are athletes)

http://www.usnews.com/news/articles/2015/03/05/state-department-honors-international-women-of-courage

18   http://www.state.gov/s/gwi/programs/iwoc/2015/index.htm

19   https://www.youtube.com/watch?v=_MweWpY47P0

"Illiteracy Rate Among Egyptian Middle Schoolers Spikes to 35 Percent," *Egyptian Streets*, October 19, 2015.

20   http://egyptianstreets.com/2015/10/19/illiteracy-rate-among-egyptian-middle-schoolers-spikes-to-35-percent/

21   http://www.theglobeandmail.com/news/british-columbia/father-of-girls-rights-activist-captivates-ted-audience/article17538451/

22   Meredith Weiss and Edward Aspinall, **eds**. *Student Activism in Asia: Between Protest and Powerlessness*. University of Minnesota Press, 2012, p. 28.

Tara Brady, "First Born and Female,?" *Daily Mail*, April 27, 2014.

23   http://www.dailymail.co.uk/news/article-2614228/First-born-female-Why-eldest-girl-means-likely-succeed.html

"Feminist Standpoint Theory," *Internet Encyclopedia of Philosophy*.

24   http://www.iep.utm.edu/fem-stan/

25   Sandra Harding. *The Feminist Standpoint Theory Reader*. Routledge, 2003.

Telephone interview, February 2015.

26   http://coalitionforadolescentgirls.org/

27   Karen Wells. *Childhood in a Global Perspective*. Polity Press, 2015, pp. 137-138.

Anna Leach and Sam O'Neill, "The Other Malalas: Girl Activists in the Developing World," *The Guardian*, December 12, 2013.

http://www.theguardian.com/global-development-professionals-network/interactive/2013/dec/12/other-malalas-girl-activists-develop-ing-world-interactive

28   https://www.youtube.com/watch?v=uB5BrUnQ6QA

James Youniss and Brian K Barber, "Egyptian Youth Make History," *Harvard International Review*, March 30, 2013.

29   http://hir.harvard.edu/archives/3079

https://www.youtube.com/watch?v=BTwT8tgoG38

30   https://youtu.be/uB5BrUnQ6QA

Robbie Couch, "The 5 Most Important Things Malala Has Done In 2014," *Huffington Post*, October 10, 2014.

31   http://www.huffingtonpost.com/2014/10/10/malala-nobel-peace-prize-winner-important_n_5965490.html

32   https://www.facebook.com/emmawatson/videos/1150256254993263/ Emma Watson

"Malala Yousafzai," NPR.org, October 15, 201

http://www.npr.org/2013/10/15/234730460/malala-yousafzai-a-normal-yet-powerful-girl

33   http://malala.gwu.edu/preface-malalas-father

www.justvision.org/budrus/about

34   http://sprachenquilt.com/tag/budrus/

35   https://globalyouthbook.wordpress.com/2014/04/16/youth-led-21st-century-uprisings/

36   Anya Schiffrin and Eamon Kircher-Allen. *From Cairo to Wall Street: Voices From the Global Spring*. The New Press, 2012, p. 33.

Adam Morrow and Khaled Moussa al-Omrani, "Women Fight for Rights in New Egypt," IDN-InDepth News, 2012.

37   http://www.indepthnews.info/index.php/global-issues/human-rights/1100-women-fight-for-rights-in-new-egypt

38   Smadar Lavie. *Wrapped in the Flag of Israel*. Berghahn, 2014.

http://globalnews.ca/news/858944/were-the-quebec-student-protests-worth-it/

[39] Isabel Ortiz, et al., "World Protests 2006-2013," Friedrich Ebert Stiftung, September 2013.

http://policydialogue.org/files/publications/World_Protests_2006-2013-Executive_Summary.pdf

[40] Katarina Tullia von Sydow, "Believing Women's Narratives in Sweden and Norway," OpenDemocracy.Net, July 29, 2015.

https://www.opendemocracy.net/5050/katarina-von-sydow/believing-womens-narratives-in-sweden-and-norway

[41] http://occupysexism.wordpress.com/

[42] Prudence "Cheers and Jeers," *Global Voices*, April 24, 2016.

https://globalvoices.org/2016/04/24/cheers-and-jeers-as-ugandan-female-researcher-undresses-to-get-her-office-back/

[43] http://www.icrw.org/sites/default/files/publications/Girls-Speak-A-New-Voice-In-Global-Development.pdf

[44] https://www.youtube.com/watch?v=WIvmE4_KMNw

https://www.youtube.com/watch?v=-Vq2mfF8puE

https://www.youtube.com/watch?v=1e8xgF0JtVg

[45] Sam Ro, "A Third of America's 18- To 34-Years-Olds Live With Their Parents," *Business Insider*, June 2, 2014.

http://www.businessinsider.com/18-34-years-olds-living-with-parents-2014-6 "Boomerang Bunch," *AARP The Magazine*, July 2014, p. 36.

[46] Editorial Board, "Millions of Men Are Missing From the Job Market," *New York Times*, October 16, 2016.

http://www.nytimes.com/2016/10/17/opinion/millions-of-men-are-missing-from-the-job-market.html?_r=0

[47] Shiv Malik, "The Dependent Generation," *The Guardian*, March 24, 2014.

http://www.theguardian.com/society/2014/mar/24/dependent-generation-half-young-european-adults-live-parents

[48] http://studentsatthecenterhub.org/toolkit/

[49] http://coalitionforadolescentgirls.org/resources-by-topic-2/

[50] Jeni Klugman et al.,*Voice and Agency : Empowering Women and Girls for Shared Prosperity*. World Bank, 2014. https://openknowledge.worldbank.org/handle/10986/19036 License: CC BY 3.0 IGO."

[51] "FAO at Work: Women—Key to Food Security," 2011, UN Food and Agriculture Organization.

http://www.fao.org/docrep/014/am719e/am719e00.pdf

[52] YWCA's Young Women's Leadership Alliance, Girls Incorporated, Girls Action Foundation in Canada, Advocates for Youth's Girls Engagement Advisory Board, Coalition for Adolescent Girls, The Girl Effect, Girls Inc., Youth United for Global Action and Awareness, UNICEF's Right to Know Initiative about HIV, and the United Nations (hereafter UN) Working Group on Girls and Girl UP.

[53] http://www.freechild.org/youth_activism_2.htm

[54] http://www.freechild.org/ladder.htm

http://www.advocatesforyouth.org/

info@girlsactionfoundation.ca

[55] http://www.bing.com/videos/search?q=severn+suzuki+youtube&FORM=VIRE12#view=detail&mid=78EC0287538F0312543E78EC0287538F0312543E

[56] http://www.truth-out.org/news/item/9931-are-you-here-to-save-face-or-save-us-brittany-trilford-17-addresses-world-leaders-at-rio-20

Democracy Now, June 21, 2012. http://www.democracynow.org/2012/6/21/are_you_here_to_save_face

[57] http://unfccc.int/cc_inet/files/cc_inet/information_pool/application/pdf/youth_in_action_on_climate_change_en.pdf

Nicole Goldin, *The Global Youth Wellbeing Index*, Center for Strategic & International Studies and International Youth Foundation, April 2014, p .2.

www.youthindex.org/reports/globalyouthwellbeingindex.pdf

[59] Kurzman, **ed.**, "The Arab Spring Uncoiled," *Mobilization*, December 2012, Vol. 17, No. 4, pp. 377-390.

http://mobilization.metapress.com/app/home/issue.asp?referrer=backto&backto=journal,1,52;linkingpublicationresults,1:119834,1;&absolute-position=1#A1,

[60] http://www.youtube.com/watch?v=gnA6qxmnsn4

[61] Emma Broadbent, et al., "Generation Z: Global Citizenship Survey," Varkey Foundation, January 2017.

https://www.varkeyfoundation.org/sites/default/files/Global%20Young%20People%20Report%20%28digital%29%20NEW%20%281%29.pdf

[62] http://writingwithmovements.com/movement-knowledge

Colours of Resistance Archive: www.coloursofresistance.org

Institute for Anarchist Studies: www.anarchiststudies.org

Punch Up Collective: punchupcollective.tumblr.com

[63] Upping the Anti: www.uppingtheanti.org

[64] http://www.wmd.org/resources/whats-being-done/women%E2%80%99s-participation-politics/womens-organizations-around-world

Caroline Howard, "The World's Most Powerful Women 2014," *Forbes*, May 28, 2014.

[65] http://www.forbes.com/sites/carolinehoward/2014/05/28/the-worlds-most-powerful-women-2014/

www.time.com/time/magazine/article/0,9171,901040927-699350,00.html

[66] https://globalyouthbook.wordpress.com/2016/03/11/what-names-do-you-hear-for-gen-y/ Check index for other posts of interest.

[67] "Pitch a Tent, Bring Your Suspenders: #Occupy Wall Street," *Transition Voice*, July 18, 2011.

http://transitionvoice.com/2011/07/pitch-a-tent-bring-your-suspenders-occupywallstreet/

[68] "Youth Speak: Powered by AIESEC. YouthSpeak Survey Millennial Insight Report. 2015." 42,257 respondents from 100 countries and territories, a majority between the ages of 18 to 25.

69 http://youthspeak.aiesec.org/wp-content/uploads/2015/07/Youthspeak-Millennial-Report-2015.pdf

70 http://www.un.org/youthenvoy/wp-content/uploads/2014/10/wethepeoples-7million.pdf

http://princess.disney.com/movies

Rebecca Hains. *The Princess Problem: Guiding Our Girls through the Princess-Obsessed Years.* Sourcebooks, 2014.

71 Peggy Orenstein. *Cinderella Ate My Daughter: Dispatches From the Front Lines of the New Girlie-Girl Culture.* Harper, 2012

Alison Flood, "Indian Comic Creates Female Superhero to Tackle Rape," *The Guardian,* December 18, 2014.

72 https://www.theguardian.com/books/2014/dec/18/india-comic-superhero-tackle-rape-women-priyas-shakti-parvati

73 http://www.winbeta.org/news/windows-10-advertisements-features-kids-will-great-things

Eliana Dockterman, "Shailene Woodly Woodley on Why She is Not a Feminist," *TIME,* May 5, 2014.

74 http://time.com/87967/shailene-woodley-feminism-fault-in-our-stars/

Roger Cohen, "The Great Unraveling," *New York Times,* September 15, 2014.

75 http://www.nytimes.com/2014/09/16/opinion/roger-cohen-the-great-unraveling.html?_r=0s

76 http://www.thetoptens.com/top-tv-shows-teenagers/

Tim Beedle, "Are You Ready for Prez's Mark Russell,?" *DC Comics,* August 27, 2015.

77 http://www.dccomics.com/blog/2015/08/27/are-you-ready-for-prezs-mark-russell

Javier Hernandez, "The 'Goddess' Yi Wan Ka: Ivanka Trump is a Hit in China," *New York Times,* April 5, 2017.

78 https://www.nytimes.com/2017/04/05/world/asia/ivanka-trump-china.html

Michelle Raffterty, "20 TV Mean Girls We Secretly Love," *Flavor Wire,* April 25, 2012.

79 http://flavorwire.com/283644/20-tv-mean-girls-we-secretly-love/7

80 Minky Worden, ed. *The Unfinished Revolution.* Seven Stories Press, 2012, pp. 315, 329.

"India's Deadly Superstition," February 25, 2016. http://www.nytimes.com/video/world/asia/100000004220390/indias-deadly-superstition.

81 html?emc=edit_th_20160225&nl=todaysheadlines&nlid=68143430

Peter Gelderloos, "The CUP: Up to its Neck in Politics," *ROAR Magazine,* January 31, 2016, p. 14.

82 https://roarmag.org/essays/cup-catalonia-spain-elections/

83 http://www.marypages.com/

84 Henry Giroux. *America At War with Itself.* City Lights Publishers, 2016.

85 Petra Rivoli. *The Travels of a T-Shirt in the Global Economy.* Wiley, 2014.

Christopher Chase-Dunn et al., "The New Global Left: Movements and Regimes," Working Paper, University of California-Riverside, August 16, 2009.

86 University of California-Riverside Transnational Movement Research Working Group.

87 http://www.irows.ucr.edu/research/tsmstudy.htm

Paul Bucheit, "More Inequality Shock," NationofChange, February 3, 2014.

http://www.nationofchange.org/more-inequality-shock-1391440735

88 http://inequality.org/author/paul-buchheit/

89 https://worldtomorrow.wikileaks.org

Ana Dinerstein and Sarah Amsler, "Women on the Verge, The Essence of Feminist Struggle," *ROAR Magazine,* January 24, 2017.

90 https://roarmag.org/essays/women-on-the-verge/

91 http://yfa.awid.org/directories/young-womens-initiatives/

Isabel Ortiz, et al., "World Protests 2006-2013," Friedrich Ebert Stiftung, September 2013.

92 http://policydialogue.org/files/publications/World_Protests_2006-2013-Final.pdf

"Brave, Creative and Resilient: The State of Young Feminist Organizing," AWID, September 21, 2016

93 https://www.awid.org/publications/brave-creative-and-resilient-state-young-feminist-organizing

94 http://www.marchemondiale.org/qui_nous_sommes/en/

"World March of Women Political Declaration,' March 28, 2015.

95 http://www.worldmarchofwomen.org

Christian Davies, "Poland's Abortion Ban Proposal Near Collapse After Mass Protests," *The Guardian,* October 5, 2016.

96 https://www.theguardian.com/world/2016/oct/05/polish-government-performs-u-turn-on-total-abortion-ban

http://www.nytimes.com/video/world/europe/100000004686970/voices-from-abortion-ban-protests.html?emc=edit_th_20161004&nl=todays-

97 headlines&nlid=68143430

Joanna Berendt, "Protesters in Poland Rally Against Proposal for Total Abortion Ban," *New York Times,* October 3, 2016.

http://www.nytimes.com/2016/10/04/world/europe/poland-abortion-black-monday.html?emc=edit_th_20161004&nl=todaysheadlines&n-

98 lid=68143430

Phoebe Lett, "Why Women Are on Strike," *New York Times,* March 8, 2017.

99 https://www.nytimes.com/2017/03/08/opinion/why-women-are-on-strike.html?_r=0

100 http://www.ted.com/talks/kavita_ramdas_radical_women_embracing_tradition.html (2009)

Scott Anderson, "Fractured Lands," *New York Times,* August 11, 2016.

101 http://www.nytimes.com/interactive/2016/08/11/magazine/isis-middle-east-arab-spring-fractured-lands.html?smtyp=cur&_r=0

David Goodman, "Deep in the Amazon, a Tiny Tribe is Beating Big Oil," *Yes! Magazine,* February 12, 2015.

http://www.yesmagazine.org/issues/together-with-earth/deep-in-the-amazon-a-tiny-tribe-is-beating-big-oil

[102] http://amazonwatch.org/news/2013/1120-patricia-gualinga-warrior-for-the-amazon

Ece Canli and Fatma Umul, "Bodies on the Street: Gender Resistance and Collectivity in the Gezi Revolts," *Interface Journal*, Vol. 7, No. 1, May 2015, pp. 19-39.

[103] http://interfacejournal.net/wordpress/wp-content/uploads/2015/06/Issue-7-1-Canli-and-Umul.pdf

Laurence Cox and Alf Gunvald Nilsen, "Social Movements Research and the 'Movement of Movements,'" *Sociology Compass*, Vol. 2, No. 2, 2007, pp. 424-442.

https://www.academia.edu/1221964/Social_movements_research_and_the_movement_of_movements_studying_resistance_to_neo-liberal_globalisation

[104] http://www.huffingtonpost.com/2011/06/06/slutwalk-chicago-turns-ou_n_872086.html

[105] https://www.facebook.com/160382763986923/photos/?tab=album&album_id=1268057506552771

[106] https://www.facebook.com/carolrossettidesign/photos_stream

[107] Afi Yellow-Duke, "Idealized? Sexy? She Draws women Who Don't Care What You Think," *Women's News*, March 13, 2016.

[108] http://womensenews.org/2016/03/idealized-sexy-she-draws-women-who-dont-care-what-you-think/

"Gendered Bodies in the Protest Sphere," *Signs*, Vol. 40, No. 1, Autumn 2014.

[109] http://www.jstor.org/stable/10.1086/673741

[110] https://www.youtube.com/watch?v=9JeWZZ39b6Y

Kamayani, "This Unique Anti-Rape Protest by women in India has Shocked Kerela," *Kractivist*, June 11, 2014.

[111] http://www.kractivist.org/tag/kerala/

[112] Jessica Taft. *Rebel Girls: Youth Activism and Social Change Across the Americas.* New York University Press, 2011.

Cristina Flesher Fominaya, "Collective Identity in Social Movements," *Sociology Compass*, Vol. 4, No. 6, 2010, pp. 393-404.

[113] https://www.academia.edu/615452/Collective_Identity_in_Social_Movements_Central_Concepts_and_Debates

[114] Ibid, pp. 178-179.

[115] Hava Rachel Gordon. *We Fight to Win: Inequality and the Politics of Youth Activism.* Rutgers University Press, 2010, p. 178.

[116] Gordon, p. 192.

[117] http://www.wmd.org/resources/whats-being-done/women%E2%80%99s-participation-politics/womens-organizations-around-world

Celia Donert, "Women's Rights in Cold War Europe," *Oxford Journals*, Vol. 208, No. 8, 2013.

[118] http://past.oxfordjournals.org/content/218/suppl_8/180.extract

[119] http://www.africa-union.org/structure_of_the_commission/women,%20gender%20and%20development.htm

Minky Worden, p. 328.

[120] https://www.youtube.com/watch?v=pFmP94NQ4jc

Elora Halim Chowdhury, "Global Feminism: Feminist Theory's Cul-de-sac," *Human Architecture: Journal of the Sociology of Self-Knowledge*, Summer 2006, pp. 291-302.

[121] scholarworks.umb.edu/humanarchitecture/vol4/iss3/

[122] http://yfa.awid.org/2014/03/demystifying-the-un-acronyms-what-csw-mdg-and-srhr-have-to-do-with-young-women/

[123] http://www.flowminder.org/about

Melinda Gates, "5 Reasons I'm Optimistic About the Future of Our Girls," Medium.com, October 11, 2016.

https://medium.com/@melindagates/5-reasons-im-optimistic-about-the-future-of-our-girls-ef0e905349a4

[124] Emily Bent, "The Boundaries of Girls' Political Participation: A Critical Exploration of Girls' Experiences as Delegates to the United Nations' Commission on the Status of Women," *Global Studies of Childhood*, Vol. 3, No. 2, 2013, p. 174.

[125] "Young Indigenous Activists in Global Advocacy Spaces," *AWID*, February 11, 2014.

http://www.awid.org/Library/Young-Indigenous-Activists-in-Global-Advocacy-Spaces

[126] http://www2.unwomen.org/~/media/headquarters/attachments/sections/news/stories/2016/youthcsw-2016-declaration.pdf?v=1&d=20160321T155235

Deniz Kandiyoti, "Disquiet and Despair: The Gender Sub-texts of the 'Arab Spring,'" *Open Democracy*, June 26, 2012.

[127] https://www.opendemocracy.net/5050/deniz-kandiyoti/disquiet-and-despair-gender-sub-texts-of-arab-spring

[128] http://blogs.state.gov/latest-stories?field_issues_tid=All&field_region_tid=All&keys=Women&=Apply

[129] https://empatsy.wufoo.com/forms/girls-research-portal-researchers/

[130] Megan Cerullo, "President Trump Picks Anti-Abortion Activist to Head Family Planning Program," *Daily News*, May 2, 2017.

http://www.nydailynews.com/news/politics/trump-picks-anti-abortion-activist-run-family-planning-program-article-1.3131370

Laura Bassett, "Trump Sends Anti-Birth Control Delegates to UN Commissiion on Women," *Huffington Post*, March 20, 2017.

http://www.huffingtonpost.com/entry/trump-sends-anti-birth-control-delegates-to-un-commission-on-women_us_58cc3dcee4b00705db4f7970

[131] http://www.unwomen.org/en/what-we-do

[132] beijing20.UNwomen.org

http://progress.unwomen.org/en/2015/pdf/SUMMARY.pdf

[133] http://wunrn.com/wurn/about-wunrn/

http://wunrn.com/2016/10/16-days-of-activism-against-gender-based-violence-2016-take-action-kit/

134 http://girlsrights.org/fact-sheets/

135 http://dayofthegirlsummit.com/wp-content/uploads/2012/07/DayoftheGirl-resourceguide.pdf Includes videos about girls internationally.

136 https://medium.com/@AhmadAlhendawi/memorable-moments-of-summer-2015-7c8d41b5b487#.e7j79w153

137 http://www.ungei.org/whatisungei/index_211.html

138 http://girlsrights.org/2015/01/take-girls-grade-beijing-survey/

Empowering Young Women to Lead Change, World YWCA, United Nations Population Fund, 2006. http://www.unfpa.org/webdav/site/global/

139 shared/documents/publications/2006/empowering-young-women_eng.pdf

140 https://www.facebook.com/UN4Youth/

www.unifem.org/attachments/products/CEDAWMadeEasy.pdf

141 http://www.un.org/womenwatch/daw/cedaw/cedaw.htm

http://teachunicef.org/sites/default/files/documents/young_people_tackle_mdgs_case_studies_9-12.pdf

http://www.un.org/millenniumgoals/bkgd.shtml

142 http://www.worldwewant2015.org/education2015

143 http://www.girleffect.org/media/139917/declaration_document_web_v6_26_9_13_copy.pdf

144 http://www.awid.org/Library/Feminist-Declaration-Post-2015-Call-for-endorsements

145 http://girlsglobe.org/2013/09/26/the-girl-declaration/

"A Post-2015 Agenda Understood by and Inspiring to Children and Young People," UNICEF, july 2015.

146 http://www.unicef.org/post2015/files/SDGDeclaration_ChildConsultationSummary.pdf

The goal's targets include elimination violence, valuing unpaid care work, access to education, education on human rights and gender equality, rights to economic resources like land, equal pay, equal opportunities for leadership, and access to sanitation and hygiene.

147 http://iwhc.org/2015/09/global-development-plan-signals-a-turning-point-for-women-and-girls/

Glen David Kuecker, "UN Sustainable Development Goals: The Matrix Reloaded," *TeleSur,* October 2, 2015.

148 http://www.telesurtv.net/english/opinion/UN-Sustainable-Development-Goals-The-Matrix-Reloaded-20151002-0012.html

149 http://youthspeak.aiesec.org/wp-content/uploads/2016/05/YouthSpeak-Preliminary-Findings-final.pdf

http://www.youthpolicy.org/nationalyouthpolicies/

150 http://www.youthpolicy.org/blog/development/ten-actions-for-the-next-unsg-to-advance-youth-issues/

151 http://www.unwomen.org/en/get-involved/step-it-up/about

Lyric Thompson, "The World's Girls: No Voice, No Rights," OpenDemocracy.Net, February 16, 2015.

152 https://www.opendemocracy.net/5050/lyric-thompson/world's -girls-no-voice-no-rights

153 http://www.un.org/ga/search/view_doc.asp?symbol=E/CN.6/2015/L.5

154 http://annualreport.unwomen.org/en/2015

"Young Feminists' Statement for the 59th CSW," *Young Feminist Wire,* March 19, 2015.

155 http://yfa.awid.org/2015/03/young-feminists-statement-for-the-59th-commission-on-the-status-of-women/

African Union Gender Policy

http://wgd.au.int/en/sites/default/files/Gender%20Policy%20-%20English.pdf

156 African Union Gender Policy, 2009. www.africa-union.org/.../african%20union%20gender%20policy.doc

Linda Etchart and Diana Athill. *The Gender Management System Toolkit: An Integrated Resource for Implementing the Gender Management System Series.* Commonwealth Secretariat, 2004.

157 http://www.womenlobby.org/?lang=fr

158 http://youngfeministfund.org/about-frida/

159 https://www.youtube.com/watch?v=Unzzh4Jh8KM

160 www.weforum.org/issues/global-gender-gap

161 http://reports.weforum.org/global-gender-gap-report-2016/top-ten/

162 http://www.weforum.org/reports/global-gender-gap-report-2013

Editorial, "U.S. Moms Deserve Better," *San Francisco Chronicle,* May 8, 2011.

163 www.sfgate.com/cgi-bin/article.cgi?f=/c/a/2011/05/07/EDEI1H5A1C.DTL

"Paid Parental Leave: How Swedish Mums and Dads Do It," *The Sydney Morning Herald,* March 20, 2014.

http://www.smh.com.au/national/paid-parental-leave-how-swedish-mums-and-dads-do-it-20140319-352gj.html

164 https://sweden.se/society/gender-equality-in-sweden/#start

Sweden GDP Growth Rate 2015

http://www.tradingeconomics.com/sweden/gdp-growth

165 http://www.topuniversities.com/student-info/choosing-university/why-study-scandinavian-university

166 http://www.socialprogressimperative.org/data/spi/findings

167 http://www.socialprogressimperative.org/data/spi/findings

www.taxrates.cc/html/sweden-tax-rates.html

168 http://articles.moneycentral.msn.com/Taxes/Advice/YourRealTaxRate40.aspx

132 http://www.nytimes.com/1995/06/12/world/unicef-asks-broader-aid-for-children.html

169 http://www.ipu.org/press-e/pressrelease201503101.htm

[170] "Nandini Rathi, The Layered Danish Pastry Called 'Borgen'," *Bitch Flicks*, July 25, 2014.

http://www.btchflcks.com/2014/07/the-layered-danish-pastry-called-borgen.html#.VHebr6TF-Ak

[171] Lars Eriksen and Luke Harding, "Helle Thorning-Schmidt Defies 'Curse of Kinnock' to Become Danish PM, *The Guardian*, September 16, 2011.

http://www.theguardian.com/world/2011/sep/16/helle-thorning-schmidt-denmark-leader

http://www.theguardian.com/world/2011/sep/16/helle-thorning-schmidt-denmark-leader

[172] Michael Booth, "Dark Lands: The Grim Truth Behind the 'Scandinavian Miracle'," *The Guardian*, January 27, 2014.

http://www.theguardian.com/world/2014/jan/27/scandinavian-miracle-brutal-truth-denmark-norway-swede

[173] Aglaea, February 24, 2016.

https://www.goodreads.com/topic/show/18025205-actual-feminist-societies

https://www.youtube.com/watch?v=Unzzh4Jh8KM

[174]

[175] Philip Lalander and Ove Sernhede, "Social Mobilization or Street Crimes," *Educare*, 2011.

http://dspace.mah.se/dspace/bitstream/handle/2043/13916/KBS%20article.pdf;jsessionid=68FA047C639675D4F8D8622D0AFA23D4?sequence=2

[176] "Sweden's Gender-Violence Shame," *Reporter*, February 22, 2013.

http://www.euronews.com/2013/02/22/sweden-s-gender-violence-shame/

Paola Battista, "Sexual Assault Affects a Third of Women in Sweden," February 5, 2014.

http://www.west-info.eu/sexual-assault-affects-a-third-of-women-in-sweden/

[177] www.thelocal.se/28968/20100913/

Dominic Hinde, "Sweden's Feminist Initiative Party is Reshaping Politics," OpenDemocracy.net, May 7, 2015.

https://www.opendemocracy.net/dominic-hinde/feminist-parties-redefining-scandi

[178] Nick Cohen, "Sweden's Feminist Foreign Minister has Dared to Tell the Truth About Saudi Arabia, *The Spectator*, March 2015.

http://www.spectator.co.uk/2015/03/swedens-feminist-foreign-minister-has-dared-to-tell-the-truth-about-saudi-arabia-what-happens-now-concerns-us-all/

[179] Crystal Shepeard, "How Sweden's Feminist Party is Changing European Politics and Possibly the World," *Care2*, September 26, 2014.

http://www.care2.com/causes/how-swedens-feminist-party-is-changing-european-politics-and-possibly-the-world.html

[180] https://en.wikipedia.org/wiki/List_of_feminist_parties

[181] George Lakey, "How Swedes and Norwegians Broke the Power of the '1 percent'," *Waging Nonviolence*, January 25, 2012. rhttp://wagingnonviolence.org/2012/01/how-swedes-and-norwegians-broke-the-power-of-the-1-percent/

[182] http://www.tradingeconomics.com/sweden/youth-unemployment-rate

[183] Matias Garrido, "Young Europeans Would Like to be Scandinavian," Cafebbel.com, January 28, 2009.

http://www.cafebabel.co.uk/article/28392/youth-european-scandinavia-education-adulthood.html

Lorenza Antonucci, "Is Sweden Perfection?" *Inequalities*, March 2, 2011. http://inequalitiesblog.wordpress.com/2011/03/02/is-sweden-perfection/

[184] Kimberly Amadeo, "U.S. Military Budget," *About News*, February 23, 2016.

http://useconomy.about.com/od/usfederalbudget/p/military_budget.htm

[185] Sara Miller Llana and Bastien Inzaurralde, "Do French Women Need Feminism?," *Christian Science Monitor*, January 8, 2013.

http://www.csmonitor.com/World/Europe/2013/0108/Do-French-women-need-feminism/s

[186] https://www.youtube.com/watch?v=4VPTulrAqAQ

[187] Jenna Goudreau, "The Container Store CEO Says 'Women Make Better Executives Than Men'," *Business Insider*, October 13, 2014.

http://www.businessinsider.com/container-store-ceo-kip-tindell-leadership-women-success-2014-10

[188] Millennials: The Challenge Generation," Prosumer Report, Europe RSCG Worldwide, Vol 11, 2011. The Euro RSCG Millennial Survey surveyed 2,500 Millennials aged 18 to 24 in China, France, India, the UK and the US in 2010.

http://www.prosumer-report.com/blog/wp-content/uploads/2011/04/MGv16no%20crops.pdf

[189] Sally Vance-Trembath, "Ban on Girl Altar Servers is Out of Step," *San Francisco Chronicle*, January 29, 2015.

http://www.sfchronicle.com/opinion/openforum/article/Banning-girl-altar-servers-takes-Catholic-Church-6049460.php

[190] Anita Harris, **ed.** *Next Wave Cultures: Feminism, Subcultures, Activism*. Routledge, 2008, p. 259.

[191] Achieve, "The 2013 Millennial Impact Report," www.achieveguidance.com

http://cdn.trustedpartner.com/docs/library/AchieveMCON2013/Research%20Report/Millennial%20Impact%20Research.pdf

[192] Nancy Dess, "Tend and Befriend," *Psychology Today*, September 1, 2000.

http://www.psychologytoday.com/articles/200009/tend-and-befriend

[193] Anna Rorem and Monisha Bajaj, "Cultivating Young Women's Leadership for a Kinder, Braver, World," The Kinder and Braver World Project: Research Series, Berkman Center for Internet and Society at Harvard University, December 17, 2012.

[194] Nikki van der Gaag, "Because I am a Girl: The State of the World's Girls 2013," Plan International, 2013, p. 95.

http://plan-international.org/files/global/publications/campaigns/biag-2013-report-english.pdf

[195] Shervin Assari, "If Men are Favored in our Society, Why do they Die Younger than Women?, *The Conversation*, March 8, 2017.

http://theconversation.com/if-men-are-favored-in-our-society-why-do-they-die-younger-than-women-71527

[196] "Depression: Men More Vulnerable to Long-Term Effects of Stress," *Michigan News*, March 25, 20116.

http://ns.umich.edu/new/releases/23629-depression-men-more-vulnerable-to-long-term-effects-of-stress

[197] Frances Jensen with Amy Ellis Nutt. *The Teenage Brain*. HarperCollins, 2015, p. 228.

[198] Gijsbert Stoet and David Geary, "Sex Differences in Academic Achievement Are Not Related to Political, Economic, or Social Equality," *Intelligence*, Vol. 48, 2015.

DOI: 10.1016/j.intell.2014.11.006

[199] "Educational Mobility Starts to Slow in Industrialized World, Says OECD," OECD, September 9, 2014.

http://www.oecd.org/newsroom/educational-mobility-starts-to-slow-in-industrialised-world-says-oecd.htm

[200] "The American Freshman," UCLA Higher Education Research Institute, February 2015.

http://www.heri.ucla.edu/monographs/TheAmericanFreshman2014.pdf

http://data.worldbank.org/indicator/SE.ENR.TERT.FM.ZS

[201] Joseph Charmie, "Women More Educated than Men But Still Paid Less," *Yale Global*, March 6, 2014.

http://yaleglobal.yale.edu/content/women-more-educated-men-still-paid-less-men

[202] Christopher Karpowitz and Tali Mendelberg. *The Silent Sex*, Princeton University Press, 2014.

http://press.princeton.edu/titles/10402.html

[203] Mayssoun Sukarieh and Stuart Tannock. *Youth Rising? The Politics of Youth in the Global Economy*. Routledge, 2015, p. 122.

[204] "No Ceilings: The Full Participation Report," Gates and Clinton Foundations, March 2015, p. 13.

http://noceilings.org/report/report.pdf

Lina Nilsson, "How to Attract Female Engineers," *New York Times*, April 27, 2015.

[205] http://www.nytimes.com/2015/04/27/opinion/how-to-attract-female-engineers.html?_r=0

[206] http://www.msn.com/en-nz/lifestyle/smart-living/women-you%E2%80%99ve-never-heard-of-but-should-have/ss-BBqr1pb#image=9

[207] Reshma Saujani, TED talk, February 2016.

http://www.ted.com/talks/reshma_saujani_teach_girls_bravery_not_perfection/transcript?language=en#t-507840

[208] Tara Sophia Mohr, "Why Women Don't Apply for Jobs Unless They're 100% Qualified," *Harvard Business Review*, August 25, 2014.

https://hbr.org/2014/08/why-women-dont-apply-for-jobs-unless-theyre-100-qualified/

[209] Alexander Hensby, "Exploring Participation and Non-Participation in the 2010/11 Student Protests Against Fees and Cuts," Ph.D. dissertation, University of Edinburgh, February 2014.

https://www.era.lib.ed.ac.uk/bitstream/handle/1842/9855/Hensby2014.pdf?sequence=1&isAllowed=y

[210] Leana Hosea, "Why do Women Outnumber Men in Technology in the Gulf?" *BBC News*, February 8, 2014.

http://www.bbc.com/news/business-26083215

[211] "A Guide to Womenomics: Women and the World Economy," *The Economist*, April 12, 2006.

http://www.economist.com/node/6802551

[212] Jonathan Woetzel et al., Report, McKinsey Global Institute, September 2015. http://www.mckinsey.com/insights/growth/how_advancing_womens_equality_can_add_12_trillion_to_global_growth

[213] John Gerzema and Michael D'Antonio. *The Athena Doctrine: How Women (and the Men Who Think Like Them) Will Rule the Future*. Jossey-Bass, 2013, p. 6., p. 18.

[214] Ibid., p. 6.

[215] Ibid., p. 255.

[216] Ibid., p. 6.

Guy Garcia. *The Decline of Men*. Harper Perennial, 2008.

hanna Rosin, "The End of Men," *The Atlantic Magazine*, July 2010.

[217] www.theatlantic.com/magazine/archive/2010/07/the-end-of-men/8135/

Andrew Moore, "The End of Men? Quite," Askmen.com

[218] www.askmen.com/entertainment/austin_500/503d_the-end-of-men-not-quite.html

Katie Rose Quandt, "Money in Politics is Darkening the Future for Millennials," Moyers & Company, April 20, 2015.

[219] http://billmoyers.com/2015/04/20/money-politics-darkening-future-millennials/

David Madland and Ruy Teixeira, "New Progressive America: The Millennial Generation," Center for American Progress, May 13, 2009, p. 14.

[220] http://www.americanprogress.org/issues/2009/05/pdf/millennial_generation.pdf

Mike Dorning, "The Slow Disappearance of the American Working Man," *Bloomberg Businessweek*, August 24, 2011.

[221] www.businessweek.com/magazine/the-slow-disappearance-of-the-american-working-man-08242011.html?campaign_id=rss_search

"Higher Education: Gaps in Access and Persistence Study," National Center for Education Statistics, August 2012, p. 162. http://nces.ed.gov/pubs2012/2012046.pdf

http://nces.ed.gov/programs/coe/indicator_cha.asp

[222] http://cnsnews.com/news/article/ali-meyer/women-now-33-more-likely-men-earn-college-degrees

Emily Inverso, "Why Women Entrepreneurs Are More Optimistic Than Ever," *Forbes*, March 12, 2014.

[223] http://www.forbes.com/sites/emilyinverso/2014/03/12/why-women-entrepreneurs-are-more-optimistic-than-ever/

Richard Reeves and Isabel Sawhill, "Men's Lib!," *New York Times*, November 14, 2015.

http://www.nytimes.com/2015/11/15/opinion/sunday/mens-lib.html?partner=rssnyt&emc=rss&_r=1

A rebuttal to the article:

http://www.returnofkings.com/74148/an-open-letter-to-two-new-york-times-writers

224 Alison Herzig and Jane Mali. *Oh Boy, Babies*. Little Brown & Co.,1980.
225 "Raising Boys, Engaging Guys, and Educating Men," Aspen Ideas Festival, July 1, 2012.
http://www.aspenideas.org/session/raising-boys-engaging-guys-and-educating-men#colorbox=transcript
226 Teddy Wayne, "Awkward Sex, Onscreen and Off," *New York Times*, October 8, 2016.
http://www.nytimes.com/2016/10/09/fashion/awkward-sex-tv-shows.html
227 Anita Harris. *Future Girl: Young Women in the Twenty-First Century*. Routledge, 2004, p. 147.
228 Harris, p. 184.
229 www.amightygirl.com
230 James Barron, "Wounded by 'Fearless Girl,' Creator of 'Charging Bull' Wants Her to Move," *New York Times*, April 12, 2017.
https://www.nytimes.com/2017/04/12/nyregion/charging-bull-sculpture-wall-street-fearless-girl.html?emc=edit_th_20170413&nl=todayshead-
lines&nlid=68143430
231 Harris, *Future Girl*, p. 1.
232 Ibid., p. 10.
233 Haydn Shaughnessy, "Who Are the Top 50 social Media Power Influencers, 2013?", *Forbes*, April 17, 2013.
http://www.forbes.com/sites/haydnshaughnessy/2013/04/17/who-are-the-top-50-social-media-power-influencers-2013/
harris, p. 127.
234 Emma Broadbent, et al., "Generation Z: Global Citizenship Survey," Varkey Foundation, January 2017.
https://www.varkeyfoundation.org/sites/default/files/Global%20Young%20People%20Report%20%28digital%29%20NEW%20%281%29.pdf
235 Katherine Zoepf, "A Troubled Revolution in Egypt," *New York Times*, November 21, 2011.
http://www.nytimes.com/2011/11/21/world/middleeast/a-troubled-revolution-in-egypt.html?pagewanted=all&_r=0
236 Tamer Nagy Majhmoud, "Egyptian Women Deserve Better," *Muftah*, June 19, 2014. http://www.aspenideas.org/session/raising-boys-engag-
ing-guys-and-educating-men#colorbox=transcript
http://muftah.org/egyptian-women-deserve-better-political-system/#.U7s7jY1dV8k
237 "The First Generation of the Twenty-First Century." *Generational Studies*, April 30, 2012.
http://magid.com/sites/default/files/pdf/MagidPluralistGenerationWhitepaper.pdfg56
238 Eileen Patten and Kim Parker, "A Gender Reversal on Career Aspirations," Pew Research Center, April 19, 2012.
239 Antonio De Wolk, "Hungering for a Tale of True Empowerment," *San Francisco Chronicle*, March 31, 2012, p. A9.
http://www.pressdisplay.com/pressdisplay/viewer.aspx
240 Caitlin Hu, "We're in a Global Feminist Movement," *Quartz*, June 6, 2015.
https://qz.com/419234/were-in-a-global-feminist-moment-mona-eltahawy-on-why-men-hate-us-and-how-they-love-us/
241 http://www.mencanstoprape.org/Resources/us-mens-anti-violence-organizations.html
242 http://www.ted.com/talks/tony_porter_a_call_to_men
243 http://www.bing.com/videos/search?q=mask+you+live+in&view=detail&mid=95A4A7B0BFA50F2EF11095A4A7B0BFA50F2EF110&FORM=-
VIRE
244 http://mic.com/articles/88277/23-ways-feminism-has-made-the-world-a-better-place-for-men#.tIgC3A8iP
245 Herbert Dyer, Jr., "Fox News Analyst: Christie's Problems Due to 'Feminized Atmosphere' of Media," *All Voices*, January 13, 2014.
http://www.allvoices.com/contributed-news/16328109-fox-news-analyst-christies-problems-due-to-feminized-atmosphere-of-media
246 https://www.youtube.com/watch?v=qIbtckx0mdw
247 Michael Stanat. *China's Generation Y*. Homa & Sekey Books, 2006, p. 45.
248 Jeffrey Jensen Arnett, ed. *Adolescent Psychology Around the World*. Psychology Press, 2012.
Celia Hatton, "100 Women: The Jobs Chinese Girls Just Can't Do," *BBC News*, October 16, 2013.
249 http://www.bbc.com/news/world-asia-24534782
Joseph Chamie, "Women More Educated Than Men But Still Paid Less," *Yale Global Online*, March 6, 2014.
250 http://yaleglobal.yale.edu/content/women-more-educated-men-still-paid-less-men
Wittgenstein Centre for Demography cited in John Poole, "Where the Girls Are (And Aren't): #15Girls. National Public Radio, October 20, 2015.
251 http://www.npr.org/sections/goatsandsoda/2015/10/20/448407788/where-the-girls-are-and-aren-t-15girls
252 https://www.dosomething.org/facts/11-facts-about-education-around-world
253 http://outspokenspeakers.blogspot.in
A.O. Scott, "The Death of Adulthood in American Culture," *New York Times*, September 11, 2014.
254 http://www.nytimes.com/2014/09/14/magazine/the-death-of-adulthood-in-american-culture.html?_r=0
Ashley Fantz, Lindsey Knight and Kevin Wang, "A Closer Look," CNN, June 19, 2014.
Adult and Youth Literacy, UNESCO, 2013. http://www.uis.unesco.org/literacy/Documents/fs26-2013-literacy-en.pdf
255 Michael Kimmel. *Guyland: The Perilous World Where Boys Become Men*. HarperCollins, 2008.
256 Niobe Way. *Deep Secrets: Boys Friendships and the Crisis of Connection*. Harvard University Press, 2013.
257 Frank Bruni, "A Star Who has No Time for Vanity," *New York Times*, October 15, 2014.
http://www.nytimes.com/2014/10/19/arts/frances-mcdormand-true-to-herself-in-hbos-olive-kitteridge.html?emc=edit_th_20141019&nl=to-
daysheadlines&nlid=68143430&_r=0
258 "Children in Single-Parent Families by Race," *National Kids Count, 2012*.

259 http://datacenter.kidscount.org/data/tables/107-children-in-single-parent-families-by#detailed/1/any/false/868,867,133,38,35/10,168,9,12,1,13,185/432,431

260 http://www.warrenfarrell.name

261 Emily Babay, "Census: Big Decline in Nuclear Family," Philly.com, November 26, 2013.
http://www.philly.com/philly/news/How_American_families_are_changing.html
December 20, 2013

262 http://yvpc.sph.umich.edu/2013/12/20/male-scarcity-linked-youth-violence/

263 http://www.state.gov/secretary/remarks/2016/03/254724.htm

264 Richard Fry, "A Rising Share of Young Adults Live in their Parents' Home," Pew Research Center, August 1, 2013.
http://www.pewsocialtrends.org/2013/08/01/a-rising-share-of-young-adults-live-in-their-parents-h

265 Andrew Yarrow, "Male Poverty Marked by Unique Set of Problem," *San Francisco Chronicle*, October 4, 2015.

266 James Poniewozik, "Sitcom Men, Grappling with a New Reality on TV," *New York Times*, September 13, 2016.
http://www.nytimes.com/2016/09/18/arts/television/white-guys-grappling-with-a-new-reality-on-tv.html?_r=0

267 Binyamin Appelbaum, "The Vanishing Male Worker: How America Fell Behind," *New York Times*, December 11, 2014.
http://www.nytimes.com/2014/12/12/upshot/unemployment-the-vanishing-male-worker-how-america-fell-behind.html?_r=0

268 Andrew Yarrow, "An Endangered Species—the American Male Worker," *San Francisco Chronicle*, April 3, 2015.
http://www.sfchronicle.com/opinion/article/The-American-male-worker-an-endangered-species-6173875.php

269 Jason DeBacker, et al., "Rising Inequality: Transitory or Permanent?" Paper presented to the Brookings Panel of Economic Activity, March 21, 2013.
http://www.brookings.edu/~/media/Projects/BPEA/Spring%202013/2013a_panousi.pdf

270 Belinda Luscome, "Workplace Salaries: At Last, Women on Top," *Time Business*, September 1, 2010.
www.time.com/time/business/article/0%2C8599%2C2015274%2C00.html

271 "The American Freshman," UCLA Higher Education Research Institute, February 2015.
http://www.heri.ucla.edu/monographs/TheAmericanFreshman2014.pdf

272 Linda Berg-Cross, et al., "Single Professional Women: A Global Phenomenon Challenges and Opportunities," *Journal of International Women's Studies*, Vol. 5, No. 5, June 2004.
http://vc.bridgew.edu/cgi/viewcontent.cgi?article=1551&context=jiws

273 Rami Khouri and Vivian Lopez, **eds.**, "A Generation on the Move: Insights into the Conditions, Aspirations and Activism of Arab Youth," report from American University of Beirut, 2011, p. 27.
http://www.unicef.org/media/files/Summary_Report_A_GENERATION_ON_THE_MOVE_AUB_IFI_UNICEF_MENARO_.pdf
Linda Berg-Cross et al., "Single Professional Women: A Global Phenomenon Challenges and Opportunities, *Journal of International Women's Studies*, Vol. 5, Issue 5, June 2004.
http://vc.bridgew.edu/cgi/viewcontent.cgi?article=1551&context=jiws

274 March 4, 2014. http://www.bbc.com/news/magazine-26391306

275 Sarah Keenlyside, "You Do Not Want to be a Single Lady Over 28 in China," *Business Insider*, July 30, 2012.
http://www.businessinsider.com/you-do-not-want-to-be-a-single-woman-over-28-in-china-2012-7

276 Isobel Yeung, "A Good Man is Hard to Find," SCMC.com, April 27, 2014.
http://www.scmp.com/magazines/post-magazine/article/1495043/good-man-hard-find-chinas-leftover-women-look-love-abroad?page=all
https://youtu.be/nDf6sOlpEDM

277 http://www.heforshe.org/en
Emma Watson, "Gender Equality is Your Issue Too," *UN Women*, September 20, 2014.
http://www.unwomen.org/en/news/stories/2014/9/emma-watson-gender-equality-is-your-issue-too
http://www.heforshe.org/#take-action

278 Colleen Curry, "Overcoming Child Marriage by Teaching Boys," *Women in the World*, July 22, 2016.

279 http://nytlive.nytimes.com/womenintheworld/2016/07/22/teaching-boys-in-india-that-girls-have-rights-too/
Angus Crawford, "Child Marriages Blight Bangladesh," *BBC News*, April 21, 2012.

280 www.bbc.co.uk/news/magazine-17779413Child

281 Joan Williams and Anne-Marie Slaughter, "Finding Balance Requires Changing the Lives of Men," *San Francisco Chronicle*, September 1, 2012.
http://www.sfgate.com/opinion/article/Family-well-being-tied-to-men-s-work-lives-3833671.php

282 http://yfa.awid.org/tag/young-feminist-activism and https://www.facebook.com/pages/AWID-Young-Feminist-Wire/206412972703108
http://blogs.state.gov/latest-stories?field_issues_tid=All&field_region_tid=All&keys=Women&=Apply

283 http://photoblog.nbcnews.com/_news/2011/03/08/6216765-women-around-the-world-mark-international-womens-day?lite

284 http://girlsglobe.org/
http://www.connecther.org/gitw/gallery?q=leadership&page=1
www.Connecther.org/gitw

285 http://www.connecther.org/projects
http://www.sfcg.org/programmes/childrenandyouth/pdf/karkarapresentation.pdf

Paris demonstration, photo by Alex Tessereau

Chapter 2

GLOBAL DESIRE FOR GENDER EQUALITY

I would change the superiority of men to women.

Monhesa, 13, Kenya

Change the traditional values of patriarchal thought thoroughly.

Ling, 14, rural China

Realize that girls have got the same rights as boys. Some adults think that girls' duty is taking care of family. I would make them realize time has changed and goes with technology.

unknown, 17, Tanzania

I want to be somebody who does what no woman did or only few do in my work. To be different in this way I need to be well educated and literate. I should have the feelings of equality between a man and woman like I can also be equal to man. I should have the ability to compete. Right now I have no interest in marriage. I am thinking to remain single in the future but if at all I am to marry, I would prefer to go by my choice. We don't have custom of selecting groom by the parents.

Chuney, 17, Bhutan

You can tell the condition of a nation by looking at the status of its women.

Jawaharlal Nehru, first prime minister of India

You may resist the invasion of an army, but you cannot stop an idea whose time has come.

Victor Hugo

Revolution has the face of a woman.

Hugo Chávez, former president of Venezuela

Contents: Equality is Desired Globally, More Females Desire Gender Equality, Girls Want Economic and Social Equality, Claims that Women Leaders are More Peaceful, Existing Models of Feminist Societies, Inequality Persists in All Countries

Equality is Desired Globally

The UN asked young people about their goals for 2030 as part of the preparation for the Sustainable Development Goals of 2015.[1] They want equal opportunity for success, no discrimination based on gender or any other factor, and no pollution. Social justice movements support each other globally to achieve the desire for equal opportunity, such as Black Lives Matter demonstrations in the US carrying banners in support of Palestinians. Egyptians like Asmaa Mahfouz traveled to New York to advise Occupy Wall Street activists, seen on video.[2] Mexican American girls write poems to raise awareness about police violence in both the US and Mexico.[3] Activist Thenjiwe McHarris of Black Lives Matter met with Mexican students in 2015 at the National Autonomous University of Mexico to discuss the disappearance of 43 Normal School students.[4] She called for global unity to end the "war on young people," especially poor people of color. McHarris envisioned an international team to research mass movements and "learn to love each other" or else nothing gets done. She noted that young people are "often the backbone of every movement" and that movements in various countries inspire each other.

Surveys discussed in this chapter indicate that generally people around the world believe in equal rights for women but report that inequality persists in their countries, especially in the Middle East and Africa. Oxfam NGO reported that just eight men-- six Americans, one Mexican and one Spaniard--own as much as 3.5 billion people in the bottom half.[5] In a study of global gender inequality, 40 of the 95 countries analyzed had high levels of inequality.[6] The most equal countries in regards to gender were in Western Europe, North America and Oceania. The report predicted that increasing women's economic opportunities could add $28 trillion to global economic growth by 2025. Women are much more likely to think gender inequality is a problem than men and be more egalitarian with positive attitudes towards ethnic minorities.

Despite global belief in equal rights, sexism persists in appalling ways such as rural Chinese practices of giving girl babies names like "looking for a little brother" or referring to a husband as a "master." Sexism contributes to suicide being the main cause of death of young women aged 15 to 19, according to the World Health Organization (WHO).[7] When asked about her future career, SpeakOut student Alex, 15, from Sweden, said, "Nothing. I'll marry a rich guy and live happily ever after." She was joking but her comment indicates the persistence of the fairy tale of the prince on the white horse who rescues the damsel in distress. Feminists aim to end the gender gap: A world map of feminists shows that they're everywhere, a project of women from five countries who met at the World Social Forum in Tunis in 2014.[8]

Although globally women are less than a quarter of the politicians, we'll see that many studies indicate that women legislators deliver more to their constituents and are more able to cooperate with their colleagues. Girls and women are the world's most underused resource, and their labor is especially needed in aging populations lacking enough workers to support retirees. Japanese Prime Minister Shinzo Abe recognized this fact in his "Abenomics" plan to encourage more women to work. He planned to develop more state-funded childcare so Japan can become "a society where all women shine."[9] A less respectful health minister in Abe's first government in 2006 described women as "baby-making machines" in an aging country with a low birth rate.

Gloria Steinem explains that many of us are uncomfortable with women leaders because we associate them with our mothers and childhood. German Neo-Freudian psychiatrist Karen Horney believed that men fear and envy women' power as pro-creators. Our ancient ancestors thought birth, lactation ad menstruation were evidence of women's magical powers. Hence, the first deities were female fertility figures. The archetype of the powerful Great Mother was described by Swiss psychoanalyst Carl Jung and a book of that title by Jung's student Eric Neumann (1955), followed by Neumann's *The Fear of the Feminine* (1994). Early civilization worshipped goddesses and more egalitarian and was more peaceful than warrior patriarchal culture, according to various authors. [10]

The shadow side of the mother is the witch. Thousands of women are still killed for being witches in Africa, India, Latin America and Papua New Guinea. The witch hunters, often young male vigilantes, may be motivated by taking the women's property.[11] The polarity of the archetypes of the virginal mother versus the evil witch still influences our reaction to women in power positions, along with our personal relationship with our own mother and religious beliefs. Images of women convey powerful impact in an age of viral global media, such as the ballerina dancing on the Wall Street bull used to publicize Occupy Wall Street, the woman in the blue bra stomped on by police during demonstrations in Egypt's Tahrir Square.[12]

Former President Jimmy Carter argues in *A Call to Action* (2013) that sexism is the "worst and most pervasive and unaddressed human rights violation on earth." He faults religious leaders who preach that women are inferior and don't allow them to serve as pastors and priests. Dr. Nawal el-Saadawi, the famous Egyptian writer and feminist, pointed out, "Whenever any external or internal power wants to abort a revolution, they control women. If women revolt, that's the end. And it's easy to control women by religion."[13] Hillary Clinton, winner of the popular vote in the US presidential election of 2016, agreed that the status of women is the unfinished business of the 21st century and that extremists everywhere share a common goal of dominating women. When she told the 1995 UN Beijing Women's Conference that women's right are human rights and proposed a 12-part plan, conservatives in the US accused her of proposing a "radical feminist agenda." Clinton observed,

> *Why extremists always focus on women remains a mystery to me. But they all seem to. It doesn't matter what country they're in or what religion they claim. They want to control women. They want to control how we dress, they want to control how we act, they even want to control the decisions we make about our own health and bodies.*[14]

Although Clinton downplayed her gender in her first bid for the presidency partly due to polls showing that people view men as better leaders,[15] she played up being a mother and grandmother in her second attempt indicating a shift in attitudes. When discussing national security, the Republican National Committee criticized her for not smiling more, but in a double standard they didn't criticize Donald Trump although he smiled less in their televised debate.

The World Economic Forum (WEF) found a clear correlation between gender equality--measured by employment, education, participation in government and health--and Gross Domestic Product. (GDP). Educating girls is especially linked to increased prosperity and healthier children. However, the WEF reported only a small improvement in the gender gap over the nine years it collected data, up only 4% from 2006 to 2014.[16] In their 2015 Global Gender Gap report, the top countries for gender equality were Iceland, Norway, Finland, Sweden, Ireland, Rwanda, the Philippines, Switzerland, Slovenia and New Zealand. The most equal countries in their regions were Nicaragua, Israel, Rwanda, Iceland, and the Philippines. The best countries for women's economic participation were Burundi, Norway, Malawi, the US, and the Bahamas. Women have the most political power in Iceland, Finland, Norway, Nicaragua and Sweden. In 2017, Sweden was selected as the best country for women.

Scandinavia is always where I look for models of equality programs. In 2015 Sweden had the first government that calls itself feminist under Social Democrat Prime Minister Stefan Lofven, with 45% women members of parliament, and a feminist political party called Feminist Initiative was founded in 2006.[17] Women earn two-thirds of the university degrees and 72% of women are employed. Employers of over 25 people are required to list their gender diversity strategies. Foreign Minister Margot Wall-strom spoke up about Saudi Arabia's violation of women's human rights despite the controversy she caused. Various NGOs work on gender issues like Men for Gender Equality to enable men to participate in their family life. A tourism website explains, "The modern Swedish man is a feminist."[18] Olika Publishing creates non-sexist and non-racists books for children and a gender neutral pronoun is *hen*.

Aglaea reported from Helsinki on the Our Shared Shelf bookclub website that Finish health care and education is free--including university if the student passes the entrance exam, free supplies are provided parents of new babies, paternity leave is increasingly being used by men, childcare for all although it may be harder to get in the crowded Helsinki, and most women are employed. She and her friends speak at least four languages. Street harassment doesn't exist. She likes about their relationships that "People don't stick their noses in other people's business nearly as much as I see on a daily basis done by foreigners." Even in such an advanced country, male-dominated professions earn more than traditional women's professions and more professors are male. Aglaea also thinks rapists should be more severely punished. The main church is Lutheran, but she reported most young people aren't religious. The endnote includes the tax structure Aglaea emailed to show the cost of all these services.[19]

Sex role stereotypes persist everywhere, even in Sweden, as Hilda, 21, a young Swedish mother explained on Our Shared Shelf in 2016:

> *Sweden is, compared to a lot of other countries, doing quite well when it comes to equality, but there is still a lot to do. Like when my partner, the father of my children, was referred to as "babysitting" when he (alone!) took care of our newborn daughter her first day. He had spent more time with her than I had. Or when my daughters, when I dress them in dresses and pink are "cute," "nice," "flirty" (!), "shy," "lovely," "beautiful," "good" etc. But when I dress them in more "boy-ish" clothes, they suddenly become "brave," "tough," "cool," "smart," "naughty," "funny" etc. Also they suddenly become "a handful." This is at only a couple of months old.*

Expectations for equal opportunity spread around the world as the media show strong female athletes and high visibility government leaders like US Secretaries of State Albright, Rice, and Clinton and German Chancellor Angela Merkel. Akra, a Cambodian high school teacher, told me, "Growing equality is influenced by media images of women in active roles such as playing sports" in the Olympics. Now, as girls go on to higher education and professional jobs, they're more valued as breadwinners then bread bakers and they can afford to escape an abusive marriage. When Akra was a Cambodian student, girls would blush and hang their heads when reproduction was taught, but now he observes girls aren't shy when learning about AIDS and other sexual topics.

The Pew Research Center's Global Attitudes Project polled people in 22 nations about gender equality. Released in 2010, it reported that solid majorities support it but say inequality persists in their countries, as many believe that men have better paid jobs.[20] Nigerian men were the only group in which a majority didn't believe in equal rights. Women are far more likely than men to think gender inequality is problematic. Muslim respondents—men more than women—are least likely to advocate equality and in fact their preference for equality in marriage decreased over time in Nigeria and Pakistan. Attitudes towards marriage became more egalitarian over the decade in seven of 19 countries that Pew surveyed, including Jordan, Lebanon, Russia, Poland, Mexico and the US.

Many people told Pew researchers that when jobs are scarce, men have more right to a job, a more frequent belief in Muslim majority countries and India, China, South Korea and Nigeria. Men are more likely to have this view that men need jobs more than women need them. When asked if it's more important for a boy to have a university education than a girl, a majority agreed only in Egypt (50%), among Nigerian Muslims (50%), in Pakistan (51%) and India (63%)--the only country without a Muslim majority. Thus, more of the respondents believe in the important of girls' education. When asked if men or women have better lives, about half agreed that men did (more women believed this than men) and about half of the respondents said there weren't gender differences in the quality of life. The exceptions were South Korea and Japan where respondents thought women have a better life, perhaps because of men's long work hours. Also, young Japanese women often delay marriage to enjoy their freedom, often portrayed as selfish by media. It's encouraging that advocacy of equality is increasing, but worrisome that it lags in Muslim countries when Islam is the fastest growing religion.

Some Muslim young women, however, don't view Western girls as more liberated. In rebuttal to the Saudi film *Wadjda* about a girl who wants to buy and ride a bicycle, a Saudi young woman sarcastically posted on a *Wadja* YouTube site, "I am REALLY worried about the OPPRESSION of young Western girls and their media stuffed minds with psychological problems, eating disorders, poor self-image, lack of respect for parents and teachers. Out of the kindness of my heart I'm going to start an aid fund and get all my Saudi girls to donate to this fantastic cause. Let's help raise the spirituality and self-confidence of these girls so they don't all end up believing you have to strip down and show your bony bits to be something."[21]

In a Pew Global Attitudes 2012 survey of Muslim countries, the majority supported equal rights for women, but women again were more likely to be supportive.[22] Jordan had the most striking gap with 82% of women but only 44% of men believing in equal rights for women. Over half of the respondents in Tunisia, Pakistan, Turkey, and Jordan said men are better political leaders, and if jobs are scarce, men should have priority. In Pakistan and Jordan, the majority believed that a woman's family should help select her husband. Not an encouraging finding, a survey of 850 ninth grade students from Amman, Jordan, reported a third believe honor killing is justified--40% of boys compared to 20% of girls, and less educated teens were more likely to have this viewpoint.[23] Around the world girls' are sheltered in order to protect their reputation and by extension their family's reputation, while boys are allowed to be wild without tarnishing their families. In the West too, boys have the freedom to play out "boys will be boys," while as the book *Girls, Feminism, and Grassroots Literacies* (2008) points out, "Girls and girl culture have become cultural flash points, reflecting both societal and particularly feminist anxieties about and hopes for the future."[24]

A brighter note in the Middle East is Sultan Qaboos bin Caraid. The absolute ruler of Oman, he advocates, "This country, in its blessed way forward, needs both men and women—because it resembles a bird in relying on both of its wings to fly high in the horizons of the sky. How can this bird manage if one of its wings is broken? Will it be able to fly?"[25] Women and men have equal education opportunities in Oman, but as in most countries, women are rarely found in higher management positions. A SpeakOut girl from Oman does not value democracy, explaining, "Opposition is not a common thing in Oman because we know how much our leader did for us in the past 40 years and we know that all he wants is the best for his people" (Afra, 17, f). However, in a country where 45% of the population is under age 25, the problem of youth unemployment causes some unrest even under the absolute rule of Sultan Qaboos.[26] Gloria Steinem said accurately that we're lurched around between medieval and modern attitudes and that we've begun to raise our daughters more like our sons, but "few have the courage to raise our sons more like our daughters."

The growing economic inequality created by neoliberal capitalism motivates current youth protests. In India, SpeakOut student Kushum reports, "Rich people are taking the poor people under their feet " (f, 15). In rapidly growing India, the richest 10% own over 53% of the wealth, leaving over one-third of the population living on less than 52 cents a day.[27] I saw the thin, barefooted, unwashed urban poor sleeping on highway meridians, on sidewalks, in their rickshaws, or in plastic tents. Their children moved about in the middle of traffic tapping on car windows to beg, making faces, turning summersaults, holding up dirty babies—seen in my photos on the book Facebook page albums.

Pope Francis caused a global stir and accusations of being a Marxist when he proclaimed in 2013 "a globalization of indifference has developed" in the pursuit of profits in the "new tyranny" of capitalism and the "idolatry of money." He stated, "Today everything comes under the laws of competition and the survival of the fittest, where the powerful feed upon the powerless. As a consequence, masses of people find themselves excluded and marginalized: without work, without possibilities, without any means of escape." He also praised "feminine genius," but doesn't seek to apply that genius to the priesthood. (The Pope declared Trump is not a Christian in his policies towards immigrants and low-income people.)

Economic equality has improved only 1.4 points from 2002 to 2008, according to the Gini coefficient measure of inequality. The emerging middle classes in China, India, Indonesia and Brazil are making gains, while Africans, some Latin Americans, and countries of the former USSR are losing out.[28] The middle class is shrinking in the US and the UK, where growing numbers of children live in poverty (20% in the US and 10% in the UK). Income inequality in the US is the greatest it's been since just before the Great Depression, a bigger gap than in other industrial nations. The gap between the rich and poor is widening throughout the Western world, even in Scandinavia. Austerity programs implemented during the recession of 2008 resulted in high unemployment (27 million out of work in the European Union) and cuts in social supports causing a "race to the bottom." Poverty is a woman's issue.

Facts about growing inequality:

*UNICEF reports that the richest 20% of the world's population controls 83% of its income, while the poorest 20% control just 1%. The richest 1% control 70% of the private financial wealth.[29]

*Globally, the 85 richest people have the same amount of wealth as the poorest 3.5 billion—half the world's population.[30]

*Only 0.15% of the world's population controls $42 trillion dollars or two-thirds of world GDP, while 0.001%, control a third of the total wealth as a result of neoliberal economic policies of deregulation and austerity cuts in government services.[31]

Discussion of the economic problems created by globalization often leave out its specific impact on women, including the "feminization of the labor force" of factory workers, feminization of poverty (60% of the world's hungry people), domestic workers employed in foreign countries with harsh conditions, the loss of female jobs after the collapse of the USSR linked to an increase sex trafficking and sex tourism, the loss of government jobs employing women caused by neoliberal privatization of previous public enterprises, women's double job at home and work. Even small female businesses funded by microfinance like Grameen Bank in developing countries charge high interest loans.[32]

Females More Egalitarian

Only 10% of all young Europeans in a large survey listed in the endnote favor keeping a strong distinction between gender roles.[26] Girls are more likely than boys to have egalitarian ideas about gender roles but are more interested in having a traditional female job in a helping profession, according to a survey of 8,000 adolescents from 20 countries that asked about their ideal woman and man.[33] Boys are more likely to be interested in the athletic and sexual qualities of an ideal person to emulate. In a similar question given to 25,000 world youths about characteristics of their ideal society, gender equity is one of the important characteristics for Westerners, with over 90% of both sexes advocating equality in the US, France, Canada, Spain, Germany, Finland, Australia, and the UK, with the least support in Morocco.[34]

Emma, age 19, is a college student in Maryland. When I asked her if she sees gender differences she said, "I think girls tend to be more accepting, maybe because girls have experienced more discrimination in the past, so they can ensure others do not have to go through similar un-acceptance. I think boys and girls are generally about the same for being motivated and caring about our world to make a difference." She thinks the reasons for this increase in caring and acceptance of controversial issues like same-sex marriage, gay people, and interracial marriage, is due to better education, more Internet activism by groups like people of color and LGBT advocates shared, and religions becoming more accepting of differences.

Gender roles are changing as more women do paid work. A growing phenomenon is the number of single women with professional careers. Some of these women said they didn't have time or energy for a family and women said there's a shortage of appropriate men who are educated and willing to share family work.[35] Making their own living, they don't have to settle for second best. This is a global phenomenon and the first new sociological phenomenon of the 21st century according to authors who studied it in India, Poland, Germany and the US. Khue (16, f) explained how gender roles have changed in Vietnam:

> About the differences in my parents' generation and mine, besides general differences in music and clothing style, I think there are two major things. The first difference is the improvement in gender equality. In my generation, the idea that boys are more important than girls is considered conservative and old-fashioned. Teenage girls now are aware of their value, so they demand respect from the opposite sex. Compared to me, my mother used to be treated unfairly as a girl. She had to do all the housework while my uncle didn't and she used to be hated because she was too ambitious.

> According to what my parents told me, I know that in their generation boys and girls were very shy in relationship and the way they approached their "target" was also more innocent and reserved than today's teenagers. Besides, at their time poverty was the common situation of my country, so their love tended to be more idealistic, instead of physical and materialistic. For me, to be honest, I don't intend to be with someone who can't make good money.

Sarah Jameel started her youth activism in Sri Lanka at the age of 11 to help after the tsunami devastation. At 15 she started a community service project to meet the UN Millennium Goals to end poverty and a year later she developed the first fashion and social media based anti-smoking campaign. Jameel is part of an international community of teen activists who are part of We are Family Foundation's Global Teen Leaders.[36] Among these young women leaders in the US are the founder of RandomKid for youth activists, a 15-year-old who started a program for the homeless in Virginia, the founder for Kids Caring 4 Kids now in five African countries, and a girl who founded FoodSync to connect leftover restaurant food with hungry people. In other countries, a Kenyan young mother started a support group for other disadvantaged young women, and a Swede founded "Seema" for Indian women near Pune to make money-making jewelry.

Jameel disagrees with the stereotype that Millennials are narcissists, saying her generation is "open-minded, liberal, self-expressive, upbeat, and overtly passionate about equality." Their special skills are multi-tasking, being tech-savvy and team players who want transparency and to know their opinions are valued. They also need recognition and instant gratification. She recommends that activists be Divergent, okay with being different, probably a reference to the *Divergent* film trilogy (2014-2016) featuring a female action hero.

The Millennial Generation in the US is more egalitarian in their attitudes and actions than previous generations, including their Gen X predecessors.[37] In 2008, the Families and Work Institute reported that for the first time since they started asking the question in 1992, women under age 29--including young mothers, were just as likely as their male peers to want jobs requiring major responsibility and time commitment. Millennial fathers spend more time with their children than Gen X fathers, an average of 4.1 hours per workday with their children under age 13, compared to mothers who average 5.4 hours. An unintended benefit of the recession was an increase in the number of unemployed fathers who regularly cared for their children under age 15 to almost one-third of dads in 2010, including 20% of fathers who served as the primary caregivers of their preschool children.[38] One of the $5 million Super Bowl ads in 2017 was an Audi ad about a father encouraging his young daughter as she competes in a cart race, questioning "Do I tell her that despite her education, her drive, her skills, her intelligence, she will automatically be valued as less than every man she ever meets?" The end ended with the statement that Audi is "committed to equal pay for equal work."[39]

Factors leading to gender equality in the US are that women earn more than half of graduate and professional degrees and even mothers of young children are often employed. Nationally, the first year students surveyed by a UCLA institute the women more likely to plan on going on after a bachelor's degree (36% vs. 29% of men).[40] In 40% of households with children, the mother is the sole or main breadwinner (up from only 11% in 1960 according to the Pew Research Center), but single mothers have one quarter of the median income of marred couples.[41] By 2008, 80% of US employees of all ages who had a spouse or partner lived in dual-earner families. In 27% of the households surveyed by Pew in 2013, the women earned more than the men, so that five million married mothers make more than their husbands. In dual-earner parent families, only 16% have a husband who is better educated than his wife. Despite these changes and the fact that 79% of Pew respondents reject the idea that children are better off if their mother stays at home and only 8% felt that way if the father stayed home.

Claims that Women Leaders are More Peaceful

IMF head Christine Legarde told BBC that exchanges between women leaders don't need to go through the first chapter of establishing turf that men jockey through. She said, "I believe that more women leaders would help society" because many studies show women leaders are more inclusive and more risk adverse. She referred to a survey of Fortune 500 companies that found companies with more women board members were more profitable. Legarde was a lawyer, French Minister of Finance, and is the mother of two sons who lived with guilt about not going to all their games and parent meetings when they were young. Twenty-four men interviewed her for the IMF job in 2011. As happens frequently, a woman is picked to replace a leader in trouble, in her case Dominique Strauss-Kahn who was involved in sex and finance scandals. Giving the level of global inequality, Legarde feels it's her responsibility to constantly bring up gender inequality even if people don't want to hear about it. In France, none of the top 40 companies have a woman CEO. She added that in 120 countries studied by the IMF, almost 90% have some legal barrier to women's advancement. If the barriers are removed, more jobs are created and GDP increases by up to 30%.[42]

World leaders look to women to bring about a more equal society. Gandhi said he got the idea of *Satyagraha*, nonviolent resistance, from 19th century suffrage activists. Former UN Secretary General Kofi Annan said, "Women who know the price of conflict so well are also better equipped than men to prevent or resolve it. For generations women have served as peace educators, both in their families and in their societies. Women build bridges, not walls." The Tibetan Buddhist Dalai Lama advocates more women leaders because he thinks women are often innately more sensitive and peaceful. He stated that the world's future is in the hands of Western women because "females have more sensitivity for others' pain and suffering," implying that women with economic resources have the motivation and power to improve the human condition. He told reporter Nicholas Kristof, "I insist that women should carry a more active role. If eventually most of the leaders of different nations are female, maybe we'll be safer."[43] Some blame male leaders for economic inequality: Icelanders blamed hyper-masculine traits for the financial crisis of 2008. They believe we all have masculine and feminine traits, but "hyper-masculine traits such as aggression, competiveness, risk-taking and a lack of emotional awareness" cause problems like the financial meltdown.[44] Feminine qualities of risk-aversion, openness, emotional awareness and empathy" might have prevented the global recession.

Various men also suggest women can save us. In *The Better Angels of Our Nature*, Steven Pinker argues for increasing equality for women because "feminization" and "the feminine style" of leadership results in less violence.[45] He states, "Traditional war is a man's game: tribal women never band together to raid neighboring villages." Professor Melvin Konner also argues that women's less testosterone-driven aggressiveness makes them better suited for modern times in his *Women After All: Sex, Evolution and the End of Male Supremacy* (2016). Hillary Clinton told a women's conference in 2017, "Despite all the challenges we face, I remained convinced that, yes, the future is female."[46] She added, "We need strong women to step up and speak out. We need you to dare greatly and lead boldly." Ana Dinerstein, editor of *Social Sciences for an Other Politics: Women Theorizing Without Parachutes* (2017), maintains that women internationally lead prefigurative efforts to actually create local utopias.

The belief that women are more likely to be peacemakers than men is portrayed in the third *Hunger Games* film *Mockinjay Part 1* that contrasts tyrannical President Snow with good President Coin. She's the president of District 13 and believes in democracy and shared resources. Her citizens wear simple uniforms in contrast with the lavish fashions worn in the capital headed by Snow. However, in Part 2 the teen heroine Katniss kills President Coin because she got corrupted by power and didn't plan to schedule elections. A black woman takes over as a good leader and the film ends with Katniss and her two children and husband having a picnic. The very feminine scene holding her baby contrasts with the warrior theme of the series.

Gloria Steinem explained that women have a "special ability to make connections between people and "Women are not more peaceful than men, but we don't have our masculinity to prove—so we are and will be good peacemakers," as they have been in Ireland and Liberia. Irish women closed doors to prevent men from leaving Northern Ireland peace talks, women defused conflicts in Guatemala and Darfur, and women in Liberia occupied a soccer field for months to insist on peace talks.[47] One of the women, Leymah Gbowee was honored with a Nobel peace prize. Colombian women organized community peace enclaves were weapons weren't allowed and demanded to be represented in peace talks with FARC guerilla fighters. However, the feminist Swedish Foreign Minister Margot Wallström bemoaned the fact that, "From 1992 to 2011, fewer than 4% of signatories of peace agreements and less than 10% of peace negotiators were women."[48] When women are represented in peace agreements, the accords are 35% more likely to last for at least 15 years.[49] Nigerian scholar Akin Iwilade thinks recent African peace talks are weakened by not incorporating women, as has also been suggested about Syrian peace talks.[50] Claims are that women are more likely to consider practical implications for ordinary people in negotiating deals.

Other examples of women's organizations that work for peace are Code Pink (and its book *Stop the Next War Now*--2005), Women's International League for Peace and Freedom (this and other women's international organizations between the two world wars are described by Marie Sandell[51]), Global Peace Initiative of Women, Nobel Women's Initiative, Madre, Peace is Sexy (founded in Mozambique by Marianne Perez de Fransius), Widows for Peace in the UK, and Nigeria's Niger Delta's Kebetkache Women Development & Resource Center.[52] Code Pink was founded in 2002 by Jodie Evans, Medea Benjamin and other activists; their website includes suggestions for how to organize a campaign. Women in Black is a "global network of feminist women peacemakers" active in at least 18 countries.[53] They hold vigils dressed in black while standing silently.

Some studies show young women are less supportive of militarism. A 2007 study by the Centre for the Study of Developing Societies interviewed 5,000 youth in locations around India about their attitudes about government policies. About 45% of young men would like the government to give top priority to strengthening the defense system, compared to only 3% of young women. Young men were also less likely to emphasize the need for greater gender equality than women. Only 31% of men versus 52% of women would like the government to give top priority to gender equality, but a majority of both sexes support reserved seats for women and for youth in Parliament. Interestingly, rural men surveyed for the study are more supportive of gender equality.

A website called Gather the Women reports on women's activism for peace and spirituality, which some call the fourth wave of feminism. Women tend to be more religious than men—especially Christian women.[54] The Pew Research Center collected massive data from 192 countries to conclude that women pray more often and are more devout: About 83% of women are affiliated with a religion, compared with 80% of men. However, only 11% of American Protestant congregations where led by women in 2012, unchanged since 1998, according to Pew.[55] Even today women are not ordained by Catholics, Southern Baptists, Later-Day Saints (Mormans) or Orthodox Jewish rabbis.

Even young girls are more interested in achieving consensus and avoiding battle, according to John Hunter, inventor of the World Peace Game and fourth grade teacher in Virginia.[56] After teaching the game for almost 30 years, he reported that students of both genders more interested in peaceful solutions and girls have become more willing to take leadership. He hopes these children will save us. The American Freshman national survey of 137,456 first-year students in 2016 reported that the gender gap is the widest ever: Young women are more liberal than men, 41% vs. 29%.[57] Women are more likely to advocate that climate change should be a government priority—82% vs. 78%, and to advocate stricter gun control laws—75% vs. 59%. Women are slightly more likely than men to say they are tolerant of people with different beliefs than their own and that they can work well with diverse people. However, men are more likely to believe that can discuss controversial issues and are more open to having their beliefs challenged. (Women are more worried than men about how to finance their college education (66% vs. 34%).

Able to transcend old divisions, women from different ethnic backgrounds have come together to make peace, as with Kup Women for Peace in Papua New Guinea, composed of four rival tribal groups.[58] When fighting broke out, the women spent two weeks camping on the battlefield using a megaphone to call for a truce. They visited the villages of the warring factions urging peace until they succeeded. Women Nobel Prize winners formed the Nobel Women's Initiative for Peace and Nonviolence to support women's activists who work for peace.[59] The film *Where Do We Go Now?* (2011) tells the fictional story of Muslim and Christian women who work together for peace in a remote Lebanese village. They used women's peaceful tactics, sedating their husbands with hashish placed inside pastries they baked and then hiding men's weapons.

Women like Leymah Gbowee, from Liberia, organized thousands of Muslim and Christian women to join in peace talks to end their country's civil war. They walked out onto the battlefield and refused to leave until a truce was reached.[60] Police were going to arrest Women of Liberia Mass Action for Peace when they protested outside stalled peace talks in Accra in 2003, but their threat of removing their clothes scared off the police who were afraid of the taboo against female nudity. The Liberian women peace activists also threatened to withhold sex, a threat repeated by women activists in Togo in 2012 to demand the resignation of the President Gnassingbe.

An exception is some women soldiers. Kurdish women fighters disagree with the emphasis on peacemaking, as they bear arms against ISIS and its femicide and sale of female sex slaves in Syria and Iraq.[61] The Kurdistan Workers' Party, called PKK in Turkey, is known for its women leaders; the most famous was Sakine Cansiz who survived years of torture in Turkish prisons but was assassinated. By 1993, about one-third of new PKK recruits were women, leading to the organization of women's guerilla units called YJA-Star. Part of the motivation was to create equality and mutual respect between men and women soldiers. The intent of PKK was to permanently change sex roles, unlike short-term expedient use of women guerillas in other revolutionary struggles, in contrast to the use of women soldiers in China, Vietnam, Sri Lanka, and Nepal; in Cuba, El Salvador, Nicaragua, and Angola, Eritrea, Mozambique, South Africa and Zimbabwe. Unlike the Kurdish forces, women in these other countries were rarely commanders and were expected to be subordinate to men and do the cooking and cleaning. Celibacy is emphasized among Kurdish soldiers of both sexes to protect female honor in a conservative region and to channel devotion into the revolution. Some PKK leaders are also suspicious of marriage as a patriarchal institution. Meredith Tax lists revolutionary struggles with women soldiers in *Road Unforseen* (2016). The unusual Zapatistas are similar to the PKK in aiming for permanent gender equality among women and men soldiers in their democratic communities in southern Mexico (discussed in Volume 2 Chapter 3).

Historically, women compose about 25% of members of terrorist groups such as the Irish Republican Army, Chechen fighters and Tamil Tigers, and some are joining the so-called Islamic State despite its extreme sexism.[62] An affiliated all-woman jihadi group affiliated with ISIS is called Al Zawraa. They fought with Chinese and Vietnamese communists, in Sri Lanka, Nepal, Angola, Eritrea, Mozambique, South Africa, Zimbabwe, Cuba, El Salvador, Nicaragua and Mexico. However, they rarely were allowed to be commanders, unlike the Kurdish troops in Rojava, discussed in Volume 2 Chapter 5.

Despite a common belief that women leaders are more peaceful, a review of psychological studies of men and women in the US concluded that gender differences are small.[63] Women may be more aggressive than men when they think they're anonymous. In a survey of support of military force in recent US conflicts, 51% of men and 43% of women supported the use of force, only an 8% difference. Female aggression tends to be indirect such as getting a teacher to punish someone rather than hitting. A survey of 805 young activists in Eastern European far left and far right groups, reported that men and women in equal numbers supported violent tactics to change the government or defend other members of their group from police violence. This was especially true of the right-wing activists, meaning that the use of violence depends more on group ideology than gender.[64]

Women Politicians Make a Difference

"Women-led movements arising around the world herald a profound shift that changes everything," according to Osprey Orielle-Lake, Leila Salazar and Lynne Twist. They point to the women leading the Green Energy Revolution in Africa, protecting the Amazonian rainforest, and peace making in Liberia.[65] In Milawi a woman chief named Theresa Kachindamoto campaigns against child marriage. She got 50 sub-chiefs to sign an agreement to end child marriage under customary law and fired four male chiefs who allowed it. She makes sure the girls freed from marriage go school and checks to make sure their parents keep sending the girls.[66] In the Philippines, the bravest opposition to President Rodrigo Duterte's extrajudicial killings of drug users are two outspoken women legislators, Senator Leila de Lima (imprisoned on false charges) and Vice President Leni Robredo.[67] An article lists 17 women who are currently changing the world.[68]

Senator Susan Collins explained that women "are used to working together in a collaborative way." In the US, women senators worked together from both parties were credited with negotiating the end of the US government shutdown in October 2013, leading Senator John McCain to joke that "the women are taking over." I heard similar that comments at my university when I organized a women's faculty association.[69] After 31 years as a US Senator and leader of the Democrats, Harry Reid observed the greatest change is the increasing number of dynamic women; they improved the Senate because women are more patient, less inclined to go to war.[70] (A report on women in US politics by the Institute of Women's Policy Research is available online.[71])

Ada Colau, the first woman mayor of Barcelona, made major changes starting with her election in 2015, at the same time that former judge Manuela Carmena became the first woman mayor of Madrid with similar goals. An article about Colau asks, "The World's Most Radical Mayor?"[72] Housing activist and PAH (Platform for Mortgage Victims) founder Ada Colau (age 41) was the first of the Spanish *indignados* to win office, the leaders of large demonstrations against austerity programs and high youth unemployment. She told her supporters, "This is the victory of David over Goliath." Her campaign included a popular music video available on YouTube with her having fun singing *El Run Run* (the buzz). She wants to "feminize" politics and avoid macho leftist rhetoric, such as Pablo Iglesias' statement that, "Heaven is not taken by consensus—it is taken by assault." He is the head of the new party Podemos that grew out of the 2011 huge demonstrations. Most of its leaders are men. In response to the 2015 immigrant crisis, Colau posted on Facebook to suggest creating a network of refuge-cities. Her "appeal to affection" went viral and families responded with offers to share their homes with refugees. She is not afraid to shed tears while making public speeches.

Colau promised to follow the Mexican Zapatista way "to govern by obeying the people." The *Barcelona en Comu* platform was drafted by over 5,000 people online and in assemblies. Neighborhood assemblies researched the needs of their areas and generated proposals for solutions. The platform advocates mainstreaming gender equality in all local government departments, including the city budget and urban planning. In office, Colau quickly reduced her pay, restored school meal subsidies for poor children, fined banks that owned vacant properties, and sought to limit the millions of tourists with a moratorium on new tourist apartments and hotels.

I asked a resident of Barcelona about Colau's administration. Vani said that Colau is an environmentalist who prevented building an ice rink in such a warm city and created a municipal solar energy company, a feminist who works for shelters for women and finding housing for low-income people in abandoned buildings. Before the paintings in City Hall were all by men, but now portraits of eight women leaders are on walls, including famous anarchist leader Federica Montseny. When opponents criticized Colau for doing what a cleaning woman could do, she said she had the highest respect for such workers.

Former Spanish Socialist Prime Minister José Zapatero believed that equality is vital for peace, so he appointed an equal number of women and men to his Cabinet, as did French President Emmanuel Macron in 2017. He explained he was raised by his mother to be a feminist. Japanese Prime Shinzo Abe appointed five women to his cabinet in 2014 in order to "conjure a fresh wind of change by bringing women's perspectives" and develop "womenomics" to enlarge the work force. However, two of the women resigned because they were plagued by scandal about campaign contributions. Neither sex is angelic but girls are generally socialized to be less overtly aggressive and more cooperative.

Female presidents in Latin America who served between 1999 and 2013 appointed 24% more female ministers to their cabinets than average for the region.[73] Brazilian President Rousseff appointed the largest number of women ministers in history including a Secretariat for Women and put women in key economic positions.[74] Rousseff campaigned against criminalizing abortion; these positions plus being a single parent led to charges that she was a lesbian. In a March 8, 2012, speech, she listed eight commitments for women in areas including work and health. She struggled with scandal though in her second term when corruption was revealed in the national oil company Petrobras, during her tenure as chair of the board from 2003 to 2010. No one accused her of taking bribes herself but she was accused of hiding the national deficit by illegally borrowing from state banks and spending government money on corporations to curry their support. The Vice President who replaced her selected an all white male cabinet in a country where whites are a minority. The Office of the Public Prosecutor found her not guilty of any crimes in July 2016.

A young Brazilian young woman replied to me about Rousseff's feminism, "She isn't a feminist, she created a law that makes a crime if someone kills a woman just because she is a woman, but apart from that she never spoke about abortion, harassment... nothing." She was accused of being autocratic, not a team player, refusing to meet with members of Congress including her own party members, harsh, having a short fuse, swearing at a mayor during a meeting and "humiliating him with a string of expletives."[75] She defended not meeting saying, "There were certain types of blackmail negotiations I would not engage in." She was the victim of a coup attempt by people who didn't like her anti-neoliberal capitalist orientation and programs to help the poor.

Women leaders have to be part of the male club of power brokers to get in power, so we don't see differences between men and women in well-known *Forbes Magazine* lists the 100 most powerful women each year; in 2015 only three of the most powerful women were politicians. Angela Merkel, Hillary Clinton, Dilma Rousseff, Melinda Gates, Janet Yellen, Mary Barra (CEO of General Motors), Christine Lagarde, Sheryl Sandberg, Susan Wojcicki (CEO of YouTube) and Michelle Obama.[76] Hawkish women leaders like Margaret Thatcher and leaders of neofascist political parties like Marine Le Pen in France, Frauke Petry in Germany, Pia Kjaersgaard in Denmark, and Siv Jensen in Norway haven't actually provided peaceful female alternative. In Israel, former general Miri Regev is a conservative Minster of Culture and Sport whose "Loyalty in Culture" initiative aims to give money only to institutions that express loyalty to Israel as a Jewish state. My personal experience with several women department chairs was they were vindictive, such as one of the women tried to move my office to a former geography map closet in retaliation for me being a witness in a discrimination suit against the department.

In response to my posting a photo of the women presidents of Argentina, Brazil and Chile on the Global Youth SpeakOut Facebook page, the German editor of Youth-Leader online magazine, Eric Schneider commented:

> *Ask the people of Argentina and Brazil about the corrupt leaders with breasts creating a corporate Monsanto state, banning WWF [World Wildlife Fund] and others from the rio+20 summit etc. You are being misled by an illusion. Think of [Secretaries of State] Albright and Rice, foreign ministers running illegal wars*

of aggression lying to the global public and saying, "The death of 250,000 Iraqi kids is okay." Think of Merkel turning the environmental wheel back 20 years. You are just being misled through a trick, ... they used George Bush as a cowboy clown to win the Republican Americans, they use smiles like Obama or female clowns to win you while the same show goes on: drone warfare, corporate Monsanto, fracking etc. and putting the corporate ex-CEOs into leading food and environmental state agencies. Stop being so naive. Ask Costa Rica and their corrupt Mafia friend politician pretty lady who criminalized Sea Shepherd for persecuting illegal shark killers in Costa Rica's marine reserves, etc. Bah!

Schneider is correct that the influence of women leaders isn't clear-cut. Conservative Prime Minister Margaret Thatcher was called the Iron Lady and Tory Prime Minister Theresa May was accused by the *Independent* newspaper of opposing equality and human rights legislation throughout her career in parliament, as did other writers.[77] When May was challenged about her request in July 2016 for parliamentary funding for nuclear weaponry that could kill a 100,000 people, she said it was a necessary deterrent to enemies. Indian Prime Minister Indira Gandhi restricted freedoms with her state of emergency, called "Dictator of India" by a member of the Janata Party. South Korean President Geun-hye Park was also criticized for suppressing freedom of speech, her hard-line approach to North Korea, and charges of corruption that led to her impeachment in 2017.

Maternal Qualities Idealized as Compassionate Leadership

When activist Bill Moyer analyzed the stages of a social movement and the factors leading to its success, he advised that leaders must be "nurturing mothers, not dominant patriarchs."[78] Some associate the motherhood role with peacefulness. The interim president of the Central African Republic, Catherine Samba-Panza told citizens, "I am your mother. You are all my children," hoping to stop fighting between Christians and Muslims. In Burma/Myanmar Aung Saan Suu Kyi is called Mother Suu. In Palestine, Raghda Abu-Shahla works for the UN on refugee issues; she observed, "Palestinian women are the strong pillar that hold our social fabric together."[79] A Liberian male university student, 24, commented about their President Ellen Johnson Sirleaf, "Since independence men have always run the country and they have failed at the job. We're looking to her to quickly bring security and to reunite our Muslim and Christian brothers. Now it's up to the mother to reconcile these different communities."[80]

President Johnson Sirleaf believes that being mothers gives women leaders "a sensitivity to humankind" that will make the world a better and safer place.[81] The unmarried former president of South Korea, Park Geun-hye campaigned with the promise that she "would govern like a mother dedicated to her family. To make you happy is the reason I do politics." Yingluck Haskin, former Prime Minister of Thailand, said she would use her feminine qualities of "strength and gentleness" to heal her country's divisions. (She was ousted in a military coup in 2014.) Both these leaders were preceded by powerful male relatives, the former her brother and the latter her father. North Korean leaders blamed Park for increasing tensions on the peninsula with her "venomous swish of skirt," a Korean term used to describe controlling women.

Women used their image as loving mothers to protest the disappearance of their children during the military dictatorship from 1976 to 1983, in Argentina's Madres de la Plaza de Mayo. The world media reported on them as they wore white head coverings as a symbol of their purity, contributing to the fall of the military junta. Similarly, Iranian "Mourning Mothers" meet weekly in Laleh Park in Tehran to protest the disappearance of their children during protests against corruption in the 2009 election. Libyan mothers carried photos of disappeared relatives in 2011, as the Mother's Front had done in Sri Lanka in the 1990s. Mothers also organize as a group in the US. Mothers Against Drunk Driving, founding by the mother whose daughter was killed by a drunk driver, successfully organized against drunk drivers in the US. The blog group Mamavation lobbied for health measures and pressured the American Academy of Pediatrics to end its "unholy alliance" with Monsanto chemical corporation.[82] Moms Demand Action for Gun Sense in America was formed in 2012 after the school massacre at Sandy Hook Elementary School in Connecticut. Moms Clean Air Force works to end air pollution. All these lobby groups use their status as mothers to convey their message as worth listening to and pure.

Tawakkol Karman, a major leader of the 2011 revolution in Yemen, also believes that women as mothers are peacemakers.[83] She advocates, "There is no solution [for peace] other than spreading the culture of coexistence and dialogue, skills that women master and possess." She explains that women can be an anecdote to terrorist violence:

> *Women have more opportunities in challenging extremism and terrorism than men due to woman's nature in having patience, containing others, hating killing and bloodshed and—more importantly—women have tremendous feelings of*

love and sacrifice towards their husbands, children, and communities that is enough to enhance the attitude of coexistence, respect, trust, and listening to the other. This, in turn, will lead to drying the roots and sources of extremism. Extremism stems from the culture of rejecting the other and the culture of hating the other. Therefore, there is no solution other than spreading the culture of co-existence and dialogue, skills that women master and possess.

A Yemeni woman cannot be part of terrorism because she herself is suffering from terrorism. She is banned from taking part in public life, fearing she will mingle with men (which is forbidden). The intellectual terrorism that is prac-ticed against woman by a large segment of men in the Yemeni society makes her ineffective in the public domain either politically or socially. A Yemeni woman without doubt has no role in recruiting or training terrorists in order to kill inno-cent people. If the policy of excluding women from public life and preventing her from effectively taking part in developing this country and challenging terrorism along with men continues, the culture of extremism will flourish and the rami-fications will be disastrous.

French nationalist Marine Le Pen created an image of mother of the nation, the "woman next door" for her campaign for the presidency in 2017. She started wear-ing pantsuits like Angela Merkel and Hillary Clinton, cut her hair, and stopped wear-ing high fashion brands such as Dior sunglasses (her opponent Emmanuel Macron stopped wearing very expensive suits but stuck to the dark suits worn by powerful men). A French professor observes that depending on how "maternal she seems, it's much easier to hear" for the audience.[84]

Perhaps the most powerful women in the world, German Chancellor Angela Merkel is referred to as *Mutti*, Mommy. The name was first used by rivals in her Chris-tian Democratic Union party as an insult, but then caught on with the public and she embraced it.[85] Germans told me it's an affectionate rather than disparaging nickname. Merkel doesn't have children, is in her second marriage, and doesn't sleep more than five hours a night. She was a brilliant student with a doctorate in quantum chemistry and approaches politics like a scientist rather than being a charismatic public speaker. She grew up in communist Eastern Germany where books were banned and newspa-pers censored. Despite her unlikely background, she won her third term in office in 2014. Myra Marx Ferree describes German feminism as conservative and materialistic, looking to the state to support equality, in a patriarchal country.[86]

Merkel is not a feminist, reporting she had no interest in her first appointment as Minister of Women and Youth. At that time Chancellor Helmut Kohl referred to her as "my girl," *mein Mädchen,* though he later regretting the appointment, telling a friend she was a snake who wanted power. Merkel feels being a woman can be an advantage, comparing her experience in the chemistry laboratory with all male colleagues: "The men in the laboratory always had their hands on all the buttons at the same time. I couldn't keep up with this, because I was thinking. And then things suddenly went 'poof,' and the equipment was destroyed." She listens more than she talks, then acts. A former US Ambassador to Germany, John Kornblum observed, "If you cross her, you end up dead. There's nothing cushy about her. There's a whole list of alpha males who thought they would get her out of the way, and they're all now in other walks of life." When Merkel met with new British Prime Minister Theresa May, she agreed with May's comment that they were two women who would get on with the job, implying that women are more direct about achieving a task.

Chile's President Michelle Bachelet emphasized being a mother, saying, " I am the mother of three. Right now I don't have a partner... I hope there will come a time for my children, for my family, and if a boyfriend, better, but otherwise I can live." Young women today are fortunate enough to grow up in a world where they can see single mothers who are governing their countries."[87] In a Catholic country, not only is Bachelet a single mother but an agnostic socialist who aims to create a society where "tolerance, understanding of diversity, integration and not discrimination, will be the main policies." Like President Rousseff in Brazil, she was detained by the military for her political activism when they were younger.

A Chilean journalist, Paul Walder wrote an article titled "Michelle Bachelet: A Mother for Chile?" in which he said the maternal image is common in Latin American politics, such as the use of cooking pots banged together to protest, but, "This image had never previously been donned by a figure with presidential aspirations and possibilities. The case of Eva Perón, who also had a strong mythical content, was incarnated at the side of masculine power," her husband.[88] He ties the appeal of a single woman to the Latin American emphasis on the Virgin Mary, appealing in a country where about half the births are to single mothers. Walder argued that great recent social and cultural changes follow from women like Bachelet moving into the public sphere when she served as Defense Minister. She represents a break with the macho tradition as Chile moves into modernity,

Ellen Johnson Sirleaf became the first African woman president in 2006 campaigning as a caring mother. She said voters told her during the campaign, "Men have failed us. Men are too violent, too prone to make war. Women are less corrupt, less likely to be focused on getting fancy cars and fancy homes for themselves." Her campaign relied on women volunteers going village to village, door-to-door campaigning. She appointed women as Ministers of Youth and Sports, Gender and Development, Commerce, Foreign Affairs, and Finance. She believes that being mothers gives women leaders "a sensitivity to humankind" that will make the world a better and safer place.[89] In Zimbabwe, Grace Mugabe is the power behind her aging husband, President Robert Mugabe, so a sycophant choir sang to her, "Be pleased to follow Mrs. Mugabe, a mother who has love, mother of the nation, the one who takes care of orphans."[90]

A recent debate about motherhood, in July 2016, UK Energy Minister Andrea Leadsom told the *Times of London* that being a mother gives her an advantage over rival for Prime Minister childless Home Secretary Theresa May. Leadsom said, "But genuinely I feel that being a mum means you have a very real stake in the future of our country, a tangible stake. She possibly has nieces, nephews, lots of people, but I have children who are going to have children who will directly be a part of what happens next."[91] A cry of protest arose and Leadsom tried to backtrack and May became Prime Minister.

"Mom" is used as a term of praise by young fans in the US for people like a Supreme Court Justice: a "Jezebel" website headline demanded, "You leave our mom Ruth Bader Ginsburg alone, you monster," and singer Beyoncé's fans declared that she is "everyone's mom."[92] Singer Taylor Swift (born in 1989) is also called "mom," although she doesn't have children. Female college roommates sometimes call each other "mom."

Women are often viewed as more caring and compassionate.

US government statistics report that women of all ages volunteer more than men do.[93] Mariana is 14 and lives in Portugal. She typifies young women's desire to do service and awareness of global issues, as she shared on Our Shared Shelf in 2016.

> I'm a volunteer in some campaigns in my city especially in my school where we collect clothes and food for the students who need these types of help. This may seem to not have anything to do with feminism but it does, these types of things make me want to end the differences that exist in our world and it makes me so happy to see that I actually make a small difference everyday just by doing

simple actions. When I discovered Malala's work I was sure I wanted to do something like that, later I found amazing TED talks about feminism and "HeforShe."

In Portugal we don't have gender inequality but for me as a woman I want to make sure everyone around the globe has the same opportunities I have. We don't live isolated in our own countries, we are all part of a bigger thing, our world and we are the ones that can change it.

"Affective politics," *politica afectiva*, was formulated in Argentina aiming to change group relationships to loving caring relationships rather than competition and dominance struggles. Authors Marina Sitrin and Dario Azzellini observe that, "Affect and emotion are too often relegated to the politics of gender and identity, and this not seen as 'serious' theory or as a potentially revolutionary part of politics."[94] They point out that "affective politics is not an expression of 'maternal responsibility' but a social responsibility to build a new society based on cooperation and mutual aid rather than competition."

Nurturing or Strict Fathers in Politics

Father figures are also part of politics, divided into the nurturing father of progressives and the strict father of conservatives, according to George Lakoff.[95] He associates the strict father with father knows best, physical discipline and the importance of winning. Another explanation for Trump's popularity is he appealed to the Stone Age brain that evolved during the Pleistocene, the last long ice age.[96] It responds to fear and anger in the most sensitive parts of the brain in the insula, making Trump seem authentic and relatable. He called Clinton a monster and weak who doesn't look presidential wouldn't be respected in Mexico like he was. In contrast, Hillary Clinton's campaign didn't have a direct emotional impact, according to author Rick Shenkman.

Trump's 2016 presidential campaign was the epitome of machismo toughness and anger, talking about how he would bomb and "beat the shit out of ISIS," would use more extreme torture than water boarding, make Mexico pay for a border wall, make China adjust its currency and be a winner. About ISIS, he said, "I think we're weak. Nobody would be tougher on ISIS than Donald Trump. I will find the right guy to make the military really work. Nobody will push us around." He added in a tweet, "I alone can solve this problem." He told followers that his movement is the most important in US history and if he lost, it would be the end of democracy. He repeatedly advocates,

"We gotta be tough." He's fine with being called "an authoritarian." Trump's father frequently told him, "You are a killer … you are a king."[97] When he first moved into the Oval Office his only family photograph featured his father.

Trump's office often released official photographs of the president flanked by white men in suits, such as when he signed the global "gag rule," that prevented US funding for health organizations that even mention abortion. *New York Times* writer Jill Filipovic suggests that the photos aren't "an error but a game plan."[98] She views the photos as a continuation of Trump's campaign of "aggrieved masculinity," and male entitlement, as men feel they've lost power. Trump's theme of make American great again can be interpreted as a desire to give power back to white men. The hatred of Hillary Clinton seen in chants to lock her up for using a private email server as Secretary of State and T-shirts saying "Trump That Bitch." Trump's cabinet is composed of the most white male members in the past 35 years. When he was asked in August 2016 about women cabinet members, the only one he could think of was his daughter Ivanka, who he said he would date if she wasn't his daughter. She ran an ad for her father's presidential campaign stating, "The most important job any woman can have is being a mother."

We've become weak, Trump said, insulting rival Senator Ted Cruz by calling him soft, weak, like a baby. Trump said to a large campaign rally, "I love the old days — you know what they used to do to guys like that when they were in a place like this? They'd be carried out on a stretcher, folks." When some white supporters punched and attempted to choke a Black Lives Matter protester at a rally, Trump said, "Maybe he should have been roughed up." At another rally he said, "I'd like to punch him in the face" and at another, if his supporters saw anybody with a tomato, "Knock the crap out of them, would you? Seriously. OK? Just knock the hell [out of them]. I promise you I will pay for the legal fees." "We've gotta fight back," he said about unruly protesters, and threatened to send his supporters to disrupt Bernie Sander's speeches, charging that Sanders was the instigator of the protests at Trump events. He said, "I am so tired of this politically correct crap." He hired "alt right" Stephen Bannon, associated with extremist Breitbart blog to be his campaign CEO and then his chief adviser. The alt-right advocates protection of white identity perceived as under assault under the guise of "political correctness" and "social justice," attacking even most Republican leaders as not conservative enough.[99]

As the protective father, Trump told Idaho potato growers, "As President, I will protect your market." He told Michigan workers before their primary in February, "If you get laid off, I still want your vote. I'll get you a new job; don't worry about it." In his messianic acceptance speech at the Republican convention in July 2016 he told voters, "I alone can fix it," referring to the dystopian picture he painted of a violent US overrun by illegal immigrants and Muslim terrorists. To low-wage workers, he said, "I am your voice" and that since no one understands the economic system better than he does, he is the only one to fix it.

He tells supporters he loves them and there are good people and bad people, and he's the greatest at everything he mentions—the presidency, the military, building walls, making money. He doesn't feel the need to research policies just makes pronouncements about how great he is, commenting on climate change that weather changes and goes up and down and he thinks that "it's very low on the list" of world problems.[100] Hence, he pulled the US out of the Paris climate agreement in 2017. His approach to voters is compared to techniques used by fascists like Mussolini, who Trump quoted in a tweet.[101] His campaign brought in pollster Kellyanne Conway to "soften" his message, but he kept repeatedly used the words "tough" and "strong." She offered excuses for his misstatements, justifying "alternative facts."

Trump seems uncomfortable with female body functions. He called Fox News reporter and lawyer Megyn Kelly a lightweight bimbo (she is trained as a lawyer) and implied her tough questions were due to menstruation, commenting on "blood coming out of her wherever." He thinks breastfeeding is disgusting and said his pregnant third wife looked like a blimp. In March 2016 he said that women should be punished for having an abortion, then changed his mind a few hours later saying doctors who perform abortions should be punished rather than women. Saying he is against "political correctness," he allowed black women to be pushed and roughed up during his rallies. He criticized Fox News women employees who spoke up about sexual harassment by Roger Ailes, stating that they should be more grateful to their former boss who "helped" them so much in their careers.

Trump told a contestant on *Celebrity Apprentice* that it would be a pretty picture to see her on her knees, implying a sexual act, and he often discussed the "hotness" female contestants and asked the men if they would like to have sex with various women. He judges women by their appearance, as when he told *Esquire Magazine*, "You know, it doesn't really matter what [the media] write as long as you've got a young and beautiful piece of ass."[102] He called Rosie O'Donnell a fat pig and condemned presidential candidate Carly Fiorina's appearance: "Look at that face! Would anyone vote for that?" About sexual assaults in the military he tweeted, "What did these geniuses expect when they put men and women together?" He slut-shamed and fat-shamed Alicia Machado, a Miss Universe winner, and constantly "maninterrupted" (similar to "mansplaining") Hillary Clinton during their first debate.[103] *Telegraph* and *New York Times* articles list more sexist actions.[104] Trump picked serial adulterers like Rudy Giuliani, Newt Gingrich, and serial sexual harasser Roger Ailes as his close advisors.

His sexist comments hit a new low when a lewd video was released close to the November elections, in which a newly married Trump said his celebrity gave him the permission to grab women's genitalia, although the word he actually used is one he used to disparage Ted Cruz.[105] He also called a female reporter a vulgar word for female genitals that starts with a "c." All of Utah's Republican leaders temporarily revoked their endorsements of him, along with other party leaders like Senator John McCain, but Trump received millions of emails from his supporters and aligned himself with the "alt-right" to continue his "revolution."

The positive outcome is Trump generated consciousness-raising about sexual assault. When Canadian author Kelly Oxford asked women to tweet about their "first assaults," in a few hours she quickly received almost 10 million stories of assault, and millions more kept coming to @kellyoxford. Michelle Obama's speech about sexual harassment also went viral.[106] Documentary filmmaker Michael Moore commented (in an open letter to Republican lawmakers on October 11, 2016) who he blamed for trying to control women's bodies and laying the foundation for Trump's campaign: "If you're against women, you're over. There's a fourth wave of feminism afoot now--and you are going to be its first casualties. Or, as I prefer to see it, its first victory," when they get voted out of office. Republican TV commentator Nicolle Wallace tweeted that "There is a hot gender war underway," including Fox anchor Meghan Kelly's verbal confrontation with Trump and with his surrogate Newt Gingrich.

The anarchist art collective INDECLINE put naked statues of Donald Trump by "Ginger" in six US cities in August 2016, titled "The Emperor Has No Balls" with only a very small male organ. In New York City, the parks department removed the statue in Union Square, making this statement, " NYC Parks stands firmly against any un-permitted erection in city parks, no matter how small." Trump and Rubio were not the first to discuss penis size, as traced in US history in a lively article that reported that President Lyndon Johnson displayed his penis, named "Jumbo," to answer a reporter's question about why the US was still involved in the Vietnam War and that[107] Hillary Clinton asked reporters to describe her policies as "muscular."[108] The mostly male characters of Silicon Valley make frequent references to male genitalia, often as an insult.

Once in office, Trump was rude to some US allies and praised strong men like stating that Russian Vladamir Putin is a better leader than Obama, praising Erdogan in Turkey after winning a fraudulent vote, said Xi in China is "a very good man" despite the lack of freedom, and he praised General el-Sissi in Egypt despite thousands of political prisoners, and invited President Duterte in the Philippines to visit, despite his war on drugs killing more than 7,000 people during the first year of his presidency and comparing himself to Hitler. Trump called the brutal leader of North Korea, Kim Jong-un, a "smart cookie" because he was able to assume power in his 20s and said he would be honored to meet with him.[109] Clearly, strength is more important than rights and justice in the macho worldview.

Trump's sexism galvanized feminist activism in the US and around the world. Feminists in a 2017 march in China wore shirts that translate as "This is what a feminist looks like." They protested against increasing sexism, referred to as spreading like "straight man cancer." Trump inflamed their activism: "He has brought solidarity to Chinese feminists. We have never stood so close to each other to fight against one person," said well-known feminist Zheng Churan. (She was one of the five activists detained before they could organize events on International Women's Day in 2015.) The Chinese Feminist Collective was organized in the US to provide support for feminists detained in China.

Women are Better Leaders?

Young people ages 18 to 24 have more faith in women's ability to lead change than men's, as described in an international Euro survey of Millennials in France, China, India, the UK and the US.[110] In India, high school student Siddhant founded an environmental group called GreenGaians in 2009.[111] The group organized a campaign in schools and government offices to plant trees. When I asked him about the girls' participation, he emailed that they are some of his best members: "They are loyal to the cause and don't get distracted, that's what I like about them." When asked if girls have different organizing styles, Taika, 18, answered in the affirmative from Ethiopia:

> *Basically, the difference comes from instincts of being a woman. Whether 18 or 81, we have the motherly feeling and the soft side that comes with it. We are more rational towards situations. We are also more dedicated to projects and more open-minded towards new ideas. From my experience, they are less dragged into the prejudice and it is always about work and nothing else. As*

leaders, even though women are more emotional, they really work hard to keep their emotions intact and away from the work area. The same can be said with their organization and prioritizing. They are more organized, because women take responsibility when they know they can do it or learn from others. Their personal background rarely affects their decisions.

Christina, 18, Trinidad and Tobago, agreed that women are more organized:

I believe that women are generally more organized than men and have a more perfectionist attitude. They know what they want the outcome to be and they know the way to get there. Whereas a man may know what he wants too but will more likely take the go with the flow approach. He may quicker delegate duties than a woman that in some ways can be considered better.

From Cambodia, SpeakOut student Kuntia, 18, observes that women are more patient than men: "Since patience is the key to success, women will become the leader of this world and make it better by using their knowledge." In my dialogue with students in a government girls' high school in South Korea in 2012, the students said women and girls have experienced discrimination so they have more ambition and desire to succeed, they're more patient, they're steady and more diligent, whereas boys and men get distracted (see videos[112]). As an aside, they said girls are better looking. Females are sensitive so they can think about details, not only the big things, but small things too. Observing her younger brother, a girl said boys like to fight, they're pugnacious, and their nature is brutal. Girls said their generation believes in women more than the older generation. Another generational difference mentioned in our dialogue in a co-ed high school in the same town was that while the older generation values politeness and, youth are more Westernized, influenced by Western media, and both sexes speak out more.

Some believe that women are less corruptible, less likely to take bribes. This is the reason that a central Mexican state organized an all female traffic police force in 2013, excluding short and fat women. The Ecatepec Police Chief wanted "tall women that render respect" and focused on women police because they calm men down.[113] Studies do indicate that women police officers in the US do rely more than men on communication and are better able to defuse potentially violent situations.[114] Journalist Hanna Rosin suggests the postindustrial management style suits women better than men because it values "social intelligence, open communication, the ability to sit still and focus" and emphasizes being "post-heroic" member of a group rather than out in front.

Christine Lagarde, president of the IMF, believes that women such as Iceland's former prime minister Johanna Sigurdardottir make better leaders in a crisis than men because women have the ability to listen (similar to women physicians), the desire to form a consensus, and pay attention to risk factors.[115] She asked, "What would have happened if Lehman brothers had been Lehman Sisters?" This is in regards to financial misdeeds leading to the long-last financial crisis of 2008. She observed women are more risk-averse and more concerned about financial exclusion although women are only 3% of bank CEOs.[116] A study of 31 countries reported that more women legislators leads to greater respect for government on the part of both men and women.[117]

California Senator Kamala Harris advised in the early days of the Trump presidency, "Support women candidates. They are the only ones in Congress right now who actually engage in reasoned, bi-partisan discussions." New York Senator Kristen Gillibrand wrote in her book *Off The Sidelines: Raise Your Voice, Change the World* (2014) that women Senators make a difference because they are better collaborators who are more interested in working together to find solutions than her male colleagues; the women want to find common ground. When asked about their role models who inspired their leadership, girls are more likely to mention their mothers than women political leaders.[118] Politicians are not highly respected. When the female majority Seattle City Council voted in 2016 to reject a land deal to build a sports arena as financially unwise, they were attacked as "ladies" who didn't understand the importance of sports who should kill themselves and rot in hell.

A *Foreign Policy* magazine survey of 43 international women politicians reported that 84% believe that having more female leaders would alter their government's policies and 65% believe they would bring more peace.[119] The Inter-Parliamentary Union reports that women's presence in parliaments (only 22% globally) and in ministerial positions significantly increases investments in social welfare and legal protection, as well as honesty in government and business.[120] Nevertheless, women held only 22% of parliamentary seats in 2015 and only 17 countries had elected female leaders in 2016, according to UN women (they're shown in a slide show[121]). Thirty-two countries don't have constitutional guarantees for gender equality.

A cooperative called CONAMURI in Paraguay is run mostly by feminist women who formed it in 2002 by joining 11 barrios with around 6,500 families combined. The full name is National Coordinator of Rural and Indigenous Women Workers. They'll work with young men but not older ones, because, as Maria explained, "We women won't sell out, we won't make pacts, we aren't going to negotiate."[122] One of the leaders,

Ada said the men are less involved with family life, working outside on cars or construction; women keep the family and the community together. They constructed their barrios themselves. Each barrio is governed by its own committee. The coordinating committee is composed of 26 women and four men. They hope to teach youth to create more equal gender relationships and a new culture. Their socialist struggle is not against men but against patriarchy and capitalism. One of their campaigns is to protect native seeds from GMOs and pesticides with an emphasis on involving young people to block "this system that trades our right to live in this planet for gold."[123] They aim to return to the indigenous system of the "good life" and work with regional associations like ALBA, the Bolivarian Alternative for the Peoples of Our Americas.

Women Business Managers and Millennial Employees

When four US women business executives were asked about the differences in women's and men's leadership, they said men are able to have a heated debate and not carry away bad feelings while women take it more to heart and are uncomfortable with conflict.[124] A study confirmed that competitive male athletes spend more time re-connecting after a competition than women. Another executive observed that women work more effectively in a group because they don't have to be the alpha top dog and possess "soft skills" cooperating with a group, as in the ability to read non-verbal cues. Studies confirm that women under stress make more rational decisions than their male peers who take more risks with slim odds of success, with different reactions to the hormone cortisol produced in the adrenal gland in response to stress.[125] The women studied became more empathetic when stressed while the men became more focused on themselves. Despite the fact that businesses with diverse management perform better than homogenous managements, and women managers tend to be better at engaging in a two-way dialogue, the percentage of senior women managers grew only 2% from 22% in 2015 to 24% the next year.[126] The highest percentages of women managers are in Eastern Europe and Southeast Asia, with the most in Russia and the least in Japan and Germany.

Corporations like General Motors and Yahoo respond to a crisis in the company with the "glass cliff" where they select a woman as the CEO in a time when failure is most likely. Another example is when corruption in the world soccer federation was revealed, in 2016 FIFA appointed a woman as their head, Fatma Samoura from Senegal, who worked for the UN. Some place the 2016 selection of Theresa May as Prime Minister to oversee the UK after the Brexit vote to leave the EU in this "glass cliff category. *The Guardian* ran an article stating, "There is an increasingly widespread sense that strong female leaders are needed to 'clean up the mess created by men.'" [127] The article quotes a Tory member of parliament who said, "I think they feel that at a time of turmoil, a woman will be more practical and a bit less testosterone [-driven] in their approach. More collaborative, more wiling to listen to voices around the table, less likely to have an instantly aggressive approach to things." But the head of the Women's Equality Party, Sophie Walker, pointed out that May and others haven't confronted sexism. (The same year as May became Prime Minister, women leaders led Scotland and Northern Ireland, as well as Germany's Angele Merkel, Croatia's President Kolinda Grabar-Kitarovic and the powerful IMF head Christine Lagarde. UN Climate Chief Christiana Figueres and former New Zealand Prime Minister Helen Clark were nominated to be UN Secretary-General but the male monopoly continued with the appointment of a Portuguese man.)

Some research reports women make better investors, earning higher returns than men because they take fewer risks, don't overtrade or "churn" their investments, and are less ego-driven.[128] The number of women on corporate boards in Fortune 500 companies is linked to more corporate profits, especially when at least three women serve.[129] A study found that internationally companies with women on their boards were less likely to lay off employees during the recession.[130] Although companies with women directors on their boards perform better than those without them, women hold only 16% of Fortune 500 board seats.[131] A survey of nearly 22,000 companies around the world found about 60% of their corporate boards have no female directors.[132] Thus, France, Norway, Spain and Germany require quotas for women on company boards.

Sodexo, a multinational company with 419,000 employees in 80 countries, studied its employees and found that units with equal numbers of men and women managers consistently generated more profits that units dominated by men.[133] A similar finding was reported by McKinsey & Co. in their survey of 366 companies. In a study of 12-member student teams, same sex teams didn't perform as well as those that were 55% female. Other studies of mixed sex teams are discussed in Nicholas Kristof's article on "When Women win, Men Win Too."[134] Companies with balanced management teams are more effective at recruiting and maintaining talented employees, have better customer relations, and make better business decisions with a more inclusive approach. However, a Harvard Business School survey of its graduates reported that women progressed more slowly in their careers because of sexism and the expectation that they manage family life.

A 2008 Internet survey of 2,277 students equally male/female from 114 countries (sponsored by AIESEC and The Career Innovation Company) asked students what they wanted from the workplace.[135] Women were more likely to mention: love, immersion, and altruism. Men were more likely than women to mention: problem solving, and risk. Respondents as a group want their work to provide: 1. Fellowship 2. Application of ability 3. Altruism 4. Discovery 5. Humor 6. Problem solving. Few experienced or wanted the following activities at work: doing physical activity, seeing or using beautiful or well-made things, competing against others, and a sense of risk or danger. The percentages are included in the previous endnote.

What claims to be the largest global generation study of Millennial employees under age 33 reviewed over 9,000 surveys of Milliennial employees, plus 300 interviews and 30 focus groups, in 2011 and 2012.[136] Their findings back up my observation they're the Relationship Generation. The young employees are more likely to leave "if their needs for support, appreciation and flexibility are not met." What's important to young workers, especially in developed countries, is time to develop their personal lives, flexibility and leverage of technology and social media at work, interesting teamwork and emotional connection at work. Frequent feedback and support from managers is more important than salary. Millennials, more than older generations, like having the possibility of assignments in another country due to being "particularly attuned to the world around them." They appreciate corporate social responsibility programs that match their values and like input into important issues more often than older generations.

Although Millennials are often said to value horizontal structures, more than three-quarters of young professionals surveyed in 22 countries believe that hierarchies are useful and a majority like a clear chain of command—many of the respondents are in management.[137] Women were 49% of the respondents. However, in all 22 countries surveyed, a majority said they prefer working in a group rather than alone, with the exception of Korea and Japan.[138] The most group-oriented countries were Spain, Mexico, China, Brazil, Germany and the Netherlands, all with over half of the Millennials in favor of working in groups. All female groups may favor equality than mixed groups.

Do Women Organize Differently than Men?

More Collaborative

In a Bioneers conversation on "Women Re-Imagining the World" women authors listed in the endnote maintained that humans lost their connection to life in the age of patriarchy, but patriarchy is dying and a revolution in valuing the feminine is occurring.[139] Psychologist Jean Shinoda Bolen said, "Women are unique as a gender. We've got compassion. We use conversation to bond." She said feminist conscious-raising circles in the 60s and 70s "changed the world," starting with more egalitarian relationships at home. She advocates for a new wave of the woman's movement to bring peace to the world. The Bioneers panel agreed that a major contribution to scholarship is feminist honoring experiences of oneself and others that "led to new theories and practices." The editors of a book about young global feminists, *Defending Our Dreams*, observe that if they want to be effective and cutting-edge, "it might mean that we run at loggerheads to the customary notions of an activist movement," including leadership style.[140]

Studies indicate that patients have better health outcomes than male physicians because they listen and cooperate: "Female physicians are more likely to practice evidence-based medicine, perform as well or better on standardized examinations, and provide more patient-centered care. Patients of female primary care physicians also experience fewer emergency department visits compared with patients of male primary care physicians."[141] However, these female doctors are promoted and paid less than their male peers. MD Sarah-Anne Schumann told NPR that women tend to be better communicators with better emotional intelligence, able to see patients as people, and more nurturing and able to work as a team with nurses and other staff.[142] A woman physician I interviewed suggested that women listen better so they learn more information to make an accurate diagnosis to treat.

Canadian Naomi Wolf, author of *Give Me Liberty: a Handbook for American Revolutionaries* (2008), teaches leadership skill to women, finding that it's difficult for many of them to speak out in a "hierarchical organizational structure."[143] They're not comfortable being the star with the megaphone directing a crowd, although I've seen such women in videos of global protests. Social media, however, gives women the chance to lead through social connections, a feeling of "us" rather than me as they've led in recent uprisings.

Feminist concepts influenced horizontal organizing in the global justice movement and feminist organizations are some of the most globalized recent social movements.[144] Feminist critique of patriarchal hierarchies in government, business, media, and the family was a major influence on direct democracy horizontal movement organizing. In consciousness-raising groups, the main tool of the Second Wave feminism, each person gets a chance to speak without interruption and arriving at consensus is valued. Women learn that their issues are socialized, that "the personal is political." "The feminist process" is inclusive. Women's Studies introduced "history from the bottom up," studying social history, folk art, and women's diaries not previously considered worthy of scholars. This academic arrogance carries over to a motivation for this book to honor the voices of youth usually not included even in books about youth.

Some girls observe that they're more interested in horizontal organizing than boys. In 2005 and 2006, Jessica Taft interviewed activist 75 girls in Vancouver (British Columbia), San Francisco, Mexico City, Caracas and Buenos Aires.[145] The girls consider themselves leftists, seeing the global struggle against neoliberalism as the background for their work. Some of them participated in "pink blocs" at global protests, starting with demonstrations against the IMF and World Bank in Prague in 2000. Queer youth organized a "silver bloc." Taft found that Latin American girls are more aware of the history of youth activism than North Americans who tended to be unaware of it.[146] Most of the girls focus on local issues, including their school governance.

Taft reported that her interviewees identify themselves as girl activists, seeing themselves as different from adults in their organizing and often critical of adults who try to dominate them, patronize them, or just ignore them in "adultism." Many of the girls organize their activism without adult involvement. Like the activists interviewed in *Citizens in the Present: Youth Civic Engagement in the Americas* (2013), the girls don't want to be treated as future leaders but as equal partners now.

The girls Taft interviewed value horizontal democracy including building supportive group relationships, listening to each other, and arriving at consensus. Girls, unlike their male peers, are socialized to engage in "touchy-feely" relationships and listening. They see themselves as different than boys who may try to dominate discussions, are not good listeners, and aren't as interested in creating group bonding and fun. Some girls report that guys talk more in meetings; studies generally show that men monologue more than women. Girls' style of organizing with its emphasis on relationships can keep boys away, according to some of the interviewees. Kayla said, "Guys, it is more socially acceptable for them not to care very much and just to, you know, not to care… Girls do things as friends more often, and guys more individually."

While in general the girls aimed for horizontal organizing, some of the groups use majority vote. A little more than half of the girls said they were part of groups where there are no leaders because everyone is a leader. Some groups valued participatory democracy but selected formal leaders to do tasks like facilitating group discussions.

Maria, 17, was involved in a student center in Buenos Aires that is committed to the participation of everyone and being a community, rather than a vertical structure with presidents and vice-presidents. She said it takes more time to make decisions, but they achieve more as a group. Azul, a member of her student center, disagrees with Maria on the merits of horizontal organizing because, "in order to not be above anyone, nothing happens," and policy is "incoherent." She thinks the emphasis shifts from ideas to personal relationships. One of the girls commented that the relationship focus can keep boys from joining.

A Mexican girl active in a Zapatista collective, Ramona reported that the first step they learn is to listen. They arrive at consensus through discussion. Another girl, Ella, observed, "I think that youth are really more open to doing things different ways, whereas older people are kind of set in certain ways." The fact that women are the majority of university graduates globally indicates their leadership style will be spread by their rising professional status.

One way to look at how change will occur as women assume more leadership and agency is to look at matrilineal societies. Small matriarchal societies exist in some tribal areas.[147] They trace descent with the mother, live with her, and children are raised by their maternal uncles rather than their fathers. Matrilineal examples from the past and those continuing in the present (the latter underlined) are listed in the endnote.[148] In some of these cultures women chose lovers as they please rather than monogamous marriage. *Cherokee Women in Crisis: Trail of Tears, Civil War, and Allotment, 1838-1907,* (2003) written by Professor Carolyn Johnston, describes equality in the matrilineal Cherokee tribes before the white men corrupted the system. She wrote,

> *Women had autonomy and sexual freedom, could obtain divorce easily, rarely experienced rape or domestic violence, worked as producers/farmers, owned their own homes and fields, possessed a cosmology that contains female supernatural figures, and had significant political and economic power. Cherokee women's close association with nature, as mothers and producers, served as a basis of their power within the tribe, not as a basis of oppression.*

The Moso are a matrilineal people who live in China near the Tibet border. They're Buddhists like the Tibetans and believe in ghosts and deities with their mountain goddess considered the mother of the Moso. In the autobiography of Yang Erce Namu, a girl who grew up in Moso culture, she explains that wealth was held communally and shared equally.[149] Although the oldest woman was the head of the household, they shared decision-making. "In ideal terms, Moso families are democratic units where all relatives expect to be included in decision making." Older people are deferred to whether male or female. Children address their biological father as "uncle" since maternal uncles raise their sisters' boys. Daughters are favored over sons and only daughters have their own bedroom, called a "flower room," where lovers may tap on a girl's window to spend the night if she agrees. They say visiting keeps relations between men and women pure and joyful, without the fights between married couples: They believe that "Love is like the seasons—it comes and goes." Harmony is highly valued, so it's forbidden to argue or gossip. Namu reported, "Nobody in Moso country today can recall either murder or beating or robbery, or a truly ugly fight between neighbors or jilted lovers." Another tribal cultural with matriarchal roots, the Jino in China worship goddesses, permit adolescents to have many lovers before marriage, don't frown on childbirth outside of marriage, and divorce is common.[150] Elders share leadership according to seniority. The implication is that women will bring more democracy, peace and sexual freedom when they're in charge.

Existing Models of Feminist Societies

Looking for models of egalitarian societies, for most of human history we were hunters and gathers who lived in fairly egalitarian bands where duties were shared. Before that our cousins the bonobos are matriarchal societies that resolve tensions with sex of all kinds rather than fighting, although we mostly hear about alpha male chimps who dominate their troops.[151] Professor Herbert Marcuse believed that adopting so-called feminine qualities such as care and tenderness "could be the beginning of a qualitatively different society, the very antithesis to male domination with its violent and brutal character."[152] He said in 1974 that the women's movement is "potentially the most radical political movement that we have." Friends of the Earth wrote a book titled *Why Women Will Save The Planet* (2015), suggesting that ecofeminists combine environmentalism and feminism in a way that strengths both. Indian ecofeminist Vandana Shiva argues that capitalist patriarchy has constricted women and that "we need another worldview that happens to be more alive in the sustaining and caring culture of womankind."[153] Activist Michal White, co-initiator of Occupy Wall Street in 2011, would like to see a matriarchal global political party, perhaps starting from a women-led backlash against sexist patriarchs including Putin (Russia), Erdogan (Turkey), Duterte (Philippines), Xi (China), Jong-un (North Korea), and Trump (US). He suggests, "Women will make the next great social movement, in a global matriarchy."[154]

Currently, the most feminist smaller communities are Kurdish Rojava in Northern Syria (discussed Volume 2 Chapter 5 and the Zapatistas in Southern Mexico (discussed in Volume 2 Chapter 3). Established countries in Scandinavia provide the Nordic Model of how to create social and economic equality and break the power of the oligarchic 1%, while also encouraging private enterprise in mixed economies. The Social Progress Index ranks countries by quality of life factors such as health, access to education, religious freedom and personal safety.[155] In 2014 Norway was at the top, while the US was in 8th place.[156] Norway also ranked at the top of the UN Development Program's Human Development Index for 12 of the last 15 years.[157] Norwegians work 37 hours a week, over half of workers are represented by unions, and workers have a year parental leave and long vacations so they have time to spend with their families. Kindergartens are available starting at age one. For these reasons, Save the Children selected Norway as the best country to raise children (the US was in 33rd place).

A British author who lives in Denmark with his Danish wife, Michael Booth wrote about his criticisms of the homogeneous Nordic countries in *The Almost Perfect People: Behind the Myth of Scandinavian Utopia* (2014). "These societies function well for those who conform to the collective median, but they aren't much fun for tall poppies. Schools rein in higher achievers for the sake of the less gifted; 'elite' is a dirty word; displays of success, ambition or wealth are frowned upon."[158] Despite their imperfections he believes as I do that they provide the best model of governments with happy citizens, "enviably rich, peaceful, harmonious, and progressive."[159] One of the key contributions to happiness is a feeling of autonomy and ability to rise up the economic ladder. Another British author, Helen Russell spent a year in rural Denmark, which she described in *The Year of Living Danishly: My Twelve Months Unearthing the Secrets of the World's Happiest Country* (2015).

Booth explained the historical background that led to this egalitarianism, mutual trust, social cohesion, economic and gender equality, rationalism, and modesty. As agrarian populations, Nordic populations learned to work together. In the 1930s, labor movements organized general strikes and boycotts and Social Democrats were elected to lead parliament for three decades before Conservatives returned to the ruling coalition in Sweden and Norway.[160] Essential to social mobility is excellent free education and social welfare programs. Scandinavia has a hybrid economy, socialist in government provision of health care, education, child and elder care, along with capitalism, similar to Britain and Canada.

Iceland is another Nordic model of equality, continuously ranked at the top of 145 countries of the global Gender Gap Index since 2009. The World Economic Forum report of 2015 ranked Iceland at the best country to live in for the seventh year in a row. A female head of state has been in power for 20 of the last 50 years. Socialized childcare allows women to progress in their careers and both sexes can use parental leave. With the long paternity leave, new fathers can take 90 days off work.

Icelandic women told Michael Moore in his documentary *Where to Invade Next* (2016) that they thought they lived in the best country for women and that when at least three women joint a board they change its culture for the better because they think about all the stakeholders not just personal gain. They said in Iceland they care about the group, the WE, compared to the ME in the US. They couldn't live with themselves if their neighbors suffered the way the poor do in the US. During the economic crash of 2008, the only bank that didn't fail was a woman's bank. They wondered if Lehman sisters would have avoided the crash. Unlike the US, the guilty male bankers were jailed. Large companies are required to have at least 40% of each sex on their boards and parliament members are 40% female.

The background is about 90% of women went on strike on October 24, 1975, to celebrate the UN's Women's Year, shutting down the country. A radical group called Red Stockings suggested the "day off." "It was, in all seriousness, a quiet revolution," reported Elin Olafsdottir who latter represented the Women's Alliance on the Reykhavik city council.[161] Within five years they elected the world's first woman president, a single mother. Direct action works, they concluded, inspiring other actions such as Polish women's Black Protests against further restrictions on abortion on October 3, 2016, when about 60% of women went on strike. In the 2013 Icelandic elections voters selected 52% women in parliament. They proceeded to abolish strip clubs and penalize those who pay for sex rather than the prostitutes, as well as refused to bail out the banks. The Minister for Welfare is responsible for supervising gender equality legislation, advised by a Gender Equality Council and the Complaints Committee on Gender Equality.

Photographs and text by Gabrielle Motola in her photobook *An Equal Difference* (2016) provide an introduction to Iceland. In an interview, she states that Iceland was selected the most gender equal in the world for seven years.[162] She wrote on Kickstarter, "I see a relationship between gender equality and intelligent thought that feels absent in most Western civilizations. Something is definitely going on in Iceland which, if harnessed, could be exported along with its tasty fish and affordable energy." She acknowledged that sexism still exists in a gender pay gap and domestic violence; the obesity rate is higher than the US (a chart compares obesity by country[163]) and Transparency International ranked Iceland the most corrupt Nordic country.

The former Prime Minister of Iceland, Johanna Sigurdardottir, campaigned to end the "age of testosterone," and blamed the banking crisis on men. Irish President Mary McAleese echoed the theme that the country's troubles were "testosterone driven" and in a poll of *Irish Times'* readers 55% agreed. It follows that the number of female heads of state increased by 250% since the recession of 2008 caused by reckless bankers and financers and their Ponzi schemes.[164]

Former prime minister, Jóhanna Sigurdardóttir, the world's first openly lesbian Prime Minister, explained, "gender equality is one of the best indicators of the overall quality of societies."[165] Iceland is the only country that recovered so completely from the 2008 financial crisis, partly because of the effort to "feminize banking." Women were appointed to head two of the failed banks. Government minister Katrina Juliusdottir explained that after the crisis, people "want balance in our lives, and a big part of that is the balance between men and women." (The documentary film *Reykjavik Rising* (2015) tells the story of the Iceland revolution against corrupt banks.) By 2015 unemployment was only 4%, the economy was growing and tourism booming, along with family supportive programs similar to Sweden's and the lowest adolescent drug use in Europe.

In the summer of 2015 the Pirate Party grew from three members of parliament who have a hacker background (including Brigitta Jonsdottir and 25-year old Asta Helgadottir) to being the leader in national polls predicted to lead the next government. But, the Pirates came in third. Jonsdottir explained, "I definitely approach this job from the perspective of the hacker.... It's better to pretend you don't know the limitations, so you can break them."[166] She explained, "People should not allow themselves to believe that we are going to save them. They are going to save themselves, and we'll give them the tools to do it. We want to look for the wisdom of the masses…through collective effort." She added, "Young people in particular find it unacceptable that they can only wield influence once every four years." She is proud that many young Icelanders are actively engaged in politics. Helgadottir worked for a tech collective and describes herself as a "boring Harry Potter fan," whose hero is the British Suffragettes. The third member, Helgi Gunnarsson, age 35, said his hero is Edward Snowden.

The Pirate Party's Core Policy advocates for increased direct democracy as in e-democracy and referendums, the right to privacy and freedom of information (they passed the Icelandic Modern Media Initiative which attracted young people like Helgadottir to the party), a new constitution and stabilizing the currency.[167] Their website states, "Pirates believe that centralization needs to be reduced in all areas and democracy needs to be promoted in all the forms that are available." Iceland became the first country to require employers of more than 25 people to prove they offer equal pay, after an October 2016 strike when thousands of women left work at 2:38 PM, to signify the time they work for free due to the pay gap.

Opposition to Prejudice

Girls are more egalitarian than boys in general, not just about sex roles. A survey of 14-year olds from 29 countries in the late 1990s, by an international education consortium, found that girls in nearly every country surveyed had more positive attitudes towards ethnic minorities.[168] Girls were more likely to want to participate in community activities and to be interested in voting in nine of the 29 countries. On the other hand, boys were more confident about their political knowledge than girls and more likely to be interested in "protest activities."

SpeakOut students report concerns about racism. "It bothers me to be discriminated by people who are rude or another color—white" (Athy, 17, f, Tanzania). An Asian-American woman in her 20s who works in public health in Dar-es-Salaam, Tanzania, reports:

> There is tons of racism here, way more than any other place I have ever been. First of all, there is a HUGE amount of racism between Indians and Blacks here. Blacks discriminate against Indians, and Indians discriminate against blacks. There are very few whites compared to Indians and Tanzanians, and in general, white people have tons of money, and all live in the same places. I can imagine how strange it would be to see a completely separate upper class of whites.

White people try to get tan and brown, while some brown-skinned people try to lighten their skin, but it would be boring if we were all the same color. With global media and advertisements, a Western beauty standard makes people who don't fit it feel inadequate, as the following quotes from SpeakOut students illustrate. I've seen billboard and print ads with Anglo looking light-skinned models in China, Tanzania, Japan, etc. You can see a photo of a light-skinned Tanzanian soap package model and a similar Chinese model on the book Facebook page. In Indian matrimonial ads fair skin is a plus and I've never seen such an ad mention beautiful dark skin--search for yourself.[169]

I will change the color of my skin just a little bit lighter.
   Celio, 9, Belize

I would change my skin color and my hair; I would love it more straight.
   Sarah, 16, Saudi Arabia

Some guys prefer fair-colored skins in girls. In Pakistan, a pretty girl has a smooth and fair skin.
   Shehroz, 17, m, Pakistan

Viola, 18, Italy, advocates, "We stay under the same sky, so we are equal. Stop racism!" In Kenya, university student Eunice Kilonzo blogs against tribalism.[170] In South Africa, Mabena (18, m) is optimistic about progress, observing, "Our parents grew up in an era of racism where they feared one another (blacks and whites), but we live in a united generation." However, all the students in his high school in the rural northeast are black. I asked Jeanette about her observation of racism because she lived in Mabena's area for seven years when she was married to a black South African.

> *The issue of racism has improved greatly since apartheid, but the main improvements are in the larger cities, like Johannesburg and Cape Town. There is still racism and tribalism in the rural areas--tribalism is also in the large cities. In many of the big gatherings the ANC [African National Congress] holds in the rural areas, speeches given by some of the blacks include negative comments about whites. White people don't go. I have felt from some of the black people in the rural area a sense of entitlement, resentment, and anger. I have also felt much love and acceptance from many. The younger generations are more accepting. I felt the racism in many different places I was in during the seven years I lived there. In some ways, it feels like what it might have been in the USA South in the 1950s.*

Despite the continued problem of racism, white Millennials' belief that race isn't significant is illustrated when Hannah tells her black boyfriend on the HBO series *Girls* season two, ""I never thought about the fact you were black once ... I don't live in a world with divisions." The formation of the most activist youth-led groups is discussed in Volume 2, Chapter 1. Groups led by people of color are the most in the news: Black Lives Matter and United We Dream for Latinx immigrants.

Caste and Class

Class divisions are found in urban neighborhoods in cities like Sydney: "Personally I think it is an awesome school. But hey it's in the west of Sydney so the typical attitude from everyone else is that we are breeding the gangsters and thugs of tomorrow, which is really not true" (Patricia, 15, Australia). Of course caste is still a major issue in India, as seen in protests against the government reserving places in universities and government jobs for lower castes and tribal people, the rise of political parties based on caste, and in ads seeking a spouse of the same caste. Soma Maiti, an upper caste Brahmin, "considered herself largely blind to the ancient system that for millenniums determined position in life in India."[171] Her parents didn't share her modernity: When she told her West Bengali parents she wanted to marry a lower caste man, "They immediately tried to get me married to someone they regarded as eligible simply because he was a Brahmin." When she went ahead with her "love marriage," her family stopped speaking to her. Other girls are killed or gang raped for the same offense of marrying outside their caste.

In Nepal, Indira Gale was the first Dalit (low caste formerly called Untouchables) girl to get a college education. She helped me gather survey responses from Dalit college students and explains:

> We have the caste system and very bad looking towards the girls' education. The family name represents the caste in Nepali society [similar to India and Pakistan]. Every person in Nepal can know what caste you belong to. Most of the parents in Nepal are farmers in the village. They are illiterate but they want to send their boys to the school rather than girls.

> Most of the students stay with their family and in Nepal we have the joint family style even after they passed the high school degree, the parents take care of them, as we do not have the state policy. In Nepal most of the people in the [Dalit] communities are uneducated. They are living without computer, telephone, television and the other modern facility. They believe like the old days people. People in the upper caste do not allow them to enter into the teashop, temple and other peoples' house. They are known as the untouchables within the society.

As a consequence of lack of opportunity for lower castes, some girls became Maoist soldiers. Nepal elected a feminist leader of the Communist Party in 2015. Bidya Bhandari, age 54, fought for a one-third quota for women in parliament.[172] She vowed to keep fighting for the rights of women and the oppressed until her last breath.

The Millennial generation tends to be less concerned about class differences. For example, in Mexico City, high-school student Pablo would be glad to go to the almost free and outstanding government university to study architecture, but his parents prefer that he go to a private Jesuit college located in Santa Fe, "which is where the rich people live. I tell you this because I think this is part of the changes between my parents' generation and mine. You can see I do not mind studying with people from different social class, but my parents do."

Socialist countries including Russia, China, Viet Nam, Laos and Cuba[173] (North Korea dropped references to Marxist-Leninism in its 1998 constitution) tried to do away with rich and poor classes and aimed to create the egalitarian New Man and New Woman. Cuba's Family Code of 1975 tried to equalize sex roles, requiring husbands to do half the family work when wives are employed. A film titled *Portrait of Teresa* (1979) illustrates personal struggles over equality issues between Teresa and her husband. She has three children, is a crew leader in the factory where she works, and is a union leader. Her husband feels neglected, they separate and he has an affair. When he wants to get back together with Teresa, she asks him how he'd react if she also had an affair. He replies, "But men are different," and so she doesn't take him back.

Cuba does an exceptional job of educating and providing health care to its citizens, the best in Latin America. But, poverty still exists. On a trip there, my teenage son traded T-shirts with a Cuban boy and was surprised that he only had a few shirts on his shelf. Many of these countries are now encouraging private enterprise, as in Cuba where government jobs are being slashed—with young workers often the first to be fired.[174] Many necessities are rationed and many people work multiple jobs, although restrictions on running your own business were lightened. Students have organizations to represent them and many blog, discussed in Chapter 3.

Discrimination Against LGBT Youth

The relatively fast turn around of opposition to same sex marriage and LGBT rights in the US is a success story of civil resistance that uses Gene Sharp's tactics.[175] Sharp explained how to succeed at peaceful civil resistance in his *The Politics of Nonviolent Action* (1973). He was criticized for not recognizing that power lies in institutions and social systems, but his emphasis on the support of the masses proved to be right. Robert Helvey developed the idea of undermining pillars of support for a regime in *On*

Strategic Nonviolent Conflict (2004). If enough pillars are removed, transformation occurs and the roof will collapse. Tools available to citizens include worker strikes, a boycott such as the United Farm Workers' campaign to not buy grapes, and protests such as at nuclear sites, segregated restaurants, or more recently, Congressional offices and city squares and parks. What motivated Katrina, a local teen activist in my town, was her concern about mistreatment of the gay and lesbians: "In other countries they're being killed and imprisoned. This hurts me, it very weights heavily on me. I really want to change that."

When public opinion was won over, President Obama, legislators, and courts followed, making change from the bottom up--not top down. Opinion was changed by likeable athletes and actors like Ellen DeGeneres coming out (1997), TV shows and movies including LGBT characters, mainline Protestant churches embracing LGBT members, international models like Canada's 2005 marriage equality law, and LGBT student support groups. "A digital TV cable for Millennials premiered in 2013, featuring an Australian series Please Like Me, about a gay young man named Josh.[176]

Youth were a "final decisive pillar that began to move early" against homophobia, according to brothers Mark and John Engler of DemocracyUprising.com, who wrote about political nonviolence. Youth are more likely to know someone who is openly gay, a strong predicator of support for marriage quality. By 2011, for the first time polls showed over half the respondents supported same-sex marriage and in that year the military ended "Don't ask, don't tell" policies for queer soldiers.

Globally, 77 countries still make homosexuality a crime, as in 2014 when India's Supreme Court upheld a colonial law criminalizing homosexuality as an "unnatural offense" punishable by 10 years in jail. The law can be used by police to blackmail LGBT Indians to pay bribes and health workers fear that the law will prevent people from seeking HIV health services. Three judges agreed to reconsider the ruling in 2016, after a Change.org petition created by Shashi Tharoor got over 40,000 signatures.

In Hungary the Radical Queer Collective teaches workshops on self-defense and queer self-empowerment. In Russia, repression against LGBT people surfaced in St. Petersburg in 2012 when homophobic activists sued Madonna and her St. Petersburg concert organizers for around $10 million due to her support for gay rights during her concerts. In 2013, the national legislature, the Duma, passed a law imposing heavy fines on those who provide information about homosexuality referred to as "non-traditional relations," to minors. They also prohibited the adoption of orphans by gay couples or by couples in countries that permit gay marriage. Lesbian journalist Masha

Gessen left Russia before the 2014 Olympics because a family had already proposed taking in her adopted teenage son. She feared repression after foreigners left Russia after the Olympics. A bill was also proposed to take biological children from gay parents, tabled until after the Olympics so as not to rouse protests. Gessen also has a biological child, a strong motivation to leave Russia.

President Vladimir Putin justified his support for homophobia in demographic terms, as "gay marriages do not produce children," although Gessen's motherhood indicates that his claim is false. He also aimed to contrast the darkness of Western immorality with the light of Russian traditional families and orthodox religion. Part of his motivation was to build allies against youthful critics of his presidency. Clashes between gay rights groups and their opponents took place in Moscow, as nearly half of Russians are against gay rights, according to a poll.[177] The Duma also agreed to punish Russians who "offend religious feeling" like Pussy Riot's song "Mother Mary, Drive Putin away" in a cathedral (discussed in Volume 2 Chapter 8). A journalist, 26-year-old Yelena Klimova was convicted under anti-gay propaganda laws in 2015 for setting up a website called Children 404 to support LGBT teens.

In Africa, 38 nations ban homosexuality, considered unnatural and unAfrican, and it can be punished by death in three countries. President Robert Mugabe in Zimbabwe refers to gays as worse than animals, specifically mentioning cats and dogs. In Ethiopia, Taika (18) reports that homosexuality is viewed with disgust in a country with "almost zero flexibility towards culture and religion, homosexuality is a concept that will cause bloodshed or even worse." The Ugandan parliament passed a "kill the gays" law in 2013, so named because a previous version permitted the death penalty, as urged on by US evangelicals. President Yoweri Museveni signed the bill in 2014, saying that gays were abnormal, a product of "random breeding" in the West when "nature goes wrong." The law allowed 14 years in prison and penalizes people who don't inform authorities about gays or who assist LGBT people, as by offering HIV counseling.

A tabloid published a front-page article titled "Top Homos Named." Parliament also passed a law outlawing miniskirts and other "suggestive clothing" for women. The Supreme Court outlawed the bill in 2014 because a quorum wasn't present when the bill passed, but Parliament passed a similar bill in January 2014. Kenyan youth wearing rainbow-painted masks and wigs to hide their identity protested the Ugandan law.

In 2014 Nigeria outlawed gay marriage and clubs, even public display of affection. One young person posted "I cannot believe GEJ [the president] took time to sign a bill into law jailing people for being gay. I don't have any electricity, dude!" Nigeria is the worst country in the world in regard to homosexuality, according to a Pew Research Center "Global Attitudes Project." [178] A young women-led organization organized "security training" "to educate and empower our sisters to take necessary steps to stay safe and secure both off and online."[179]

South Africa is the only African country that permits gay marriage, but after Nelson Mandela's death, gays worried about backlash as two husbands discuss in a video.[180] A South African SpeakOut boy, age 15, reports:

> *Without a chick or guy [to date] at 14 you're gay. Peer pressure is what bothers me in my daily life. The most famous saying that teens use to pressure their friends is "practice makes perfect." This involves kissing and you know what. But what happened to Christianity and the Ten Commandments? I desire to take action and start a Soul Buddies Club at my school where I teach teens about such matters.*

In Egypt, an anonymous girl asked me, "How many 'out' homosexuals do you know in Egypt?" She emailed her coming out story:

> *A huge part of my teenage years was spent fighting away depression, melancholy, and a dangerously low self-esteem. Soon enough, however, I had managed to pull myself out of it. By the time I was 16, I had come out to some people and I was even ready to tell my parents. I realize now that even though I managed to go through a hard experience and emerge with a decent amount of strength, I had in fact made a terrible mistake. Too caught up in the whirlwind of my sexual orientation, I had skipped the most essential part of anyone's teenage years: Self-identification. Until then, whether I accepted it or rejected it, "gay" was the only identity I had. I hadn't exactly paid much attention to anything else.*
>
> *People often labeled me. I was the nerd, the socially awkward, the overly-mature, the apathetic, and lately the gay. Their assumptions were compatible with my eagerness to find any identity whatsoever to fill the blanks, so I accepted and embraced their definitions. I did well at school, just because I was supposed to. I acted as though I didn't care, because it seemed to be expected. I even followed right-wing politics, left-wing politics, communism and anarchism at different points just because someone thought I should. I had let people define me and in doing so I had lost sight of my true self. I couldn't even answer the question "Who are you?" I have no idea, and that's okay.*

Coming out publically is a form of resistance to prejudice.

Discrimination Against Immigrants

Migrant struggles are another equality issue, although Greek activist Hara Kouki pointed out that similar to race and gender issues, migrants' rights are viewed as secondary. She created a map of racist and anti-migrant attacks in Athens called "The City at a Time of Crisis."[181] Citizenship politics emphasizes the power of ordinary people in politics regarding issues like immigration, refugees, and human rights.[182] From Barcelona, Carlos Delcós said at the 2013 Global Uprisings conference in Amsterdam, "Migrant rights in fortress Europe is the dividing line for all anti-fascist struggles," but social movements haven't done much to tackle this problem. Love means we're willing to take risks for other people, he said, as we're all migrants. Neighborhood assemblies in Barcelona are working with about 3,000 unemployed African workers without official status who squatted in an abandoned factory. If migrants remain undocumented, they don't get health care or other benefits. They created an informal city with shops, bars, and restaurants but received an eviction notice in 2013. A similar story is playing out in Amsterdam in another squat occupied by Africans.

Comments about immigrants are a theme for European SpeakOut students since about 12% of Europe's population is composed of recent immigrants.[183] Of those, 25 million are Muslim, the majority of the non-European immigrants. In England, Spain, France and Germany, most immigrants come from Turkey and many new arrivals also come from Asia. The European Union Commission reported that in 2014 "more than 276,000 migrants illegally entered the EU, which represents an increase of 155 percent compared to 2013."[184] In the first half of 2017, 13,546 refugees were relocated in Europe.[185] Although an aging Europe needs an immigrant workforce, "A wave of xenophobia has washed across Europe in the last decade," says Professor Peter O'Brien, as evidenced by a 2004 poll in which one-third of Europeans described themselves as "racist" and 52% of respondents feared "a collective ethnic threat from immigration."[186] They believe that immigrants threaten jobs and their country's culture, as well as increase the crime rate.

O'Brien pointed to the growing influence of right-wing politicians like Jean-Marie Le Pen replaced by his daughter Marine Le Pen as the head of the anti-immigrant National Front. Similar to Le Pen are Geert Wilder in the Netherlands, the late Jorg Haider in Austria, and the German Alternative for Germany headed by Frauke Petry.

In England the English Defense League wants to expel Muslims and prevent Sharia law. Even moderate leaders like British Prime Minister David Cameron, German Chancellor Angela Merkel, and French president Nicolas Sarkozy attacked the previous policy of "multiculturalism," the right of all groups to live by their traditional values. They changed their minds because the policy led to segregated communities and a lack of integration.

Youth culture in places like Germany is sometimes anti-immigrant.[187] Torsten, a German secondary student who wants to be a nurse, told me he enjoys his friends from Turkey or Africa. He finds them warm and friendly (see our video[188]). He worries about racism, as when his African friend was attacked from behind in school and the principal shrugged it off with the comment, "These things happen." He adds that Germany has many immigrants who some people view as aggressive and associate with terrorism. But,

> *It's not only foreigners who are aggressive, it's my generation, we see so many films with drugs and violence, and listen to angry hip hoppers who say f*** this bitch. German history wasn't that good with Nazis, but I think its over, but maybe some people are against foreigners, I don't really know. But we're all human, whatever skin color we have, we have the same blood. We don't really know their traditions, anything about them, because we don't speak to them face-to-face. But they're Germans: The Turkish girls say I'm German, why should I wear a headscarf?*

In Norway, the anti-immigrant Progress Party got nearly a quarter of the seats in Parliament in the 2009 elections but was put on the defensive in 2011 after one of its members, Anders Breivik (age 32) massacred 77 young people. He wanted to make an anti-immigrant statement against the Labor Party at its summer youth camp after his party leader Siv Jensen warned that Muslim immigrants were eroding Western civilization. Without adequate social support, immigrant youth have rioted in Sweden, as well as progressive Denmark, Holland, Germany, and France and right-wing nationalist political parties are growing. A theory about the rise of anti-immigrant right-wingers is that the freedom associated with modernization "stimulates anti-modernist reactions among marginalized parts of the population", who blame immigrants for job and wage losses. [189]

European SpeakOut students are concerned about immigrant violence, as in Switzerland:

No more foreigners; I have nothing against nice foreigners, but those who knife others shouldn't come into the country.
Michallea, 11, f, Switzerland

I would change my homeland Bosnia so many poor people would be helped. I would help the poor in Switzerland where I was born as well and would try to decrease the racism.
Barigha, 14, f, Switzerland

A Swiss mother explained to me,

> *When the students are talking about knives, ex-Balkan people are meant, Koso-vars and Albanians mainly, who have a macho mentality and often not much education, nor a chance to integrate themselves easily since they came here as teenagers and not as children. Their parents come from what's called "removed from education" type situations. Ignorance is the problem, to put it bluntly.*

In 2007, the Swiss People's Party called for a law to deport entire immigrant families if a child breaks national laws. Party posters showing white sheep kicking out a black sheep sparked protest, but the People's Party picked up seats in the lower house. In 2009 a law was passed banning building new Muslim minarets in Switzerland.

Some European SpeakOut students, but fewer, support immigrants:

I would strongly support the integration of all minorities: In Bulgaria at present there are many conflicts on ethnic basis, but all the people in a multi-cultural society should be together as a nation. Also, I would make sure disabled people and orphans are properly looked after, because I think their current position is rather unenviable. I would try to create job opportunities for the poor people: poverty is a very serious problem, which should be eliminated as effectively as possible.
Marina, 18, f, Bulgaria

I would allow immigration, make health insurance free and lower taxes.
K., 11, m, Belgium

I would allow more immigrants.
Max, 14, m, Sweden

It's encouraging that advocacy of equality is increasing globally, with some exceptions in Muslim areas. But this chapter demonstrates that, despite evidence that women leaders are effective and quotas for females assist the movement toward equality (as in Nicaragua, Bolivia and France), gender equality is rare. China and Pakistan have a higher percentage of women in their national assemblies than the US, because of quotas.

We've seen a dichotomy between beliefs in equality, girls' academic achievements, beliefs that women leaders are more likely to bring peace, and the reality of degradation of girls and women. A Finish member of Girls' Globe, Emma Saloranta wrote about tactics to achieve gender equality: speak up about sexism, vote, raise money for causes like Catapult that crowd-fund gender equality or Global Fund for Women, have faith that equity can be achieved, and educate yourself and others using social media, letters to the newspaper editor, speak on the local radio station, etc.[190]

Frances Hesselbein, CEO of the Leader to Leader Institute in the US and former head of the Girl Scouts, asks, "What actionable ideas will help us inspire a new generation to lead and innovate?" She answers,

- *Provide Meaningful Work: The workforce of the future was brought up in a fast-moving world. They had their fingers on the pulse of changing technology. They multi-task and enjoy a challenge. They need projects that utilize their knowledge and skills that can connect with their philosophical or deeper interests.*

- *Recognize the Importance of teamwork and Inclusion: This generation is considered the most open generation of all. Inclusion and diversity are a way of life. Millennials see themselves as part of a global community and believe that everyone belongs to this community. They want to be connected with teams at work and with customers.*

- *Provide Opportunities to Lead Sooner: This is one thing our military does very well. Look for projects and assignments where Millennials have a chance to lead.*

- *Find Ways for Millennials to Serve Society: Being true to themselves equates to personal and social responsibility. They advocate to reduce, reuse, recycle, repurpose, rescue, and remember. Reduce their carbon footprint; re-*

use wrapping paper, clothes, and goods that are no longer useful to others; recycle paper, plastic, and aluminum cans; repurpose everything from pill bottles to entire rooms; rescue cats and dogs from shelters; and remember those around the world who need their support, their concern. We must find ways to support this deeply felt need to help others. This is the generation for whom "to serve is to live."[191]

How to Increase Women's Influence on Government

Established models of how to include more women in office include quotas and reservations as in India, equal rights legislation including family law as in Scandinavia, a Minister for Women, economic incentives such as food or cash payments for girls to be educated, quality childcare, and a gender-responsive budget. The evidence indicates that women improve the quality of life of their constituents; however, in 2013 only 21% of legislators globally were women, up from 11% in 1995.[192] At the current rate of progress, it will take 40 years to reach gender parity in the world's national legislatures.[193] The highest numbers of women legislators in 2015 were in Rwanda, Bolivia, (these two have more women than men), Cuba, Sweden and the Seychelles, according to the World Bank.

Nine legislative bodies lack any women at all. Israel's two Orthodox parties don't include women legislators, so Orthodox women formed a lobby group called "No Voice, No Vote" that won't vote for parties that don't include women. The first country to give women the right to vote was New Zealand, in 1893.[194] Since then women have led countries including Australia, New Zealand, India, Iceland, Sri Lanka (the first country to have a woman Prime Minister), Bangladesh, Liberia, Haiti, Philippines, Ireland, United Kingdom, Israel, Norway, Finland, Argentina, Brazil, Thailand, Jamaica, Lithuania, Denmark, Germany, Scotland and the UK. A website lists current women presidents and prime ministers.[195]

The lack of equal representation of women in governments is not due to lack of female ambition or ability, but "arises from men choosing men," explains Margot Wallström, former chair of the Council of Women World Leaders.[196] She suggests that women need to support each other and publicize gender discrimination perpetrated with "master suppression techniques." She explains, "I have lost count of how many times I have experienced or witnessed men ridicule or ignore women at meetings or in public, and exclude them for the decision-making process." Wallström says laws are needed to stop discrimination—such as quotas for female candidates--and to enable a better work-life balance with parental leave, childcare, and other family programs.

The international Organization for Economic Co-operation and Development (OECD) found gender equality is encouraged by laws about legal age to marry; and women's access to credit, inheritance, the right to own property; and prohibiting discrimination against girls.[197] OECD observed that laws aren't enough to change discrimination, as community awareness programs are necessary such as using social media to involve young men in ending violence against women. OECD reported that the worst discrimination against women was in Africa and the Middle East, although South Africa and Morocco show improvement, with inheritance law in the former and Family Code reforms and quotas for political representation in the latter. Armenia's Equal Rights and Equal Opportunities for Men and Women implemented in 2013 is an example of equal rights legislation that generated backlash like posting photos of young men wearing makeup and transgendered couples kissing. These images were attributed to "warped Western values."

Training programs are helpful for women leaders. As Secretary of State, Hillary Clinton began the Women in Public Service Project to train global women leaders with the goal that women will hold half of public service jobs by 2050. Their website features global women leaders who participated in a WPSP training program.[198] Another effort begun in 2011 to encourage young women's leadership is the Global Shapers, ages 20 to 30, an offshoot of the World Economic Forum held yearly in Devos, Switzerland.[199] Half of the young leaders are women and the Shapers represent 37 countries.

The NGO Oxfam's "Raising Her Voice: The Power to Persuade" instruction trained women to influence policy (from 2008 to 2013).[200] They reported the program assisted over one million marginalized women in 17 countries to influence decision makers, evidenced by new laws to protect against violence against women and more public money for local services. Oxfam found that the greatest leverage is gained through building alliances, creating relationships with powerful male leaders, and providing factual evidence for the need for action. When women are involved in decision-making, public money is better spent; they create more accountability and transparency and reduce violence against girls and women.

A third model of how to train women politicians, The Center for Women's Global Leadership at Rutgers University teaches women leaders to use a human rights framework to achieve their goals.[201] Rutgers students discuss feminist leadership on a video titled "Feminist Leadership: Transforming Boundaries," 2013.[202] Twenty-one young women described as "feisty" graduated from the Leadership Scholars program between 2000 and 2008. Ten of the young women were immigrants or had immigrant parents. All the students learned that they could be taught how to be leaders. They identified women's leadership as "collaborative, community-based, intergenerational, and fueled by passion and humility."[203] "I learned the value of collaborative leadership and its strength to facilitate positive change," wrote Courtney Turner in her *Leading the Way* book chapter. In contrast they defined traditional masculine leadership as aiming for personal power and the cult of the individual leader. They embraced the feminine tradition of nurturing disadvantaged people including children and the poor, were influenced by role-models of their female relatives and by intersectional women's studies to do "local problem solving" in teams. They also sought allies in young male peers, disavowing stereotypes of their generation as apathetic and aiming to transcend identity politics.

A fourth model, Vital Voices Global Partnership Policy Advocates program also trains women leaders, reporting that after 15 years of work, they discovered women are "multipliers." Acting as mentors and role-models, they share their new expertise and new access to information and networks. They "play it forward to the next wave of women leaders" in a powerful ripple effect.[204] Their website includes a video about global women leaders. They partner with the Women in the World Foundation to support women leaders and nonprofit organizations. Women's Campaign International coaches grassroots activists about how to achieve their goals and run for office.

In Uruguay UN Women and other UN agencies led a training program to encourage young women to enter politics by job shadowing political leaders. These examples offer abundant ideas for how to enable women to assume more equal representation in government.

Quotas are usually needed to get to the 30% of women legislators necessary to create policy changes, according to attorney Amber Maltbie.[205] The Atlas of Electoral The Quota Project provides a database of global quotas for women.[206] Gender Quotas reports on the regulations in 85 countries.[207] Over 97 countries use gender quota systems that result in women being nearly 33% of their legislatures, compared to an average of 12% in countries without quotas, according to UN data. However, if women end up at the bottom of the lists for national elections, they have no chance of being elected. Sweden has a quota system and women held 45% of its parliamentary seats in 2014.[208] Argentina passed a law in 1991 requiring that one in three candidates nominated for election to the legislature must be women. In France, a 1998 law required political parties to nominate an equal number of male and female candidates for elections, but parties often pay fines rather than comply. Pakistan requires a small quota of 17% women in the National Assembly, but women legislators recently passed more pro-women legislation than in any time in the past because they worked together.

The Indian government changed the constitution in 1993 to require that one third of village *panchayats* chiefs be women. Villages headed by women have better infrastructure such as access to drinking water and improved roads and reduced corruption.[209] Girls' career aspirations rise as well. A reporter comments, "In rural India, which is by any measure more patriarchal and conservative than urban India, the promotion of women to public positions of power constitutes nothing short of a revolution."[210] However, a male pharmacist I interviewed in Delhi said that often wives of influential men are elected. Studies show, however, that in villages run by women, more water pumps or taps were installed and were better maintained.[211] Because fewer than 11% of members of the country's parliament are women, a proposal in 2010 to extend the one-third reservation for women in parliament caused uproar. It was passed by the upper house, but not the lower house.[212] Despite this activity, an Indian activist told me in 2010, "India never had a feminist movement! I think that is the problem with the 'women's movement' in India. It does not have a feminist foundation."[213]

An Indian SpeakOut boy (Sambhav, 14) advocates that quotas be established for young people too, suggesting that "20% of the seats should be reserved for people between the age of 21 to 30," even though he thinks his generation is "faster and impatient, often short tempered." Some countries do mandate quotas for youth: Uganda reserves five seats in parliament, in Rwanda two members of the Chamber of Deputies are elected by the national Youth Council, Morocco reserves 30 seats for candidates under age 40, and Tunisia requires each party list to include one candidate below age 30. The Philippines stipulates that youth should be included on party lists, as described in a UN report "Enhancing Youth Political Participation throughout the Electoral Cycle."[214]

Some look to women's political parties to address equality issues. These parties aren't new: Suffragette Alice Paul led the Woman's Party in the US in 1913. In Turkey, women's rights activist Benal Yazgan organized the Woman Party (*Kadin Partisi*) party in 2014 because: "Once again, hegemony is being passed from man to man. The patriarchy is the same; they always leave women out and pass the roles amongst themselves."[215] She drew on the legacy of the influential People's Party of Women created in 1923 but not recognized by the Turkish government. Aiming for equality, the nine founders of Kadin Partisi included two men who established a quota for male candidates. Actions to increase the number of women in government include quotas, equal rights legislation including family law, a Minister for Women, a Youth Minister, quotas, a gender-responsive budget, training programs and government campaign funding.

Since young people tend to be more comfortable with women's rights, equality should increase in the future; we've seen many global examples of outspoken girls like Yara. Millennials don't like discrimination against any group, including men. With more women getting an education and entering professions worldwide, will they change the workplace and politics from business as usual? The next chapter looks at problems faced by young women globally that they'll need to solve.

Discussion Questions and Activities

Questions

1. Do you agree or disagree with President Jimmy Carter that sexism is the "worst and most pervasive and unaddressed human rights violation on earth?" Why does it persist in such horrendous ways if the majority of humans value equality?

2. Girls appear to have more egalitarian or horizontal values and ways of organizing than boys. As they're the majority of university students, how do you predict they'll change traditional systems as they assume more power?

3. Gloria Steinem stated, "Women are not more than men, but we don't have our masculinity to prove—so we are and will be good peacemakers." Do you agree or disagree based on what you've read in this chapter about women leaders?

4. Neoliberalism is the main target, the source of economic inequality, to young activists who led recent global uprisings, starting with the Arab Spring in 2011. Do you agree or disagree that this is the root cause of current gaps between the rich and poor?

Activities

1. How are women portrayed in TV series about high-level women politicians? Compare the Danish series Borgen about an effective prime minister with US series about often sleazy women politicians. In *Political Animals* Sigourney Weaver plays a Secretary of State, as does Tea Leoni in *Madam Secretary*. Women senators are played by Cynthia Nixon and Wanda Sykes in *Alpha House Chasing the*

Hill. In *Veep* Julia Louise-Dreyfus plays a goofy vice-president who runs for president telling her staff, "I can't identify myself as a woman. People can't know that. Men hate that, and women who hate women hate that—which I believe is most women." Kate Burton plays another Vice President in *Scandal*. Women presidents are portrayed in *Commander in Chief* with Geena Davis and Cherry Jones in *24*. Robin Wright plays a manipulative First Lady in *House of Cards*, as does Bellamy Young in *Scandal*. *Miss Sloane* (2016) portrays a ruthless, powerful and successful lobbyist in Washington, DC. How are the women politicians portrayed differently than male politicians?

2. Be a changemaker to address a local problem, checking out activist guidelines.[216]

3. What themes do you find in girls' articles on Teen Voices? http://womensenews. org/category/teen-voices/

4. Read some science-fiction novels about gender-equal societies.[217] What themes do you find? Would you like to live in any of these societies?

Films

What do the following films show about females influence on peace and equality?

1. *Women, War & Peace* is a five-part documentary about women as peacekeepers in Bosnia, Liberia, Afghanistan and Colombia. http://www.pbs.org/wnet/women-war-and-peace/category/full-episodes/

2. *Where Do We Go Now?* Christian and Muslim women work together for peace in their village in Lebanon. 2011

3. *The Girl in the Café*. A British film about a young woman who becomes friends with a British civil servant and accompanies him to the G-8 summit, where she becomes obsessed with the plight of children all over the world who are dying from preventable causes. She keeps interrupting their formal G-8 social events to confront them about their refusal to take action. Includes information about child poverty. 2005

4. *Bruno*. Girls can wear jeans. What happens when a boy wants to assume a dress? An 8-year-old boy has a dream about an angel and concluded that like angels, he should wear dresses, which he calls holy vestments, even in spelling bees. There's lots of resistance from the nuns at his Catholic school and from his police officer father, but his mother and grandmother back him up and he wins the national bee. 2000

Endnotes

1
http://www.un.org/sustainabledevelopment/sustainable-development-goals/https://issuu.com/aiesecinternational/docs/report_youthspeak_2016

2
https://www.youtube.com/watch?v=kbXE3ZaZwXk

3
Aurora Ellis, "This Ayotzinapa Poem Shows How Mexican Youth Embrace Resistance," *TeleSur*, October 2, 2015.

http://www.telesurtv.net/english/opinion/This-Ayotzinapa-Poem-Shows-How-Mexican-Youth-Embrace-Resistance-20150926-0012.html

4
"Ayotzinapa and Black Lives Matter: Shared Resistance Movements," *TeleSur*, September 28, 2015.

http://www.telesurtv.net/english/bloggers/Ayotzinapa-and-Black-Lives-Matter-Shared-Resistance-Movements--20150928-0003.html

5
"Just 8 Men Own as Much as the Bottom Half," Oxfam, January 16, 2017.

https://www.oxfam.org/en/pressroom/pressreleases/2017-01-16/just-8-men-own-same-wealth-half-world

6
Jonathan Woetzel, et al., "The Power of Parity," McKinsey Global Institute, September 2015.

http://www.mckinsey.com/global-themes/employment-and-growth/how-advancing-womens-equality-can-add-12-trillion-to-global-growth

7
Jessica Valenti, "Worldwide Sexism Increases Suicide Risk in Young Women," *The Guardian*, May 28, 2015.

http://www.theguardian.com/chttp://www.un.org/sustainabledevelopment/sustainable-development-goals/-women

8
https://feministnetworkproject.wordpress.com/

renee Kasinsky, "'Otro Mundo Es Possble,' Women Power of the VI Caracas World Social Forum and the Bolivarian Revolution," *Journal of international Women's Studies*, Vol. 8, No. 3, April 2007.

http://vc.bridgew.edu/cgi/viewcontent.cgi?article=1393&context=jiws

9
Jonathan Soble, "To Rescue Economy, Japan Turns to Supermom," *New York Times*, January 1, 2015.

http://www.nytimes.com/2015/01/02/business/international/in-economic-revival-effort-japan-turns-to-its-women.html?_r=0

10
Marija Gimbutas and Joseph Campbell. *The Language of the Goddess*. Thames and Hudson, 2001.

Leonard Shlain. *The Alphabet Versus the Goddess*. Pengui Merlin Stone. *When God Was a Woman*. Mariner Books, 1978.

11
Mitch Horowitz, "The Persecution of Witches, 21st-Century Style," *New York Times*, July 4, 2014.

http://www.nytimes.com/2014/07/05/opinion/the-persecution-of-witches-21st-century-style.html?_r=0

12
Agata Lisiak, "The Ballerina and the Blue Bra: Femininity in Recent Revolutionary Iconography," *View: Theories and Practices of Visual Culture*. No date.

http://pismowidok.org/index.php/one/article/view/162/29

13
Katherine Zoepf, "A Troubled Revolution in Egypt," *New York Times*, November 21, 2011.

http://www.nytimes.com/2011/11/21/world/middleeast/a-troubled-revolution-in-egypt.html?pagewanted=all&_r=0

14
May 2012, remarks to the Women in the World Summit. http://content.usatoday.com/communities/onpolitics/post/2012/03/hillary-clinton-ex-tremists-control-women-/1#.T-ePnStYv-I

15
"Sexism Rules in the Ballot Booth Unless Voters have More Information," *Research News@Vanderbilt*, November 9, 2015.

http://news.vanderbilt.edu/2015/11/sexism-rules-in-the-ballot-booth-unless-voters-have-more-information/

16
Global Gender Gap Report 2014, World Economic Forum.

http://www.weforum.org/issues/global-gender-gap

17
Sally Howard, "The Genderpreneurs," *Ms. Magazine*, Summer 2016, pp. 14-15.

18
http://www.visitsweden.com/sweden/Featured/Sweden-Beyond/Society/

t depends on your income, this year income tax is as follows:

16 700€ - 25 000€: 6,50%

25 000€ - 40 800€: 17,50%

40 800€ - 72 300€: 21,50%

72 300€ - : 31,75%

1 Euro equals $1.10

19
"Gender Equality Universally Embraced, But Inequalities Acknowledged," Pew Research Center, July 1, 2010.

20
http://pewglobal.org/2010/07/01/gender-equality/

21
http://www.youtube.com/watch?v=hck7q_OnJag

22
"Most Muslims Want Democracy, Personal Freedoms, and Islam in Political Life," Pew Global Attitudes Project, July 10, 2012.

http://www.pewglobal.org/2012/07/10/most-muslims-want-democracy-personal-freedoms-and-islam-in-political-life/

23
Manuel Eisner and Lana Ghuneim, "Honor Killing Attitudes Amonst Adolescents in Amman, Jordan," *Aggressive Behavior*, Vol. 39, Issue 5, September 2013.

24
Mary Sheridan-Rabideau, *Girls, Feminism, and Grassroots Literacies*. State Univeristy of New York Press, 2008, p. 2.

25
Scott Jaschik, "Worldwide Paradox for Women," *Inside Higher Ed*, March 14, 2011.

www.insidheighered.com/news/2011/03/15/educators_com

26
Brain Whitaker, "Oman's Sultan Qaboos," *The Guardian*, March 4, 2011.

http://www.guardian.co.uk/commentisfree/2011/mar/04/oman-sultan-qaboos-despot

27
Aseem Shrivastava and Ashish Kothari, "Why is India Still Poor?" *Yes! Magazine*, June 18, 2012.

http://www.yesmagazine.org/new-economy/why-is-india-still-poor

28
Joseph Stiglitz, "Inequality is a Choice," *New York Times*, October 13, 2013.

29 http://opinionator.blogs.nytimes.com/author/joseph-e-stiglitz/
    Pat Garofalo, "China's Richest 1 Percent hold 70 Percent of their Nation's Private Wealth," *Think Progress*, August 17, 2012.

30 http://thinkprogress.org/economy/2012/08/17/708521/china-1-percent/?mobile=nc
    Ricardo Fuentes-Nieva and Nicholas Galasso, "Working for the Few," Oxfam, January 20, 2014.

31 http://www.oxfam.org/en/policy/working-for-the-few-economic-inequality
    "State of Power 2013," *Transnational Institute*, January 23, 2013.

32 http://www.tni.org/report/state-power-2013

33 Mary Hawksworth. *Globalization and Feminist Activism*. Roman and Littelfield, 2006.
    Judith Gibbons and Deborah Stiles. *The Thoughts of Youth: An International Perspective on Adolescents' Ideal Persons*. Information Age Publishing:
    Greenwich, CN, 2004, pp. 220-228.

34 *Dominique Reynié*, **ed.**, *"World Youths," Fondation Pour L'Innovation Politique," 2011. Electronic survey in 2010 by TNS Opinion of 25,000 youth
    born between 1981 and 1994 in 25 countries, plus 7,714 respondents aged 30 to 50.* http://expeng.anr.msu.edu/uploads/files/83/2010%20Youth%20
    leadership%20in%20a%20Globalized%20World%20Survey.pdf

35 Linda Berg-Cross, et al., "Single Professional Women: A Global Phenomenon Challenges and Opportunities, *Journal of International Women's
    Studies*, Vol. 5, No. 5, June 2004.

36 https://www.questia.com/library/journal/1G1-131430452/single-professional-women-a-global-phenomenon-challenges
    Sarah Jameel, "Being an Inconvenient Youth," Medium.com, May 8, 2014.

37 https://medium.com/@sarahjameel/being-an-inconvenient-youth-fbc2eaa81712#.t914l5ekd
    Families and Work Institute, "National Study of the Changing Workforce," 2009.

38 www.familiesandwork.org/site/research/.../Times_Are_Changing.pdf
    "One-Third of Fathers with Working Wives Regularly Care for Their Children, Census Bureau Reports," Census Bureau, December 5, 2011.

39 http://www.census.gov/newsroom/releases/archives/children/cb11-198.html

40 https://www.youtube.com/watch?v=G6u10YPk_34&feature=youtu.be
    "The American Freshman," UCLA Higher Education Research Institute, February 2015.

41 http://www.heri.ucla.edu/monographs/TheAmericanFreshman2014.pdf
    Wendy Wang, Kim Parker and Paul Taylor, "Breadwinner Moms," Pew Research Social & Demographic Trends, May 29, 2013.

42 http://www.pewsocialtrends.org/2013/05/29/breadwinner-moms/
    Christine Lagarde, "Fair Play," *IMF Direct*, February 23, 2015.

43 https://blog-imfdirect.imf.org/2015/02/23/fair-play-equal-laws-for-equal-working-opportunity-for-women/
    Nicholas Kristof, "Kalai Lama Gets Mischievous," *New York Times*, July 16, 2015.
    http://www.nytimes.com/2015/07/16/opinion/nicholas-kristof-dalai-lama-gets-mischievous.html?emc=edit_th_20150716&nl=todayshead-
    lines&nlid=68143430

44 "Iceland's Proposed Fix for its Banking Crisis? Feminizing an Entire Industry," excerpt from G.S. Motola's *An Equal Difference*. Restless Machinery
    Ltd, 2016.

45 https://medium.com/the-coffeelicious

46 Steven Pinker. *The Better Angels of Our Nature*. Viking Adult, 2011.
    Louis Nelson, "Clinton: The Future is Female," Politico.com, February 7, 2017.

47 http://www.politico.com/story/2017/02/hillary-clinton-video-message-future-is-female-234723
    Elizabeth Weingarten, "Where are all the Women Peacekeepers?" *The Weekly Wonk*, June 30, 2014.

48 James Rupert, "Sweden's Foreign Minister Explains Feminist Foreign Policy, United States Institute of Peace, February 9, 2015.

49 http://www.usip.org/olivebranch/2015/02/09/sweden-s-foreign-minister-explains-feminist-foreign-policy
    Matthew Rycroft and Swanee Hunt, "Want Peace in Syria?," Defense One, January 29, 2016.

50 http://www.defenseone.com/ideas/2016/01/want-peace-syria-put-women-negotiating-table/125536/
    Akin Iwilade. "Women and Peace Talks in Africa." *Journal of International Women's Studies*, 2011, 12(1), 22-37.

51 Available at: http://vc.bridgew.edu/jiws/vol12/iss1/2
    Marie Sandell. *The Rise of Women's Transnational Activism: Identity and Sisterhood Between the World Wars*. International Library of Twentieth
    Century History, I.B. Tauris, 2015.

52 www.kebethachewomen.org

53 http://globalgendercurrent.com/2014/04/org-spotlight-women-in-black/
    "The Gender Gap in Religion Around the World," Pew Research Center, March 22, 2016.

54 http://www.pewforum.org/2016/03/22/the-gender-gap-in-religion-around-the-world/
    David Masci, "The Divide Over Ordaining Women," Pew Research Center, September 9, 2014.

55 http://www.pewresearch.org/fact-tank/2014/09/09/the-divide-over-ordaining-women/
    http://www.worldpeacegame.org/connect/contact-us/john-hunter

56 A film about the project is *World Peace and Other 4th-Grade Achievements*.
    he described student changes over the decades in a TED radio interview.
    http://worldpeacegame.org/world-peacegame-foundation/news/item/john-hunter-on-npr-s-ted-radio-hour

57 The American Freshman: National Norms Fall 2016," Higher Education Research Institute, UCLA, 2017.

58 https://www.heri.ucla.edu/monographs/TheAmericanFreshman2016.pdf

59 www.wunrn.com/news/2008/12_08/12_08_08/120808_papua.htm

60 http://www.nobelwomensinitiative.org/

Documentary film, *Pray the Devil Back to Hell, 2008* http://www.praythedevilbacktohell.com/v2/

61 www.pbs.org/independentlens/ironladies

62 Meredith Tax. *A Road Unforeseen: Women Fight the Islamic State.* Belleview Literary Publishers, 2016, p. 141.

Steven Erlanger, "In West, ISIS Finds Women Eager to Enlist," *New York Times*, October 23, 2014.

63 http://www.nytimes.com/2014/10/24/world/europe/as-islamists-seek-to-fill-ranks-more-western-women-answer-their-call.html

Rosa Brooks, "Women Are from Mars Too," *Foreign Policy*, August 9, 2013.

64 http://www.foreignpolicy.com/articles/2013/08/08/women_are_from_mars_too

Jeffrey Murer, "Youth Violence and Group Identity," *The Conversation*, September 29, 2011.

65 www.theconversation.com/youth-violence-and-group-identity-understanding-radical-protest-2900

http://media.bioneers.org/listing/the-sophia-century-when-women-come-into-co-equal-partnership-osprey-orielle-lake-leila-salazar-and-lynne-twist/

http://media.bioneers.org/listing/the-next-wave-of-women-and-power-cultivating-womens-leadership-rha-goddess/

"Want Peace in Syria? Put Women at the Negotiating Table," Women's UN Report Network, February 1, 2016.

66 http://www.defenseone.com/ideas/2016/01/want-peace-syria-put-women-negotiating-table/125536/

Makers Team, "This Fierce Female Chief Terminated Nearly 850 Child Marriages," Makers.com, April 11, 2016.

67 http://www.makers.com/blog/female-chief-child-marriages-malawi

Janice Raymond, "The Women Who Are Staring Down Duterte," *TruthDig*, May 4, 2017.

68 http://www.truthdig.com/report/item/the_women_who_are_staring_down_duterte_20170504

Kristin Williams, "17 Women Changing the World," *Inclusive Security*, January 28, 2015.

69 https://www.inclusivesecurity.org/17-women-changing-world/

Jonathan Weisman and Jennifer Steinhauer, "Senate Women Lead in Effort to Find Accord," *New York Times*, October 14, 2013.

70 http://www.nytimes.com/2013/10/15/us/senate-women-lead-in-effort-to-find-accord.html

"Rachel Maddow Inteviews Senator Harry Reid," MSNBC.com, April 17, 2015.

71 http://www.msnbc.com/rachel-maddow-show/rachel-maddow-interviews-senator-harry-reid-full-video-and-transcript

"Status of Women in the States," Institute for Women's Policy Research, 2015.

72 http://statusofwomendata.org/explore-the-data/political-participation/political-participation-full-section/

Dan Hancox, "Is This the World's Most Radical Mayor?" *The Guardian*, May 26, 2016.

73 https://www.theguardian.com/world/2016/may/26/ada-colau-barcelona-most-radical-mayor-in-the-world

Sheryl Sandberg and Adam Grant, "The Myth of the Catty Woman," *New York Times*, June 26, 2016.

74 http://www.nytimes.com/2016/06/23/opinion/sunday/sheryl-sandberg-on-the-myth-of-the-catty-woman.html

Tatiana Farah, "Brazil: Life for Women Under Dilma," *Latin America Bureau*, March 14, 2012.

75 http://lab.org.uk/brazil-life-for-women-under-dilma

Andrew Jacobs, "Dilma Rousseff, Facing Impeachment in Brazil, Has Alienated Many Allies," *New York Times*, May 1, 2016.

76 http://www.nytimes.com/2016/05/02/world/americas/brazil-president-dilma-rousseff-impeachment-allies-alienated.html?_r=0

77 http://www.forbes.com/power-women/

Andrew Griffin, "Theresa May," *The Independent*, July 11, 2016.

http://www.independent.co.uk/news/uk/politics/theresa-may-what-the-mp-set-to-become-prime-minister-believes-on-human-rights-a7130861.html Ellie Mae O'Hagan, "Iron Ladies: The False Choices of Theresa May and Andrea Leadsom," Verso blog, July 11, 2016.

78 http://www.versobooks.com/blogs/2766-iron-ladies-the-false-choices-of-theresa-may-and-andrea-leadsom

Bill Moyer, "The Movement Action Plan: A Strategic Framework Describing the Eight Stages of Successful Social Movements" in an 1987 article, expanded into a book *Doing Democracy*. New Society Publishers, 2001.

79 Heideman et al., **eds.**, *MENA Women: Opportunities and Obstacles in 2014*, Wilson Center, 2014.

80 http://www.wilsoncenter.org/sites/default/files/mena_women_opportunities_obstacles_2014_1.pdf

Hipployte Marboua and Krista Larson, "Central African Republic Leader Sworn in Amid Looting," Associated Press, January 23, 2014.

81 http://bigstory.ap.org/article/widespread-looting-hits-c-african-republic

82 Deborah Solomon, "Questions for Ellen Johnson Sirleaf," *New York Times Magazine*, August 23, 2009.

http://www.madd.org/about-us/

http://ecowatch.com/2015/10/06/aap-cuts-ties-with-monsanto/

83 http://www.mamavation.com/2015/09/the-american-academy-of-pediatrics-cuts-ties-with-monsanto.html

"Letter from Tawakkol Karman to Women Without Borders," February 2, 2010. http://womenwithoutborders-save.blogspot.com/2010/02/letter-from-twakkol-karman-chairwoman.html

84 Vanessa Friedman and Guy Trebay, "The Look of the French Election," *New York Times*, May 3, 2017.

85 https://www.nytimes.com/2017/05/03/fashion/marine-le-pen-emmanuel-macron-france-presidential-election.html?mcubz=1&_r=0

George Packer, "The Quiet German," *New Yorker*, December 1, 2014.

http://www.newyorker.com/magazine/2014/12/01/quiet-german

[86] Myra Marx Ferree. *Varities of Feminism: German Gender Politics in Global Perspective*. Stanford University Press, 2012.

[87] Tracey-Kay Caldwell, "Michelle Bachelet, President and Single Mom," Bella Online, 2015.
http://www.bellaonline.com/articles/art17426.asp

[88] Paul Walder, "Michelle Bachelet: a Mother for Chile? *Punto Final*, November 25, 2005, republished in *Envio Digital*, 2011.
http://www.envio.org.ni/articulo/3203

[89] Deborah Solomon, "Questions for Ellen Johnson Sirleaf," *New York Times Magazine*, August 23, 2009.

[90] Norimitsu Onishi, "In Zimbabwe, a First Lady Exerts Her Power," *New York Times*, January 7, 2017.
https://www.nytimes.com/2017/01/07/world/africa/in-zimbabwe-a-first-lady-exerts-her-power.html?_r=0

[91] "Debate erupts: Is motherhood an advantage for UK's next PM?" Associated Press, July 9, 2016.
http://finance.yahoo.com/news/debate-erupts-motherhood-advantage-uks-next-pm-100441308.html

[92] Jessica Bennett, "On the Internet, to Be 'Mom' is to Be Queen," *New York Times*, December 3, 2016.
https://www.nytimes.com/2016/12/03/fashion/how-teens-use-the-word-mom-online.html?_r=0

[93] http://www.bls.gov/news.release/volun.nr0.htm

[94] Marina Sitrin and Dario Azzellini. *They Can't Represent Us! Reinventing Democracy From Greece to Occupy*. Verso, 2014, p. 29.

[95] George Lakoff, "Why Trump?" *Common Dreams*, March 3, 2016.
http://commondreams.org/views/2016/03/03/why-trump

[96] Rick Shenkman. *Political Animals: How Our Stone-Age Brain Gets in the Way of Smart Politics*. Basic Books, 2016.

[97] Richard Conniff, "Donald Trump and Other Animals," *New York Times*, October 15, 2016.
http://www.nytimes.com/2016/10/16/opinion/donald-trump-and-other-animals.html

[98] Jill Filipovic, "The All-Male Photo Op Isn't a Gaffe. It's a Strategy," *New York Times*, March 27, 2017.
https://www.nytimes.com/2017/03/27/opinion/the-all-male-photo-op-isnt-a-gaffe-its-a-strategy.html?_r=0

[99] Althernative Right, Southern Poverty Law Center,
https://www.splcenter.org/fighting-hate/extremist-files/ideology/alternative-right

[100] Philip Lewis, "Donald Trump on Climate Change," *Huffpost*, September 22, 2015.
http://www.huffingtonpost.com/entry/trump-global-warming_us_5601d04fe4b08820d91aa753

[101] Robert Reich, "The American Fascist," *Nation of Change*, March 9, 2016.
http://www.nationofchange.org/news/2016/03/09/the-american-fascist/

[102] Alan Rappeport, "Donald Trump's Trail of Comments About Women," New York Times, March 25, 2016.
http://www.nytimes.com/2016/03/26/us/politics/donald-trump-women.html?emc=edit_th_20160326&nl=todaysheadlines&nlid=68143430

[103] Megan Garber, "Seeing Red: The Rise of Mensesplaining," *The Atlantic*, April 28, 2016.
http://www.theatlantic.com/entertainment/archive/2016/04/periods-pop-culture-red-devil/480417/

[104] Michael Barbaro and Megan Twohey, "Crossing the Line: How Donald Trump Behaved with Women in Private," *New York Times*, May 14, 2016.
http://www.nytimes.com/2016/05/15/us/politics/donald-trump-women.html ?
Claire Cohen, "Donald Trump Sexism Tracker," *The Telegraph*, October 8, 2016.
http://www.telegraph.co.uk/women/politics/donald-trump-sexism-tracker-every-offensive-comment-in-one-place/

[105] https://www.washingtonpost.com/news/powerpost/wp/2016/10/07/ryan-mcconnell-silent-on-lewd-trump-video/

[106] http://www.npr.org/2016/10/13/497846667/transcript-michelle-obamas-speech-on-donald-trumps-alleged-treatment-of-women?utm_campaign=storyshare&utm_source=twitter.com&utm_medium=social

[107] "Chinese Feminists Stand Against Trump's 'Straight Man Cancer,'" *TeleSUR*, February 9, 2017.
http://www.telesurtv.net/english/news/Chinese-Feminists-Stand-Against-Trumps-Straight-Man-Cancer-20170209-0024.html

[108] Stacy Keltner and Ashley McFarland, "On Pricks and Politics: How to Measure Up This Election Season," *Common Dreams*, September 9, 2016.
http://www.commondreams.org/views/2016/09/09/pricks-and-politics-how-measure-election-season

[109] Domenico Montanaro, "6 Strongmen Trump Has Praised—And the Conflicts it Presents," National Public Radio, May 2, 2017.
http://www.npr.org/2017/05/02/526520042/6-strongmen-trumps-praised-and-the-conflicts-it-presents

[110] "Millennials: The Challenge Generation," Prosumer Report, Europe RSCG Worldwide, Vol. 11, 2011. The report surveyed 2,500 Millennials aged 18 to 24 in China, France, India, the UK and the US in 2010. http://www.prosumer-report.com/blog/wp-content/uploads/2011/04/MGv-16no%20crops.pdf

[111] http://greengaians.blogspot.com/

[112] https://www.youtube.com/watch?v=bXuXYoh-lFA co-ed high school https://www.youtube.com/watch?v=bXuXYoh-lFA

[113] http://www.npr.org/2013/09/28/226903227/mexican-state-s-anti-corruption-plan-hire-women-traffic-cops

[114] National Center for Women & Policing
http://www.womenandpolicing.org/
http://www.womenandpolicing.org/pdf/NewAdvantagesReport.pdf

[115] Will Yakowicz, "Women Leaders Have Attention to Detail," Inc.com, October 23, 2013.
www.inc.com/will-yakowicz/christine-lagarde-on-the-female-leader.html

[116] William Greider, "What Would Happen if Women Were in Charge of the Global Economy?," *The Nation*, May 8, 2015.
http://www.thenation.com/blog/206737/what-would-happen-if-women-were-charge-global-economy#

[117] Leslie Schwindt-Bayer and William Mishler, *Journal of Politics*, Vol. 67, No. 2, May 2005.

[118] http://www.jstor.org/discover/10.1111/j.1468-

Nikki van der Gaag, "Because I am a Girl: The State of the World's Girls 2013," Plan International, 2013, p. 98.

[119] http://plan-international.org/files/global/publications/campaigns/biag-2013-report-english.pdf

Margaret Slattery, "The FP Survey: Women in Politics," *Foreign Policy*, May 2012. http://www.foreignpolicy.com/articles/2012/04/23/the_fp_survey_women_in_politics

[120] Claire Devlin and Robert Elgie," The Effect of Increased Women's Representation in Parliament: The Case of Rwanda," *Oxford Journals*, February 3, 2008

[121] http://pa.oxfordjournals.org/content/61/2/237.full

[122] http://www.refinery29.com/2016/03/105325/female-world-leaders-2016#slides

Raul Zibechi, "Paraguay: Women at the Center of Resistance," *Americas Program*, December 30, 2013.

[123] http://www.cipamericas.org/archives/11255

Diana Viveros, "CONAMURI: Developments and Challenges in the Struggle Against Agrochemicals in Paraguay," *Environmental Justice*, Vol. 5, No. 2, 2012.

[124] DOI: 10.1089/env.2011.0022

Adam Bryant, "Four Executives on Succeeding in Business as a Woman," *The New York Times*. October 12, 2013.

[125] http://www.nytimes.com/interactive/2013/10/13/business/women-corner-office.html

Therese, "Are Women Better Decision Makers?" *New York Times*, October 17, 2014.

[126] http://www.nytimes.com/2014/10/19/opinion/sunday/are-women-better-decision-makers.html

Dina Medland, "Today's Gender Reality in Statistics," *Forbes*, March 7, 2016.

http://www.forbes.com/sites/dinamedland/2016/03/07/todays-gender-reality-in-statistics-or-making-leadership-attractive-to-women/#5cce26526255

[127] Ester Addlely, "May, Sturgeon, Merkel: Women Rising From the Political Ashes of Men," *The Guardian*, July 5, 2016.

[128] http://www.theguardian.com/politics/2016/jul/05/sturgeon-may-leadsom-women-to-the-rescue-amid-political-turmoil

Michael Trudeau, "Should Men be Investing like Women?" *Moneywise*, October 7, 2014.

[129] http://www.moneywise.co.uk/investing/first-time-investor/should-men-be-investing-women

Lois Joy, et al., "The Bottom Line," *Catalyst*, October 2007.

[130] http://www.catalyst.org/system/files/The_Bottom_Line_Corporate_Performance_and_Womens_Representation_on_Boards.pdf

David Matsa and Amalia Miller, "Is There a Female Leadership Style?" *Kellogg Insight*, September 4, 2012.

[131] http://insight.kellogg.northwestern.edu/article/is_there_a_female_leadership_style

Mary Curtis, "Gender Diversity and Corporate Performance," *Credit Suisse Research Institute*, August 2012.

[132] Andre Chanavat and Katharine Ramsden, "Mining the Metrics of Board Diversity," Thomson/Reuters, June 2013.

Leslie Picker, "Hedge fund Targets Companies' Weakness: The Gender Gap," *New York Times*, October 4, 2016.

[133] http://www.nytimes.com/2016/10/05/business/dealbook/hedge-fund-targets-companies-weakness-the-gender-gap.html?_r=0

Danica Kirka, "For Business, More Women in Charge Means Bigger Profits," Associated Press, March 23, 2015.

[134] http://www.theheraldbusinessjournal.com/article/20150323/BIZ02/150329602

Nicholas Kristof, "When Women Win, Men Win Too," *New York Times*, July 30, 2016.

[135] http://www.nytimes.com/2016/07/31/opinion/sunday/when-women-win-men-win-too.html

[136] https://www.slideshare.net/guest50fdb1/digital-generation-survey-2008-technology-part-1-presentation

Dennis Finn and Anne Donovan, "PwC's NextGen: A Global Generational Study," 2013.

http://www.pwc.com/en_GX/gx/hr-management-services/pdf/pwc-nextgen-study-2013.pdf

Engaging and Empowering Millennials

[137] http://www.pwc.com/gx/en/hr-management-services/publications/assets/pwc-engaging-and-empowering-millennials.pdf

[138] Jennifer Deal and Alec Levenson. *What Millenials Want From Work*. McGraw-Hill Education, 2016, p. 121.

[139] Ibid., p. 121.

"They Don't Call Her Mother Earth for Nothing," Bioneers Radio Series, April 23, 2013.

http://media.bioneers.org/listing/they-dont-call-her-mother-earth-for-nothing-alice-walker-jean-shinoda-bolen-nina-simons-sarah-crowell-joanna-macy-and-akaya-winwood/

[140] Shamillah Wilson, Anasuya Sengupta, Kristy Evans, **eds**. *Defending Our Dreams: Global Feminist Voices for a New Generation*. Zed Books and AWID, 2005, p. 237.

[141] Nicole Lou, "Older Hospital Patients Get Better Care from Female Docs," *MedPage Today*, December 19, 2016.

[142] http://www.medpagetoday.com/hospitalbasedmedicine/generalhospitalpractice/62156

Patients Cared For By Female Doctors Fare Better Than Those Treated By Men," NPR, December 19, 2016.

[143] http://www.npr.org/sections/health-shots/2016/12/19/506144346/patients-cared-for-by-female-doctors-fare-better-than-those-treated-by-men

Naomi Wolf, "The Middle East's Feminist Revolution," Project Syndicate, February 28, 2011.

[144] http://www.project-syndicate.org/commentary/the-middle-east-s-feminist-revolution

Janet Conway, Transnational Feminisms Building Anti-Globalization Solidarities," *Globalizations*, Vol. 9, No. 3, June 2012, pp. 379-393.

[145] http://dx.doi.org/10.1080/14747731.2012.680731

Jessica Taft. *Rebel Girls: Youth Activism and Social Change Across the Americas*. New York University Press, 2011.

146
Ibid., p. 4.
147
http://mentalfloss.com/article/31274/6-modern-societies-where-women-literally-rule
148
Cherokee, Choctaw, Gitksan, Haida, Hopi, Iroquois, Lenape, and Navajo of North America; the Minangkabau people of West Sumatra, Indonesia; the Nairsand the Bunts of Kerala and Karnataka in South India; the Khasi, Jaintia and Garoof Meghalaya in Northeast India; the Mosuo of China; the Basques of Spain and France; the Akan including the Ashanti of West Africa; and the Tuaregs of West and North Africa. http://en.wikipedia.org/wiki/Matrilineality in Alaska, the Tlingit and Haida clans are often matrilineal. Deb Vanasses's book *Wealth Woman: Kate Carmack and the Klondike Race for Gold* (2016) discusses the matrilineal traditions of the Tagish people. Yang Erce Namu and Christine Mathieu. *Leaving Mother Lake: a Girlhood at the Edge of the World*. Little Brown & Company, 2004.
149
Ibid., p. 277. Search Namu's name to see photos.
150
Pedro Ceinos Arcones. *China's Last But One Matriarchy: The Jino of Yunnan*. Papers of the White Dragon, 2013.
151
Natalie Angier, "In the Bonobo World, Female Camaraderie Prevails," *New York Times*, September 10, 2016.
http://www.nytimes.com/2016/09/13/science/bonobos-apes-matriarchy.html?_r=0
152
"Herbert Marcuse," *Stanford Encyclopedia of Philosophy*, December 18, 2013.
http://plato.stanford.edu/entries/marcuse/
153
Rob Sidon, "Vandana Shiva: Ecofeminism and the Sanctity of Seed," *Common Ground Magazine*, October 2012, p. 48.
154
Micah White. *The End of Protest: A New Playbook for Revolution*. Knopf Canada, 2016, p. 198.
155
http://www.socialprogressimperative.org/data/spi/findings
156
Ami Sedghi, "Norway has been Named the Most Prosperous Country in the World," *The Guardian*, November 3, 2014.
http://www.theguardian.com/news/datablog/2014/nov/03/european-countries-dominate-in-global-prosperity-rankings
157
http://hdr.undp.org/sites/default/files/hdr15_standalone_overview_en.pdf
Ann Jones, "American Democracy Down for the Count," *The Nation*, January 28, 2016.
158
http://www.tomdispatch.com/post/176096/tomgram%3A_ann_jones%2C_social_democracy_for_dummies/
Michael Booth, "Dark Lands: The Grim Truth Behind the 'Scandinavian Miracle,'" *The Guardian*, January 27, 2014.
159
http://www.theguardian.com/world/2014/jan/27/scandinavian-miracle-brutal-truth-denmark-norway-swede
160
Michael Booth. *The Almost Perfect People*. Picador, 2014, pp. 367-369.
George Lakey, "How Swedes and Norwegians Broke the Power of the '1 percent,'" *Waging Nonviolence*, January 25, 2012. rhttp://wagingnonviolence.org/2012/01/how-swedes-and-norwegians-broke-the-power-of-the-1-percent/
161
Annadis Rudolfsdottir "The Day the Women Went on Strike," *The Guardian*, October 18, 2005.
http://www.theguardian.com/world/2005/oct/18/gender.uk
162
Interview with Gabrielle Motola by Emily von Hoffmann and Polarr, "What the Icelandic Know," *Medium,* February 25, 2016.
163
https://medium.com/the-coffeelicious/what-the-icelandic-know-9f34c9d827cf#.omirvbg21
164
https://grapevine.is/news/2016/01/25/iceland-out-ranks-america-in-obesity/
Claire Gordon, "Women Make Better Leaders Than Men, If you Give Them the Chance," AOL Jobs, August 23, 2011.
165
http://jobs.aol.com/articles/2011/08/23/women-make-better-leaders-than-men-if-you-give-them-the-chance/
"Is Iceland the Best Country for Women," *The Guardian*, October 3, 2011.
166
http://www.theguardian.com/world/2011/oct/03/iceland-best-country-women-feminist
John Rogers, "Hacking Politics: An In-Depth Look At Iceland's Pirate Party," *Grapevine Magazine,* November 19, 2015. http://grapevine.is/mag/feature/2015/11/19/hacking-politics/
167
http://www.piratar.is/policies/core-policy/?lang=en
168
Verla Husfeldt, et al., "Adolescents' Social Attitudes and Expected Political Participation," Working Paper from Civic Education Data and Researcher Services, December 2005.
169
http://www.terpconnect.umd.edu/.../CEDARS%20new%20scales%20report....
170
http://top10matrimonysites.in/
171
http://iamnotmytribe.blogspot.com. She also interned at http://www.newsfromafrica.org.
Mian Ridge, "India's 2010 Census Considers Taboo Question," *Christian Science Monitor* June 9, 2010
172
www.csmonitor.com/World/Asia-South-Central/2010/0609/India-s-2010-census-considers-taboo-question-What-s-your-caste
173
http://www.quotaproject.org/uid/countryview.cfm?CountryCode=NP
An American who lived in Havana with her family described life there in the 1990s. Isadora Tattlin. *Cuba Diaries*. Broadway Books, 2002.
174
Mary Murray, "Cubans Deal with the Unimaginable: Pink Slips," *MSNBC*, May 4, 2011.
www.msnbc.msn.com/id/42803466/ns/world_news-americas/t/young-cubans-deal-unimaginable-pink-slips
175
Mark Engler and Paul Engler, "When the Pillars Fall," *Waging Non Violence*, July 9, 2014.
http://wagingnonviolence.org/feature/pillars-fall-social-movements-can-win-victories-like-sex-marriage/
176
https://www.youtube.com/user/PivotTVnetwork
177
Steve Rosenberg, "Russian Duma Passes Law Banning 'Gay Propaganda,'" *BBC News*, June 11, 2013.
http://www.bbc.com/news/world-europe-22862210
178
"The Global Divide on Homosexuality," *Pew Research Global Attitudes Project*, June 4, 2013.
http://www.pewglobal.org/2013/06/04/the-global-divide-on-homosexuality/
179
Johnson, "Claiming Rights, Facing Fire: Young Feminist Activists," s*50.50 OpenDemocracy*, October 20, 2014.

180 https://www.opendemocracy.net/5050/ruby-johnson/claiming-rights-facing-fire-young-feminist-activists

181 http://www.nytimes.com/video/world/africa/100000002590361/gays-worry-about-post-mandela-s-africa.html?nl=todaysheadlines&emc=edit_th_20131215

182 http://crisis-scape.net/

183 http://www.cpn.org/tools/dictionary/citizenpolitics.html

"Europe Needs More Immigrants, But Sees Spike in Racism," April 26, 2005.

184 www.finalcall.com/artman/publish/article_1950.shtml

Sylvain Charat, "Illegal Immigration: Is Europe Losing Control of its Borders?" *Human Events*, January 19, 2015.

185 http://humanevents.com/2015/01/19/illegal-immigration-is-europe-losing-control-of-its-borders/

186 http://www.cnn.com/2017/03/02/europe/european-countries-not-meeting-refugee-resettling-obligations/index.html

187 Paolo Pontoniere

Eva Kolinsky, "Party Governance, Political Culture and the Transformation of East Germany since 1990," *German Politics*, Vol. 10, Issue 2, August 2001, pp. 169-183.

188 https://www.youtube.com/watch?v=wYgBT_NL1Kc

189 Ronald Inglehart and Christian Welzel. *Modernization, Cultural Change, and Democracy: The Human Development Sequence*. Cambridge University Press, 2005, p. 45.

190 Emma Saloranta, "Five Ways to Promote Gender Equality in 2016," *Girls' Globe*, December 25, 2015.

191 http://girlsglobe.org/2015/12/25/five-ways-to-promote-gender-equality-in-2016/

192 USAID internet discussion, http://www.hesselbeininstitute.org/#!bookshelf/c6uq

193 United Nations, "The Millennium Development Goals Report," June 15, 2010, p. 25.

Helen Clark comments about the impact of women in government. http://content.undp.org/go/newsroom/2010/march/helen-clark--international-womens-leadership-conference.en;jsessionid=axbWzt...?categoryID=593043&lang=en

194 http://en.wikipedia.org/wiki/Timeline_of_women's_suffrage

195 http://www.guide2womenleaders.com/index.html

196 www.cwwl.org/index.html

Margot Wallström, "A Womanly Virtue: Female Representation as Global Security Strategy," *Harvard International Review*, May 1, 2011.

197 http://hir.harvard.edu/print/women-in-power/a-womanly-virtue

www.oecdbetterlifeindex.org/topics/life-satisfaction

198 *A 2008 film called Number One illustrates gender issues in a Moroccan clothing factory of female workers with a male boss*

199 http://womeninpublicservice.wilsoncenter.org/about-us/50-x-50-changemakers/

200 http://globalshapers.org/

201 file:///Users/gaylekimball/Downloads/er-rhv-evaluation-summary-081113-en.pdf

202 http://www.cwgl.rutgers.edu/about-110/history

203 https://www.youtube.com/watch?v=zuLnhjOivoI

Mary Trigg, editor. *Leading the Way: Young Women' Activism for Social Change*. Rutgers University Press, 2010, pp. 1-16.

204 Lia Jervis, "Goodbye to Feminism's Generational Divide," in Melody Berger's *We Don't Need Another Wave*. Seal Press, 2006.

Vital Voices Global Partnership Policy Advocates program

205 http://www.vitalvoices.org/how-we-do-it

"Arab Spring Democracy: A Win for Women?" *The Media Line*, March 8, 2012.

206 http://www.genderconcerns.org/article.php?id_nr=3040&id=Arab+Spring+Democracy:+A+Win+for+Women

207 http://www.quotaproject.org/uid/countryview.cfm?CountryCode=PK

208 www.quotaproject.org

Women in National Parliaments, May 2014. http://www.ipu.org/wmn-e/classif.htm

209 Michelle Nichols, "Share of Female Lawmakers Hits New Global High," March 1, 2007.

Viveka Hulyalkar, "The Emergence and Effects of Political Quotas in India," *The Women in Public Service Project*, October 16, 2013.

http://womeninpublicservice.wilsoncenter.org/2013/10/16/the-emergence-and-effects-of-reservations-in-india-panchayati-raj-as-a-precedent-for-political-quotas-and-female-representation/

210 Mian Ridge, May 11, 2010

211 www.csmonitor.com/World/Asia-South-Central/2010/0511/Some-Indian-villages-prefer-to-put-women-in-power/(page)/2

212 Nicholas Kristof and Sheryl WuDunn. *Half the Sky: Turning Oppression into Opportunity for Women Worldwide*. Alfred A. Knopf, 2009, p. 197.

213 www.csmonitor.com/World/Asia-South-Central/2010/0511/Some-Indian-villages-prefer-to-put-women-in-power/(page)/2

214 Rita Banerji, www.ritabanerji.com The 50 Million Missing Campaign http://50millionmissing.wordpress.com/

January 1, 2013. http://www.undp.org/content/undp/en/home/librarypage/democratic-governance/electoral_systemsandprocesses/enhancing-youth-political-participation-throughout-the-electoral/

215 Rossalyn Warren, "18 Badass Women You Probably Didn't Hear About In 2014," BuzzFeed, December 8, 2014

216 http://www.buzzfeed.com/rossalynwarren/badass-womenalert#.rk2PPq3Peg

217 http://schoolgirlsunite.org/wp-content/uploads/2015/03/Activist-Gameplan1.pdf

https://www.goodreads.com/list/show/97563.Books_Set_in_a_Gender_Equal_Society

Mashal, 18, photo by Hassan Saeed, Pakistan

Chapter 3

GLOBAL STATUS
OF WOMEN AND GIRLS

I will introduce equal opportunity to stop violence against women.

Saygee, 11, f, Liberia

I would improve women's rights involving sexual abuse, labor, etc.

Rose, 15, f, Tanzania

I want to empower the youth as the bone of development of Nepal and eradicate discrimination, inequality, and eliminate social evils like early child marriage of girls, dowry, trafficking in girls, drug addiction and the bonded labor system (Almost like slave labor, farmers are perpetually in debt to landowners).

Anzel, 16, f, Nepal

I'd like to stop the apocalypse and save the world; we are the new generation and it's up to us.

Miriam, 16, f, Israel

Policymakers in both rich and poor countries have treated women and children, quite frankly, as if they matter less than men.

Melinda Gates, Gates Foundation

Contents: Neoliberalism, Rural Vs. Urban Sex Roles, Feminization of Poverty, Education, Health, Violence

Inequality

Young people generally lack power, living in consumerist cultures that rely on money and neoliberal capitalist policies directed by the WTO, IMF, and World Bank since the debt crises of the 1970s. Government austerity programs needed to pay back loans to these international lenders rob social service programs in developing countries. Young women are more disadvantaged and are more likely to be low-wage workers. They do more of the world's work than men but earn less.[1] The world's poor are likely to be women and children. One person in eight on earth is a female ages 10 to 24, but in many places young women can't vote, inherit land, or go to school. They do the heavy, time-consuming, and unpaid work in rural areas like hauling firewood and water—650 million people lack access to clean water.[2] The widespread lack of toilets faced by 2.5 billion poor people exposes females to danger from animals and humans as they go into the fields to find privacy to relieve themselves. They do a double shift in industrialized nations, doing more of the family work in addition to paid work. Michelle Obama told youth leaders in South Africa in 2011 that they can make history by ensuring that girls aren't treated as second-class citizens, that they get an education, and make sure that violence against women is regarded as a human rights issue.

The large majority of young women share a sense of unfairness about the "institutions and ideologies that structure our lives and our world," according to Canadian Alison Symington, a researcher at the Association for Women's Rights in Development (AVID).[3] She added that human rights include the right to food and health care. Symington observed, "Many young women are facing up to this challenge, mastering a crucial analysis of economics and developing skills in advocacy, policy-formulation, public protest and mobilization. It's up to us to decide how to address the neoliberal global economic system—whether to challenge it, work within it, attempt to reform it or disengage from it."[4] The goal is to think globally, act locally, a slogan that has been around since the late 1960s.

The Global Gender Gap Report 2015 reported on the lack of progress in that the gender gap decreased by only 4% in the last decade.[5] The World Bank's Little Data Book on Gender compiles recent gender statistics.[6] An additional quarter of a billion women entered the workforce since 2006 but their average pay equals what men earned a decade ago. If progress continues at the same rate, it will take 128 years for women to earn the same wages as men. More women than men are university students in 97 countries, but they're the majority of skilled workers in only 68 countries and the majority of leaders in only four countries. Women were only 23% of legislators in 2016 (an increase from 11% in 1995). There are more women legislators in countries with quotas like Rwanda, which has 64% of women in the lower house and Bolivia, with 53% women legislators, as well as the Nordic countries that highly value equality.[7] As of January 2017, 19 women were heads of state or government.

All the recent democracy uprisings point to the root oppression as globalized neoliberal capitalism, in opposition to Prime Minister Margaret Thatcher's widely quoted statement that "there is no alternative!" to the current capitalist system. "Neo" refers to the revival of liberalism by Professor Milton Freedman at the University of Chicago. Friedman turned Marx on his head, stating, "To each according to what he and the instruments he owns produces," not according to human need as Marx desired. The neoliberal approach is the free market, deregulation of finance, reduction of taxes on the wealthy, and privatization of national resources. The individual is expected to make it on her own, in a kind of social Darwinian survival of the fittest. Yet girls are socialized to be nice, cooperative, not be bossy or get angry, or be too assertive, which minimizes success in a competitive environment.

The editors of *Occupy! A Global Movement* described the global uprisings mentioned earlier as "a novel and noisy intervention in the recent capitalist crisis in developed economies."[8] The protests were characterized by the creation of a mass identity of the 99%--versus the 1% elite--and the strategic importance of using occupation of public spaces. Although the latter wasn't a novel tactic, what was new was including almost everyone except the richest 1%, rather than a specific group like students or union members, feminist-style assemblies where anyone could speak, an increasing number of women leaders, and the emphasis on prefigurative action to create direct democracy and cooperatives in the occupied areas. Meditation, therapists and drumming spaces are often provided along with free food, first aid, libraries, workshops, and childcare in this generation's concern about caring relationships.

An activist organization called "The Rules," headquartered in New York City, wrote *The One Party Planet* pamphlet in 2014. It outlines the impact of neoliberal capitalist elites, what they refer to as the Neoliberal Party governing the world.[9] In an increasingly unequal economic system, 60% of the population lives on less than $5 a day, according to the World Bank. The richest 1% owns almost half of the world's wealth, surpassing elected governments in their control.[10] Women comprise only 11.5% of the 1% globally and are only 16% of the richest 1% in the US, defined as earning over $394,000 a year. Of the nearly 2,500 billionaires in the world, women are only about 12% of them and only 49 of the 294 female billionaires are self-made, with Asia having more women who made their wealth on their own rather than inheriting it. Women represented few of *Forbes'* "The World's Most Powerful People" in 2015; the nine women out of 73 leaders are listed in the endnote.[11] Angela Merkel was second most powerful, behind Putin, and Janet Yellen, Ph.D. (head of the US Federal Reserve Board) was in seventh place.

Most of the largest economic entities (1101 out of 1752 entities in 2011) are corporations rather than nations and they are skilled in not paying their fair share of taxes.

Corporations have the rights of persons in the US--thanks to the Citizens United Supreme Court decision, one of the grievances of the large Democracy Spring protests in Washington, DC in 2016 that advocated a constitutional amendment to overturn the decision. Since the oil industry comprises seven of the 10 biggest global corporations, they continue to increase the amount of carbon dioxide. Oil companies like Exxon and Koch Industries have paid millions for false "science" reports denying human impact on climate change as a time when half the coral reefs have died.[12] (See the 2006 documentary *Who Killed the Electric Car?*) This is similar to tobacco company ads that paid doctors to testify that smoking was good for your health.

The One Party Planet authors call for multiplication of popular global uprisings like the ones in Gezi Park, Tahrir Square, Occupy Wall Street, and Paris' Place de la Republique. In addition to some of the democratic models mentioned in this book, they mention the Ekta Parishad land reform in India,[13] the Project for the Advancement of our Common Humanity think tank at New York University, the farm labor coalition of the Immokalee Workers in Florida, and Kenyans for Tax Justice in Nairobi. They point to leaders such as Uruguay's President José Mujica, who rejected neoliberal policies and reduced poverty as by promoting cooperatives. They believe that "something like a cohesive movement is taking place." The Rules authors value a new paradigm of systems theory to understand how to correct inequality, explained in *The Systems View of Life* by Fritjof Capra and Pier Luigi Luisi (2014). An alternative to neoliberal economics is the growing field of "steady state" or "no growth economics" as taught by the New Economics Foundation.

Neoliberal austerity cuts of social services and government jobs impact women in developed nations as well as in poorer countries. In response, the European branch of The World March of Women network organized their first young feminist camp in France in 2011. The EU's Youth in Action Program funded it because:

> *Unemployment, precariousness and poverty have been growing and mortgaging the lives of most people, including thousands of women. The right to health and sexual and reproductive rights are increasingly becoming a mirage for many of us. In the last ten years Portugal was one of the only European countries to see the wage gap between men and women decrease [along with Latvia]. Gender based violence has also been growing and intensifying.*[14]

Feminists fight "the forces of imperialism, colonialism, racism, sexism and poverty."[15] The anthology Defending Our Dreams: Global Feminist Voices for a New Generation (2005) identified feminist issues such as new technologies, HIV and sexuality, religious belief and families (which they felt weren't explored by earlier feminists), feminist men, using the International Criminal Court and other ways to enforce women's human rights, and the main Third Wave theme of the intersection of multiple oppressions. Sexism leads to violence, including suicide.[16] It's the leading cause of death for girls ages 15 to 19 worldwide, according to the World Health Organization.[17] Girls' Globe NGO calls for a mental health revolution to recognize and treat depression and other disorders and the UN included promoting mental health in its Sustainable Development Goals established in 2015.

The developed world faces these problems as portrayed in the US film *Precious* (2009) about Claireece, a poor, obese, illiterate, HIV+ and abused black 16-year-old girl living in the Harlem ghetto in New York City. The film was based on the novel *Push* (1994) by Sapphire. National research estimates that 6.8 million young people ages 10 to 17 live in food-insecure households. The Urban Institute interviewed 193 teenagers in poor areas because teen problems are often overlooked by policymakers who focus on children five and younger.[18] In 13 out of 20 focus groups in the US the teens reported sexual exploitation.

The world's greatest unused resource isn't minerals, but uneducated girls and women, as pointed out by the authors of *Half the Sky* (2009). They stated that in the 19th century, the moral challenge was slavery, in the 20th it was totalitarianism, and in this century it's violence against women. One in every three girls is married off before age 18, with lifetime consequences limiting their education and autonomy.[19] Poor women are also used to sell their uteruses in surrogacy or eggs for couples who can't conceive, sell their breast milk, babies, and hair.[20] Women and girls suffer from sex trafficking acid attacks on schoolgirls (as in Pakistan and Afghanistan), domestic violence in every country, harassment on the street and at work and at school, bride burnings to collect more dowry (i.e., India), child marriage (i.e., Saudi Arabia), being forced to marry their rapists (i.e., Kyrgyzstan), being sold into prostitution (i.e., Thailand), and gang rape by soldiers and others.[21] The notion of "rape culture" started to be discussed in 2013 with the gang rape of a young woman in New Delhi and the problem is illustrated in a video by a 16-year-old California girl, Annie Lu.[22] Girls are around 40% of the world's 250,000 child soldiers, especially in Africa and Asia.[23] Many of those girls are raped by other soldiers.

Because boys are preferred In India and China, more than 1.5 million fewer girls are born each year than statistics would predict,[24] leading to millions of missing women—more than all the men killed in all the wars and genocides of the 20th century. Ultrasound technology followed by abortion of female fetuses is practiced in parts of East and South Asia, leading to more men than women, and a shortage of women to marry.[25] This is problematic because single men are associated with a higher crime rate than married men.

Scholar Deniz Kandiyoti traces the global increase in violence against women as a defensive reaction of patriarchy under attack; "We are witnessing a profound crisis of masculinity leading to more violent and coercive assertions of male prerogatives where the abuse of women can become a blood sport—whether it takes place in the slums of Soweto, outside the factories of Ciudad Juarez, in the streets of Delhi or the alleyways of Cairo."[26] Any suggestion that the need for feminist action is over is dispelled by the facts that women are most often poor and more abused than men in both developed and developing countries.

A reminder that sexism is alive and well globally, the president of Turkey, Recep Tayyip Erdoğan said in 2014 that it's impossible to think of equality between the sexes because of biological differences and God's design. He said, "Our religion gives women a place—motherhood," but feminists do not accept motherhood.[27] This in a country that has sought to be part of the European Union since 1987 where violence against women is increasing. When Nigerian President Muhammadu Buhari's wife criticized his leadership, he responded, "I don't know which party my wife belongs to, but she belongs to my kitchen and my living room and the other room."[28] His comment resulted in the hashtag #TheOtherRoom and criticism of older men marrying girls.

Of course, Donald Trump's comments about his star status giving him the right to grab women's genitalia are infamous.[29] Elected by a landslide to be president of the Philippines in 2016, Rodrigo Duterte stated that as mayor of Davao he should have been the first in line when prisoners gang raped an Australian missionary who he described a beautiful.[30] He also bragged about shooting criminals, saying "it's going to be bloody" if he became president and that he would restore the death penalty.

Rural vs. Urban Sex Roles

The main difference between young people is not their nationality, but whether they live in urban or rural areas.[31] The largest global organization for university students conducted a survey of 160,292 global youth, 55% female, most of them ages 16 to 24, in 2016. The survey reveals few differences in attitudes by region, and generally an altruistic, global, and relationship-focused generation.[32] Support for gender equality is highest among urban young people, women, well-educated and more secular people, according to Ronald Inglehart and Pippa Norris.[33] The exception is uneducated young people in rural societies who may retain traditional sexist beliefs. As of 2008 a majority of the world's population lived in cities, with more girls migrating to cities than boys in countries like China, where they may not feel safe. In a video interview with rural farm women in Kenya they say they're happy because they can count on each other for help and they grow their own food.[34]

Maria, a high school student, posted from Lebanon on Our Shared Shelf feminist book club in 2016, "I think that women are not as equal as men are not because of the religion but because of the family's education and culture. A farmer or someone who lives in the mountains will be more strict and old fashioned than people who live in the city, so of course he won't let his daughter be totally free." Harshita confirmed from India, "People in villages still don't feel comfortable if a girl child is born in the family. Not a day goes by without hearing, 'You're a girl, you cannot do this or that.' Thus a girl child is prevented from going to school, and the killings of the females as soon as they are born cause a lower sex ratio. Many people have the belief that women are not suitable for the same job as men, hence the pay gap."

Brick Lane (2003), a novel by Monica Ali, tells the story of an uneducated rural Bangladeshi girl who is married off to a man she doesn't know and moves to London with him when she is 18. Being in the city changes her. Nazneen's husband, 20 years older, describes her as an unspoiled girl from the village who will bear children for him. She submits to her fate but gradually gains her own voice while living in the city, deciding, "I will say what happens to me." She learns English and even has a love affair.

The Turkish film *Bliss* (*Mutluluk*, 2007) contrasts the differences between rural and urban lifestyles and shows the passive rural girl's increasing resolve to stand up for herself after being removed from her rural home. It tells the story of an ex-commando who is ordered by his family to kill his 17-year-old cousin, an "honor killing," because she was raped and therefore "tainted." He can't bring himself to kill her but can't bring her back to the village. She is shocked when she sees a woman in a bikini but becomes more assertive.

The Chinese film *The Cremator* (2003) illustrates problems faced by rural women: suicide, migration to cities to do sweatshop labor, and poverty leading to prostitution.[35] Millions of Chinese young women rely on sex work to get away from farm life.[36] A local actress named Sijia Yang, who starred in the film, personally experienced rural poverty.

When her family moved from the countryside to Xian to earn more money her dialect made her an outsider and the same problem occurred when she moved back to grandparents' rural home. Feeling isolated, she studied a lot and passed the *gaokao* test that enabled her to go to college, but was traumatized by being raped by her father's boss. She never told her family and became suicidal until she became a Buddhist. Both Buddhism and Christianity have grown in rural areas for the last two decades, as has sexual abuse of women like Yang— who are outnumbered because of the one child policy and parents' preference for boys. She played a character with a similar past named Xiuqiao, and then moved to Beijing to live with a boyfriend she met on the film set. The film director Peng Tao observed, "People from the countryside in China have the hardest lives. …I hope that my film can say something about the complex relationship in China between money, morals and tradition."[37]

I asked SpeakOut student Hassan to film villages outside his home in Pakistan. I told him I was surprised that the people on the street, the children playing, were all male except for two women in purdah walking down the street. Hassan explained,

> *I was new to the village. They saw me for the first time with the camera. The women outside quickly went to their homes because they are scared of their men and they know that they are supposed to be inside at such times. We are talking about people who are absolutely confined to their own homes and not go out a lot. I live in Peshawar and we do have some exposure to girls. For example, we have co-education here. Women go out of their homes to markets, interact in schools, colleges, universities, cafes, etc. Villages have different lives than cities.*

We see again the vast differences between the lives of rural and urban women and also the Muslim theme of a girls' place is in the home, despite the fact that the Prophet's first wife was a businesswoman who rode camels and was a widow who proposed marriage to the younger man.

Because I've found a greater difference between urban and village life in the same country than between urban dwellers in different countries, I wanted to hear about a girl's daily life in a rural area. Pakistan is second-to-last place in worldwide rankings of gender equality, according to the Global Gender Gap Report of 2012. Rural girls have very different aspirations, as you'll read in Hassan's interview with Mashal. She's an illiterate girl in northern Pakistan where 71% of the people live in villages. Neelam Ibrar Chattan started working for education and peace in Swat Valley as a teenager, the year that Malala Yousafzai was shot there by the Taliban because of her advocacy for girls' education. She reported, "If a girl is getting an education [away from her parents' protection], she's not considered a good girl."[38]

Hassan interviewed Mashal with the SpeakOut questions and translated her answers from Pashto (the language of the Taliban). He introduced her as "a person who comes to my friend's house in Peshawar on a weekly basis, and cleans up the house with her little sister. Her parents let her go because that way she earns a few rupees and that's how they live. Her father works at a construction field, runs cement and stones." The entire interview is on th2 book website.[39]

Women and girls like Mashal are the face of poverty in Pakistan where 70% of the people living in extreme poverty and most of the about 25 million children ages five to 16 aren't in school. Poverty is associated with powerlessness and breeds violence against women and children. Half the school-age children in Pakistan don't have access to government schools and 41% of young women age 15 to 24 are illiterate, one of the lowest literacy rates in the world. Part of the problem is that 42% of primary schools don't have working toilets and over half don't have working electricity.[40] Village girls I Skyped with as Hassan translated didn't go to school either because the government provided no girls' schools or teachers didn't show up or they hit the students when they were in class.

Hassan points out that some "ghost schools" exist in the records but don't have teachers who come to class. A popular singer, Shehzad Roy (born in 1977), rides on a motorcycle filming schools to show his TV viewers the deplorable condition of schools. His show is called *Chal Parha*, meaning "Come, Teach."

Tell me a little about your background.

I am 18 and have eight siblings including seven sisters and one brother. Two of my sisters are married. We are very poor. My parents didn't go to school or anything, which they regret. My father earns 50 rupees a day (60 cents) and that is when he works from day to night. In my whole day, I am so busy in the household chores and activities that I don't even get a single moment for me to spend free. If, by chance, I get any, I sit with my sisters and talk. Lie down in bed and do nothing.

How is your generation different from your parents'?

Actually our thoughts don't match. They always stop me and tell me to do a

specific thing in a specific way, but I get annoyed and I try to make them under-
stand that I know my work better and I can do it. My uncles (mother's brothers)
are very strict and they try to rule us. They don't let us go out and try to make
sure we stay at home. It's a small village so for girls to go out very often is not
appropriate. Small issues can lead to disasters [regarding public opinion about
a girl's reputation].

What are the major problems facing humans today? [Her answer illustrates
the frustration of rising expectations.]

For me, the biggest problem that humans are facing today is poverty. Poor people
have no money, no food, no happiness. They can do crimes for money, like my
very own cousin who was involved in a house robbery that lead him to jail be-
cause he would look at his master's kids who had everything! Cars, cell phones,
money, new clothes, everything! This made my cousin do robbery despite the fact
that he knew it's wrong but he couldn't control his personal desires and went on
doing it. He's in jail today and it's been three years now. He's young and strong
and was the sole earner of the family. His family is having a very hard time living
these days. It shouldn't be this way. I think government should do enough things
for the poor on yearly basis so that we don't do such crimes.

What do you like to do for fun?

We don't do anything for fun. We don't have extra time for extra activities. I just
sit back at times in my home and talk to my sisters about life. That's all my life is.

When have you felt most loved by someone else?

Never. As I said, my parents have not studied much so they don't show their
emotions. In fact, they don't understand. I have never felt loved by anyone. Ev-
eryone orders me to do work for them.

Why do you think you're here on earth; what's your purpose?

I don't really understand the reason. I have not studied Quran, the religion, or
the school so I don't know why I am here. I don't like this pattern of life. I wish
my life was better.

How would your life be different if you were born a boy and would you like

your future to be the same or different from your mother's?

> *If I was a boy, that could have settled everything for me. I would have done everything. I would go out with friends, stay outside, spend time with my buddies, play cricket, have fun, make long distance travels, make phone calls with friends. It would have been awesome. I wouldn't just stay home, do the household chores everyday, listen to my parents complain about food, work, money, etc. I would get the most attention in the house and people would love me. Being a boy is very cool.*

> *I want my future to be exactly like my mother's. I love her and respect her so much. She gave me good manners. Today, no one can say that I am a bad girl because of my mother. She brought me up well and that's why I adore her. So I'd grow up to be like her and take care of our family and live happily.*

What kind of media do you use?

> *We don't have a TV or computer in the house. We just have one cell phone in the whole house. I don't even know how to use it. I just know how to pick up a call by pressing the green button and turn the cell off my pressing the red button. I cannot even send a message. We are not too much into media. We can't afford too much electricity and that's why we can't use it.* [Many poor women without electricity bend over simple stoves that burn polluting fuels like kerosene, wood or cow dung, about 2.8 billion people worldwide.[41] The indoor black carbon toxins cause more deaths than malaria, TB and HIV combined and contribute up to 20% of global warming. The Global Alliance for Clean Cookstoves is gradually supplying new stoves.]

How do you think life would be different if you grew up in a city like Peshawar?

> *I'd have all the facilities in the world. Life would have been much better. I could easily go out, go to school, have friends and enjoy being with them. I wouldn't worry about doing too much work and listen to my parents complain about food and work. It really annoys me.*

What would you like in a marriage partner? Will your parents arrange your marriage?

I would like my husband to keep me happy, don't scold me, agree with what I say, respect my thoughts, and my mother-in-law to love me and take care of me. I just want both families to get along well and spend a happy life. I want to take some rest and don't want more miseries in the world. I want him to be understanding and understand me, my emotions. That's all!

My marriage is arranged. My engagement was done last year after Ramadan and Eid. I will get married in the next six months. I don't even know how old he is. I just saw him once and that was when his family came to ask for me. I talked to him thrice on the phone but never in person. That's all the interaction I had with him. But my parents did ask me before saying yes and I had no other option than saying yes, so I am happy the way life is. Yousaf's family wants gold and expensive clothes in the marriage. My parents make 60 rupees a day. How can we even think of gold? Let's hope he understands the situation and makes his parents understand and compromise.

Very moved by reading this interview, I asked if Mashal would like to learn to read. She said yes so we decided to start a literacy program with Hassan as teacher. Because of Mashal, we set up the Open Door Literacy Project (ODLP) with Hassan teaching and me fundraising to pay his salary (it helps pay his college tuition), buy Urdu (similar to Hindi) adult literacy workbooks, and rickshaws to bring students from their villages or him to theirs. Photos of the students and Hassan are available on the ODLP website and on YouTube.[42] However, before the first class met, her mother said Mashal couldn't attend. She did allow her younger children to come to Hassan's classes in his parents' home. Hassan explained, "Mashal's mother said she won't be able to join the classes because her fiancé doesn't like her to go out very much. But her sisters would join." I asked how Mashal felt about this: "She said her mother is right and she can't come to class, though she so much wants to come, but her marriage is more important than learning to read and write."

Teacher Hassan (age 18) described the first 100-day course, for two-hours a day, with both girls and boys attending:

First class went awesome. They learned about 15 pages, writing skill. Mashal's sister brought her cousin (male) with them as well. So altogether it's 7 people now. I will do different practices with them so that their writing skills develop. You can't even imagine how good it feels once they learn something. Today, I showed them how to write the date as well. It was great!

After teaching his ninth literacy class of mainly girls, he described his frustration over early marriage interfering with girls' education:

Hira, 14, has a little background of literacy since she went to school in her early age but she was soon taken out of school after she was promised to the boy of local merchant, who is pretty well off. Though Hira's parents had the vision of educating her, they were pretty speechless in front of the family of the boy, as they've already given their word to them. Their engagement has happened and there's no way back now, although Hira's family mourn their decision of engaging their daughter. As for Hira, she is a very bright individual. She has dreams to climb high and achieve but for being a girl in a village like Turnham, this doesn't become a possibility.

I asked Hassan why an engaged girl can't go to school: "Because they consider it a disgrace that their girl will go in public to school to modernize her thoughts. Boys in the streets [who might harass her] and the fear of asking for her rights after studying more can be two other reasons. I feel so bad for her. I could see her willingness to study and do something, yet she can't." When I asked when Hira is to be married, he said it's completely up to her future father-in-law.

Another ODLP student, Sabina, told me on Skype that she didn't stay in the government school in her village (some areas have schools only for boys) because "teachers beat them for small things." She's excited to learn in ODLP so she can serve the nation and do good deeds for the village, a comment repeated by many of the other girls. Her parents are supportive although her mother is illiterate. Hassan says he also teaches the girls manners like saying please and thank you and he brings them snacks. A radio interview is available, conducted when Hassan was teaching his eleventh literacy group.[43] Group 14 was taught by Maheen, a university friend of Hassan's. Maheen posted photos of her formerly illiterate students on the ODLP website,[44] reporting,

These unfortunate kids spend their life helping their family to earn a living, bring water from the well, clean the house and help in cooking. Without education, youth cannot achieve their maximum human, intellectual and personality development necessary for the optimal blossoming of their potential. Thus, ODLP put forward its efforts to enable these kids to read and write. Upon meeting these kids I saw the shine in their eyes reflected the high spirit to learn.

When I suggested that Maheen start a microlending group for village women, she said Islam prevents collecting interest, but the program started in Muslim Bangladesh and there are ways to collect fees rather than interest.[45] Because mothers are more likely to spend their earnings on their children than fathers, most micro-finance loans target female entrepreneurs. Hassan and I tried to create a finance group, but without adequate instruction and support, the first woman to get a loan didn't pass it forward. A teenager in West Bengal, India, also teaches girls and boys who can't afford to go to school, teaching hundreds in his back yard with nine other young teachers when he gets back from attending school.[46]

In contrast to the village girls, Hassan's urban university peers often don't wear the hijab and can be in mixed groups of young men and women. I asked him about his Facebook photos where I saw the city girls without headscarves:

> *The country doesn't follow the traditional religion anymore though they should. But I don't see it bad. The country has revolutionized. It's more or less a personal choice. And it's a refreshing breather for the people. It doesn't represent an extremist view of things but it shows a better happy picture.*

When I read the 70 book survey responses from educated Pakistani girls in Peshawar that Hassan gathered from his acquaintances, none of them mentioned wanting to be housewives. Typically they wanted to help the poor, teach, design clothes, or be in business. I asked Hassan about this: "Deep down, 80% of them would get married and remain housewives or have a very nominal job at the most. This is how the role of women shapes up in this society to take care of their homes, have a wonderful family and are well-settled so their parents feel satisfied." I asked about his two sisters who grew up with him in Peshawar. "One of my sisters finished her MBA and is currently working for a non-profit organization in the Human Resource section. She earns well and her husband is very supportive. (Her husband is my first cousin). My other sister just started university. My father believes in education-before-everything policy. We've faced some hard times but education has always remained our priority, even before food."

Another sign of changing urban attitudes, although it's Pashtun custom to marry cousins in order to keep the bloodline pure, Hassan hoped for a love marriage with a girl he texted with frequently: "Our families will definitely accept. She lives in Karachi and I live in Peshawar but at the end of the day, we love each other. I have developed as an individual and I know how I want my future. She is the most important part of everything. I am very certain and positive." However, their friendship didn't last because she said their parents would never approve of a Punjabi and Pashtun marriage, so why continue when it took time away from her studies? As he gives public workshops, other urban girls "appreciate" Hassan, and contact him on social media and call him on his phone. He got engaged in 2015 to a medical student from another city who will change from Shia to Sunni Islam for him after getting approval from their parents. They married in 2017 and live in a room that's part of his office.

Two female Pakistani teachers told me love marriages are rare and frowned upon, as people ask, "Why would you leave your family group for one person?" The two teachers are not married because they don't have suitable cousins and they're not willing to settle for other suitors, so they live with their parents of course. (In other Muslim countries like Egypt, about a third of young people follow tradition and marry a relative, usually a paternal cousin.[47]) Married cousins tend to be poor, rural, and less educated.

Three out of four Chinese women still live in the countryside, where traditional customs breed prejudice, domestic violence, and a high rate of female suicide, often by swallowing pesticides. "Becky," a Chinese SpeakOut college student, reports that although China has a legacy from Chairman Mao's teaching that "women hold up half the sky," sexism still exists especially in rural areas:

> *Though the government said boy and girl are equal, there still exist a phenomenon that people like boy and don't like girl; such as in rural area, parents don't allow girls to learn more education because they think it's useless for girls who have high education, they make girls to do work and make boys continue to study.*

"Wendy," a Chinese high school student from Beijing said,

> *Girls in rural area seem to live a miserable life. They fight with hunger, with cold weather (their parents don't give them thick clothes, thick clothes are for boys), and with education problems. Usually they could read in schools until Grade 9, but their parents think girls should not get that much education and plus their parents can't afford the education fee when they are Grade 10. But still, some girls from rural get the chance to learn and go to collage.*

She added that rural areas have more problems with domestic violence and abuse: "Almost every woman that lives in a rural area has been beaten by her husband," especially in the east. On the other hand, Chinese SpeakOut students said the countryside is less polluted and life is more relaxed.

The editor of the Chinese magazine *Rural Women*, Xie Lihua experienced bias first hand as the second girl born to her disappointed parents.[48] "The rural thinking is that it's a woman's fault if she is beaten," Xie said. "She's not trying hard enough to please her master," the term for husband. The husband's family has to pay a dowry to buy the new couple household gifts, leading to a belief that a wife is a purchased possession. A saying is that marrying a woman is like getting a horse you can ride and beat at will. Xie's readers are country women given names such as Zhaodi ("looking for a little brother") and Aidi ("loving a little brother"). Xie says, "I encourage them to follow one simple rule: "You are yours. You are not anybody else's." (In India, girls are also given names meaning unwanted, such as Nakusa. A central Indian district organized a renaming ceremony with names the girls selected, like Asmita which means very tough, or the names of goddesses or Bollywood stars.)

Feminization of Poverty

No country can develop if half its human resources are devalued or repressed.
  Madeleine Albright, Former US Secretary of State

Most of the world's poor are women and their children. The main obstacles to alleviating poverty are gender inequality, climate change, destruction of natural resources, and the global recession, according to Melanne Verveer, the US Department of State Ambassador-at-Large for Global Women's Issues.[49] Globalization is widening the gap between the rich and the poor, but on the other hand, it spreads information about gender equality, directs attention to abuses and in some places provides jobs for women in factories and call centers. However, the growth of women in the labor force has stagnated and on average women earn a fourth less than men do globally.[50] Regions that don't utilize female workers lose out in earnings, estimated to cost Asia and the Pacific and MENA over $40 billion each year, according to World Bank estimates.[51]

Women and girls comprise around 70% of the 1.2 billion people who live in abject poverty on less than $1.25 a day in an era when wars in Iraq and Afghanistan cost US taxpayers nearly $5 trillion.[52] In the US, the child poverty rate increased from 18% in 2008 to 22% in 2013, according to the "Kids Count" report by the Casey Foundation in 2015. About 250 million adolescent girls live in poverty: Some describe their lives in a Girl Effect report that assembled 508 girls living in poverty from 14 countries.[53]

Women own only 1% of the wealth and 2% of the global land, according to a women's development NGO called New Course.[54] An Oxfam report titled "An Economy for the 1%" (2016) discovered that the richest 62 people have the same wealth as the poorest half of the global population—only nine of the richest are women (from the US, Germany and Chile). *Forbes'* list of the world's 1,645 billionaires reported only 172 women are on the list.[55] Only 32 of the rich women didn't inherit their fortune and only 31 of the list are under age 40.[56]

The World Bank reported that women perform two-thirds of the world's work hours, but only earn 10% of the income, and own less than 1% of the property. The World Economic Forum estimated it will take 118 years to shrink the gender pay gap. Ranking developed nations, the pay gap is highest in South Korea, Estonia, Japan, Israel, the Netherlands, Turkey, Canada, Finland, Switzerland, Austria, Australia, and the US—in that order.[57] Women in the US still earn only an average of 77 cents for every dollar that a man earns for full-time work. The gap hasn't narrowed for more than a decade. In the US, the wage gap is larger for employed mothers and women of color, despite the passage of the Equal Pay Act in 1963 and the Lily Ledbetter Fair Pay Act, the first bill signed by President Obama in 2009. Female college grads earn 93 cents for every dollar paid to their male peers. The pay gap between women and women who graduate from the best MBA programs is widening rather than narrowing.[58]

A Pew Research poll showed that Millennial women earned about 93% as much as their male peers in 2013, although the pay gap usually increases as women take time off to care for children. After college women and men's salaries are about equal, but women only earn about 55% as much as men at age 45 partly due to the responsibilities of marriage and parenting.[59] The average man with a college degree improves his earnings by 77% from age 25 to 45, but it's only 31% for their female peers. A study found that the bulk of the pay gap is women not getting the same raises and promotions in companies. Part of the problem is women are less likely than men to negotiate for higher pay.

Brazil loses about $17 billion a year as a result of girls' unemployment, according to the Girl Effect NGO, whose mission is "To change the world for girls, so girls can change the world." The Asia Society's survey reported that Asia lost $89 billion a year due to limits on female education and employment, as the majority of women are illiterate in Pakistan, Nepal and Bangladesh.[60] Few women were in high-level corporate positions, even in prosperous Japan and South Korea. In 2016 only 37% of young women were employed globally compared to 54% of young men, with the biggest gap in MENA and South Asia, according to the ILO (International Labour Organization).

Globally, women who don't have a husband are more likely to be poor, including child widows and grandmothers caring for AIDS orphans. At least 245 million women are widows and more than 115 million of them live in poverty, often forced from their homes along with their children after the death of their husbands.[61] "Across the world, widows suffer dreadful discrimination and abuse," said Cherie Blair, president of the British Loomba Foundation for widows: "In too many cases they're pushed to the very margins of society, trapped in poverty and left vulnerable to abuse and exploitation," along with their children.

Women and children are the majority of refugees and internally displaced people who suffer from poverty: Many are raped along the way to Europe and some forced to prostitute themselves to survive.[62] Amnesty International interviewed 40 refugee girls and women in northern Europe; some reported the sexual harassment they experienced and being forced into early marriage to have some safety.[63]

Access to toilets is an index of poverty and discrimination against women who can't relieve themselves in public like men do. In India, for example, poor city dwellers rely on rare and filthy government toilets. Cities provide many more men's toilets than women's toilets although men can urinate on the streets. More than half of Indian households don't have a toilet--cell phones are more common than toilets. In some rural areas women are forbidden from defecating in daylight, as well as bathing in public baths, according to an Australian who lived in India and described her observations.[64] Women have to walk further to find privacy relieve themselves. Taking the train in India, I saw men squatting near the tracks but of course no women. Two lower caste teenage cousins who went to the fields to relieve themselves in the privacy of night were gang raped and hung by their scarves from a mango tree in their small village in Uttar Pradesh in 2014. The mother of the younger girl said she wanted to go to college and get a job, to do more with her life than get married. [65] Perhaps that's one of the reasons she was killed. Poor women also suffer from lack of toilets in the US.[66]

Work

An AWID Forum emphasized that women's economic contribution is too often invisible.[67] Globally women work longer hours, get lower pay, and own less property than men. India loses $100 billion over women's lifetimes due to teen pregnancy that keeps them from paid work and Brazil loses about $17 billion a year as a result of girls' unemployment, according to the Girl Effect NGO whose mission is "To change the world for girls, so girls can change the world." The Asia Society's survey reported that Asia lost $89 billion a year due to limits on female education and employment, as the majority of women are illiterate in Pakistan, Nepal and Bangladesh.[68] Few women were in high-level corporate positions, even in prosperous Japan and South Korea. In 2016 only 37% of young women were employed compared to 54% of young men, with the biggest gap in MENA and South Asia, according to the ILO (International Labour Organization).

Only 64 countries have constitutions providing women with protection against job discrimination and 32 national constitutions don't guarantee gender equality, including the US where the Equal Rights Amendment failed to pass.[69] In 2013, 128 countries had at least one legal difference between the rights of women and men.[70] In some developing countries, over 80% of workers have informal jobs without benefits. In most of these countries, women are more likely to have these insecure jobs. Some women and girls in developing nations spend hours each day just fetching water for their families. The founder of World Pulse women's news source reports women spend 40 billion hours a year getting water. In response programs like Barefoot Solar Engineers teach illiterate women to install solar energy to electrify their villages in India, Afghanistan, and Africa so they can pump water and have lights.[71]

Michelle Bachelet (director of UN Women until she was re-elected president of Chile in 2013) pointed out that the UN's MDG (Millennium Development Goals) Report for 2010 indicated that South Asian and Sub-Saharan Africa women workers suffer most. More than 80% of women workers worked in informal employment, with no benefits or security, and low pay or no pay. An open access forum called Women In and Beyond the Global investigates the exploitation of women's labor.[72] Global industry disproportionately harms women who work in sweatshop factories, are discriminated against in foreign countries and trafficked across borders

Women make up more than 40% of the global workforce, partially because they're having fewer babies, but top jobs are still dominated by men. A UN report found progress towards gender equality is sluggish on all fronts.[73] The rate of women's paid employment--outside of farming--increases slowly, reaching 41% by 2008.[74] But in Southern Asia, Northern Africa and Western Asia, women are only 20% of those employed outside agriculture and in Sub-Saharan Africa they're one-third of paid workers.

Highly paid jobs are still dominated by men: Globally, only one in four senior officials or managers are women.[75] Only three countries have a majority of women managers: Jamaica, Columbia, and St. Lucia. Rae, a Jamaican business owner, observed, "Caribbean men are a lot more relaxed that the women." The Philippines has 48% women managers and the US leads developed countries with 43%, trailed by the UK at 34% and Japan at 11%.[76] During a 2011 speech to APEC (Asia-Pacific Economic Cooperation), Hillary Clinton pointed out that less than 3% of the Fortune Global 500 CEOs are women.[77] More men named John run big companies than there are women CEOs. She also mentioned a World Bank study that suggested discrimination against female workers and managers could increase productivity by 25% to 40%.

Earning a degree doesn't lead to pay equity. Globally, the average women's pay is 20% to 30% less than men's. Brazilian women are the majority of students at every level of education, but they earn 30% less than men, and hold only 56 of the 594 seats in the Congress. Women tend to work in female-dominated jobs such as clerical or childcare, often with lower pay, while responsible for family work as well. Women are less than a third of workers in science and technology jobs in Europe (compared to 46% in the US).[78] Numbers are even lower in developing countries.[79]

In the US, 10 years after graduation from college, women earn 69% of what comparable men earn, controlled for hours and occupation.[80] A documentary called *Code: Debugging the Gender Gap* (2015) explores the lack of women in tech jobs in Silicon Valley.[81] In the US women are 41% of science and engineering Ph.D.s, but are not quite a quarter of STEM (science, technology, engineering, math) workers. More women enter engineering and other STEM fields when they see how they can help alleviate poverty or some other humanistic goal. Young women have higher unemployment rates than young men, especially in the Arab world, and the economic recession hit women harder than men, destroying 13 million jobs for women with no hope for change in the near future.[82] The ILO reported that in 2015 little change had occurred, as women were 25% less likely to be employed than men: "Between 1995 and 2015, the global female labour force participation rate decreased from 52% to 49.5%. The corresponding figures for men are 80% and 76%. Worldwide, the chances for women to participate in the labour market remain almost 27 percentage points lower than those for men."[83]

Brazilian Professor Fulvia Rosenberg explained that childcare is required in order for women to achieve parity in the workforce, and that countries should follow the model of equality provided in the Scandinavian countries. Olga Derguova, the chair of the Moscow City Court, explained, "In Russian society the role of mother and housekeeper, in the absence of many basic services, distracts women from professional development, and they need help finding themselves."[84] More than half of Japanese women quit their jobs after giving birth to their first child because it's very difficult to find childcare. To encourage more women to contribute to the economy, Prime Minister Shinzo Abe promised to create 220,000 more daycare openings by 2020, and a total of 3320,000 by 2022 in order to do away with waiting lists.[85]

Scandinavia equality programs were discussed in Chapter 1. Canada is another model of gender equity providing one year of paid parental leave that can be split between the parents, a monthly child benefit, and childcare allowances. In France, mothers get 112 days of paid maternity leave. Corporations can help fill the gap by providing support for working parents like the MAS Company in Sri Lanka where employees have access to on-site banking, nursing stations, health education and company buses.[86]

The US group MomsRising formed in 2006 to lobby for paid parental leave, flexible work hours, childcare, equal pay, etc. It has over a million members, providing an outlet for over 1,000 bloggers. The two co-founders wrote the *Motherhood Manifesto* book with a DVD.[87] The US is at the bottom of industrial nations in family support although the percent of working mothers jumped from only 20% of mothers with children at home in 1966 to 60% by the late 1990s. Former Labor Secretary Robert Reich points out that this is one of the greatest transformations of the American family, yet the US doesn't provide paid family leave or universal childcare.[88] Despite profession of belief in family values, there's a five-year limit on aid to single women with children, the minimum wage remains low, and technical job training is lacking although the talents of both sexes is needed.

Role of Women in Development

The World Bank reported that global poverty declined rapidly over the past three decades, though more than 1 billion people are still destitute.[89] In 2012 the Bank launched the Gender Data Portal and most of its operations were "gender informed" by 2013.[90] It now publishes the "World Development Report on Gender Equality and Development" and it organized a "Think Equal" social media campaign. The realization that women are the key to development because of their devotion to family over self, particularly in regards to population control, resulted in more international focus on women's issues and support for women from international agencies. The number of NGOs devoted to girls are increasing.[91] Despite the fact that international financial lenders acknowledge the importance of including women in development projects, less than two cents of every international development dollar is spent on adolescent girls and spending on gender issues was less than 2% of the World Bank's 2011 budget. Therefore, it announced in 2016 that the Bank would invest $2.5 billion over five years in education for girls as part of its "Gender Strategy."[92]

World Bank interviews with almost 2,000 women in 19 developing countries revealed that what women need to be powerful and free is earning potential. Thirdly, they selected personality traits such as confidence and involvement in social networks like community women's organizations that provide support.[93] In the bank's 2010 report on girls in developing nations, "Girls Speak: A New Voice in Global Development," girls said they want an education, they want to be healthy, to choose when to marry and have children, and have jobs.[94] The World Bank provides a gender data portal, including UN and Bank data.[95]

The Girl Effect, a movement to raise the status of girls (started by the Nike Foundation with partners including the United Nations Foundation in 2008) provides resources for elevating the status of girls.[96] The Girl Declaration launched in 2013 was an effort to include solutions in the post-2015 development agenda. The Coalition for Adolescent Girls: Poverty Ends with Her includes more than 40 international organizations working to lift girls out of poverty, providing reports on its website.[97] The International Center for Research on Women aims to empower girls and women in developing nations with reports and toolkits.[98] Betsy Teutsch collected "One hundred tools for empowering global women" in her book *100 Under $100* (2015).

Women organize to alleviate their poverty. Women formed the Association of Women's Rights in Development and the United Nations Development Fund for Women (UNIFEM) to advocate for gender equality in the Global South. Women are forming global grassroots groups to reduce urban poverty such as Shack/Slum Dwellers International (SDI), which began in 1996. SDI has members in 34 countries that share information with each other, such as how to form collectives to pool savings and provide loans to each other. They work to improve housing security so children don't have to stay home from school to stand guard to run to their working parents to warn that a demolition squad is in the neighborhood to bulldoze slum dwellings. They lobby to make sure residents are counted in the census and on voter lists. In Delhi's slums, for example, only 55% of children attend primary schools, partly because there's no official record of their births. The Indian government has turned to fingerprint readers and iris eye scanners to establish identity since many citizens don't have birth certificates, and thus can't get a mobile phone connection, open a bank account, or receive government subsidies directly in a bank account.

On the local level, women's groups pool their resources for saving and loaning money and for growing crops. For example, a mothers' group in Aviation, Peru, works together to farm a three-acre plot. An NGO to lift Bangladeshi women out of poverty is called NERDS, the Noakhali Rural Development Society. It provides job skills training, teaches women how to make pottery, garments and carpets, and helps market their products. When husbands understand that their wives can make money, they allow them to work outside the home. Then mothers have money to send their children to school and the cycle of poverty is alleviated (more on women's development organizations in Volume 2 Chapter 4).

A University of California at Berkeley senior, Komal Ahmad was struck by the food waste in the dining halls when homeless people and others went hungry; 15.9 children go to bed hungry in the US, according to the US Department of Agriculture. Ahmad said, "Waste is literally the world's dumbest problem" and that food is a fundamental human right. In 2013 she developed a phone app to connect leftover food to hungry people. In its first two years Feeding Forward distributed around 700,000 tons of excess food in San Francisco.[99] Interested people contacted her from around the world including Nairobi, Bangalore, and Hong Kong. The app shows photos of food, a virtual marketplace, when it needs to be picked up, and how big a vehicle is needed to pick up the food. The site includes nearby volunteers who can transport the food quickly.

Talking with UNICEF staffers in Seoul, South Korea, they described programs that gather youth in leadership conferences to empower them to create sustainable development. Staff said the teens they work with are very creative, with more girls than boys volunteering. For example, the Rainbow Project themes are peace, human rights, cultural diversity, environment, globalization, local culture, economic justice, and global citizenship. Students who participated in the project that began in 2008 reported at the end of the year-long program that they felt more motivated to make change. A young activist UNICEF staffer in charge of youth programs told me when she was in high school she would be in class until 5:30, come home and eat dinner, study until midnight and then get up at 7:00 am. In her family her father was the absolute boss, but she's a feminist who now lives on her own in a different city. She works on telling the story of the Korean "comfort women" sex slaves used by the Japanese troops during World War II. She pointed out the same kind of practice still occurs around US military bases in Korea with Philippina prostitutes. She's not optimistic about finding a feminist husband but likes being in charge of her own life.

Education is the Key

Aid groups emphasize that education is the engine of change to improve girls' lives, but girls are two-thirds of the children who don't go to school.[100] (The previous endnote includes resources about educating girls globally.) The 600 million adolescent girls in developing nations are often a wasted resource because a girl is more likely than her brothers to be uneducated, be exposed to HIV (2.1 million new infections in 2013), and marry young. Education teaches skills needed to earn money, which raises women's status and is more likely than men's earnings to be funneled into their children's education. Each year of secondary school increases a girl's earning power by up to 25% and delays marriage and childbearing.[101] In 2012, 31 million girls weren't attending school, according to the World Bank's World Development Report on Gender Equality and Development. The Bank developed "Education Strategy 2020" and participates in the Global Partnership for Education. In developing countries more than 35 million girls (and 31 million boys) don't attend school and minorities are less likely to be enrolled, especially problematic in Africa and South Asia although enrollment in primary school is increasing.[102]

In a survey by The Global Fund for Women every aid NGO emphasized that education is the engine of change to improve girls' lives. Not just formal education, but teaching girls to be empowered economically, involving their mothers in educational programs, and increasing their self-worth. The girls were well aware of systemic sexism; over two-thirds of the 149 girls surveyed said the most difficult thing about being female is cultural oppression against women. A girl said, "Being a female in my community, I feel really low. I have a low status because they see me as a girl who will soon get married." Girls appreciated learning about their human rights. One girl said, "I learned a lot about my body, society, that we women are capable and have rights."[103] Because of their participation in educational programs they saw themselves as leaders who can make social change. "Even my father asks why I want to make myself better with education. But our generation, the new generation, especially the female, we want to change the thinking," said Liza, a Kabul University student in Afghanistan where two-thirds of the adults are illiterate and 60% of the girls are married before age 16.[104]

Young women are 51% of the world's university students, yet more than 62 million girls don't attend school in developing countries and one in five adolescent girls isn't in school. Minorities and the 215 million child laborers are less likely to be enrolled.[105] Not being in school is related to early marriage and childbirth.[106] Understanding the multiplier effect of girls' education on development progress, Michelle Obama started a campaign called Let Girls Learn whose website features girls' stories and ways to help them, along with a site to exchange information about girls' education.[107] Yuan, a Chinese university student, emphasized the importance of education for women;

> *I feel more and more clarity that it is my karma to fight for women's equality in education in developing countries. I see more and more clearly how the women in my family react to their fate and how their lives are different because their education. I see how a women's education impacts her whole life, her whole family--and that impacts her society. Remember I always said I didn't find my calling? Well, now I feel it's standing in front of me. How amusing that the destiny waits around the corner to see that you are ready.*

Women like Mashal, interviewed above, are most of the world's illiterates, including a third of young African women. About 20% of women are illiterate, which is nearly two-thirds of the 781 million adults who can't read or write. Co-educational schools can be worrisome to parents of girls, especially if far from home, without toilets, and expensive. About one-third of developing countries haven't achieved gender parity in primary education, part of the reason women are only 41% of paid workers globally.[108]

By the end of 2015 fewer than half of the world's countries achieved gender equality in secondary school, with one in five adolescent girls in school partly because of 15 million child brides.[109] Girls' graduation rates are even lower than boys, less than 25% in many African countries.[110] Income often determines who graduates from school, with girls from low-income families much less likely to graduate and more likely to marry early. Every day 39,000 girls under 18 are married and thereby forced to drop out of school.[111] In developing countries, 20,000 girls younger than 18 give birth every day.

Less than one in three girls in Sub-Saharan Africa and fewer than half in South Asia are enrolled in secondary school. Lack of quality education and safety are issues for both boys and girls; a "learning crisis" means many children leave school without basic literacy skills, according to the "No Ceilings" report cited in the previous endnote. Only 22% of nations guarantee the right to free secondary education, with little change since the Beijing Platform for Action in 1995. Various NGOs encourage girls to attend secondary school,[112] perhaps one of the reasons that the 2015 report by the Gates and Clinton Foundations concluded, "There has never been a better time to be born female."

A teacher in Istanbul, Hazal Ozilhan explained during an Internet course on girls' education that while the privileged kids in her neighborhood have tutors and nannies, too many children can't afford both dinner and school. Boys have priority when income is limited and sending girls to college is suspect because, "Girls who go to college lose their dignity and respect" by mingling with boys in a Muslim country. If a girl does make it through college and has connections to get a job, she will probably be paid less.

The education board in Muslim South Sumatra, Indonesia, proposed that high school girls be subject to annual virginity checks of their hymens, although it's not clear how this body part influences scholarship and many virgins don't have intact hymens. It's not just Muslims who focus on virginity: since 2012, prospective unmarried female teachers in Brazil's most populist state of Sao Paulo are required to take virginity tests or have a doctor certify they're virgins.[113]

Another example of unequal access to education is provided by Lydia, age 19, who lives in Athens and goes to university in London. When I asked her to characterize her generation she said, "I don't have hope for my generation because they're used to bribery." For example, parents will pay money to a child's school to prevent disciplinary action for a bully. Many schools are bad, she said, because teachers may not come to school or teach when they're present. Families who can afford it send their children to private schools. Paid tutors are required to help study for the important college entrance exams to get into the free public universities. Once in university, she said her peers can be lazy. Most students don't go to class, just show up for exams. Many of the unemployed youth hang out in cafes, smoking and drinking coffee. They cope with the economic crisis by relying on family support. Whoever has an income shares it with others. (Most young people aren't religious, except for the major celebration of Easter. Also her friends don't discuss politics or social issues like feminism because they don't want to be stereotyped. Like many in her generation, Lydia is interested in volunteering to help unaccompanied minor refugees connect with their families.)

Indira Ghale is one of the few college-educated Dalit (outcaste) Nepali women. Dalit women's literacy rate is only 12%.[114] She answered my questions in response to issues raised in Nepali student responses she collected for me. She explained,

> Not only my dad, but most of the parents in Nepal, have the belief that educating the girl child is like pouring the water into the sand. I was highly encouraged by my mum and she was my energy to go to the university, as she wants my life not to be like her. Her belief is that only the education will make the change of the people's mind and the attitude.

In Nepal, girl children are treated as a second child in the patriarchal society. Because of the traditional culture and values, the people think girls or the women are nothing for them. In Nepal we have the saying that girls do not have to laugh, do not educate the girl, as they have to go with the man one day. According to a UNICEF report, about 5,000-7,000 Nepali girls were sold to India for brothels every year.115 If girls die nothing happens. But local organizations such as SA-HAYATRI NEPAL are working for women's rights.

That attitude is typical of many poor families as education costs money in developing countries: parents may have to pay for textbooks and uniforms even if no tuition fees are charged. In Nepal, some girls are kept out of school in huts when menstruating, fearful they could cause harm to family members or livestock.

School Visits to Unequal Systems

Wanting to see schools for myself, I visited Tanzania (see photos on the book Facebook page) and then Switzerland. The contrast with the open-air windows, four students to a desk, and no textbooks in the classrooms in Tanzania to the well-equipped schools in Zurich was stark. Swiss students have access to many computers, musical instruments, books, gyms and playground equipment. They come to school, not on foot, but by bike or scooter, train or auto.

In Brazil, I was told that teachers are not well paid (around $350 to $750 a month, compared to $1000 for a university professor) and there aren't enough spaces for the students, so some schools are in staggered double or triple sessions, which is common in Latin America.[116] Instructors with bachelor's degrees who work for state secondary schools in a middle-ranking system only earn about $7,000 per shift per year, so many work at least a double shift. Public schools face teacher shortages, absenteeism and lack of teacher preparation, so parents who can afford it send their kids to private schools (around $500 a month).

To send a child to the private school in the costal town of Buzios when I visited costs around $1,500 if paid in advance and includes access to a room full of computers, English instruction, and lunch. About 15% of Brazilians were in private secondary schools in 2014, mostly white students (the World Bank provides this information by country).[117] Therefore only 13% of black and mixed race young people are enrolled in a university despite government Affirmative Action programs.[118] Brazil's schools have risen from the bottom of the rating list in the International Student Assessment in

2000, to eighth from the bottom in 2012.[119] (Chile scored the highest of Latin American countries but all of them were in the bottom third globally.) If students do well on the college entrance exam, they can go to public universities, which are sought after because they are free. A class system is reinforced, as poor families can't afford to send their kids to private schools to get the preparation they need to do well on the entrance exam. In Rio de Janeiro, 19-year-old Joao told me in all of Rio there are only two or three good public high schools and those require doing well on preliminary exams to be admitted. Some politicians argue for quotas to set aside university slots for low-income students and students of color.

I interviewed a former high school physical education teacher named Claudia, who told me the public schools are often divided into a morning and an afternoon session, and some have triple sessions. Kids get breakfast and lunch at school, an incentive for parents to send them. But the kids get the worst quality rice and beans because of government corruption. The schooling, books, and uniforms are free and students only pay for copybooks and pencils. She taught PE in a high school in Rio in a good residential area, but her equipment consisted of one ball and no money to buy more. The other PE teacher at her school told her not to bother coming to school when it rains and she could still collect her salary. But Claudia did go to class, and the unattended students came to her classroom to do exercises, causing other teachers to resent her. Teacher absenteeism is a problem in Brazil, as in other emerging and developing nations. The government developed a new mode for high schools in 2017 doing away with mandatory subjects to prevent dropping out, except for math and Portuguese, so that students can select what to study. The plan included extending school hours. Critics said the reform didn't "address structural issues such as infrastructure of schools, appreciation of education professionals, adequate number of students per class and a new way of teaching" (Daniel Cara of the National Campaign for the Right to Education).[120]

South Korean schools are among the best in the world, so I visited three of them in the interior province and talked with students, including at two girls' schools. The main theme in written responses to SpeakOut questions from South Korean students from the interior province Cheongju is that they don't like the education system. Students are at school until 11 PM every day studying with lots of pressure to do well on the college entrance exam to get into a good university in order to get a good job. Reading this chapter, teenager Kevin in Trinidad was surprised at the long hours; "Is this for real??? If so, please reference this awe-striking statement." Many Korean students mentioned this schoolwork burden to me and many Asian students take extra tutoring classes after school and arrive home in the evening to do homework.[121] The Korean students agreed that their generation excels in technology and is more expressive and outspoken than previous generations. The current political issue they mentioned is Japanese claims to small islands they consider Korean, as resentment against Japan still lingers long after World War II. As I hear from teachers in other countries, a Korean teacher told me girls work harder and do better in school, and since 2009 they've been the majority of university students in Korea.

In Seoul, I visited a private girls' middle school called Duksung where I was able to talk with two English teachers and some of their students. The students weren't in class because of exams, and were loud and boisterous, more outgoing than the Japanese students I observed near Toyko. Japanese teachers in exchange programs told me they are surprised that the Korean students have more freedom to speak up in class. Students talked about the "heat" on them to study for the college entrance exams. The exams are three to four days; students have some choice of subjects drawn from Korean, English, history, math and science. Over 85% of high school students go on to university; families want their children to attend the best ones, but students with connections more easily get into top universities. The focus on passing exams is criticized for diminishing creativity, so the government allows some universities to include other admission criteria such as a record of volunteer work, awards, and personal interviews. Teacher Lim said this creates additional pressure on students to study to ace the interview. The girls said they're at school until 8 PM, except Wednesdays, to take extra courses.

Graduating from a good university is necessary to get a good job in this recession, creating a lot of pressure on students. A university student from Algeria told me that now you need a graduate degree to hope for a job. Some students who don't do well on the three or four day exams resort to suicide. UNICEF staff people, mostly in their 20s, told me that school violence and bullying has increased due to school pressure, what teacher Lim described as "our horrible education system." I asked how the girls in Seoul how they cope with the pressure and they said they talk with their friends and listen to music. College is where students can relax and have fun. High school students get support from homeroom teachers who spend several hours a day working with the students and some schools have counselors to help students.

The girls and teachers in Seoul agreed that girls are better students than boys because they're more mature, but they still create discipline problems. Teachers used to be able to use corporal punishment to ensure order, but now have to find different tactics. Lim sends girls who create discipline problems to older stricter teachers to get them in line. She said she tries to make learning English fun as the girls get bored with grammar, so she includes film and music. The high school curriculum is more advanced than the US, according to Korean teachers I spoke with. A few alternative schools exist and vocational schools are available for students who don't get into university. The government helps fund private schools so teacher Lim said girls from poor families are able to attend her school.

I asked how the girls are different from their parents' generation. A middle-aged teacher said they feel freer to have their own opinions, like about how they are taught, while in her youth she was expected to obey her parents absolutely. She said change is slow, but the girls agreed it's easier to talk with their parents than their grandparents. Of course they mentioned their use of technology, the Internet and phones. One of the teachers said she thinks teens today are more independent and less obedient than her generation, but schools still expect conformity by requiring uniforms and prohibiting nail polish, short skirts, and dyed hair.

Visits to schools in the Punjab in India revealed major disparities for children with money or without it. In a government high school in Anandpur Sahib (see photos), free lunch is provided for grades 1-8. When a guest enters, the students stand and recite a greeting. To respond to a question they stand and speak in very quiet voices that don't carry around the room, with the few girls on one side. The room was dark with only an old blackboard. High school costs 100 rupees a month plus textbook fees, but is free for low castes. When I came back the next day the teacher was missing and the students were standing around or sitting on the desks chatting.

I shared my PowerPoint about global youth with an elite government academy in Anandpur Sahib that gets funding from the military and charges 1 lakh (100,000 rupees) a month for boarding and 475 rupees for day school. The school has 575 students, only 30% female. School begins with a morning assembly with prayer, a positive thought for the day, and new vocabulary words. Boarding students study 1½ hour after school with tutors, then eat dinner and study until 11 PM, similar to South Korean schools. Classrooms are well equipped with smart technology. The Sikh principal and director are former military officers who check on everything, they said, unlike free government schools where some teachers pay to get a job. The principal gets up at 4:30 to prepare for work. They only hire teachers who passed exams with merit and they closely supervise and evaluate teachers.

I also shared my global youth findings with a high school on rural Lanai, a Hawaiian island with only 3,000 inhabitants. Students are a mixture of Pilipino, Hawaiian, Japanese and European backgrounds whose ancestors came to work in Castle and Cooke's pineapple fields. The problem the school faces is a lack of funding for small schools, without enough teachers. The students are reluctant to speak out, similar to other Asian background students I interacted with in guest lectures at the University of Hawaii at Hilo, but they agreed their generation excels in technology. Similar to students in developing countries, they said they have more opportunities than their parents did and don't work as hard. They wished their parents gave them more freedom and didn't hit them. A girl said they're accused of being lazy, but she'll work hard if not pushed by adults. A single mother who grew up on Lanai said that islanders are good at hunting, planting, and using their hands--kinesthetic learners who are not good at school and writing reports. She said she barely got through high school but seemed very bright and articulate. My visits highlight the vast differences in quality education in poor and richer areas.

Solutions

The Global Solutions Lab brings young people aged 15 to 26 together to research solutions to world problems.[122] To improve education they suggest UNICEF's "School-In-A-Box" packed with supplies, lesson plans, and other resources for the over 100 million children not in school. Other ways to expand education are mobile schools in buses, the UN Girls Education Initiative,[123] peer teaching, Wi-Fi for Education to provide Internet access, and the WE CAN website for educators to share resources. Schools can be used as community education hubs in "Education for All for Life" including gardening, water catchment and energy production in SEED (Synergetic Educational Experience and Development). The researchers estimated that $15 billion would fund these programs for a year, including a self-sustaining demonstration school in each region.

Various courses and organizations address global girls' education issues, such as Johns Hopkins University online course syllabus "Educating Girls" and Girl Rising."[124] Professor Fred Mednick, author of a book-in-progress about girls' education in process, collected resources on this topic available online.[125] Girls Learn International was founded in 2003 by Lisa Alter and her two teenage daughters to link secondary schools in the US with schools in developing countries. They aim to encourage girls' access to education. The UN Girls' Education Initiative also promotes gender equality. For example, it provided scholarships for schoolgirls in Nepal and worked in Uganda to formulate policies to keep pregnant girls and child mothers in school. UNESCO partners with companies to fund programs such as teacher training in Senegal.

The key ingredient to keeping girls in developing nations in school is safety: safe access to toilets, proximity to the girl's home, boundary walls, preventing sexual abuse by school staff, as well as parent involvement and well-trained female teachers.[126] Parents are more likely to educate girls for paid work when they see a benefit in earning potential. Many girls don't go to school when menstruating because they are fearful of standing up to answer a question with a stained skirt. A Ugandan company addressed this problem by developing reusable and affordable sanitary pads that help girls stay in school during their menstrual periods.[127] Many girls in developing countries like India aren't informed about periods and or told to keep it secret, made to feel ashamed, harming their confidence. Orthodox Jews teach that women's sphere is the home where she is not to touch people during her menstrual period and must be cleansed in a ritual bath after her period. Women don't count in the *minyan*, the requirement that men pray daily in a group of ten men and Perhaps this is part of the reason Israeli women have not been very active in government, with the exception of Golda Meir, Israel's fourth prime minister.[128]

It helps to prove to parents that education will lead to employment and more earnings. Other incentives to keep girls in school are free textbooks and uniforms, and giving families food or cash payments when they send children to school as in Brazil and Mexico. UNESCO reported that free lunch is an effective motivation to attend school as for some children it may be the only proper meal of the day.

Indian high school principal Colonel Sekar emailed, "If you go back into the 1980s, and analyze the southern Indian state of Tamil Nadu, you will realize that the chief minister of the state introduced the concept of midday meals into all government schools. The scheme, universally decried when it was introduced, is now regarded as a game changer for primary education in the country," because such rewards motivate parents to keep girls and boys in school. Like free lunch programs, offering something as simple as a bicycle enabled girls in Bihar, the least literate state, to travel to school safely and without cost. The first year the bicycles were distributed for free, 170,0000 more girls were in school. (Bicycles also give mobility to young women in Afghanistan--it has an Afghan national Women's Cycling Team, and bikes give more range of movement to health workers in Zambia. Pakistan's government is teaching women to ride motorcycles, traditionally only driven by men.)

Progress

Increasing participation of educated women in the workforce can mitigate some of the economic problems of an aging population, indicating that women are "a key driver of success for many countries" according to the US National Intelligence Council's (NIC) examination of global trends leading to 2030. A megatrend is rapid aging of the world's population, especially in Europe, Japan, South Korea and Taiwan.[129] This demographic trend strains economies with a large retired population. The NIC report predicts that the fastest growth in closing the gender gap in the workforce will be in East Asia and Latin America and stated that better governance occurs as women assume political leadership. Making the case for gender equity, a 2015 report stated that $28 trillion could be added to global annual GDP in 2025 if gender parity is achieved with women's workforce participation equal to men's, matching the progress of the best country in their regions such as Chile, Spain, and Singapore.[130] However, the 2015 Global Gender Gap report produced by the World Economic Forum found that the gap in health, education, economic opportunity, and politics closed by only 4% in the past 10 years. The economic gap closed by only 3%. Progress has occurred in that almost a quarter of a billion more women are in the workforce than a decade ago and in many countries more women are graduating from university than men.

Amal, an English teacher in a government school near Cairo, Egypt, told me there are as many girls as boys in her language school because in urban areas parents value girls' education. They realize young women may need to support themselves as a marriage could end in divorce. However, she said President Hosni Mubarak and then the Islamist President Morsi didn't invest in education because illiterate people are easier to control. Some of the money meant for education is siphoned off in corruption, without improvement after the 2011 revolution so schools are short-changed.

In Amal's case, as with other educated girls and women such as Pakistani activist Malaya Yousafzai, her father values education for girls. Amal's father is a self-made man who became a teacher and respected school administrator. He helped support his siblings and encouraged his children to be well-educated. He wanted freedom for his daughters as well as his sons, but he was active in selecting her husband. A colleague at her school had a prospective husband in mind for her after she broke an engagement in a love match with a very intelligent professional who turned out to be too controlling and jealous. Amal demurred, so her friend called back a month later and said she wanted to talk to her father and then to her mother who convinced her to invite the suitor over to their home. Her father interviewed the prospective groom's employer and others to make sure his character was worthy of his daughter and he proved to be an excellent husband. Amal encourages her daughters to think for themselves. She tells them, "This is what I think is right, but it's up to you to decide, knowing you are responsible for the consequences." She respects her 15-year-old daughter as a friend, confidant and adviser. Education gives women like Amal more self-esteem and freedom, referred to as agency. The longer a girl stays in school, the less likely she is to get pregnant; therefore the highest birth rates are among poor families in sub-Saharan Africa and South Asia.

Health Issues

Health care for the poor is nonexistent or inadequate, as described in Catherine Boo's *Behind the Beautiful Forevers* (2012) about Mumbai slum dwellers. In their local hospital staff steal the medicines and don't care for patients. Poor girls and women are much more likely to die than males, especially in early childhood and reproductive years.[131] Girls are the victims of genital cutting (more than 125 million),[132] early marriage (1 in 7 girls in developing countries is married before age 15), early motherhood, plus sexual violence and human trafficking that leads to AIDS.[133] The Woman Stats research team compiles global statistics about violence against women.[134] Jimmy Carter stated in his book *A Call to Action: Women, Religion, Violence and Power* (2014) that 160 million girls are missing because they were aborted or killed at birth by parents who wanted boys (compared to 35 million killed in World War II). He says that sexism is the world's most serious unaddressed problem and offers 23 solutions in his book.

A woman who lives in a slum in the capital city of Bangladesh reports:

> *We spend lots of time bringing water from a hand pump about 20 minutes'*
> *walk away.135 You have to queue for at least two hours to get the water. I earn*
> *between 500-1000 taka per month and I have to spend about 100 taka on water.*
> *At least we are surviving. Our biggest fear is that we get evicted from the slum by*
> *the government. Many people get very ill here and I think it all stems from the*
> *open latrines. Smell the stench, it's disgusting. We get fevers, coughs and terrible*
> *diarrhea and there are no healthcare facilities that we can use.*

One of eight humans doesn't have access to clean water.[136] This problem kills more people than all forms of violence. By 2030, the need for water will exceed the supply by 40%. Project Access Water brings six young women from six continents to visit rivers and discuss how to protect fresh water. Led by Ann Bancroft, the women first visited the Ganges in 2015, shown in photos in the previous endnote.

Melinda Gates, co-head of the Gates Foundation, observed, "Policymakers in both rich and poor countries have treated women and children, quite frankly, as if they matter less than men. They have squandered opportunities to improve the health of women and babies."[137] She also pointed out that women suffer from "time poverty" globally, working longer hours than men especially in families with children at home. Girls often do more family work than boys, leaving them less time and energy for education. To save the 350,000 mothers and 3 million newborns who die every year, the Gates Foundation invested $1.5 billion through 2014. Their goal was to call attention to the problem, as their foundation did previously with malaria and AIDS. Ms. Gates praised UN Secretary-General Ban Ki-moon for designing a global action plan for maternal and child health to help achieve UN Millennium Development Goals 3 (empowerment) and 5 (lower maternal mortality), which remain the farthest from achieving the goal.

The Secretary General commented, "We are seeing a global movement for an end to the silent scandal of women dying in childbirth." In 2008 he also launched a campaign to end violence against women. WHO developed a Global Strategy for Women's, Children's and Adolescents' Health to accompany the UN's Sustainable Development Goals in 2015.[138] However, Ban Ki-moon reported in his ten goals for UN youth policy as he left office in 2016 that every resolution "stalls" at the issue of sexual and reproductive rights: "It's high time to take a stance," he advocated.[139]

Child Marriage and Pregnancy

Child marriage is one of the most harmful traditional practices for girls, undermining their chances for education and health, illustrated in a short video "Too Young to Wed"[140] and opposed by the global coalition of hundreds of organizations called "Girls Not Brides." Globally, a girl marries before she is 15 every seven seconds, according to Save the Children. Many don't realized it's a problem in the US, especially in states like Idaho and Kentucky, often used to prevent legal action about rape of a minor or in religious fundamentalist families.[141] When a Girl Scout in New Hampshire heard that a 13-year-old girl was allowed to marry in her state, she found a legislator to sponsor a bill to raise the age of marriage from 13 to 18. Republican legislators made fun of Cassandra Levesque's "Girl Scout project" and killed the bill.

A group of world leaders called The Elders founded an organization in 2011 to lobby for girls' rights.[142] Elders included Nelson Mandela, Kofi Annan, Mary Robinson and Gro Harlem Brundtland. They successfully lobbied for child marriage to be included in the UN's Sustainable Development Goals. More than 140 million girls will become child brides from 2011 to 2020, reported the UN Population Fund. Malawi has one of the highest rates of early marriage in Africa; in response a law was passed in 2015 to raise the minimum age without parental consent to 18. But enforcement is difficult in rural areas, so a community theater group portrays the hazards of early marriage to educate and raise awareness about its harmful effects and to ask fathers to sign a pledge that they'll keep girls in school.[143] Volunteers are also trained to advocate for girls who don't want to marry.

The rate of early marriage (under age 18) has declined but still remains at 26%, higher for girls from low-income families.[144] Nearly one in every four adolescent girls aged 15 to 19 in the developing world (excluding China) is married, compared to only 5% of the boys.[145] Early marriage is associated with teen pregnancy and a more powerful older husband, which is not conducive to going to school. In the developing world, nearly 40% of girls marry before age 18 and almost one-quarter of young women give birth before age 18.[146] Often the girl has little choice. Nada, a very articulate 11-year-old girl in Yemen, ran away from her parents' as they tried to marry her off for a hefty sum, saying on an online video that child marriages "have killed our dreams. This is criminal, simply criminal."[147] She didn't want to end up like her maternal aunt, married at 13, beaten by her husband with chains, who committed suicide a year after her wedding. Nada's uncle protected her and reported the abuse to authorities, an example of a male ally. The film *Difret* (2015) is based on the true story of an Ethiopian girl who was kidnapped to be a child bride and the lawyer who defended her.[148] The autobiography *I Am Nujood, Age 10 and Divorced* (2010) tells the story of a Yemeni girl who managed to escape her marriage. She wrote, "I'm a simple village girl who has always obeyed the orders of my father and brothers. Since forever, I have learned to say yes to everything. Today I have decided to say no."

Young women campaign against the early marriage of over 60 million girls married before their 18th birthday, as in Nepal's Radio Udayapur run by girls and women, Collectif Vivre Ma Vie in Burkina Faso, Gaunubia Hora in Egypt, and Salud Mujeres in Ecuador. All of these groups received grants from the Young Feminist Fund that encourages collective approaches to organizing for girls.[149] International groups educating against early marriage include Girls Not Brides, Girls Learn International, The UN

Foundation's Girl Up, the International Women's Health Coalition, CARE, Plan International's Because I am a Girl, and the International Center for Research on Women.[150]

Hadqai Bashir, age 14, campaigns in Pakistan's Swat Valley to stop child marriage although it's the norm. One of her classmates was married when she was in sixth grade and Hadqai saw how she suffered. She said, " It's a patriarchal society so I try to spread awareness, especially to parents."[151] With her parents' approval she goes after school to talk with girls and families in their neighborhoods. A BBC interview with her and a 16-year old named Shabana revealed that her husband's family beat her often, including her husband hitting her with a pipe. When she tried to go back to her parents' home, they returned her. But when her seven-year-old sister was to be married, Hadaqi talked them out of it. The mother said she won't repeat the mistake she made with her older daughter. Awareness is growing that early marriage inhibits girls' potential.

Around 15 million adolescent girls ages 15 to 19 give birth every year.[153] Maternal health is one of the widest gaps between rich and poor countries. Teen pregnancy and complications during childbirth are the second highest cause of death for girls aged 15 to 19.[154] The highest proportion of teen births are in Latin American and Sub-Saharan Africa. In Africa, childbirth is the leading killer of teen girls. Poor girls and women are much more likely to die than males, especially in early childhood and reproductive years due to early marriage. [155] Young mothers also have higher infant mortality rates than older mothers. Maternal health is one of the widest gaps between rich and poor countries.

One woman dies in childbirth every minute due to inadequate health care and the low status of women harms their children's well-being as well. In 2013, almost 300,000 women died due to their pregnancy or childbirth, with no improvement two years later.[156] Nigeria and India account for over one-third of the maternal deaths. The leading causes of maternal mortality in developing nations are hypertension and hemorrhage.[157] Nearly 800 girls and women die each day from pregnancy and childbirth-related complications partly because only half of pregnant women in developing regions get the minimum of four prenatal medical check-ups and a quarter of their babies are delivered without medical care.[158]

In India, up to 60% of the population doesn't have adequate health care and half of babies born in rural areas are permanently stunted physically and intellectually due to lack of proper nutrition.[159] About half of pregnant women in developing countries are anemic. Lack of food is the main cause of child death, killing 3.1 million children a year and stunting from malnutrition harms one in four children.[160] Often men eat meals first and women and children eat what's left over.[161] India has the highest rate of child malnutrition in the world—48%, according to UNICEF. The UN's Sustainable Development Goals passed in 2015, for the first time committed to ending malnutrition, not just cutting it in half, although an estimated 800 million people aren't adequately nourished.[162] Since women are the primary food producers, more resources for farmers would help nourish more people. This is especially needed when climate change makes farming and accessing water much more difficult. In response to these difficulties, men leave their families to look for work in cities or try to migrate to the North. Some villages in Africa lack young men because of this migration.

The leading causes of maternal mortality in developing nations are hypertension and hemorrhage.[163] Nearly 800 girls and women die each day from pregnancy and childbirth-related complications. The leading cause of death of teenage girls in developing countries is complications of pregnancy and childbirth. One woman dies in childbirth every minute due to lack of adequate health care and the low status of women harms children's well-being for the long-term—around 160 million children are stunted.

Only one in three rural women in developing regions receives the recommended care during pregnancy and the use of contraceptives is very low in Sub-Saharan African and Oceania. Often without adequate medical care, young mothers develop major health problems like fistula (permanent loss of control of feces and/or urine). About two million women suffer from fistula incontinence. For the few with access to doctors, the damage can be surgically repaired as seen in the documentary *A Walk to Beautiful* about young Ethiopian mothers with fistula. Since educated women have fewer and healthier children, logic indicates the importance of educating girls to alleviate the burden of global poverty when we're headed towards 10 billion people by the end of the century.

Even in the wealthy USA, maternal death rates doubled between 1990 and 2008, according to UN data, even though many other countries reduced their national mortality rates. Author Jennifer Margulies blames the increase of C-sections to almost one-third of births in the US as one of the contributors to maternal health problems.[164] Lack of access to health care is also problematic in the US (especially for the 9% without health insurance in 2017[165]), although Republicans tried to cut funding for Medicare for children, the elderly, and the disabled in their efforts to repeal "Obama Care."

Lack of Contraception

Conservative countries and the Holy See often block commitment to sexual rights in policies such as those formulated by the International Conference on Population and Development. Feminists warned of the growing strength of fundamentalists--Christian, Hindu, Jewish, as well as Muslim--since the 1990s. To provide a historical perspective, when Margaret Sanger started fighting for US women's rights to information about birth control in 1912, the Comstock laws made it illegal to mail any information about birth control. Even medical textbooks couldn't mention "erotic" topics. The effect of the Catholic Church's disapproval of birth control on poor families is explored in a documentary *Sex and the Holy City* (2004). European countries, Russia, Turkey and Japan are worried about low birth rates, leading to campaigns to have more babies and efforts to restrict contraceptives in Turkey. Few Russian women, just 14%, take birth control pills and 20% use an IUD, but others use unreliable methods such as withdrawal, leading to the high abortion rate of 50 abortions per 1,000 women of childbearing age.[166]

Without access to condoms, most of the new HIV infections (6,000 young people every day) are girls in Sub-Saharan Africa and Asia. Female mortality is increasing in sub-Saharan Africa where HIV/AIDs is the main cause of death for women ages 15-44, followed by childbirth. Every minute a young woman is infected with HIV; WHO reported AIDS is the second cause of death for adolescents. A study of a drug called Truvada that reduces the risk of HIV by as much as 94% if taken regularly, found that young African unmarried women were the ones most at risk for infection but the least likely to use the medicine.[167] They were deterred by the stigma associated with AIDS and some Truvada side effects such as nausea or dizziness that usually clear up over time.

In Pakistan, Muslim clerics preach that contraception is a sin and could lead to immorality: "if a woman's fear is removed," says mufti (Islamic scholar) Mohammad Zakariashe, "they will stray into bad behavior and offend God."[168] When asked about alleviating poverty by having fewer children, he replied, "Every society has its own value system. You should not judge us by yours. Children in the West lead a luxurious life. Earth is their heaven. Our children should not be compared with them. Muslims don't pay much heed to the mundane pleasures of this world. Our reward will come in the next life." As a consequence, the Pakistani government reports that 70% of married women don't use contraceptives. With many children (the average is four births per mother), the World Bank found that 60% of Pakistanis live on less than $2 a day.

As an example, Hassan reports from rural Pakistan where he teaches in our Open Doors Literacy Project; "One of the workers in the village, his wife died today giving birth to his 15th child. They already had 14 kids but the man wouldn't stop despite of the fact that she was a patient of sugar [diabetes] and high blood pressure. This is a murder. I didn't even look at his face while I was at the funeral. I hate him so much now." When I Skyped with one of his classes (ages 10 to 22) I asked if they had any choice in a future husband. They said no, their parents have their best interests at heart and it would be of no use to express a preference. Hassan added, "They can't think of disobeying their parents just like usual villagers." I asked if they would like to learn about fertile times of the month and they said no, they were too young. One of the ODLP students, the mother of nine children, age 36, told me they don't use birth control because babies are a result of the passion of the parents and up to Allah. Her tenth child was stillborn.

Around 215 million married women in the global South lack access to contraception like Hassan's friend, so hundreds of thousands die in childbirth or from unsafe abortions. The population explosion is the foundation for poverty with 80 million babies born each year and 215 million women without birth control, reported UNFPA. A new self-injectable Depo-Provera contraceptive that lasts for three months was under trial in African countries in 2016. Since the woman can inject it herself, it can lead to major changes, although the disposable device costs a $1. The Philippines is a leader in overcoming the fierce opposition of the Catholic hierarchy to a family planning policy. The Church portrays it as a US plot to reduce the population and create a market for contraceptive companies, but legislation passed in 2012 established free or low-cost contraceptives for poor couples, sex education for students from sixth grade on up, and maternal care facilities in state hospitals.

Young activists fault the lack of policies about sexuality and reproductive health because the topic is considered too controversial or in opposition to local traditions. It is "unacceptable to use culture as a justification to deny young people our rights, specifically our sexual and reproductive health and rights," stated the Arab Youth Network's Dareen Abu Lail.[169] African activists fault the ABC approach to preventing AIDs common in many African countries: "abstain, be faithful, condomize" as unrealistic. A South African activist organization called Treatment Action Campaign pointed out the only way many girls can afford to buy textbooks is to have sex with a sugar daddy so abstention is too simplistic. Some young people don't want to abstain, and asking to use a condom is "frequently interpreted as an insult." [170] TAC also works for HIV+ people's access to antiretroviral medication; the majority of them are poor black women.

Unsafe Abortions

WHO reports that 47,000 women die from unsafe abortions each year.[171] Approximately 47,000 women died from unsafe abortions in 2008, down to 22,000 women in 2016, according to estimates from WHO, with the highest rates in Africa and South-Central Asia.[172] Ironically, abortion rates are higher in countries where it's illegal; almost half of all abortions are unsafe.

In the US, extremist Christian fundamentalist Republicans systematically expand state power to limit access to abortion and birth control in states like North and South Dakota, Indiana, Oklahoma, Mississippi, North Carolina, Alabama, Virginia, Utah, Louisiana, and Texas.[173] They try to eliminate funding for Planned Parenthood clinics and Virginia has a law on the books outlawing oral and anal sex between consenting adults. Conservative young women organized to oppose sexual and reproductive rights at the 58th session of the UN Commission on the Status of Women in 2014.[174] Fundamentalists typically recruit young people with expert Internet campaigns, generally a main form of youth activism. However, boys are much more likely to have access to the Internet than girls in developing countries.

President Donald Trump resurrected and expanded President Ronald Reagan's 1984 gag rule, called the Mexico City Policy, which prohibits US funding for charities that provide information about abortion. Trump expanded the gag from family planning to all US global health assistance, such as to prevent AIDs or provide maternal and child health care. In response, the Netherlands organized an international fund for family planning and safe abortions, quickly joined by Nordic countries, Belgium, Canada, Cape Verde, and Luxembourg.

The Catholic Church views abortion, contraception and homosexuality as mortal sins.[175] When the conservative government in Spain moved to restrict abortion access in 2014, a feminist artist named Yolanda Dominguez started a protest called Register, where women line up at Chamber of Commerce offices to register "ownership" of their bodies, as shown in a video on her website.[176]

Abortion is used to eliminate female fetuses in countries like China and India that value a boy as social security for the parents' old age. About 3.9 million females under 60 are "missing" each year in developing nations due to selective abortion in favor of males, lack of medical care and violence.[177] The World Bank estimates about 1.4 million girls are missing due to "gendercide" abortions, mostly in China and India.[178] By the year 2020, China will have 30 to 40 million more males than females under age 20 although naturally around 105 boys would be born for every 100 girl babies. The ratio in China is 926 girls per 1000 boys. Millions more girls who aren't aborted don't get as good an education and health care as their brothers receive.[179] This bias is found in wealthy areas as well as poor ones, such as South Korea, Taiwan, and the nations of the Caucasus such as Armenia. Sons are needed for religious rituals for their ancestors, to inherit land, and to care for their elderly parents as daughters go to live with husbands' families.

In India, where millions of baby girls are aborted every year, the result is 914 girls per 1,000 boys. It's been illegal to reveal the gender of a fetus since 1994, but parents with money use ultrasound technology to learn the gender of the fetus and then abort a girl. Some without money for this technology purposefully neglect the baby girl once she is born until she dies. They resort to letting the girl baby's umbilical cord get infected or abandon he, leading the Indian government set up safe drop spots for these babies as you can see in photos.[180]

To provide safe abortions, young women organize hotlines to provide women with information, like the Salud Mujeres phone line in Ecuador. In Chile, where abortion is illegal, a feminist hotline called Safe Abortion Information Hotline provides information about how to use illegal Misoprostol medication in pill form to induce abortion. A similar young feminist hotline in Quito is called Salud Mujeres Ecuador, which struggles with government harassment. Youth Coalition is a global organization of young people dedicated to youths' sexual and reproductive rights, referred to as SRHR—sexual and reproductive health and rights.[181] Realizing Sexual and Reproductive Justice (RESURJ) is a "global alliance of younger feminist activists who work across generations to secure young people's and women's sexual and reproductive rights and health."[182] Youth Coalition is" committed to promoting adolescent and youth sexual and reproductive rights."[183] Sister Song: Women of Color Reproductive Justice Collective is a US activist group, formed in 1997. They remind each other to be like geese that share the work flying in V formation. NGOs such as CHANGE address these health issues globally.[184]

The majority of Polish women went on strike in 2016 after the Polish legislature tried to outlaw most abortion, with penalties of up to five years in jail for the woman. In response, over 60% of women surprised the government by going on strike on October 3, boycotting work and school, wearing black and carrying black flags in demonstrations in large cities. They chanted "Stop the fanatics!;" "My body, my choice;" "My Uterus, My Opinion;" and "Women Just Want to Have FUN-damental Rights." One of the protesters on the street explained, "You cannot change the world from your couch, you know." A Millennial protester observed, "In previous anti-government protests, it was our parents" generation on the streets. But with this, they have managed to mobilize the young, and we are very angry."[185] Many men joined in the protests and solidarity protests were held in other European countries and the US, as seen in a video.[186] The Polish protesters were inspired by Iceland's "Women's Day Off" on 1975 when about 90% of women went on strike to protest economic inequality.

Polish Foreign Minister Witold Waszczykowski commented derisively, "Let them have their fun." He added, "There is no such problem as a threat to women's rights." However, the ruling Law and Justice Party backed down three days later when Jaroslaw Gowin, Minister of Science and Higher Education, said the Black Protests "caused us to think and taught us humility."[187] The government was "scared by all the women who hit the streets in protest," said former female Prime Minister Ewa Kopacz. However, the anti-abortion group "Voice for Life" petitioned for stricter laws, including outlawing emergency contraception and contraceptives that prevent the implantation of a fertilized egg. Their proposed legislation included promoting pro-life curriculum in schools. Pro-choice groups organized on Facebook and broadened their campaign to reducing the influence of the Catholic Church in government and education and fight violence against women.

Genital Mutilation

Each year an estimated two million girls undergo some form of genital mutilation (FGM) wherein parts of their labia or clitoris are removed to make the girl "clean." Female genital cutting is practiced in 28 African countries and parts of the Middle East and Asia. At least 200 million girls and women have suffered from cutting, according to UNICEF, the majority of them before age five.[188] FGM remains high in areas where it's widely practiced.[189] Half of them live in Egypt (where FGM has dropped to 70%), Ethiopia and Indonesia. Indonesian Muslims believe that an uncut girl risks "developing mental problems and disabilities," that FGM prevents them from becoming promiscuous, and some even believe Allah won't accept their prayers.[190] Opponents say it is not advocated in the Quran. A woman in Jakarta explained she supports the practice because, "If we don't, then we can't be whole as women and we can't marry."[191] In Somalia and Guinea almost all females have been cut, as described in books by Somali women victims of FGM.[192] The UN predicts that the number will increase as population increases if present trends continue. In Egypt a father of two daughters tried to minimize the practice by telling me it's usually just the tip of the clitoris and happens before the girl is six.

Sohair al-Bataa, a 13-year old Egyptian girl, died in Mansoura after being circumcised in 2014. Although it was outlawed in 2008, her uncle explained that it's necessary because girls are "full of lust,"[193] a common belief in Islamic countries like Saudi Arabia and Pakistan. Her grandfather said, "It is God's will." Her brave friend Amira told reporters FGM is wrong and dangerous for girls, but a neighbor woman said the use of doctors makes it a modern practice. The doctor paid the father not to pursue a case, but it was the first FGM case to be taken to court in Egypt with both the doctor and father on trial, pressured by the international organization Equality Now and local rights groups. Dr. Fadl and her father were acquitted but in 2015 an appeals court gave the doctor two years in prison for manslaughter and the father got a suspended sentence.

An Ethiopian teenager who was cut when she was 10, Meaza Garedu now campaigns against FGM, telling parents in her village how traumatic it was and how it made her not trust her parents.[194] A Kenyan woman who was painfully circumcised at age 13 works with other women to develop alternative coming-of-age rituals, such as shaving the girls' head, pouring milk on her thighs, and presenting her with a woman's headdress and bracelet.[195] In Africa, 18 countries passed laws criminalizing FGM, according to the Center for Reproductive Rights. Rappers are uniting to protest against FGM, as in Senegal, shown in an *Al Jazeera* documentary.[196] *A New Agenda for Global Health* focuses on improving the health of adolescent girls.[197]

In terms of specific goals to keep youth women healthy, the authors of the best-seller *Half the Sky* suggest starting with three specific grassroots campaigns:

1. A $10 billion effort over five years to educate girls.

2. A global drive to iodize salt in poor countries, to prevent tens of millions of children from losing approximately ten I.Q. points each as a result of iodine deficiency while their brains are still being formed in utero.

3. A twelve-year, $1.6 billion project to eradicate obstetric fistula (urine and or feces leak uncontrollably due to girls giving birth too young), while laying the groundwork for a major international assault on maternal

mortality. They suggest charities and organizations to support women.[198]

Violence Against Women

People feel that a girl is meant to be used—either as a doormat, a maid, a birth-giving machine or as a source of physical pleasure. Something CONCRETE seriously needs to be done to change the current scenario because now a girl does not feel safe even in her own house, let alone the streets.[199]
Anonymous, 16, f, India

Professor Deniz Kandiyoti blames the increase of violence against women on the backlash against increasing freedom for women in what she calls "masculinist restoration." Young male unemployment leads to a "crisis of masculinity."[200] The director of WHO said, "Violence against women is a global health problem of epidemic proportions." Violence is a greater threat to women aged 15 to 44 than cancer, traffic accidents, malaria and war combined.[201] Violence is a major cause of death and disability for women aged 15 to 44, higher than deaths caused by motor vehicle accidents, cancer, and malaria. One in four women will experience domestic violence, as shown in a video about Thai violence titled *Men Are Human, Women Are Buffalo* (2008).[202] The UN reports that each year 60 million girls are sexually assaulted on their way to school, in response the UN organized a campaign called "UNITE to End Violence Against Women." In the US, 1,615 women were murdered by men in 2013 and on average 288,820 women are raped or sexually assaulted each year.

The authors of *Half the Sky* pointed out that more girls were killed in the last 50 years than all the men killed in 20th century wars (co-author Sheryl WuDunn discusses the status of women on TED[203]). For the first time in history, more men are alive than women. A short video called the "World Hates Women" went viral in 2014, giving examples of the suffering women endure around the world.[204] The best indicator of whether a country is violent internally or externally is not the degree of democracy, but the degree of violence against girls and women, as described in *Sex and World Peace* (2012) by four authors including Valerie Hudson.

Since the Beijing Conference in 1995 awareness about violence shifted from being a private matter to public policy. The number of countries recognizing that domestic violence is a crime has risen from almost none to 76 countries in the past 37 years, but still more than 700 million women are hurt by their male partners.[205] In 33 low- and middle-income countries, almost a third of women report they can't refuse sex. Domestic violence is problematic in developed nations as well: In 2014, 13 million women experienced physical violence in the European Union.[206]

Gloria Steinem explained that and that violence in the home is the single most powerful influence on national violence and also the original violence, while controlling reproduction is central to patriarchy.[207] Femicide is the most common crime in the world. She quoted former Swedish Prime Minister Olaf Palme who said that gender roles are the deepest cause of violence so it's the duty of every government to work for equality. He appointed Sweden's first equality committee in 1972. Conversely, the root of democracy is democracy inside the home. Steinem is hopeful that the world is reaching a turning point where the paradigm is the circle, not the pyramid, and where linking is more valued than ranking and horizontalism rather than vertical hierarchy.

Author Chris Hedges notes that sexism and racism exist independently of capitalism and that male violence is the main force used to keep women oppressed.[208] Violence includes pornography and prostitution, but Hedges maintains that most men, including most men on the left, refuse to acknowledge or fight this oppression. He believes, "The object of corporate culture, neoliberal ideology, imperialism and colonialism is to strip people of their human attributes" and reverence for life, especially respect for girls and women. Hedges concludes that a resistance movement must recover the "capacity for awe and reverence for the sources that sustain life," including girls and women. Tens of thousands of women and thousands of their male supporters marched in Madrid in November 2015 to demand the end of violence against women, one of the largest marches in Spain.

Feminist advocates for human rights are targeted, leading the UN to pass an International Resolution on WHRDs (women human rights defenders) in 2013.[209] Women's rights groups reported an increase in fundamentalist attacks, according to an AWID study.[210] For example, during a Women's History Month celebration, the Bishkek Feminist Collective in Kyrgyzstan was attacked by a group of men who destroyed their displays yelling, "Why do you need rights?" Editors of an Afghan feminist magazine, *Ruidad Weekly*, were told "shut this or we will shut you." Women who stand up to violence in Mexico, Myanmar, Sudan, Iraq and Ukraine are featured in an article from Security.org.[211] Girls and women suffer slavery, sex trafficking, street harassment, honor killings and punitive rapes to punish their families, domestic violence, rape, and forced abortions.

Slavery still occurs today with trafficked women and children kidnapped or sold by poor families to be used in prostitution or domestic labor without pay.[212] The UN's

International Labour Organization (ILO), believes that between 700,000 and two million women and children are trafficked across international borders every year, feeding an industry with profits estimated at somewhere between $12 billion and $17 billion per year.[213] About $32 billion is earned each year in human trafficking with over 3,000 people sold and forced into slavery every day, including 5.5 million children annually.[214] Worldwide, including in the US, girls are sometimes sold into slavery as servants or prostitutes without pay. A similar practice in Haiti refers to the child servants as *restaveks*. Over 12 million people are in forced labor, according to the ILO, the including about 1 million children in Asia.

UNICEF reported that the 1.2 million known annual cases of child trafficking a year are a gross understatement.[215] In Africa and the Middle East more than two-thirds of the victims of trafficking were children, often sold as sexual slaves. The documentary *International Boulevard* (2013) by Rebecca Dharmapalan shows sex trafficking in the San Francisco Bay Area.[216] Teen activist Dharmapalan raises awareness about the problem, as in her documentary and a TED talk.[217] Authorities reported an epidemic of sex trafficking of children in the US in 2015; despite the epidemic, only 600 children were rescued the previous year.

Most of the sex slaves are girls. The total number of prostituted children could be as high as 10 million, according to the *Lancet* medical journal.[218] Trafficking of girls for the sex industry is the fastest growing criminal business in the world.[219] At least 20.9 million adults and children are bought and sold into sex work or forced and bonded labor, including two million children in the sex trade. Most of the prostitutes are girls and women. In India thousands of girls are kidnapped and trafficked into brothels—Asia alone has about one million children working in the sex trade and kept captive as slaves.[220]

Lack of work and poverty often leads to this cruelty.[221] A Pakistani village mother of nine, one of our Open Door Literacy Project students, told me on Skype that some parents sell their daughters when they can't afford to care for them, as is common in Nepal. "Trafficking of girls from my country to India bothers me," said Megharaj, 19, m, Nepal. Some of the Nepali girls are sold to older South Korean men as brides and UNICEF reports that thousands of girls are sold each year to Indian brothels. In northwest Thailand parents may sell their 12-year-old daughters into sexual slavery so they can pay for their sons' education.

Women form organizations like Girls Educational and Mentoring Services (GEMS), headquartered in New York, and Freedom Connect to prevent trafficking of young women.[222] GEMS was founded by 23-year-old Rachel Lloyd in 1998, when she did missionary work with women who wanted to leave prostitution. *Remote Sensing* (2001) documents women sex workers who travel across the globe. A young Cambodian woman, who said she was sold into sexual slavery at age 16, escaped and founded an organization called Somaly Mam Foundation—her name.[223] She said she saved over 6,000 girls from slavery. However, she resigned from leading the foundation in 2014 due to charges she made up the story of her early life as a sex slave when she actually had a normal village life. She was also accused of telling girls to give false stories of slavery to media, despite the fact that actual trafficking is a problem in Cambodia.

A California woman, Olga Murray, set up the Nepalese Youth Opportunity Foundation to change this practice of selling girls. Over 3,000 families were given a pig or goat when they promised not to sell their daughters to be servants called *kamlari*.[224] The foundation also helps pay for girls' school fees and provides families with a kerosene lamp. Their website and newsletter share the stories of some of the rescued girls.[225] Urmila Chaudhary, whose father sold her at age six, escaped at age 18 with the help of her brother. A year later she became the leader of the largest kamlari resistance movement. She speaks on radio programs and goes door to door in villages to convince parents not to sell their daughters. She's in fifth grade in school now and would like to become a journalist.

Tania Mostari, a young activist from Bangladesh, is working to make a difference for girls. She reports that violence against girls is rampant in Bangladesh. Sexual harassment comes in all forms, and in all spheres of a woman's life. From ogling, winking, and sexual comments, to touching, groping, eve teasing (the term in this region for harassment), stalking, sending lewd text messages, prank calls, displaying pornography, threatening and intimidation, acid attacks and unwanted love proposals. Women from all walks of life have accepted such sexual harassment as part of their daily lives.

> *Bangladesh is one of the world's worst places for women and girls. It is a living hell for women. About 70% of Bangladeshi adolescent girls are married off at or before 16 and 90% of them become mother of one or two children by the age 19. Every year thousands of women are killed by their husbands for dowry. Women have no agency and no voice in Bangladesh. Their voices are never heard. They are not regarded as human beings. Their simple identity is someone's wife, daughter, servant or girlfriend. A man can marry as many as he wants [up to four]. He can demand as much as he wants. He is the supreme authority of the*

family, society and the country and women has nothing to do with family with society. She is simply a woman without any voice.

I believe that by empowering young women through developing their leadership capacities we are advancing women to lead the change. Changes must come by women in Bangladesh. I am a college student and President of Bangladesh Adolescent Girls' Rights Forum (BKAF) and Program Director of Promoting Human Rights and Education in Bangladesh (PHREB). BKAF is a project of PHREB (www.phreb.org), which aims to give agency to girls and young women so that they can raise their voices, seek and ensure access to their basic human rights.[226]

People think of women being harassed on the streets in India and Egypt, so it's important to point out that 20% of college women in the US have been sexually assaulted, leading the White House to set up a task force to study the problem in 2014.[227] The term sexual harassment was coined in the 1970s in the US and used in the legal system in the 1980s, given wide media coverage in Anita Hill's testimony to all male Senators about her experience with sexual harassment by Supreme Court nominee Clarence Thomas. President Obama initiated the "It's on US" campaign to encourage bystanders to stop assault.[228] Despite the awareness of sexual harassment in the workplace, the head of Fox News was allowed to harass many women reporters until enough of them spoke out in 2016, when he was fired but given a $40 million exit bonus. Fox anchor Bill O'Reilly lost many advertisers when a similar pattern of harassment and expensive settlements was reported about him, so he too was fired.

Rita Banerji describes the harassment even middle-aged women experience in India as a way men assert their dominance in public so that women like her don't feel comfortable even to queue up in a government building such as a post office.[229] The harassment experienced by women servers in Delhi restaurants is detailed in the book *The Beautiful and the Damned: a Portrait of the New India*.[230] Some of the women turn to prostitution to pay their bills. A young woman in Tokyo told me about men rubbing against her in packed trains; she responds by reaching behind her to pinch the perpetrator. Mexico City ranked worst in a survey of 16 international cities for harassment on public transportation.[231] In response, a city program gives whistles to women to break the silence and some young women video record harassment and post it on the Las Morras YouTube channel. Another Mexican feminist group confronts harassment with loud punk music and shooting a confetti cannon at the perpetrator. UN Women's "Safe Cities and Safe Public Spaces for Women and Girls" program advocates more women-only buses and train cars, similar those found in India, Egypt, Iran, UAE, Indonesia, and so on. Websites like Hollaback and Safecity warn women about street harassment hotspots. Hollaback! uses social media to oppose street harassment in 26 countries and 79 cities and to share experiences.[232] Their vlog is called "Love and Revolution." A growing trend is taking photos of harassers on mobile phones and some Japanese women carry buzzers to scare off harassers.

In Afghanistan, Pakistan and some Middle Eastern countries, it's OK to punish girls and women who supposedly dishonor their families with acid attacks, honor killings, and executions. In the Middle East sexual honor leads to violence, including rape as a way to punish a girl's family by dishonoring them. The UN Population Fund estimates over 5,000 honor killings occur each year, especially in Middle Eastern and South Asian countries.[233] *A Girl in the River* (2015) documents the story of a Pakistani young woman who was shot by her father and uncle for marrying a man of her choice; it got the Academy Award for Best Foreign Film in 2016. They threw her body in the river, but she survived and was eventually pressured to reconcile with her family although her father didn't express remorse. His honor was most important to him. To escape draconian punishment, Middle Eastern girls who engage in premarital sex and can afford it may have an operation to replace the hymen. Honor killings happen in the US too. An Iraqi immigrant in Arizona ran over his daughter with his car in 2009 because he felt she was too Westernized.

Old customs die slowly: A Russian proverb says, "A beating man is a loving man," and this practice of wife beating continues. Six in 10 children (one billion) aged two to 14 are regularly beaten by caregivers, according to a 2014 UNICEF report that drew on data from 190 countries. The first major global study of violence against women by WHO found that 35% women have been assaulted by a partner and 40% of murdered women were killed by a partner.[234] The abuse rates were highest in poor countries in Africa, the Middle East and Southeast Asia. Because of their low status, Amnesty International reports that at least one third of women are abused in their lifetime. In 2017, a minister in the Indian state of Gopal Bhargava gave bats to hundreds of brides in a mass wedding in Madhya Pradesh to defend against violent husbands or other drunk family members.[235] Some of the paddles included inscriptions such as "For beating drunkards." He ordered hundreds of thousands more bats.

The United Nations reports that at least one out of every three women around the world has been beaten, raped, or otherwise abused in her lifetime, usually by someone she knows.[236] A partner committed over a third of female homicides. One in 10 girls under age 18 were raped. These statistics indicate that societal violence is a bigger problem than civil wars, leading to an estimated social cost of $4 trillion a year globally.[237] But, despite these global problems, about 100 countries don't have laws against domestic violence and women's rights are absent from the goals of key NGOs, although progress can't occur without including half the population. In response, the UN adopted the Declaration on the Elimination of Violence Against Women in 1993. UN programs aim to educate young people and link women to micro-credit loans and information about how to prevent domestic violence.[238] UN Women manages grants financed by the UN Trust Fund to End Violence against Women. UN Women helped develop a website and app to lessen violence against women in Brazilian slums called favelas by providing hotline numbers and the locations of support centers for health and for women's refuges.

WHO reports that over a third of women experience sexual violence in their lifetimes. One in 10 girls worldwide suffers from sexual assault (mainly from men close to them). Nearly one in five women in the US report being raped at some time (42% before age 18), according to the Centers for Disease Control and Prevention; many rapes happen on university campuses and in the military—university students are more likely to be assaulted than other women, as discussed on a documentary.[239] A *Ms. Magazine* article lists resources for preventing campus sexual assault.[240] A documentary titled *The Invisible War* (2013) reported that one in five female military officers have been assaulted, but only 5,061 cases were reported to authorities in 2013.[241]

Women are fighting back and acceptance of violence against women as normal is changing. In protest, young feminists in the US wrote books like *Yes Means Yes! Visions of Female Sexual Power & A World Without Rape;* and *The Revolution Starts at Home: Confronting Intimate Violence Within Activist Communities.*[242] Senator Barbara Boxer tried again in 2013 to pass her bill called the International Violence Against Women Act, citing the fact that violence against women is the most widespread human rights violation, experienced by over one-third of women, according to WHO.[243] After years of debate, it did pass in 2013 although conservative organizations such as Concerned Women for America opposed it.

In Kenya, where a woman is raped every 30 minutes, "Kaia" was only 11 when she was raped on the way to school. When a teacher took her to the hospital, police demanded a bribe to write up her statement. With the help of human rights lawyers, she sued the police, chanting with other girls "I demand my rights," and won.[244] South Africa is sometimes called the rape capital of the world, made even worse by the high AIDS rate. A young man involved in the gender justice MAP Network explained that he was raised that if you hit a girl two or three times, she will have sex with you, which he carried out until he realized men should "reach a consensus" with their partners.[245] A trainer for One Man Can for gender justice reported, "If you don't somehow get violent with your girl, she thinks that you don't love her. You need to prove you're a man. So how do they prevent gender-based violence when they're expected to appear as strong and masculine? How do they practice that change in their own relationships?"[246]

Model programs to reduce male violence are found globally. After a high school student was brutally gang raped and murdered in Argentina in October 2016, women wearing black went on strike for an hour in 80 Argentinian cities and in 58 other cities globally, similar to the Polish Black Monday strikes against restrictive abortion legislation. Demonstrators used the well-known slogan *ni una menos*, not one woman less. Earlier in the year President Mauricio Macri announced measures to prevent more violence against women, including electronic tags for violent men and building women's refuges. Argentina was one of 16 countries in Latin America that passed anti-femicide legislation establishing harsher penalties when gender is involved in a crime. *Mensajes de Paz* (Messages of Peace) was organized by Justice for My Sister women's collective in Guatemala where nearly 6,000 women were murdered in the last decade. In both Egypt and Guatemala neighbors formed local safety groups and media savvy youth lead outreach programs.

An example of a local group to stop violence against women is the Young Feminists Movement Namibia.[247] The Guy-to-Guy Project of Instituto Promundo in Rio de Janeiro organizes young men who live in poor areas to do outreach to other guys with a play about reducing violence against women and providing educational materials. A similar group in Mumbai, India, called Men Against Violence and Abuse teaches young men through street plays, essay and poster competitions, newspapers posted on walls, radio plays, and discussion groups. Other organizations of men against violence against women are the White Ribbon Campaign that began in Canada, and 3N1 Men to fight trafficking. Both men and women are organizing to prevent violence against women, such as Man Up, a global campaign to activate youth to stop violence against women and girls.[248]

Eve Ensler, of Vagina Monologues fame, organized the One Billion Rising annual demonstration with flash mobs and dances against violence against women. The official song was "Break the Chain" by Tena Clark. It took place in over 200 countries on Valentine's Day, supported by over 13,000 organizations. A video posted by *The Guard-*

ian shows global participation during the first year in 2013.[249] Ensler explained that Congolese women taught her that dancing is the more liberating form of energy, seen in videos on onebillionrising.org. Annual global protests are organized by an organization called *Stop Street Harassment* directed by Holly Kearl, also the author of a book with that title (2012). Her *Stop Global Street Harassment* was published in 2015. In 2014, 24 countries participated in the protests. Activists chalked slogans on sidewalks, plastered posters saying "Stop Telling Women to Smile," marched, and organized Internet campaigns posting maps of reported violence.[250] For example, The Egyptian Center for Women's Rights created HarassMap to show hotspots for harassment and its 500 volunteers do consciousness-raising.

Equality Now works for human rights of girls and women around the world, as through the Women's Action Network that includes over 35,000 groups and individuals in over 160 countries.[251] One of the international board members is Gloria Steinem. Equality Now focuses on changing the law, sexual violence (up to 50% of sexual assaults are committed against girls who are less than 16), female genital mutilation and trafficking. Charitable organizations for women include Women For Women, which helps survivors of war, and The Global Fund for Women. The GFW has given grants to women's groups since 1987 that adds up to over $71 million to more than 3,800 women's groups in 167 countries.[252] Tactics to end widespread violence against girls and women are school education programs, microfinance groups that include gender equity training, community programs that teach communication skills, and campaigns like "From Peace in the Home to Peace in the World" sponsored by the Center for Women's Global Leadership at Rutgers University.[253] UN Women's Safe Public Spaces Global Initiative works with local women's groups, mayors and civic organizations to implement projects to increase safety.[254]

The statistics in this chapter paint a grim picture of women being treated as sub-human, somehow deserving of violence, illiteracy, and lack of health care. All countries struggle with violence against women and their exclusion from positions of power. Proven solutions provide models for how governments can implement equality through policies such as quotas and in so do doing improve the quality of governance. A report titled "The State of the World's Girls" concluded that legislation is useful, but in a time of backlash against women's rights, grassroots organizing of social movements supported by both sexes "will bring about a tipping point for gender equality."[255] The world needs the talents of half its population enhanced by access to good education. The next chapter looks at pressures on youth by created by global consumerism.

Discussion Questions and Activities

Questions

1. Do you agree or disagree that living in a poor rural area or in a city has more influence on youth than their nationality? Why?
2. If you had a chance to talk with Mashal in Pakistan, what would you ask her?
3. How does sexism contribute to poverty? Neoliberalism? What solutions do you think are most effective?
4. Is education the key to improving girls' inferior status? What incentives are needed to keep girls in school in developing countries? How can child marriages be prevented? See a video on Bangladeshi child-marriage free zones.[256]
5. What kinds of support systems enable mothers to do paid work?
6. Why do you think violence against women is so widespread and cruel?
7. Do you think cultural beliefs like the importance of female circumcision should be respected to honor cultural relativism?

Activities

1. Read The Girl Declaration written by girls living in poverty in 14 countries. What are their goals?[257]
2. The endnote includes resources of organizations working to improve the status of women.[258] How do they compare with the goals in the Girl Declaration?
3. What issue facing girls globally is most important in your judgment? Start with the Coalition for Adolescent Girls' list of resource topics.[259]
4. What does the Coalition emphasize to involve girls?[260]
5. For a breakdown of the gender gap by country see a 2013 report by the World Economic Forum.[261]
6. Enact Chelsea Clinton's suggestions for actions we can take to solve some of the problems described in this chapter in her book for young people, *It's Your World* (2015), pp. 174 to 175. Examples are: girlsnotbrides.org, letgirlslead.org, the Global Alliance for Clean cookstoves, Girls Who Code, girleffect.org, Shinning Hope for Communities, and noceilings.org.
7. Check out the game "Half the Sky Movement: The Game," available on Facebook. See the DVD *Half the Sky: Turning Oppression Into Opportunity For Women Worldwide* (2012). Nicholas Kristof and Sheryl WuDunn's 2014 book is *A Path Appears:*

Transforming Lives, Creating Opportunity about global altruism.

8. Read science fiction books about utopian or dystopian societies.[262] What themes do they emphasize as most influential?

Films:

1. A BBC documentary concludes there's no country where girls and boys are equal. It explores limitations on girls In the UK, Jordan, Iceland and Lesotho and includes interviews with girls.[263] Also look for key issues in the BBC series *100 Women* that began in 2013.[264]

2. What issues are featured in Global Voices documentaries about young women? http://worldchannel.org/programs/global-voices/

Endnotes

Anup Shah, "Women's Rights," *Global Issues*, March 14, 2010.

http://www.globalissues.org/article/166/womens-rights#WomenWorkMoreThanMenButArePaidLess

Deirdre Fulton, "People's Water Summit," *Common Dreams*, March 22, 2016.

http://www.commondreams.org/news/2016/03/22/peoples-water-summit-women-and-girls-bear-brunt-global-crisis

Shamillah Wilson, Anasuya Sengupta, Kristy Evans, **eds**. *Defending Our Dreams: Global Feminist Voices for a New Generation*. Zed Books and AWID, 2005, p. 34.

Ibid., p. 46.

http://reports.weforum.org/global-gender-gap-report-2015/report-highlights/

ttps://openknowledge.worldbank.org/bitstream/handle/10986/23436/9781464805561.pdf?sequence=1&isAllowed=y

"Facts and Figures," UN Women, August 2016.

http://www.unwomen.org/en/what-we-do/leadership-and-political-participation/facts-and-figures

Jenny Pickerill, et al., editors. *Occupy! A Global Movement*. Routledge, 2014.

https://platform-production.s3.amazonaws.com/therules-191-One_Party_Planet_simple_text_final.pdf

Robert Frank, "Why Aren't There More Female Billionaires?" *New York Times*, December 30, 2017.

https://www.nytimes.com/2016/12/30/business/why-arent-there-more-female-billionaires.html

Heads of State: Angela Merkel, Dilma Rousseff, and Park Geun-hye; NGO heads Christine Lagarde, Janet Yellen and Margaret Chan; CEOs Virginia Rometty, and Mary Barra, and politician Hillary Clinton

http://www.forbes.com/powerful-people/list/

Alexander Kaufman, "Exxon Continued Paying Millions to Climate Change Deniers Under Rex Tillerson, *Huffington Post*, January 9, 2017. http://www.huffingtonpost.com/entry/tillerson-exxon-climate-donations_us_5873a3f4e4b043ad97e48f52

http://www.who.int/tobacco/media/en/TobaccoExplained.pdf

http://ektaparishad.com/en-us/about/vision.aspx

https://www.indiegogo.com/projects/european-young-feminists-camp

blog: http://youngfeministcamp.wordpress.com/

Wilson, *Defending Our Dreams*, p. 136.

http://www.unwomen.org/en/what-we-do/ending-violence-against-women/facts-and-figures

Sarah North, "Mental Health: The Health Crisis of Our Time," *Girls' Globe*, September 22, 2016. https://girlsglobe.org/2016/09/22/mental-health-the-health-crisis-of-our-time/

Jessica Valenti, "Worldwide Sexism Increases Suicide Risk in Young Women," *The Guardian*, May 28, 2015. http://www.theguardian.com/commentisfree/2015/may/28/worldwide-sexism-increases-suicide-risk-in-young-women

Natasha Hakimi Zapapta, "How Can America's Wealthy Sleep at Night When Some Teens Must Sell Sex or Drugs in Order to Eat?," *TruthDIG*, September 12, 2016.

http://www.truthdig.com/eartotheground/item/how_can_wealthy_elites_sleep_at_night_american_teens_selling_sex_20160912

Julie Cornell, "Ending Child Marriage within a Generation," *Crowd 360*, September 27, 2016.

20   http://crowd360.org/ending-child-marriage-within-generation-ensuring-representation-girls-everywhere/

Julie Bindel, "The Selling of Subordination: How the Female Body is Reduced to Products," *TruthDig*, September 15, 2016.

21   http://www.truthdig.com/report/item/the_selling_of_subordination_how_the_female_body_20160915

Nicholas Kristof and Sheryl WuDunn, "The Women's Crusade," *The New York Times Magazine*, August 23, 2009, p. 28. See their book *Half the Sky: Turning Oppression Into Opportunity for Women Worldwide*. Alfred A Knopf, 2009.

22

23   https://www.youtube.com/watch?v=8nBrGbrSHYc&feature=youtu.be

"Young Feminists' Statement for the 59th Commission on the Status of Women, Young Feminist Wire, March 19, 2015.

http://yfa.awid.org/2015/03/young-feminists-statement-for-the-59th-commission-on-the-status-of-women/http://yfa.awid.org/2015/03/young-feminists-statement-for-the-59th-commission-on-the-status-of-women/ Pat Hynes, "Girl Soldiers: Forgotten Casualties of War," *TruthDig*, October 19, 2016.

24   http://www.truthdig.com/report/item/girl_soldiers_forgotten_casualties_of_war_20161019

Tina Rosenberg, "The Daughter Deficit," *The New York Times Magazine*, August 23, 2009, p. 23. Statistics are from Goretti Nyabenda, p. 33-34, also in the *Times*.

25

26   Mara Hvistendahl. *Unnatural Selection: Choosing Boys Over Girls, and the Consequences of a World Full of Men*. Public xAffairs, 2011.

Deniz Kandiyoti, "Fear and Fury," OpenDemocracy.Net, January 10, 2013.

27   https://www.opendemocracy.net/5050/deniz-kandiyoti/fear-and-fury-women-and-post-revolutionary-violence

"As Turkish Women Struggle for Freedom from Violence, Their President Tells Them: Give Up on Equality," *Global Voices*, November 25, 2014.

http://globalvoicesonline.org/2014/11/25/as-turkish-women-struggle-for-freedom-from-violence-their-president-tells-them-give-up-on-equality/

28   Nwachukwu Egbunike, "Nigerian President Says First Lady 'Belongs to My Kitchen' and 'The Other Room,'" *Global Voices*, October 16, 2016.

29   https://globalvoices.org/2016/10/16/nigerian-president-says-first-lady-belongs-to-my-kitchen-and-the-other-room/

"Trump Recorded Having Extremely Lewd Conversation about women in 2005," *Washington Post,* October 8, 2016.

https://www.washingtonpost.com/politics/trump-recorded-having-extremely-lewd-conversation-about-women-in-2005/2016/10/07/3b9ce776-8cb4-11e6-bf8a-3d26847eeed4_story.html?utm_term=.08a8c6a3e1b5

30   Iris C. Gonzales, "Will Filipinos Elect an Emblem of Rape Culture as President Today?" *Women's News*, May 9, 2016.

31   http://womensenews.org/2016/05/will-filipinos-elect-a-rape-culture-leader-as-president-today/

32   Ruth Panelli, et all, editors. *Global Perspectives on Rural Childhood and Youth*. Routledge, 2007.

(my summary) http://wp.me/p47Q76-r4

33   http://youthspeak.aiesec.org/wp-content/uploads/2016/05/YouthSpeak-Preliminary-Findings-final.pdf

34   Ronald Inglehart and Pippa Norris. *Rising Tide: Gender and Cultural Change Around the World*. Cambridge University Press, 2003.

"Harvesting Happiness on a Kenyan Farm," BBC News, August 5, 2015.

35   http://www.bbc.com/news/magazine-33728876

Eric Fish. *China's Millennials: The Want Generation*. Roman and Littlefield, 2015, p. 136.

36   http://asianwiki.com/The_Cremator

37   Ibid., pp. 142-143.

Clare Pennington, "Indie Director Peng Tao on His Latest Film 'The Cremator,'" Blouinartinfo, January 24, 2013.

38   http://encn.blouinartinfo.com/news/story/859679/indie-director-peng-tao-on-his-latest-film-the-cremator#

Sonia Narang and Ameera Butt, "In Malala's Hometown, One Young Woman Fights for Childhood Education," *News Deeply Women & Girls' Hub*, September 14, 2016.

39   https://www.newsdeeply.com/womenandgirls/in-malalas-hometown-a-peace-activist-stands-up-for-girls-education

40   https://globalyouthbook.wordpress.com/2014/04/07/interview-with-an-illiterate-pakistani-girl/

Mosharraf Zaidi, "How Pakistan Fails Its Children," *New York Times*, October 14, 2014.

41   http://www.nytimes.com/2014/10/15/opinion/how-pakistan-fails-its-children.html

Katy Daigle, "Experts Push for Cleaner Stoves in Poor Countries to Cut Pollution," *Canadian Business*, April 8, 2015.

42   http://www.canadianbusiness.com/business-news/experts-push-for-cleaner-stoves-in-poor-countries-to-cut-pollution-reduce-deaths/

http://opendoorsliteracyproject.weebly.com

https://www.youtube.com/watch?v=KtJ-oSuYlx0

This is a short video of ODLP students we've moved on to private schools.

https://vimeo.com/76195912

43   http://gaylekimball.wordpress.com/open-doors-literacy-project-in-pakistan/

44   http://www.mediafire.com/?q7tv6j63knny977

45   http://opendoorsliteracyproject.weebly.com/group-thirteen-from-ramdas-peshawar.html

46   http://bailsf.org/2014/07/30/microlending-and-islam/

"Hungry to Learn Across the World," BBC News, October 12, 2009.

47   http://news.bbc.co.uk/2/hi/8299780.stm

48   Shereen El Feki. *Sex and the Citadel: Intimate Life in a Changing Arab World*. Pantheon Books, 2013, p. 32.

John M. Glionna, "A Voice for Rural Women of China," *Los Angeles Times*, January 2, 2008. http://articles.latimes.com/2008/jan/02/world/fg-women2

49 Charundi Panagodam, "Despite Rhetoric, Women Still Sidelined in Development Funding," *Terraviva Europe Newsletter,* February 6, 2012.
http://ipsnews.net/newsTVE.asp?idnews=106663
50 "Progress of the World's Women 2015-2016," UN Women, 2015
http://progress.unwomen.org/en/2015/
51 Global Economic Forum, "The Global Gender Gap Report 2015."
http://reports.weforum.org/global-gender-gap-report-2015/
52 Nadia Prupis, "Post-9-11 Wars Have Cost Nearly $5 Trillion: Report," *Common Dreams*, September 13, 2016.
http://www.commondreams.org/news/2016/09/13/post-911-wars-have-cost-nearly-5-trillion-and-counting-report
53 http://www.girleffect.org/media/139917/declaration_document_web_v6_26_9_13_copy.pdf
54 http://www.anewcourse.org/Our_Work/Lessons_Learned.aspx
55 Luisa Kroll, "Inside the 2014 Forbes Billionaires List," *Forbes*, March 3, 2014.
http://www.forbes.com/sites/luisakroll/2014/03/03/inside-the-2014-forbes-billionaires-list-facts-and-figures/
56 The article profiles some of the women:
http://www.forbes.com/sites/connieguglielmo/2014/03/03/the-class-of-2014-leans-in/
57 http://www.oecd.org/gender/data/genderwagegap.htm
58 Alison Damast, "A Pay Gap for Female MBAS Has Reemerged," *Bloomberg Business Week*, December 20, 2012. http://www.businessweek.com/articles/2012-12-20/a-pay-gap-for-female-mbas-has-reemerged.
59 Claire Cain Miller, "The Gender Pay Gap is Largely Because of Motherhood," *New York Times*, May 13, 2017.
https://www.nytimes.com/2017/05/13/upshot/the-gender-pay-gap-is-largely-because-of-motherhood.html
60 Elaine Kurtenbach, "Women's Lower Status Risks Asian Future," *Asia Society*, April 20, 2012. http://www.irrawaddy.org/archives/2766
61 "Invisible Forgotten Sufferers: The Plight of Widows around the World," a 2010 study commissioned by the Loomba Foundation.
http://dailytimes.com.pk/default.asp?page=2010%5C06%5C24%5Cstory_24-6-2010_pg4_9
62 Lori Robertson, "Stretching Facts on Syrian Refugees," *Fact Check*, September 15, 2015.
http://www.factcheck.org/2015/09/stretching-facts-on-syrian-refugees/
http://www.un.org/en/globalissues/briefingpapers/refugees/index.shtml
Janice Raymond, "Women Seeking Refuge: A Crisis Within a Crisis," *TruthDIG*, September 23, 2016.
http://www.truthdig.com/report/item/women_seeking_refuge_a_crisis_within_a_crisis_20160923
63 Amnesty International, "Female Refugees Face Physical Assault," January 18, 2016.
https://www.amnesty.org/en/latest/news/2016/01/female-**refugees-face-physical-assault-exploitation-and-sexual-harassment-on-their-journey-through-europe/**
64 here's Malala's video about refugee girls: https://www.facebook.com/MalalaFund/videos/1442849959062185?source=medium_091316
65 Sarah Macdonald. *Holy Cow: An Indian Adventure*. Broadway Books, 2003.
"Our Ambitious Girl," BBC News Asia, May 30, 2014.
66 http://www.bbc.com/news/world-asia-27622236
http://www.huffingtonpost.com/2015/01/14/homeless-women-tampons_n_6465230.html
67 http://www.huffingtonpost.com/ranit-mishori-md-mhs/women-and-toilets-a-tale-_b_8575622.html
Jennifer Allsopp, "Women Defining Economic Citizenship," *Open Democracy*, April 20, 2012.
68 https://www.opendemocracy.net/5050/jennifer-allsopp/women-defining-economic-citizenship
69 Elaine Kurtenbach, "Women's Lower Status Risks Asian Future," *Asia Society*, April 20, 2012. http://www.irrawaddy.org/archives/2766
UCLA World Policy Analysis Center
70 http://worldpolicycenter.org/topics/gender/policies
"Voice and Agency: Empowering Women and Girls for Shared Prosperity, The World Bank," October 10, 2014.
71 https://openknowledge.worldbank.org/handle/10986/1903
72 http://www.barefootcollege.org/about/
73 http://www.womeninandbeyond.org/?page_id=8
United Nations Department of Economic and Social Affairs (DESA), June 2010, p. 24. unpan1.un.org/intradoc/groups/public/documents/un.../unpan039616.pdf p. 4.
74 United Nations Department of Economic and Social Affairs (DESA), June 2010, p. 24. unpan1.un.org/intradoc/groups/public/documents/un.../unpan039616.pdf
75 United Nations Department of Economic and Social Affairs (DESA), June 2010, p. 24. unpan1.un.org/intradoc/groups/public/documents/un.../unpan039616.pdf
76 Maybelle Morgan, "Who's the Boss," *Daily Mail*, April 1, 2015.
77 http://www.dailymail.co.uk/femail/article-3019701/Only-three-countries-world-boss-likely-woman.html
Stach Finz, "Hillary Clinton Argues for End to Sexism in Workshop," *San Francisco Chronicle*, September 17, 2011.
78 www.sfgate.com/cgi-bin/article.cgi?f=/c/a/2011/09/16/BUQN1L5JEG.DTL&type=business
79 https://www.weforum.org/agenda/2016/04/where-are-the-women-in-computing/
https://www.weforum.org/agenda/2016/04/where-are-the-women-in-computing/
80 American Association of University Women, "Behind the Pay Gap," 2007. (In response, the Paycheck Fairness Act was proposed in 2009.)

[81] Mario Osava," Women More Educated, Not More Equal," *IPS/TerraViva*, March 8, 2012.
http://ipsnews.net/print.asp?idnews=50494

[82] "Global Employment Trends for Women 2012," The International Labor Organization, 2013.
http://www.ilo.org/global/publications/books/forthcoming-publications/WCMS_190354/lang--en/index.htm

[83] "Women at Work: Trends 2016," International Labour Office, 2016.
http://www.ilo.org/wcmsp5/groups/public/---dgreports/---dcomm/---publ/documents/publication/wcms_457317.pdf

[84] Delphine d'Amora, "Top Female Government Leaders Balance State and Family Obligations," *The Moscow Times*, March 7, 2014.
http://www.themoscowtimes.com/article/495806.html

[85] Tomoko Otake, "Prime Minister Abe Unveils Government Push to Solve Day Care Crunch," *The Japan Times*, May 31, 2017.
http://www.japantimes.co.jp/news/2017/05/31/national/prime-minister-abe-unveils-government-push-solve-day-care-crunch/#.WWlnxYqQzm0

[86] http://www.masholdings.com/responsibility/work_life_balance.php

[87] https://action.momsrising.org/cms/donate/storefront

[88] Robert Reich, "The Gradual Devaluation of Women in the Workforce," *San Francisco Chronicle*, May 19, 2013.

[89] World Bank Annual Report, 2013.
http://siteresources.worldbank.org/EXTANNREP2013/Resources/9304887-1377201212378/9305896-1377544753431/1_AnnualReport2013_EN.pdf

[90] http://www.worldbank.org/en/topic/gender

[91] The Nike Foundation, the NoVo Foundation, the UN Foundation, the Coalition for Adolescent Girls, the International Center for Research on Women, CARE, the Center for Global Development, Plan International, the Girl Effect, etc.

[92] https://openknowledge.worldbank.org/handle/10986/23425

[93] Ibid, p. 94.

[94] http://www.icrw.org/publication-search?title=girls&text=youth&author=&region=All&subject=All&type=All&year%5Bvalue%5D%5Bdate%5D=

[95] http://datatopics.worldbank.org/gender/

[96] www.girleffect.org/learn/more-resources

[97] http://coalitionforadolescentgirls.org/about-us/#

[98] http://www.icrw.org/publication-search?title=girls&text=youth&author=&region=All&subject=All&type=All&year%5Bvalue%5D%5Bdate%5D=

[99] https://www.feedingforward.com/

[100] http://blogs.state.gov/stories/2014/09/08/power-classroom
http://girlsneedtoknow.org/
https://docs.google.com/spreadsheet/ccc?key=0Au3H3pEsgusadDFEYVc2VVRBUmMzbGozb2Y4Smg3X2c&usp=sharing#gid=0
https://www.scribd.com/collections/4449612/Educating-Girls
http://www.oxfam.org.uk/education/
http://www.unicef.org/publications/index_21344.html
http://www.unicef.org/progressforchildren/2007n6/index_41798.htm

[101] www.girleffect.org/uploads/documents/2/Girl_Effect_Media_Kit.pdf

[102] *Finance & Development*, Vol. 49, No. 1, March 2012.

[103] www.imf.org/external/pubs/ft/fandd/2012/03/revenga.htm

[104] *Girls Need to Grow, Impact Report No. 2*, The Global Fund for Women. Study conducted from 1998-2000. www.globalfundforwomen.org

[105] Karin Ronnow, "Rising Stars," Central Asia Institute's *Journey of Hope*, Vol. IV, 2010, p. 31.
Ana Revenga and Sudhir Shetty,"Empowering Women is Smart Economics," *Finance & Development*, Vol. 49, No. 1, March 2012.

[106] www.imf.org/external/pubs/ft/fandd/2012/03/revenga.htm
Ibid., p. 39.

[107] https://www.whitehouse.gov/letgirlslearn

[108] https://www.globalinnovationexchange.org/topic/adolescent-girls-education
Sam Jones, "UN: 15-Year Push Ends Extreme Poverty for a Billion People," *The Guardian*, July 6, 2015.

[109] http://www.theguardian.com/global-development/2015/jul/06/united-nations-extreme-poverty-millennium-development-goals
Anne-Birgitte Albrectsen, "Women and Girls Can't Wait 100 Years for Global Goal Results," *Devex*, September 13, 2016.

[110] https://www.devex.com/news/women-and-girls-can-t-wait-100-years-for-global-goal-results-88740
"No Ceilings: The Full Participation Report," Gates and Clinton Foundations, March 2015, pp. 11-13.

[111] http://noceilings.org/report/report.pdf

[112] http://www.unfpa.org/sites/default/files/pub-pdf/MarryingTooYoung.pdf

[113] Education for Equality International, Girl Pride Circle
"Anger Over Gynecological Tests for Teachers," *Daily Telegraph*, August 9, 2014.

[114] http://www.telegraph.co.uk/news/worldnews/southamerica/brazil/11023395/Brazil-anger-over-gynaecological-tests-for-teachers.html
Nepal Youth Foundation newsletter, November 2010. www.nepalyouthfoundation.org

115   Prostitution is not illegal in Nepal. http://drdivas.wordpress.com/2008/09/19/sex-in-kathmandu-city/ CNN produced a documentary on "Nepal's Stolen Children," 2011.

116   http://cnnpressroom.blogs.cnn.com/2011/06/06/downloadable-images-for-nepals-stolen-children/

117   Seth Kugel, "Brazil's Unequal Education System Amounts to Big Problems," *GlobalPost,* September 22, 2010. www.thehawaiiindependent.com/story/brazils-unequal-education-system-amounts-to-big-problems/

118   http://data.worldbank.org/indicator/SE.SEC.PRIV.ZS?locations=BR

Cleucide Oliveira, "Brazil's New Problems with Blackness," *Foreign Policy,* April 5, 2017.

119   http://foreignpolicy.com/2017/04/05/brazils-new-problem-with-blackness-affirmative-action/

"No Longer Bottom of the Class: Weak and Wasteful Schools Hold Brazil Back," *The Economist,* December 9, 2010. www.economist.com/node/17679798/print

120   http://nces.ed.gov/surveys/pisa/pisa2012/pisa2012highlights_6a.asp

Lise Alves, "Brazilian Government Announces New Education Model," *The Rio Times,* September 23, 2016.

121   http://riotimesonline.com/brazil-news/rio-politics/brazilian-government-announces-new-education-model/

Amanda Ripley, "Teacher, Leave Those Kids Alone," *TIME Magazine,* September 25, 2011. http://www.time.com/time/magazine/article/0,9171,2094427,00.html

122   Medard Gabel. *Designing a World that Works for All.* BigPictureSmallWorld, 2015, pp. 223-271.

123   http://www.ungei.org/whatisungei/index_2593.html

124   http://www.scribd.com/doc/169580881/Syllabus-Educating-Girls

http://girlrising.pearsonfoundation.org/#college

125   www.scribd.com/collections/4449612/Educating-Girls

126   Greg Mortenson, "Why is Girls' Education so Important?" *Journey of Hope Magazine,* Fall 2013. https://www.ikat.org/publications/2013JOH.pdf

127   "The Innovation Keeping Ugandan Girls in School, " *Girl Effect,* January 9, 2014.

128   http://www.girleffect.org/news/2013/04/the-innovation-keeping-ugandan-girls-in-school

Naolim Chazan, "Women in Israel: Women in Public Life," *Jewish Virtual Library,* March 2013. http://www.jewishvirtuallibrary.org/jsource/Society_&_Culture/Women_in_public_life.html

129   "Global Trends 2030: Alternative Worlds. National Intelligence Council," 2012, p. 11. www.dni.gov/nic/globaltrends

130   Jonathan Woetzel, et al., "The Power of Parity: How Advancing Women's Equality Can Add $12 Trillion to Global Growth," McKinsey Global Institute, September 2015.

http://www.mckinsey.com/insights/growth/How_advancing_womens_equality_can_add_12_trillion_to_global_growth

131   Bruce and Lloyd 1997; Eisler, Loye, and Norgaard 1995; Hausman, Tyson, and Zahidi 2009.

* 9.2 million children die every year before they reach their 5th birthday,

* 97 percent of child deaths occur in 68 developing countries,

* A quarter of all children are underweight,

* A third have stunted growth, and

* 75 million primary-school-age children—mostly girls—are not enrolled in school (Hague 2008).

132   www.urban.org/publications/412101.html

Female Genital Mutilation (FGM) affects nearly 170,000 girls and women in the United States and 140 million around the world. FGM is currently illegal in the US but the Girls Protection Act (H.R. 5137) of 2010 would make it a crime to transport minors outside the U.S. for the purpose of performing FGM.

133   http://amirahsvoice.org/about_fgm.html

MDG   www.globalhealthmagazine.com/guest_blog/mdg_5_3_billion/

134   [UN Millennial Development Goal] 5: 3 Billion Reasons to Invest in Young People's Sexual and Reproductive Health

135   http://www.womanstats.org/WomanStatsOverview2015.pdf

136   www.wateraidamerica.org/what_we_do/the_need/default.aspx

137   http://www.slideshare.net/yourexpedition/bae-access-water08sep

www.huffingtonpost.com/melinda-gates/a-new-vision-for-the-heal_b_603337.html, www.gatesfoundation.org/press-releases/Pages/women-deliver-2010-100607.aspx

138   http://www.who.int/life-course/partners/global-strategy/global-strategy-2016-2030/en/

139   Ban Ki-moon, "Ten Actions for the Next United Nations Secretary General to Advance Youth Issues," *Youth Policy,* 2016.

140   http://www.youthpolicy.org/blog/development/ten-actions-for-the-next-unsg-to-advance-youth-issues/

141   http://bit.ly/1QVetXD

Nicholas Krisof, "11 Years Old, a Mom, and Pushed to Marry Her Rapist in Florida," *New York Times,* May 26, 2017.https://www.nytimes.com/2017/05/26/opinion/sunday/it-was-forced-on-me-child-marriage-in-the-us.html?emc=edit_th_20170528&nl=todaysheadlines&nlid=68143430

142   www.girlsnotbrides.org

143   Didem Tali, "It Takes a Village to Not Marry a Girl," *The Development Set,* February 25, 2016. https://medium.com/the-development-set/it-takes-a-village-to-not-marry-a-girl-1aea49299f19#.vlfc9fin9

"Teaching Parents in Malawi Why Girls Need Education, Not Marriage," The World at School, February 19, 2016.

144 www.aworldatschool.org/news/entry/Tearfund-charity-changes-views-on-child-marriage-and-school-in-Malawi-2534

"No Ceilings: The Full Participation Report," Gates and Clinton Foundations, March 2015, p. 14.

145 http://noceilings.org/report/report.pdf

"Progress For Children: A Report Card on Adolescents," No. 10, UNICEF, April 2012, p. 19.

146 http://www.unicef.org/publications/files/Progress_for_Children_-_No._10_EN_04232012.pdf

147 Demographic and Health Survey

http://gawker.com/brave-little-girl-flees-forced-marriage-records-powerf-866434307?utm_campaign=socialflow_gawker_facebook&utm_source=gawker_facebook&utm_medium=socialflow

148 http://www.cnn.com/2013/07/30/world/yemen-child-marriage/

149 http://www.difret.com/press/

"Meet FRIDA's New Grantees," Young Feminist Fund, January 21, 2014.

150 http://youngfeministfund.org/2014/01/meet-fridas-new-grantees/

Gayle Tzemach Lemmon, "Too Young to Marry," *Ms. Magazine*, Winter 2015.

151 http://msmagazine.com/blog/2015/02/20/too-young-to-marry/

"The Girl Fighting to Stop Child Marriage in Pakistan," BBC News, May 18, 2015.

152 http://www.bbc.com/news/world-asia-32776484

153 Demographic and Health Survey

UNP, "Framework for Action on Adolescents and Youth: Opening Doors with Young People: 4 Keys," 2007.

154 UNFPAwww.unfpa.org/public/pid/396

"No Ceilings: The Full Participation Report," Gates and Clinton Foundations, March 2015, p. 14.

155 http://noceilings.org/report/report.pdf

Bruce and Lloyd 1997; Eisler, Loye, and Norgaard 1995; Hausman, Tyson, and Zahidi 2009.

* 9.2 million children die every year before they reach their 5th birthday
* 97% of child deaths occur in 68 developing countries
* A quarter of all children are underweight
* A third have stunted growth
* 75 million primary-school-age children—mostly girls—are not enrolled in school (Hague 2008).
www.urban.org/publications/412101.html UNP, "Framework for Action on Adolescents and Youth: Opening Doors with Young People: 4 Keys,"

156 2007. UNFPAwww.unfpa.org/public/pid/396

The Millennium Development Report 2014.

http://www.un.org/millenniumgoals/2014%20MDG%20report/MDG%202014%20English%20web.pdf

157 https://data.unicef.org/wp-content/uploads/2015/12/MMR_executive_summary_final_mid-res_243.pdf

158 United Nations, "The Millennium Development Goals Report," June 15, 2010. pp. 34, 36.

Sam Jones, "UN: 15-Year Push Ends Extreme Poverty for a Billion People," *The Guardian*, July 6, 2015.

159 http://www.theguardian.com/global-development/2015/jul/06/united-nations-extreme-poverty-millennium-development-goals

Graham Peebles, "Healthcare in india," *Albany Tribune*, November 29, 2013.

160 http://www.albanytribune.com/29112013-health-care-india-sick-distorted-development-oped/

Linda Poon, "A Booming Economy Doesn't Save Children From Malnutrition," *WSYU Radio*, March 27, 2014.

161 http://wysu.org/content/npr/booming-economy-doesnt-save-children-malnutrition

Nicholas Kristof, "Women as a Force for Change," *New York Times*, July 31, 2014.

162 http://www.nytimes.com/2013/08/01/opinion/kristof-women-as-a-force-for-change.html?_r=0

163 Steve Godfrey, "Better Nutrition for Women and Girls is Crucial to Achieve the SDGs," *The Conversation*, October 18, 2016.

164 United Nations, "The Millennium Development Goals Report," June 15, 2010. pp. 34, 36.

165 Jennifer Margulis. *The Business of Baby*. Scribner, 2013.

166 http://www.businessinsider.com/uninsured-rate-for-american-health-insurance-all-time-low-2017-5

Svetlanaa Smetanina, "High Abortion Rates Drive Debate on Contraceptive Methods in Russia," *Russia Beyond the Headlines*, March 28, 2013.

167 http://rbth.com/society/2013/03/28/russian_women_prefer_abortion_to_the_pill_24379.html

Shannon Pettypiece, "AIDS Drugs' Usefulness Questioned," *The Chronicle with Bloomberg*, March 6, 2013. http://www.pressdisplay.com/press-

168 display/viewer.aspx

Julie McCarthy, "In Pakistan, Birth Control and Religion Clash," NPR, August 10, 2011.

169 www.npr.org/2011/08/10/139382653/in-pakistan-birth-control-and-religion-clash

"Young People Speak up for their Sexual and Reproductive Rights at 47th CPD," *Youth Coalition*, April 16, 2014.

170 http://www.youthcoalition.org/un-processes/young-people-speak-sexual-reproductive-rights-47th-cpd-2/

Katarina Jungar and Elina Oinas, "A Feminist Struggle? South African HIV Activism as Feminist Politics," *Journal of International Women's*

171 *Studies*, Vol. 11, Issue 4, May 2010, p. 184.

172 www.lpch.org/aboutus/news/releases/2009/yen.html Suzanne, Petroni, "Global Population," *Ms. Magazine*, Summer 2011.

Gilda Sedgh, et.al, "Induced Abortion: Incidence and Trends Worldwide from 1995 to 2008," *The Lancet*, January 19, 2012.

http://www.thelancet.com/journals/lancet/article/PIIS0140-6736%2811%2961786-8/abstract

[173] http://www.who.int/reproductivehealth/news/440KeyAbortionFactsFinal.pdf

Sarah Kliff, "All States Except Oregon Now Limit Abortion Access," *The Washington Post*, January 31, 2013. http://www.washingtonpost.com/blogs/wonkblog/wp/2013/01/31/all-states-except-oregon-now-limit-abortion-access/

[174] "CSW58: Young Feminists Speak Loudly and clearly," *AWID*, March 28, 2014.

[175] http://www.awid.org/news-and-analysis/csw58-young-feminists-speak-loudly-and-clearly

Liz Olson, "Global Abortion Rates"

[176] http://www.infoplease.com/science/health/global-abortion-rates.htmlp://www.catholic-pages.com/morality/fatal.asp

[177] http://www.yolandadominguez.com/en/register-2014.html

[178] Ibid.

"No Ceilings: The Full Participation Report," Gates and Clinton Foundations, March 2015, p. 14.

[179] http://noceilings.org/report/report.pdf

[180] www.globalhealthmagazine.com/conference_blog/a_radical_proposal_fighting_for_women_and_girls/

http://photoblog.msnbc.msn.com/_news/2010/10/01/5214051-undesired-in-india-boys-are-prized-over-girls-with-violent-results?p-c=25&sp=50

[181] http://www.youthcoalition.org/about/who-we-are

[182] http://www.resurj.org/

[183] http://www.youthcoalition.org/about/who-we-are/

[184] Center for Health and Gender Equity, founded in 1994. www.genderhealth.org It seeks to implement the US Global Health Initiative begun in 2009 with a "human rights approach."

[185] Christian Davies, "Poland's Abortion ban Proposal Near Collapse After Mass Protests," *The Guardian*, October 5, 2016.

https://www.theguardian.com/world/2016/oct/05/polish-government-performs-u-turn-on-total-abortion-ban

[186] http://www.nytimes.com/video/world/europe/100000004686970/voices-from-abortion-ban-protests.html?emc=edit_th_20161004&nl=todays-headlines&nlid=68143430

[187] Joanna Berendt, "Protesters in Poland Rally Against Proposal for Total Abortion Ban," *New York Times*, October 3, 2016.

http://www.nytimes.com/2016/10/04/world/europe/poland-abortion-black-monday.html

[188] Rosin Davis, "Number of Victims of Female Genital Mutiluation is 70 Million Higher Than Thought," *TruthDig*, February 5, 2016.

http://www.truthdig.com/eartotheground/item/number_of_female_genital_multilation_victims_found_to_be_70_million_higher_?utm_source=feedburner&utm_medium=feed&utm_campaign=Feed%253A+Truthdig+Truthdig%253A+Drilling+Beneath+the+Headlines

[189] Juhie Bhatia, "Doctors Push Controversial Strategy to Fight Female Genital Mutilation," *Women's eNews*, February 22, 2016.

http://womensenews.org/2016/02/doctors-push-controversial-strategy-to-fight-female-genital-mutilation/

[190] "Indonesia Grapples with Female Circumcision Problem," *South China Moring Post*, March 28, 2017.

http://www.scmp.com/news/asia/southeast-asia/article/2082455/indonesia-grapples-female-circumcision-problem

[191] Pam Belluck and Joe Cochrane, "UNICEF Report Finds Female Genital Cutting to Be Common in Indonesia," *New York Times*, February 4, 2016.

www.nytime.com/2016/02/05/health/indonesia-female-genita…html?emc=edit

[192] Waris Dirie. *Desert Flower: The Extraordinary Journey of a Desert Nomad*. Harper Perennial, 2011.

[193] Patrick Kingsley, "Egypt Launches First Prosecution for Female Genital Mutilation After Girl Dies," *The Guardian*, March 14, 2014.

http://www.theguardian.com/society/2014/mar/14/egyptian-doctor-first-prosecution-fgm-female-genital-mutilation

[194] https://www.facebook.com/BetterLIFEonEARTH/timeline

[195] Sarah Tenoi, "An Alternative to Female Genital Mutilation that Prevents Girls Suffering," *The Guardian*, February 6, 2014.

http://www.theguardian.com/commentisfree/2014/feb/06/alternative-to-circumcision-prevents-girls-suffering-kenya

[196] http://interactive.aljazeera.com/aje/2016/breaking-cycle-fgm-senegal/index.html#17

[197] Miriam Temin and Ruth Levine, *Start With a Girl: A New Agenda For Global Health*, Center for Global Development, 2009.

http://www.cgdev.org/files/1422899_file_Start_with_a_Girl_FINAL.pdf "Why is Girls' Education important for Public Health and Vice-Versa?" Global Partnership for Education, September 15, 2014.

[198] http://www.globalpartnership.org/blog/why-girls%E2%80%99-education-important-public-health-and-vice-versa

www.globalgiving.org, www.kiva.org, Plan International, **Women for Women International**, World Vision, or American Jewish World Service. Get email updates on www.womensenews.org and www.worldpulse.com Join the CARE Action Network at www.can.care.org.The *Girl Fund* (www.thegirlfund.org), Equality Now (www.equalitynow.org), Global Fund for Women (www.globalfundforwomen.org), Grameen Bank (www.grameen-info.org), International Women's Health Coalition (www.iwhc.org), Women for Women International (www.womenforwomen.org), Women's Campaign International (www.womenscampaigninternational.org)

[199] *Voices of Youth*, March 5, 2006.

www.unicef.org/voy

[200] Deniz Kandiyoti, "Promise and Peril: Women and the 'Arab Spring,'" *Open Democracy*, March 8, 2011.

https://www.opendemocracy.net/5050/deniz-kandiyoti/promise-and-peril-women-and-%E2%80%98arab-spring%E2%80%99

[201] The first three facts are mentioned in Bianca Jagger, "Ending Violence Against Women and Girls: If Not Now, When?" CommonDreams, November 11, 2016.

[202] http://www.commondreams.org/views/2016/11/25/ending-violence-against-women-and-girls-if-not-now-when

www.vday.org/take-action/violence-against-women Includes more resource information, plus action guides for students.

[203] http://www.girleffect.org/explore/breaking-the-cycle-of-violence-against-girls/in-numbers-why-tackling-violence-will-unleash-the-potential-of-millions-of-girls/

[204] http://www.ted.com/talks/sheryl_wudunn_our_century_s_greatest_injustice?language=en

[205] http://www.youthkiawaaz.com/2014/08/world-hates-women-video-chilling-account-women-face-world/

"Voice and Agency: Empowering Women and Girls for Shared Prosperity, The World Bank," October 10, 2014, p. 3.

[206] https://openknowledge.worldbank.org/handle/10986/1903

[207] http://fra.europa.eu/sites/default/files/fra-2014-vaw-survey-factsheet_en.pdf

Gloria Steinem, "Escaping Control," Talk to *Bioneers* conference, 2012.

[208] http://media.bioneers.org/listing/escaping-control-linking-gender-social-movements-and-democracy-gloria-steinem/

Chris Hedges,"No One is Free Until All Are Free," Speech at Simon Fraser University in Vancouver, *TruthDig*, March 29, 2015.

[209] http://www.truthdig.com/report/item/no_one_is_free_until_all_are_free_20150329

[210] http://www.un.org/en/ga/search/view_doc.asp?symbol=A/RES/68/181

Cassandra Balchin, "Religious Fundamentalisms on the Rise: A Case for Action," AWID.

[211] http://issuu.com/awid/docs/rfs_on_the_rise_-_a_case_for_action

Kristin Williams, "16 Women Who Are Standing Up to Violence," The Institute for Inclusive Security, February 11, 2016.

[212] https://www.inclusivesecurity.org/16-women-who-are-standing-up-to-violence/

See the documentary *Trading Women*, a 2003 documentary filmed in Asia. A Nigerian report in 2010 stated as many as 40,000 girls and women were trafficked to West African countries as sex slaves.

[213] www.iast.net/thefacts.htm The website for a 2011 documentary about sex trafficking of Eastern European women includes many resources: http://priceofsex.org/content/resources

[214] "Human Trafficking Facts," Force 4 Compassion

http://www.f-4-c.org/slavery/facts.asp Rebecca Theodore, "Human Trafficing," *Nationof Change,* January 27, 2015.

http://www.nationofchange.org/2015/01/27/human-trafficking-curse-modern-civilization/

[215] human Trafficking 101—The Presenter's Kit, 2007. It includes two films and a training video.

Rick Gladstone, "Real Threat in a Known Market for Children," *New York Times*, May 7, 2014.

[216] http://www.nytimes.com/2014/05/08/world/africa/real-threat-in-a-known-market-for-children.html

[217] https://www.youtube.com/watch?v=VYMWn4JsO00

https://www.youtube.com/watch?v=gL49DREHr20

[218] https://www.youtube.com/watch?v=VYMWn4JsO00

[219] Nicholas Kristof and Sheryl WuDunn. *Half the Sky: Turning Oppression into Opportunity for Women Worldwide.* Alfred a. Knopf, 2009, p. 9.

[220] "Global Sex Trafficking Fact Sheet," Equality Now. http://www.equalitynow.org/node/1010

[221] Statistics about women in India http://sigi.org/gv_india.html Information about trafficking of women and children. www.csuchico.edu/stop/reports.php

[222] Girls Count: A Global Investment & Action Agenda (PDF) Center for Global Development, 2008 Clinton's Global Initiative

[223] http://www.freedom-connect.com/about

[224] www.somaly.org/whoweare/

[225] www.nyof.org

[226] www.nyof.org/meetTheChildren/index.html

[227] www.worldpulse.com/user/1204

Glen Kessler, "One in Five Women in College Sexually Assaulted," *Washington Post*, May 1, 2014.

[228] http://www.washingtonpost.com/blogs/fact-checker/wp/2014/05/01/one-in-five-women-in-college-sexually-assaulted-the-source-of-this-statistic/

[229] Itsonus.orgs

[230] http://ritabanerjisblog.files.wordpress.com/2011/08/usa-india-puzzle_0.jpg

[231] Siddhartha Deb. *The Beautiful and the Damned: A Portrait of the New India.* Faber and Faber, 2011.

Lauren Ferreira Cardoso, "Street Harassment is a Public Health Problem," *The Conversation*, March 19, 2017.

[232] http://theconversation.com/street-harassment-is-a-public-health-problem-the-case-of-mexico-city-73962

http://www.ihollaback.org/share/

[233] http://www.ihollaback.org/resources/vlog/

[234] Nicholas Kristof and Sheryl WuDunn, op.cit, p. 182.

"WHO Report Highlights Violence Against Women," *World Health Organization*, June 20, 2013.

[235] http://www.who.int/mediacentre/news/releases/2013/violence_against_women_20130620/en/

Evann Gastaldo, "Indian Wedding Gift: Paddles to Beat Drunk Husbands," Newser, May 1, 2017.

[236] http://www.newser.com/story/242084/indian-wedding-gift-paddles-to-beat-drunk-husbands.html

[237] www.worldpulse.com/pulsewire/programs/action-**blogging-campaign-gbv**

Bjorn Lomborg, "Why Domestic Violence Costs More than War," *World Economic Forum Agenda*, September 19, 2014.

238 https://agenda.weforum.org/2014/09/domestic-violence-cost-war-development-goals/

239 http://www.unicef.org/zimbabwe/media_15384.html

240 http://www.cdc.gov/violenceprevention/pdf/sv-datasheet-a.pdf *The Hunting Ground*, 2015, about sexual assault on US college campuses.

Caroline Heldman and Danielle Dirks, "Blowing the Whistle on Campus Rape," *Ms. Magazine*, Winter, 2014.

241 http://msmagazine.com/blog/2014/02/18/blowing-the-whistle-on-campus-rape/

Helene Cooper, "Pentagon Study Finds 50% Increase in Reports of Military Sexual Assaults, *New York Times*, May 2, 2014.

242 http://www.nytimes.com/2014/05/02/us/military-sex-assault-report.html

243 Mako Fitts, "Where Do We Go From bell?" September 10, 2010. http://msmagazine.com/blog/blog/2010/09/10/where-do-we-go-from-bell/

244 http://www.who.int/mediacentre/factsheets/fs239/en/

245 Avaaz.org, November 21, 2013. https://secure.avaaz.org/en/take_kaias_win_global_donate/

Shamillah Wilson, Anasuya Sengupta, and Kristy Evans, **eds.** *Defending Our Dreams: Global Feminist Voices for a New Generation*. Zed Books and AWID, 2005, p. 188.

246 Kimberly Burge, "How Men in South Africa are Trying to Stop Violence Against Women," *The Atlantic*, December 28, 2012.

247 http://www.theatlantic.com/sexes/archive/2012/12/how-men-in-south-africa-are-trying-to-stop-violence-against-women/266689/

248 http://youngfeministnamibia.wordpress.com/

Man Up is a global campaign to activate youth to stop violence against women and girls. On July 5-11-2010, the Man Up Campaign held their very first global summit to stop violence against women. www.worldpulse.com/pulsewire/programs/action-blogging-campaign-gbv

249 "Violence Against Women: 1bn Rising," 14, 2014.

http://www.theguardian.com/society/2014/feb/14/one-billion-rising-to-end-violence-against-women-global-day-of-action-and-dancing-live-coverage

250 http://www.stopstreetharassment.org/about/

251 http://www.equalitynow.org/about-us

Gloria Steinem was interviewed on *BBC Hardtalk*, February 27, 2013. http://www.bbc.co.uk/programmes/p014rsrm

252 http://www.womenforwomen.org/

www.globalfundforwomen.org/

253 http://16dayscwgl.rutgers.edu/2014-campaign/2014-theme-announcement

254 https://www.youtube.com/watch?v=4S7EwZ-yGQI&nohtml5=False

255 "The State of the World's Girls 2014," Plan International, p. 14 plan-international.org/girls/reports-and-publications/the-state-of...

256 https://www.youtube.com/watch?v=FPA1rTrPuzw&feature=share&list=UUVLkqTvsRpm46RDmM4SYf6Q

257 http://www.girleffect.org/media/139917/declaration_document_web_v6_26_9_13_copy.pdf

258 http://www.oxfam.org.au/world/gender/index.html

http://www.unmillenniumproject.org/press/press2.htm

http://www.icrw.org/html/quickfacts/quickfacts.htm UN Millennium project- work on women

http://www.unmillenniumproject.org/press/press2.htm Oxfam gender work and statistics

http://www.oxfam.org.au/world/gender/index.html UNESCO- statistics on women's progress

http://www.uis.unesco.org/ev.php?ID=6265_201&ID2=DO_TOPIC

http://www.uis.unesco.org/ev.php?ID=6098_201&ID2=DO_TOPIC Oxfam International, ActionAid International, Education International www.oxfam.org www.socialwatch.org www.actionaid.org www.whiteband.org International Center for Research on Women (ICRW) 1717 Massachusetts Avenue, NW | Suite 302 | Washington, D.C. 20036

259 http://coalitionforadolescentgirls.org/resources-by-topic-2/

260 http://coalitionforadolescentgirls.org/resources-by-topic-2/

261 http://www3.weforum.org/docs/WEF_GenderGap_Report_2013.pdf.

262 http://www.feministsf.org/bibs/recommended.html

263 http://www.bbc.com/news/magazine-26664736

264 http://www.bbc.com/news/world-29763582

http://www.bbc.com/news/world-29758796

Doaa, Egyptian graduate student, Aswan

Chapter 4

CONSUMERISM TARGETS "GIRL POWER"

I hope I'll have a lot of money because I don't want to work. But I like traveling around the world. I want to go anywhere. I think everything on the earth is interesting and magical. I don't like to know everything from books. It's too boring, so I want to see everything with my own eyes. I wish I were born rich and pretty. Anyway, I want to become a well-known person.

Ko-Yun, 15, f, Taiwan

I would stop wars, make peace, make sure no one is living on the streets, and people not dying all the time. Not everything is about money and being number one.

Talia, 15, f, Australia

I bet you every girl here is so much looking forward to escaping away to wearing jeans and adopt Western culture as soon as they get a chance. If someone would be proud of wearing salwar kamiz [a tunic worn over loose pants with a scarf around the neck] and eating at local restaurants rather than big fancy American-style ones and wearing all those lovely sparkly jingly dresses and bangles, that person is traditional.

Sahar, 17, f, Pakistan

When it comes to being corrupt, immoral and materialistic, those are the words that describe this generation. We have lost our humanity and our focus really seems to be on MONEY!!!!

Taika, 18, f, Ethiopia

"Bart, with $10,000, we'd be millionaires! We could buy all kinds of useful things like... love!"

Cartoon character Homer Simpson to his son Bart

Globalization is producing a global youth culture. Urban landscapes in developed and developing countries alike feature many of the same shopping malls, fast food chains, clothing stores, music clubs, and reality TV shows. Mass media shapes young people's tastes and trends. Music Television International (MTV), for example, which has a presence in most countries of the world, transmits music but also aspirations, codes, *values, behaviours and tastes. Internet cafes have become meeting places, especially for young men. Cellular phones are found everywhere in urban centres, and as a communal service in villages and poor communities. [The world has more than 5 billion mobile phones, including more than one billion smartphones.] Rural areas have less access to the global youth culture, though mobile phones and the Internet are spreading information, ideas and popular culture still travel largely through radio and sometimes TV.*

Globalization and the global culture have made everyone aware of consumption possibilities, including the people least able to satisfy them; for example only 1% of young people in Ethiopia have access to the Internet, compared to 50% in China. This sense of exclusion and frustration can turn into crime, violence and civil unrest.

Quote from AIESEC youth leaders of the world's largest youth-run leadership organization representing 110 countries.[1] It's composed of university students and recent graduates.

Contents: Consumer Youth Religion?, Teen Identity Through Consumption, Social Unrest from Rising Expectations, How Youth Are Manipulated by Multinational Corporations, Negative Consequences of Consumerism, Youth Views about Materialism and Getting Rich, Traditional and Modern Beliefs: Moving Towards the Middle

Consumer Youth Religion?

SpeakOut youth from various backgrounds are critical of materialism, although some want to have a lot of money to support their future families and do good. This chapter looks at how consumerism is manipulated by advertisers and asks if Generations Y and Z buy into the sales pitches. A Dutch critic warns, "Tasteless American youth culture rules all." The planet can't sustain the current rate of consumption of resources, especially water and land. Global media stimulate desire for possessions, yet almost one billion people live in abject poverty. A Dawson College student in the US, Annika explained, "Consumer and pop culture raised us to be the way they want us to be, rather than spend time on issues like abortion, gender-based violence, AIDS and the like. The younger generation of feminists are less likely to speak up because of the pressure pop-culture puts on us to conform."[2] Until recently she was afraid to tell people she was a feminist; her fears were verified because when she started speaking up all she got was "the stink eye and whispers." Keeping in mind the lag between rural and urban dwellers, will youth in developing countries adhere to consumerism or foment unrest because they can't afford to buy and shop?

Increasing numbers of government and NGO programs for girls are focusing on girls' loss of voice in adolescence, encouraging girls to speak up online and at conferences and other spaces supervised by adults where they are open to surveillance and control. Australian scholar Anita Harris warns that the problem with encouraging girls to express themselves is that it's channeled through adult mediators and authorities who provide guidance: "It could be argued that the more young women speak, the less power they have."[3] To subvert this control, girls turn to the new media-based politics of "border work" between the public and private, without adult supervision: on their websites (i.e., "Ms. Mediocre," "Losergrrl," and "Big Bad Chinese Mama"); zines ("I'm So Fucking Beautiful"); in alternative music (punk, grunge, and hip-hop); performance art; graffiti; stickering (pasting political stickers on sexist ads); culture jamming "ad busting;" art and comics (i.e., "Re: Vulva Girl").

A group called Brandalism replaces corporate ads in public spaces with political messages and art by international artists, as happened during the Paris climate change conference in November 2015.[4] Some young political activists also use traditional tactics including demonstrations, petitions, letter writing, and lobbying.

Since the late 1990s, advertisers have defined "Girl Power" as the action of being savvy consumers and they frequently use the term in ads (online photos show sexist ads from the 1930s to 1960s[5]). The British group The Spice Girls introduced this concept without using the word feminism; girl power was reinforced by the *Buffy the Vampire Killer* TV series (1997 to 2003), and in films discussed in the next chapter. Girls are targeted in various countries to practice "self-invention" through buying things.[6] Youth citizenship and power is defined as rooted in their spending power as consumers with disposable income and their knowledge of style to create personal identity. The campaign is mainly concentrating on girls and what Anita Harris calls the "feminization" of the workforce in service and communication industries.[7] Interviews with 70 teen girls in New York City revealed that the girls adopted the belief that they had power as consumers, but realized it would be difficult to succeed as women in the work world with their future family responsibilities.[8] They accepted the neoliberal "girl power media culture" belief that they have the individual choice of when to be feminine and when to exert their power assertively. In a post-feminist era, the girls didn't have a sense of organized efforts to make change. This was especially true of low-income girls of color in New York, who tended to view themselves as liberated in contrast to oppressed women in other countries like Afghanistan.

Products aimed at the achieving girl include Goldie Blox engineering toys, Lego Friends, and the Nerf Rebelle toy gun for girls. *Sports Illustrated* usually shows scantily clothed and probably airbrushed women on its covers, but the magazine featured 13-year-old Little League pitcher Mo'Ne Davis in uniform on its August 2014 cover. US academic Christia Brown observes that girl power aims for girls to be more like boys in math and science, in sports, and in boldness. She suggests that boys also need a movement to free them from restrictive roles.[9] Studies of consumerism usually don't report on how girls resist these definitions of feminine attractiveness or "girl power," such as K-Mart underpants for little girls with the logo "I heart rich boys." When parents protested the slogan, K-Mart withdrew the underwear. It is surprising that amid scholarship about youth activism, there are so few empirical examinations of young feminists' resistance to the contemporary gender stereotypes."[10]

Globalization is accompanied by consumerism. Taking advantage of a natural adolescent desire to establish an identity different from their parents, corporations sell goods that signal subcultural identity. Teens wearing brand logos are "globalizations' most powerful symbols," said Canadian author and activist Naomi Klein. She explains, "More than anything or anyone else, logo-decorated middle-class teenagers, intent on pouring themselves into a media-fabricated mold, have become globalization's most powerful symbols." She argues in her book *No Logo* (2009) that corporations manipulate an international youth identity based on the brand of a "global teen" to sell the same "cool" products around the world through MTV and other multi-national media.[11] Advertisers aim to create a hybrid "third notion of nationality—not American, not local, but one that would unite the two, through shopping." Sometimes youth blend tradition and Western consumerism: a hybrid example is the chapter photo of an Egyptian young woman I interviewed in Aswan who wears a three-layered black and white hijab scarf, jeans and a black and white T-shirt with the slogan, "A Sexy Dress Spiral Girl Product."

Consumer mentality is rampant. Reyna, 17, reported from California, "Teenagers today are concerned the most with being marketable so they can collect a larger friend database." She reports on how advertising psychology influences her peers' desire to market themselves as if they are popular brands:

> *The thing that characterizes youth culture is the importance of image. With the help of Internet communities and technology you can "sell" yourself to other*

teenagers based on all the things that comprise image. These would be interests, hobbies, friends. The more interesting your image is, the more "marketable" you are to other friends. These friends are also marketing themselves on these Internet communities. Being a teenager is about consumerism and standing out. The more unique you are, the more favorable in the eyes of the youth.

I present my fashion image virtually through Tumblr, a blog that lets you post images to your webpage.[12] *A lot of the images I post are fashion images that I like. Other people can look at my page and decide to subscribe to my blog if they have similar interests. The two biggest fashion fads at this moment are piercings [she has two studs in her cheeks] and thrift clothing, which is a good thing because it helps save a lot of money! [She reports what's trendy on Tumblr.]*[13]

Neoliberal capitalism can be viewed as a new religion that preaches happiness through buying "Happiness inside" is written on the can of my coconut water. In its ads, Subaru claims, "Love. It's what makes a Subaru, a Subaru." When the Thai military took over the government in a coup in 2014, they tried to distract protesters with their "Return Happiness to the People" campaign including free concerts, food, and sexy female dancers in miniskirts. Advertisers, entertainers, and the media took over from preachers to tell us how to obtain paradise on earth through consumption. Neal Gabler maintains in his book *Life the Movie: How Entertainment Conquered Reality* (1998) that celebrity culture is a hostile takeover of religion by consumer culture. It defines how we live our lives, how to look young and glamorous like celebrities, exploiting our desire to be famous—if only on social network sites. "I want to be a dancing teacher and a celebrity," said Zijun, a rural Chinese girl (age 13). Another of her ambitious goals is to "see all the wonders in the world."

Celebrities become our gods and personality is valued over character in the "cult of the self," as discussed by Katrina (19, f, California).

You can't generalize to all young people, but it's concerning when I see people at school who talk about celebrities who aren't even celebrities. They're reality TV stars like Paris Hilton, Jersey Shore, and the Kardashians. It's really scary that a lot of young people would rather discuss someone else's life who is rich rather than talking about real social issues. Maybe there's some fear in discussing social issues; sometimes it's easier to live in ignorance and not face the problem. It's really scary that they find other people's lives so interesting. I don't want to make excuses for my generation, but the mass media creates these characters on TV.

"Individual consumption is the defining experience of our age," according to sociologist Zygmunt Bauman in his book *Freedom* (1989). What results is, "a homogenized set of consumption practices and ways to think about identity." "I think global media influences us to care about accumulating things and caring too much about status," said Raia (20, f, Pakistan). Partly as a consequence of media definitions of beauty, over half of US girls age 13 are unhappy with their bodies, and this rises to 78% by age 17; other facts about girls and media are on "The Representation Project" website, which aims to change stereotypes.[14]

Advertisers tell us that the modern meaning of life and the way to obtain fulfillment comes through buying things like technological gadgets, brand name clothes, entertainment, and food from trendy restaurants. As a result, the average person bombarded with advertising in the West consumes as much as 32 Kenyans consume each year.[15] Martin Luther King, Jr., warned a year before his assassination in 1968 that, "If we are to get on the right side of the world revolution, we as a nation must undergo a radical revolution of values. We must rapidly begin the shift from a 'thing-oriented' society to a 'person-oriented' society," but this shift was opposed by the Trump Administration emphasis on making money over values like environmentalism or health care for all.

Media stars are themselves turned into commodities: "I hate being thought of as a product," reported singer Miley Cyrus when she was 17. Regarding the last season on her TV show *Hannah Montana*, seen in many countries, she said, "Now I just want to be chill and have my private life. When they're putting me in sparkles and in pink this final season, I have to grit my teeth. I can't breathe looking like that anymore. I'm feeling claustrophobic in all these frills."[16] She said she was insecure as a teen because she had "bad skin" and tried every possible product, but her parents allowed her to be herself. "I think you just should be who you are." She moved on to slinky adult fashion or wearing very little, as shown online,[17] happy to express "the bad bitch that I am" and to twerk, use drugs, and be nude in reaction to good girl stereotypes.

Cyrus refers to herself as a feminist because, "I'm just about equality, period."[18] At age 22, she said, "I think we've overused it so much that it's getting confusing to girls as to what a feminist actually is. Being a feminist is just about we want to be equal, not above, not below. Equal."[19] "So yes, I'm a feminist because I'm female-empowered, and I want to give fucking women jobs and I want us to be out there, being leaders and being badass, totally, but I want the same thing for men as well. Totally." The lack of political and social awareness epitomizes the weakness in young feminist emphasis on doing your own thing.

Girls called the "Influencers" can gain enormous followings with popular blogs and Internet presences like Tavi Gevinson's style blog called Rookie. Cyrus said about them fame-seekers, "I do think it's true that my generation is in crisis. Everyone is trying to get Instagram famous and a lot of it is purely what they're wearing, what they look like." This creates a crisis in self-esteem for the girls who look at the photos because, "People are chasing something that doesn't exist." For Cyrus equality seems to be superficial matters of clothing or lack of it although she founded a charity in Los Angeles called the Happy Hippie Foundation for homeless youth.

An example of how to manufacture a celebrity, In *Branding Obamessiah: The Rise of an American Idol* (2011), Cal Thomas maintains that starting in 2004 the Obama campaign deliberately used advertising branding tactics--similar to those used to sell Apple products--to create an image of a messianic leader, "The One." The term was used in the *Matrix* films about the hero, Neo, a series that portrays social illusion to an extreme so that virtual images are believed to be reality. Some say this refers to our own manipulation by media, such as the Russian use of bots and social media to influence the 2016 presidential election in favor of Trump's candidacy. The way branders reach the American "cultural unconscious" or the "virtual-hive mind" is to appeal to the concept of dreams, a concept used by Latino immigrant activist Dreamers.

Cal Thomas believes that savvy media experts created a religious brand for Obama, with a creation story told in his book *Dreams from My Father,* celebrity true believers like Oprah Winfrey, sacred words ("hope" and "change"), sacred images (halos of light over his head in photos), pilgrimages to holy places, and use of rituals and relics. Thomas writes that Obama was careful to avoid taking strong stands on issues in a "pattern of ambiguity" and that he sometimes changed his story to curry favor with various audiences. Of course this is not unique to Obama. A later addition to the theme, David Garrow's 2017 book *Rising Star: The Making of Barack Obama*, describes how Obama manipulated his image in order to fulfill what he believed was his destiny.

Youth Studies professor James Côté explains that the debate about youth participation in politics is between those who worry about youth's lack of involvement in old formal politics such as voting and political parties and its replacement, the new "techno-politics" of informal involvement using ICT.[20] More than half the world's people use a smartphone (4.9 billion), more than half of the 3.7 billion Internet users access via their phones, and 2.8 billion are active social media users.[21] Facebook has over two billion monthly users. Africa has the least connectivity, with only 29% Internet users, followed by South Asia with only one-third of Internet users. More than one in five people shopped online in the last 30 days.

Some dismiss youth political resistance in social media campaigns as motivated by group conformity that doesn't threaten the neoliberal economic system and is manipulated by the system. The economic system aims to keep youth consuming, distracted and uninvolved in critiquing neoliberalism's reduction of social programs for youth, lower wages and higher tuition fees. This important area of economic study of media influence is "underdeveloped" and divided between "internet idealists" and those who are skeptical about the distractions of "cocooning," clicktivism and being "cool" that is enabled by the Internet. Côté states in his *Youth Studies* (2014) book that, "There does not appear to be a political revolution on the horizons in the West that would eradicate the problems facing contemporary youth that stem from their exploitation under neoliberal conditions." The illusion of resistance is manipulated with superficial "badges of rebellion" such as tattoos and piercings.

A documentary explores *#ReGeneration: The Politics of Apathy and Activism in the Me Generation*: The transcript of interviews with young people and older experts is available online.[22] On the video reporter Tucker Carlson says, "We do our best to affect youth culture because that's where the ad dollars are." A high school girl also quoted in the film says, "We may not demonstrate and aren't as active as generations of the 60s and 70s, but a big part of that is because we haven't gone outside for our entire lives. We've been inside, on the Internet." Some models of youth activism exist: Côté cites Sweden as a model for effective youth political involvement, with a high voting rate and knowledge about political issues, indicating that the use of ICT and traditional political arenas are not mutually exclusive.

Teens told *BuzzFeed* in 2015 that fads change and that they don't know about current fads, except for fashion trends: hippie clothes, choker necklaces, crop tops, and silver or lilac hair color.[23] They report that Netflix replaced MTV and they listen to music and watch TV online. They don't like Facebook but most use it, mostly to connect with their parents, while the preferred teen platform is Instagram. They think technology helps them connect with friends and family. What is uncool is speaking in text lingo and bad boy Justin Bieber. The most popular celebrities are women: Kim Kardashian, Taylor Swift and Beyoncé. What the teens want is to be taken seriously by adults and they like talking with them. I asked a high school senior named Sacha in my town about the accuracy of this survey, she said, "Ha ha, most of those seem pretty spot on."

Scholars focus on girls as passive consumers rather than producers of media, according to *Girls Make Media* by Mary Kearney (2006), but the blogosphere is full of Third Wave feminists. A European website called "grassroots feminism.net" corrects the view of young women as vapid consumers: "The preconception of youth, and in particular of girls and young women, as culturally unproductive and as passive consumers of mass culture and media is still very much ingrained today. However, girls and young women are capable cultural producers who create a wide variety of their own films, music, media, and festivals." Their website (grassrootsfeminism.net) features these feminist creations and activities, mainly European. Two of the members edited a book on *Feminist Media: Participatory Spaces, Networks and Cultural Citizenship* (2012). Some teens, like many adults, accept consumerism's values, while others subvert media and create their own.

Some girls do "culture jamming" adbusting, and Internet blogging to criticize consumer culture. The band Negativland coined the term culture jamming in 1984 meaning to subvert popular culture with guerrilla communication by altering ads and logos, and doing performance art like the older Guerrilla Girls in the art world who began in 1985,[24] graffiti, and hacktivism. Canadian "girl activists" explain, "The response among many youth, including eco-grrrls, is to target the culture industry directly. This new generation of activists play with cultural images and challenge them through a production of their own independent, consumer-free spaces." Three sisters formed the Radical Cheerleaders in 1996, creating cheers as protests, and published a zine the following year, which states, "It's screaming fuck capitalism while doing a split."[25] Squads spread around the US and in some international cities; one of the activists explained, "It's a safe space to feel feminine and badass."

Teen Identity Through Consumption

Taking advantage of a natural adolescent desire to establish an identity different from their parents, corporations sell goods that signal subcultural identity. Brands of clothing and types of music are used to mark group membership, such as hip-hop fans wearing baggy pants and gold chains. In an article, Sandy Banks quotes a young woman who observes, "What's wrong is that the 'consumer culture' has become such a defining force in young women's search for identity. It's what you're wearing, what your weight is, rather than what you believe in, how you think." The popular TV reruns and movie series *Sex and the City,* and its prequel, *The Carrie Diaries* about Carrie as a high school fashionista, illustrate how status and joy come from the brand of shoe and purse you display.[26] However, the young women friends in the HBO series Girls that ended in 2017 don't focus on expensive brands.[27] The main character Hannah, expresses herself with tattoos, and revealing a lot of skin wearing shorts or less.

As former president Jimmy Carter warned, "Human identity is no longer defined by what one does but by what one owns...too many of us now tend to worship self-indulgence and consumption." The ad message is if you don't buy this product, you're out of it. From Italy, Carlotta (also 17) reports, "I think that TV and Internet have an important place in my everyday life but I don't think I'm influenced by them because I have a lot of critical sensibility. The only thing that influences me are advertisements, because if I see something beautiful on TV I would like to have it, and, if I can, I buy it." Manmehak (17, f, India) explained, Global media "makes me feel connected to the world and advertisements make me buy better products." Some ads challenge the usual sexist messages. An video ad for a laundry soap called #SharetheLoad features a father visiting his married daughter as she cooks, cleans, and talks on the phone all at the same time while her husband just sits.[28] She serves him tea and he asks her to wash his shirt. Observing this, her father tells her he is sorry he just let her play house as a girl and let his wife do all the housework. He then goes home and surprises his wife by doing the laundry.

A new identity was created in the 20th century--the consumer. Identity is signaled by what we own and display to others, our clothes, phones, and vehicles. Although not usually recognized by historians, US girl "bobby soxers" created the identity of the teenager during World War II as a "subcultural resistance."[29] They wore overalls and were fans of Frank Sinatra. Since then, "young female fans continue to be the subject of simultaneous moral panic and patronizing scorn." Teens' new heroes are media stars, some of them manufactured by promoters like The Spice Girls or One Direction singing groups, or airbrushed and heavily made-up anorexic fashion models who've had plastic surgery. We're supposed to buy their CDs or fashion styles to be like them. A study of young Indonesian bloggers reported they often write about singers, movie stars, and soap opera plots.[30]

An example of the result of the commercial propaganda that identity and self-worth is based on owning the latest fad is the near riots in US malls among young people fighting to buy the new Nike Foamposite Galaxy Shoe in 2012. Some "sneakerheads" spend thousands of dollars on their favorite shoes; one of them explained, "It's like I'm wearing art on my feet."[31] What's cool changes, with trends often starting in the US. Teens in 2014 changed from wanting to dress like their sub-culture to wanting "to put an individual spin" on their look, according to a 16-year-old in Washington, DC. In response, retailers selling to teens replaced their logo T-shirts, struggling to make their products more exciting than the latest iPhone.[32]

In a materialistic culture, what you consume signals your style, your sexual attractiveness, your social class and power, connects you with friends, and is how you find pleasure. For example, how would you judge someone who spends their money going to museums and concerts and drinks wine versus someone who goes to car races and drinks beer? Drives a Porsche or a truck or VW bug? Although many youth aspire to the lifestyle sold by Western media, older leaders fear its impact. In Burma, the ruling generals tried to undermine middle-aged Aung San Suu Kyi's political charisma by referring to her as a "Western fashion girl."

Global youth are critical of consumer culture yet they define themselves by their role as consumers, according to a 2003 global electronic survey of 1,400 youth conducted by an international youth NGO, TakingITGlobal.[33] Many (76%) felt consumerism has too much influence on youth, making them materialistic and self-centered. Yet they often saw themselves as consumers. When asked about the roles that youth play in society, all regions selected the student role as the most important, but "consumers" was second place in North America, Europe and Oceania, third in South America, and seventh in Asia. Respondents identified youth as trendsetters in their region except for Africa. They approved of technology as a way to share information and communicate, with a positive effect on youth, although they were concerned about the digital divide leaving out poor children.[34]

Four characteristics of global youth were identified in Elissa Moses' marketing research survey of 34,000 mainly middle-class teens in 44 countries. In addition to being consumers, respondents like sports, value relationships, and have a passion for technology and entertainment.[35] As consumers they desire brand names and are influenced by television shows about wealthy people and their possessions. When global youth were surveyed by AIESEC (the largest global college student organization) about what field they would like to work in, their goals were mainly business and tech-oriented, in this order: own a business, entertainment, high-tech, government, manufacturing, charity, financial services, energy/utilities, and retail.[36]

Half of American teens use brands to help express their individuality and make them stand out, according to a survey of 112,258 global teens active on the Habbo virtual world. Fewer teens in other countries have this goal--38%.[37] Overall, about the same number--30%--use brands to fit in with their friends rather than trying to be different. Much of their favorite entertainment is American: Their favorite TV shows are *The Simpsons, Hannah Montana,* and *SpongeBob SquarePants.* Their favorite Internet sites also originated in the US—YouTube and Facebook. Young people questioned in another large global survey are slightly more concerned about looking good (83%) than older people ages 30 to 50 (77%).[38] Since the 1920s the fashionable Modern Girl in global cities has been expected to buy cosmetics, high heels, and sexy clothes.[39] However, young women are only 5% more focused on their appearance than men, according to the Habbo poll. A majority of respondents are not concerned about being fashionable but 49% do think it's important. In the face of pressure to look like airbrushed anorexic models, described by Natasha Walter in *Living Dolls: The Return of Sexism* (2011), the poll results are encouraging in that the majority don't try to fit fashion norms.

Style and image now include not just clothes but virtual avatars or icons to represent oneself in cyber culture, on the more than 60 youth-oriented virtual worlds.[40] One of the more popular worlds, *Second Life,* offers a "Teen Second Life." Youth can also create avatar images to represent themselves on the virtual *World of Warcraft.* The young "Digital Natives" experienced the first social networks and blogs in 2000. Media also popularize the latest styles in teen magazines like *Qingnian Yizu,* the Mandarin version of *Seventeen.* Researchers who analyzed children's TV commercials in Hong Kong and South Korea expected differences between the two areas, but the gender stereotyping was similar. The researchers suggested the similarity might be due to "the emerging homogeneous youth market using a standardized advertising strategy" that transcends nationalities.[41]

A consumer study called "The Phoenix Generation: Insights into Chinese Consumers" focused on Chinese youth ages 16 to 30, based on 200 interviews and online surveys.[42] They found that what's popular with Chinese youth is Western sports like the National Basketball Association (NBA) and music like hip-hop, which has been called the largest youth movement in the world.[43] These fads benefit brands such as Nike, Adidas and Li Ning because young people want to look like their favorite sports and music superstars. The Phoenix Generation report says "Chuppies" (Chinese Yuppies) are increasingly common. They buy homes and cars and invest in stocks and bonds. By 2009, more cars were purchased in China than in the US, so McDonalds responded with drive-in restaurants (they have restaurants in over 100 countries).

From China, SpeakOut student Yuan reports, "About consumerism and materialism, some people who can't afford an iPhone even sold their kidney to black market just to buy one. iPhone's marketing is so successful in China that iPhone has a unique position among cell phones. It became a symbol of fashion and trend." A rural Chinese girl (age 13) agreed that ads do "stimulate my desire to buy stuff." A survey of 2,000 Arab youth asked what they did with their leisure time: Watching TV is the most popular activity for young people, which of course sells consumerism with ads and product placement in shows. Their next favorite activities are going to malls and dining out that require expenditures.[44]

Style is an important way youth with money create their identity, as did earlier Western subcultures like the corseted Gibson Girls in the 19th century, followed by in the 20th century by flappers, beatniks, hippies, punks and hip-hop "gangstas."[45] Hybrid identity is expressed in clothes, music preferences, use of communication technology and in going to certain hangouts with friends, as studied in Subcultural and Post-Subcultural Studies. When I worked on developing youth programs in my town, administrators at teen centers I interviewed in other cities told me they had to schedule different kinds of music on different nights of the week to attract various subcultures. Youth aim to establish their individual identity or brand with their music preferences, Internet pages, and their appearance. A Danish boy, Christoffer said, "I think it's kind of cool that you don't just look like the others," but an Icelandic girl interviewed in a BBC documentary about girls in four countries, said girls generally face pressure to look sexy and attractive.[46]

I asked Reyna, 17, about the global teen uniform of jeans, T-shirt, sweatshirt, and sneakers/trainers, as well as groups like preppies or Goths that don't seem to want an individual style but prefer to be identified as a group member through wearing similar clothes.

> *No matter what social clique you're in, every teen wants to stand out and be recognized, to receive positive attention. It seems like teens thrive on it.*

> *All social cliques differ from each other but within each group it's hard not to notice that they each have their own brand. Preps wear Hollister, Abercrombie, and play sports. Punks are anti-fashion and wear anything that offends traditional society or fashion in some way. If you identify yourself with a group you most likely look like the others that are in the same group as you.*

US songs demand "look at this body," while "Show Off" is the name of a make-up brand, in sharp contrast to indigenous cultures and Nordic countries where standing out is considered rude and deviant. Being a "tall poppy" is frowned upon in Nordic countries where conformity is expected, as explained about Denmark by Helen Russell in her book *The Year of Living Danishly* (2016).

MTV developed a website called "mtvsticky" that includes fashion stories like "Become a Reccessionista" and another site called "districtmtv" where viewers can share fashion styles. MTV surveys found that Millennials' number one spending priority is to buy clothes to express themselves through fashion. Typical high school clothes are shown in a student's photographs of Santa Monica High School.[47] Interestingly, they haven't changed since my friend Califia graduated in 1995.

Rhys, 15, lives in my town and educates me about teen culture. He evolved from identifying with the "emo" style of expressing emotion and angst to the "scene" group who may have unusual hair colors, piercings, and makeup. He can also identify with punk defiance of norms and hipster attempts to not follow what's currently popular. He likes websites such thetripatorium.com. Rhys says most of the teens he knows feel entitled, people he calls "the normals." They want to look like the people in their group— perhaps punk, Goth, or scene, and listen to the same music. (Check the online Urban Dictionary for current definitions of teen groups and search the Internet for photos of their recent fashion styles.[48]) Maybe only 10% of local teens are like him, teens who don't want to conform to a clique and don't think life is about having things. A UK critique of what Rhys calls "the normal" is a book titled *What the **** is Normal?!* (2014) by Francesca Martinez who calls for a "wobbly revolution" to accept people like her, born with cerebral palsy.[49]

Rhys would like to be involved in making a revolution to prevent filmmakers and other media from putting us into a mold. He'd like to see more local autonomy through growing food in community gardens and providing housing for the homeless. In our conversation with Joe, 16, he agreed with Rhys that youth are brainwashed by TV and school to want to grow up fast. Girls use makeup and sex to try to be adult, while guys like Joe fight, do random acts of violence, and get high.

Reading about an HBO documentary series *American Hipster Presents*, I asked Kirby, a college senior in Boston, about the difference between hipsters hippies, and indies in the 21st century:

> *Hippies are all about free love and drugs and spirituality, to strongly generalize,*
> *and came from the counterculture of the 60s, combating the materialism of the*

50s. Hippies are all about love; hipsters are often standoffish and like to connect over shared interests in pop culture and music, as opposed to values. An indie is much like a hipster, very focused on independent media, which ties into their desire for an independent identity. The similarity here is that most youngsters want to feel special and so try to be different from their peers (but they consequently all do similar things, which is what happens with hipsters), but hippies and hipsters came out of vastly different historical contexts.

Another type of style is seen in Santiago, Chile, where hundreds of Pokémon teens gather in a park, some wearing Japanese T-shirts.[50] This androgynous "urban tribe" dyes and waxes their hair and wear low-rise jeans and thick black eyeliner. Their look is what defines them, not an ideology; "It's basically a fashion thing. A Pokémon has a certain style and does *ponceo*," (making out and oral sex) explained Raul, a 19-year-old with piercings down the side of his nose. Both sexes compete to have multiple partners including same-sex hookups. They use instant-messaging and share videos and photos on YouTube and Fotolog. Other urban teen subgroups in Chile are Goths, sharps, darks, punks, and thrashers who distinguish their identities by their clothes and appearance. At least they have more variety than global businessmen in dark suits whose only real choice of style is their tie color, with the exception of Arab men—mainly Saudis, who wear white robes and headcoverings. Youth are simultaneously influenced by advertising styles and are "cool hunted" for new styles to copy and manufacture.

In our style scanning around the globe, we end with Europe. Inga reports from Berlin that in her high school it costs a lot of money to buy clothes to fit in with the style of a particular group, in her case the Goths or wannabe-gangsters who listen to Heavy Metal music. Goth buckles, lace and leather clothing, and shoes costing 200 euros can be purchased in special shops, but Inga just wears affordable black. Music that began in the US, like rap, is adapted to the German language and scene. Similar to teens in most other countries, she watched US cartoons, children's shows from Nickelodeon, and dubbed US movies.

One of the differences Inga sees (one I've heard from many nationalities) is that the US stands alone in its fast pace, especially when it comes to eating.[51] In contrast, Sunday meals at her grandparents' house are leisurely and relaxed. Her family spends a whole afternoon in a café, eating, drinking coffee, talking and people watching. Their conversation is not about personal growth and emotional issues as it might be in California. Another difference she notices is the bigger size of meals, vehicles, and people in the US.

Adolescents want to establish an identity distinct from their parents so they can leave home, assisted by bonding with their friends to create a style and identity for themselves. Corporations have taken advantage of this natural process of becoming adult by selling clothes, vehicles, makeup, electronic devices, magazines and food that supposedly provide identity, acceptance by the tribe, and happiness. For some, consumption assumes the locus of life purpose. Some adults oppose gender stereotyping by manufacturers, such as when comedian Ellen DeGeneres started a clothing brand for tweens (and other ages) called E.D., with quotes like Shakespeare's "And though she be but little she is fierce." The girls who model her clothes are selected for their skills such as skateboarding. The same year, Target stores stopped dividing toys by gender. Books advise parents on nonsexist parenting, such as *Redefining Girly: How Parents Can Fight the Stereotyping and Sexualizing of Girlhood, From Birth to Tween* (2014) by Melissa Atkins Wardy and my *50/50 Parenting*.

Social Unrest from Rising Expectations

As Western media--the "global imagination industries"--permeates the world, they generate frustration about not being able to afford the lifestyle shown on TV and films. Young people want to make money in order to experience what they see on television and film dramas. Ads teach that viewers should act on "impulse: love it, want it, get it now," as urged in a Macy's Department store print ad, with no mention of sticking to a budget or plan. Many songs have "gimme, gimme, gimme" as their title and refrain as seen on YouTube: "Gimme" usually refers to sex. In Italy, Lucrezia (16) compares her generation with her parents' peers: "At the time of my parents, things were very different and much more beautiful. Now social networks, mobile phones, TV and computers have replaced relationships. Now-a-days, among young people, those who don't have designer clothes, an iPhone and the scooter are out!!" A young Indian student reported about her cool new expensive iPhone, "When I use my blue-colored iPhone, I draw attention." It took her half a year to convince her father to buy her the $698 phone.

Some youth lose touch with traditional values to avoid being judged as "geeks." An Indonesian SpeakOut university student, Narsika reported,

> *As our generation becomes more consumerist, like a hedonist, firstly they look out to the role models, perhaps the celebrities or the media that show every model of the technologies, fashions, and all of the pleasure, that makes the youth start*

to think to get one, to show that they aren't geek. But we can say the positive of this is they're high tech and modern, even though they need to get a loan to buy the new technology. They become poor when they don't know how to get the new gadget to look stylish, so they need loans. I think they don't care anymore about the environment. They throw a gum on the street. That's why we have to filter this modern era to make a better generation in the future.

An Indian girl, Pratibha, 14, reports, "TV and the Internet has totally changed our life. I can't think of life without the imagination of the Internet and TV." In regards to Indian young women in particular, the Grey Global Group surveyed 3,400 unmarried women aged 19 to 22 from various income and social levels.[52] Altogether, the project involved 40 focus groups in five large metro areas and five smaller cities. Nisha Singhania, senior director of Grey Worldwide India, reported that 51% of young single women in major metro areas said it's necessary to have a big house and big car to be happy. In smaller cities, 86% agreed with this materialist statement: "This shows that the less women have, the greater are their aspirations," Singhania concluded. "A typical comment in recent interviews with young women was, 'I want money, fame and success.'" One of the materialist influences on the respondents was satellite and cable that brought American music videos and TV shows to India in the early 1990s. They feature Western imports like passionate kissing, sensitive guys, independent women and new products that influence viewers.

The main goal of young Indians is to "become rich," according to a survey by Co-ca-Cola. MTV's first "Youth Icon of the Year," in 2003, was an industrialist named Anil Ambani. When he was asked what is the one thing that stands out about today's young people, Ambani said: "India's youth are very, very ambitious. Very competitive. There is a great spirit to achieve success and reward."[53] But he added, "They're losing touch with some of the grassroots principles of our society, our culture, our systems. I think we need to harness our core values, our religion, our spiritualism. This is what the whole world wants to learn from us. Indian youth shouldn't give up on that."

Right-wing Hindu nationalists protest the type of sexuality brought by foreign/modern consumerism, which is seen in the popularity of "cinema culture," beauty contests, fashion shows, and celebration of Valentine's Day. Beauty is big business. When Indian women win Miss Universe and Miss World contests (the last Indian winners of the two major contests were both in 2000), it enhances India's reputation as a major "beauty machine." Major newspapers like the *Times of India* cover the winners.[54] Opposition to the beauty business links Hindu nationalists with the feminist left. Feminists decry the contests as demeaning to women: "There are clear links between glo-balization and the accelerated commodification of women," states the leader of the All India Democratic Women's Association.[55] Although both the right and left attack consumerism, it is spreading nonetheless. Women's clothing, sexuality, and freedom of movement in public are "central to struggles over the cultural meaning and impact of globalization."[56]

At the same time that media is raising consumer expectations, the rate of youth unemployment is rising. Factory workers' wages are also going down to compete with huge companies like Wal-Mart as firms move production to countries with lower wag-es. With the evolution from agriculture to manufacturing to information and service jobs, fewer workers are needed. Some youth do benefit from outsourcing jobs as in call centers in Delhi and Mumbai that employ more than a million people, mostly women, but more people know about consumer items who can't take part in the consumer culture. Some worry about not being able to meet youth's rising expectations, as when young people go into debt to buy the latest mobile phone. Indrani Vidyarthi of ORG-MARG, a major market research agency, asks, "But how to get more when there ain't more?" According to India's 2001 census, about 78 million rural households had no access to electricity, so how can they have Internet access? More than 40% of India's population depends on kerosene for lighting and uses batteries to watch DVDs.[57] Some have solar-powered cell phones that can access the Internet, the first such phone, called the "Solar Guru," was launched by Samsung in 2010.

Some of the discontent and frustration about being poor gets funneled into funda-mentalist religions, which can stir up prejudice and hatred. Aalamata Ly from Senegal reported in a USAID Internet dialogue, "Nowadays we all realize that young people are no longer interested in studies. What interests them is making money." Mary Patricia Williams, a university student in Trinidad and Tobago, replied to Ly,

> *You mention the situation with young people in Senegal; truth be told this sit-uation is everywhere. I am of the firm belief that it exists because of the high value that is placed on money. It gives you access, open doors, gives you the ability to travel extensively, acquire material possessions, and most importantly it increases your status within the social rankings of society. From a sociological perspective, they are only doing what the society as a whole has taught them.*

The authors of *Being Young and Muslim* report that music is "perhaps the most effective venue for outraged and excluded youth [like Muslims in France and Germany] who feel the overbearing inequities of host societies, and find, through music, a way to attain a social capital of hipness and respect on the streets."[58] Thus, global youth culture shares hip-hop, rap, rock, and heavy metal. Examples of "multicultural national identity" are Moroccan "Maroc-hop" music in the Netherlands or hip-hop lyrics for Lebanese-Australian youth by Sleek the Elite:

> *Your culture, given from Allah*
> *Remember your history 'cause it helps you work harder*
> *Helps you respect more your mother and your father*
> *Your parents or grandparents came from another land*
> *You might be Australian now, but it's not your motherland.*[59]

In a case study of youth frustration in response to new media, a researcher did fieldwork in a leather-worker community of low-caste people called the Rabi Das, in West Bengal. She found that young people struggle against tradition; for example, when some young women speak out against arranged marriage. Influenced by media images of the "new woman" and by Hindi films, girls want to wear fashionable clothes and go to school. However, school is expensive and neighbors criticize girls who leave home and suspect that the girls might "do something wrong" with boys. Mothers frequently say, "What is the use of going to school? She will just get married and have a family anyway."

Most Rabi Das girls drop out after primary school and help their mothers or work as domestic servants, while boys have more time to hang out under the banyan tree or on street corners to chat about film stars, sing pop film songs, and tell tall tales. Most girls are married off and leave home when young, but boys have more freedom to rebel and criticize their elders for spending money on alcohol and not saving money for the future. Influenced by consumer culture, young Rabi Das people long for the "sweet life" but they don't have the education or skills to get it, leading to frustration and resentment.[60]

Consumerism fueled by global media harms the environment and increases migration to cities to get jobs to buy things--which weakens social supports, results in isolation sitting in front of electronic screens, and causes discontent among those who desire but can't afford the lifestyle they see in the media. Yet as the middle-class is predicted to grow globally, consumerism will also grow, along with environmental hazards. Will Gen Y and Z be willing to give up pollutants like cars and beef?

How Youth Are Manipulated by Multinational Corporations

Despite all the time they spend engaging with media, US Millennials are less likely than any other generation to be attached to a brand, product or company, according to Gallup.[61] High school activist Zoe Willingham believes her generation is shrewd. She observes,

> *Corporate power is increasing around the world and our Congress as well. That's very scary to me. The Citizens United Supreme Court decision in 2010 opened the floodgates for corporate money to pollute our democracy. It removes the individual from their political representative. This is increasingly a country controlled by the wealthy. Third World America by Arianna Huffington outlines the economic poverty in this country. We're not far from being a third world nation.* Banana Republic *is another useful book.*
>
> *In this economy it's becoming more apparent that households are on the brink of bankruptcy if they lose their job, their car breaks down, or have an illness or injury. The Koch brothers, Super PACS, Fizzer, these kind of wealthy groups will completely control the government if we don't get mad enough.*

A young Sikh man in North India, is married, with a toddler, and has a master's degree. When I visited his home, he told me how he's manipulated to consume and believes he's influenced negatively. He lives in his parents' compound in a small city. Contrasting his life with his parents, he said,

> *I spend on trendy brands, my belt cost nearly $20 and I'm wearing good shoes. I'm a little addicted; shopping malls change our ideas about shopping. We read fashion magazines, which influence us to buy. My parents had no electricity; they used candles and oil kerosene lamps, and didn't have shoes. My parents walked many kilometers and lived a very simple life. They shared food with neighbors and begged. Then they got jobs, my father worked for the government and my mother was a teacher. Now we have electricity, AC, and good medicines. We have become lazy and materialistic; we use a scooter instead of walking. We've become soft; we don't exercise or do yoga. We wear good brand clothes and go to good places to eat, while my parents don't like to spend money in restaurants.*

But, 70% of Indians are still in the village. They live hand to mouth; they don't have good schools, and have a problem with drugs and alcohol. Pot grows wild. In any home in the Punjab at least one person is on drugs, maybe only 10% of families don't have drugs. I had to say no to friends who offered me drugs, pot, alcohol, and opium. We have more freedom, as we no longer have to do our father's profession, but changes also makes for imbalance. We've gotten more greedy and spoiled.

We've seen that youth identity and style is influenced by consumerism. How do advertisers succeed in raising lifestyle expectations? A powerful influence shaping youth identity is multi-national corporations and their "culture industry" of global advertising, entertainment, news, books, magazines, music and fashion. Estimates are that 500 multinational corporations control 70% of world trade.[62] They unsuccessfully tried to institute a Trans-Pacific Partnership that critics such as former US Congressman Alan Grayson say makes corporations more powerful than governments.[63] Youth internationally are influenced by media images in the global economy's Americanization or McDonaldization. It's caused by "The growth of the most centralized forms of power accumulation and transnational centralization of culture that humankind has ever seen."[64] Roohi, a 17-year-old girl of Indian ancestry who lives in Singapore observes:

With regards to consumerism and youth, I feel that we can be divided into two main categories. Those who accept it and integrate it into their lives and those who don't. It's difficult to be in the middle, because once you see the impacts of consumerism around the world, it's hard to be accepting of it. There are many times where having the right clothes, the right look, things like these are given more emphasis and importance than what used to be more valued, such as friendships.

I mean no offence to America, but in so many cases people are losing their culture and tradition to adopt a foreign one. In this globalized world, it's definitely important to have international interactions and be accepting and integrate with people of other cultures, but youth should not forget their roots and the more important things in life.

The working class is controlled by creating "false needs" through consumerism and the false belief in personal freedom, according to Herbert Marcuse's *One-Dimensional Man* (1964). Marcuse explained we're manipulated into thinking we can buy happiness, which makes us work longer hours to earn more money to buy more things with less time and energy to enjoy them. Similar to drug addiction, the addict is "happy" for a short time until the drug wears off, then the craving starts again, as it does for compulsive shoppers. Arias (18, m, California) says, "What bothers me most in daily life is how we have fallen victim to our society, how we work in cubicles all day long, then come home and sleep just to wake up and do it the next day. Our media has trained our world how to be violent and vulgar and to obliterate true peace." Some Asian countries have a word for dying of overwork: Japanese *karoshi* and Chinese *guolaosi*.

Cultural icons often originate in the US, Europe, and Japan: A video shows young fashionistas in Tokyo.[65] Corporations are always "cool shopping" for new youth styles and trends to commercialize and sell globally, yet we've seen youth are often marginalized and ignored. Multinational corporations and advertising agencies compete with family and school to become the most influential institutions in young people's lives. Efforts to ensure the ideological dominance of consumerism reinforce social divisions between the haves and the have-nots."[66]

US-based transnational companies dominate the global production and distribution of popular culture.[67] They create a mythology around buying. Children are raised to celebrate holidays with things, like getting gifts from Santa Claus. We're expected to buy gifts to celebrate media-created holidays such as Valentine's Day and Mother's Day. Fashion trends in clothes, cars, and electronic gadgets are designed with planned obsolescence so we'll buy more. "The way people over here take everything for granted bugs me. For a girl's precious Louis Vuitton purse, she could be using that money to be feeding loads of families in another country," complains Michelle (15, f, Washington).

Children's TV programs and ads were developed in the US in the 1950s to create new beliefs. The message was shared things, like the family TV, are more important than shared values. Advertisers continue to shape how adults think about kids so "the child is a social construct."[68] Advertisers give parents the message that good mothering includes shopping for products for optimal child development, as you can see in toy store ads. At the same time they encourage kids to be "bratz," like the line of dolls with that name,[69] as well as disrespectful like Bart in the cartoon series *The Simpsons* and the crude fourth-grade boys in *South Park*. At the same time as portraying homemakers dressed like TV's June Cleaver in apron and heels, advertising images of US women became sexualized dumb blonds like Marilyn Monroe in the late '50s, part of the strategy to get women home after World War II. Portraying women as sexual objects has grown more explicit.[70]

Fathers are often portrayed as ignorant and vulgar anti-heroes including bigoted Archie Bunker in *All in the Family* in the 1960s and early 70s, ignorant Al Bundy in *Married with Children* in the 1980s and 90s, and bumbling Homer Simpson in *The Simpsons*, on the air since 1987. In one episode, Homer tells his son, "Bart, with $10,000, we'd *be* millionaires! We could buy all kinds of useful things like...love!" *Family Guy's* Peter Griffin is another man-child, an overweight, intellectually challenged, blue-collar husband and father who frequently gets drunk. Phil in *Modern Family* is described by his wife as "the kid I'm married to." (Melania Trump said in a CNN interview that she as two boys at home, her son and her husband.) In the same show, stay-at-home-dad Cameron is a fun and devoted dad to the daughter he adopted with his partner Mitchell, an over-protective dad.

Bill Cosby in *The Cosby Show* may be one of the few good dads many men would want to emulate since the days of Ward Cleaver in *Leave it to Beaver*, although a friend who watches more TV than I do suggested other good dads.[71] It's ironic that Cosby turned out to be a disgusting married sexual predator who admitted he drugged young women who he wanted to have sex with.[72] Is the subliminal message, "Don't listen to dad as he's a goofball; listen to the advertisers?' Super Bowl ads in 2015 signaled a small change with Dove and Nissan featuring good fathers.[73] The next year an ad called "First Date" showed an overly-protective father supervising and ruining his daughter's date, while an Axe ad called "Find Your Magic" encouraged men to flaunt their individuality, whether it be having a large nose or dancing in high heels.[74] An Audi car ad in 2017 portrayed a feminist father supporting his daughter's effort to win a go-cart race, aware of the obstacles she'll face as a woman.[75]

In the 1950s, advertisers developed a new market for adolescent shoppers, including teen fashion and clothing—the top expenditure for both boys and girls. A 2013 market research survey of US teens reported that teens spend about 40% of their budgets on fashion and that about 18% of their spending is online. Their purchases are most strongly influenced by their friends, followed by the Internet.[76] Over half of the teens surveyed own a smartphone and almost half buy organic food. Other large US teen expenditures are for beverages and food (the most frequent purchase), music, magazines (8 out of 10 teens read them and their numerous ads), films and other entertainment, electronic devices and games, buying things at meeting places like shopping malls, sports equipment, and skin care and cosmetics. Tweens, ages 11 to 14, (others define the as age 8 to 14) are a recent example of a manufactured youth culture and market. They influenced $1.88 trillion in global spending in a year, both on their own and through their parents' purchases.[77] The book *Tweening the Girl* (2014) by Canadian Natalie Coulter argues that advertisers manufactured the concept of the tween in the 1980s as one of "capitalism's most valuable consumers."

The documentary *I Am Eleven* (2014) interviews 11-year-olds from around the world because, as Australian filmmaker Genevieve Bailey explained, "When you're 11, your blinkers (blinders) are off. There's a sense of clarity in the ideas these 11-year-olds shared with me, and a sense of honesty as well—none of the self-censoring that often comes after that period."[78] Fictional tweens are portrayed in the 2012 film *Moonrise Kingdom* where a 12-year-old boy and girl run away to escape the unhappy adult world they see around them. They illustrate shortening of the time children have to be innocent playful kids. Sam is an orphan and Suzy's mother communicates with her family by yelling through a bullhorn. The film takes place in 1965 on a New England island.

We see Suzy and Sam move back and forth from being children to adolescents, as when Sam warns Suzy that he may wet the bed and she reads children's fantasy novels out loud to a group of Boy Scouts, like Wendy reading to Peter Pan and his Lost Boys. To run away from home Suzy fills her suitcase with novels and takes a record player rather than more practical items. Then Sam smokes a pipe and refers to Suzy as his wife, while she wears heavy green eye shadow and instructs him on how to kiss and says he can touch her chest. She understands that her mother is having an affair with the local policeman and lets her know she doesn't like him.

An Australian manager for SUPRE, a chain-store for tweens, describes the girls who shop there: "They love to shop, hang out with friends in shopping centres and spend more time online and flicking through mags like *Dolly* than they do on school work. They're searching for what's hot, giving them the edge among their friends."[79] (Why are popular things either hot or cool?) They get their fashion styles from American and British celebrities. SUPRE's website says, "SUPRE culture is everything that is fun, fast and funky! It is great music, making things happen, laughing out loud, dancing on ladders and doing it with a BIG smile!!" That's a useful summary of consumer youth culture, as advertisers portray it--fast and fun. Females in general are expected to smile more than men; Hillary Clinton was criticized for not smiling during a televised discussion of national defense, judged as unlikeable, although she smiled more than Trump. Studies show we believe that women are more governed by their emotions and men by rational reaction to a situation.[80]

After interviewing 50 Gen Y Australians, Rebecca Huntley found them to be similar to American youth, influenced by American media and consumerism, optimistic like their US peers but also worried about their job prospects. She concluded, "I have seen the potential in this generation for both radical transformation and terrible conformism."[81] From Pakistan, Sahar (17, f) is concerned about this focus on superficial appearance and fame: "People are being driven more and more towards how you show off to the world, while the importance of the beauty of your heart and soul have lost its importance, even though these should be more important."

Advertisers get us to buy by showing role models of happy, beautiful, successful people using their products or by making us feel insecure so we'll buy their products to make us look more fashionable and enhance our femininity or masculinity. Advertising seeks to "generate dreams and desires, fears and fantasies, repressions and displacements."[82] Ads "remake the meaning of goods in order to sell them," inventing new needs and desires with fantasy virtual images, a "hyperreality" of intense emotion and action.[83]

Corporations analyze our emotional imprints from childhood and what we associate with things in order to get us to buy their products. For example, Clotaire Rapaille found Americans unconsciously want a car with the freedom of the Wild West and the code words "horse," and "identity," while Germans want fine engineering.[84] For teens, a phenomenon on YouTube is "haulers," teen fashionistas who videotape what they've purchased on a shopping spree and post it on social media for their thousands of fans.[85] Retailers picked up on this and use haulers in their ads. Another trend is YouTube beauty tutorial sites by beauty bloggers, stars in their teens to or early 20s, such as Gigi Gorgeous (age 22) and Bethany Mota (age 18).[86] They sometimes meet their fans in person at BeautyCon conferences, sponsored by *Elle* magazine. YouTube often supersedes beauty magazines partly because watching a how-to video is easier than reading print instructions on arranging hair or applying makeup.

Even schools are used as a market for consumption of computers, books, and food. They're "doing a great job at indoctrinating students to be slaves to corporate masters," observed Dan, 19, m, Alberta. Schools should include analysis of media manipulation techniques and discussion of values. Values curriculum is available, such as that written by Bahá'í teachers or by the Institute of Noetic Sciences.[87] To counter the focus on a conformist beauty image, the *Empowering Young Women Manual* produced by UNFPA and the YWCA that stated, "Beauty is slowly narrowing down to a single image—a blond anorexic woman with breast implants," not a healthy or realistic model.[88] The manual provides "good practices" like the Australian YWCA campaign that uses stickers proclaiming "Be Real—NO Body's Perfect."[89]

Negative Consequences of Consumerism

The consequences of global consumerism include increased use of non-renewable resources—including minerals, liquid fossil fuels, and fresh water as aquifers are pumped dry—and a drain on the environment with more trash and industrial pollution. Some young people migrate to cities or other countries in search of paid work, which weakens social support provided by their extended family, neighbors, and religious groups. For example, for the first time in India an increasing number of paid non-family members care for elders because the younger generation doesn't live in or near the ancestral home.

Almost a third of the world's population (2.1 billion) is obese; as people have more income they eat more processed and sugary foods and exercise less.[90] Obesity rates for children nearly doubled between 1980 and 2013, with the highest increase in MENA, especially for girls. The US has the highest percentage of fat people of any country, leading to health problems such as diabetes and pancreatic cancer, followed by emerging nations of China, India, Russia, Brazil and Mexico.

Consumerism contrasts with traditional cultures that value the group rather than the individual, duty over indulgence, living lightly on the land over mining its resources for profit, and spirituality over materialism. Industrial consumer societies aren't happier, as having lots of stuff doesn't buy enjoyment.[91] I drew from Sulak Sivaraka's definitions (a Thai Buddhist activist and NGO director) and added some with the help of Krishna Deep, an Indian student, to make the following comparisons:

TRADITIONAL SOCIETIES	WESTERN CONSUMER CULTURE
Community center:	
Religious center	Shopping malls
Personal success:	
Cooperative, generous	Rich
Identity:	
Family, clan	Individual and the products she or he displays, such as clothes and car

Status:

Inherited   Wealth, fame

Environment:

Respect, balance   Exploit, believe food comes in packages

Values:

Cooperation, piety, self-control   Competition, material success,
                                                              hard work, pleasure now

Rebirth:

Through religion   Consume new products

Heroes:

Religious leaders, scholars   Rich entertainment and business figures

Happiness:

Harmony, love, family   Consumption of goods and experiences

Music:

Classical, inspiring, personal   Violent, sexual, heavily marketed

Pace:

Slow, drink tea ceremonially   Instant gratification, now
to establish relationships, patience, aware of seasons

Work:

Hands   Machines

Education:

For the elite   Literacy increases for girls too, Internet opens up information access

Communication:

Local   Global, cell phone access even in rural areas so information spreads rapidly

Age:

Elders respected   Aspire to youthful appearance and style

A Nigerian Chief, Dr. Iwowarri Berian James, contrasted his experiences with traditional and consumer society in an email.

The Nigerian youth of yesteryears had a very humble beginning, loved parents, was obedient and God fearing. Resulting from parental limited income, such things as television, cable news and videos were either not there at all or in few elite homes in the cities. They never defined the moment of the youth's life. Religious activities were in most homes the centre of activities and living. Family values and community expectations served as deterrents for many youths even when peer pressure defined living to the contrary.

Today it is different. There is CNN, BBC, Cable News, DSTV, and Cartoon Networks, which begin early to influence the way a modern child begins to see his or her environment. The schools and colleges are now grounds of high immoral breeding that has attracted the attack of contemporary families. [Republican Presidential candidate Rick Santorum brought up this same issue in 2012.] Youths now define the status in terms of the worth of their wristwatches, shirts, pants, etc. The type of school now determines the child's social class. Parents who depended upon communal support now seek avenues to amass, so much so that youths now define their own status according to the amount of wealth amassed by their parents.

The type of freedom enjoyed by youths of today never existed when we were growing up. Parental and family control was sharp and to the point. Every child belonged to the community as against now when the child belongs only to the nuclear family, some members of whom may not even be available for the child's upbringing, as both father and mother are away on business or office work to fetch the much needed money. The result is a youth that has developed without the soul training and inner wisdom that supports one in real life situations. So they play to the winds, wishing for the make-believe life of the TV celebrities who seem to get everything going with ease. When the challenge comes, the result is crime and more crime. That is where we now see the majority of our youths.

The speed of technology is crashing into other traditional societies, according to Andy Lehto, an American who teaches in Jordan: "It creates a shock to the collective senses of this society which until relatively recently, remained a rather closed society." A teacher in a village school in Jerash, Jordan, told him, "The only thing that your technology has brought us is 10,000 new ways to sin.'" Julia, a 14-year-old South Korean girl reported that because of Western media, "I tend to sometimes think as if I AM from a Western heritage. It disappoints my parents a lot." They grew up in small towns while she is growing up in a large city.

In Iran, the police tried to prevent the Trojan Horse of permissive Western culture by confiscating Barbie dolls. "I think every Barbie doll is more harmful than an American missile," warned an Iranian woman.[92] Banned for more than a decade, they're sold illegally in stores. Dara and Sara were promoted as dolls to promote traditional values but weren't as popular as Barbie—see photos of them.[93] The authorities also worry about satellite dishes that enable viewers to watch foreign films and TV programs.

Barbie dolls have long been contentious issues although many girls have loved them since 1959. The Barbie Liberation Organization exchanged Barbie doll voice boxes with G.I. Joes' and put them back on store shelves in the early 1990s. After 56 years of popularity, Barbie lost popularity in the US since 2012, despite new models carrying a briefcase or driving a sports car.[94] German youth activists demonstrated in 2013 at the opening of Berlin's "Barbie Dreamhouse Experience" that provides visitors with fashion and baking experiences for girls. The demonstrators, including youth organizations like Left Youth and Socialist German Workers Youth, wanted to stimulate a debate on how corporate consumerism targets kids, as explored in a book about black children and Barbies.[95]

The most recent Barbie can carry on a spoken conversation with a child and she's been modified in various ways. In 2015, Barbie came in seven different skin colors and the next year choices of three different body types were added to the line: tall, curvy, and petite.[96] (A variety of Ken dolls with different body types and hairstyles, including the "man bun," came out in 2017.) The focus on buying dolls illustrates reports from all over the world that elders worry about the shift from valuing one's family's moral reputation to valuing how much stuff an individual can buy, a shift from modesty and generosity to conspicuous consumption without "soul training." We'll all need to investigate what Barbie is programmed to say to children using Artificial Intelligence. A Mattel vice-president explained, "The subtext that is there that we would not do for boys is: 'You don't have to be perfect. It is O.K. to be messy and flawed and silly.'"[97]

Youth Views about Materialism and Getting Rich

Combining Materialism and Altruism

The debate between Generation We or Me is discussed in my *Ageism in Youth Studies* and *Global Youth Values Transforming Our Future* (2017). On the We side of the discussion, a 2012 survey of over 700 Europeans under age 30 reported none of them think that making a lot of money is central to life's meaning. Only 4% said money motivated them most.[98] Their most important value is love and they believe that the meaning of life is to help and inspire others. The most pressing issues they see are community problems and youth unemployment. Over one-third think the best way to make an impact on the community is to do volunteer work. These findings are more typical of survey results I've read than in Lost in Transition.

A Burmese student (Htet, 18, f, Burma/Myanmar) points that youth can be interested in making money to put it to good use: "My aim is to set up my own business when I'm an adult. I want to do many volunteer organizations for the people who need help, so I'll need a lot of money. That's why I want to set up my own business first, a CSR (Corporate Social Responsibilities). We youth will become the leaders for the future" Millennials value being of service as taught in the schools that require service learning or regions where governments pay small stipends for service work such as GroundBREAKER in South Africa, Americorps in the US, and Youth Initiative in Nepal. Young people today want to make money to have a secure family life and they also want to contribute to the good of others. As Ben (20, m, California) pointed out, "I think my generation has a huge emphasis on making a difference in their career options. I feel in the past the norm has been to have a steady job and provide for a family, while now individuals are going above and beyond to make as big as an impact as possible."

Some Youth Buy Into Consumerism

Some SpeakOut students buy into consumerism and want to get rich, but they're the exception. In the minority is Megh, a 15-year-old boy from India, who says he plans to become an engineer and "make loads of money and live a life of luxury and comfort" like celebrity lifestyles he knows from the media. When asked about his life purpose, he explains, "I think I am here on earth to do my bit and enjoy my life. I don't think I am here on earth to make a difference to the world; that is all philosophy and I don't believe in all that." He replaces traditional beliefs with the typical youth focus on relationships: "For me, friends are everything. I have a very big friend circle and they are a very crucial part of my life. Sometimes to satisfy my friends I have to go against my parents' wish and make them unhappy, so in those situations I get very confused and am not able to decide what to do."

From Addis Ababa, Ethiopia, Taika (age 18) told me in a Skype conversation,[99] that her generation faces increased competition in a corrupt world, which makes them selfish: "Money, money and more money has become the focus of everyone because without it, seems like nobody can survive."

Before people would die for honesty or their beliefs, while now it's all about money. When it comes to honesty, life has become really hard to get by, cheating and lying has become a way to get by. Their goal is more money, more pretty cars, better clothes, a better house. It's not about education, friendship, and family any more, it's about being better than others, just the life style. Before using head sets, people socialized, and talked about issues, now they ignore each other.

About 40% of teens are indeed materialistic, according to a global marketing survey of over 50,000 teens from 31 countries who are active in the Habbo virtual world.[100] Their responses fell into five typologies of roughly about 20% each. Achievers and Rebels want to be rich and famous--the Rebels are committed to having fun in the process. In contrast, Traditionals and Creatives are less ambitious and more interested in helping others, while Loners are more introverted and open-minded. This survey indicates that a majority of teens don't place a high value on getting rich.

A Millennial blogger, Sarah Flanagan observes that the characters on the HBO series *Girls* illustrate the insecurity caused by high unemployment rates. Only Charlie did well financially, after inheriting money to start a tech company, but in the 2016 season legal troubles caused him to walk away from his app company with no money and turn to being a drug seller and user.[101] Coupled with their high aspirations and narcissism, Flanagan says, "The result is a self-reflective and self-involved group of people who just don't know what to do with their great selves. So we go to Facebook." Even more critical, Professor William Deresiewicz describes American youth as a "post-emotional" generation lacking the focus on love, angst or anger of previous generations.[102] He observes growing up in the age of dot.com entrepreneurship, Generation Sell has the personality and values of a salesperson. These nice, moderate, friendly hipsters value starting a small business; "What's really hip is social entrepreneurship," reports Deresiewicz. This ties in with Flanagan's observation about the impact of the high unemployment rate on Gen Y.

Youth are often criticized for being materialistic, as in the scholarly book *Lost in*

Transition: The Dark Side of Emerging Adulthood (2011).[103] Fewer than one in ten of their 230 interviewees (ages 18-23) were critical of mass consumer materialism. Their US respondents felt buying things helps the American economy, as President George Bush urged Americans to do after the 9-11 terrorist attack. Shopping was mentioned as a source of pleasure and happiness for 61% of them, while only 30% expressed concerns about consumerism. They felt there is nothing they can do to change the system so they might as well enjoy buying things. As one young woman said, "There's a lot of people who need shoes and I have over 100 pairs that I don't need. So yeah, I'm worried about how consuming we are as a society, but not worried enough to change my ways yet."[104] Only a small percent of all interviewees were concerned enough to take action, even something easy like shopping in a second-hand store instead of a mall. Their primary solution is to be a more discriminating consumer, which doesn't inhibit their identity as consumers. Only about one-quarter said they wanted to help others or have a positive influence on others.

In a much larger 2011 national survey of US college freshmen, the main motive for going to college was to get a better job, but a close second was to learn. Before the 2008 recession, learning was the main motivation, indicating that fear about future security trumps more abstract goals, as Abraham Maslow's hierarchy of needs predicts. As the unemployment rate has fallen, so has the number of students motivated to attend college to get a good job, down from a high of 88% in 2012 to 85% in 2016.[105] An all-time high of 75% of students said that getting a general education and appreciation of ideas was very important to them. Pleasing their family by going to college was especially motivating for nearly half (46%) of first-generation college students. About three-quarters of both groups of students plan on earing a graduate degree, women more ambitious than men.

More college students (52.5%) rely on loans so they need a good job to pay them back. The increasing gap between rich and poor is showing up in US universities as the university attendance gap between children from high- and low-income families is about a third greater among children born in 2001 than those born 25 years earlier.[106] Current freshmen come from wealthier families than in the past, with incomes 60% higher than the national average. This may be a factor in students' emphasis on earning money to be able to duplicate their parents' lifestyle. They're also faced with rising tuition fees and an average of $37,172 owed to lenders by the average Class of 2016 graduate, a total of $1.4 trillion—more than credit card debt.[107] With youth unemployment at around 18%, 74% of over 3,000 young people selected jobs and the economy as their top issue in a 2011 Harvard survey.[108] At the same time, many (69%) regard community service as an "honorable thing to do."

In the Dominican Republic, a college student, Lidia, 22, comments that materialism is a problem there too:

> *I do believe my generation is too focused on material gains and that we waste too much time on useless things. People are no longer committed to the greater cause, to social service, to making a better nation. This isn't the 60s when we had the civil war. Young men and women would go to the streets and fight the occupation, would risk their lives for freedom.*

Lidia points out, however, that her generation can be both materialistic and socially aware and activist, and that people need something to push against to be motivated to act:

> *I believe there can't be heroes without something to save. For example, I've found a lot of young people in my country are actually interested in working towards social development and taking care of the environment. If not actively volunteering then at least donating. I come from a third world country and poverty is everywhere and very visible but children are growing up with a better sense of the world.*

Countries like China and Russia replaced their Marxist ideology, which valued serving the working people and creating a classless society, with a focus on getting rich, being able to afford fashionable clothes, an apartment and a car. A Chinese girl (Xiaoxiao, 18, f, rural China) complains, "Ignorant adults in poor areas seek fashion blindly, as extravagant and wasteful as the adults in the cities. I hope I can be as simple as in childhood and not be afraid of anything, speak what I want to speak." A Russian urban youth trend that emerged at the end of the 1990s is the attempt to be glamorous in reaction to Soviet drabness and post-Soviet bleakness: "Russian glamour has become the cultural equivalent of unchallenged globalized capitalism."[109] A Russian scholar wrote that interest in "mass glamour signals the desire for social change, but this longing has been redirected into the sphere of consumption."[110] (See more about Russian glamour in Volume 2 Chapter 8.)

Yuan (20, m, China) comments about materialist Chinese young people he knows:

> *I am not really sure my fellows have any religious beliefs at all. They are less*

superstitious than their parents. I don't hear "spirit, afterlife, Heaven." I hear carpe diem, money, luxury brands. I'd say almost all the peers I know are quite realistic. They believe in money and power. There are two groups of them. One is all about money. They believe more money will make their life better. The other is all about politics, positions and power, maneuver, climbing the social ladder [of the Communist Party].

Backing up Yuan's observations, in a survey of global teens, Chinese teens are the most likely to value entrepreneurship as a quality that children should learn—89% compared to the next highest, which was 57% of teens in Spain. A survey of over 2,000 respondents in Shanghai concluded that young people had shifted from traditional values to modern ones, focusing on personal success rather than making a contribution to society.[111] They are more individualistic and secular than older generations. An economics professor at the Beijing Institute of Technology, Hu Xingdou agrees with Yuan that modern Chinese, "don't have beliefs, although China has indigenous religions like Taoism and Buddhism. China is actually an atheist country, and Chinese people are never afraid of God's punishment."[112] Professor Hu added: "The Chinese government has made economic development its central task, which means everything is money-centered. Both the legal system and the moral system have been sacrificed to moneymaking."

The catalyst for Hu's comments was a national discussion about a child who was injured in an accident on the street but no one stopped to help her. In response to this and similar incidents, the Communist Party newspaper *Global Times* worried that, "Cracks can be seen in the moral framework of Chinese society. Many are asking: What's wrong with China?" An opinion writer for the English-language *Shanghai Daily* asked,

Why has the East followed the West in abandoning its Eastern core values for near-religious faith in money and the market? In 30 years of embracing a market economy, China has changed from a haven of honest love to a haven of flirtation, fun and infidelity. Chinese media outlets compete with each other in sponsoring brazen women who shout slogans like "I would rather weep woefully in a BMW car than laugh merrily on a bike."[113]

The "brazen" young woman, who made the BMW statement on a TV dating show where a bachelor interviews glamorous girls, said it was a joke.[114] However, the government added a censor to the show to prevent such materialist messages in the future. Former President Hu Jintao (much like the Supreme Leader Khamenei of Iran) explained, "hostile foreign powers are intensifying strategies and plots to Westernize and divide our country, the ideological and cultural sphere is the focus sphere in which they conduct long-term infiltration...the international culture of the West is strong, while we are weak."[115] Professor Hu commented that young people have already been Westernized. A film professor commented that the government has a "persecution complex; it always feels people are infiltrating us, attacking us, Westernizing us." Of course, the government wants to keep youth in line with Communist Party ideology.

The Chinese government introduced a new policy in 2012 to reduce "low taste vulgar" entertainment shows on satellite channels to two a week and require at least two hours of news each evening in order to "promote traditional virtues and socialist core values."[116] For example, *Ordinary Hero*—a show about people doing heroic deeds--replaced a popular dating show called *Take Me Out*. This is ironic because some believe the government encouraged light entertainment to distract viewers from political issues. China has the largest number of TV viewers in the world, as about 95% of the population of 1.3 billion has TV access.

SpeakOut student Krishna, in his early 20s, comments on consumerism in formerly socialist India under Jawaharlal Nehru, the first prime minister in 1947 (neoliberalism was introduced in 1991):

> *The problem with modern comforts is that everyone is hankering after more and nobody seems to be content. The root of this "culture" is the almost sub-conscious desire of instant gratification. In some cases, things are so bad that kids think veggies just grow on shelves in a department store! In a frantic search for the next best "in--thing," we are taught to neglect what is right before our eyes and live in an illusion of past and future. Most of the things in the article you sent me [about urban Indian youth]--the sex, the drugs, the social networking, etc. are true, yet not very rampant.117 All of that is still a luxury to most teens here because they involve money. Kids from poor families cannot afford to indulge in such vices because if they do so, they are putting their family's future at stake. So they work hard and try to be responsible bread earners for their family when they grow up.*

Arun Maira, Chairman of Boston Consulting Group India, comments on youth materialism in India where some equate riches with success:

> *In my younger days, wealth did not automatically or easily give you high esteem.*

Now, wealth seems to have become the most important indicator of a person's worth. In those days, a question one had about rich people was, "I wonder what else is good about this person for me to respect him?" Jobs and careers are valued mostly in money terms, whereas in those earlier times, "service to the nation" was an important source of status, compensating greatly for less money.[118]

The focus on materialism and self at the expense of traditional moral values and concern for others is portrayed in the Bollywood movie *Bunty and Babli*. A hit film in India in 2005, the film is about two rebels. As Babli's Punjabi parents plan an arranged marriage, her mother tells her than in her new family, "You'll eat, die, walk, and sleep the way they want you to." But Babli wants to be a model and try out for the Miss India beauty pageant. Her father threatens her, "Don't make me hurt you." She covers her room with posters of international models like Aishwarya Rai, Naomi Campbell and Cindy Crawford, dreaming of being famous and rich like them and analyzing how to apply makeup. She decides to sneak away from home to enter a beauty contest.

She meets Bunty, another young rebel. His father tells him he needs to get a job as a train ticket-taker like him and not try to be rich like Tata (the car manufacturer). His son refuses to work 9 to 5 taking petty bribes like his father. He too leaves home, hoping to get rich with an investment scheme and "be someone important and famous." He says young people can waste time in school or learn on their own—his choice. The new friends need money to go to Mumbai, the city of opportunity, so they start a series of revenge scams on people who didn't treat them well. With their illegal riches, they buy fancy clothes, makeup, and a car—and of course as they are in a Bollywood film they dance a lot. They end up falling in love, but don't have sex until they perform their own marriage ceremony around an outdoor fire. All we see on their wedding night is mild kisses, more than in many Bollywood films that avoid any kissing but do allow rape scenes and violence.

A policeman who is on their trail complains that young people look to Bunty and Babli as "new age heroes" who make money and commit crimes for fun, and forget about values of good and bad. He says he'd like to cure their generation. After Babli gives birth to their son she has a change of heart, insisting they give up crime. They decide to go back to traditional life living with his parents, but they're bored; she says she's so tired of making mango chutney she could scream. The police officer offers them a job tracking down other scam artists and they film ends with the couple in black business suits dancing away from the traditional emphasis on the extended family.

Aishwarya, an Indian college student, emailed an update on movies in 2014,

Kissing is common in movies here now. Though, internationals do not kiss or do glamorous roles any more because they're married. Actress Kareena Kapoor (now suffixed Khan) said in an interview "I am very modern. Saif and me are a very modern couple. Why should I cook, he will cook for me. Why would I leave the film industry?" But she said so without realizing that it was her who suffixed Saif's surname, not him to suffix hers. So all this boasting of her Modernity is hollow. Movies both in Hollywood and Bollywood show men sitting at the "head of the family table" and making important decisions while females cook.

Another Indian film, *Like Stars on Earth*, (2007) criticizes the obsession with material success, as the film song lyrics ask, "Work your fingers to the bone, do exactly as you're told. Why this steady striving towards a goal?" In the film, the father of two boys is so obsessed with his sons being "toppers" at the head of their class and winning sports events that he's cruel. Ishaan, the younger son, is imaginative and "thinks outside the box," but his parents and teachers criticize him harshly, not understanding that he's dyslexic. Sent off to a boarding school at age eight, he shuts down in depression until his art teacher recognizes his learning disability and helps him overcome it. The boy wins the school's art contest, making his parents proud of his unique gifts. We've seen that Indian films tackle the issue of too much focus on getting ahead.

A US public health officer, Nora observes that the reach of Western consumerism is patchy. She has worked in Tanzania, Thailand, Pakistan and Kyrgyzstan, where she observed:

Central Asia is quite isolated, and while you do see some American and European brands here, Western media is definitely not the dominant force here. In general, it really depends on the geographic location and level of development. In places with a higher level of infrastructure in Asia, such as Thailand, and even India, the influence of Western culture is huge. Most of what I have seen in Africa is that Western culture greatly influences sports, but not so much consumerism or culture.

With the increasing availability of mobile phones, Internet connection and battery-powered TVs, ads and the consumer religion they preach are spreading even to rural villages.

Some young people have materialistic aims, as indicated in these SpeakOut comments.

I feel more loved by someone when they buy me something, because then I don't feel invisible.
    Kyla, 10, f, Belize

I want to know the ways or steps of getting myself to be a rich person if there is a formula I can then follow through and reach my target.
    Catherine, 11, f, Hong Kong

I want to become a mechanical engineer and establish a company of automobiles and become a big shot like Ratan Tata [car manufacturer].
    Sandee, 13, m, India

How can I become easy a millionaire?
    Flow, 16, m, Germany

How do I make a **** load of money?
    Anthony, 16, m, Quebec

My friends want to do community work just because it would help them get admission in good colleges. No one is ready to put their future at stake by taking out time for something besides fun and studies and I am honest enough to admit that I am one of them. Islam focuses a lot on Modesty and Simplicity (principles which are against Consumerism), which means that Islam tells us to live clean, simple and non-extravagant lives. The question "Is consumerism going to stray people away from their religion?" Would the rise of consumerism in teenagers mean decline of religion in future since teenagers are the future?

I have observed in my college that all those materialistic teenagers who run after branded items and expensive consumer products are not so religious (this is true in big cities). They do not pray or fast. Even I can call myself one of those teenagers but not to an extreme extent. But there is another angle to that question. What if once the teenagers have grown to adulthood, they become more sensible and less inclined towards consumerism and thus go back on track of their religion? That is a possibility which only time can tell.
    Shehroz, 17, m, Pakistan

Others Reject Consumerism

Many SpeakOut youth criticize adults' materialism. They're backed up by studies showing that people who focus on getting more money and possessions are less happy than people who have less materialistic values.[119] The former are more anxious, narcissistic, more likely to be depressed, and less concerned about protecting the environment. A marketing study of US Millennials reported the main influences on their purchasing decisions were anxiety and empowerment.[120] SpeakOut youth from various backgrounds are critical of materialism. In Chile, Florencia, 18, states about adults, "I would change their materialistic mentality. They rather prefer a big house or an expensive car, to prove that they are better than others, and sometimes those things just show that adults have a physical perspective about life, and they do not appreciate it as they should."

Two young feminists in the UK critiqued consumerism's negative effect on women. University students Rhiannon Lucy Cosslett and Holly Baxer poked fun at women's magazines with their focus on appearance and pleasing men, then critiqued them on their blog "Vagenda" in 2012. It grew into a book of the same name published two years later. They point out that sexism in media has gotten worse rather than better. A socialist critique of the tyranny of "the patriarchal capitalist machine" was provided by British student activist Laurie Penny in *Meat Market: Female Flesh Under Capitalism* (2011). She was 24 when the book was published and had suffered from anorexia from ages 12 to 17. She read feminist blogs online, concluding, "The Internet has revived feminist debate for a new generation of women and men."[121]

Jessie J is an English singer whose song "Price Tag" topped the charts in 19 countries. The lyrics include "Why is everybody so obsessed? Money can't buy us happiness. Can we all slow down and enjoy right now?"[122] She altruistically shaved off her hair to raise money for charity; "It's just hair," she said. Typical of her generation in the West, she is also frank about her sexuality, namely, bisexuality.

Generally surveys usually find young people value family over getting rich. A marketing survey of US teens asked them how they define success in their adulthoods: When asked about their future goals, making a lot of money was in eighth place. Being really good at your job was number one with 82%, followed by having a really good relationship with your kids and being in control of your life in a tie with 78%.[123] At the top of their priorities were, in this order: go to college, enjoy life, buy a house, have a good relationship with friends and family, have a successful career and marriage—but not to get rich.

Because they grew up in a global recession, young people want material security but they don't think money buys happiness. Their focus on loving relationships as the source of happiness is proven correct by the longest longitudinal study of human development, which followed 268 male Harvard students beginning in 1938. After 75 years and millions of dollars spent on the Men of Harvard study, author George Vaillant concluded in his *Triumphs of Experience* (2012), "Happiness is love" and warm relationships. Youth do desire money to create charitable projects and start green businesses as well as to take care of their families.

A survey of US youth didn't find them to be enchanted by wealth either. Asking about sex and romance in an online survey of 355 respondents ages 18 to 34, (by marketing agency Euro RSCG Worldwide), the survey found they were most attracted to someone with intelligence, similar to the older generations surveyed, with physical strength in second place.[124] They were less likely than older respondents to be attracted by money as a turn-on, as only one in 20 felt this way. Millennials were more likely to choose "power" (14%) as attractive, compared to 6% of the middle-aged group. The researchers think this interest in power is explained by their previous surveys indicating that Millennials want to create meaningful change.

In Central China, Zheyu's father was raised in a farm family, but acceptance into university propelled him into a very successful banking business. He stresses frugality to his son, who reports,

> *I'm not willing to spend one more dollar except for necessities, that's not because I don't have that money, that's because I want to save. I'm not the guy who spoils money and is living in a heaven-like house as some believe. The whole family, my parents and grandparents, told me to rely on myself and support myself after graduation. With my children I wouldn't care about their grades, but about their personality, they shouldn't be selfish and mean. I won't expect my son to be very powerful and rich.*

"People were made to be loved and objects were made to be used. The problem is, people are being used and objects are being loved. Why?" criticizes Dhawal (16, m, India). Despite Western media influence, the pull towards traditional family values continues. A popular Indian TV show, *Sasural Genda Phool*, is about a daughter-in-law [*bahu*] who adjusts her lifestyle to suit her in-laws' simple and modest living.[125] She can wear modern clothes but her priority must be her family. Gaurav Banerjee, a manager of STAR Plus TV network, said the character represents,

... the face of the 'modern bahu' in terms of dressing and thought but still adhere to Indian ethics. We are trying to redefine the 'Indian bahu' on TV with this show. But when it's about a commitment to the family and how fiercely protective this bahu should be towards the family--that is something we wouldn't want to change. Those values must always resonate and be constant and yet getting refreshed and replenished by the experiences of today.

Krishna, 21, satirically describes the materialistic focus of middle class life in his blog, "A Salute to the MC [Middle Class] Yogis of India."[126] He prefers a spiritual focus.

An alarm clock goes off. Women from the neighboring houses get up early and start sweeping their front yards. Newspapers are delivered, milkmen are all over the place. You hear a cow moo. You hear the hens and roosters. You know it's time to get up. This is an average morning for the average Ram in our billion-plus strong country, India. He wakes up everyday with thoughts of bills to pay, debts to clear, work to do, distances to travel, food to eat and of the one precious thing that he treasures the most: settling down. Yes, one day, he will earn enough money to solve all his problems and he will be happy ever after. That is the common dream of every middle-class family that I've seen so far (mine included).

Well, what does our average Ram do in life? He works in one of the many industries that we have. I am yet to see someone from the middle-class (let's call it MC) who runs a business. When you grow up in a MC family, the words that are tossed around the most are "job" and "settle down." So little Ram gets into an English medium, if possible International school, and starts cramming his brain. He is looking at 12-17 years of "education." After all, only when he gets an education will Ram have enough money to solve his problems (where did they come from in the first place...one wonders!) and settle down.

Ram gets a job. But, he realizes that he can only settle down when he is retired. This is because Ram has a family to look after and that's no easy task, considering the fact that his boss demands major chunks of time in his daily life! Ram's middle age is spent looking after his family--the kids, their education, the furniture, the friends and relatives, the festivals, the holidays, the picnics and the knick-knacks and the what-nots.

Ram is old now. His kids are in the USA [the mobility theme]. He's bought as many pieces of property as he could. He's bought all the gold that he could and hid them safely in the multiple bank accounts that he has. He is retired. He just attended a nice retirement party. He is happy. Ram is old now.

Poor Ram. Just when he thought he could settle down at last, the idle crowd in the retirement party started asking him questions about his kids' marriages. Ram started asking himself the same questions. He found out the answers soon enough, thanks to the many middle-aged "aunties" who miraculously descended on his humble cottage to help him find them. They showed Ram dreams of a "settled down" life, where he is happily playing with his grandchildren...not a care in the world! He loved this idea. Well, he got what he wanted. More than half of his savings were wiped out for the weddings. (The laddus and the shahi paneer [food] were the talk of the town for three days, they say.)

I've seen many Rams like this, with wrinkles on their faces, bitterness in their voices and haunting dreams of "settling down." About the only place where they seem to settle down is on their deathbed! That too, isn't much respite, for life goes on again, on another planet, in another plane.

Being a kid from the MC block, I asked myself if it was worth all the strife to settle down like others around me. Something in me told that there's more to life than just having a low profile all through and living it complacently within the walls that we've built ourselves. My questions led me to the spiritual path and obviously, my Guru said that life does have a meaning and that perfect contentment (another word for settling down) and bliss are possible. Whenever I travel and look out of the window of my bus or train, I wonder...If only our MC Yogis learned to divert their energies to find that joy that they always carry within themselves, they'd be much happier than they are now.

Thus, for some youth, making money is the top priority, but more, like Krishna, focus on spirituality and doing good:

I think adults should not be trusting success and money. People don't want to hear anything about God because they think they are going to make it with their money.
Joe, 13, m, Quebec

I would remove greediness and materialistic attitude from people.

Gleb, 14, m, Russia

The main aim is money. I want to change it, because money is not the main thing in our life.
Marjana, 15, f, Ukraine

Why is the world focusing on money?
Marie, 17, f, France

I would change that adults do everything for money. I think they must have their spirit and opinion, and should insist on their childhood dreams.
Deng Yawen, 19, f, China

Big companies are the cause of the world's problems.
Joao, 19, m, Brazil

I would remove adult's greed about money.
Mi-Hyeon, 19, f, Korea

Other young people campaign against how their shoes and clothes are made in unsafe sweatshops, including groups like United Students Against Sweatshops. Founded in 2009, it has chapters on over 150 university campuses. Their website explains, "We seek to use a diversity of tactics, especially nonviolent direct action and civil disobedience, which fundamentally challenge the oppressive power structures that exploit the majority of the world's population. We believe that substantive change is created through movements of oppressed people organizing to develop and use their own power."[127]

Another approach Is to create an economy with shared resources like cars and houses, as discussed in books like Rachel Botsman's *What's Mine is Yours: The Rise of Collaborative Consumption* (2010) and Robin Chase's *Peers Inc.: How People and Platforms Are Inventing the Collaborative Economy and Reinventing Capitalism* (2015). Chase is the founder of Zipcar. The CEO of My Swirl, Tracy Saville believes that "In the emerging, collaborative economy we not only have a leg up, we are the drivers," because women "control the consuming economy" and are "inherently collaborative."[128] Do you agree or disagree?

Businesses based on peer-to-peer capitalism that utilize existing resources are increasing in the 'sharing economy," like Airbnb that rents out private rooms to travelers, as described in various books.[129] Other sharing businesses are car-sharing or informal taxi services like Lyft, Uber, Sidecar and RelayRides; household jobs on TaskRabbit, Fiverr or Mechanical Turk; and deliveries on Favor or grocery shopping on Instacart. Vayable matches tourists with local non-professional guides. Peer-to-peer financing, crowdfunding, and community shares fund local projects such as a solar co-op or a ferryboat service in Bristol, England. Crowdfunding platforms like Kickstarter and Lending Club provide loans outside the banking system. *Forbes* magazine estimated that the sharing economy raised over $3.5 billion in the US in 2013, a growth rate of over 25%.[130] (Robert Reich discusses it in a video.[131])

Traditional and Modern Beliefs: Moving Towards the Middle

Rather than asking if consumerism is eradicating traditional customs and values, perhaps we need to think of humans as complex, capable of multiple identities based on intersecting factors like where we live, religion, class, gender, race, and our age. The authors of *Globalization: Debunking the Myths* believe that the future depends on "how successfully the components of globalization (cosmopolitan, individualized, democratized, and secularized) are 'grafted' into preexisting local cultural values, traditions, and practices that are communal, hierarchical, and sacred."[132] SpeakOut youth reveal the contemporary continuum between traditional values in developing nations and postmodern values in developed countries, with Latin America in the middle combining traditional and newer attitudes.

Satellite TV, Internet and shopping malls lead to consumerism, all sold in the name of individual freedom of choice and fulfillment at the expense of the environment, religious values, public service and lasting happiness.[133] Can we find a way to teach young people to respect the traditional values of caring for others, simplicity, and living in harmony with nature and regional traditions? Fiona Ngarachu, in Kenya, points out, "Modernization is sometimes confused with Westernization. Some authors see it as a cultural change that is desperately needed to pull 'Africa out of the dark ages.' It is essential for any development programs to take into account the existing system of beliefs, culture and way of life and not belittle them." [134]

Traditional values are alive in our survey responses. Surveys of young North Americans indicate they are becoming more conservative in valuing their families and spending time with them and place great value on becoming parents in the future. Kirby, a Boston college student, explains that, "Hipsters are, interested in family and financial responsibility, in reaction to their Baby Boomer parents, but are often sarcastic, focused on 'original' concepts like indie music and movies, and feel lost in a world where things were mostly easy for them."

Like the rural Chinese SpeakOut students, Indian students frequently mentioned their social duty to care for parents and help their country develop and eradicate poverty and corruption, rather than just being motivated by personal success. The Indian students often mentioned joking and teasing their friends for fun, rather than playing electronic games. An Indian boy Abhinar, 18, comments,

> *I am here on the earth because of my parents. So, I have to fulfill their hopes for me, their dreams, share their problems and be with them till the end of my life. Till my last breath, I have to help others, make the most of them happy without any selfishness. Living for ourselves is not a life, living for the society is a complete life.*

Mary, 14, reports that in Mexico City, "We don't often live together--just in some cases, but I often see my cousins and grandparents once a week." Stephanie Tarrago, an American married to a Cuban, who has lived in Yucatan, Mexico for a decade, emailed,

> *In Mexico, it is normal for families get together every week and cook together (women cooking, men drinking beer and kids playing). It is not uncommon for children to live with their parents in the same house for their whole lives. Many people raise their families in their parents' house--or their in-law's house (which ever house is bigger). I have a friend who owns her own house, but because her parent's house is bigger she lives there with her husband and her two kids. She feels better in her parents' house and she feels like she can look after her parents too as they get older. That is really common here.*
>
> *As far as love and marriage, people seem to choose their partners for the most part. There is a lot of American influence here. Young people are more and more like Americans. They watch movies from the US, listen to American songs and most of them have family living in the US. So, some of our culture has rubbed off on them.*
>
> *Cubans are similar in that they also live with their families for a long time, but mostly because there is not enough housing nor jobs to accommodate anything different. Cubans are very individualistic and the parents do not have much*

control over their children when they become adults. People love who they want to and live together out of wedlock if they want and there is really not much of a taboo about it. With the revolution, religion was scorned and even made illegal so many religiously influenced traditions that try to put rules on male and female relationships no longer have any power.

The mandate for our future well-being is for adults to facilitate youth's hopefulness, energy, and willingness to do volunteer work into development as caring global citizens. The know-how and the resources to educate all children and provide them with health care are available, but instead industrialized nations spend millions on ice cream, pets and weaponry. Governments need to invest in schools, health care, job creation, and youth organizations such as the Youth Ministry in Senegal that set up teen guidance centers with reproductive health services. The goal is to spread the advantages of global technology to kids living in poverty, including education for both girls and boys.

We've seen that globalization heightens the pace of change and global media stimulates desire for consumerism. Although many live in poverty they may have access to radio, smartphones, and battery-powered TV with all the products they sell, indicating that rising expectations can lead to frustration and anger. The United Nations Sustainable Development Goals adopted in 2015 should be put into place if we care about human well-being, including access to education for all children.[135] Former Communist countries seem to have bred the most materialistic youth, as many weren't raised either with strong religious beliefs or the Marxist emphasis on serving the people. If more young critics like Zoe and Krishna are disgusted by consumer culture, Millennials won't be as easily controlled by advertisers as previous generations, and will help protect the environment from increased consumption devices that drain world resources. People of all ages are saturated with electronic media and its focus on consuming expensive products and lifestyles; we'll see media influences on youth in the next chapter.

Discussion Questions and Activities

Questions

1. Do you agree or disagree that a materialistic focus on money has corrupted youth, warping them into "Generation Sell" with the personality and values of salespeople?
2. How do corporations and their media campaigns influence our values and behaviors? Use print ads to illustrate your observations.

3. Most people can't achieve the lifestyle shown on TV and movies, leading to frustration. Will this lack of money to consume lead to positive change, rebellion, or a resigned bitterness and escape into drugs and alcohol?
4. The planet can't sustain the current consumption of resources, let alone accommodate growing middle classes who want cars and meat. How can the planet be saved?
5. A defining quality of youth today is closeness to their parents and friends. Will this counter materialistic consumerism?

Activities

1. Analyze print ads and those on television to see how they manipulate viewers, as in making them feel inadequate and unhappy by not consuming the product advertised.
2. Read a Mongolian young man's blog about cycling across the US and his impressions of the US, including the obsession with things like yard sales and lawns.[136]
3. See videos about how various cultures oppose or adopt Valentine's Day.[137]
4. Look at photos of children's favorite possessions to examine sex role socialization and differences between developed and developing nations.[138]

Films

1. *The Truman Show* tells the story of a man who doesn't know his life is a reality TV show. Fake media is fed to him to manipulate his thinking and prevent him from wanting to leave home. How does this apply to people you know who are manipulated by the media? US, 1998
2. *The Joneses* about "stealth marketers" who pretend to be a family. US, 2009
3. *Bro Code: How Contemporary Culture Creates Sexist Men.* 2011 (transcript available[139])
4. *Killing Us Softly 4: Advertising's Image of Women*[140] 2010
5. *Consuming Kids: The Commercialization of Childhood*[141] 2008

Endnotes

[1] http://goglobal.virb.com/overview
[2] "How Do You See Feminism?" Muse Syndrome, Dawson College, November 24, 2013. http://musessyndrome.wordpress.com/2013/11/24/how-do-you-see-feminism/

3 Harris, pp. 140-142.
4 http://www.brandalism.org.uk/artists Angela Natividad, "600 Fake Outdoor Ads in Paris," *Adweek*, November 30, 2015.
http://www.adweek.com/adfreak/600-fake-outdoor-ads-paris-blast-corporate-sponsors-cop21-climate-talks-168358
5 http://kindakind.com/sexist-vintage-ads-illustrate-why-the-world-needs-feminism/
6 Anita Harris and Michelle Fine, eds. *All About the Girl: Culture, Power, and Identity*. Routledge, 2004, pp. 164-169.
7 Anita Harris, "Jamming Girl Culture," in *All About the Girl*, p. 165.
8 Emilie Zaslow. *Feminism, Inc.: Coming of Age in Girl Power Media Culture*. Palgrave Macmillan, 2009.
9 Christia Brown, "Girl Power is the New 'It' Movement," *Psychology Today*, January 1, 2015.
https://www.psychologytoday.com/blog/beyond-pink-and-blue/201501/girl-power-is-the-new-it-movement
10 Ruth Lewis and Susan Marine, "Weaving a Tapestry, Compassionately: Toward an Understanding of Young Women's Feminisms," *Feminist Formations*, Vol. 27, Issue 1, Spring 2015, p 121.
11 Naomi Klein. *No Logo*. St. Martin's Press/Picador, 2009, pp. 118-121. She sees Barack Obama as the first president who is a brand with an Obama logo, viral marketing, product placement, brand alliances, etc. (p. xxiv)
12 http://subtleuniverse.tumblr.com/archive
13 "What people like on Tumblr"
hipsters/Indies. Vintage pictures, a.k.a, film pictures. Pictures of girls without their heads showing, in cute outfits. Triangles and space. Pictures of people smoking. Guys with tattoos. Harry Potter. Mean Girls. Quotes. Movie scenes, with the words written on it. Pictures of girls holding some sort of alcohol. People wearing animal masks. Pictures of people holding a camera over their face. Lol Pictures of people flipping off the camera. People kissing. Hot guys with piercings and nice bodies. Pretty girls.
14 http://therepresentationproject.org/about/#mission
15 Jared Diamond, "What's Your Consumption Factor?" *New York Times*, January 2, 2008.
http://www.nytimes.com/2008/01/02/opinion/02diamond.html?pagewanted=all
16 Kevin Sessums, "Nobody's Teen Queen," *Parade* magazine, March 21, 2010, p. 4.
17 http://www.eonline.com/photos/gallery.jsp?galleryUUID=554#174932
18 Stephanie Marcus, "Miley Cyrus Talks Feminism," *Huffpost Celebrity*, June 23, 2014.
http://www.huffingtonpost.com/2014/04/08/miley-cyrus-feminism-disney_n_5110669.html
19 Jennifer O'Connell, "Miley Cyrus, "I Think My Generation is in Crisis," *Irish Times*, January 30, 2015.
http://www.irishtimes.com/life-and-style/people/miley-cyrus-i-think-my-generation-is-in-crisis-1.2077486
20 James Côté. *Youth Studies: Fundamental Issues and Debates*. Palgrave Macmillian, 2014, pp. 194-2010.
21 Simon Kemp, "Digital in 2017: A Global Overview," We are Social, January 24, 2017.
https://wearesocial.com/special-reports/digital-in-2017-global-overview
22 The Media Education Foundation
23 http://www.mediaed.org/assets/products/160/transcript_160.pdf
Logan Rhoades, "16 Random things You Should Probably Know About Today's Teens," *BuzzFeed*, April 21, 2015.
http://www.buzzfeed.com/mrloganrhoades/16-random-things-you-should-probably-know-about-todays-teens#.pkx5Ywyaa
24 http://www.guerrillagirls.com
25 http://hemisphericinstitute.org/journal/1_1/cheerleaders_print.pdf
26 http://observer.com/2017/02/girls-hbo-wardrobe-marnie-michaels-hannah-horvath/andy Banks, "A Younger View of Feminism," *Los Angeles Times*, April 20, 2009.
27 Emma Fraser, "The Clothes They Wore," *The Observer*, February 8, 2017.
http://observer.com/2017/02/girls-hbo-wardrobe-marnie-michaels-hannah-horvath/
28 https://www.facebook.com/sheryl/videos/10156510941810177/
29 Tim Snelson, "Grrrls: How Female Teens Invented Youth Culture," International Day of the Girl, website, October 14, 2014.
http://dayofthegirlnorwich.org/2014/10/14/the-original-riot-grrrls-how-female-teens-invented-youth-culture/
30 Merlyna Lim, "Many Clicks but Little Sticks: Social Media Activism in Indonesia," *Journal of Contemporary Asia*, February 2013.
http://www.academia.edu/4951916/Lim_M._2013_Many_Clicks_but_Little_Sticks_Social_Media_Activism_in_Indonesia
31 "Meet the 'Sneakerheads,'" *Daily Mail*, March 20, 2012.
http://www.dailymail.co.uk/femail/article-2117667/Meet-sneakerheads-pay-5-000-pair-old-trainers-queue-street-overnight-them.html
32 Anne D'Innocenzio, "Retailers Get Cold Shoulder from Teens for Holidays," *Associated Press*, December 11, 2014.
33 http://bigstory.ap.org/article/f9a2ce77adec4a858a7a169d6d807c15/teen-retailers-get-cold-shoulder-holidays
34 http://research.tigweb.org/roleofyouth/
The number of Internet users doubled between 2003 to 2009. John Ribeiro, May 27, 2010
www.businessweek.com, www.sikhnet.com/news/more-one-four-use-internet-worldwide-says-it By May 2017, 49.6% of the world's population was online, with over 3.7 billion users.
https://www.internetworldstats.com/stats.htm
35 Elissa Moses. *The $100 Billion Allowance: Accessing the Global Teen Market*. John Wiley and Sons, 2000.
36 A 2008 Internet survey of 2,277 students from 114 countries equally male/female sponsored by AIESEC and The Career Innovation Company.

37. www.aiesec.org/.../Digital_Generation_Survey_2008_-_Technology_xPart_1x.pdf

Global Habbo Youth Survey 2009 of over 112,000 youth on Habbo virtual world site. http://www.prweb.com/releases/2009/06/prweb2493344.htm

38. *Dominique Reynié, ed., "World Youths," Fondation Pour L'Innovation Politique, 2011. Electronic survey in 2010 by TNS Opinion of 25,000 youth born between 1981 and 1994 in 25 countries, plus 7,714 respondents aged 30 to 50.* http://expeng.anr.msu.edu/uploads/files/83/2010%20Youth%20leadership%20in%20a%20Globalized%20World%20Survey.pdf

39. Alys Eve Weinbaum, et al., **eds.** *The Modern Girl Around the World*. Duke University Press, 2008.

40. Alycia de Mesa. *Brand Avatar*. Palgrave, 2009, pp, 26-27.

41. Young Sook Moon and Kara Chan, "Gender Portrayal in Hong Kong and Korean Children's TV Commercials: A Cross-Cultural Comparison," Asian Journal of Communication, Vol. 12, Issue 2, 2002, pp. 100-119.

42. www.researchandmarkets.com/research/9443a8/phoenix_generation

43. See the DVD documentary *Five Sides of a Coin* in which the rapper Aesop Rock guesses that if God had to choose one religion that best articulated His own intentions, "He would choose hip-hop."

44. Asda'a Burson-Arab Youth Study 2010, 2,000 interviews face-to-face with respondents ages 18-24. videwww.slideshare.net/BMGlobalNews/asdaa-bursonarab-youth-study-2010

45. Dannie Kjeldgaard and Soren Askegaard, "The Globalization of Youth Culture: The Global Youth Segment and Structures of Common Difference," *Journal of Consumer Research*, Vol. 33, September 2006, p. 233.

46. http://www.bbc.com/news/magazine-26664736

47. Nico Young, "Inside Santa Monica High School," *New York Times*, September 11, 2016. http://www.nytimes.com/interactive/2016/09/11/magazine/11mag-santa-monica-high-photo-essay.html?emc=edit_th_20160911&nl=todays-headlines&nlid=68143430

48. www.urbandictionary.com/define.php?term=youth+sub-culture

49. kerman Andrews, "I Want to Start a Wobbly Revolution, *Advertiser*, May 23, 2013. http://www.advertiser.ie/galway/article/61138/i-want-to-start-a-wobbly-revolution

50. Ashley Steinberg, "Rebels Without Cause," *Daily Beast*, March 17, 2008. www.newsweek.com/id/124098 http://www.bing.com/videos/search?q=Pok%c3%a9mon+teens+&view=detail&mid=8915DCFE1A1B53E266058915DCFE1A1B53E26605&FORM=VIRE

51. The slow-food movement began in 1986 in Italy. Founder Carol Petrini called for a return to the "pleasures of a slow life rather than a fast life." By 2010 there were nearly 450 slow food chapters world-wide.

52. Pete Engardio, *Businessweek*, October 3, 2005. www.businessweek.com/magazine/content/05_34/b3948530.htm

53. "If You Dream, You Can Do It" http://www.outlookindia.com/article.aspx?222591

54. http://timesofindia.indiatimes.com/specialcoverage/5868107.cms

55. Ibid, p. 59.

56. Lukose, Op.Cit., p. 13.

57. www.cnn.com/2010/WORLD/asiapcf/02/14/india.village.no.electricity/index.html

58. Linda Herrera and Asef Bayat, **eds.** *Being Young and Muslim*. Oxford University Press, 2010, p. 21.

59. Kurt Iveson, "Partying, Politics and Getting Paid—Hip-hop and National Identity in Australia." *Overland*, No. 147, Winter 1997, pp. 39-47.

60. Ruchira Ganguly-Scrase, "Globalization and Gendered Social Transformation: Young People in an Urban Artisan Community in India," *Children, Youth and Environments*, Vol. 14, No. 2, 2004.

61. "How Millennials Want to Work and Live," Galllup Poll report, 2016. http://www.gallup.com/reports/189830/millennials-work-live.aspx 25% are fully engaged, compared to 33% of Baby Boomers.

62. "Share the World's Resources," http://www.stwr.org/multinational-corporations/key-facts.html

63. Zach Carter, "Alan Grayson on Trans-Pacific Partnership," *Huffington Post* blog, June 18, 2013. http://www.huffingtonpost.com/2013/06/18/alan-grayson-trans-pacific-partnership_n_3456167.html

64. Garcia Canclini, 1995. p. 2

65. http://www.nytimes.com/video/fashion/100000003575605/intersection-harajuku-style-in-tokyo.html?emc=edit_th_20150318&nl=todaysheadlines&nlid=68143430

66. "Young People in a Globalizing World," Chapter 11, *World YOUTH Report*, 2003. http://www.un.org/esa/socdev/unyin/documents/ch11.pdf

67. Sarah Anderson and John Cavanagh. "Top 200: The Rise of Global Corporate Power," *Global Policy Forum*, 2000. http://globalpolicy.org/component/content/article/221/47211.html. *Field Guide to the Global Economy*. The New Press, 2005.

68. Kenway and Bullen, p. 35.

69. www.youtube.com/watch?v=Tr_B4Nv4RKo

70. NPR Staff, "Wordless Ads Speak Volumes in 'Unbranded' Images of Women," *NPR*, April 18, 2015. http://www.npr.org/2015/04/18/400396747/wordless-ads-speak-volumes-in-unbranded-images-of-women

71. Lisa Currier listed: Bill Bixby in *Courtship of Eddy's Father*, Tom Selleck in *Blue Bloods*, Ralph Waite in *The Waltons*, Michael Landon in *Bonanza*

[72] *and* Little *House on the Prairie*, Phillip Banks in *Fresh Prince of Bell Air*, Mike Brady in *The Brady Bunch*, and Damien Wayans in *My Wife and Kids*.

Dave McNary, "Bill Cosby Admits to Drugging Women for Sex," *Variety*, July 6, 2015.

[73] http://variety.com/2015/biz/news/bill-cosby-admits-to-drugging-women-for-sex-report-1201534649/

Maura Judkis, "Super Bowl Commercials Still Sassy," *The Washington Post*, February 1, 2015.

http://www.washingtonpost.com/lifestyle/style/super-bowl-commercials-still-sassy-but-a-little-more-classy-as-sexism-fades-in-

[74] 2015/2015/02/01/696093a6-a89a-11e4-a06b-9df2002b86a0_story.html

Bethonie Butler and Maura Judkis, "The 10 Best Commericals of Super Bowl 50," *Washington Post*, Feburary 8, 2016.

[75] https://www.washingtonpost.com/news/arts-and-entertainment/wp/2016/02/08/the-10-best-commercials-of-super-bowl-50/

[76] https://www.youtube.com/watch?v=6DO3rT0I4hE

"Piper Jaffray Completes 25th Semi-Annual 'Taking Stock with Teens' Marketing Research Project," April 10, 2013.

[77] http://www.piperjaffray.com/2col.aspx?id=287&releaseid=1805593

Martin Lindstrom, et al. *BRANDchild: Insights into the Minds of Today's Global Kids*. Kogan Page, 2003. A marketing survey by Millward Brown

[78] of several thousand tweens in 15 countries. The tweens are exposed to 8,000 brands a day.

Michael Ordona, "'Eleven' Gives Voice to Wisdom of Children," *San Francisco Chronicle*, September 21, 2014.

[79] http://www.sfchronicle.com/movies/article/Eleven-gives-voice-to-wisdom-of-children-5762695.php#/0

Cathy Van der Meulen is international brand manager of the Sydney-based chain clothing store called SUPRE. www.theage.com.au/news/

Fashion/Tweenage-**idols**/2005/05/20/111653353. Fiona Brookes and Peter Kelly, "Dolly Girls: Tweenies as Artefacts of Consumption," *Journal*

[80] *of Youth Studies*, Vol. 12, Issue 6, December 2009, pp. 599 to 613.

Lisa Feldman Barrett, "Hillary Clinton's 'Angry' Face," *New York Times*, September 23, 2016.

[81] http://www.nytimes.com/2016/09/25/opinion/sunday/hillary-clintons-angry-face.html?_r=0

Rebecca Huntley. *The World According to Y*. Allen & Unwin, Australia, 2006, p. 188.

[82] Ibid, p. 31.

[83] Ibid, p. 9

[84] Clotaire Rapaille. *The Culture Code: An Ingenious Way to Understand Why People Around the World Buy and Live As They Do*. Broadway Books, 2006.

[85] http://articles.latimes.com/2010/aug/01/business/la-fi-teen-haulers-20100801

[86] https://www.youtube.com/user/Macbarbie07

[87] https://virtuesshop.com/index.php?option=com_virtuemart&Itemid=98

www.noetic.org/about/case-studies/worldview/

[88] "Empowering Young Women to Lead Change," UNFPA and World YWCA, 2006.

http://www.unfpa.org/public/home/publications/pid/378

[89] http://www.qvwc.org.au/wp-content/uploads/2012/05/QVWC_YoungWomenBodyImageandtheDigitalAgeKit_2009.pdf

[90] "Fat is the New Normal," *Science 2.0*, May 29, 2014.

http://www.science20.com/news_articles/fat_is_the_new_normal_nearly_onethird_of_the_worlds_population_is_overweight-137319

[91] Peter Stearns, "Teaching Consumerism in World History," *World History Connected*, Vol. 1, No. 21, p. 5. http://worldhistoryconnectedpress.

illinois.edu/1.2/stearns.html Annie Leonard radio discussion. http://www.bioneers.org/radio/series-archives/2009-series/episode-8-can2019t-

[92] buy-me-love

"Muslim Dolls Tackle 'Wanton' Barbie," BBC News, March 5, 2001.

[93] http://news.bbc.co.uk/2/hi/middle_east/1856558.stm

[94] http://xavl.com/blog/iran/9976-iran-seizes-barbie-dolls-only-dara-and-sara-allowed.html

Shelly Banjo, "What Mattel's CEO Departure Means for the Future of Barbie," *Quartz*, January 27, 2015.

[95] http://qz.com/333459/what-mattels-ceo-departure-means-for-the-future-of-barbie/

Elizabeth Chin. *Purchasing Power: Black Kids and American Consumer Culture*. University of Minnesota Press, 2001. Gary Cross. *Kids' Stuff:*

[96] *Toys and the Changing World of American Chlldhood*. Harvard University Press, 1997.

http://kids.barbie.com/en-us

[97] James Vlahos, "Barbie Wants to Get to Know Your Child," *New York Times*, September 16, 2015.

[98] http://www.nytimes.com/2015/09/20/magazine/barbie-wants-to-get-to-know-your-child.html?_r=0

[99] www.facebook.com/wealthofeurope

[100] https://www.youtube.com/watch?v=BTwT8tgoG38

"Habbo Reveals Results of the 2008 Global Youth Survey of Teens," Habbo press release, April 3, 2008. http://www.prweb.com/releases/2008/04/

[101] prweb827874.htm

Sarah Flanagan, "NY Girls on Girls," Huffingtonpost.com, March 29, 2013. http://www.huffingtonpost.com/sarah-flanagan/girls-millenni-

[102] als_b_2971463.html

William Deresiewicz, "Generation Sell," *The New York Times*, November 12, 2011.

[103] http://www.nytimes.com/2011/11/13/opinion/sunday/the-entrepreneurial-generation.html?pagewanted=all

Christian Smith, et al. *Lost in Transition*. Oxford University Press, 2011. Discussed further in my *Global Youth Values Transforming Our Future*.

[104] Cambridge Scholars Publishing, 2017.

[105] *Lost in Transition*, p. 83.

"The American Freshman: National Norms Fall 2016," Higher Education Research Institute, UCLA, 2017.

[106] https://www.heri.ucla.edu/monographs/TheAmericanFreshman2016.pdf
Bill Boyarsky, "Income Inequality Goes to School, " *Truthdig*, February 24, 2012.

[107] http://www.truthdig.com/report/item/income_inequality_goes_to_school_20120224/

[108] https://studentloanhero.com/student-loan-debt-statistics/
Spring 2011 poll, Harvard Institute of Politics

[109] http://www.iop.harvard.edu/Research-Publications/Survey/Spring-2011-Survey

[110] Birgit Menzel, "Russian Discourse on Glamour," *Kultura*, December, 2008.

[111] Kseniya Gusarova,"The Deviant Norm: Glamour in Russian Fashion," *Kultura*, December 6, 2008, p. 19.

[112] Jiaming Sun and Xun Wang, op.cit., pp. 65-81.
Keith Richburg," An Injured Toddler is Ignored, and Chinese Ask Why," *The Washington Post*, October 19, 2011.

[113] www.washingtonpost.com/world/asia_pacific/an-injured-toddler-is-ignored-and-chinese-ask-why/2011/10/19/gIQAxhnpxL_story.html

[114] Wang Yong, "East Meets West in Love of Lucre," *Shanghai Daily*, January 12, 2011.

[115] http://video.nytimes.com/video/2011/12/31/world/asia/100000001227148/a-date-with-the-censors.html
Louisa Lim, "China Targets Enertainment TV in Cultural Purge," *NPR*, January 22, 22011.

[116] www.npr.org/2012/01/11/144994861/china-targets-entertainment-tv-in-cultural-purge
88 "China Campaign Cuts Entertainment TV by Two-Thirds," *BBC News*, January 4, 2012.

[117] http://www.bbc.co.uk/news/world-asia-china-16405804

[118] http://indiatoday.intoday.in/site/article/secret-life-of-indian-teens/1/130880.html

[119] August 22, 2005 www.businessweek.com/magazine/content/05_34/b3948401.htm
Tim Kasser. *The High Price of Materialism*. Bradford Book, 2003. Carmen Lawrence, "What Rising Inequality and Materialism Does to Us, " *Shaping Tomorrow's World*, June 30, 2011.

[120] http://www.shapingtomorrowsworld.org/lawrenceInequality.html
Hilary Stout, "Oh, to be Young, Millennial, and so Wanted by Marketers," *New York Times*, June 20, 2015.

[121] http://www.nytimes.com/2015/06/21/business/media/marketers-fixation-on-the-millennial-generation.html?_r=0
"Feminism is an Incomplete Revolution," posted on *Huffington Post*, June 21, 2012.

[122] http://www.independent.co.uk/arts-entertainment/books/reviews/meat-market-female-flesh-under-capitalism-by-laurie-penny-2273989.html

[123] www.metrolyrics.com/price-tag-lyrics-jessie-j.html, 2011. She was born in London in 1988.

[124] www.magazine.org/content/files/teenprofile04.pdf
Naomi Troni, "Love and Lust," *Huff Post Culture*, February 16, 2012.

[125] http://www.huffingtonpost.com/naomi-troni/millennials-romance_b_1280380.html
Radhika Bhirani, "Modernity a Far Cry for Women on Small Screen," *AOL Bollywood*, March 06, 2010

[126] www.aol.in/bollywood-story/modernity-a-far-cry-for-women-on-small-screen-march-8-is-international-womens-day/819838

[127] http://krishnadeepananda.blogspot.com/ July, 2009

[128] http://usas.org/about/mission-vision-organizing/
Tracy Saville, "Why Women Are Leading the Global Collaborative Economy," *MySWIRL*, February 13, 2016.

[129] https://medium.com/the-internet-of-women/why-the-global-collaborative-economy-is-women-why-our-technology-will-define-the-future-today-48b215295327#.absaj3m1x
Chris Anderson's *The Long Tail*, Van Jones' *The Green Collar Economy* or Malcolm Gladwell's *The Tipping Point*, Robin Chase's *Peers Inc*, and Rachel Botsmand and Roo Rogers, *What's Mine Is Yours: The Rise of Collaborative Consumption*.

[130] Tomio Geron, "Airbnb and the Unstoppable Rise of the Share Economy," *Forbes*, January 23, 2013.

[131] http://www.forbes.com/sites/tomiogeron/2013/01/23/airbnb-and-the-unstoppable-rise-of-the-share-economy/

[132] https://www.facebook.com/moveon/posts/10153124665965493

[133] Lui Hebron and John Stack, Jr., p. 98.

[134] http://www.imamreza.net/eng/imamreza.php?id=5513
Fiona Ngarachu, "Understanding Young People's Perspectives on Ethnic Politics in Kenya," 2012.

[135] https://www.academia.edu/6579804/Understanding_young_peoples_perspectives_on_ethnic_politics_in_Kenya?auto=download
http://oprahsangelnetwork.org/our-work/overview/leadership/about-o-ambassadors TV personality Oprah Winfrey started a group to teach about the UN goals.

[136] www.zilong.be/2013/07/thousand-mile-reflections.html

[137] http://globalvoicesonline.org/specialcoverage/love-is-in-the-air/

[138] http://www.featureshoot.com/2013/03/photos-of-children-from-around-the-world-with-their-most-prized-possessions/

[139] www.mediaed.org/assets/products/246/transcript_246.pdf

[140] http://www.mediaed.org/assets/products/241/studyguide_241.pdf

[141] http://www.mediaed.org/assets/products/134/transcript_134.pdf

A subway ad in Shanghai for weight loss products.

Chapter 5

GLOBAL MEDIA BOTH INHIBITS AND HELPS GIRLS

Media are going to make us stupid little by little.

Susi, 13, f, Costa Rica

I fall into the stereotypes about what beauty is and how one should be.

Lydia, 16, f, Greece

I think you have to give us a little bit of credit. We're not just mindless sponges sitting in front of the TV for hours. We're able to discern, we're disgusted by it. Corporate power is increasing around the world and our Congress as well. That's very scary to me. There are a lot of passionate, intelligent, angry youths out there who are willing to do stuff and make change.

Zoe, 17, f, California

It was obvious that my generation was losing ground on reality by being overwhelmingly filled with "ego highs" to float up the dark tunnel of consumerism, cigarettes, alcoholism, rampant pornography, and criminal media. These thought-patterns and action-patterns are reinforced by our capitalist "culture" which my age group has grown up to enjoy and, if still possible, support and strengthen, with the backing of the internationally renown American Ego.

Miranti, 20, f, Indonesia, on Facebook

Teenagers today are under a lot of pressure from everyone. Pressure to be perfect, pressure to perform.

Julie Andem, Norwegian creator of the TV series about teens called Skam.

Contents: Global Media is Pervasive, Hollywood Films Provide Global Activist Symbols, Global Media Provides New Information for Activism, Media Exposure Makes Youth Opinionated and Brave, Media Sells Consumerism, Media Addiction Creates Dumb Zombies

Global Media is Pervasive and Changes Attitudes

Global media has massive impact; as billions of young people become aware of increasing economic inequality resistance occurs. Global media brings information and creates networks of support for youth activism, as well as pressure to define our identity by what we consume. Global media culture targets youth as the most tech-savvy group worth trillions of dollars in potential sales, which some criticize as leading to McWorld hybridization of traditional cultures. If the Millennial critics of consumerism win out, our future looks good, but youth are growing up in a post-millennial, post-modern, post-industrial, post-colonial era with instant global communication and pressure to consume trendy hot or cool items. A Millennial pointed out the impact of their generation on the US: They've "already steered the country to a place where diplomats tweet, gay marriage is turning mainstream, and running a blog can be more financially secure than a company gig."[1] But, if newly middle-class young adults in the Global South continue the consumption habits of the West, we'll be in even deeper environmental trouble.

Mimi Ito, involved in a Digital Youth study, reports it's important to reveal "how adults often unreasonably curtail young people's freedom and voice." She states that, "Age is one of the most naturalized forms of oppression that we have," the least questioned among racism, sexism, and classism despite ongoing "generational tension and moral panics." In modern times adolescents are segregated in schools, but electronic media allows them to access adult worlds, to be unsupervised, and have more private conversations than phones may permit. Ito studies girls' mobile phone culture to explore "girl-led tech innovation."[2] She advocates that now that more adults join youth in using social media, traits that were attributed to youth such as "drama, oversharing, narcissism, attentional fragmentation, are certainly not age specific." Ito and co-author dana boyd (she uses lower case) look to electronic media use as a source of freedom and innovation for young people.

What local traditions and values will youth retain as media facilitates global groupthink? The Millennial Generation "takes for granted interaction, collaboration, and community building on-line."[3] A girl from Greenland, age 19, compares her life to that of teens in different countries: "We sleep, we watch television, we listen to music, we party and go to school. I ride a snow scooter; they ride a motorcycle or a scooter. It's the same." Even Australian media tycoon Rupert Murdoch questioned in 1992, "Are we not creating a homogenized world culture and at the same time destroying indigenous cultures?" Western cultural imperialism promotes its particular values about how life is to be lived, thus undermining local traditions as well as local film and TV. In South Africa, Siphila (15, m) reports the media is "a very big part of my life. This is how I make my decisions, how I dress and how I speak is what I copy from the media, if it is a good habit." Altruistic like many of his generation, as an adult he would like to work as a peacekeeper between conflicting communities and start an international NGO to assist disadvantaged children.

Teens spend nine hours a day in front of electronic devices, while tweens (ages 8 to 12) spend six hours, which is more time than they spend with human beings, according to a 2015 study by Common Sense Media.[4] Boys spend more time playing male-dominated multiplayer online video games like "World of Warcraft" and "Grand Theft Auto" and girls spend more time on social media. Teens spend more time with music and tweens with TV. Communication giants like Verizon, Condé Nast, Hearst, ABC's Freeform and HBO's Now created online video channels aimed at the almost 80 million Millennials in the US. They're trying to appeal to the most diverse generation in history. Alfie Brown relates the popularity of the mobile phone and the Pokemon GO game to corporate control of our lives, "turning the mobile phone into a new kind of unconscious; an ideological force driving our movements while we remain only semi-aware of what propels us," not realizing that "what you want is itself set in motion by the phone;"[5] literally in the search for Pokemon game fad.

Impact of Global Media

Marshall McLuhan explained in the 1960s that "the medium is the message;" it changes how we think--not only with its content, but also with the specific characteristics of the medium. Sherry Turkle, author of *Alone Together* (2012) said that Apple products like the iPod and iPad are meant to be an extension of the user's body and can interfere with human communication. Observe parents and children at a park and see how many of the adults are looking at their phones rather than their children. British singer David Bowie observed in 1999 that the Internet is like an alien life form permitting interplay between the user and the medium. Estimates are that half a million kids suffer from Internet addiction in the US and China has officially recognized it as a mental disorder.[6]

Film critic Mick Lasalle thinks that the US has become so secular that "We've chosen to worship silly things, or at least to see in silly things (i.e., the meeting of *Batman v Superman*) emblems of significance. Thus the overuse of the work 'icon.'" (A list of the most spiritually and theologically important recent films was compiled by J. Ryan

Parker.)[7] Hedges quotes Daniel Boorstein's *The Image: A Guide to Pseudo-Events in America* (1992), which charges that we live in a "world where fantasy is more real than reality. We are the most illusioned people on earth." The illusions are cleverly created by corporations and their advertising, as explained in the pioneering studies of corporate propaganda by Australian scholar Alex Carey and illustrated in the *Matrix* film series (1999 to 2003) about a virtual reality created by machine ovelords.

Author Nicolas Carr argues that our time spent in front of electronic screens actually changes how our brains work, making us less able to focus to think deeply about a topic. He believes that the Net is "chipping away my capacity for concentration and contemplation" and refers to scientific studies that back up his personal observation in his chapter titled "The Juggler's Brain."[8] He maintains that the brain cells that are harmed are those that "support calm, linear thought." The Pew Research Center surveyed over 1,000 tech experts about the future effects of "hyperconnected" young people by 2020. Over half of the experts (55%) think young people's brains will be wired differently and they'll be able to "supertask" and access Internet information to answer "deep questions." The other experts think the effect will be to reduce the ability to do deep thinking and relate to people face-to-face, making young people impatient and wanting to be entertained in instant gratification.[9]

A series of studies discovered that greater use of social media sites like Facebook results in an increase in self-esteem due to friends' positive comments and "likes," but also in less self-control manifested in binge eating, weight gain, and higher levels of credit-card debt.[10] This may apply more to girls, as women are more likely to post comments and photos on Facebook, Twitter, and Pinterest.[11] Facebook employees check flagged posts; those who seem suicidal are given suicide prevention information and asked to contact a friend or suicide hotline.

A study examining the effect of electronic media on 12-year-olds discovered that playing video games is associated with higher creativity, but using the Internet or a computer did not increase creativity.[12] (Internet Studies developed around 1999 as an academic discipline.) By May 2017, there were 3.7 billion Internet users out of 7.3 billion people, with over half of the users in Asia, 17% in Europe, and 9% of the users in North America.[13] Pew Research Center studies find that social media use helps women, but not men, cope with stress by providing social support and that women report more stress than men.[14] Women who use social media to communicate with others report less stress than women who don't use social media. However, in England, Deana, 16, worries, "The more time we spend online, on our phones and whatever technologies are coming, the more trouble we can get into. And stuff can come back to haunt you,"[15] if sharing embarrassing stories and photos.

Rebecca Hains explored the influence of media on girls in *Growing Up with Girl Power: Girlhood on Screen and in Everyday Life* (2012). She featured these influential girl's groups: the Riot Grrrls DIY music and zines, the band Spice Girls singers (they made a comedy film called *Spice World* in 1997), the *Powerpuff Girls* (a 1995 animated TV series, movie, and videogame about girls with superpowers who fight bad guys. It returned to the Cartoon Network in 2016[16]). Books like *Reviving Ophelia* about negative sex-role socialization of girls and feminist movements like Take Our Daughter to Work Day (initiated by Ms. Foundation in 2003) were also influential. (Hain's website includes illustrations.[17])

The neoliberal approach to post-girl power is part of a postfeminism that emphasizes individual self-expression as freedom and takes equality for granted without the need for social movement pressure or further exploration of sexism. Contemporary girl power supposedly comes from fame, wealth, and from wearing sparkly fashion, so that marriage is no longer what girls dream about.[18] This is true even for the poor abused overweight black girl in the film *Precious* (2009) who fantasizes about being a star on stage cheered by the audience and in a fashion photo shoot. A website called "A Mighty Girl" claims to have the world's largest collection of books, toys and movies to raise "smart, confident, and courageous girls." Girls' Studies analyzes these kinds of themes via The International Girls' Studies Association, journals *Girlhood Studies* and *Girls' Studies: The Interdisciplinary Journal*, and books such as the two volumes of *Mediated Girlhoods: New Explorations of Girls' Media Culture by* Mary Celeste Kearney and Morgan Genevieve Blue (2011 and 2017).

From Indonesia, Diandra, 15, told me in our video interview that global media gives freedom to young people like her.[19] She has learned information her parents wouldn't want her to know but it also enlarges her worldview.

> *The media has definitely played a large role in my life, and it's not entirely negative. I've seen various things on the Internet and TV and that definitely opened my eyes about what is going on in the world. It changed my views about life, even though very slightly. I've befriended interesting people through the Internet; I've got pen pals from New York and Reunion Island thanks to the Internet. I got to know the worldwide music and pop culture (although a lot of things are mainly derived from USA). However, the Internet and television are very addicting;*

probably that's why it is such a huge problem in the society.

An Indian girl, Kavyashree, 13, agrees: "From global media I've come to know many things that I need not know and also it has given me a lot of information. It has influenced me in both ways—good and bad." By May 2017 Internet access increased globally to half the population.[20] However, almost 4.4 billion people don't have access to the Internet, most of them in developing countries.[21] In 2017, 80% of Euroepeans were online but only 25% of Africans had access. Also at least 1.8 billion Web users live in countries that censor the Internet: Almost 40% of countries censor the Web. Facebook CEO Mark Zuckerberg commissioned *The Economist* magazine to carry out a global study of Internet users in 2016:

> *While connectivity is improving around the world, the gender gap is widening: Women make up a smaller proportion of Internet users today than in 2013. The data shows that women in developing countries are not only less likely to have data-capable phones than men, but are also less likely to have even heard of the internet. By definition, if women are not online, the internet is not inclusive, and more needs to be done to decrease the gender gap in connectivity.22*

From Egypt, Yostina (17, f) has a mixed view of global media:

> *I'm influenced a lot, because they are the reason for making me in a bad mood by knowing about hunger, poverty, destroying planet earth, rapists, bullies, shooters, terrorists, and politicians, but global media also can make my day. I love chatting to people from different sides of the world; we share thoughts and feelings. Also watching science fiction and cartoons broaden my mind, watching international programmes helps me know more about cultures, so I think global media is a mixed blessing to me.*

About 95% of US teens are online and 80% of them use social networks, especially Facebook (started in 2004), although Twitter (since 2006) is becoming more popular. Most (94%) teen respondents to a Pew Internet and American Life survey have a Facebook account, but fatigue is setting in as many said checking their page is a chore.[23] According to a Piper Jaffray report, teenagers are shifting their focus from "me" pages to social networks that provide discussion forums such as Reddit, 4chan, Snapchat, Whisper, Vine (6 second videos), Tumblr, We Heart It (80% of users are under 24), Let and Instagram (photo sharing owned by Facebook).

A CNN interview with over 200 US 13-year-olds from six states and the accompanying scholarly report concluded the teens are addicted to what their peers think of them on social media—mainly photos on Instagram, Twitter and Facebook (with two billion monthly users) in that order--checking their phones frequently, even at school.[24] Instagram (owned by Facebook) grew from 500 million to 700 million by April 2017—80% of users are outside the US. The teens are very anxious about what their peers say about them or fear getting excluded from social events. According to the CNN report, they reported their main reasons for checking their accounts are they're bored, want to connect with friends, and to see if their posts get reactions. They're very upset if their parents take away their phones, a frequent concern from young people I've interviewed. One girl said she'd rather go without eating for a week than give up her phone and it feels like she's going to die without it. The researchers were surprised by the amount of social media use of profanity, "revenge porn" (publicizing sexual videos to shame an ex-partner), "sexting" nude photos, self-harm vlogs,[25] and reference to drug use.

The CNN report concluded that some of the negative effects of social media negativity are eased by parents' involvement with their teens, but parents tended to underestimate the pain caused by "social combat" and bullying or feeling left out. The parents, especially the mothers, are also engaged in social media as you can probably see in any public space. A review of 50 of the most watched children's TV shows found most of the shows included "social aggression," at an average of 14 acts of an hour.[26] Nine out of 10 of the shows contained this kind of rude or sarcastic verbal aggression. An example is a bully, ironically named Angelica, who torments other characters on the cartoon Rugrats. Providing a global perspective, *Youth Cultures in the Age of Global Media* (2014) explores the impact of new global technologies on youth cultures around the world.[27] Max, a Ukrainian teacher, reported, "Most of the cartoons kids watch here in Ukraine are Disney and Pixar animation. Popular are: *How to Train your Dragon, Planes, Rio, Cars, Up, Wall-E, Shark Tale, Finding Nemo, Cloudy with a Chance of Meatballs* and others.")

Despite media focus on sexuality and "sexting," Gen Y is less sexually active than Baby Boomers. For the Baby Boomers and Gen X, the age of first intercourse steadily fell and the trend continuing from the beginning of the 1950s and peaking in the early 1990s.[28] But the trend reversed itself with Gen Y: For the past 25 years, teens have been waiting longer to have intercourse and fewer teens report losing their virginity. From 1991 to 2013 the percentage of high school students who had engaged in sexual intercourse dropped from 54% to 47% and condom use increased from 46% to 59%.

The percentage that had sex with four or more partners decreased from 19% to 15% and teen sexual assault also decreased. There's more awareness that date rape is rape and young women have a right to say no, although Peggy Ornstein's interviews with over 500 girls discussed in *Girls and Sex* (2016) found that they didn't think in terms of their own sexual gratification, but with pleasing boys as by performing oral sex that isn't reciprocated.

Digital Divide

Nearly 1.3 billion people still don't have electricity, half the world's population doesn't have mobile phones, and over half don't have Internet access.[29] New industries are creating fewer jobs than in the previous technological revolutions and with "on demand" economies more employers are using the "human cloud" of temporary workers called the precariat. Millennials set the tone for these consumer trends in a "now world" of peer sharing and user-created content, where 87% of young people in the US report their smartphone is always with them.[30] However, progress towards gender equity is slow and possibly stalling under the Trump Administration's global influence, such as cutting funding for international health clinics that mention abortion as an option. Another problem is the global population is aging, requiring changes in retirement practices and in other issues

About half of the world's population has access to the World Wide Web, but new advances increase the gap between the rich and the poor, according to the Web's founder, Sir Tim Berners-Lee while speaking to the BBC. The gap between rich and poor is increasing, at the same time that people have more access to information with the widespread use of inexpensive cell phones with Internet connections and solar-powered and battery-powered TVs in rural areas. The mobile Internet has enabled developing countries to skip fixed landlines for radio waves that transmit phone messages, although Africa and parts of Latin America lag behind. Mobile broadband connections number over two billion, nearly three times the number of fixed-line subscriptions. Surfing the Internet and hanging out with friends are the most popular leisure activity for middle-class youth aged 15 to 25 from 16 countries—especially in China and India.[31] Listening to music comes in third, followed by watching TV and video gaming—all media-based except face time with friends.

Global media is part of a digital revolution that's changing the world. A fourth industrial revolution began at the turn of this century building on the digital revolution, according to Klaus Schwab, German engineer and founder of the World Economic Forum. [32] (Previous economic revolutions were agricultural, industrial, computer-driven.) The new revolution depends on smart technology: mobile devices that can connect billions of people; AI (artificial intelligence, self-driving vehicles, robotics, drones and virtual assistants like Apple's Siri); 3D printing that can manufacture a new human liver or a gun; quantum computing; new materials; virtual reality goggles;[33] and IoT (the internet of things such as connected computer chips in household appliances). Nanotechnology and biotechnology will change medical practices and permit genetic engineering, implanted memories in brains, and designer babies. Moore's Law accurately predicts that computer processor speeds and processing power will double every two years.

Schwab is concerned about traditional leaders' low level of preparedness for the rapid changes in entire systems that the fourth revolution is bringing, and the increased inequality and social unrest that can result from failure to collaborate. Talent is now the basis for success, requiring flexible networks rather than hierarchies in order to best utilize it. He thinks there's never been a time of greater promise or potential danger. With growing economic inequality, half of all assets are controlled by the richest 1% while the lower half owns less than 1% of the world's wealth, according to Credit Suisse's Global Wealth Report 2015. The authors of *The Spirit Level: Why Greater Equality Makes Societies Stronger* prove that more equal societies have higher well-being, less violence and stress, and better health.[34]

The fourth revolution leads to what Schwab believes is a disruptive "transformation of humankind" in a global civilization. Some of the changes in identity are people are willing to be mobile as in moving for work, families may be separated by these moves in a "trans-national family network," and people are more comfortable with "multiple identities" that come from exposure to other cultures. A "me-centered" society creates "new forms of belonging and community."[35] Spending so much time being interrupted by multiple electronic messages can impact our ability to relax and reflect. More polarization can result between those digitally connected and those not connected. Schwab's book is a plea to adapt to the fourth revolution so that too many people don't get left behind in a digital and education divide.

In developing countries, 28% of girls and 17% of boys aged 15 to 19 don't watch TV, listen to the radio or read a newspaper on a weekly basis.[36] For those who have access to media in rural areas, radio and battery-powered TV are the most common forms. In Southern and Eastern Africa, only 22% of youth ages 15 to 19 watch TV at

least once a week. Radio reaches more villagers than TV and can be a positive influence when soap operas teach health information about AIDS and contraception in
countries like Ethiopia and Mexico. A Tanzanian government-sponsored radio show
increased contraception use[37] and in Brazil, soap opera viewing is linked to reduced
birth rates. A Turkish soap opera titled *Bumus* (changed to *Noor* for Arab audiences),
about an egalitarian dual-career couple, attracted 80 million views in the Middle East
and Northern Africa.[38] In a nod to tradition, the couple's marriage was arranged and
they observe Ramadan and other religious practices. The series discusses premarital
sex and other issues avoided in mainstream Turkish media.

Zan TV is the first TV channel by and for Afghan women that includes talk shows
and information about women's health and education, in a country that scores 169 out
of 189 in the UN's ranking of gender equality. In rural areas of India women who watch
cable TV are less likely to prefer a male baby or to say it's acceptable for a husband to
beat his wife.[39] Villages with TVs have lower birth rates because TV provides a dis-
traction from sex and shows modern role models of smaller families, as seen in Brazil
and India.[40] However, Venezuelan President Nicolas Maduro blamed TV soap operas,
video games and Hollywood movies like *Superman* for glamorizing violence, guns, and
drugs, in violation of a 2004 law mandating "socially responsible" programming.

SpeakOut student Hafsa Oubou reminds us of the rural/urban split in access
to media in Morocco where she is a university student:

*In Morocco, middle-class youth like to listen to Western music a lot, watch
American movies, follow the latest trends and fashion, etc. But that can vary
from one region to another; in some rural places youth still drop out from school
to help their parents in farming and household. Some of them have no access to
the Western world. They still wear traditional clothes and girls still get married
at a younger age.*

The revolution of rising expectations leads to unrest and political upheaval aggra-
vated by high young adult unemployment including many college graduates who are
un- or underemployed in precarious work. Youth in developing regions want more
access to media and information, according to a 2009 survey of 15,000 youth, ages 23
to 28.[41] In Central and South America, 90% of young people want greater freedom of
information. In Africa and the Middle East, 89% share this same demand, as do 78%
of Asian youth. The United Nations' Millennium Development Goals include increasing women's access to ICT and broadband. An example of a program to implement

this goal, UNICEF's Techno Girls program aims to empower disadvantaged girls in South Africa by matching them with mentors in various corporations where they can job-shadow and use ICT.[42]

Teachers Compare their Generation With Their Students

Teachers globally told me that students have changed because of global media; they're more independent and disrespectful than when the teachers were in high school. A school administrator in South Korea, Cheol Yu told me change is underway. Students were naïve and innocent in his youth, while today students are "very clever, they're socially informed, they know a lot of information, but they're worse in their personalities. Even bad students in the past were obedient, but not now." Bullying and school violence are a problem and students "say anything" to adults. He said things started to change around at the end of the 1980s. Students have more money compared to when he was a boy and walked three miles a day to school because he couldn't afford bus fare. Parents are also more aggressive in their interaction with schools, whereas in a more Confucian-based society teachers were highly respected. He observes that girls are better students than boys, less likely to get in trouble or smoke cigarettes and drink alcohol.

Three high school teachers from Peru, Cambodia and Tajikistan told me that although youth want to be independent, they often aren't willing to work hard to achieve success. The teachers agreed students are lazier than in their school days. The Cambodian said in his day students cleaned the classroom and maintained the grounds, but students today want to push a button rather than carry water. On one hand, youth are worried about getting good jobs in the future, but on the other they seem not to care enough to work hard academically. More materialistic than previous generations, they crave the lifestyle they see in American TV and films. Drug use is a problem.

I asked the three teachers how this generation of students is different than when the teachers were in school. They didn't have TV and computers and agreed that exposure to the Internet and international media has made a big difference. This generation values freedom, believes they have rights (as in Peru where some young people know to get help when parents are abusive), and they are less obedient. (A rural father in Upper Egypt told a *National Geographic* reporter, "When my father said, 'Stop speaking,' I stopped speaking. I can't do that with my own children.")

However independent in their thinking, students in other countries are not as disrespectful as US students. Foreign teachers and students visiting Chico, are shocked to see California students informally put their feet up on a desk, chat to each other or text in class, wear shorts and revealing clothes, and speak very casually to the teacher. When the foreign teachers were students, their teachers were revered and feared, but this has changed. To instill discipline, Peruvian schools often include an hour of instruction about how to behave in class, how to march, and so on. Several Indian teachers told me discipline became more difficult after the government outlawed corporal punishment. An Indian high school principal told me his children are his parents when it comes to using technology, a common reversal of authority.

In an example of student informality, comfort with vulgarity, and use of social media, students at the University of Texas at Austin protested the state's legislation permitting carrying concealed handguns on campus by carrying dildos on their backpacks. Companies donated the dildos internationally. Jessica Jin and Ana Lopez led the "Cocks Not Glocks" campaign. Jin posted music videos with dildos hanging from the ceiling, after she was inspired by her unscripted comment during a radio discussion of gun violence, "What a bunch of dildoes!" She started a Facebook page that surprised her by going viral, stating, "You're carrying a gun to class? Yeah well I'm carrying a HUGE DILDO!" The page includes a photo of young women extending their middle finger to the state flag. She got a lot of hate mail, but encouraged students to display dildos as long as others could carry guns in their backpacks. Student Rosie Zander, age 20, commented, "We wanted something fun that people could really engage in. Because it's hard to get involved in the political process at our age, people our age don't tend to vote or get involved, and this is so easy. Strap a dildo on and you're showing the Texas legislature this is not a decision we wanted."[43]

Confucian emphasis on obedience to the teacher lingers in Asia, as Khue (16) spells out from Vietnam (similar to other Asian countries in their respect for elders). Keep in mind she spent her last year in high school in the US:

> I wish the educational system in my country could provide more space and opportunity for students to raise their voice and to be creative. When the teacher says that this is A, the students just need to remember, not to question why it is not B. And sometimes they must follow a trite, uniform pattern in writing in order to pass the test, even though what they put down on paper is not their idea and feeling. In short, students are taught to say and write what their teachers like

to hear and read, not what they really think. I would establish special courses to train teachers in psychology before they start their careers. I must say that teachers in my country are very excellent in their field, however not all of them are good at understanding teenagers. I hope these courses would encourage them to reduce their adult pride, to open their minds to accept novel ideas from their students.

In Cambodia, young people learned from violent Western media to fight over something like being looked at the wrong way. As a consequence, wedding parties may have to hire a guard because of the fighting that accompanies drinking alcohol. Outside life and friends now influence young people more than their families, said a Tajik teacher who has four sons in their 20s. She said with stimuli on the street and in front of a computer, school is less important to youth than in her generation when parents had many children and not much time to spend with a dozen children, as in her family. School was the center of her life. Schools aren't as well equipped as in the US, so she thinks pupils now may be bored with the lack of books and computers.

I asked four Pakistani teachers about generational differences. With access to information on the Internet and TV, students learn very quickly and are very aware of global issues—unlike American students who aren't well informed about international issues, according to foreign teachers' classroom observations in California. Used to fast change, youth are less accepting of longstanding problems like corruption. This critical view of the mess elders have made is typical of SpeakOut youths; those from developing and emerging nations are especially critical of adults' bad habits like smoking cigarettes and drinking alcohol. As Justice (17, m) writes from South Africa, "Adults are supposed to be loving and caring for their kids. I would change alcohol-drinking and casino-playing so that they could use the money to support their kids financially." His schoolmate (16, f) adds, "Most adults, especially those who are drinking, disrespect the young ones. I wish they would stop disrespecting us as children so that we can learn from them."

In developing nations, youth are still taught to respect elders. In India, I often saw people reach down to touch the feet of elders who graciously intercepted the younger person's hands in a greeting. A physician from Amritsar, a Brahmin grandmother with two sons, told me the younger generation is more liberal, more honest than their elders. She thinks the prevalence of media "is a bad influence, with a lot of exposing dresses which common people can't wear anywhere. The positive effect is that each person can get knowledge about things we were ignorant about." When she was a girl, love marriages were not allowed, and you were not supposed to talk to a boy. The only reason she got to peek at her fiancé before her marriage was that her mother allowed it without telling her father. Now young people talk to anyone they want. "We were scared and concealed our feelings," she said, while "my husband and I encouraged our sons to say what they want. They do what they like, we don't object. My second son gets so irritated if told what to do. The elder one is more likely to seek advice. I never told them to do this or that and they moved to Australia where they chose their wives."

Indian Media: The County with the Most Youth

Rapidly becoming the most populated country and already the one with the largest amount of young people, India has a large divide between rich and poor, and between urban and rural. Indian media aims to capture the huge youth market. Asianet, a private satellite TV channel in the southern state of Kerala, added "Rosebowl" programming for young people in 2007 to offer music, interviews with young celebrities, English language movies, and short videos on current issues.[44] The Indian magazine with the most readers is targeted at youth. *Saras Salil*, a Hindi language publication, discusses Hindi cinema and gossip and shows a lot of female flesh, as seen on its website,[45] but the focus is on politics, economic and social issues, and short stories.

An educated girl reports, "I am positively influenced by global media, TV, Internet, advertisements, etc.—through these we come to know that nothing is impossible: This shows that possibility lies in every particle (Ramanjit, 17). An excellent blog describes the Indian media's impact on sex roles, written by SpeakOut student Rosni, age16, in Chennai.[46] She and her co-writer Vaishnavi's blog posts discuss Indian gender issues. Saurav Adhikari, a tech business executive, reports about youth:

> *They are exposed to satellite TV (there was only one or two state-run channels in India when I grew up), the Internet (DSL/cable access is growing, but cyber cafes remain a key access point), freer access to social interaction, and mobility (global and virtual). They are global citizens. Adoption of styles and fashion from anywhere (America still dominates) is quick.*[47]

Hindi language films made in Bollywood and TV soap operas are popular with Indian youth (as is Bollywood music in the US), often portraying themes of romantic love with the parents' marriage choice portrayed as the wisest. Close ties between newlyweds may not be encouraged, as a strong bond is forged between a mother and her first-born son who raises his mother's status. Films address contemporary issues like working women and government corruption. Film actor Kalki Koechlin did a widely viewed video performance against sexism in which she asks men not to look at women as objects.[48] In another video titled *The Printing Machine* she raps about media excesses and rape and in *It's Your Fault* she condemns rape. Aamir Kahn, a superstar actor, also tackles sexism, dowry (which he says impacts over 90% of marriages), and other social issues in his popular TV show titled *Satyarnev Jayate*, "with love." He discussed gender issues in a video interview[49] and his first show tackled gender-selective abortion in 2011. To counter the traditional portrayal of women, the first feminist women's documentary film collective in India, Mediastorm, was organized in Delhi by Shohini Ghosh.

A common theme in TV soap operas is the relationship of the daughter-in-law and mother-in-law living in the same home and shown working in the kitchen with full makeup and expensive saris. Reality shows are also popular; for example, filming 15 young people isolated in a house for three months or a bachelor show where women compete to be selected by the young man. Gender activist Rita Banerji commented on TV portrayal of women from where she lives in Kolkata in an email:

The impact of Western culture on the Indian youth is largely through T.V., Hollywood movies, and the Internet. And it is commercial and cosmetic. It is largely because many of the brand names, style of clothing, and a projected lifestyle that is American implies wealth and power to the youth of India. If tomorrow China becomes the global number 1 power, I can guarantee you Indians will start eating with chopsticks and Mandarin will become the most popular language.

But underneath it all, the Indian youth accept tradition, custom and belief by rote. India is not a culture that is based on the idea of individuality, innovation and change like the American culture is. This is reinforced by the popularity of T.V. shows that emphasize traditionalism--soap operas. Soap operas like "Balika Badhu" (Child Bride) have very high trps [Television Rating Points]. There are many other like them. This one follows the life of a child bride who then settles into a very contented marriage. In one interview a young college woman said the lesson she gets from this is that if we want to avoid Western-type break up of marriages it is better to marry younger, that way girls are more adjusting!50

Here is an interesting article on why women characters must be tradition-

al on TV--taking hardship and abuse subserviently.51 It says, "The makers of these serials say TV gives as good as it gets--women are usually appreciated by audiences as subservient, overtly loyal and moralistic or evil, conniving and home-breaking characters. Television cannot be about superwomen. It has to be about the average Indian women; otherwise it will lack identification," written by Ekta Kapoor, the creator of India's most watched 'bahus' [beautiful young daughter-in-laws named] Tulsi and Parvati.

We've seen that Indian TV is a driving force for change, starting in the early 90s when cable and satellite television became available in 50 million Indian homes, including Rupert Murdoch's STAR TV music channel, Channel V and Viacom's MTV.[52] "The old Brahmanical code of 'lofty thinking and simple living' went out of style, to be replaced by the MTV culture of youth anywhere in the world," observes Vibha Rishi, marketing director for PepsiCo Inc. India. Revealing this TV influence, a SpeakOut girl's goal is to "live like a legend" (Akhila, 15). But another Indian teenager questions, "Why do most of the people want to be famous?" (Archana, 17, f).

Graphic novelist Ram Devineni and illustrator Dan Goldman, created a modern legend, a superhero named Priya, to respond to the 2012 gang rape of a Delhi young woman that shocked the world with its brutality and her death. Priva and her tiger are on the cover of Volume 2. After Priya is raped, she is shunned by her family and village and makes the jungle her home. The goddess Parvati grants her powers including fearlessness and a magical mantra to change people's minds. She tames a tiger that stalks her, and the *Priya's Shakti* graphic novel shows her riding it back to her village and around India to fight against sexual violence.[53] The comic next addressed acid attacks on women in *Priya's Mirror* with a 3d app that allows readers to see more content.

Starting in 2002 in India, low-caste rural women wrote a feminist newsletter called *Khabar Lahariya* (New Waves) that went digital in 2016 and includes video reports--pertinent because 350 million Indians can access the Internet, usually through a smartphone.[54] (The government of India mandated that starting in 2017 all mobile phones sold in the country must have a panic button to call for help in an emergency.) The writers often report on local sexism such as the gang rape of the daughter to punish her mother who ran for local office and won. The local police were not helpful, a familiar story in regards to abuse of women. The newsletter also reports on achievements of Indian women such as female fighter pilots, indicating the power of the digital revolution to give even village women the chance to be heard.

Going against the grain of Bollywood movies where a happy marriage is featured,

Dangal (2016) became very popular in both India, China, and around the world. Based on a true story, it tells about an Indian wrestler and coach who trained his two daughters to be champions after they beat up guys who harassed them. The girls cut their hair short like a boy in a country where most women wear long hair. Daughter Geeta Phogat is fact won a gold medal in wrestling at the Commonwealth Games in 2010 and qualified for the Olympic Games. The Hindi language film was produced by the Walt Disney Company India. The government encouraged viewing the film as part of its campaign to educate girls and prevent femicide, but some criticized the film for featuring the father's fulfillment of his dream to be a champion through his daughters. Media has a lot to do with changing gender roles in India and other emerging nations.

Mobile Phones and Social Media

Any youth with a smartphone with video capacity can be a citizen journalist, like rural migrants to Chinese cities who document their lives on video. In Rio de Janeiro, UNICEF gave a group of teens living in the *favelas* smartphones to map the problems and assets of their urban slum communities, as they discuss in a video.[55] The documentary *Hari Gets Married* (2012) tells the story of a North Indian taxi driver whose father arranges a marriage to a girl he has never seen, as tradition dictates. But he finds a way to get to know her by talking on their mobile phones and then falls in love with her, a hybrid courtship process combining the old and the new. Pakistani young adults told me they also use cell phones in courtship to get to know each other without parental supervision. Because of this kind of communication, Muslim village councils in the Indian state of Uttar Pradesh prohibited single girls from using mobile phones (and wearing jeans). A villager explained, "We don't think it is good for unmarried girls to use mobile phones. God forbid, if they talk to someone (men), it results in increase of crimes and mischief, so we have banned it. In fact, I think only the married men, the responsible men should carry mobile phones."[56]

Biz Stone, who co-founded Twitter in 2006 when he was 32, believes that five billion mobile phones with instant messaging capacity enable global citizenship.[57] He observes,

> *I can be waiting in line at the grocery store and I can take out my iPhone and scan the tweets and see what's happening halfway around the world, and I can put myself in the shoes of someone who is trying to overthrow a repressive re-*

gime, and I can suddenly have an empathy with that person that I would not otherwise necessarily have had. People all around the world are realizing that we're not just necessarily citizens of a particular state or a particular country, but citizens of the world.

An example of young women using Twitter for activism is the thousands of women in Turkey who organized a campaign to own their own space on mass transit where men "manspread" their legs wide to touch the girls sitting next to them.[58] The Istanbul Feminist Collective started it by tweeting photos of men's legs spread out on trains. In the Ukraine, the protests against government corruption and Russian influence became the top trending topic on Twitter because of US journalist Andrea Chalupa who founded #DigitalMaidan in January 2014. A third example of the power of Twitter is a single tweet by a radio reporter Marcela Ojeda stating, "They're killing us," which generated hundreds of thousands marching against *femicidio* in Argentina.[59] Her campaign called #NiUnaMenos (Not One Less) went viral. In response, the government set up task forces to study the fact that a woman is killed every 36 hours, most (70%) by a lover or ex-lover.

The Argentinian feminists also protested another component of machismo, street harassment and vulgar comments called a *piropo*. The mayor of Buenos Aires, Mauricio Macri, said, "Deep down, all women like being told a piropo." In the US, a video by journalist Elon James documented the catcalls and comments directed at a young woman walking down a New York City street for 10 hours. (It's no longer on YouTube.) James asked if men think they're being complimentary, why not do the same for each other? He started the #DudesGreetingDudes Twitter movement.

A survey of 11,000 girls from 11 countries who log into the virtual world Stardoll found that even tweens have their own phones, 65% of those 12 and younger.[60] A study of global youth found they use phones less for talking than texting. Older girls are the most frequent texters, as illustrated in "#Selfie," a vapid song popular worldwide, by The Chainsmokers.[61] One of the singers asks her friend while they're in the bathroom, "Do you think I should go home with him? I guess I took a good selfie." She proceeds to criticize the appearance of other women in the club. The song went viral with millions of views in the Western world due to young Internet microcelebrities called Influencers who sent in their own selfies and re-posted the song to their networks.[62]

In the US, three-quarters of young people age 12 to 17 have their own cell phones. Advertisers spend billions on advertising their apps on these phones. A Pew Research survey of US teens found that 24% go online "almost constantly," and most go on daily, mainly with smartphones (the most popular social media platforms are Facebook, Instagram, Shapchat and Twitter).[63] A feminist Instagram account called "Feminist Thought Bubble" shows drawings of women "who don't buy into your casual sexist BS." It's drawn by Molly Williams, a 20-year-old college student.[64] An example of a thought bubble is, "So…a bunch of old white men get to decide what I'm allowed to do with my body? When did I sign up for that?"

College women in the US spend an average of 105 minutes a day texting and an unbelievable 10 hours with their smartphones, compared to men's 84 minutes texting and eight hours with their phones.[65] Typical teens text 30 times a day. The amount of time US kids spend online has tripled in the last decade; the average teen spends about two hours a day, texting more than 50 times a day, and a majority of teens chat on a social network daily.[66] As a result of teen reliance on texting, crisis-counseling programs have formed such as Crisis Text Line, a nonprofit group in New York that relies on texts between counselor and client.

I asked Marin (13, f, California) what there is to write about so frequently: She actively texts with four girls and two boys and she doesn't often email or talk on the phone.

> *My friends and I talk about a lot. There is always drama to talk about with my friends, even if its drama having to deal with other people or drama/problems with our own lives including families. Such subjects are very private. After we get the drama talk over with (which takes from about 3 o'clock after school to 5 o'clock in the afternoon because there is so much drama that you wouldn't believe), we usually talk about what we are doing at that moment in time. Usually when one of my friends or myself asks "so…what's up?" we would respond with something like "listening to music." That always starts a conversation. Also we each respond back with a text within about 10 minutes of when the first text was sent. Or other times it's just who will write the most random letters and numbers.*

Chinese youth text frequently, as SpeakOut student Yuan reports: "One of the reasons why it is so popular is that this service is free. All you need is a device connected to the Internet. Most cell phones can access the Internet. By the way, you cannot imagine how many people are using iPhone and iPad." The most popular app is Weixin/Wechat and they also enjoy using a walkie-talkie phone application.

"A Teenager's View on Social Media," written by Andrew Watts, a 19-year-old male student at the University of Texas at Austin, reported that Facebook was cool in middle school, but is not anymore, but teens still use it because it's so functional.[67] Instagram is the most popular social media platform where his peers actually post because it "hasn't been flooded with the older generation yet," so It's cool. They don't see the point of Twitter, but Snapchat is becoming the most used, especially "My Story." The site called Medium is used by bloggers like him, rivaling WordPress for popular blogging sites. A popular app with girls is called Wishbone, which posts polls about teen culture because teens like apps where everyone can create content and not be criticized.[68] Their phones become their security blankets for coping with high school drama.

    #StopGamerGate criticized sexism in video games. Minecraft is a popular (100 million users) online game that involves creativity; it's mostly boys, but more girls are getting involved. Sexist male-dominated video games prevail. Feminist critics like Anita Sarkeesian and Brianna WU receive death and rape threats and other abuse from gamer opponents much more often than male gamers, including those who Tweet at #GamerGate to oppose "social justice warriors."[69] Games that feature women like Lara Croft are rare, but her first Tomb Raider adventure began in 1996 and she became both a sex icon and feminist icon, outlasting Xena the Warrior Princess. Feminist Frequency, an organization that studies women's images in pop culture, viewed Croft as a sex object in hot pants until the 2013 version where she looks real as she slaughters dozens of enemies.[70] She discusses her guilty feelings with a therapist, which would probably not be part of a male killer's story line. Gender roles express themselves in choices of social media and other Internet use.

The Internet Creates Global Youth Culture

President Obama's landmark Cairo speech in 2009 advocated instant global contact, as he proposed to "create a new online network, so a teenager in Kansas can communicate instantly with a teenager in Cairo." Media has already created a global youth culture with common slang (hang out, chill with friends), clothes (jeans, T-shirts and sweatshirts with a Western logo, and athletic shoes or plastic sandals), and electronic communication (mobile and smartphones). A 17-year-old Angolan activist was detained in 2013 after ordering 20 T-shirts stating "Jose Eduardo out! Disgusting dictator!" You can see teens wearing T-shirts and jeans, and listening to hip-hop on an iPod in any city in the world, illustrated in a video of a young Indian woman rapping in English strongly denounces sexism or in a documentary about hip-hop in Morocco.[71]

Kevin (18) in Trinidad and Tobago commented after critiquing this chapter that these examples need to be updated as youth fashions change: "Just walk within one mile of any developed city's shopping center and it's not difficult to spot a teenager parading through the promenade, face fixated on the latest version of Temple Run (a widely successful and publicized game for Android and iOS markets) with a pair of Beatz (popular headphones) planted firmly in their ears." Global teens use Wanelo, Vine, Snapchat, Kik, and 4chan, in that order.[72] The largest sites for users of various ages are (in this order) Facebook (over a billion users monthly), YouTube, Qzone (China), Sina Weibo (China), and WhatsApp.[73] Twitter is in ninth place but is the fastest-growing social network for teens.

Growing up in Lagos, as described in the novel *Americanah* by Chimamanda Adichie, young Nigerians listened to American R&B singer Toni Braxton, and "everybody watched American films and exchanged faded American magazines."[74] The novel's main character, Ifemelu, mentions watching American TV shows about African Americans like *The Cosby Show, the Fresh Prince of Bel Air*, and *A Different World*, although they struggled with power outages and reading by kerosene lamps. After being a student in the US, Ifemelu says what she most misses about the US is NPR, fast Internet, and soymilk. What she doesn't like is how informal American children are with elders; they "feed on praise and expect a star for effort and talk back to adults in the name of self-expression." (A discussion of charges of narcissism among US Millennials is featured in my *Ageism in Youth Studies*.)

Tech entrepreneurs are global heroes: A South Korean (Taegyeong, 16, m) quotes Apple co-founder Steve Jobs, "Stay hungry, stay foolish." He explains, "This is one of Steve Job's words who is my role-model and it is my favorite phrase." Middle-class youth are linked to each other by access to television, films, and the Internet, but Netflix reported that scripted entertainment for teens is rare and MTV has declined in popularity with youth.[75] Netflix aimed in 2015 to become the entertainment hub for tweens and teenagers among its nearly 63 million global subscribers. SpeakOut youth praised it for providing global information and criticized it for trying to make them want to buy things. A Pakistani young man relates, "I am massively influenced by global media, it is like a part of my body because without Internet and TV, life is just not the same" (Hayan, 20, m). Another Pakistani, Hassan adds, "The addiction of teens to cell phones and iPods is the same in Pakistan as the US."

A minority among SpeakOut youth, Ahmed, a 17-year-old Iraqi boy, suggests a return to traditional practices in resistance to the West: "The world is in change so any parent should do the same thing that their parent was doing to them." The evils of Western influence are feared by Qaiser Sharif, leader of a conservative Islamic student organization. He told a National Public Radio reporter that, "two kinds of people live here in Pakistan nowadays. First kind likes Western civilization and Western culture, Western traditions, and the second kind is very different, and likes Eastern civilization. I think, in the near future, the war of thoughts on campuses will begin."[76] He plans to open a chain of schools to promote his conservative Islamic beliefs against Western influences.

From Accra, Ghana, Maame (age 23) is a recent college graduate who hopes to go to law school and is influenced by the West. She emailed:

> *I am influenced by Western Media a lot. I am constantly reading American blogs, news, listening to Western music, etc. My mindset is affected by what I read and I see. I choose what I need to adopt and I do away with the negative stuff. (Might be negative in my culture but not necessarily in the West.) I am also influenced by the Western view of women. The idea that a woman has to be slender and thin with no folds is fast seeping into Ghanaian culture. Before I left for college, I thought big women were gorgeous because that's how they were viewed in my society. A woman who was big was seen as wealthy and a skinny woman was not attractive. Four years later, I think every big woman needs to lose weight not just for aesthetic reasons but for their health. I take my weight very seriously now and take better care of my body. [More from Maame in Volume 2 Chapter 5.]*

At the top of all YouTube channels is PewDiePie, created by a Swedish young man named Felix Khelberg (born in 1989), who dropped out of college when it bored him and concentrated instead on posting a daily video, some with animation. He puts on shows with frequent use of the f word and playing video games. He calls his fans "Bro Army," with about 43 million subscribers. *TIME* magazine named him one the world's 100 most influential people in 2016.[77] His post on "How to Respect Women," directed at his dog as his audience, has over two and a half million views. One of his suggestions is don't open doors for women because it makes them feel weak. I would imagine his appeal is mainly to young men. In contrast, a feminist young woman is third on the list of YouTube subscribers (with over 11 million). Canadian comedian (born in 1988) Lilly Singh's channel is IISuperwomanII. She also wrote a bestselling book *How to be a Baswe* [a confidant person]: *A Guide to Conquering Life* (2017). She is also a filmmaker and sells bracelets to raise money for Kenyan girls' education, although her background in Indian. (TED Teen features teen speakers on YouTube.[78])

As media consumers, sports are important to young people, especially soccer/football in many countries—as evidenced during the World Cup matches when people around the world are glued to TVs to cheer on their favorite teams. Cricket is popular in the UK and former British colonies, as shown in the film *Bend It Like Beckham*, about an Indian Sikh family and their two daughters who migrated to London. The younger daughter is an excellent soccer player while her father likes cricket. The film illustrates generational frictions; the immigrant girls' mother has traditional notions about what's proper for her girls and how they get around her restrictions, to play on a team for the younger sister, while the older sister has sex in a car and then marries her boyfriend overcoming his parents' objections.

SpeakOut student Srinath, 15, in India, listens to US pop singers Justin Bieber and Kesha, and R&B artist Akon as he chats with friends on Facebook. Other young Indians listen to the Icelandic rock band Sigur Ros, which "speaks to their pain." A girl in Ecuador (age 11) mentioned liking Justin Bieber. A young Saudi actor chose to sing a Bieber song when she auditioned for the Saudi film *Wadjda* (2012), about a girl's non-traditional efforts to buy a bicycle. Japanese bands play heavy metal music and Mexican teens are fans of Korean K-Pop music and videos.[79] Korean girls want to look like girl bands such as Girl's Generation who are tall and thin and are attracted to boys who look like cute boy band members, illustrating theorist Judith Butler's claim that gender is a socially constructed performance.[80] Japanese manga comic books and anime TV shows are popular globally; for example, *Sailor Moon* is about very long-legged girls with various hair colors and big eyes wearing high heels or boots who travel to space and fight evil.[81] One Western fan said the series inspired her to enter a career in aerospace engineering. Over 70 million global youth create virtual pets on the Japanese anime-inspired website Neopet.[82]

Japanese entertainers and fashionistas experiment with gender-bending in their clothes and makeup, including androgynous boy bands.[83] Acrush is a similar group of five young women in China who dress like boys, intended to replace the popular South Korean bands that were unofficially banned by Beijing in 2016. A promoter explained, "there are so many androgynous-looking girls these days, we thought they would be more relatable."[84] One of the singers said, "My family has always thought that girls should look and act like girls. But for my generation, we think: My life is my own life."

From Giza, Egypt, English teacher Amal's students Skyped with students in a small

Northern California town. They were surprised that they listened to the same music, watched some of the same TV serials, and used the same slang. The difference was their knowledge of world issues: Egyptian students asked what the California students thought about the Arab Spring, but they hadn't heard of it! Their ignorance is similar to other students and adults I've talked with in various US states.

English is the common world language for educated youth with the prevalence of American music, film, television and textbooks in cities. Academic high school classes are often taught in English, for instance, Egyptian public "experimental schools" where math and science are taught in English. University classes offer online extension educational opportunities available to anyone with access to the Internet, including some free courses called MOOCs (massive open online courses) offered by excellent universities. Starbucks made news by announcing in 2014 that they had partnered with the University of Arizona's online program to provide scholarships for Starbucks employees, and paid their expensive tuition for their junior and senior years.

English is also the most common language used in global graffiti, including frequent use of the f-word,[85] which can be seen in *F*** Mao" in photos of Chinese graffiti,[86] "Morsi F*** You" in Egypt, or in the slogans written on the bare torsos of members of the feminist group FEMEN that started in the Ukraine. I saw a Swiss German girl with a tattoo on the back of her neck that read, "The earth has music for those who listen;" she told me she hadn't thought about translating it into German (see the photo on the book Facebook page). Yang, a young mother in China, reports that she constantly surfs the Internet for information on the latest trends.[87] As a result, her two-year-old son can already speak a smattering of English; it's one of the five required topics on the all-important university entrance examinations (*gaokao*).

Youth passion about technology and entertainment, including video games and TV, can be applied to the classroom. Educators Rita King and Joshua Fouts point out that educators can use this new platform with new ideas and leaders rising in the virtual world, to create a new path for public diplomacy. As an example, they created a virtual world on the international site *Second Life* (only 30% of users are in the US) to help viewers understand Islam, accompanied by a graphic novel and report.[88] Their project is called "Digital Diplomacy: Understanding Islam through Virtual Worlds" and includes collaborators from 25 countries. Computer games also can be used as teaching tools about issues such as reducing obesity or protecting the environment. King and Fouts advocate that schools should encourage young people's ability to collaborate, and be agile and creative, rather than using the hierarchical model developed in the industrial era with desks in rows and the teacher lecturing. A peace education program uses a film series with a female superhero peace builder who teaches conflict resolution skills in the new island nation of Timor-Leste, near Indonesia.[89] An activist guide for girls written in English and French is *Girls Gone Activists! How to Change the World through Education.*[90]

Global Media Sells Consumerism

A middle-class Indian father of three discussed generational media issues with me when I stayed in their home in 2012. Rakesh, a Hindu pharmacist in Delhi, said kids are different now as they want branded everything. "If I buy sweets I go for the sweets, not the brand," he said. "In our time we were focused on study only and family. We want them to spend time with elders, but they're too busy on the Net, chatting, using iPhone. Gadgets eat up their time." They no longer follow their parent's jobs--his son (15) wants to be a painter. Rakesh explained that youth are exposed to Western movies, and the Internet has even more impact. "In my generation," Rakesh said, "We prefer a small village, but youth like cities and big cars like Ferrari. We go to a friend's Muslim restaurant that's run by the fifth generation cooking with the same recipes. We like that, it's a good place, so bonded as a family."

His daughter, Ninni, 22, explains the influence of the global media on her family's activities and values as seen in our video:

> We've been influenced by Western culture, because of the media. Youth are not as reserved due to westernization. We have the freedom to go out and study and establish a profession, while my mother's generation married at 20. More women are aware of women's rights. They know more about health but don't use the word feminist. TV shows educate and motivate women. People then were more involved with the extended family, now we're more nuclear family. We don't live jointly as much, although my uncles live below us [in a four story flat with stairs—elevators are rare]. We're more money-oriented, instead of values. We're influenced by the Internet. As kids, we were more likely to go out and play and now kids use IPod and Xbox and gain weight. Little kids know the world because of the Internet. We hardly see family because we're so busy, although my father tries to get the family together every weekend [all three young people live at home; the two in their 20s work and take classes].

SpeakOut student Yuan reports from China about the appeal of South Korean media and fashion:

> *South Korean TV programs STRONGLY influence not only young but also people like my mom! If you switch channels on TV in China, you will be amazed how popular the South Korean TV dramas are. You can find them on almost every channel, and mostly they are soap operas. People like them so much that they are imported and broadcasted a lot. I can use the word "horrifying" to describe the cultural invasion. A woman can feel proud that her dress is South Korean style, which she considers very fashionable and supreme.*

These South Korean and American TV shows are smuggled into North Korea on USB sticks; the black market thrives in a country where food and running water can be hard to get and skinny jeans are illegal.[91]

The burden of living up to the Western media image of the sexy achieving woman is a global theme. Maya, 15, London, being treated for anorexia, told the author of *Generation Z* that, "being female is awful and is going to get so much worse. There's girls being attacked online for every possible thing." She advises girls, "stay offline, don't read fashion magazines, don't talk to guys." [92] Professor Jean Twenge traces some of the increase in symptoms of increased depression and anxiety in US young people to isolation in "modern life."[93] Working so much doesn't give us as much time to connect with family and friends as we're more isolated and there's more emphasis on "money, fame, and image" (discussed in *Ageism in Youth Studies*).

Like many in her generation Khue, (17, f, Vietnam) is active on ICT and concerned about the isolation it produces:

> *I was sitting in the car with my parents and brother as we went to the countryside for vacation. My brother and I both plugged our ears with earphones of our devices, leaving our parents sitting silently in the front seats. And I was surprised by my own questions: Then what's the point of this vacation? Wasn't vacation a time for family member to connect with each other more? I wonder how can we expect to be understood if we do not spend enough time with each other?*

Middle- and upper-class young people are influenced by Western commercialism and global media, as in the romanticism of Valentine's Day. Examples of sexism appear in widely-seen Super Bowl ads in 2015 like a Carl's Jr.'s ad featuring a naked woman eating a hamburger in a suggestive way and Kim Kardashian wearing just her underwear for T-Mobile. However, a few positive ads showed an athletic young woman and confident girls in an "Always" brand of female hygiene products that advocated rewriting the rules for girls. The ad encouraged father involvement to encourage daughters to be strong.[94] GEICO ran an ad where a sleeping beauty defies the prince by pretending to be asleep when the prince comes to wake her up with a kiss. She'd rather watch TV.[95]

In a book of essays by teenage girls in the US, the editor reported that by far the majority of essays were about body image and, "They know more about style, music, and culture than any young people in history."[96] They may have read books like Kate Schatz' *Rad American Women A-Z: Rebels, Trailblazers, and Visionaries* (2015) and her *Rad Women Worldwide: Artists and Athletes, Pirates and Punks* (2016).

In reaction to Western criticism of Saudi restrictions on women, a Saudi young woman posted on the *Wadja* film YouTube site,

I am REALLY worried about the OPPRESSION of young Western girls and their media-stuffed minds with psychological problems, eating disorders, poor self-image, lack of respect for parents and teachers. Out of the kindness of my heart I'm going to start an aid fund and get all my Saudi girls to donate to this fantastic cause. Let's help raise the spirituality and self-confidence of these girls so they don't all end up believing you have to strip down and show your bony bits to be something.[97]

In Fiji, girls who were exposed to Western images on TV were 60% more likely to have eating disorders.[98] Women's concern with body image in Egypt can be problematic, as it is globally.[99] Japanese, Chinese, Indians and other nationalities spend billions on skin-whitening products. A Japanese SpeakOut girl, Haruno, 15, stated, "I think medias have an effect on a lot of people, especially people of a young age. Now a lot of young girls want to be skinny, but a long time ago plump is better. It is because a lot of skinny girls are shown in media. I know media is not always truth but media has strong power."

In Costa Rica, Koylux (14, f), reports, "Media made me sensitive, a little insecure because the magazine and commercials always demonstrate a woman with perfect curves and I'm a little bit skinny." She thinks the popular stylish group of students in her school in San Jose gets preferential treatment. Her high school teacher, Giovanna responded to my question about the problem of popular high school cliques getting special treatment and excluding students with less money and popularity that showed up in their SpeakOut responses; "The problem is they see TV programs about USA and they believe that it is true that in the schools over there the students are divided in popular and not popular. The students have rich kids with newly rich moms and dads that give them everything they want. The laws to protect minors are very strong and spoiled children and their parents use that a lot since they could lawsuit the school if they are expelled."

In India, Unilever (UL) ran a successful but controversial TV ad for its Fair and Lovely line of skin-lightning beauty products.[100] The commercial shows a young woman talking with her father, who complains about not having sons to provide for him. The daughter uses the UL cream to lighten her skin, so she gets a better-paid job as a flight attendant and is able to help out her parents. The ad was controversial because it disparages dark skin, but it's positive in that portrays a woman providing for her family. Ishita Malaviya is India's first well-known female surfer but her friends worried her tan would reduce her marriage chances by darkening her skin, but she kept on surfing as she described in a short video.[101] Her parents wanted her to focus on her journalism studies and not surf. A "Dark is Beautiful" campaign was started by social worker Kavitha Emmanuel in Chennai to oppose the skin lightening creams and denigration of darker skin.[102] Ads can create unrealistic romantic expectations. An Indian teen reports on TV's impact on her: "Watching TV serials, I feel like my life would be just like one of them with a prince charming coming on the horse and singing for me. It gives a kind of satisfaction that even I will get somebody who will love me," (Ashiesha, 16, f). Her's is seemingly a traditional attitude but it may be modern not to mention the role of her parents in an arranged marriage.

In China, "Ads never build the image that women should be strong or successful, just that they should be pretty," observed Zhang Zheng, a 25-year-old brand manager.[103] She reported professional women are only shown using beauty care products: "There are only two images of women: the pretty girl and the good mother. The pretty girl predominates, and invariably is dangerously thin, scantily clad, and listlessly passive," as demonstrated in my photo at the beginning of the chapter of a very thin movie star in shorts in a subway ad in Shanghai. These kinds of ads may contribute to the fact that Chinese spend $27 billion a year on Internet pornography.[104] But a rural SpeakOut Chinese girl (age 12) aims to "be a boss, drive my own car and have my own air-conditioned office," so girls are also getting the message that women can have good jobs and be independent. (A documentary shows the lives of rural Chinese women.[105])

Consumers also have power: Outrage about a 2015 German insurance company ad featuring a girl who doesn't skateboard and loves taking photos of boys and also featuring a 50s style housewife, resulted in the company removing the ads.[106] *Ms. Magazine* always includes a "No Comment" page of outrageous ads and encourages readers to write to the offending companies. The *Ms.* blog includes photos of culture-jamming sexist ads with stickers and graffiti.[107]

Media Addiction Creates Dumb Zombies

TV turns some teens into zombies rather than critical thinkers: Russians therefore refer to their TVs as "the zombie." From El Salvador, Gustavo, 17, reveals the negative impact of media: "I am always watching the news and watching Facebook, and they said things that are very strange and sometimes I believed. I feel like a zombie watching all day the screen and I try to distract myself with sports but it's difficult." Interestingly, since 9/11 Hollywood has produced many films about zombies and dystopian apocalypses, which some call an obsession.[108] Maria, also from El Salvador (16), reports, "The global media makes me lazier and a little unsociable because I spend a lot of time with it." Kalwane, an English university student (m, 20), reports, "I try to take everything on TV with a pinch of salt, but the news and documentaries have a huge effect on me both positively and negatively. It stirs my imagination and makes me learn new things, but the news also gives me an unpleasant feeling of frustration and hatred."

Keerthana, 14, in India reveals: "I'm thoroughly influenced by global media. Time evades me just like that. It mesmerizes me." "Global media mutilates our mind such that we are condemned to follow what it says and no longer become what we are," reported Sagar, 15, m, also in India. A young Russian man complained that his peers are shallow: "People prefer to consume everything, the simplest things, and the faster, the better. Books are something that forces you to think, reading a book requires some effort. But they prefer entertainment."[109]

Japanese youth seem to be especially isolated by media access. A Japanese term *kuribotchi* describes young people who interact with others mainly online. The term *hikikomori* refers to young people who isolate themselves from others. In a survey of Tokyo young adults in their 20s, nearly 60% were not dating or in a relationship.[110] I asked college student Haruna to explain this phenomenon: "Most of young Japanese make online relationship. Because they might feel easily to contact with unknown people (escape from real) or they may expose themselves and share fun time with someone who has same hobby, fitting characteristics, etc." The Japanese have a word for "geeks" (*otaku*) who live in a virtual world, leading the government to develop "immersion projects" aimed to get youth into communication with real people. Twitter has a higher percentage of users in Japan than in the US, surpassing Japan's top social-networking site Mixi in 2010.

"We're forgetting what it means to be intimate with another human," warns social scientist Sherry Turkle.[111] She says children are learning that it's safer to talk to a computer than to a person. Young men who isolate themselves are called "herbivores" in Internet slang. A survey by the Ministry of Health in 2010 found that over one-third of Japanese men aged 16 to 19 had no interest in sex with a real woman, while some enjoyed virtual girlfriends provided by computer games like Nintendo's Love Plus.[112] Some attribute this withdrawal to pessimism about their futures. In China, millions of young Chinese chat with a software program, a chatbot called Xiaoice. The next version will include a woman's voice--not just text-messaging. This phenomenon is similar to a film titled *Her (2014)* where the main character is in love with a computer operating system he calls Samantha. He's hurt when she tells him she has thousands of other relationships. In the film *Lars and the Real Girl* (2007) Lars falls in love with a blow-up doll. US fictional films explore the hazards of connecting more to electronic devices than humans, including *Disconnect* (2013) and *Men, Women and Children* (2014). The latter includes lonely young people who are addicted to video games, pornography, or weight-loss.

A teen named Mason, the main character in *Boyhood* (2014) cancels his Facebook page to protest media-obsessed people turned into cyborgs melded to their devices. Like Mason, Khue (17, f, Vietnam) disconnected from Facebook because of its materialistic and superficial impact on her:

> I think media also leads to the need for attention. In my country, some girls show off their fashion styles, attractive bodies and relationships just to be called "hotgirl," leading to many other girls trying the same way to earn the deceptive feeling of being admired. Recently, I have decided to deactivate my Facebook because it has led me into other's life, but only on the surface. I got to know a person from their gorgeous, stylish photos and the status that reveals the happy sides of their life or relationships. I confess that it did lead me to compare myself to others and feel left behind. It created an unnecessary need to upload my photos and keep my page updated as if I were very famous. Yet, I realized it was a time-consuming illusion. Also, it creates a time-consuming habit of checking the latest image of others' latest pictures or status – something that I don't think

necessarily betters a relationship. I'm not saying that social network is bad, but it does lead some to abandon the quality of real life for the quality of an unreal one on the Internet.

Rudy Koursbroek, a Danish writer, attacked media influence on youth culture: "American culture is vulgar rubbish, the free market is killing literature, tasteless youth culture rules all and civilization as we know it must be protected against the barbaric businessman."[113] The Cuban government agreed, shutting down private 3D movie theaters in 2013 because they showed "banal and frivolous" American films. Lack of depth is revealed in the top Google searches in 2014, which were not about science or social science but entertainers and entertainment. The foremost search was Robin Williams' suicide, followed by topics like the "Flappy Bird" game and Austrian drag queen Conchita Wurst.

Girls like Acacia Brinley and Julia Kelly get paid to influence their thousands of Internet followers. While Gen Y blogs, the younger generation responds to images on Tinder and Instagram, using emoji symbols, so now "Grammers" (Instagrammers) with hundreds of thousands of followers are more important for advertisers than some entertainment celebrities.[114] Research on Millennials by the Deep Focus agency found that four in 10 Millennials would rather communicate with pictures than words.[115] Another advertising agency reported, "This is the most challenging group to target because they really are the first demographic group that isn't as predictable as others. When it comes to this generation, they're moving around, and they're so much savvier." Millennials spend an average of 30 hours a month on social apps, especially Instagram and Snapchat, using mobile devices almost half the time (41%).

In China, young people earn money by performing from their homes on Internet webcams to produce interactive web entertainment, more spirited than state-run TV game shows and dramas.[116] Some receive money to spread pro-government posts (In Russia, paid hackers and computer bots spread propaganda to influence elections, such as Russian efforts to elect Donald Trump, as well as their efforts to influence European countries such as the Ukraine.) Millions watch karaoke performances, comedy skits and talk shows, and women doing erotic dancing. The women performers often wear scanty clothes. The audience can stream text messages and buy virtual gifts such as roses; the performer gets a percentage of the purchases. The viewers tend to be single men in smaller cities who have money to spend on these "gifts."

A young woman from the Dominican Republic criticizes the impact of media on progressive change:

Mainstream media has ruined us. I personally think MTV is one of the worst things out there because we are shaping a culture around superficiality and money only. As Oscar Wilde said, people nowadays know the price of everything and the value of nothing. They ask why the suicide rate is going higher everyday. How wouldn't it be? We are so empty, so careless! Magazines sell you impossible standards of beauty, the radio sells music about partying, sex, drugs, etc. TV sells you 60/30 minutes of collective stupidity and nonsense! When did we go from [singing] "How many times can some people exist before they're allowed to be free? to "you a stupid h@#!" Lidia, 22

The HBO Series *Girls* portrays narcissistic people in their mid-20s who could be called empty, to use Lida's word. The show is about four young women several years out of college, inspired by *Sex and the City* (1998 to 2004) except that they live in Brooklyn rather than Manhattan. *Girls* aired from 2012 to 2017. It strengthens the narcissistic side of the debate about Generation WE or ME, a devolution away from the confidence and humor of the older friends in *Sex and the City*. The creator and writer of *Girls* and lead actor, Lena Dunham, stated in an NPR radio interview, "Each character is a piece of me or someone close to me."[117] In an interview with the *New York Times* she said, "I'm probably the most neurotic sexual partner you could inherit. Anyone who dates me is not getting some dreamy 30-year-old. They're getting someone with so much baggage that they can just watch *Girls* to find out."[118]

Her character Hannah describes herself as a narcissist who is "more of a dumpling than a woman," in the opening of Season Six. In Dunham's book of essays published when she was 28 (similar to her character Hannah's proposed book), titled *Not that Kind of Girl* (2014) Dunham described herself as, "I am a girl with a keen interest in having it all." A girl at 28? Dunham commented on delayed adulthood in 2015, "I think a big part of being in your 20s is realizing that your parents are people, and that they're not just in the world to serve you. Realizing that your parents have their own issues and their own anxieties, it can be traumatic, because you still feel like a child. You don't feel ready for it."[119]

Dunham describes her character Hannah as a brat who usually makes the wrong decisions, as when she bombs a job interview by making a joke that the rape rate went up after the interviewer entered his university. She drinks opium tea and then passes out while trying to convince her parents to continue supporting her two years after graduation. Hannah tells her friend, "No one could ever hate me as much as I hate myself, okay? So any mean thing someone's gonna think of to say about me, I've already said to me, about me, probably in the last half hour!" The narcissistic wrong decisions continue in Season 3 when Hannah gets fired from a writing job at *GQ* magazine and springs news that she may leave NYC on her boyfriend Adam just before his Broadway debut as an actor. Her friends are equally clueless: Shoshanna fails a college class so she can't graduate, Marnie seduces Shoshanna's ex-boyfriend (who Shoshanna wants back) and flirts with a musician who is in a committed relationship. Jessa is a drug addict who loses jobs. Hannah says the last four years of her life were "a total wash" full of "ridiculous mistakes."

In Season 4 Hannah drops out of creative writing graduate school because she has writer's block. Dunham explained that Hannah has an authority problem, as she did in accepting criticism in her college writing classes. However, she stated that the girls made more adult decisions in Season 4. She ranked their judgment at a "B" compared to a fail in the first seasons, although Hannah is reprimanded by her principal for inappropriate behavior with students in the school where she is a substitute teacher.[120]

In Season Five Hannah is shown taking nude photos to replace her boyfriend's photos of former girlfriends and deleting them from his phone. She also alienates her boyfriend by taking him out of the class he's teaching to berate him for writing on one of her student's papers. When the principal scolds Hannah for inappropriate comments to students about other teachers, she silences him by opening her legs in her chair to reveal she isn't wearing underwear. She calls her friend Jessa a very vulgar word, so Jesse sleeps with Hannah's ex-boyfriend. Working in Japan, Shoshannah hooks up with her boss after whipping another employee in a sado-masochistic sex club.

The reaction to *Girls* from peers in feminist blogs such as *Jezebel* "staffed largely by people Dunham's age, can't kick her enough. The biggest complaint about her is that she represents all that is wrong with an over-privileged, nepotistic, Caucasian-focused slice of America," writes Ha in 2017, Dunham told *Nylon* magazine, "I wouldn't do another show that starred four white girls." (Other TV series about New York Millennials are more diverse, such as *Broad City*, *Search Party*, and *Master of None*.) In Season Six in 2017, Hannah has a brief affair with Pakistani-American man while on vacation and decides to keep the baby boy when she gets pregnant. Her friend Marne and her mother help her: Dunham explained, "It's all about trying to reconcile that anxious, addled, selfish person with the fact that someone else needs her now. I think Hannah needed that in order to get to the next step of her maturation."[121] Hannah still makes everything about herself, interpreting baby Grover's difficulty breast feeding as due to hating her, but she tells a teenage girl that mothers are always there for their children no matter how difficult. More examples of self-absorbed and foolish characters from *Girls* are described on the book website.[122]

Some consider Dunham the "de facto figurehead" for feminism, as when she wrote in her book about being raped in college and supported Planned Parenthood in her book tour. *Girls* characters discuss pertinent women's issues like abortion, body image and social media. The increase in advertising by fashion, beauty and fitness corporations has led to increased attention to the ideal body, contrasted to a society like Cuba where ads don't exist and amply endowed women proudly reveal their curves in spandex clothes. Revealing your most painful and degrading experiences seems more masochistic then feminist, but *TIME Magazine* selected her as one of the 100 most influential people of 2014. Not a fan, activist Deva Cats-Baril started a Twitter campaign #DropDunham in reference to her role as a spokesperson for Planned Parenthood; Dunham is criticized for racist comments like "I'm thin for Detroit."[123]

In a TV series about another seemingly irrational 28-year old, *Crazy Ex-Girlfriend* is about a lawyer who runs into an old boyfriend from summer camp on the streets of New York City and decides to follow him to the Los Angeles suburb of West Covina. *Girlboss* (2017) is a Netflix series about a 23-year-old who develops an online fashion business. Sophia is portrayed as lost, angry, smart and dumb, and weird—like Hannah and Megan.

Another HBO series, beginning in 2014, features equally self-involved and clueless men about the same age as *Girls*. Three techie geeks live in *Silicon Valley* in the "Hacker Hostel" home of a more experienced app creator, Erlich, who gets 10% of what his tenants sell; he is arrogant and insulting. The guys are socially awkward, struggle with masculinity, are amazed if girls show up at a party and wonder why they always end up together at one side of the room. Richard programmed the algorithm that created his Pied Piper start-up; he has anxiety attacks and vomits when under pressure. His only sexual contact is initiated by a woman who tells him the next day how awful it was. One woman is an assistant to her boss and a loyal friend to Richard, but we don't see other employed women until the Season 2 when Richard hires a woman programmer who later blackmails them.

A 2014 film *Laggies* features another confused and narcissistic young woman who is 28. Megan, played by Keira Knightley, buys alcohol for teens, pals around with 16-year-old Annika and lies to the teen's father, goes to Annika's high school prom, gets drunk with her father and has sex with him while engaged to her boyfriend since high school. Although she has a graduate degree in psychological therapy, she didn't relate to her clients during training, and is working part-time for her father waving a sign and dancing in front of his office to attract clients. In the end she breaks up with her fiancé in the airport on the way to elope in Los Vegas because he sent their photo to their group of friends since high school. That act makes her decide to break away from her friends and boyfriend. She then brings liquor to Annika's father and is embraced by him and the movie ends. The only bright note is she is supportive of Annika and seems to be interested in being a school counselor after pretending to be Annika's absent mother in a required meeting with the counselor.

A popular Norwegian series about teens, *Skam* is shown on TV and online, the most popular web TV show in Norwegian history.[124] Many Internet fan sites indicate international interest in the show. Each character has an Instagram account. Each season focuses on one character, such as Isak who comes out as gay. Few adults are in the picture, as the teens work out their own issues. Julie Andem, 34, the show's creator and writer, spent half a year interviewing teens. She identified their main problem as: "Teenagers today are under a lot of pressure from everyone. Pressure to be perfect, pressure to perform." She was surprised to discover that girls today use sex to be more popular on Instagram, while when she was a teen, girls used sex to get love. (The English language version is titled *Shame.*)

In Israel, filmmaker Talya Lavie's film *Zero Motivation* (2014) features more inept young women conscripts stationed at a remote desert base doing boring clerical work poorly and serving coffee to the male officers in charge. A TIME Magazine critic provided more TV examples of "self-centered young women who consistently make self-defeating decisions: *Two Broke Girls, The New Girl, The Mindy Project,* and *Don't Trust the B---- in Apartment 23.*"[125] Bill Persky notes, " All of these shows portray characters who, week after week, take the uninspiring path of casual, empty sex and small aspirations." He adds young men are portrayed as "sex-crazed slackers, nerds and underachievers as featured in *Two and a Half Men, How I Met Your Mother* and *Happy Endings.*" Why do you think young adults are portrayed is such confused, awkward, and unstable characters?

The media provides virtual friends and experiences via TV dramas with characters whose personalities and histories viewers know better than actual neighbors or acquaintances. Of course people also collect virtual friends on social networking groups like Facebook (started by a Harvard student in 2004), with 70% of Facebook users outside the US. The British show *The Office,* and American shows *Friends, Cheers, Sex and the City* and *Grey's Anatomy* provide examples of virtual flawed friends whose biographies are well known by global viewers, as well as a diverse cast of characters. Newer series about women friends are *Orange is the New Black* about women in prison, and *Broad City* about two young women living in New York City. *Modern Family* is acclaimed for including a gay couple and a Hispanic woman, but none of the women work outside the home. *Glee* is another TV show that included LGBT youth and people of color as talent in a high school performance group led by a Hispanic teacher.

These TV shows change attitudes about LGBT and gender issues, as does the film *Hidden Figures* (2016) about African-American women mathematicians who helped develop the US space program. *The Mis-Adventures of An Awkward Black Girl* started on YouTube in 2011, created by Issa Rae.[126] The show was picked up by HBO, leading to comparisons with the *Girls* series. The main character, called J, is described as quirky and bright. She works at a call center with co-workers. Issa Rae created a similar series beginning in 2016: *Insecure* is about a black woman and her friends who climb the corporate ladder while searching for a job and boyfriend that would inspire her more. Rae wanted to explore black female friendship because she didn't find other shows like *Sex and The City, Friends,* and *Girls* that featured women of color.

Critical thinking skills are essential in analyzing media brainwashing techniques, but a report on US high school students who took the ACT (American College Testing Program) test for college admission revealed that only 26% passed all four subject areas (English, social studies, math and natural sciences) and almost one-third were not proficient in any area.[127] Only 43% of high school students who took the SAT (Scholastic Aptitude Test) were college-ready in 2013—continuing a downward five-year trend. This lack of basic knowledge doesn't bode well for overturning the sway of media consumerism.

An Australian teen worries about the neglect of pressing human problems as people focus on TV. What bothers her is:

> . . . *the ignorance that surrounds me everyday. How people just turn their backs on the insanities of the world, they know what's going on but refuse to care. Poverty: 30,000 thousand kids die every single day because of preventable causes and we know but our response is simply, "Ow, that's horrible," then we turn back on our TVs and care about who Paris Hilton is dating. People don't believe change can happen. Maybe we just like being ignorant, but for how long will this continue? How many more people will have to contract HIV/AIDS before it holds our attention for more than just 30 seconds?* Patricia, 15, f, Australia

In Costa Rica, Jose, 21, told me multinational corporations keep us stupid, watching insipid TV shows and drinking beer. He believes consumerism is making slaves out of workers, who work long hours to buy things from outside the country. None of the clothes he was wearing when we talked were made in Costa Rica. He added that the US "War on Drugs" hurts poor people, such as the violent drug gangs in Mexico who satisfy the drug habits of North Americans. He has learned interesting theories from DVDs like *Zeitgeist* about how a cabal of bankers runs the world.

Media conveys corporate influence that distracts us from the destruction of the planet and growing inequality. Economist Joseph Stiglitz reports that from 2009 to 2010, 93% of income growth in the US went to the top 1% of earners. Author Chris Hedges states that "cultures that cannot distinguish between illusion and reality die," like many fallen empires that were taken over by a corrupt elite.[128] Hedges predicts a bleak future due to neoliberals "who sold us the perverted ideology of free-market capitalism and globalization." They have "dynamited the foundations of our society" and created turmoil that is a setup for fascism.

Hedges critiques US media for featuring sadistic professional wrestling, pornography (with annual sales of around $10 billion), inane reality TV, and talk shows whose combativeness "mirror the emotional wreckage of the fans." He believes American TV viewers feel hopeless and angry about their economic decline, which sounds like the Romans distracting the masses with cruel spectacles in the Coliseum in the days of Emperor Nero. Updating Plato, Hedges says, "We are chained to the flickering shadows of celebrity culture, the spectacle of the arena and the airwaves, the lies of advertising, the endless personal dramas, many of them completely fictional."[129] Interest in celebrity is not confined to the West: from India, Vaishnavi (f, 16) combined her generation's altruism with a seeming contrasting theme, "I would love to teach and help the underprivileged. But for me, I would love to become a celebrity stylist or fashion designer. I would also love to advocate for women's rights."

The crude vulgarity is manifested in the popularity and media coverage of the presidential campaign of tycoon Donald Trump, who referred to women as dumb bimbos, losers, dogs, fat pigs, and disgusting animals. "Blimp" was the word he used for his pregnant third wife. He describes himself as smart, good-hearted, and popular--a tough savior correcting the country's efforts for political correctness.[130] Trump called young protesters at his rallies "thugs" who should "Go home to mommy and get a job." He delights in urging his supporters to push and hit demonstrators of color. He told a Los Vegas rally "I'd like to punch him in the face," as a young man was expelled. As a reality show producer, he understands the use of violence: At a St. Louis rally on March 11, Trump said about the protests, "Can I be honest with you? It adds to the flavor. It really does. It makes it more exciting. I mean, isn't this better than listening to a long boring speech?" [131] His were the only rallies with violence.

The influence of consumerism leads to health problems as well as detracting from critical thinking. Advertising shifts the traditional focus from caring for nature and people to eating unhealthy processed sugary food and acquiring things that don't bring health or happiness over time and do waste limited resources. Ads raise obesity rates as kids eat junk food and sit in front of electronic screens rather than exercising. A British Heart Foundation study revealed that 80% of children in the UK aren't eating a healthy diet and young adults already suffer from heart problems. Nearly half of US schools sold sweet or salty snack foods in 2010.

In Pakistan, Hassan, 18, worries about the impact of media on health and values.

Previous Generations (PGs) were outgoing; now teens sit in front of their laptops 24/7 and even forget they have to eat/drink. PGs worked hard in fields; no matter what happened, they would work in fields and don't let their boss down, but teens today are lazy. They can't even make it to school/colleges on time and have lame excuses for that. PGs were healthy because there was no pollution, so the food was clean and pure; we have artificial food these days, which doesn't help us grow at all. That's why PGs were tall while this generation is short. PG were polite, welcoming, and hospitable. These things are vaporizing slowly in this generation.

When I asked Zoe, 17, about the impact of so much violent, crude, inane media, she corrected me as you can see in our interview on The Global Youth YouTube channel.[132]

Jersey Girl follows this party girl who goes around and gets drunk and throws up in people's hair, but we're seeing documentaries like Killing Us Softly *[a second wave feminist film about sexism in advertising].* South Park *and* Family Guy *are really popular [animated TV shows]. I think the reason it's so popular is it appeals to both men and women and tackles social issues.* Family Guy *wrote a brilliant musical about the Securities Exchange Commission, they discuss legalization of marijuana legislation and gay marriage and tackle other social issues on these programs. People get distracted by the violent scenes, which* Family Guy *does to make fun of other shows with violence and its exhausting and boring. A lot of adults don't take the time to absorb the media as we're doing and they don't see what we see. The same thing with social media, they're not seeing the posts about current issues. They just see what they expect.*

Young people like Zoe don't think of themselves as dumb zombies but as critical thinkers, but Zoe is an exceptionally outstanding student.

Media Exposure Makes Youth Opinionated and Brave

Comics

A list of the best 19 female cartoon characters was compiled by *The Telegraph* newspaper.[133] A Pakistani TV cartoon series called *Burka Avenger* spread to India and other countries in 2015. The heroine is a teacher named Jiya who wears a burka as a disguise to fight the ban on girls going to school, attacks on polio health workers by Taliban extremists, child labor, environmental destruction and other current issues.[134] Some feminists criticize showing the burka as a symbol of liberation but Jiya is powerful. Despite progress, few girls submit their films to youth film festivals, despite film schools like Reel Girls for girls nine to 19.

Wonder Woman is the favorite female comic book superhero (since 1941), according to *The Secret History of Wonder Woman* (2015). The UN even appointed her as honorary ambassador for gender empowerment in October 2016 in an effort to reach young people. The campaign called "All the Wonder We Can Do" received some criticism and petition against it for picking a white woman cartoon figure in hot pants with an US flag design. One of her DC writers noted that Wonder Woman is queer due to her origins in Themyscira, an all-female island in Greek mythology. A movie about her was released in 2017, part of a long history of sexy warrior goddesses and heroines.[135]

However, female superheroes are rare. Some are listed online, along with film superheroines.[136] A website called Girl-Wonder.org collects positive female comic characters. The Marvel comic titled *Ms. Marvel* features a Pakistani-American teenager called Kamal Khan, the first Muslim girl hero in mainstream comics, collected in a book by G. Willow Wilson (2014). Marvel's Riri Williams took over from Iron Man. She's a science genius who went to MIT age 15. Kamal talks about women's rights with the imam at her local mosque in Jersey City. The first Latina superhero called *La Borinqueña* was created by Puerto Rican artist Edgardo Miranda-Rodriquez.[137] Also at DC

Comics, Beth Ross is the first female and teen president in *Pres,* elected on Twitter in 2036.[138] (The comic can be purchased online.) Boom Box comics publishes *The Lumberjames* about a diverse group of girls at a summer camp including queer girls, *Goldie Vance* about a teenage black girl who solves mysteries, *Giant Days* about three female university students, and *Jonesy* about a Latina teenager.

Television

Female movie superheroes are rare but television shows do a better job than films of providing smart women in starring roles. The TV series *Buffy the Vampire Slayer* has been called feminist because, "Buffy stands next to Wonder Woman as a figure of feminine strength and potential: she is a superhero, one that is able to both defend herself and others."[139] Netflix's *Jessica Jones* series features a superhero who despite her alcoholism gets the bad guy. The young adult fantasy novel series called *The Mortal Instruments* by Cassandra Clare is also about teens with superhuman or angelic powers compared to ordinary humans called "mundanes." (In the popular *Twillight* film series, Bella turns into an immortal vampire, but Edward made all her choices for her.[140])

Teen girls are often portrayed as mean girls on television, like the US TV show of the same name or the Australian series *Ja'mie: Private School Girl* about a spoiled girl played by a male comedian. The TV series *Veep* portrays a rather mean politician who becomes the first woman president after the elected president resigns. When her dying mother and pregnant daughter needed her attention, she put politics first. Described as a narcissist, she is not a feminist role-model, as when discussing a possible presidential library she dismissed the idea of a woman architect because "we're not remodeling a kitchen here." Other TV shows featured high-level women government leaders with more intelligence, especially the Danish show *Borgen* about a woman prime minister. US shows with women leaders with integrity include *Parks and Recreation* and *Madam Secretary.*

The Handmaid's Tale dystopian novel by Margaret Atwood was made into a TV series on Hulu in 2017, about a future where pollution reduced women's fertility so much that the few women who can bear babies are enslaved to bear babies for the elite. These kinds of political shows taking on prejudice are referred to by youth as "woke," including liberal TV political comedians such as Samantha Bee, Stephen Colbert, Bill Maher, and John Oliver who've had a heyday making fun of Donald Trump.

Game of Thrones, the HBO TV series since 2010, is discussed globally, with numerous articles about the increasing number of strong women characters by Season 6.[141] Along with various queens and warriors, a ten-year-old girl named Lady Lyanna Mormont plays an important political role, initiating the selection of Jon Snow as King of the North with a stirring speech. She also appears on the battlefield. *Game of Thrones* is a symbol of political intrigue, often referred to in relation to actual politics, as when the leader of the new Podemos Party in Spain gave DVDs of the show to the king. The series is extremely violent. Another media influence on young demonstrators for democracy who show great courage in the face of police violence (like Yara in Egypt) may be that they've seen many violent scenes in media where the hero is usually not harmed or the cartoon character gets squashed and bounces back. This may give young people an unrealistic sense of immunity from harm.

Reality TV shows are often about groups of young people who compete with each other: A Palestinian reality show called *The President* featured young adults campaigning to be virtual president, which was a criticism of the lack of elections for the previous decade.[142] A young woman, age 22, was one of the top three candidates, with her campaign managed by her father. She was of course the only candidate whom the judges criticized for her clothing. The show was mostly funded by a US State Department grant to an NGO called Search for Common Ground. US and British TV shows about young people are often raunchy, in that young women use their sexuality to influence men, including *The Bachelor, The Bachelorette, 16 and Pregnant* and *Teen Mom* in the US. British TV shows about wild teens include *Skins, Misfits, Some Girls,* and *Fresh Meat*.[143] We see that TV shows have mixed outcomes for providing girls with positive options and goals.

For little girls, TV series feature girls as superheroes like the *Powerpuff Girls* (beginning in 1998), Hispanic *Dora the Explorer* (began in 2000), *WordGirl* (2006), and African-American *Doc McStuffins* (2012). However, In British children's TV 44 out of 50 television shows shown from 1950 to 2013 have only male or mostly male characters.[144] Do you think TV's overall the effect is more positive or negative?

Music

Lesley Gore's 1963 song "You Don't Own Me," is a feminist statement of autonomy, stating she's not a toy to be put on display or owned, she's young and loves freedom.[145] Her song came out the same year as Betty Friedan's *The Feminist Mystique*, so Gore was a vanguard voice.[146] In the same assertive tone, Meghan Trainor's 2016 song "No" encourages women to assertively say no to unwanted attention from men, as repeated in the lyrics like "my name is no, my number is no."[147] A motivation for these songs is the extensive history of sexism in popular music, including emo that is supposedly anti-macho.[148] The girlfriend is both the enemy and the prize to be won, as seen in songs by Adam Lazarra and his band Taking Back Sundays or violent songs by Chris Conley and his band Saves the Day. He sings about sawing off flesh from a woman's thighs "If I could somehow make you mine." John Lennon talked about hitting his first wife in "Getting Better" ("I used to be cruel to my woman. I beat her and kept her apart from the things that she loved.") "Under my thumb" Mick Jagger sings about a man raping a young black slave in "Brown Sugar." In his song "Kim," Eminem says, "Sit down bitch. If you move again I'll beat the shit out of you," an exceptionally hateful and violent song—search the lyrics online.

The punk music scene in the West generated a DIY spirit where musicians produced their own albums. A feminist offshoot beginning in the late 1980s was the Riot Grrrl movement led by punk bands like Bikini Kill and Bratmobile. Their songs discussed rape, sexual harassment, eating disorders and other young women's issues. Girls created their own media with feminist zines (homemade magazines) and independent punk rock music albums in the 80s and early 90s, as documented in *Grrlyshow*.[149]

Bikini Kill band was influential, led by lead singer Kathleen Hanna, with its Riot Grrrl Manifesto published in 1991 and movies about the band.[150] Their goals were "creating non-hierarchal ways of being AND making music, friends, and scenes based on communication + understanding, instead of competition + good/bad categorizations." The Manifesto stated that grrrls hate capitalism and are "angry at a society that tells us Girl = Dumb, Girl = Bad, Girl = Weak." The bands Nirvana and Pearl Jam were male feminists, as when Pearl Jam's Eddie Vedder displayed "pro-choice" written on his arm with a marker pen 25 years ago and he sang feminist songs like "Daughter" and "Better Man." Nirvana's Cobain sometimes wore a dress and sang to protest rape. Punk style gave new meaning to objects such as a safety pin made into a decorative item, which academics call cultural bricoleursl. A Swedish film, *We Are the Best!* (2013) portrays rebellious 13-year-old girls who start a punk band in 1982 Stockholm to irritate the boys at their local youth center.

Feminist rap and hip-hop singers followed with artists like Queen Latifah, Salt-n-Pepa, and TLC in the US and Pussy Riot in Russia. A St. Louis, Missouri, male feminist rapper, Tef Poe likes feminist hip-hop artists like Nicki Minaj, Young M.A., Rapsoddy and Bates.[151] He raps lyrics like "I am sure God is a woman" that he says offends some men. He points out that queer women are leaders in the Black Lives Matter movement and outnumber men in organizing protests. He said feminism in hip-hop has "forced people to recognize the feminine energy in the culture." M.I.A. is a British-Sri Lankan Tamil rapper (born in 1975) who exposes violence against women, especially among immigrants, as well as opposing global capitalism and patriarchy. Her songs refer to her as a warrior and a fighter in "guerrilla warfare," leading to interest in her songs by transnational, post-colonial, and queer scholars.[152]

Teen singer Lorde (from New Zealand) said about feminism, "A lot of girls think it's not shaving under their arms and burning bras and hating boys, which just seems Stone Age to me." Lorde promotes healthy body image to her over one million Twitter followers, such as sharing a photo of herself before and after being photoshopped. The dominant singers in US pop music are young women—Lady Gaga, Beyoncé, Rihanna, Katy Perry, Taylor Swift, and Miley Cyrus. They project an a message of being powerful and in control, frequently using the word "boss." Niki Minaj titled a song "Boss Ass Bitch." (An article describes other feminist singers including Kurt Cobain and the Beastie Boys."[153]) However, Taylor Swift has been criticized for "faux feminism," using it to further her career but not support feminist issues.[154]

Beyoncé performed with the words "boss" and "hustler" flashing on the screen behind her, along with a video of her mashing a vacuum cleaner and sewing machine. She also sang behind a large sign proclaiming feminism and her dancers formed the woman's symbol at various VMA award performances. A Pakistani fashion company called Do Your Own Thing hired two students to choreograph a flashmob of five girls dancing on the streets of Lahore to Beyoncé's song "Run The World (Girls)." The video generated much social media protest about shameless dancing on the street as not being feminism. See what you think of the video.[155]

A rap song saved an Afghan girl from early marriage. While living in Iran, Sonita Alizadeh's parents told her when she was 14 they needed her dowry money to pay for her brother's wedding. To protest, she made a music video called "Brides for Sale."[156] She dressed as a bride with a bruised face and a barcode on her forehead. Her parents got the message and backed down. She advocates "girls need to have hope for their future, even if it is hard. If a girl loses hope, she'll feel dead inside and this is the worst thing." Her music led to a scholarship in the US.[157] Central American feminist hip-hop artists link their art with activism and their personal healing working together to tour in *Somos Guerreras* (We are Warriors). Feminist Brazilian funk singer Valesca reported that, "Nowadays it's easy to speak the language of feminism," compared to when she started singing about her sexuality in the 1990s.[158] "We used to only listen to men's side of the story" singing about women as sex objects.

Music can be a political tool. Hip-hop songs are often the theme songs of youth-led uprisings, as in Egypt's "Ezay" (How come?") by Mohamed Mounir, referred to as "the Voice of Egypt."[159] An Australian young woman living in Rangoon put together the first girls' singing group in the country called the Tiger Girls, who insert political messages in their songs, as shown in a video about them.[160] An international rap protest video titled "Multi_Viral" includes a Puerto Rican rap group singing in Spanish "The State fears us because we're at once 132 and 15-M." The video references uprisings in Spain (15-M), the Arab Spring, the Occupy Movement and Mexico's Yosoy132, discussed in Volume 2. The eclectic group includes US guitarist Tom Morello, Arab-Israeli protest singer Kamilya Jubran (the only woman) and spoken word by Julian Assange, plus a video of a Palestine boy who chooses music over violence.[161] Some of the lyrics were solicited from fan tweets. Assange noted, "From Cairo to Quito a new world is forming, the power of people armed with the truth." (He garners criticism for his WikiLeaks publishing of sensitive information.)

Female rappers like Angel Haze attack sexism in the US, although she describes herself as a "real-ass bitch."[162] The Swedish group Femtastic produced tracks like "FAT-TA" to expose stories of sexual violence and rape. Other advocacy music videos in 2015 are collected online, supporting Black Lives Matter (the Russian Riot punk band's song "I Can't Breathe"), immigrants (M.I.A), prevention of sexual assault (Lady Gaga) and domestic violence (Melanie Fiona), LGBT rights (Jennifer Hudson), and Macy Gray's advocacy for health care, gun control, and ending global warming.[163] Two Pussy Riot members were jailed for their "Punk Virgin" song filmed in an orthodox cathedral, but continued to criticize the state and church. They created an anti-Trump English-language video in 2016 titled "Make America Great Again" and included clips of the presidential candidate.[164] Around the same time they put their "Straight Outta Vagina" rap song on YouTube and released a video performance about Russian corruption, titled "Chaika," to support the main theme of the Russian opposition to Putin. An English version came out the following year.

The widely watched Eurovision talent contest in 2016 was won by Jamala, a Ukrainian young woman who indirectly attacked Russian annexation of Crimea by singing "1944" about Russian deportation of her Crimean ancestors. Russian media and politicians criticized the song for being political and anti-Russian. Songs were an important part of the 2011 Arab Spring and the uprisings that followed, including Nuit

Debout in France in 2016, and will continue to encapsulate a political message and motivate protesters.

Hollywood Films Provide Global Activist Symbols

Hollywood films influence attitudes globally, comprising most of the top grossing films internationally (the top five most viewed are *Gone with the Wind, Snow White, Star Wars, The Ten Commandments* and *The Sound of Music*).[165] Even Putin's government in Russia used themes from Western movies, portraying young protesters as orcs, monsters from the *Lord of the Ring* films. Disney cartoons like *The Lion King* inspired Egyptian activists to rebel. Films influence the political debate, with *V for Vendetta* (2005) being the most influential in the recent global uprisings. It describes an anarchist rising up against totalitarianism in a fictional England, the inspiration for demonstrators who wear the Guy Fawkes mask. The masked hero, called V, says, "Ideas are bulletproof" and "People should not be afraid of their governments. Governments should be afraid of their people." He does not advocate peaceful resistance. His protégé is Evey, age 16, the young woman who leads the insurrection after V is killed.

In 2016 Missouri Representative Blaine Luetkemeyer called Senator Elizabeth Warren the "Darth Vader of the financial services world" who should be neutered. She responded,

> *They can call me Darth Vader or Voldemort or the Wicked Witch of Massachusetts for all I care—but I won't be neutered. I've always seen myself more as a Princess Leia-type (a senator and Resistance general who, unlike the guys, is never even remotely tempted by the dark side). Clearly the Force is not strong with Congressman Luetkemeyer (maybe he's a Trekkie).[166]*

Around the world, kids with access to TVs and movie theaters watched cartoons and *Harry Potter* films where the young hero defies authority. Harry Potter films are unusual blockbuster films for their positive role-models like smart Hermione and helpful and compassionate boy Neville, in contrast to the *Twilight* series with unequal and unhealthy romantic relationships between Bella and Edward and Jacob. Yara, 17, lives near Cairo, as you read in Chapter 1. She said that Hogwarts (Harry Potter's school created by series author JK Rowling) was "my safe place, a sanctuary. It was the world I could go to by closing my eyes when the here-and-now had too many conflicts, arguments, confusion and noise. I never really felt I'd fit into the real world." When she was in ninth grade she found the study of physics was real magic: "Getting a rocket into the air proposed the same challenge as sending a broomstick zooming through it. Physics made me realize that the real world is just as magical as the wizarding one."

Andrew Slack organized the Harry Potter Alliance in 2005 with 190 chapters in eight countries and 35 US states in order to use popular culture to "fight injustice in our world." He said the Potter films changed his life. The Alliance joined with *Hunger Games* film fans and the NGO Oxfam to organize the "Hunger is Not a Game" campaign. In 2013 *Hunger Games* fans relaunched the "Odds in Our Favor" campaign against inequality first launched by the Harry Potter Alliance, asking fans to share their experiences on #MyHungerGames and post a photo making Katniss' three-fingered salute. They also feature community activists on the #WeAreTheDistricts tumblr.[167] In Bangkok, Thai protesters against a military coup used the three-fingered salute that young rebels used to signal dissent in *The Hunger Games*.[168] The military banned the salute in political gatherings and pressured a cinema chain to cancel showing the film after anti-coup students planned to attend the opening of the third film in the series.

Egyptian activist Esraa Abdel Fattah said that as a child she watched animated movies where the hero takes on the power structure: "I loved *The Lion King, Finding Nemo,* and *Antz;* I was always wondering why we weren't doing this in Egypt."[169] Responding to criticism about passive Snow White princesses, Disney offered heroines of color including Pocahontas, Mulan, and Moana. Lacking a Latina heroine, Disney offered a TV series called *Elena of Avalor.* At age 16 she saved her kingdom from a sorceress, and rules it with the help of a Grand Council.

Studios might be surprised to learn of their influence on revolutionaries since critics fault Disney films for their passivity, challenged in a youth activist campaign to tweet drawings of active princesses.[170] The Anti-Princess Collection for Children tells the stories of achieving women, including the difficulties they overcame.[171] With the similar intent, Nadia Fink wrote a series of books about famous Latin American women like Mexican artist Frida Kahlo, Chilean folk singer Violeta Parra and Bolivian independence leader Juana Azurdy. The books were adopted by publishers in other Latin American countries.

Disney spent four billion dollars on buying the *Star Wars* films, an indication of their financial reach. In line with their recent featuring of young women in films like *Brave, Frozen,* and *Inside Out,* the Disney-produced Star Wars movie *Return of the Force* stars Rey, a young woman. (Pixar only produced two girl-centered animated movies, *Brave* and *Inside Out.)* Publicity for the film features a man, but Rey is clearly the central character.

For the first time in the *Star Wars* series, the action hero of episodes VII (2015) and VIII (2017) is a young woman. Rey is played by Daisy Ridley who stars with a black hero played by John Boyega—both are British and 22. Her father described her as "an extraordinary lady, though not an easy one." Fans were angry that she was left out of the Hasbro Star Wars Monopoly game that included Darth Vader, who wasn't even in *The Force Awakens*. They started a campaign called #WhereisRae? that succeeded in adding Rae to the game in 2016. Other important female characters in *Star Wars: The Force Awakens* are Carrie Fisher's character General Leia, and a small wise woman over 1,000 years old named Maz Kanata who replaces Yoda.

Traditional gender roles are challenged by female heroines in action movies such as the *Hunger Games* trilogy outdating literary critic's Leslie Fielder's conclusion that the "The mythic America is boyhood." Role reversal occurs with kind boys like Peeta in *Hunger Games* who accepts the heroine's Katniss' strengths. Other revolutionary teen girls star in *V for Vendetta* (2006) and *Divergent* (2014). The heroine of the 2016 film *Arrival* wins with her intelligent empathy as a linguist and her courage when she takes off her biohazard suit to communicate with aliens, without any physical fights.

Fictional heroines that inspired young women who posted on Emma Watson's feminist book club on Goodreads included Hermione Granger and Ginny Weasley, Catwoman, Princess Leia, Disney princesses Jasmine and Merida, and perhaps less famous ones: Luna Lovegood, Melody Brooks, Furiosa, Minerva McGonagall, Skeeter Phelan, and Arwen. Other young adult heroines suggested by Serene on the bookclub's message board are featured in *The Testing, Reboot, The 5th Wave, In the End, Heroes of Olympus,* and *Cinder*.

After being ignored in film since she was created in 1941, *Wonder Woman* finally was featured in a 2017 film, the first superhero action film directed by a woman. The main character is played by Gal Gadot, an Israeli veteran, born in 1985, the mother of two children. She gained 17 pounds of muscle to train for the part.

A teen British feminist blogger who campaigns against genital mutilation of girls liked the 2015 film *The Diary of a Teenage Girl*, about Minnie, a 15-year old who has an affair with her mother's boyfriend. June Eric-Udorie wrote on her blog that she identified with Minnie, liked that her imperfect naked body wasn't airbrushed, that she cried and "overshared" with her friends, and that she demonstrated that, "Girls like sex, want to talk about sex and have sex. I read Judy Blume's *Forever* when I was 10 or 11. It was the first book I read that featured sex and blowjobs and all that jazz, and *deep breath* I loved it."[172] A French film titled *Young and Beautiful* (2013) depicts teen sexuality, first with a German tourist, then as a prostitute. The film director said, "Adolescents today are very aware of their power. We're in a society that celebrates adolescent beauty. Just look at the magazines. Youth is given a high value, and the youth in our society are leveraging that. The character Isabel is exploiting that."[173] Is choosing to sell one's body an act of power?

Sleepover (2004) is one of many US teen dramas about mean popular girls versus the smart nicer girls in high school. The film is about girls graduating from eighth grade, worried about how they'll fit in high school and if they'll be able to eat lunch at the spot for popular kids by the school fountain. They do one kind act by including a girl who is slightly chubby and is used to being invisible. Otherwise, their concerns are trivial with two cliques of girls in competition to sit at the fountain. The main character's big moment is kissing a hunky guy she has a crush on. He was attracted to her when she expertly skateboarded past him wearing her mother's sexy red dress.

The Bechdel Test (named after an American cartoonist) was created to rate movies for their gender balance, then used to test other media. The bar is set low: An "A" rating goes to a movie that includes two women talking to each other about something other than a man. Sometimes a requirement is added that the women be named. Women certainly are not heard equally, as documented by the Geena Davis Institute on Gender in the Media. More Hollywood films are passing the Bechdel test than before, but the institute reported the percentage has "flatlined at about half over the last 20 years, and women don't make up any more than 20 percent of producers, directors and writers across the board."[174] Films with a female director or writer had more girls and women on screen and the countries with the most female leads (40%) were Australia, China, and Japan. When an Australian radio station published an all-male list of the "Hottest 100 of All Time" popular singers, women used social media to generate the "Hottest 100 Women."

Despite feminist criticism, the media has many more male characters who have more speaking time, and female actors are five times as likely to be shown in sexy clothes.[175] Women were 28% of featured roles in Hollywood's most popular films in 2012, an increase of only 7% since 2007.[176] Over a third of these women were dressed to be sexy or shown partially nude, including well over half of the teenage actors. Women directed only 1.9% of the popular films.

A review of the 100 most popular fictional films released in the US from 2007 to 2014 found that only 30% of all characters who spoke or were named were women, and most were young, white and heterosexual.[177] A Tumblr site called "Every Single Word" by Dylan Marron shows video clips of the few words spoken by nonwhite characters.

Women were only 29% of major characters in the top-selling films of 2013, were only 30% of characters who said something, and were more likely to be identified by their marital status than men.[178] Only 28% of characters in family films were women. In children's PG movies, only 17% of the people were female with very little progress over the last two decades.[179] Are there strong female film characters that should be added to our list?

Media Facilitates Activism

In Saudi Arabia, Manal al-Sharif (born 1979) is an example of someone who radically changing her worldview because of media, as she explained in a TED video and her dramatic book *Daring to Drive* (2017), discussed in Volume 2 Chapter 5. She was so fundamentalist in her religious views, she burned her paintings of people and her brother's music tapes for violating Islam. She covered herself because fundamentalists view women as seductive and sinful, including their names, voices, and faces. Women are thus called mother of Mr. X or wife of Mr. Y, because men can't control their instincts, not a flattering view of males. A revolution in her thinking was sparked by the introduction of the Internet in 2000. She said, "It was the first door to the outside world for youth. I realized how small a box I was in and my phobia about getting my purity polluted. I was 21 when for the first time I allowed myself to listen to a song, as music was Satan's Flute and the path to adultery."[180] The first song she heard was by the Backstreet Boys and it seemed sweet and innocent to her. Watching the TV video of the attack on the World Trade Center made her realize, "No religion on earth can accept such cruelty. My heroes were nothing but bloody terrorists."

Al-Sharif was inspired by news coverage of the Arab Spring to start a campaign called Drive Your Own Life on June 17, 2011. She recorded a video revealing her name and face to explain the campaign and show herself driving. Her Facebook video got 700,000 views the first day she posted it and she was jailed the next day in a horrendous crowded room with many other women in cots and literally crawling with cockroaches, although 100 other women drivers weren't arrested. Two camps sprang up between men and women on Facebook. A photo showed men throwing their headgear at women drivers and women responded with a photo of them throwing high heels. A rally led to her release nine days later. The harsher the attacks the greater her impact, she concluded, motivating her to campaign for full citizenship for women "to be in the driver's seat of our destiny" because "society is nothing if women are nothing."

In 2012, Al-Sharif filed suit against the Ministry of Interior for not issuing her a driver's license. She was fired from her good job as one of few women working at Aramco and cleric Shaikh Abdul Aziz Al Tarifi issued a fatwa declaring Manal a "hypocrite" and questioning her status as a Muslim. The waves of women driving cars starting in 2011 were documented on YouTube despite harsh penalties including job loss. Women drivers also use Twitter to create what has been called the best-organized social campaign in Saudi Arabia. Another media leader in Saudi Arabia, Muna AbuSulayman founded and co-hosts a popular TV show in the Arab world hosted by women that discusses controversial topics such as gender equality and LGBT rights in a country where homosexuality is illegal along with mixing of the sexes in most environments.

Social media is used by feminists, such as the Twitter Youth Feminist Army--#TYFA--organized by British 15-year-old Lili Evans and two of her friends. She and a friend also organized a blog to connect young feminists.[181] Her goals are better sex education and contraception information for young people. An app called Juicebox provides answers to questions about sex and provides comments, developed by Brianna Rader, age 24, because she was frustrated with the lack of sex education in schools. Her interviews with young people found they got sex education from Google, their friends, and from movies. (Other digital information sources are TeenSource and Scarleteen.) A survey of female college students in Guangzhou reported more than half learned about sex on the Net, although over a quarter were bothered by their lack of sexual information—only 17% learned about sex from their parents.[182] (About 60% depended on their parents to approve of a future marriage partner.) Kelly Oxford's call for women to tweet their experiences of being sexually assaulted in response to Donald Trump's making light of his sexual harassment of multiple women quickly resulted in over 30 million tweets under the hashtag #NotOkay.

Women—mainly young—sent about a third of the Twitter messages during the 2011 Arab Spring in Tunisia and Egypt and were a large presence on Facebook (41% in Tunisia and 36% in Egypt).[183] During the uprisings in 2011, over two-thirds of the Internet users in Egypt and Tunisia were under age 34. A Bahraini civil rights activist, Esra'a Al Shafei founded the online forum Mideast Youth when she was 20, in 2006. The project includes CrowdVoice.org to crowdsource reports on social justice movements and Ahwaa.org for LGBT people to discuss their issues in countries where it's illegal and punishable (by death and stoning) to be homosexual. Mideast Tunes provides a platform for underground musicians.

An international network of bloggers called Girls' Globe is headquartered in Sweden. Their website lists some of their feminist bloggers from around the world, including: Ripple Effect about the effect of climate change on poor women, Akili Dada leadership training for young African women, Girl Pride Circle (also for African girls), Honor Diaries about Muslim women's activism, Education for Equality International, and Educate Girls in India.[184] Outstanding women bloggers from around the world are recommended in an article.[185]

Their technology skills give young people an advantage. The Internet's cyberactivism provides international support for groups like the Zapatistas and anti-GMO movements, alternative reporting as on YouTube, hactivism (e.g., revealing Nation Security Administration secret documents or denial of service to punish a corporation), and culture jamming. The Zapatistas were pioneers in using "tactical media" for a political goal. They explained, "The important thing is the spectacle that you make out of an event in the media, as opposed to the event itself," as demonstrated by the Chiapas Media Project.[186] Also in Mexico, artist Valeria Gallo started a project to create portraits of 43 missing students who were killed in 2014. The portraits of the young men in a rural teacher training college were posted on Facebook, Twitter and Tumblr.[187] The remains of only one student were found, leaving uncertainty as to their killers.

A New York University student, 18-year old Rachel Brown, took a break from studying for final exams in 2015 to create a fake Facebook page to protest Chicago police shooting Laquan McDonald, age 17. They shot him 16 times. Her page stated, "Citywide walkout! Rahm Emanuel's [mayor] and Anita Alvarez's [the first Hispanic state attorney for Cook County] resignation party!" She photoshopped a photo of them waving goodbye together. She invited "tons of people" to attend the event at the Civic Center, thinking it would be a viral joke, but almost 3,000 posted acceptance. The actual protest rallies that resulted while she was sleeping in her dorm made national news and led to more calls for Emanuel to resign. Another example of organizing on social media, a student took a break from final exams to use her computer to connect food pantries and soup kitchens with donors giving food away. Maria Rose Belding, age 20, calls her system MEANS Database.[188]

Women led social movements against corruption and inequality in the "Bosnian Spring," in 2014, using active Internet sites written by women.[189] "For the first twenty days, it was all women. Then the men started slowly seeping in," reported Italian feminist Valentina Pelizzer. She started a feminist portal to discuss current issues. Journalist Paulina Janusz explained that Bosnian women were outspoken, such as about the government's inadequate response to floods, because, "They're not predefined in their roles like men are," and live outside the patriarchal structure.

An inspiring youth activist model of using the Internet is the website MideastYouth.com set up by a young woman in Bahrain, Esra'a Al Shafei, when she was a 19-year-old university student. Her goal is to "start a fierce dialogue among ethnic and religious minorities and see what happens." The site initiates campaigns (for example, to free a jailed Egyptian blogger who criticized the government) and its CrowdVoice records global protests.[190] The site utilizes comics, videos and podcasts including local musicians to attract young people. The site provided eyewitness accounts of the 2011 protests. In Tunisia, Lina Ben Mhenni is a 27-year-old cyber activist whose blog "A Tunisian Girl" and photographs kept people informed about the Tunisian uprising. Tunisian's ousted their despot, President Zine al-Abidine Ben Ali, who stepped down in January 2011, after weeks of protests. Eleven days later the uprising spread to Egypt showcasing the importance of the Internet (especially Facebook and Twitter) and cell phones in organizing, tools available to both sexes.

Iran jailed cartoonist Alena Farghadani, age 28, for criticizing Parliament members for restricting access to contraception and attempting to pass a bill criminalizing voluntary sterilization. She drew legislators as cows, monkeys and other animals. She also created an exhibition of people killed in the 2009 protests against voting fraud in the presidential election. The court sentenced her to 12 years in prison for "insulting members of Parliament through paintings" and insulting her prison interrogators. Also in 2015, Iranian activist Atena Daemi, age 27, was sentenced to 14 years in prison for her postings on Facebook and Twitter advocating an end to the death penalty and alleging human rights violations.

In Iran in 2016, anonymous developers created a crowdsourced *Gershad* phone app to pinpoint the location of the *Ershad* morality police vans on street so young people can avoid them if they're wearing fashionable clothes or walking with a person of the opposite sex.[191] The developers asked on the Gershad webpage, "Why do we have to be humiliated for our most obvious right which is the right to wear what we want? Social media are full of footage and photos of innocent women who have been beaten up and dragged on the ground by Eershad patrol agents." The app designers said that in 2014 about three million were issued official warnings about their appearance or conduct and 18,000 people were prosecuted. Similarly, in the US, some schools mandate dress codes against "distracting" clothes that reveal too much skin or underwear.[192]

Girls encouraged by the #YesAllWomen Twitter campaign and SlutWalks retort, "Don't tell us what to wear; teach boys not to stare." Access to social media gives protesters a way to organize and publicize their activities without having to risk police breaking up meetings in person. It's liberating for women who can be radical leaders from their bedrooms using their phones and computers, as was common in the Arab Spring when parents kept daughters from joining street demonstrations.

Another example of using Change.org, a website for petitions that calls itself "the world's platform for change." Shelby Knox creates campaigns for women's rights.[193] Care2 is another social activism site; its petitions succeeded in getting gender-neutral bathrooms in several high schools and vegetarian options in school cafeterias.

Culture Jamming

Culture jamming manipulates corporate advertising with "spoof sites" like PinkLoves-Consent.com, which seemed to feature Victoria's Secret underwear printed with anti-rape slogans advocating consent (other spoof ads are shown online.[194]) Australian Anita Harris argues in *Next Wave Cultures* (2007) that activism in Third Wave feminism is different in a neoliberal global culture that values individualism, consumer citizenship and a breakdown of class identification. She views girl media creators as activists so that Third Wave feminism expands the definition of resistance to the patriarchal system. Pranksters do "culture jamming" or "pranking" to expose advertising tactics used to sell products. The term was coined in 1984 by a band called Negativland. Examples of tactics are "stickering,"[195] which is pasting stickers such as "This insults women" on billboards, altering company logos, performance art, graffiti, and hacktivism. In Brazil, Panmela Castro organized a graffiti group for women called *Rede Nami* to educate women about their rights. In Puerto Rico young women artists paint murals to protest austerity measures and violence against women. When vandals painted underwear on murals with bare breasted women, the bare breasted artists protested in front of the mural.[196]

The Guerrilla Girls, created by New York City feminist artists in 1985, wore gorilla masks in their demonstrations against exclusion of women in art and film, as shown on their website and in a recent video.[197] Two French art students started a campaign to remedy the fact that only 1.3% of public spaces such as streets are named after women. They put up posters saying, "Too few streets are named after women" and suggesting women's names.

The blog and Facebook page *Teen Feminist* includes images of phone cases for feminists with slogans like "Feminism is the Radical Notion that Women are People" and "I hate patriarchy, not men." The blog also includes photos of feminist singers. Slogans like "Enough!" or "We are the 99%" become memes, a symbols that have widespread appeal and are "rhizomatic" and easy to share with others on the "hive mind," common memes among activists.

To fight "nerd discrimination," teenage girls in a Winnipeg, Canada Grrlz Club drew trading cards with superheroes like "Click" who has the power to make uncool teens cool without changing them and the power to end gossip. The "Masked Peacock" turns racists into people who "see the beauty in diversity," as seen online.[198] Global Citizen organized a do-it-yourself media campaign called #ShowYourSelfie to send messages to policy makers to take action for young people living in poverty. They want to end global problems discussed in Chapter 3, like 71 million young people leave school before age 16, youth are 40% of the unemployed people and the new HIV infections, 130 million women and girls suffered genital mutilation, and youth lack representation in decision-making.[199]

Campaigns Against Sexualization of Girls

A study of 120 films from 11 countries released between 2010 and 2013 reported that women had only 31% of the speaking roles and only 23% of the films had a female protagonist.[200] Women and teen girls were sexualized, showing more skin, while women were also rarely shown in STEM jobs. A book advised parents on how to deal with sexual sell--Jane Levin and Jean Kilbourne's *So Sexy So Soon: The New Sexualized Childhood and What Parents Can Do to Protect Their Kids* (2009).[201] Professor Susan Douglas argues that antifeminist attitudes are manufactured by a media that defines women by their sexuality:

> *Enlightened sexism is a manufacturing process that is constantly produced by the media. Its components—anxiety about female achievement; renewed and amplified objectification of young women's bodies and faces; dual exploitation and punishment of female sexuality; dividing of women against each other by age, race and class; and rampant branding and consumerism—began to swirl around in the early 1990s, consolidating as the dark star it has become in the early 21st century.[202]*

Media sexualization of girls compromises their thinking abilities and leads to depression and poor self-esteem, according to an American Psychological Association report.[203] The report includes remedies to correct problems like Mattel's Teen Talk Barbie who said "Math class is tough" in 1992. (The documentary *Barbie Nation: An Unauthorized Tour* explores the world's most popular toy and a teen gives a TED talk about Barbie and the perfect body image.[204])

In her book *American Girls: Social Media and the Secret Lives of Teenagers* (2016), Nancy Jo Sales reports on her interviews with more than 200 teenage girls in 10 states. She recognizes that too often reports on teenagers don't include their voices. For the first time in history girls of various classes and backgrounds are doing the same activities although they told her they are hurt by the frequent cyber bullying, sexual harassment, requests for nude photos, and critical judgments of their photographs. Sales blamed the "hypersexualization" of girls on the availability of online pornography. She concludes that, "Now more than ever, girls need feminism" and its critical tools to understand the socialization of girls in a digital age. However, few of the girls quoted in her book mentioned using social media for activism. The 2016 film *Audrie and Daisy* reveals the bullying on social media that led Audrie to commit suicide.[205]

Olive Bowers, 13, got media attention for writing to *Tracks Surf Magazine* in 2014, "I would subscribe to your magazine if only I felt that women were valued as athletes instead of dolls." She pointed out that women surfers should be included as more than just pretty bystanders. Members of the Girls Project 2013 included Kentucky girls who challenged the media misrepresentation of girls through their art and performance piece, shown on video.[206] About-Face Media Literacy aims to change sexism in media, with the theme of "don't fall for the media circus."[207]

A famous campaign against sexism in women's media, the *Seventeen Magazine Project* was launched by 18-year-old Jamie Kelles in 2010. She blogged daily to report on her plan to only live by the magazine's tips for a month.[208] She included analysis of how women of color are portrayed and other significant issues, using "playful activism." She didn't use the word "feminist" to avoid being labeled "militant." Her blog generated international comments. In 2012 SPARK Sexualization, Protest: Action, Resistance, Knowledge, (founded in 2010) led another successful petition drive for *Seventeen Magazine* to include at least one spread a month of untouched photographs. SPARK opposes the sexualization of young girls by the media, which they illustrate in photos on their webpage.[209] Julia Bluhm, 14, wrote the petition and got over 86,000 signatures on Change.org, as she and another blogger described to a TEDx audience.[210] Over 13,000 people viewed their online video. SPARK held a mock photo shoot in front of the magazine and got media coverage and a meeting with the editor. They next targeted *Teen Vogue* where staff told them they already included some natural non-models (the magazine later moved into the vanguard of politics). Gloria Steinem, co-founder of the Women's Media Center that serves on SPARK's leadership committee, said they "triumphed over false standards that contribute to eating disorders and self-hatred."[211] Their activism echoed the 1970 take over of the *Ladies' Home Journal* office to lobby for a female editor-in-chief.

The international SPARK team put together an activists guide for girls titled Spark-It! *SPARKing Change, Encouraging Activism.* The SPARK Movement coordinates the efforts of over 60 organizations in the US and Canada to "demand an end to the sexualization of women and girls in the media."[212] Their website reports on a study by Rachel Calogero that found feeling objectivized hinders activism, by keeping girls' focus on appearance and traditional gender roles, but, "As activists, we are living, breathing proof that existing in a sexualized world doesn't keep *all* of us from fighting back."[213]

Covering Women's News In Zines, Magazines and Blogs

Women's issues are left out of newspapers and magazines. According to Vida, a research group that tracks women's representation in print media, over 75% of US magazines like the *Nation* and the *Atlantic* bylines are male.[214] To compensate, feminist magazines in the US include *Bitch, BUST, Jezebel, make/shift* and *Off Our Backs* (1970 to 2008), and of course *Ms.*, founded in 1972. More magazine are listed in Women in Media & News and the Feminist Majority websites; the latter also lists LGBTQ and women-of-color magazines.[215] *Herizons* is a Canadian feminist magazine and *Mxlexia* features young British women writers. Internet news sources like Young Feminist Wire and South Feminist Voices provide coverage of current issues, including a section of college writers on the Wire.[216] According to Women's Media Center, US male reporters, columnists, and editors dominate mainstream journalism. In response, women are starting independent ventures such as Laura Poitras' *Intercept* and Kara Swisher at *Re/code*.

Millennials are likely to get their news from the Internet or TV rather than reading and going to the library.[217] Although most Millennials own a smartphone (83%), a Pew survey from only 5% of people under 30 said they follow political news very closely.

Their views of mainstream news media and religious organizations are growing more negative.[218] New news media is available, as listed by Eleanor Goldfield.[219] The Mic website aims to be the leading news source by and for Millennials, based in New York (Mic.com). The Mic CEO is Chris Altchek, age 28; and he defined the characteristics of his young college-educated audience as having a sense of entitlement, oversharing on social media, and "frankness verging on insubordination."[220] They also use the word "literally" a lot. The staff of over 100 workers ride hoverboards and shoot dart guns at work and are encouraged to "say anything." They may communicate over Twitter when they're in the same office; one employee warned that his age group is "taking over" as the largest cohort of workers.

Rival news sources are Vice Media and BuzzFeed. Women and Girls Hub reports international news stories.[221] Other news networks are the International Women's Tribune Center, the International Women's Media Foundation, and the ISIS International Women's Information and Communication Service.[222] *Truthdig* launched "Global Voices: Truthdig Women Reporting" to create a network of female foreign correspondents in collaboration with the International Women's Media Foundation." The World Economic Forum website provides "must-read gender stories of the week."[223] *Ms. Magazine* and *Women's News* provide updates on global women's issues.[224] Girls' Globe, headquartered in Sweden, provides a network for bloggers and advocates for girls' and women's rights and health.[225] Their website lists organizations that work for these goals. Youth-Leader.org Magazine reports on global youth activism.[226] Other progressive online newsletters are listed in the previous endnote. Chris Hedges recommends Democracy Now radio, Link TV, The Real News, Occupy websites and *Revolution Truth*. I would add email newsletters and magazines *NationofChanges, TeleSur, Roar Magazine, Yes! Magazine, Truthdig* and *Open Democracy*. The latter has the most articles on women's issues and feminism.[227] Occupy.com recommends 20 media sources listed in the previous endnote.

World Pulse was founded to report on women's news by Jensine Larsen, who quoted Stella Paul in India, "This is what technology is all about: empowering one woman to help empower another, bridging a gap between the urban and the rural, the vocal and the voiceless." Larsen was a shy Wisconsin girl who went to the Amazon to work with native women when she was 19. Then she went to Burma to assist refugees. At age 23 she had a vision to increase media's coverage of women because she found only 10% of central stories are about women and only 1% of the world's editors are female. By the time she was 28 she was able to raise the funds to start World Pulse, which draws from local reporters in over 140 countries. They tell women's stories in a print magazine and website where women from all over the globe can talk with each other.[228] Larsen quotes Beatrice Achieng, a young rural leader from Uganda: "If I did not find World Pulse, I would still be boiling, my voice was always indoors, burning, longing for a way out. I am grateful I found not only a channel but listeners too. I will speak for change until my very last breath."

The first global feminist radio program was founded in 1991 at the UN women's conference in Nairobi and is headquartered in Costa Rica. Its website includes news on women in Central America and internationally.[229] Young women run Radio Udayapur in Nepal with the goal of ending patriarchy.

Mary Celeste Kearney reported zines were the dominant form of media production, as described in *Girl Zines* by Alison Piepmeier (2009), but were replaced by Internet zines and blogs such as "Girls Get Busy Zine" in London.[230] Kearney pointed out in 2006 that scholars focused on girls as consumers of culture, rather than producers, when in fact girl media creators are a "disruptive force." Self-published paper Zines continue to be made now, covering topics like coming-of-age, gender nonconformity, immigrants, and ethnicity.[231] The author of *Girls Make Media* (2006) believes the greatest advance in girls' media is the increased activity of young girls of color in zines like *Evolution of a Race Riot*, films like *Share Our World* (about three Muslim girls in New York City), and websites like *C/SDistro*, although their numbers remain too few.[232] Blogs include *Black Girl Dangerous*.

Bitch Magazine was founded by Third Wave feminists to comment on popular culture.[233] The three founders, two young women and a man, were recent college graduates in 1996 who described themselves as "pop culture obsessives." They wanted to do fun feminist analyses of sexism in the media. A compilation of their favorite articles is called *Bitchiest: Ten Years of Cultural Criticism from the Pages of Bitch Magazine* (2006). Their website is "Bitch: Feminist Response to Pop Culture." An example of their approach to issues is *Bitch's* response to the Supreme Court decision in 2014 that permitted some corporations, like Hobby Lobby, to eliminate some kinds of birth control from their medical coverage. *Bitch* suggested fun ways to protest: chalk slogans on the street in front of Hobby Lobby stores, produce a zine with the addresses of craft stores, or put images of Justice Ruth Bader Ginsberg on finger nail polish because she wrote the dissent in the case.[234]

An online magazine written by Millennials, *Young[ist]* explains their purpose but leaves out the word feminist. It rather lists "gender" in its list of topics of interest:

Youngist was born in response to the scapegoating of our generation in main-stream, corporate media narratives. As we are burdened with the economic crisis, a broken immigration system, and the rampant violence on young Black, Brown, queer, and transgender youth across the globe--we pursue storytelling not only as a vehicle to spread news, but also as a vital organizing tool to combating oppression. We see youth-led publishing and cross-pollination of ideas and strategies as a political necessity in this digital age.[235] *(Other youth-led media are listed on Wikipedia but only about 15% of the editors are female.*[236]*)*

The term cyberfeminist was first used in the early 1990s to refer to activists interested in thinking about and using the Internet and other new media. "Global Girl Media" was set up by women broadcasters and journalists to assist girls in "under-served communities" to become journalists, to correct the problem that "young women pass silently under the radar" of mainstream reporting.[237] Their webpage includes videos by girls. The Women's Rights Campaign put together an "Info-Activism Toolkit" to teach how to create a successful campaign by telling a story, inspiring action, and grabbing attention.[238]

Today cyberfeminist girls write Internet blogs and make videos about their issues, as posted on Young Feminist Wire (YFW), created in by 300 English-speakers in 2010 at the Association for Women's Rights in Development (AWID).[239] YWF expanded to include Spanish and French essays and provide trainings both online and in person on topics such as movement building and how to counter religious fundamentalism. *New Moon* is a magazine edited by and for girls ages 8 to 14, since 1992.[240]

Magazines by and for teens include *Rookie* (online), *Shameless Magazine, Teen Voices* at Women's eNews, and *Womxn Magazine*.[241] A girl from Peru, Alessandra reported on the Our Shared Shelf feminist book club that the main influences on her becoming a feminist were reading *Rookie* articles and seeing the video of Emma Watson's 2014 speech to the UN that defined feminism.[242] *Girl Talk* magazine in the UK includes a Girl Talk Promise in each issue including, "I will love myself the way I am," and "I believe girls are equal to boys." The magazine organized a feminist campaign for tweens called #Girls Are Amazing.[243] Editors realized that "the media for girls is rotten and we're part of it," referring to sexualized pop stars and makeover computer games that teach girls their main goal is to be attractive.

GirlZone is an advice blog, launched in 1997, which claims to be one of the first and few independent websites for teen girls.[244] *Scarleteen: Sex Ed for the Real World* is a site for girls to get accurate information about sex, including a place to ask specific questions about relationships, sexuality, and gender issues.[245] Young adults gain huge numbers of followers like "sexuality geek" Laci Green, 25, who attracts over a million subscribers to her YouTube channel. She discussed sexism, popular media, and sexuality issues since she was 19.[246] When she was 16, Juliette Brindak created a social media site called "Miss O & Friends" that attracts about 3.5 million unique monthly visitors.[247] She now earns millions from her social media. In an episode called "Why I'm a …Feminist *gasp*," she lists many problems faced by girls and women, including being called bossy and the fact that her father did nothing to help around the house. The video got over 2.5 million views. Her YouTube show led to an MTV show called *Braless*.

"Girl vlog" refers to personal video blogs posted on YouTube or other video-sharing sites like Vine. Californian vlogger Brittany Jayne Furlan, born in 1986, had nearly nine million followers on Vine where she posts six second videos. *TIME Magazine* named her as one of the most influential Internet personalities. Bloggers usually ask for comments and interaction: examples are on YouTube.[248] Blogs can be looked at as creating a public self and a room of one's own (as Virginia Woolf explained the need for personal space in 1929) for girls who feel excluded by what Kearney called the "adult-centric approach taken by mainstream feminism."

In 2009, teenager Julie Zeilinger started writing the *FBomb* blog, which she says was the first blog for teen feminists.[249] Her blog reached girls in over 190 countries, including a Middle Eastern girl who happily reported that she was able to read about feminism online without her parents' knowing. Zeilinger explained how she came to feminism: "When I was a freshman in high school, I read Jessica Valenti's book *Full Frontal Feminism* and it changed my life. It's what sent me to *Feministing,* which introduced me to the feminist blogosphere, which in turn inspired me to start a blog for teenage feminists" (her blog includes resource lists). Still a teen, Zeilinger went on to write a book for teens, *A Little F'd Up: Why Feminism Is Not a Dirty Word* (2012), which Seal Press claims is the first such handbook written by a young woman. A 17-year-old girl, Natalie, wrote to FBomb, "The first challenge for teen feminists is community— finding a supportive environment, and that's where things like the FBomb come it," filling in for what zines used to provide. This positive environment contrasts with adult moral panics over sexual predators in chat rooms, the pornography industry, and cyber-bullying. (Lists of feminist blogs are online.[250])

Other teen feminists started blogs such as *Experimentations of a Teenage Feminist* (2010 to 2012 when she was a university student), *GrrrlBeat* (focused on music), *Teen Feminist,* (by 14-year-old girl Jules Spector), *Rookie* (started by a feminist fashionista*), Feminist Stuck in Suburbia* (by a girl of color in Ohio), *Star of Davida* (by an Orthodox Jewish feminist, begun in 2010), and Teen Feminist (by 14-year-old Jules Spector). Spector, who lives in Brooklyn, wants to "get teenagers more involved in learning about who they are and not being ashamed of being a woman." The blog *Adios, Barbie* deals with body images. Examples of international blogs are *the Youth Activist Network, Gender Across Borders,* and *UK Feminista.* Blogger Alida Nugent collected her own humorous essays for girls including issues like body image and becoming a feminist in *You Don't Have to Like Me: Essays on Growing Up, Speaking Out,* and *Finding Feminism* (2015).

If the young critics of media fueled consumerism win out, our future looks good, but youth are growing up in a post-millennial, post-modern, post-industrial, post-colonial era with instant global communication that pressures them to consume trendy hot or cool items. Keeping in mind the lag between rural and urban dwellers and educational deficiencies, will Millennials in developing countries adhere to the new religion or rebel against it because they can't afford to shop or don't want to pollute the earth? If newly middle-class young adults in the Global South are incited by global media to want to continue the consumption habits of the West, we're in trouble. The first chapter in Volume 2 provides feminist theory based in the West that attempts to remedy some of the problems discussed in the previous chapters.

Discussion Questions and Activities

Questions

1. Some youth are being treated for addiction to electronic media as is happening in China, Japan and the US. Does spending many hours a day in front of a screen interfere with young people's ability to relate face-to-face? With their understanding of reality? Does it interfere physiologically with calm linear thinking?

2. Deandra in Indonesia says she learns a lot from global media, some of which her parents would forbid. Does media interfere with local values and traditions? If so, what remedies would you suggest?

3. Several Arab young women said global media gave them the courage to rebel against dictators and sexism. Is it accurate to say that the youth revolutions that started with the Arab Spring in 2011 wouldn't have happened without global media?

4. Media created a new identity, a way of defining ourselves by what we buy and

consume, such as wearing clothing with brand logos or driving a certain brand of automobile. A Danish commentator said, "Tasteless youth culture rules all." Do you agree or disagree? What do your consumption practices say about your identity and thought processes?

5. Do you consider yourself a cyberfeminist? Explain.

6. Some critics say consumerist global media takes the place of religion in defining our goals and values. Do you agree or disagree?

Activities

1. Look through print media and at TV ads to see how they manipulate us into buying, as by making us feel inadequate without their product to make us more feminine or masculine. Post your findings on the Global Youth SpeakOut website.

2. Keep a time diary of how you actually spend your time. The average teen in the US spends over nine hours a day in front of electronic media. How much time do you spend?

3. Various sites discuss the role of girls and women in media.[251] What themes do you find? What's on the minds of teen girls who've given TEDx talks (the endnote selects the top 10 TED talks by girls.)[252]

4. Check out Stop!t website to report cyber bullying and other "inappropriate behaviors." [253]

5. How did protesters use media in a collection of the 18 most creative protests?[254]

6. Are women's issues featured in the 100 best documentaries? Films for Action selected the 100 most influential and provocative documentaries. All of them are available online, either free or to rent. [255]

7. You can stay current with *Women in the World* and *GlobalGirls Media* and other newsletters. [256]

Films

1. Look at Disney cartoons for examples of youth going against older tyrants as in *The Lion King, Finding Nemo* and *Antz.*

2. Listen to Manal al-Sharif discuss the impact of media on her revolution from traditional to advocate for women's right to drive in Saudi Arabia.[257]

3. See Jean Kilbourne's *Killing us Softly: Advertisings Image of Women* (1979), Still

Killing Us Softly (1987), *Spin the Bottle: Sex, Lies and Alcohol* (2004), *Slim Hopes: Advertising and the Obsession with Thinness (1995)*, and update with recent ad images. Study guides for the films and others are available online www.mediaed.org/assets/products/241/studyguide_241.pdf

4.   See *Miss Representation* (2011) about how media portrays women in a way that keeps them from aspiring to power positions. *The Mask You Live In* (2015), shows how masculinity limits and men.[258]

5.   Look at films and TV shows about female superheroes. How are they portrayed differently than male superheroes? You could start with *Buffy the Vampire Slayer* (1997 to 2003, also a 1992 film about a high school girl). *Hanna* (2011) is about a 14-year-old genetically bred to be a super warrior. Not only an outstanding warrior, she also has a super memory and knows many languages. She is a killer who wants to stop the killing as she travels from Finland to Morocco to Germany. The actress who played her is 18 and grew up in Ireland.

6.   See films about teenage girls to look for themes and changes over time: *Time Square* (1980), *Ladies and Gentlemen, the Fabulous Stains* (1982), *Valley Girl* (1983), *Sixteen Candles* (1984), *Pretty in Pink* (1986), *Heathers* (1988), *Now and Then* and *Clueless* (1995), *She's All That* (1999) *The Virgin Suicides* (2000), *Thirteen* (2003), *Mean Girls* (2004), *Juno* (2007), *Easy A* (2010), the *Hunger Games* series (2012-2015).

7.   Watch *Meet Corliss Archer* on YouTube (a radio show from 1943 to 1956, a TV show in 1952, and a comic[259]) and *My So-Called Life*, 1994 to 1995, to see how teen issues have changed from when Corliss and Angela were both 15 and starting to date.

8.   *Freedom Writers.* A true story, it answers the question "what was so great about Anne Frank's writing?" The other theme is that seeing kids as gifted people can turn the worst racist gang members into inspired creators. The kids and the teacher started a foundation to spread her methods. 2007

Endnotes

1   Selena Simmons-Duffin, "Why You Should Start Taking Millennials Seriously," NPR.org, October 6, 2014.

2   http://www.npr.org/2014/10/06/352613333/why-you-should-start-taking-millennials-seriously
    P.37

3   Linda Herrera, "Egypt's Revolution 2.0: The Facebook Factor," *Jadaliyya*, February 12, 2011.

4   www.jadaliyya.com/pages/index/612/egypts-revolution-2…
    "Landmark Report," Common Sense Media press report, November 3, 2015.

https://www.commonsensemedia.org/about-us/news/press-releases/landmark-report-us-teens-use-an-average-of-nine-hours-of-media-per-day
5   Alfie Brown, "Google's Lemmings: Pokemon Go Where Silicon Valley Says," *ROAR Magazine*, July 24, 2016.
    https://roarmag.org/essays/pokemon-go-where-google-says/
6   Lesley McClurg, "Is 'Internet Addiction' Real?" NPR, May 18, 2017.
    http://www.npr.org/sections/health-shots/2017/05/18/527799301/is-internet-addiction-real
7   J. Ryan Paarker, "Ten Spiritually/Theologically Significant Films of the Decade," *Pop Theology*, January 4, 2010.
    http://www.patheos.com/blogs/poptheology/2010/01/ten-for-the-decade/
8   Nicholas Carr. *The Shallows*. W.W. Norton, 2011.
9   Janna Anderson and Lee Ranie, "Millennials will Benefit and Supper Duet to their Hyperconnected Lives," Pew Research Center, February 29,
    2012.
10 "Social Networks May Inflate Self-Esteem, Reduce Self-Control," Columbia Business School, January 14, 2013.
    http://www8.gsb.columbia.edu/media/newsn/2243/Social+Networks+May+Inflate+Self%26%238211%3BEsteem%2C+Reduce+-
    Self%26%238211%3BControl
11 Britney Fitzgerald, "More Women on Facebook, Twitter and Pinterest Than Men," *The Huffington Post*, July 9, 2012.
    http://www.huffingtonpost.com/2012/07/09/women-facebook-twitter-pinterest_n_1655164.html
12 "Video Game Playing Tied to Creativity," *Michigan State University News*, November 2, 2011. http://news.msu.edu/story/9971/
13 "Internet Users in the World," Internet World Stats
    http://www.internetworldstats.com/stats.htm
14 Keith Hampton, et al., "Social Media and the Cost of Caring," Pew Reearch Center, January 15, 2015.
15 http://www.pewinternet.org/2015/01/15/social-media-and-stress/
16 Chloe Combi. *Generation Z*. Windmill Books, 2015, p. 276.
17 http://www.bustle.com/articles/141335-11-feminist-the-powerpuff-girls-moments-you-notice-when-you-rewatch-the-series-as-an-adult
18 www.GrowingUpWithGirlPower.com
    Mary Celeste Kearney, "Sparkle: Luminosity and Post-Girl Power Media," *Continuum: Journal of Media & Cultural Studies*, 2015. DOI:
19 10.1080/10304312.2015.1022945 Sarah Projansky. *Spectacular Girls: Media Fascinations and Celebrity Culture*. NYU Press, 2014.
20 https://www.youtube.com/watch?v=UyZdHiQX3HE
    "2015: An Year of Digital Darwinism?," *I am Wire*, February 8, 2015.
21 http://www.iamwire.com/2015/02/2015-year-digital-darwinism/109585/comment-page-1
    "The Web and Rising Global Inequality," *Web Index*, December 2014.
22 http://thewebindex.org/report/#1._executive_summary:_the_web_and_growing_global_inequality
    FaceBook & Mark Zuckerberg, "State of Connectivity 2016: Using Data to Move Towards a More Inclusive Internet," February 28, 2017. https://
23 info.internet.org/en/blog/2017/02/28/state-of-connectivity-2016-using-data-to-move-towards-a-more-inclusive-internet/
    Lee Rainie, "How American Teens Navigate the New World of 'Digital Citizenship,'" Pew Internet, November 9, 2011.
24 http://pewinternet.org/Reports/2011/Teens-and-social-media/Summary/Findings.aspx
    Chuck Hadad, "Why Some 13-Year-Olds Check Social Media 100 Times a Day," CNN, October 5, 201.
    http://www.cnn.com/2015/10/05/health/being-13-teens-social-media-study/index.html Marion Underwood and Robert Faris, "#Being
    Thirteen."
25 https://www.documentcloud.org/documents/2448422-being-13-report.html
26 Amy Adele Hasinoff. *Sexting Panic: Rethinking Criminalization, Privacy, and Consent*. University of Illinois Press, 2015.
    Salynn Boyles, "Social Bulllying Common in TV Shows Kids Watch," WebMD, September 27, 2012.
27 http://www.webmd.com/parenting/news/20120924/social-bullying-prevalence#1
    David Buckingham, et al., ed. *Youth Cultures in the Age of Global Media*. Palgrave Macmillan, 2014. Bill Osgerby. *Youth Culture and the Media:
28 Global Perspectives*. Routledge. 2016.
    Malcolm Harris, "When It Comes to Sex, Baby Boomers Aren't Normal," *Pacific Standard Magazine*, August 16, 2016.
29 https://psmag.com/when-it-comes-to-sex-baby-boomers-arent-normal-39c5dcfc38d4#.e6awov02b
30 Klaus Schwab. *The Fourth Industrial Revolution*. World Economic Forum, Geneva, 2016, p. 77.
31 Ibid, p. 54.
    "Generation Y Around the World: Global Youth Research," InSites Consulting surveyed 4,056 young people.
32 https://insites.wetransfer.com/downloads/f54071de1cae1f4fdb1a90035e2d974220130715162508/93559f
33 Klaus Schwab
    Ian Sherr, "Facebook, Samsung Prepare to Sell Virtual Reality to the Masses," CNet, November 20, 2015.
34 http://www.cnet.com/news/facebook-samsung-prepare-to-sell-virtual-reality-to-the-masses/
35 Richard Wilkinson and Kate Pickett. *The Spirit Level Why Greater Equality Makes Societies Stronger*. Bloomsbury Press, 2011.
36 Ibid., p. 94.
    "Progress For Children: A Report Card on Adolescents," No. 10, UNICEF, April 2012, p. 11.
37 http://www.unicef.org/publications/files/Progress_for_Children_-_No._10_EN_04232012.pdf
    "World Bank Development Report 2012: Gender Equality and Development," p. 314.
    https://openknowledge.worldbank.org/handle/10986/4391

38 Lindsey Weedston, "The Middle Eastern TV Show bringing Feminist Views on Marriage to 80 Million People," *Yes! Magazine*, February 4, 2016.
39 http://www.yesmagazine.org/happiness/the-middle-eastern-tv-show-bringing-feminist-views-on-marriage-to-80-million-people-20160204
40 World Bank World Development Report 2012, p. 268.
"Evidence: TV Shows Can Lower Fertility Rates," *Legally Sociable*, August 26, 2012.
41 http://legallysociable.com/2012/08/26/evidence-tv-shows-can-lower-fertility-rates/
42 www.oneyoungworld.com/press/study/
43 http://www.unicef.org/infobycountry/southafrica_60527.html
Tom Dart, "Cocks Not Glocks," *The Guardian*, August 25, 2016.
https://www.theguardian.com/us-news/2016/aug/25/cocks-not-glocks-texas-campus-carry-gun-law-protest
44 https://www.facebook.com/cocksnotglocks/
45 http://acv.in/index.php/ente-nadu-ente-vartha/view/14
46 See photos http://sarassalil.delhipress.in/index.aspx
47 http://outspokenspeakers.blogspot.com/2016_02_01_archive.html
Saurav Adhikari, Corporate Vice-President, HCL Technologies India
48 www.businessweek.com/magazine/content/05_34/b3948426.htm
http://indiatoday.intoday.in/story/kalki-koechlin-womens-day-exclusive-performance-india-today-conclave/1/347480.html An interview:
49 https://www.youtube.com/watch?v=TYoJ3FHsMBA
50 https://www.youtube.com/watch?v=vNyj4ZMhxm0&feature=youtu.be
http://in.movies.yahoo.com/news-detail/34628/Balika-Badhu-TV-gets-good-audience-response.html and http://www.indiastudychannel.com/
51 forum/26952-Balika-vadhu-india-s-no-serial.aspx
52 http://www.aol.in/bollywood-story/modernity-a-far-cry-for-women-on-small-screen-march-8-is-international-womens-day/819838
53 Article about STAR TV in India and China http://lass.calumet.purdue.edu/cca/gmj/sp07/gmj-sp07-chang.htm
Rhitu Chatterjee, "India's new Comic Book Hero Fights Rape, Rides on the Back of a Tiger," *NPR*, December 16, 2014.
http://www.npr.org/blogs/goatsandsoda/2014/12/16/371209381/indias-new-comic-book-hero-fights-rape-rides-on-the-back-of-a-tiger
54 http://www.priyashakti.com/portfolio/comic-book/
Emma Niles, "Truthdiggers of the Week," *TruthDig*, August 20, 2016.
55 http://www.truthdig.com/report/item/truthdiggers_women_khabar_lahariya_feminist_newspaper_rural_india_20160820
56 http://www.theguardian.com/sustainable-business/digital-mapping-young-people-video
"UP Village Council Bans Jeans, Mobile Phones for Girls," *Times of India*, September 21, 2015.
57 http://timesofindia.indiatimes.com/india/UP-village-council-bans-jeans-mobile-phones-for-girls/articleshow/49043739.cms
Terry Gross interview with Biz Stone, NPR, February 17, 2011.
58 www.npr.org/2011/02/16/133775340/twitters-biz-stone-on-starting-a-revolution
59 http://yfa.awid.org/2014/04/turkish-women-use-twitter-to-fight-sexual-harassment
Uki Goni, "Argentine Women Call Out Machismo," *New York Times*, June 15, 2015.
60 https://www.nytimes.com/2015/06/10/argentine-women-call-out-machismo.html
61 "Stardoll and Carat Network Join Forces in Global Survey on Gen Z Girls' Digital Behavior," PR Newswire, January 27, 2011.
62 2014, https://www.youtube.com/watch?v=kdemFfbS5H0
Taffy Brodesser-Akner, "Turning Microcelebrity Into a Big Business," *New York Times*, September 19, 2014.
63 http://www.nytimes.com/2014/09/21/magazine/turning-microcelebrity-into-a-big-business.html?_r=0
Amanda Lenhart, "Teens, Social Media & Technology Overview 2015," Pew Research Center, April 9, 2015.
64 http://www.pewinternet.org/2015/04/09/teens-social-media-technology-2015/
65 https://instagram.com/feministthoughtbubble/
James Roberts, et al., "The Invisible Addiction," *Journal of Behavioral Addictions*, June 7, 2014. DOI: 10.1556/JBA.3.2014.015
66 http://akademiai.com/content/b288753537587502/fulltext.pdf
Amanda Lenhart, et.al., "Teen and Mobile Phones," Pew Internet, April 20, 2010.
http://pewinternet.org/Reports/2010/Teens-and-Mobile-Phones/Chapter-2/The-typical-American-teen-who-texts-sends-1500-texts-a-month.
aspx Emily Listfield, "Generation Wired," *Parade*, October 9, 2011.
www.parade.com/health/2011/10/generation-wired.html Lindsey Tanner, "Docs Urge Limits on Kids' Texts, Tweets," ABC News, October 28, 2013.
67 http://abcnews.go.com/Health/wireStory/docs-urge-limits-kids-texts-tweets-internet-20702343
Andrew Watts, "A Teenager's View on Social Media," Medium.com, January 2, 2015.
68 **https://medium.com/backchannel/a-teenagers-view-on-social-media-1df945c09ac6#.dz5gh1itu**
Conor Dougherity, "App Makers Reach Out to the Teenager on Mobile," *New York Times*, January 1, 2016.
69 http://www.nytimes.com/2016/01/03/business/app-makers-reach-out-to-the-teenager-on-mobile.html?_r=0
Nick Wingfield, "Feminist Critics of Video Games Facing Threats in 'GameGate' Campaign," *New York Times*, October 15, 2014.
70 http://www.nytimes.com/2014/10/16/technology/gamergate-women-video-game-threats-anita-sarkeesian.html
"Rise of the Tomb Raider Review," Feminist Frequency, November 8, 2015.
https://feministfrequency.com/video/rise-of-the-tomb-raider-review/

71 Rene Sharanya Verma raps in 2015
http://www.youthkiawaaz.com/2015/01/open-letter-to-honey-singh-poetry-slam/
http://www.snagfilms.com/films/title/i_love_hip_hop_in_morocco?%26utm_content=newsletter&utm_source=Sailthru&utm_medium=e-mail&utm_term=SnagFilms%20Contacts%20Master&utm_campaign=1-24&utm_content=Final&&utm_content=newsletter I Love Hip Hop in Morocco, 2015.

72 Jordan Crook, "Facebook Still Reigns Supreme With Teens, But Social Media Interest Dwindling," *Tech Crunch*, April 10, 2013.

73 http://techcrunch.com/2013/04/10/facebook-still-reigns-supreme-with-teens-but-social-media-interest-dwindling/
Marcelo Ballve, "Our List of the World's Largest Social Networks Shows How Video, Messages, and China Are Taking Over the Social Web," *Business Insider*, December 17, 2013.

74 http://www.businessinsider.com/the-worlds-largest-social-networks-2013-12

75 Chimamanda Ngozi Adichie. *Americanah*. Anchor Books, 2014, pp. 80, 502, and 564.
Emily Steel, "Netflix to Add Films and TV Series for Teenagers," *New York Times*, August 24, 2015.

76 http://www.nytimes.com/2015/08/25/business/netflix-to-add-films-and-tv-series-for-teenagers.html

77 Steve Inskeep, May 19, 2010. http://www.npr.org/templates/story/story.php?storyId=126395475&jump=12
http://time.com/4302406/felix-kjellberg-pewdiepie-2016-time-100/

78 https://www.youtube.com/watch?v=NsevBxOWFXs

79 https://www.youtube.com/playlist?list=PLiiPPqU92mNvKNx3bp7TZEPWtv0pxpdtF

80 http://www.youtube.com/watch?v=tu_XJidrGLI

81 Judith Butler. *Gender Trouble: Feminism and the Subversion of Identity*. Routledge, 1990.
N'Donna Russell, "What Sailor Moon Means to Women all over the World," *Global Voices*, June 24, 2015.
http://globalvoicesonline.org/2015/06/24/what-sailor-moon-means-to-women-all-over-the-world/

82 http://sailormoonnews.com/

83 http://www.neopets.com/explore.phtml
Jennifer Robertson, "Japan's Gender-Bending History," *The Conversation*, February 28, 2017.

84 http://theconversation.com/japans-gender-bending-history-71545
Amy Qin, "The 5 'Handsome Girls' Trying to be China's Biggest Boy Band," *New York Times*, May 20, 2017.

85 https://www.nytimes.com/2017/05/20/world/asia/china-acrush-pop-music-gender-boy-band.html
Ingrid Piller, "The F-Word on the Move," May 22, 2010.

86 www.languageonthemove.com/recent-post/the-f-word-on…
www.google.com/images?client=firefox-a&rls=org.mozilla:en-US:official&channel=s&hl=en&q=graffiti+china&um=1&ie=UTF-8&source=univ&ei=-SZYTKmEBom-sQOm95yqCw&sa=X&oi=image_result_group&ct=title&resnum=1&ved=0C-CMQsAQwAA&biw=1307&bih=873A

87 www.womenofchina.cn/Data_Research/Latest_Statistics/212822.jsp

88 http://secondlife.com/whatis/
http://dancinginkproductions.com/2010/06/22/understanding-islam-through-virtual-worlds/
http://dancinginkproductions.com/2010/06/23/brookings-institution-the-doha-forum/

89 http://bafuturu.homestead.com/Article_for_Peace_Newsletter.pdf Sierra James works on peace building in Timor-Leste. She reports, "On a recent program we also let them [youth] focus on drama, media or art during a 5-month training program. More than half of the at-risk youth [who were in gangs or violent] involved in the program enrolled in university or found a job with in a few months of when the program ended. http://www.internationalpeaceandconflict.org/profiles/blogs/peace-education-transforming-situations-or-transforming-societies?xg_source=activity#.U--zwbxdWQM

90 http://www.schoolgirlsunite.org/PDF/GGAExcerpt.pdf

91 "Why Young North Koreans Are Daring to Wear Skinny Jeans," *Global Voices*, October 4, 2015.
https://globalvoices.org/2015/10/04/why-young-north-koreans-are-daring-to-wear-skinny-jeans/

92 Chloe Combi. *Generation Z*. Windmill Books, 2015, p. 268.

93 Jesse Singal, "For 80 Years, Young Americans Have Been Getting more Anxious and Depressed," *New York Magazine Science of Us*, March 13, 2016.

94 http://nymag.com/scienceofus/2016/03/for-80-years-young-americans-have-been-getting-more-anxious-and-depressed.html
Maura Judkis, "Super Bowl Commericals Still Sassy," *The Washington Post*, February 1, 2015.
http://www.washingtonpost.com/lifestyle/style/super-bowl-commercials-still-sassy-but-a-little-more-classy-as-sexism-fadein-2015/2015/02/01/696093a6-a89a-11e4-a06b-9df2002b86a0_story.html

95 https://abancommercials.com/vid/9213/det/geico-sleeping-beauty-its-what-you-do-commercial

96 Amy Goldwasser, **Ed.** *Red: Teenage Girls*. Plume, 2007. P. xv.

97 http://www.youtube.com/watch?v=hck7q_OnJag

98 Rick Nauert, "Eating Disorders from Secondhand TV?" *Psych Central*. January 7, 2011.
http://psychcentral.com/news/2011/01/07/eating-disorders-from-secondhand-tv/22387.html

99 Jorgen Baek Simonsen, **ed.** *Youth and Youth Culture in the Contemporary Middle East*. Aarhus Universtiy Press, Denmark, 2005, p. 99.

100 www.trentarthur.ca/index.php?option=com_content&view=article&id=1053%3Aonslaught-of-the-dove&Itemid=100002

101
102 http://www.youthkiawaaz.com/2014/05/know-surf-india-meet-indias-first-surfer-girl/
Swati Sanyal Tarfdar, "India's 'Dark is Beautiful" Campaign Force, *We News*, May 26, 2015.
103 http://womensenews.org/story/cultural-trendspopular-culture/150522/indias-dark-beautiful-campaign-builds-force
104 Lisa Movius, "Cultural Devolution," *The New Republic*, March 2004. www.movius.us/articles/TNR-sexism-original.html
Internet Pornography Statistics
105 http://internet-filter-review.toptenreviews.com/internet-pornography-statistics.html
106 https://www.youtube.com/watch?v=qUSLXjzmgMs
"German Company's Videos Image Modern Women as Passive and Dependent," *Global Voices*, March 27, 2015.
107 https://globalvoices.org/2015/03/27/german-companys-videos-imagine-modern-women-as-passive-and-dependent/
http://msmagazine.com/blog/2011/07/08/culture-jamming-sexist-ads/
108 http://womenandmediafa2011.blogspot.com/2011/10/0-0-1-561-3203-nyu-26-7-3757-14.html
http://www.whatweekly.com/2014/05/28/the-art-of-the-modern-apocalypse-a-cultural-love-affair/
http://www.livescience.com/27287-zombie-apocalypse-world-war-ii.html
109 http://interactive.nydailynews.com/2016/02/why-hollywood-obsessed-with-apocalypse/
Jessica Sequeira, "The New Censorship," *Harvard International Review*, August 12, 2008.
110 http://hir.harvard.edu/print/blog/jessica-sequeira/the-new-censorship
Nevin Thompson, "Spending Christmas Eve Alone? Japanese Has a Word for That," *Global Voices*, December 6, 2014.
111 http://globalvoicesonline.org/2014/12/06/spending-christmas-eve-alone-japanese-has-a-word-for-that/
Fable, "Sherry Turkle and Her Plea to Technology Junkies,"
112 http://you.stonybrook.edu/christylau/2014/02/14/sherry-turkle-and-her-plead-to-technology-junkies/
Anita Rani, "The Japanese Men who Prefer Virtual Girlfriends to Sex," *BBC News Magazine*, October 23, 2013.
113 http://www.bbc.co.uk/news/magazine-24614830
114 Lui Hebron and John Stack, Jr, p. 92.
Katherine Rosman, "Your Instagram Picture, Worth a Thousand Ads," *New York Times*, October 15, 2014.
115 http://www.nytimes.com/2014/10/16/fashion/your-instagram-picture-worth-a-thousand-ads.html?_r=0
Sydney Ember, "Brands Woo Millennials With a Wink, and Emoji or Whatever it Takes," *New York Times*, September 27, 2015.
116 http://www.nytimes.com/2015/09/28/business/media/brands-woo-millennials-with-a-wink-an-emoji-or-whatever-it-takes.html?_r=0leeann
David Barboza, "Lucrative Stardom in China, Using a Webcam and a Voice," *New York Times*, April 17, 2014.
117 http://www.nytimes.com/2014/04/18/business/media/lucrative-stardom-in-china-using-a-webcam-and-a-voice.html
118 http://www.npr.org/2012/05/07/152183865/lena-dunham-addresses-criticism-aimed-at-girls
https://www.nytimes.com/2017/02/11/fashion/lena-dunham-and-judd-apatow-on-girls-geeks-and-trolls.html?emc=edit_th_20170212&nl=to-
119 daysheadlines&nlid=68143430
120 http://girlshbo.tumblr.com/
Ree Hines, "Lena Dunham Talks 'Victim Blaming' after Revealing Sexual Assault," NBC News TODAY, Jan. 7, 2015.
121 http://www.today.com/popculture/lena-dunham-talks-victim-blaming-after-revealing-sexual-assault-1D80409191
Amanda Hess, "The Final Shot of 'Girls' Was Judd Apatow's Idea," *New York Times*, April 16, 2017.
https://www.nytimes.com/2017/04/16/arts/television/lena-dunham-on-the-girls-finale-and-that-last-shot-of-hannah.html?&moduleDetail=sec-
tion-news-1&action=click&contentCollection=Television&region=Footer&module=MoreInSection&version=WhatsNext&contentID=WhatsN-
122 ext&pgtype=article
123 http://earthhavenchico.wix.com/theglobal-youth#!millennials-are-narcissistic--anxious/c1fyr
Samnatha Allen, "Will White Feminists Finally Dump Lena Dunham?" *The Daily Beast*, November 4, 2014.
124 www.thedailybeast.com/articles/2014/11/04/will-white-feminists-finally-dump-lena-dunham.html
Rachel Donadio, "Will 'Skam,' a Norwegian Hit, Translate?" *New York Times*, December 9, 2016.
125 https://www.nytimes.com/2016/12/09/arts/television/will-skam-a-norwegian-hit-translate.html?_r=0
Bill Persky, "Viewpoint: The Problem with Lena Dunham's Girls," *TIME Magazine*, February 8, 2013.
126 http://ideas.time.com/2013/02/08/viewpoint-the-problem-with-lena-dunhams-girls/
127 https://www.youtube.com/watch?v=xv0ahGRkaKE
Philip Elliott, "Only 1-in-4 ACT Test-Takers have College, Career Skills," NBC News, August 21, 2013.
128 http://www.nbcnews.com/business/only-1-4-act-test-takers-have-college-career-skills-6C10962838
Chris Hedges, "Thank You for Standing Up," *Nation of Change: Progressive Journalism for Positive Action*, January 24, 2012.
129 www.nationofchange.org/thank-you-standing-1327425435
Alex Carey. *Taking the Risk out of Democracy: Propaganda in the US and Australia. University of New South Wales*, 1995.
130 http://www.hartford-hwp.com/archives/25/006.html
Madeleine Morenstern, "Donald Trumb Goes All-Out Against Megyn Kelly Over Alleged Debate Bias," *The Blaze*, August 7, 2015.
http://www.theblaze.com/stories/2015/08/07/donald-trump-goes-all-out-against-megyn-kelly-over-alleged-debate-bias-heres-what-he-tweeted-
131 about-her/
Michael Finnegan, "Donald Trump has a History of Endorsing Violence Against Protesters," *Los Angeles Times*, March 11, 2016.
http://www.latimes.com/politics/la-na-trump-protester-violence-20160311-story.html

132 https://www.youtube.com/watch?v=FcU8iBpXduk

133 http://www.telegraph.co.uk/culture/pixar/10488378/The-19-best-female-cartoon-characters.html?frame=endScreen

134 FP Staff, "Burka Avenger Cartoon Series Coming to India to Empower Girls," *First Post*, April 15, 2015.

http://www.firstpost.com/india/pakistans-burka-avenger-cartoon-series-coming india-empower-girls-2197218.html

135 Christian-Georges Schwentzel, "Selling Sex: Wonder Woman and the Ancient Fantasy of Hot Lady Warriors," *The Conversation*, May 25, 2017.

136 http://theconversation.com/selling-sex-wonder-woman-and-the-ancient-fantasy-of-hot-lady-warriors-78059

http://www.hitfix.com/news/girl-power-10-female-superheroes-who-deserve-their-own-movie

137 http://www.film.com/photos/female-superheroes

138 http://www.laborinquena.somosarte.com/

Tim Beedle, "Are You Ready for Prez's Mark Russell,?" *DC Comics*, August 27, 2015.

139 http://www.dccomics.com/blog/2015/08/27/are-you-ready-for-prezs-mark-russell

"Feminism and Buffy the Vampire Slayer," *Media Chick*, May 9, 2014.

140 http://themediachick.com/2014/05/09/feminism-and-buffy-the-vampire-slayer/

"Weak Women In *Twilight*," Burke Museum

http://www.burkemuseum.org/static/truth_vs_twilight/gp-01.php The most successful films with female leads: http://www.gamesradar.com/20-most-successful-movies-with-a-female-lead/

141 http://www.harpersbazaar.com/culture/film-tv/news/a16251/game-of-thrones-female-characters-season-6/

142 http://www.bing.com/videos/search?q=Palestinian+reality+show+called+The+President+&view=detail&mid=B57FA511FB7A8A954704B-57FA511FB7A8A954704&FORM=VIRE

143 Ashley Reese, "7 Teen British TV Shows That Everyone Should Watch," *Girl*, July 22, 2013.

http://www.gurl.com/2013/07/22/best-teen-british-tv-shows-drama-comedy/#1

144 Viv Groskop, "Is UK Children's TV Really Sexist?" *The Guardian*, June 5, 2014.

http://www.theguardian.com/tv-and-radio/tvandradioblog/2014/jun/05/is-uk-childrens-tv-sexist

145 http://www.metrolyrics.com/you-dont-own-me-lyrics-lesley-gore.html

146 http://www.metrolyrics.com/you-dont-own-me-lyrics-lesley-gore.html

147 http://www.directlyrics.com/meghan-trainor-no-lyrics.html

148 Matthew Reyes, "Why Did We Justify Misogyny in the Emo Scene?" *The Earlier Stuff*, November 4, 2016.

149 https://theearlierstuff.com/why-did-we-justify-the-misogyny-in-the-emo-scene-a9dbda5ba396

150 http://www.grrlyshow.com/description.htm

http://onewarart.org/riot_grrrl_manifesto.htm *The Punk Singer*, 2013, a feature length film about Kathleen Hanna.

151 Marion Deschamps Interviews Tef Poe, "'You'll Never Kill their Music:' The 'Voice of Ferguson' Tef Poe Talks BLM, Feminism in Rap," *TeleSUR*, February 23, 2017.

152 http://www.telesurtv.net/english/opinion/The-Voice-of-Ferguson-Tef-Poe-Talks-BLM-Feminism-in-Rap-20170222-0034.html

Lisa Weems, "M.I.A. in the Global Youthscape: Rethinking Girls' Resistance and Agency in Postcolonial Contexts," *Girlhood Studies*, December 1, 2009. DOI: http://dx.doi.org/10.3167/ghs.2009.020205

153 Kelsey Whipple, "10 Proudly Feminist Musicians," *LA Weekly*, January 3, 2014.

154 http://www.laweekly.com/westcoastsound/2014/01/03/10-proudly-feminist-musicians

Rebecca Bohanan, "Taylor Swift and Her Brand of Feminism," *The Huffington Post*, July 25, 2016.

155 http://www.huffingtonpost.com/rebecca-bohanan/taylor-swift-and-the-bran_b_11101662.html

156 http://tribune.com.pk/story/1178015/fashion-brand-comes-fire-female-flash-mob-lahore/

157 http://bit.ly/1QVetXD

Shuka Kalantari, "Afghan Rapper Escaped Teen Marriage by Singing About It," *PRI*, May 12, 2015.

http://www.pri.org/stories/2015-05-12/afghan-rapper-escaped-teen-marriage-singing-about-it

https://www.youtube.com/watch?v=n65w1DU8cGU

158 Kamille Viola, "Songs of the Slums: Meet the Feminist icons of Brazilian Funk," *News Deeply Women and Girls*, February 1, 2017.

159 https://www.newsdeeply.com/womenandgirls/songs-slums-meet-feminist-icons-brazilian-funk/

160 http://www.npr.org/2011/02/11/133691055/Music-Inspires-Egyptian-Protests

Miss Nikki and the Tiger Girls, Global Voices, 2014.

161 http://www.itvs.org/films/miss-nikki-and-the-tiger-girls

Sarah Doughterty, "Millions are Watching this Puerto Rican Rap Video," *Global Post*, December 17, 2013.

162 http://www.globalpost.com/dispatch/news/regions/americas/united-states/131216/multi-viral-calle-13-julian-assange-rage-against-machine

163 http://www.youtube.com/watch?v=n7BeH2PC1Hc

Samatha Cowan, "6 Powerful Music Videos that Tackled Pressing Social Issues in 2015," *TakePart*, December 27, 2015.

164 http://www.takepart.com/article/2015/12/27/music-videos-2015

https://www.youtube.com/watch?v=s-bKFo30o2o&feature=youtu.be

https://www.youtube.com/watch?v=Bp-KeVBNz0A

165 Sierra Rayne, "The Best Movies Gross the Most," *American Thinker*, May 31, 2015.

http://www.americanthinker.com/blog/2015/05/the_best_movies_gross_the_most.html

166 Deirde Fulton, "Sen. Elizabeth Warren: 'I'm Not Darth Vader, I'm Princess Leia,'" *Common Dreams*, March 18, 2016.
167 http://www.commondreams.org/news/2016/03/18/sen-elizabeth-warren-im-not-darth-vader-im-princess-leia
168 http://wearethedistricts.tumblr.com/
169 et_agony_of_the_young_doves_thailand_after_the_coup_20150122
Katherine Zoepf, "A Troubled Revolution in Egypt," *The New York Times*, November 21, 2011. http://www.nytimes.com/2011/11/21/world/mid-
170 dleeast/a-troubled-revolution-in-egypt.html?pagewanted=all
http://feministdisney.tumblr.com/post/8143040245/the-disney-princess-identity
171 https://www.dosomething.org/campaigns/realprincess
"'Anti-Princess' Collection for Children Launched in Argentina," *TelSur*, August 26, 2015.
172 http://www.telesurtv.net/english/news/Anti-Princess-Collection-for-Children-Launched-in-Argentina-20150826-0042.html
June Eric-Udorie blog, August 23, 2015.
173 http://june-writes.com/2015/08/23/lessons-i-learnt-while-watching-the-diary-of-a-teenage-girl/
David D'Arcy, "Teen Chooses Prostitution in French Hit," *San Francisco Chronicle*, 'April 30, 2014.
174 http://www.sfgate.com/movies/article/Fran-ois-Ozon-discusses-his-film-Young-and-5444176.php#photo-6217405
Adam Sherwin, "Bechdel Tested," *The Independent*, April 2, 2014. /films/news/bechdel-tested-women-talking-to-each-other-on-screen-equals-
a-bigger-box-office-hit-analysis-finds-9233617.html
175 The Geena Davis Institute on Gender and the Media. A 2005 study of G-rated movies and children's TV. www.thegeenadavisinstitute.org/
research.php
176 Tracy Bloom, "Hey Hollywood, Remember the Ladies?", *Truthdig*, May 16, 2013.
177 http://www.truthdig.com/report/item/hey_hollywood_remember_the_ladies_20130516/
Jake Coyle, "Study Throws Harsh Light on Inequality in Popular Movies," WRAL.com, August 5, 2015.
178 http://www.wral.com/study-throws-harsh-light-on-inequality-in-popular-movies/14812928/
Martah Lauzen, "It's a Man's (Celluloid) World," *The Guardian*, March 11, 2014.
179 http://www.theguardian.com/world/2014/mar/11/mans-celluloid-world-study-finds-women-under-represented-film
180 http://www.seejane.org/downloads/GDIGM_Gender_Stereotypes.pdf
http://www.youtube.com/watch?v=0PXXNK-3zQ4
181 http://www.facebook.com/pages/Teach-me-how-to-drive-Lets-all-support-the-Saudi-women-basic-rights/221552737857010
182 jellyandlilipop.wordpress.com
Xu Jingxi, "Female Students Learn About Sex from Internet," *China Daily*, March 4, 2014.
183 http://www.chinadaily.com.cn/china/2014-03/04/content_17322468.htm
Phillip Howard, et al., "Opening Closed Regimes: What was the Role of Social Media During the Arab Spring?" Project on Information Technology and Political Islam, Working Paper 2011.
184 www.piTPI.org.
185 http://girlsglobe.org/featured-organizations/
http://suggestive.com/15-amazing-women-you-should-follow-on-social-media/15/
186 Bloggers from US, UK, Mexico, Brazil, Austrlia, Singapore, India, Pakistan, Iran, Saudi Arabia, Ghana,
187 Lee Tusman. *Really Free Culture*. Pedia Press, 2014, p 176.
188 http://ilustradoresconayotzinapa.tumblr.com/
189 https://www.meansdatabase.com/
Nedium Hadrovic, "Women are at the Forefront of Grassroots Movements in Bosnia," *Muftah*, October 20, 2014.
190 http://muftah.org/women-forefront-grassroots-movements-bosnia/#.VHP7z1XF-Ak
191 www.crowdvoice.org
Amir Azimi, "Iranian Youth Get App to Dodge Morality Police, BBC News, February 9, 2016.
192 http://www.bbc.com/news/blogs-trending-35533287
Peggy Orenstein, "The Battle Over Dress Codes," *New York Times*, June 13, 2014.
193 http://www.nytimes.com/2014/06/14/opinion/the-battle-over-dress-codes.html
194 www.change.org/users/shelbyknox
195 https://www.adbusters.org/spoofads/
196 http://www.stickersisters.com/activism.html
Torey Van OOt and kaelyn Forde, "These Women had the Perfect Response for Vandals who Destroyed Their Mural," *Refinery29*, October 29,
2015.
197 http://www.refinery29.com/2015/10/96605/mural-puerto-rico-vandals-violence-women
http://www.guerrillagirls.com/
198 http://www.nytimes.com/video/arts/design/100000003836847/guerrilla-girls-going-and-going-.html?playlistId=1194811622313
http://winnipegarts.ca/images/uploads/files/Press_pages/Public_Art/PA_The_Craftastics/BLOG_-_Autostraddle-June-7-2013-Team-Pick-Ge-
nius-young-women.pdf
199 http://showyourselfie.org/resources
http://showyourselfie.org/issues

200 Stacy Smith, et al., "Gender Bias Without Borders," Geena Davis Institute on Gender in Media, 2014.

201 http://seejane.org/wp-content/uploads/gender-bias-without-borders-executive-summary.pdf
Jane Levin and Jean Kilbourne. *So Sexy So Soon: The New Sexualized Childhood and What Parents Can Do to Protect Their Kids.* Ballantine Books, 2009.

202 Susan J. Douglas. *Enlightened Sexism: The Seductive Message That Feminism's Work is Done.* Times Books, 2010.

203 "Sexualization of Girls," American Psychological Association, 2007.

204 http://www.apa.org/pi/women/programs/girls/report.aspx
Leeann Schudel, "The Female Body Perfect, TED Talk, 2013.

205 https://www.youtube.com/watch?v=qxS5UfhJz7w
Barbara Coloroso. *The Bully, the Bullied, and the Bystander.* William Morrow, 2016.

206 http://www.thegirlprojectusa.org

207 http://www.about-face.org/educate-yourself/get-the-facts/ founded in 1995 in San Francisco.

208 http://theseventeenmagazineproject.blogspot.com/

209 http://www.sparksummit.com/category/research-blog/

210 http://tedxwomen.org/speakers/juliabluhm-izzy-labbe/
Women's Media Center, July 3, 2012.

211 http://www.womensmediacenter.com/press/entry/the-womens-media-center-congratulates-spark-partners-and-girl-activist-for

212 http://www.sparksummit.com/who-we-are/#join

213 http://www.sparksummit.com/2014/06/05/research-blog-objects-dont-object-or-how-objectification-discourages-activism/

214 http://www.vidaweb.org/category/the-count/the-2013-count/
http://wimnonline.org/education/resource_guide.html#feminist

215 http://www.feminist.org/research/zines.html
http://yfa.awid.org/category/activist-tools-resources/
https://paper.li/RESURJ/1307854061#!headlines

216 http://thefeministwire.com/category/college_feminisms/
Morley Winograd and Michael Hais, *Millennial Makeover: My Space, YouTube and the Future of American Politics.* Rutgers University Press, 2008, p. 195. Ben Rigby. *Mobilizing Generation 2.0: A Practical Guide to using Web 2.0 Technologies to Recruit, Organize and Engage Youth.* Jossey-Bass, 2008.

217 values/posts/millennials-on-religion-and-interfaith-work Hannah Fingerhut, "Millennials' Views of News Media, Religious Organizations Grow More Negative," *Pew Research Center,* January 4, 2016.

218 http://www.pewresearch.org/fact-tank/2016/01/04/millennials-views-of-news-media-religious-organizations-grow-more-negative/
Eleanor Goldfield, "20 News Sites Kicking Our Generation Into Action," *Popular Resistance,* August 25, 2014.
https://www.popularresistance.org/20-news-sites-kicking-our-generation-into-action/

219 women of the World reports on global news: http://nytimes.us8.list-manage.com/subscribe?u=dd2ebd95b929cf4d18cc1f4b08&id=cd99fc85ee
Ben Widdicombe, "What Happens When Millennials Run the Workplace?" *New York Times,* March 19, 2016.

220 http://mobile.nytimes.com/2016/03/20/fashion/millennials-mic-workplace.html?_r=1

221 www.newsdeeply.com/womenandgirls

222 http://www.iwtc.org
http://www.isiswomen.org

223 http://www.weforum.org/agenda/2016/02/17-must-read-gender-stories-of-the-week-2109c252-7aa8-44ed-866d-d0f7e4f6c4b6

224 http://msmagazine.com/blog/blog/category/global/
http://womensenews.org/home/series
http://girlsglobe.org/about/

225 http://girlsglobe.org/featured-organizations/

226 http://www.global1.youth-leader.org/ www.occupytogether.org, OccupiedStories.com, Occupy.com, OccupyWallSt.org
http://the99spring.com/materials http://roarmag.org/2011/11/the-global-square-an-online-platform-for-our-movement/http://wiki.theglo-balsquare.org/wiki/Main_Page
http://billmoyers.com/spotlight/take-action/ Truthdig.com MoveOn.org http://pol.moveon.org/keepmeposted/ NationofChange info@nationofchange.org
http://www.telesurtv.net/english/news/ Popular Resistance http://www.popularresistance.org
http://www.popularresistance.org/popular-resistance-newsletter-communities-standing-up/ Democracy Now http://www.democracynow.org
ZNet http://zcomm.org/znet The Commoner: A Web Journal for Other Values http://www.commoner.org.uk/ Z Magazine: The Spirit of Resistance Lives http://zcomm.org/zmag/ Red Pepper: Spicing up Politics http://www.redpepper.org.uk/ Indymedia https://www.indymedia.org/or/

227 index.shtml Upside Down World http://upsidedownworld.org/main (Latin America) Occupy.com global Voices, http://globalvoicesonline.org/
https://www.opendemocracy.net/5050
https://www.popularresistance.org/20-news-sites-kicking-our-generation-into-action/

228 http://cultureandyouth.org/global-youth-news/
www.worldpulse.com/pulsewire/

229 http://worldpulse.com/about/what

230 http://www.fire.or.cr/indexeng.htm

231 http://issuu.com/ggbzine

Jenna Wortham, "Why the Internet Didn't Kill Zines," *New York Times*, February 28, 2017.

232 https://www.nytimes.com/2017/02/28/magazine/why-the-internet-didnt-kill-zines.html

233 Mary Celeste Kearney. *Girls Make Media*. Routledge, 2006, p. 292.

234 http://bitchmagazine.org/blogs/social-**commentary**

235 http://bitchmagazine.org/post/eight-new-lobbying-hobbies-that-fight-against-hobby-lobby

236 http://youngist.org/about/

237 https://en.wikipedia.org/wiki/List_of_youth_empowerment_organizations

238 http://globalgirlmedia.org/about-us/

239 https://womensrights.informationactivism.org/

240 http://yfa.awid.org/about-us/

241 https://www.newmoon.com/help/

242 http://www.womxnmag.com/about-us.html

243 https://www.youtube.com/watch?v=p-iFl4qhBsE

Bea Appleby, "Feminism for Pre-Teens," *The Guardian*, May 4, 2014.

244 http://www.theguardian.com/theobserver/she-said/2014/may/04/feminism-for-pre-teens-delivered-along-with-pink-nail-stickers

245 http://www.girlzone.com/who-we-are

246 http://www.scarleteen.com/bb/viewtopic.php?t=427&p=2089#p2089

247 https://www.youtube.com/user/lacigreen

248 http://www.businessinsider.com/juliette-brindak-created-miss-o-and-friends-2012-6

https://www.youtube.com/user/marinashutup

249 http://womenofyoutube.tumblr.com/

250 http://thefbomb.org/category/feminism/

251 http://sherights.com/2015/03/02/top-20-feminist-blogs-all-boats-rise/

http://mediagirl.org/whoetc

http://wimnonline.org/WIMNsVoicesBlog/

http://www.igc.org/index.html

252 http://www.jeankilbourne.com/resources-for-change/

253 http://womensenews.org/2016/11/top-10-ted-talks-by-teen-girls/#

254 http://stopitcyberbully.com/

255 http://www.trueactivist.com/18-of-the-most-amazingly-creative-protests-ever/

256 http://www.filmsforaction.org/articles/the-top-100-films-for-action/

257 https://www.globalgiving.org/donate/3611/global-girl-media/reports/

258 www.youtube.com/watch?v=0PXXNK-3zQ4

259 https://www.youtube.com/watch?v=hc45-ptHMxo

https://www.youtube.com/playlist?list=PLMLvwwZgiTJgiLxJz5ElkdXmATrDMIiFf

BIBLIOGRAPHY

Manal Al-Sharif. *Daring to Drive: A Saudi Woman's Awakening.* Simon and Schuster, 2017.

Lila Abu-Lughod. *Do Muslim Women Need Saving?* Harvard University Press, 2013.

Ayaan Hirsi Ali. *The Caged Virgin: An Emancipation Proclamation for Women and Islam.* Free Press, 2004.

Rubina Ali. *Slumgirl Dreaming: Rubina's Journey to the Stars.* Delacorte Press: NYC, 2009.

A.P.J. Abdul Kalam. *Mission India: A Vision for Indian Youth.* Puffin Books, 2005.

Aravind Adiga. *The White Tiger.* Free Press, 2008.

Ama Ata Aidoo. *Changes: A Love Story.* The Feminist Press, 1993.

Uwem Akpan. *Say You're One of Them.* Tells the fictional stories of five children from different African countries. Little, Brown and Company, 2008.

Maytha Alhassen and Ahmed Shihab-Eldin, eds. *Demanding Dignity: Young Voices from the Front Lines of the Arab Revolutions.* White Cloud Press, 2012.

Ann Anagnost, Andrea Arai, and Hai Ren, eds. *Global Futures in East Asia: Youth, Nation, and the New Economy in Uncertain Times.* Stanford University Press, 2013.

Jorgen Baek Simonsen, ed. *Youth and Youth Culture in the Contemporary Middle East.* Aarhus Universtiy Press, Denmark, 2005.

David Baker and Gerald Letendre. *National Differences, Global Similarities: World Culture and the Future of Schooling.* Stanford Social Sciences, 2005.

Asef Bayat. Life as Politics: *How Ordinary People Change the Middle East.* Stanford University Press, 2013.

Rita Banerji. *Sex and Power: Defining History, Shaping Societies.* Penguin Press, 2008.

Marwan Bishara. *The Invisible Arab: The Promise and Peril of the Arab Revolution.* Nation Books, 2012.

Katherine Boo. *Behind the Beautiful Forevers: Life, Death, and Hope in a Mumbai Undercity.* Random House, 2012.

B. Bradford Brown, R. Larson and T. Saraswathi, eds. *The World's Youth: Adolescence in Eight Regions of the Globe.* Cambridge University Press: Cambridge, UK, 2002.

Victoria Bromley. *Feminisms Matter: Debates, Theories, Activism.* University of Toronto Press, 2012.

Lyn Mikel Brown. *Powered by Girl: A Field Guide for Supporting Youth Activists.* Beacon Press, 2016.

David Burstein. *Fast Future: How the Millennial Generation is Shaping Our World.* Beacon Press, 2013.

Dorothy Sue Cobble, Linda Gordon, and Astrid Henry. *Feminism Unfinished: A Short, Surprising History of American Women's Movements.* Liverwright Publishing, 2014.

Andy Carvin. *Distant Witness: Social Media, the Arab Spring and a Journalism Revolution.* CUNY Journalism Press, 2012.

Manuel Castells. *Networks of Outrage and Hope: Social Movements in the Internet Age.* Polity Press, 2012.

Paul Clark. *Youth Culture in China: From Red Guards to Netizens.* Cambridge University Press, 2012.

Leslie Chang. *Factory Girls.* Spiegel and Grau, 2008.

Chelsea Clinton. *It's Your World: Get Informed, Get Inspired & Get Going!* Philomel Books, 2015.

Isobel Coleman. *Paradise Beneath Her Feet: How Women are Transforming the Middle East.* Random House, 2010.

Mathew Collin, *The Time of the Rebels: Youth Resistance Movements and 21st Century Revolutions.* Profile Books, 2007.

Chloe Combi. *Generation Z.* Windmill Books, 2015.

Colette Daiute, et. al., eds. *International Perspectives on Youth Conflict and Development.* Oxford University Press: Oxford, UK., 2009.

William Dalrymple. *Nine Lives: In Search of the Sacred in Modern India.* Alfred A. Knopf, 2010.

Marcel Danesi. *Forever Young: the 'Teen-Aging' of Modern Culture.* University of Toronto Press: Toronto, 2003.

Tsitsi Dangarembga. *Nervous Conditions.* Ayebia Clarke Publishing, 1988.

Siddhartha Deb. *The Beautiful and the Damned: A Portrait of the New India.* NYC: Faber and Faber, 2011.

Maria De Los Angeles Torres, Irrene Rizzini, and Norma Del Rio. *Citizens in the Present: Youth Civic Engagement in the Americas.* University of Illinois Press, 2013.

Peter deSouza, Sanjay Kumar, Sandeep Shastri, editors. *Indian Youth in a Transforming World.* Sage: Los Angeles, 2009.

Susan Dewey and Karen Brison, eds. *Super Girls, Gangstas, Freeters, and Xenomaniacs.* Syracuse University Press, 2012.

Rachel Dewoskin. *Foreign Babes in Beijing.* W.W. Norton, 2005.

Nadine Dolby & Fazal Rizvi, eds. *Youth Moves: Identities and Education in Global Perspective.* Routledge: NYC, 2008.

Adama and Naomi Doumbia. *The Way of the Elders: West African Spirituality and Tradition.* Llewellyn Worldwide: St. Paul, MN, 2004.

Lena Dunham. *Not That Kind of Girl: A Young Woman Tells You What She's "Learned."* Random House, 2014.

William Easterly. *The White Man's Burden: Why the West's Efforts to Aid the Rest Have Done So Much ill and So Little Good.* Penguin Books, 2006.

Hester Eisenstein. *Feminism Seduced: How Global Elites Use Women's Labor and Ideas to Exploit the World.* Paradigm Publishers, 2009.

Shereen El Feki. *Sex and the Citadel: Intimate Life in a Changing Arab World.* Pantheon Books, 2013.

Cristina Flesher Fominaya and Laurence Cox, eds. *Understanding European Movements: New Social Movements, Global Justice Struggles, Anti-Austerity Protest.* Routledge, 2013.

Cristina Flesher Fominaya. *Social Movements and Globalization: How Protests, Occupations and Uprisings are Changing the World.* Palgrave Macmillan, 2014.

Andy Furlong. *Youth Studies: An Introduction*. Routledge, 2013.

Nawal El Saadawi. *Reader*. Zed Books: London, 1997.

A Daughter of isis, Zed Books, 1999.

Walking Through Fire. Zed Books, 2002.

Eve Ensler. *I am an Emotional Creature*. Villard, 2010.

Johanthon Epstein, ed. *Youth Culture: Identity in a Postmodern World*. Blackwell: London, 1989.

Deborah Fallows. *Dreaming in Chinese: Mandarin Lessons in Life, Love, and Language*. Walker & Co, 2010.

James Farrer. *Opening Up: Youth Sex Culture and Market Reform in Shanghai*. University of Chicago Press: Chicago, 2002.

Eric Fish. *China's Millennials: The Want Generation*. Roman and Littlefield, 2015.

Frederick Franck, J. Roze and R. Connolly, eds. *What Does It Mean to be Human?* Circumstantial Productions,1998.

Friends of the Earth. *Why Women Will Save The Planet*. Zed Books, 2015.

Medard Gabel, ed. *Designing A World That Works for All: How the Youth of the World are Creating Real-World Solutions for the UN Millennium Development Goals and Beyond*. BigPictureSmall World, Media, PA, 2010.

Neal Gabler. *Life: The Movie: How Entertainment Conquered Reality*. Vintage, NYC, 2000.

John Gerzema and Michael D'Antonio. *The Athena Doctrine: How Women (and the Men Who Think Life Them) Will Rule the Future*. Jossey-Bass, 2013.

Masha Gessen. *Words will Break Cement: The Passion of Pussy Riot*. Riverhead Books, 2014.

Judith Gibbons and Deborah Stiles. *The Thoughts of Youth: An International Perspective on Adolescents' Ideal Persons*. Information Age Publishing: Greenwich, CN, 2004.

Janice Gibson-Cline, ed. *Youth and Coping in Twelve Nations*. Routledge: London and NYC, 2000.

Henry Giroux. *Youth in Revolt: Reclaiming a Democratic Future*. Paradigm Publishers,

2013.

Al Gore. *The Future: Six Drivers of Social Change.* Random House, 2013.

Eric Greenberg. *Generation We: How Millennial Youth Are Taking Over American and Changing Our World Forever.* Pachatusan: Emeryville, CA, 2008.

Wael Ghonim. *Revolution 2.0.* Boston: Houghton Mifflin Harcourt, 2012.

Rha Goddess and JLove Calderon. *We Got Issues! A Young Woman's Guide to a Bold, Courageous and Empowered Life.* Inner Ocean Publishing, 2006.

Hava Rachel Gordon. *We Fight to Win: Inequality and the Politics of Youth Activism.* Rutgers University Press, 2010.

Mikki Halpin. *It's Your World—If You Don't Like It, Change It; Activism for Teenagers.* Simon and Schuster: NYC, 2004.

Alexandra Hanson-Harding. *Activism: Taking on Women's Issues.* Rosen Publishing, 2013.

Joel Harden, *Quiet No More: New Political Activism in Canada and Around the Globe,* **James Lorimer & Co.,** Toronto, 2013.

Willis Harman. *Global Mind Change.* Berrett-Koehler Publications, 1998.

Anita Harris, ed. *Next Wave Cultures.* Routledge, 2008.

Anita Harris and Michelle Fine, eds. *All About the Girl: Culture, Power, and Identity.* Routledge, 2004.

Anita Harris. *Future Girl: Young Women in the Twenty-First Century.* Routledge, 2004.

Anita Harris, ed. *Next Wave Cultures: Feminism, Subcultures, Activism.* Routledge, 2008.

Chris Hedges. *Empire of Illusion: The End of Literacy and the Triumph of Spectacle.* Nation Books: NYC, 2009.

Death of the Liberal Class. Nation Books, NYC, 2010.

Lui Hebron and John Stack, Jr. *Globalization: Debunking the Myths.* Prentice Hall: NYC, 2009.

Matt Hern and the Purple Thistle Centre editors. *Stay Solid! A Radical Handbook for Youth.* AK Press, 2013.

Linda Herrera. *Revolution in the Age of Social Media.* Verso, 2014.

Linda Herrera and Asef Bayat, eds. *Being Young and Muslim.* Oxford University Press, 2010.

Leta Hong Fincher. *Leftover Women: The Resurgence of Gender Inequality in China.* Zed Books, 2014.

Alcinda Honwana. *The Time of Youth: Work, Social Change and Politics in Africa.* Kumarian Press, 2012.

Youth and Revolution in Tunisia. Zed Books, 2013.

Phillip Hoose. *It's Our World, Too! Young People Who Are Making a Difference.* Little, Brown and Company: NYC, 1993.

Christine Horansky. *Girl Power in the Age of the Millennials.* Ivy and Airwaves, 2014.

Neil Howe and William Strauss. *Millennials Rising: The Next Great Generation.* Vintage Books, NYC, 2000.

Zach Hunter. *Generation Change.* Zondervan: Grand Rapids, MI, 2008.

Lose Your Cool. Zondervan, 2009.

Ronald Inglehart and Christian Welzel. *Modernization, Cultural Change, and Democracy: The Human Development Sequence.* Cambridge University Press: NYC, 2005.

Frances Jensen with Amy Ellis Nutt. *The Teenage Brain.* HarperCollins, 2015.

Karen Tranberg Hansen, ed. *Youth and the City in the Global South.* Indiana University Press, 2008.

Rebecca Huntley. *The World According to Y: Inside the New Adult Generation.* Allen & Unwin: NSW, Australia, 2006.

Ronald Inglehart and Christian Welzel. *Modernization, Cultural Change, and Democracy.*

Maryam Jamshidi. *The Future of the Arab Spring.* Elsevier, 2014.

Craig Jeffrey and Jane Dyson, eds. *Telling Young Lives: Portraits of Global Youth.* Temple University Press, Philidelphia, PA, 2008.

Jeffrey Jensen Arnett, ed. *Adolescent Psychology Around the World.* Psychology Press, 2012.

Sally Howard. *The Kama Sutra Diaries.* Nicholas Brealey Publishing, 2013.

Malalai Joya. *A Woman Among Warlords*. Scribner: NYC, 2009.

Reynol Junco and Jeanna Mastrodicasa. *Connecting to the Net Generation: What Higher Education Professionals Need to Know about Today's Students*. National Association of Student Personnel Administrators. Washington DC: 2007.

Samir Khalaf and Roseanne Saad Khalaf. *Arab Youth: Social Mobilization in Times of Risk*. Saqi Books, 2011.

Cindi Katz. *Growing Up Global: Economic Restructuring and Children's Everyday Lives*. University of Minnesota Press, Minneapolis, MN, 2004.

Mary Celeste Kearney. *Girls Make Media*. Routledge, 2006.

Jane Kenway and Elizabeth Bullen. *Consuming Children: Education-Entertainment-Advertising*. Open University Press, 2001.

Jomo Kenyatta. *Facing Mt. Kenya*. Vintage: NYC, 1965.

Salman Khan. *The One World Schoolhouse: Education Reimagined*. Twelve, Hachette Book Group, 2012. www.khanacademy.org

Parag Khanna. *How to Run the World: Charting a Course to the Next Renaissance*. NYC: Random House, 2011.

Alex Khasnabish. *Zapatistas: Rebellion for the Grassroots to the Global*. Zed Books, 2010.

Michael Kimmel. *Guyland: The Perilous World Where Boys Become Men*. HarperCollins: NYC, 2008.

Hilary Klein. Compañeras: *Zapatista Women's Stories*. Seven Stories Press, 2015.

Naomi Klein. *No Logo*. St. Martin's Press/Picador: NYC, 2009, pp. 118-121.

The Shock Doctrine: The Rise of Disaster Capitalism. Picador: NYC, 2007.

Gudrun Kochendorfer-Lusius and Boris Pleskovid, eds. *Development and the Next Generation*. The World Bank: Washington, DC, 2007.

Fawzia Koofi. *The Favored Daughter*. Palgrave, 2012.

Nicholas Kristof and Sheryl WuDunn. *Half the Sky: Turning Oppression into Opportunity for Women Worldwide*. Alfred A. Knopf: NYC, 2009.

Nur Laiq. *Talking to Arab Youth: Revolution and Countrrevolution in Egypt and Tunisia*. International Peace Institute, 2013.

Barbara Lewis. *The Teen Guide to Global Action.* Free Spirit Publishing: Minneapolis, MN, 2008.

Elline Lipkin. *Girls' Studies.* Seal Press, 2009.

Ritty Lukose. *Liberalization's Children: Gender, Youth, and Consumer Citizenship in Globalizing India.* Duke University Press, 2009.

Sunaina Maira and Elisabeth Soep, eds. *Youthscapes: The Popular, the National, the Global.* University of Pennsylvania Press, 2005.

Mike Males. *The Scapegoat Generation: America's War on Adolescents.* Common Courage Press: Monroe, ME, 1996.

Framing Youth; 10 Myths About the Next Generation. Common Courage Press, 2002.

Firoze Manji and Kosari Ekine. *African Awakening: The Emerging Revolutions.* Pambazuka Press, 2012.

Veronica Box Mansilla and Anthony Jackson. *Educating for Global Competence.* Asia Society and Council of Chief State School Officers, 2011.

Courtney Martin. *Do It Anyway: The New Generation of Activists.* Beacon Press, 2010.

Jennifer Martin, et al., eds. *Feminist Pedagogy, Practice, and Activism: Improving Lives for Girls and Women.* Routledge, 2017.

Paul Mason. *Why It's Still Kicking Off Everywhere: The New Global Revolutions.* Verso, 2013.

Mavis McCovey and John Salter. *Medicine Trails: A life in Many Worlds.* Heyday Books, 2009.s

Bill McKibben. *Eaarth: Making a Life on a Tough New Planet.* Times Books: NYC, 2010.

Ritu Menon, ed. *Making a Difference: Memoirs for the Women's Movement in India.* Women Unlimited, New Delhi, 2011.

Pankaj Mishra. *Temptations of the West: How to be Modern in India, Pakistan, Tibet, and Beyond.* Picador: NYC, 2006.

Valentine Moghadam. *Globalizing Women: Transnational Feminist Networks.* The Johns Hopkins University Press, 2005.

Valentine Moghadam. *Globalization and Social Movements: Islamism, Feminism, and*

the Global Justice Movement. Roman & Littlefield, 2009.

Rosario Montoya, Lesslie Jo Frazier, and Janise Hurtig, eds. *Gender's Place: Feminist Anthropologies of Latin America.* Palgrave Macmillan, 2002.

Greg Mortenson and David Relin. *Three Cups of Tea.* Penguin, NYC, 2006. *Stones into Schools.* Viking: NYC, 2009.

Elissa Moses. *The $100 Billion Allowance: Accessing the Global Teen Market.* John Wiley and Sons, NYC, 2000.

Bharati Mukherjee. *Miss New India.* Houghton Mifflin Harcourt: NYC, 2011.

Caryle Murphy. *A Kingdom's Future: Saudi Arabia Through the Eyes of its Twentsomethings.* Wilson Center, 2013.

Yang Erce Namu and Christine Mathieu. *Leaving Mother Lake: a Girlhood at the Edge of the World.* New York: Little Brown & Company, 2004,

Nandan Nilekani. *Imagining India: The Idea of a Renewed Nation.* Penguin Press, 2009.

Pam Nilan and Carlos Feixa, eds. *Global Youth? Hybrid Identities, Plural Worlds.* Routledge: NYC, 2006.

Jacqueline Novogratz. *The Blue Sweater: Bridging the Gap Between Rich and Poor in an Interconnected World.* Rodale Press, 2009.

Kennedy Odede and Jessica Posner. *Find Me Unafraid.* Ecco, 2015.

David Ornstein. *The Price of a Dream: The Story of the Grameen Bank.* Oxford University Press: Oxford, UK, 1996.

Peggy Orenstein. *Girls and Sex: Navigating the Complicated New Landscape.* HarperCollins, 2016.

Richard Osmer and Kenda Creasy Dean, eds. Youth. *Religion and Globalization.* Transaction Publishers, 2007.

John Palfrey and Urs Gasser. *Born Digital: Understanding the First Generation of Digital Natives.* Basic Books: NYC, 2008.

Victoria Pepe, et al., eds. *I Call Myself a Feminist.* Virago, 2015.

Linda Perlstein. *Not Much Just Chillin': The Hidden Lives of Middle Schoolers .* Ballentine, 2004.

Hilary Anne Pilkington, Elena Omel'chenko, Mona Flynn, and Uliana Bliudina.

Looking West? Cultural Globalization and Russian Youth Culture. Pennsylvania State University Press, 2002.

Geraldine Pratt and Victoria Rosner, eds. *The Global and the Intimate: Feminism in Our Time.* Columbia University Press, 2012.

Mona Prince. *Revolution is My Name: An Egyptian Woman's Diary from Eighteen Days in Tahrir.* The American University in Cairo Press, 2014.

Werner Puschra and Sara Burke, eds. *The Future We the People Need: Voices from New Social Movements.* Friedrich Ebert Stiftung, February 2013.

Margaret Randall. *Gathering Fage: The Failure of 20th Century Revolutions to Develop a Feminist Agenda.* Monthly Review Press, 1992.

Clotaire Rapahille. *The Culture Code.* Broadway Books: NYC, 2006.

Thom and Jess Rainer. *The Millennials: Connecting to American's Largest Generation.* Nashville, TN: B&H Publishing Group, 2011.

James Marshall Reilly. *Shake the World.* NYC: Portfolio Hardcover, 2011.

Oksana Robski. *Casual.* Regan: NYC, 2006.

Amélie Le Renard. *A Society of Young Women: Opportunities of Place, Power and Reform in Saudi Arabia.* Stanford University Press, 2014.

Anuradha Roy. *The Folded Earth.* Free Press, 2011.

Srila Roy. *New South Asian Feminisms.* Zed Books, 2012.

Jeffrey Rubin and Emma Sokoloff-Rubin. *Sustaining Activism: A Brazilian Women's Movement and a Father-Daughter Collaboration.* Duke University Press, 2013.

Jeffrey Sachs. *The End of Poverty: Economic Possibilities for Our Time.* Penguin Press, 2005.

Rob Salkowitz. *Young World Rising: How Youth, Technology, and Entrepreneurship are Changing the World from the Bottom Up.* John Wiley & Sons, 2010.

Yoani Sanchez. *Havana Real: One Woman Fights to Tell the Truth About Cuba Today.* Melville House, 2009

Ziauddin Sardar and Borin Van Loon. *Introducing Cultural Studies.* Icon Books, Cambridge, UK, 2004.

Jon Savage. *Teenage: The Creation of Youth Culture.* Penguin Group: NYC, 2007.

Timothy Shary and Alexandra Seibel. *Youth Culture in Global Cinema.* University of Texas Press, 2007.

Anya Schiffrin and Eamon Kircher-Allen. *From Cairo to Wall Street: Voices From the Global Spring.* The New Press, 2012.

Ellen Johnson Sirleaf. *This Child Will Be Great.* HarperCollins: NYC, 2009.

Marina Sitrin, ed. *Horizontalism: Voices of Popular Power in Argentina.* AK Press, 2006.

Tracey Skelton and Gill Valentine, eds. *Cool Places: Geographies of Youth Cultures.* Routledge: NYC, 1998.

Marina Sitrin. *Everyday Revolutions: Horizontalism and Autonomy in Argentina.* Zed Books, 2012.

Sitrin, ed. *Horizontalism: Voices of Popular Power in Argentina.* AK Press, 2006.

Christian Smith, et. al. *Lost in Transition: The Dark Side of Emerging Adulthood.* Oxford University Press, NYC: 2011.

Malidoma Some'. *Ritual, Healing, and Community.* Penguin, NYC, 1993.

Valerie Sperling. *Sex, Politics, and Putin.* Oxford University Press, 2015.

Michael Stanat. *China's Generation Y.* Homa & Sekey Books: Paramus, NY, 2006.

Starhawk. *Truth or Dare: Encounters with Power, Authority and Mystery.* Harper San Francisco, 1990.

William Strauss & Neil Howe. *Generations: The History of America's Future.* William Morrow, 1991.

Manfred Steger, *Globalization: A Very Short Introduction.* Oxford University Press, 2009.

Shirley Steinberg, et. al, eds. *Contemporary Youth Culture: An International Encyclopedia,* Vols. 1 & 2, Greenwood Press, 2006.

Marcelo Suárez-Orozco and Desirée Baolian Qin-Hiliard, eds. *Globalization Culture and Education in the New Millennium.* University of California Press: Berkeley, CA, 2004.

Marcelo Suárez-Orozco, ed. *Learning in the Global Era.* University of California Press: Berkeley, CA, 2007.

Mayssoun Sukarieh and Stuart Tannock. *Youth Rising? The Politics of Youth in the*

Global Economy. Routledge, 2015.

Nicholas Sullivan. *You Can Hear Me Now: How Microloans and Cell Phones are Connecting the World's Poor to the Global Economy.* John Wiley & Sons, 2007.

Jessica Taft. *Rebel Girls: Youth Activism and Social Change Across the Americas.* New York University Press, 2011.

Chandra Talpade Hohanty. *Feminism Without Borders: Decolonizing Theory, Practicing Solidarity.* Duke University Press, 2003.

Don Tapscott. *Grown Up Digital.* McGrawHill: NYC, 2009.

Isadora Tattlin. *Cuba Diaries.* Broadway Books, 2002.

Meredith Tax. *A Road Unforseen: Women Fight the Islamic State.* Belleview Literary Press, 2016.

Marta Tineda and William Julius Wilson, eds. *Youth in Cities: A Cross-National Perspective.* Cambridge University Press, 2002.

James Tooley. *The Beautiful Tree.* Cato Institute: Washington DC, 2009.

Mary Trigg, ed. *Leading the Way: Young Women' Activism for Social Change.* Rutgers University Press, 2010.

Minky Worden, ed. *The Unfinished Revolution.* Seven Stories Press, 2012.

Muhammad Yunus. *Banker to the Poor.* Perseus Books: NYC, 2003.

Annie Zaidi and Smriti Ravindra. *The Bad Boy's Guide to the Good Indian Girl.* Zubaan, 2011.

Emilie Zaslow. *Feminism, Inc.: Coming of Age in Girl Power Media Culture.* Palgrave Macmillan, 2009.

Katherine Zoepf. *Excellent Daughters: The Secret Lives of Young Women who are transforming the Arab World.* Penguin Press, 2016